Butterworths New Law Guides

The Land Registration Act 2002

Butterworths New Law Guides

The Land Registration Act 2002

Gregory Hill MA BCL (Oxon), Barrister,
10 Old Square, Lincoln's Inn, WC2

Richard Wallington MA (Cantab), Barrister,
10 Old Square, Lincoln's Inn, WC2

Timothy Harry MA BCL (Oxon), Barrister,
Maitland Chambers, 7 Stone Buildings, Lincoln's Inn, WC2

Richard Dew LLB (Reading), Barrister,
10 Old Square, Lincoln's Inn, WC2

LexisNexis®
Butterworths

Members of the LexisNexis Group worldwide

United Kingdom	LexisNexis Butterworths, a Division of Reed Elsevier (UK) Ltd, Halsbury House, 35 Chancery Lane, LONDON, WC2A 1EL, and 4 Hill Street, EDINBURGH EH2 3JZ
Argentina	LexisNexis Argentina, BUENOS AIRES
Australia	LexisNexis Butterworths, CHATSWOOD, NEW SOUTH WALES
Austria	LexisNexis Verlag ARD Orac GmbH & Co KG, VIENNA
Canada	LexisNexis Butterworths, MARKHAM, ONTARIO
Chile	LexisNexis Chile Ltda, SANTIAGO DE CHILE
Czech Republic	Nakladatelství Orac sro, PRAGUE
France	Editions du Juris-Classeur SA, PARIS
Germany	LexisNexis Deutschland GmbH, FRANKFURT, MUNSTER
Hong Kong	LexisNexis Butterworths, HONG KONG
Hungary	HVG-Orac, BUDAPEST
India	LexisNexis Butterworths, NEW DELHI
Ireland	LexisNexis, DUBLIN
Italy	Giuffrè Editore, MILAN
Malaysia	Malayan Law Journal Sdn Bhd, KUALA LUMPUR
New Zealand	LexisNexis Butterworths, WELLINGTON
Poland	Wydawnictwo Prawnicze LexisNexis, WARSAW
Singapore	LexisNexis Butterworths, SINGAPORE
South Africa	LexisNexis Butterworths, DURBAN
Switzerland	Stämpfli Verlag AG, BERNE
USA	LexisNexis, DAYTON, Ohio

© Reed Elsevier (UK) Ltd 2005
Published by LexisNexis Butterworths

A CIP Catalogue record for this book is available from the British Library.

Gregory Hill, Richard Wallington, Richard Dew and Timothy Harry, have asserted their rights under the Copyrights, Designs and Patents Act 1988 to be identified as the authors of this work.

ISBN 0 406 95764 9

Printed & bound in Great Britain by William Clowes Ltd, Beccles, Suffolk.

Middle image on the cover is reproduced with the kind permission of The National Archives (PRO): ref E31/1/3

Visit LexisNexis Butterworths at www.lexisnexis.co.uk

Preface

Land registration has come a very long way since its beginnings in the nineteenth century as a possible solution to the formidable complexity of the then law of title to land (Land Registration Acts of 1862 and 1875). The power to declare areas of compulsory registration was first introduced in the Land Transfer Act 1897, but was used sparingly, in relation to London only, before 1925. The framers of the 1922 to 1925 property legislation thought of the reforms to the general law of land which they were introducing as being an alternative to land registration. They hoped that their reforms of unregistered conveyancing would make it unnecessary to extend compulsory registration further. That is why under Land Registration Act 1925, s 122 as originally enacted there was a ten-year deferment of the power of the central government to declare new compulsory registration districts. The idea was that the reforms to unregistered conveyancing would have ten years in which to show their effectiveness, after which extension of compulsory registration could be reconsidered. In the preface to Wolstenholme and Cherry's Conveyancing Statutes, 12th edition (1932), it was stated "Among some of the older practitioners there appears to be still a tendency to make inquiries respecting equities which are intended to be placed behind the curtain, thus playing into the hands of the advocates of registration of title. This tendency is, however, likely to disappear when the younger generation assume control. At the same time it is fair to note that the bitter hostility to compulsory registration appears, at any rate in London, to be wearing down; no doubt this is attributable to the broad minded manner in which the Land Registration Act, 1925, is being administered in practice."

The bitter hostility had declined sufficiently by 1935 for there to be some modest extensions of compulsory registration in the late 1930s, but the process was interrupted by the war. The last stand of the opponents of land registration was probably the public inquiry in 1951 as to whether compulsory registration should be extended to Surrey— s 122 of the 1925 Act as originally enacted entitled opponents of any proposed extension of compulsory registration to require a public inquiry, and three local law societies in Surrey exercised this right. The inquiry reported in favour of compulsory registration, and it was extended to Surrey in 1952. There were then modest extensions of compulsory registration in the 1950s and early 1960s, but the turning point in favour of the general extension of land registration was probably the announcement in 1964 by the Conservative government that there would be a special measures to extend compulsory registration to the majority of urban areas, a policy which was continued by the succeeding Labour government. The process of extension of compulsory registration was given fresh impetus by the Conservative government in the 1980s, and as from 1 December 1990 the extension of compulsory registration to the whole of England and Wales was completed. The Land Registration Act 1997 then extended the categories of transaction which gave rise to compulsory registration. The Land Registry's estimate is that by 1 October 2003 (ie just before Land Registration Act 2002 came into force and much extended the number of registrable titles) around 85 per cent of registrable titles were registered. Apart from the inherent advantages of economy and efficiency of conveyancing under the registration system, there are social, economic and constitutional changes since 1925 which have favoured the spread of land registration, in particular the tremendous increase in home ownership, and the acceptance of state intervention in everyday life in ways undreamt of in the 19th century, by comparison with which a system of compulsory land registration is extremely modest.

The governing statute throughout the period of the triumph of land registration has been the Land Registration Act 1925. It is generally agreed to have been the worst drafted part of the 1925 property legislation. It was unnecessarily complex in some respects, while lacking logical coherence in others. Despite the shortcomings of the

Land Registration Act 1925, what mattered was the way in which it operated in practice, and the Land Registry managed to make it work, and to gain the confidence of the public and the legal professions in the system of registration. However, after 1990, with registered conveyancing having become the predominant system of conveyancing, the pressure increased for a general extension and improvement of the system, and replacement of the 1925 Act with something better. Also, growing computerisation meant that there was a need to adapt the system for the possible introduction of electronic conveyancing. The Law Commission and the Land Registry beavered away on this project for years, producing a consultative document in 1998, Law Com No 254, and then a draft Bill and report of recommendations in 2001 in Law Com No 271. The Land Registration Act 2002 is, subject to very minor amendments, the Bill proposed in Law Com No 271. It completely replaces the Land Registration Act 1925, restating the basic principles in a clearer and more coherent form, and making changes of substance in several important respects. It came into force on 13 October, 2003. The redrafting of the basic structure of the legislation is a most impressive piece of work, and an outstanding intellectual achievement. The 2002 Act was accompanied by new Land Registration Rules 2003, which replace completely the 1925 Rules.

The main changes of substance made in the Land Registration Act 2002 are to pave the way for electronic conveyancing (see Chapter 3 of this work), to extend registration to leases of between seven years and 21 years duration (see Chapter 6), to reduce the number and scope of overriding interests (see Chapter 7), to rewrite the law of adverse possession of registered land in a way which much reduces the chances of a squatter obtaining title (see Chapter 13), and to provide an adjudicator to decide registration disputes (see Chapter 15). The changes to the law of adverse possession are particularly noteworthy, as showing the self-confidence of the registration system: it is no longer thought necessary or important that the law in this respect in relation to registered land should be the same as it is in relation to unregistered land. There are numerous other changes throughout the legislation, on the whole making the law clearer and more user-friendly. See Chapter 1 of this work for a fuller account of the background to the Act and a more detailed summary of the changes made by it.

This book attempts to give a full account of the Land Registration Act 2002 and the accompanying statutory instruments, and the Act and all the statutory instruments are set out in Appendix 2, with the exception of the forms in Schedule 1 to the Land Registration Rules 2003. The numbers and titles of the forms are there set out, however. The forms did not lend themselves to reproduction in this format, and can be readily obtained from the Land Registry, or downloaded from its web site (www.landregistry.gov.uk/publications/). Also included in Appendix 2 are the provisions of the Law of Property Act 1925, ss 1 and 205, which are referred to in Land Registration Act 2002, ss 27(2) and 132(1).

The work on this book has been carried out as follows. Richard Dew: Chapters 1–3, 10–12, 14 and 15; Richard Wallington: Chapters 4–6; Gregory Hill: Chapters 7–9; and Timothy Harry: Chapter 13.

We would like to acknowledge the help and patience of each other, and of the staff of LexisNexis Butterworths. The law is stated as at 31 December 2004.

Gregory Hill
Richard Wallington
Timothy Harry
Richard Dew

May 2005

Contents

Table of Statutes

PARA

Table of Statutory Instruments

Table of Cases

1 Introduction

1.1 The Land Registration Act 2002 (LRA 2002) is a major reform of the system of land registration. This chapter outlines the history of the reforms, the aims and objectives of the legislation and introduces the reader to the legislation and to the rules, as well as outlining the major changes created by the Act.

HISTORY OF THE REFORMS

1.2 The LRA 2002 is the culmination of two reports by a Joint Working Group made up of the Law Commission and HM Land Registry.[1] It is the largest single law reform project and Bill that has been undertaken by the Law Commission since its foundation in 1965.[2]

---

[1] *Land Registration for the Twenty-First Century, A Consultative Document* (1998) (Law Com No 254) and *Land Registration for the Twenty-First Century, A Conveyancing Revolution* (2001) (Law Com No 271).

[2] Law Com No 271, para 1.1.

1.3 The reports are part of a much larger programme of reform of the system of land registration which began with Working Papers in the 1970s.[1] In total the Law Commission has produced seven reports concerning land registration.[2] The first and second[3] were implemented by relatively modest amendment to the 1925 legislation.[4] The third and fourth reports[5] were considerably more ambitious and proposed major reforms to the legislation,[6] not all of which appeared to be based on proposals contained in, or responses to, the original Working Papers.[7] They involved reforms which (perhaps in hindsight) appeared unworkable.[8]

---

[1] *Transfer of Land: Land Registration (First Paper)* (1970) Working Paper No 32; *Transfer of Land: Land Registration (Second Paper)* (1971) Working Paper No 37; *Transfer of Land: Land Registration (Third Paper)* (1972) Working Paper No 45; *Transfer of Land: Land Registration (Fourth Paper)* (1976) Working Paper No 67.

[2] *Property Law: Land Registration* (1983) (Law Com No 125); *Property Law: Second Report on Land Registration: Inspection of the Register* (1985) (Law Com No 148); *Property Law: Third Report on Land Registration: A. Overriding Interests: B. Rectification and Indemnity: C. Minor Interests* (1987) (Law Com No 158); *Fourth Report on Land Registration* (1988) (Law Com No 173); *Transfer of Land: Land Registration (First Report of a Joint Working Group on the Implementation of the Law Commission's Third and Fourth Reports on Land Registration)* (1995) (Law Com No 235); *Land Registration for the Twenty-First Century: A Consultative Document* (1998) (Law Com No 254) and *Land Registration for the Twenty-First Century: A Conveyancing Revolution* (2001) (Law Com No 271).

3 *Property Law: Land Registration* (1983) (Law Com No 125) and *Property Law: Second Report on Land Registration: Inspection of the Register* (1985) (Law Com No 148).
4 See the Land Registration Act 1986 and the Land Registration Act 1988.
5 *Property Law: Third Report on Land Registration: A. Overriding Interests: B. Rectification and Indemnity: C. Minor Interests* (1987) (Law Com No 158); *Property Law: Fourth Report on Land Registration* (1988) (Law Com No 173).
6 The three areas covered by the third report were overriding interests, rectification and indemnity and minor interests. The fourth report was a vehicle for a draft Bill.
7 See Law Com No 254.
8 Particularly the proposal, in the third report, that purchasers should be indemnified in respect of overriding interests.

1.4 In 1994 the Joint Working Group was established to consider ways in which the third and fourth reports could be implemented. The first report of this group,[1] published in 1995, proposed three reforms: an increase in the triggers for first registration; fee concessions to promote first registration; and amendments to the rules on indemnity. Of these, only the third was contained in the third and fourth Reports. All three were implemented by the Land Registration Act 1997.

1 *Transfer of Land: Land Registration—First Report of a Joint Working Group on the Implementation of the Law Commission's Third and Fourth Reports on Land Registration* (1995) (Law Com No 235).

1.5 In September 1998 the Joint Working Group produced a considerably more ambitious report entitled 'Land Registration for the Twenty First Century'.[1] Although nominally a report on the implementation of the third and fourth reports it contained very different proposals. This was the first report to contain proposals for the reform of adverse possession in registered land and the first to identify electronic conveyancing as a major reason for reforming the 1925 legislation. Many of the proposals, for example in respect of overriding interests, were the complete opposite of proposals made in the third and fourth reports. For that reason the report was published as a consultation paper.

1 *Land Registration for the Twenty-First Century: A Consultative Document* (1998) (Law Com No 254).

1.6 The proposals were welcomed by the Government who, amongst other things, considered that the electronic conveyancing proposals would simplify house buying and reduce the delays involved in residential conveyancing. By the time the final report of the Joint Working Group[1] was published,[2] (entitled 'Land Registration for the Twenty First Century; A Conveyancing Revolution') the Bill attached to the report had already had its second reading in the House of Lords.[3] The Government, having found space for the Bill in the Parliamentary timetable, were unwilling to miss the opportunity through waiting for the publication of the report.[4]

1   Law Com No 271.
2   On 10 July 2001.
3   On 3 July 2001. See Hansard 626 HL Official report (5th Series) col 776 and in particular the speech of Lord Goodhart at col 790.
4   See the speech of the Baroness Scotland (the Lord Chancellor's Parliamentary Secretary) at 626 HL Official report (5th Series) col 798.

1.7   The Bill proceeded through all stages with a consensus of support from all parties although a number of amendments were tabled from all sides.[1] It passed through its third reading in the Commons on 11 February 2002 and received royal assent on 26 February 2002. Thereafter, a period of time passed for the various Rules and Orders to be drawn up and consulted upon. The LRA 2002 came into force on 13 October 2003.[2] Apart from a few minor amendments of a technical nature, the LRA 2002 is the same as the draft bill set out in Law Com No 271.

1   Perhaps the most contention arose out of the proposal to reduce the length of non-registrable leases from 21 years to seven. The opposition pressed for the length to be 14 years, as had been proposed in the third report. The Government did not give way on this point and it stands as seven years.
2   The Land Registration Act 2002 (Commencement No 4) Order 2003, SI 2003/1725. Certain of the rule making powers and other provisions were brought into force before this date, see the Land Registration Act 2002 (Commencement No 1) Order 2003, SI 2003/935; the Land Registration Act 2002 (Commencement No 2) Order 2003, SI 2003/1028; and the Land Registration Act 2002 (Commencement No 3) Order 2003, SI 2003/1612.

AIMS AND OBJECTIVES OF THE REFORMS

1.8   The reforms are probably the most ambitious undertaken by the Law Commission. Both they and the Land Registry saw the opportunity presented by the Joint Working Group as a means to consider all aspects of the system of land registration and, as the titles of the reports suggest, bring it into the twenty-first century.

1.9   The starting point for the Joint Working Group, and ultimately the fundamental objective of the Bill, was that:

'the register should be a complete and accurate reflection of the state of the title of the land at any given time, so that it is possible to investigate title to land with the absolute minimum of additional enquiries and inspections.'[1]

1   See Law Com No 254, para 1.14; Law Com No 271, para 1.5 and the speech of the Lord Chancellor during the second reading at 626 HL Official report (5th Series) col 777.

1.10 The concept that underlay this objective was that of electronic conveyancing. By the fourth report the Joint Working Group considered that a system of conveyancing conducted in 'dematerialised form' was inevitable.[1] As a result it was imperative that the register that would appear on the conveyancer's computer screen would be as accurate a reflection of title as possible since otherwise it would be necessary to resort to 'paper' enquiries to discover the true position. The desire to introduce an efficient and workable system of electronic conveyancing was the basis for a number of the proposed reforms including, for example, the reduction of the scope of overriding interests.[2] It was also the justification of a number of decisions to make no change, including the area of priorities[3] and of the problem of the 'registration gap'[4] between application and registration, which should be eliminated by an electronic system.

[1]   See Law Com No 271, para 1.4.
[2]   See Law Com No 271, para 1.8.
[3]   See Law Com No 271, para 5.3. The LRA 2002 does set out the rules of priority in the legislation and does alter the priority rules for certain interests, see Chapter 7.
[4]   See Law Com No 271, para 1.7.

1.11 Some of the reforms are difficult to justify purely on the grounds of electronic conveyancing or as part of steps required to achieve the fundamental objective. Whilst some of these are reforms that can be justified as useful amendments to unfortunate oddities[1] this cannot be said of all of them. This is particularly true of the adverse possession reforms[2] where it would certainly have been possible to introduce less radical changes without fundamentally altering the system of acquisition of land by possession. It is apparent, from the depth and breadth of the reforms, that the Law Commission and the Land Registry used the opportunity of the reports and the Bill to consider all aspects of land law affected by land registration and to reform all those areas that were perceived to be in need of it.[3] Underlying these reforms is a belief that registration of land is itself a worthwhile objective, and should be the basis of a reliable and predictable system of conveyancing providing as much protection to the purchasers of land, or interests in land, as possible.

[1]   For example, the replacement of the caution against dealings with a new 'unilateral' notice achieves clear benefits but it is difficult to state that the caution could not have been retained without endangering either electronic conveyancing or the fundamental objective.
[2]   See Chapter 13.
[3]   In addition to the adverse possession reforms see, for example, the reform of the priority of rights of pre-emption (paras 11.6–11.10).

1.12 This belief is reflected in another feature of the LRA 2002—the divergence between the registered and unregistered system. The LRA 2002 makes changes that affect only registered land[1] although in a number of cases the legal principles which were altered applied to both forms of land.[2] This divergence was deliberate, it was stated that 'unregistered land has had its day'.[3] It is clear that the policy decision was that the limitations of the unregistered system should not inhibit the registered system. In addition it was perceived that improving the registered system would encourage the voluntary registration of unregistered land so achieving the objective of all land being registered.[4]

---

[1] Although the alterations to the system of first registration will have also have an impact on unregistered land.
[2] Eg the priority of rights of pre-emption.
[3] See Law Com No 271, para 1.6.
[4] See Law Com No 271, para 2.10.

1.13 Finally the LRA 2002 reflects a number of objectives that were identified by the Joint Working Group in their second report:[1]

- it is a clear and well drafted piece of legislation that sets out the principles and concepts in a straightforward manner. This is in clear contrast to the Land Registration Act 1925 (LRA 1925), which was extremely difficult to follow and whose drafting made the concepts difficult to understand;
- the LRA 2002 contains all the principles of the system of land registration. The mechanics are left to rules and there are very few instances where the rules do anything more than provide the workings of the system;[2]
- the system, whilst involving major changes is designed to 'follow on' from the old and does not require a fundamental overhaul of the existing structures.[3] The changeover involved the Land Registry shutting down for no more than 2½ days.[4]

---

[1] See *Land Registration for the Twenty-First Century, A Consultative Document* (1998) (Law Com No 254), para 1.12. It is difficult to assess whether the final objective, that the reforms took account of resource implications, has been met.
[2] The provisions regarding the provision of information held by the registrar are perhaps one such example, see paras 2.65 et seq.
[3] See, for example, the LRA 2002, s 1: 'There is to continue to be a register of title'.
[4] From midday on 10 October 2003 until Monday 13 October 2003.

THE LEGISLATION

1.14 The LRA 2002 wholly repeals the LRA 1925 (LRA 2002, s 135, Sch 13). It contains a completely new scheme of land registration. In contrast to the LRA 1925 it is a clear and logically rigorous piece of legislation. The overall scheme is to establish, in 12 parts, the fundamental principles of the system of land registration. Detailed schemes, such as those in respect of adverse possession or electronic conveyancing, are left to Schedules. The mechanics of implementing the principles of the Act are left to rules.

THE LAND REGISTRATION RULES 2003

1.15 The Land Registration Rules 2003, SI 2003/1417 (LRR 2003) govern the practical implementation of the LRA 2002. In drafting the Bill the Law Commission were keen to draw a clear line between the LRA 2002 and the LRR 2003 with any major legislative matters being set out in the Act rather than the rules.[1]

---

[1] See Law Com No 254, para 1.12.

1.16 The LRA 2002 contains wide ranging rule making powers. In broad terms the rules can be divided into:
- 'land registration rules' (LRA 2002, s 132(1)).[1] These are the major body of rules and establish and set out much of the practice of the Land Registry in implementing the legislation. They set out extensive prescribed forms in Sch 1. They are supplemented by the Fee Order and Proper Office Order;[2]
- the adjudication rules.[3] These govern the principles and practice of the adjudicator. In fact there are two sets of rules, one governing referrals to the adjudicator by the registrar and the other concerning the principles and practice of the exercise of the adjudicator's jurisdiction;
- transitional orders;[4]
- electronic conveyancing rules and network access agreements. These have yet to be devised.[5]

---

[1] Set out in Appendix 2, except that a list of the Forms in Sch 1 is provided instead of the Forms themselves.

[2] The Land Registration Fee Order 2003, SI 2003/2092 and the Land Registration (Proper Office) Order 2003, SI 2003/2040, both set out in Appendix 2.

[3] Set out in Appendix 2.

[4] The Land Registration Act 2002 (Transitional Provisions) Order 2003, SI 2003/1953; and the Land Registration Act 2002 (Transitional Provisions) (No 2) Order 2003, SI 2003/243; see Appendix 2. Note that some transitional provisions are set out in the LRA 2002 (Sch 12) and the LRR 2003 (rr 218–224), and there is also one in the LRA 2002 (Commencement No 4) Order 2003, SI 2003/1725; see Appendix 2.

[5] See Chapter 3.

1.17 The power to make the rules is exercisable by the Lord Chancellor with the advice and assistance of the Rule Committee (LRA 2002, s 127(1)). The members of this are the Registrar, persons nominated by the Lord Chancellor (one of whom must be a Chancery judge), and persons nominated by interested bodies (LRA 2002, s 127(2)).

THE MAIN CHANGES

1.18 It is hard to overestimate the scale of the reforms introduced by the LRA 2002. It represents a fundamental reform of land law which is at least as, if not more, significant than that brought in by the 1925 legislation and its precursors. Even in those areas that are not changed, the LRA 2002 imposes clear principles, in notable contrast to the old LRA 1925.

1.19 In summary, the most significant changes introduced by the LRA 2002 are:
- provisions for the implementation of entirely paperless conveyancing (electronic conveyancing) (see paras 3.1–3.4);
- an entirely new system of adverse possession with the effect of significantly restricting the possibilities of obtaining registered land by adverse possession (see paras 13.6 et seq);
- the abolition of cautions and inhibitions and the introduction of a system of notices and restrictions for the protection of interests in registered land (see paras 7.20–7.61);
- a reduction of the range of interests that are overriding, including a narrowing in the scope of interests protected by occupation of land (see paras 7.62 et seq);
- extension of registration of leases to all leases of a length of term exceeding seven years (previously only those exceeding 21 years were registrable) (see paras 6.1, 6.2);
- allowing, for the first time, all land belonging to the Crown to be registered (see paras 12.16–12.25);
- a clear statutory scheme of priorities of interests in registered land (see paras 7.17–7.19);
- the abolition of land and charge certificates (see paras 2.57–2.64);
- extension of the information held by the registrar that will be publicly available to leases and charges (see paras 2.65 et seq);
- clarification and reform of the status of certain rights in registered land such as rights of pre-emption, equities by estoppel and mere equities (see Chapter 11);

- a redefining of the principles of rectification of the register, distinguishing between alterations and rectification (see paras 14.3–14.31);
- the introduction of the office of adjudicator and detailed provisions governing the implementation of that jurisdiction (see paras 15.24–15.11).

2 The registrar and the register

THE REGISTRAR

2.1 The registrar is described as the keeper of the land register (Land Registration Act 2002 (LRA 2002), s 1(1)) and the LRA 2002 makes frequent references to acts to be taken by, or applications to be made to, the registrar. The role is filled by the Chief Land Registrar.[1] The Chief Land Registrar has power to delegate any of the functions of the registrar to the staff of the Land Registry (LRA 2002, ss 99(2) and 100(1)). The Land Registry is itself described as being charged with 'the business of registration' under the LRA 2002 (s 99(1) and (2)) and consists of the Chief Land Registrar, who is its head, and the staff appointed by him. In practice these provisions mean that all functions of registration are carried out by the staff of the Land Registry overseen by the Chief Land Registrar.

---

[1] He is appointed by the Lord Chancellor and must hold and vacate his office in accordance with the terms of his appointment. He may at any time resign his office by written notice to the Lord Chancellor and may be removed from office by the Lord Chancellor if he is unable or unfit to discharge the functions of office. The Lord Chancellor has power to pay him such remuneration, pensions, allowances or gratuities as he may determine and may compensate him for a loss of office. He is disqualified from being a member of parliament. See the LRA 2002, s 99(3) and Sch 7, paras 1, 2 and 7. The person who held the position prior to 13 October will continue to do so thereafter, see the Land Registration Act 2002 (Transitional Provisions) Order 2003, SI 2003/1953, art 2.

THE REGISTER

Conclusiveness

2.2 The entry of a person in the register as the proprietor of a legal estate deems that estate to be so vested whether or not the legal estate would be otherwise vested in him (LRA 2002, s 58(1)). This is the central principle underlying the concept of registration—registration is the ultimate source of a person's title and third parties are entitled to rely upon it without investigating the underlying conveyances. It is subject only to the possibility of rectification of the register (see paras 14.3–14.31).

2.3   The deeming provision referred to in para 2.2 above does not apply where requirements, set out in the LRA 2002, Sch 2, for registering registered dispositions are not met (LRA 2002, s 58(2)). These requirements relate to the provision and recording of sufficient information for the disposition to be accurately registered, in particular to make sure that a disposition (such as a lease or easement) which burdens a registered estate is noted against the title to that estate (see, for example, paras 6.20, 7.25–7.27). The exception is designed to ensure that the accuracy of the register cannot be undermined.[1] For example, it is a requirement that a grantee of a lease must be entered in the register as the proprietor of the lease and a notice in respect of the lease must be entered in the register (Sch 2, para 3). If the requirement for registration of a notice were not met, but the lessee were nevertheless deemed to be registered with a leasehold title, it could be possible for the freehold title to be sold without a record of its being subject to a leasehold title existing on the register. If the requirements are met at a date later than the date of registration the deeming provisions will then apply.

---

[1]   Law Com No 271 stated 'But for this exception … the provisions of Schedule 2 would not be registration *requirements* at all', see para 9.5 (their emphasis). Of course, it would be possible for requirements to be enforced without such drastic sanctions, so suggesting that the Sch 2 requirements are fundamental to the accuracy of the register.

2.4   The rule and its exception can produce some interesting anomalies. For example, if a 21-year lease of registered land to John Smith is fraudulently created and then registered in accordance with LRA 2002, Sch 2, para 3, John Smith will be deemed to own a leasehold interest in the land.[1] This is so irrespective of the forgery. However, if the lease had been validly granted, but by an administrative error no notice in respect of the lease had been entered on the freehold title, John Smith would not have been deemed to be the registered proprietor unless and until the defect was corrected.[2] In the first example John Smith would have no right to an interest whereas in the second he would have every entitlement, yet in the first example John Smith is deemed to be the owner and in the second he is not.[3]

---

[1]   Unless and until the register is rectified, see para 14.19.
[2]   See Law Com No 271, para 9.6.
[3]   Although in the second example the transfer would take effect in equity, see para 4.10.

Form and arrangement

2.5   The register may be kept in electronic or paper form, or partly in one form and partly in another (Land Registration Rules 2003, SI 2003/1417 (LRR 2003), r 2). In fact, the current register is fully computerised.

2.6   The register is made up of individual registers of registered estates.[1] The definition of a registered estate includes all (registered) legal estates except registered charges (LRA 2002, s 132). It follows that the vast majority of registered estates are estates in land (that is fee simples and leaseholds) but there are also registered rentcharges, franchises, manors and profits à prendre in gross.[2]

---

[1]   See the LRR 2003, r 2. The registrar has wide powers to amalgamate and/or divide registered estates, see the LRR 2003, r 3.
[2]   See Chapter 12.

2.7   Each individual registered estate is identified by a title number and divided into three parts, a property register, a proprietorship register and a charges register (LRR 2003, rr 4–9):
   •   the property register contains a description of the registered estate with reference to a plan based on the Ordnance Survey Map (the title plan). This part of the register also includes details of rights benefiting the estate, such as easements and covenants. For leases it will include sufficient information for the lease to be identified. It will also include any defect in title recorded by the registrar;[1]
   •   the main function of the proprietorship register is to identify who owns the estate ('the registered proprietor'). It will also include the price paid by that registered proprietor. In addition, this part of the register includes details of the class of title, the address for service of the registered proprietor and restrictions on the ability of the proprietor to dispose of the estate;
   •   the charges register records those interests which are adverse to the registered estate. Most commonly this will be details of the proprietor of any registered charge over the land and the address for service of that proprietor. It will also include details of any leases, charges, easements, restrictive covenants or other interests adverse to the proprietor's title, subsisting at the date of first registration or created subsequently, and any dealings with those interests or matters affecting their priority capable of being noted.

---

[1]   Pursuant to the LRA 2002, s 64, see the LRR 2003, r 125.

Dependent estates

2.8   Dependent estates are estates which subsist for the benefit or detriment of a registered estate and so are registered in relation to the registered estate itself. There are two classes of dependent estates:
- the first consists of estates which exist for the benefit of a registered estate, such as easements and profits à prendre. The entry of a person as the proprietor of such an estate must be made in relation to the registered estate that is benefited (LRA 2002, s 59(1));
- the second class is that of registered charges and sub-charges. The entry of a person as the proprietor of a charge on a registered estate must be made in relation to the estate over which the charge exists. Proprietors of a sub-charge on a registered charge must be made in relation to the registered charge (LRA 2002, s 59(2) and (3)).

Qualities of title

2.9   The proprietorship register will record the class of title held by the registered proprietor. In the case of freehold title this may be absolute, qualified or possessory (see paras 5.10–5.15). In the case of leasehold title, title may be absolute, good leasehold, qualified or possessory (see paras 6.10–6.18).

Defects in title

2.10 Most defects in title will be apparent from the quality of title or from other details recorded on the register. Other defects are specifically overridden by the terms of the LRA 2002.[1] Nevertheless, defects arising from acts or omissions of the registered proprietor whilst registered proprietor will affect the title but may well not be apparent from the register. As a result, the LRA 2002 provides that, where it appears to the registrar that a right to determine a registered estate in land is exercisable, he may enter the fact in the register (LRA 2002, s 64). Thus, the register could record a breach of covenant by a tenant giving rise to a right of re-entry or a failure to pay a rentcharge where the rentcharge contains a right of re-entry in circumstances of non-payment.

---

[1]   For example, the registered proprietor is deemed to be the owner whether or not there were defects or even forgeries in the transfer to him.

2.11 The LRR 2003 place a duty on the registrar to make such an entry where an application for it is made and is supported by evidence sufficient to satisfy the registrar that the right to determine the estate exists and is exercisable (LRR 2003, r 124). At present there is no requirement for a conveyancer to inform the Land Registry of a defect in his client's title. However, Law Com No 271, para 9.35, suggested that network access agreements may require the disclosure of this information (see paras 3.19–3.24). This, ominously, suggests that conveyancers will be required to act as 'whistle blowers' in order to maintain the ideal of a complete register.

2.12 Where there is sufficient evidence to satisfy the registrar that the right to determine the registered estate is not exercisable (for example the arrears of rent are paid or the claim compromised) an application may be made for removal of the entry (LRR 2003, r 125(5) and (6).

Maps and boundaries

2.13 The property register of a registered estate must contain a description of the registered estate. In the case of a registered estate in land, rentcharge, or a registered franchise,[1] the description must refer to a plan based on the Ordnance Survey map and known as the title plan (LRR 2003, r 5(a)).

---

[1] Relating to a defined area of land and which is an adverse right affecting (or capable of affecting) the title to an estate or charge.

2.14 The title plan will provide a good basis of reference for the physical scope and extent of the registered estate. However, as in the previous system, any boundary shown for the purposes of the register does not determine the exact line of the boundary (LRA 2002, s 60(1), (2)). Thus, it is not possible to rely upon the title plan in order to decide upon the line of the boundaries of the registered property.

2.15 It is possible to apply to the registrar for the exact line of the boundary to be determined and fixed (LRR 2003, rr 117–121). The application is made in Form DB. Where the applicant is able to provide sufficient details of the exact line of the boundary as to establish an arguable case and where he is able to identify all the owners of the land adjoining the boundary, the registrar will give notice of the application to all those owners. The owners then have until 12 noon on the twentieth business day after the date of the issue of the notice (or such longer period as the registrar shall decide) to object to the application or to request an extension of time. The application will be completed unless an owner objects to it within the time limit or any extended time limit. It appears (but is not clear)[1] that if an owner does object the matter will be referred to the adjudicator for determination.

---

[1] On one view the application simply fails if an objection is made to it.

2.16 In circumstances involving transfer of part of the registered title, or the grant of a lease over part of the estate and where there is both a common boundary and sufficient information in the disposition to enable the registrar to determine the boundary, the registrar is able to determine the exact line of the boundary without an application (LRR 2003, r 122).

Accretion and diluvion

2.17 When land is conveyed it is conveyed subject to and with the benefit of such subtractions and additions as may take place over the years. So where land is bounded by water it is likely that, over time, the forces of nature will cause changes in the boundary between the land and the water. These gradual additions and subtractions to the land alter the physical extent of the land itself and form part of the title to the land.[1]

---

[1] *See Southern Centre of Theosophy v South Australia* [1982] AC 706, 716.

2.18 The LRA 2002 preserves these principles, so that the delineation of a particular boundary for a registered estate in land will not affect that boundary shifting through either accretion or diluvion (LRA 2002, s 61(1)).

2.19 It is possible for the principles to be expressly excluded in an agreement or transfer of land. Such an agreement is of no effect unless registered (LRA 2002, s 61(2)). An application to register the agreement requires the consent of the proprietor of the registered estate and of any registered charge, although no consent is required from a party to the agreement. When the agreement is registered the registrar must make a note in the property register of the registered estate (LRR 2003, r 123).

Indexes

2.20 The LRA 2002, s 68 requires the registrar to keep an index from which it will be possible to ascertain in relation to any parcel of land whether any registered estate relates to the land, how any registered estate so related is identified for the purposes of the register, and whether the land is affected by any (and if so what) caution against first registration.

2.21 The LRR 2003 require that the index kept under s 68 must comprise (LRR 2003, r 10):
   - an index map from which it is possible to ascertain, in relation to a parcel of land, whether there is a registered estate, charge,

rentcharge or other estate as well as whether there is a caution against first registration or a pending application either for first registration or for a caution against first registration;

- an index of verbal descriptions related to registrations, pending applications and cautions against first registrations in respect of franchises and manors.

2.22 In practice the part of the register most frequently searched is probably the index map. This provides vital information as to whether a piece of land is registered and, if so, who the registered owner of the land is, or of any charges over that land. It is essential for conveyancing in relation to any land not yet registered since it is necessary to know whether any estate in the land is already registered, whether any conflicting interests are recorded on the register, and whether there are any cautions against first registration or pending applications for such cautions. It is also important for the process of first registration, as it enables the registrar to identify estates or interests already registered in relation to the land in question, so that, for example, any existing lease may be noted against the title to the freehold in a case where the latter comes to be first registered after the lease has been first registered.

2.23 The LRR 2003 also require the registrar to keep an index of proprietors' names (LRR 2003, r 11). This will show, for each individual register, the name of the proprietor of the registered estate and the proprietor of any registered charge together with the title number. In order for a person to search this register in respect of the name of a person other than himself,[1] he must satisfy the registrar that he is interested generally in that other person's property. The examples given by the LRR 2003 are searches by a trustee in bankruptcy or a personal representative.

---

[1] No restriction is placed on searches against the name of the person making the search.

The day list

2.24 The registrar is required to keep a record, known as the day list, showing the date and time at which every pending application under the LRA 2002 or the LRR 2003 was made and of every application for an official search with priority (LRR 2003, r 12). As will be seen, the entry of an application on the day list will frequently be determinative of the time on which it was made and so the priority of that application or search in relation to other applications or searches (see para 7.17).

ADDRESSES FOR SERVICE AND SERVICE OF NOTICES

The address for service

2.25   Much of the system of land registration relies upon the service of notice of various matters by the registrar upon persons interested in those matters. For example:

- the proprietor of a caution against first registration is entitled to be given notice of any application for first registration and thereafter to object to the application;[1]
- restrictions may specify persons upon whom notice of a disposition, or a particular kind of disposition, of the land must be made before the disposition can be registered (see paras 7.40 et seq);
- under the new system of adverse possession the registrar must serve notice of an application by an adverse possessor for registration of his title upon the persons listed in Sch 6, para 2, including the proprietor of the estate and of any registered charge on the estate.[2]

Crucial to the working of this system, therefore, is the mechanics of the address for service and of deemed service of such notices.

---

[1]   See LRA 2002, s 16(1) and paras 4.3 et seq.
[2]   See the LRA 2002, Sch 6 and Chapter 13.

2.26   Providing, and maintaining, a current address for service is a central obligation of any proprietor of registered land, or of an interest in that land protected by registration, since this is the means by which notice of any challenge to that estate or interest or any other matter adverse to that interest will be communicated by the registrar. A function of the new adverse possession regime is that it will be particularly important that the registered proprietor and any registered chargee keep their address for service up to date since without this an application for registration of a title acquired by adverse possession might succeed without any objection.[1]

---

[1]   See Law Com No 271, para 14.34 and paras 13.12–13.16. It is possible to argue that the requirement, imposed by a system that was fundamentally 'possession based', of using land and evicting other users or trespassers in order to keep that land has been replaced by a requirement of maintaining a current address for service.

2.27   The following persons are required to give the Registrar an address for service to which all notices and other communications may be sent (LRR 2003, r 198):

- the registered proprietor of a registered estate or charge;

- the registered beneficiary of a unilateral notice;
- a cautioner named in an individual caution register;
- a person whose name or address is set out in a restriction or whose consent or certification is required or upon whom notice is required to be served by the registrar or any other person by a restriction;[1]
- a person entitled to be notified of an application for adverse possession as a person who has satisfied the registrar that he has sufficient interest to be so notified;[2]
- a person who, having received notice of an application for registration by an adverse possessor, serves notice on the registrar, under Sch 6, para 2, of his or her opposition to such a registration;[3]
- a person who objects to an application;[4]
- any person requested to provide such an address in the course of dealing with the registrar in connection with registered land or a caution against first registration.

---

[1] Although this requirement may be satisfied by the service of the address for service within the application for the restriction, see the LRR 2003, rr 198(11) and 92(2)(b).

[2] Under the LRR 2003, r 194.

[3] See para 13.14. In most cases this will be unnecessary since the person will already have received notice of the application through his or her address for service. However, since actually receiving the notice is neither a pre-requisite for the objection nor determinable of the time limit for lodging the objection (see LRR 2003, r 189), it is possible that the registrar will not hold a current address for service for the objector.

[4] See paras 2.55, 15.4–15.8.

2.28 It is possible to give the registrar up to three addresses for service (LRR 2003, r 198(4)). Where the provision of an address for service is required because the person is one of those listed above, one of the addresses must be a postal address (although not necessarily in the UK) (LRR 2003, r 198(3)). The other addresses may be a postal address, a document exchange box number[1] or an electronic address.[2]

---

[1] The document exchange must be one to which delivery can be made on behalf of the Land Registry under arrangements already in existence between the Land Registry and a service provider at the time the box number details are provided (LRR 2003, r 198(7)).

[2] An electronic address means an e-mail address although the registrar also has power to issue a direction to the effect that some other form of electronic address is a suitable form of address for service (LRR 2003, r 198(8) and (9)).

Service of notices

2.29 All notices which the registrar is required to serve may be served by any one or more of the following (see LRR 2003, r 199):

- posting[1] to a postal address (whether inside or outside the United Kingdom) entered in the register as an address for service;[2]
- leaving the notice at a postal address in the United Kingdom entered in the register as an address for service;
- directing the notice to the relevant box number at a document exchange entered in the register as an address for service;
- electronic transmission to the electronic address entered in the register as an address for service;
- fax;
- by posting to, or leaving the notice, at an address which the registrar believes the addressee is likely to receive it or by directing the notice by document exchange to such an address.

---

[1] 'Post' means pre-paid delivery by a postal service which seeks to deliver documents within the United Kingdom no later than the next working day in all or the majority of cases, and to deliver outside the United Kingdom within such a period as is reasonable in all the circumstances (LRR 2003, r 199(5)).

[2] The requirement that the address be one 'entered in the register as an address for service' appears to be different from the requirement (set out above) to provide an address for service to the registrar. Note that addresses provided by persons requested to do so by the registrar in the course of dealing with the registrar in connection with registered land or a caution against first registration (LRR 2003, r 198(2)(h)) are treated as if they were within this definition (LRR 2003, r 199(2)).

2.30 In order for service by fax to be sufficient, the recipient must have informed the registrar in writing that he or she is willing to accept service of the notice by fax and of the fax number to which it should be sent (LRR 2003, r 198(3)). It should be noted that a general statement of willingness to accept service by fax will not suffice—the registrar requires written consent for the particular notice to be sent by fax.

2.31 The fact that the registrar may choose to serve a notice at an address at which the registrar believes the addressee is likely to receive it is something of a peculiarity. It appears to undermine the efficacy of providing the registrar with addresses for service if the registrar is then able to validly serve at a different address provided he has a belief (however misguided) that the addressee will receive it. However, it is probable that this rule will be rarely used and then only in circumstances where it appears to the registrar that the addressee would be unlikely to receive the notice if sent to the addresses provided for service.

2.32 Where more than one address for service has been provided or is entered on the register, the registrar is not required to serve the notice on more than one of these addresses. For this reason if more than one address has been provided to the registrar it is important to ensure that all these addresses are kept up to date.

2.33 The date upon which service is deemed to have taken place depends upon the form of service used (LRR 2003, r 199(4)):

Table 1:

Method of Service	Time of Service
Post to an address in the United Kingdom	The second working day[1] after posting
Leaving at a postal address	The working day after it was left
Post to an address outside the United Kingdom	The seventh working day after posting
Document Exchange	On the second working day after it was left at the registrar's document exchange
Fax	The working day after transmission
Electronic transmission to an electronic address	The second working day after transmission

---

[1] 'Working day' means any day from Monday to Friday (inclusive) which is not Christmas Day, Good Friday or any other day specified or declared by proclamation under the Banking and Financial Dealings Act 1971, s 1 or appointed by the Lord Chancellor.

Content of notices

2.34 The content of any notice will vary according to its nature and purpose. However, every notice given by the registrar must (LRR 2003, r 197(1)):

- fix the time within which the recipient is to take any action required by the notice;
- state what the consequences will be of a failure to take such action as is required by the notice within the time fixed;
- state the manner in which any reply to the notice must be given and the address to which it must be sent.

2.35 Unless otherwise specified by the Rules the time fixed by the notice will be the period ending at 12 noon on the fifteenth business day after the date of issue of the notice (LRR 2003, r 197(2)).

FORMS

2.36 The LRR 2003 are highly prescriptive in their requirements of the use of standard forms. The general rule is that where the LRR 2003 require a form to be used, whether for a disposition, application, objection or any other transaction or communication, that form must be used (LRR 2003, r 206). The LRR 2003 also prescribe the size of the paper and the layout of the information although certain flexibilities are allowed where the form is being produced by computer (LRR 2003, rr 210 and 211). If no form exists the form must be in such form as the registrar may direct or allow, but it must not bear the number of a form in the LRR 2003, Sch 1, and must bear the title number if it relates to a registered title.[1] Wherever a scheduled form is required for a disposition the LRR 2003 also prescribe the forms of execution that should be used.[2]

---

[1]   LRR 2003, r 212. Note that where no form exists for an application the application must be in Form AP1 (r 13).

[2]   LRR 2003, r 206(3) and Sch 9.

2.37 Using the right form could be very important. Where there is a prescribed form for a disposition of registered land, the disposition will not be effective if the prescribed form is not used,[1] and where an application for registration is in the wrong form it could be rejected (LRR 2003, r 16(3)). In either case priority could be lost. The Sch 1 forms are not printed in Appendix 2, because in the format of this work they would be too small to be useful, but a list of them is provided in place of Sch 1. They can be obtained from law stationers or downloaded from the Land Registry's website at www.landregistry.gov.uk/publications/.

---

[1]   LRA 2002, s 25(1). LRR 2003, r 58 prescribes compulsory forms for transfers. The form of charge in the LRR 2003, Sch 1 is permissive rather than compulsory (LRR 2003, r 103), and there is no prescribed form for leases, as yet.

2.38 Where an application should be accompanied by a scheduled form and a person wishes to make an application relying instead upon some other document, that person may make a request to the registrar, either at the time of the application or before, that he be permitted to rely upon the alternative document (LRR 2003, r 209(1), (2)). In order to succeed in such a request he must provide evidence sufficient to satisfy the registrar that it is not possible for him to obtain and lodge the relevant scheduled form at the Land Registry, or it is only possible to do so at unreasonable expense (LRR 2003, r 209(1)(b) and (3)).

2.39   Since the prescribed forms are widely available, both from the District Land Registries and freely on the internet, it is difficult to imagine how it would be possible to provide evidence in support of an application to use an alternative to a prescribed form. Even then the request will only be granted if the registrar is satisfied that neither the rights of any person, nor the keeping of the register, are likely to be materially prejudiced by allowing the alternative document to be relied upon instead of the relevant scheduled form and the registrar may attach conditions to the grant of the request (LRR 2003, r 209(4), (5)). It is likely that, no matter how much trouble or expense might be required to obtain and lodge the proper form, it would involve less trouble and expense than making the application to use the alternative form.

2.40   The rationale behind this highly prescriptive regime is almost certainly that of electronic conveyancing. In a world where all documents will be made and submitted by computer, it will simply not be feasible to allow for the proliferation of different forms of document for any given type of transaction. As a result, it is necessary to begin the process of ensuring that all documents, whether in paper form or electronic, are set out in the manner required by the registry.[1]

---

[1]   *The LRR 2003—A Land Registry Consultation* proposed a standard form of lease, which was not proceeded with in the LRR 2003 because of adverse reactions from consultees, but the registry still hope to provide one in the reasonably near future.

2.41   For the present all applications and other requests must be delivered by post, document exchange or personal delivery. However, in the future, the registrar will be able to make provision for dealing with such matters electronically. This will be done by publishing notice of the arrangements (LRR 2003, Sch 2). This is separate from the provisions in the LRA 2002, s 93 which will require certain registered dispositions to be carried out electronically (see paras 3.56–3.58).

2.42   Although the new forms became the required forms on 13 October 2003, the transitional provisions allowed a three month 'grace period' during which the old forms might be submitted: Land Registration Act 2002 (Transitional Provisions) Order 2003, SI 2003/1953 (set out in Appendix 2), art 26(1)(a). Now that that period has expired, the old forms will only be allowed if required by law or required under the terms of a valid contract entered into before 13 October 2003 (art 26(1)(b)). Even where the use of an old form is still permitted, its use may be subject to restrictions or additional requirements set out in the Schedule to SI 2003/1953.

APPLICATIONS

Forms

2.43   There are many types of applications that can be made. Some have specific prescribed forms, for example, applications for the first registration of a legal estate, for the registration of an agreed notice, for the entry or withdrawal of a unilateral notice, and to upgrade the title of land.[1] For applications with no specific prescribed form, including registration of a transfer of registered land, the application must be made in form AP1 ('Application to change the register'),[2] subject to certain exceptions.[3]

---

[1] See LRR 2003, Sch 1, Forms FR1, AN1, UN1, UN2, and UT1 respectively.
[2] LRR 2003, r 13(1).
[3] See LRR 2003, r 13(2).

Timing and priority

2.44   An entry in, removal of an entry from, or alteration of the register pursuant to an application under the LRA 2002 has effect from the time of the making of the application (LRR 2003, r 20). Therefore, on occasions it will be important to determine the time on which an application is made. This will be particularly so where two applications are made in respect of the same land and those applications are in conflict.

2.45   An application is taken to be made at the earlier of:

(a) the time of day on which it is entered on the day list; or

(b) (i) midnight on the day of receipt[1] if received before 12 noon,

(ii) midnight on the day following the day of receipt if the application was received at or after 12 noon on that day.

If the application is not received on a business day (that is a day when the Land Registry is open to the public) it is taken to be made at the earlier of: the time of a business day that notice of it is entered on the day list, or midnight marking the end of the next business day after the day it was received. In other words if the application is received on a Sunday it will be deemed to have been made at the time on Monday that the Registry employee enters it on the day list or, if no such entry is made on the Monday, at Midnight on Monday (LRR 2003, r 15).

---

[1] See the LRR 2003, r 15(3) and paras 2.49 and 2.50 as to when an application is received.

2.46 Where two or more applications related to one registered title are treated as having been made at the same time, the order in which they will rank in priority is determined as follows (LRR 2003, r 55):

- if the two applications are made by the same applicant the applicant may specify the priority;
- if made by different applicants they will rank in such order as the applicants may specify that they have agreed;
- if the applicants have not agreed the registrar will notify them that their applications are regarded as having been delivered at the same time and request them to, within a specified time, agree the order of priority. The registrar will act upon such agreement;
- if the applicants do not agree the registrar will propose the order of priority and will serve notice on the applicants of his proposal. The applicants have no power to appeal this decision but one applicant may object to the other's application in which case the objection will be determined either by the registrar (if agreement can be reached) or by the Adjudicator;[1]
- if one transaction is dependent upon the other, the registrar will assume that the applicants have specified their agreement that the applications shall have priority, so as to give effect to the sequence of the documents effecting the transfer.

---

[1] See Chapter 15.

Outline applications

2.47 Prior to making a formal application using the prescribed form it is possible for an applicant to make an informal 'outline application'.[1] The purpose of such an application is to provide a period of priority during which time a detailed formal application can be made. Thus, if a conveyancer wishes to apply to register a unilateral notice in order to protect an unregistered interest he may first make an outline application by telephone. Provided the full application is lodged at the proper office (see para 2.49) before 12 noon of the fourth day[2] following the telephone call, the application will be treated as having been made at the date and time of the telephone call.[3] As a result, provided the application is granted (and that the notice is not later removed), any disposition that took place between the telephone call and the lodging of the full application will nevertheless be subject to the interest protected by the unilateral notice.[4]

---

[1] This does not apply to applications which can be protected by an official search with priority, an application for the first registration of land, an application for a caution against first registration, an application dealing with part only of land in a registered title or an application under the LRR 2003, Pt 13 (for information from the register or to designate documents as

exempt information documents), see the LRR 2003, r 54. It will also not apply where the right, interest or matter which is the subject of the application does not exist at the time of the delivery of the application.

2   Quoting the official reference number of the outline application and including the relevant fee.

3   This is the effect of the LRR 2003, r 54(2), which states that any application may be made by outline application if it satisfies the conditions there set out and r 54(6) which states that an outline application will be cancelled unless the form, fee and documentation are filed within the 'reserved period' (defined in r 54(9)). If the outline application is cancelled the formal application will be treated as an application made in its own right.

4   An entry in, removal of an entry from, or alteration of the register pursuant to an application under the LRA 2002 has effect from the time of the making of the application, see the LRR 2003, r 20.

2.48   An outline application cannot be used for an application that could be protected by an official search, (see paras 7.82 et seq) nor for applications for first registration, cautions against first registration,[1] dealing with part only of land in a registered title or for information from the register (LRR 2003, r 54(2)(a)). In addition the interest must exist at the time the application is made (LRA 2003, r 54(2)(b)). The outline application must contain the particulars of the title number affected, the name or names of the proprietor or applicant for first registration, the nature of the application, the name of the applicant and the name and address of the person or firm lodging the application (LRA 2003, r 54(4)).[2]

1   Or any other application made in respect of the cautions register.

2   Where a notice under the LRR 2003, Sch 2 (regarding alternative means of making the application) exists the application must also contain such particulars as are required by the notice.

Proper office

2.49   All applications must be delivered to the 'designated proper office' (LRR 2003, r 15(3)(a)). This is a reference to the power of the Lord Chancellor to designate particular offices of the Land Registry as the proper office for the receipt of applications or a specified description of applications (LRA 2002, s 100(3)). This power has been exercised so as to designate each District Land Registry as the proper office in relation to land in specified local authority areas.[1]

1   The Land Registration (Proper Office) Order 2003, SI 2003/2040, set out in Appendix 2. Most registries are responsible for the area in their vicinity or surrounding them (for example the Tunbridge Wells Office is responsible for Kent and Midway). However, this is not the case for all registries (for example, the Swansea Office is responsible for Barnet, Ealing, Enfield, Harringey, Hillingdon and Hounslow).

2.50   It is important to comply with the requirement of sending an application to the proper office, because an application is only made when it has been delivered to the proper office, and has priority over other applications by reference to the time when that happens (LRR 2003, r 15(3)(a)). The two exceptions to the requirement are where the registrar has entered into a written arrangement as to the delivery of an application with the applicant or the applicant's conveyancer, or under the provisions of any notice given under the electronic conveyancing provisions (r 15(3)(b) and (c)).

Accompanying documents

2.51 Some rules, and some forms, require documents or other evidence to be lodged with the application. Where it appears to the applicant that the document or other evidence is unnecessary, or can be achieved by lodging other documents or evidence, the applicant may request the registrar to be relieved of the requirement (LRR 2003, r 215). Where the Rule requires the document to be an original it is, in general, possible to lodge a certified copy or office copy of the document in place of the original,[1] although the registrar may decide to require the applicant to lodge the original (LRR 2003, r 214(3)). The registrar may retain documents (or copies of them) which accompanied an application (LRR 2003, r 203). There is public access to such documents: see paras 2.66 et seq.

---

[1] This does not apply to applications for first registration, documents that are themselves registrable dispositions, or where the original is required by a standard form, see LRR 2003, r 214(2).

2.52 Where a document lodged with the Land Registry deals with part of the land in a registered title it must have attached to it a plan clearly identifying the land dealt with (LRR 2003, r 213). Thus, for example, an application for the registration of a disposition of part of a registered title must have a plan identifying which part of the land is being disposed of. If, however, the land dealt with is clearly identified on the title plan it is possible to refer to the land by reference to the title plan (LRR 2003, r 213(4)). Similarly, if a disposition contains a sufficient plan the application accompanying the disposition need not contain a separate plan (LRR 2003, r 213(5)). Where the document is a disposition or application, the plan must be signed by the disponor or applicant (LRR 2003, r 213(2), (3)).

Requisitions

2.53 Where an application is substantially defective the registrar may simply cancel it. Rather than doing so the registrar may choose to raise such requisitions as he considers necessary and specify a period (of not less than 20 business days) for those requisitions to be complied with. If the requisitions are not complied with within the time period, the registrar may either cancel the application, or extend the time period. In the event that the answers to the requisitions show that the application is substantially defective the registrar will cancel it (LRR 2003, r 16). However, if the requisitions are complied with and show that the application is in order, the registrar will proceed with the application.

2.54   If at any time the registrar considers that the production of any further documents or evidence, or the giving of any notice is necessary or desirable, he may refuse to complete or proceed with an application until such documents, evidence or notices have been supplied or given (LRR 2003, r 17).

Objections

2.55   Any person may object to an application to the registrar (LRA 2002, s 73(1)).[1] The objection is made by way of a written statement signed by the objector or his conveyancer stating the grounds of the objection and the full name and address of the objector (LRR 2003, r 19(1)).[2] Once made the registrar must, unless satisfied that the objection is groundless, give notice of the objection to the applicant and may not determine the application until the objection has been disposed of (LRA 2002, s 73(5), (6)). If the objection cannot be disposed of by agreement the registrar must refer it to the adjudicator (LRA 2002, s 73(7)).[3]

---

[1]   There are two exceptions. First, the only person who may object to an application to cancel a caution against first registration is the person who lodged the caution. Second, the only person who may object to an application to cancel a unilateral notice is the person shown in the register as the beneficiary of the notice to which the application relates. See s 73(1) and (2).
[2]   The definition of conveyancer includes a solicitor, thus a solicitor will be able to make an objection on behalf of an individual notwithstanding that he is not involved in conveyancing.
[3]   See Chapter 15.

2.56   An objection to an application must not be made without reasonable cause. Where an objection is made without reasonable cause the objector will be liable for a breach of statutory duty to any person who suffers damages as a consequence of the breach (LRA 2002, s 77).[1]

---

[1]   See para 15.77.

LAND AND CHARGE CERTIFICATES

2.57   A feature of the 1925 system was the use of land and charge certificates. The certificate was, essentially, a certificate of the registered title. To a significant extent it took the place of a proprietor's title deeds as proof of entitlement to the land or charge and as evidence of the title. In order for any significant dealings with the land or charge to take place the proprietor was (with exceptions) required to lodge the certificate—thereby indicating his consent to the dealing.

2.58   In practice the certificates became less significant because:

- whilst there was any registered charge outstanding over the land the proprietor would be required to lodge the certificate at the Registry. In practice the Registry would not create a certificate for land registered subject to a charge unless and until that land was free from charges;[1]
- there were circumstances where dealings with the land could occur without the production of the certificate (although the proprietor's consent might be required). As a result the land certificate could not be relied upon as a true reflection of the title held by the proprietor;
- the abolition of the creation of informal mortgages by deposit of title deeds[2] reduced the importance of the certificate as a means of security;
- charge certificates were increasingly retained, by arrangement, at the Registry so in many cases the charge certificate was never seen by lender or borrower;
- the usefulness of the charge certificate was further reduced by the introduction of a scheme allowing for charges to be discharged electronically.

---

[1]   See Law Com No 271, para 9.85
[2]   Law of Property (Miscellaneous Provisions) Act 1989, s 2 and *United Bank of Kuwait v Sahib* [1997] Ch 107.

2.59   Furthermore, the use of paper documents as certificates of title and ownership would not accord with the move to an electronic system which underlay the whole of the new scheme.

2.60   The Law Commission proposed abolishing charge certificates and the LRA 2002 contains no reference to them.

2.61   In respect of land certificates the Law Commission proposed a form of document more akin to an 'indicium of title', certifying that a registration had taken place and that a named person was the registered proprietor. The LRA 2002 contains a power for the rules to make provision about when a certificate of title to a legal estate may be issued, the form and content of such a certificate, and when such a certificate must be produced or surrendered to the registrar (LRA 2002, Sch 10, para 4). In fact this power has not been not exercised and land certificates will no longer be issued.

2.62   For the time being both land and charge certificates issued under the old regime will continue to exist. From 13 October 2003 they ceased to have any legal status. There is no requirement for the certificates to be lodged. If one has been lodged this will have no legal effect and the registrar will destroy it.[1]

---

[1]   See Land Registration Act 2002 (Transitional Provisions) Order 2003, SI 2003/1953, art 24 (set out in Appendix 2) and Land Registry *Practice Bulletin 2* (March 2003).

2.63   The Registry have decided that in place of a land or charge certificate they will on completion of the registration of a disposition or other change to the register, issue an official copy of the title, an official copy of the title plan where the plan has been created or amended, and a 'Title Information Document' which explains why the official copy has been issued and how to obtain further copies.[1] It will provide a buyer with confirmation that he has been registered as proprietor, a record of the title details, which will, for example, be useful to the proprietor's personal representatives or receiver in the event of his death or mental incapacity, and guidance as to how to obtain more information about the individual register.

---

[1]   See Land Registry *Practice Bulletin 2* (March 2003) para 3.

2.64   In addition it is possible to apply for an official copy of the register, which is then admissible in evidence to the same extent as the original register (LRA 2002, s 67; LRR 2003, rr 134 and 135). Any person who relies upon a mistake in an official copy is not liable for loss suffered by reason of the mistake (LRA 2002, s 67(2)). Proprietors of registered estates will therefore demonstrate their ownership of the land by producing an official copy of the register.

ACCESS TO THE REGISTER

Open register

2.65   Historically, access to the register has been restricted. Prior to 3 December 1990 the only person who could inspect the register of a registered title was the registered proprietor or an authorised person, although an index and a parcels index could be searched by anyone. On 3 December 1990 the Land Registration Act 1988 substituting a new s 112 of the Land Registration Act 1925, and the Land Registration (Open Register) Rules 1990 (SI 1990/1362),[1] came into force. These allowed any person to inspect the register itself and any documents referred to in the register which were in the custody of the registrar apart from leases or charges and copies of leases or charges.[2] There was no right to inspect documents in the custody of the registrar, but not referred to in the register, although the registrar had a discretion to allow the inspection and copying of such documents.

---

[1] Revoked and replaced by Land Registration (Open Register) Rules 1991 (SI 1992/122) with effect from 30 March 1992.

[2] The Law Commission described s 112 as 'one of the most important provisions' and stated that it was this provision that was the springboard for electronic conveyancing and that the provision had changed the perception of the register itself from that of a private matter to a public information source. See Law Com No 271, para 9.37.

2.66 The LRA 2002, s 66 continues the provisions of the substituted LRA 1925, s 112 in allowing the inspection and copying of the register of title by any person. It then goes considerably further by giving a right to the inspection or copying of:

- any documents kept by the registrar which are referred to in the register of title, including leases and charges and copies of them;
- any other document kept by the registrar which relates to an application to him;
- the register of cautions against first registration.

2.67 There is a considerable difference between permitting the inspection and copying of the register of title and the inspection and copying of documents kept by the registrar. The register itself is widely regarded as a public resource and the ability to access it without the permission of the registered proprietor is essential if electronic conveyancing is to function properly. However, the documents supplied to the registrar are documents that record the full details of the transaction that led to the registration or application itself. Such documents will include considerably more information than is needed to register the disposition, including information that has no relevance to a register of title.

2.68 The right set out in the LRA 2002, s 66 is subject to the LRR 2003. In *The LRR 2003—A Land Registry Consultation* the Land Registry proposed allowing exemption from public access only in respect of information of which the disclosure would, or would be likely to, prejudice a person's commercial interests. A number of concerns were raised about the narrowness of this, and in the LRR 2003 the exemption was widened to include information of which disclosure will or is likely to cause substantial unwarranted distress or damage to an individual, as well as commercially sensitive information as previously proposed. Nevertheless, as discussed further in para 2.78

below, there is much information of a solely personal or private
nature which the definition does not seem to exempt.[1]

---

[1]   Such as the value of the charge on a person's property at the date of its creation. There is a
question whether Article 8 (or Article 1 of the First Protocol) of the European Convention for the
Protection of Human Rights and Fundamental Freedoms is infringed by these provisions.

Inspecting the register and documents

'Unofficial' copies

2.69   It is possible to simply attend at the registry and to inspect and copy
both the register and the documents held by the registrar set out
above. In order to do so an application must be made in Form PI and
the application must take place at the 'proper office' in relation to the
land in question.[1]

---

[1]   See paras 2.49, 2.50 above for this, and the Land Registration (Proper Office) Order 2003,
SI 2003/2040 (set out in Appendix 2).

Official copies

2.70   Alternatively an official copy of the register or the documents held by
the registrar set out above can be obtained by application in paper, in
Form OC1 (for copies of the register) or OC2 (for copies of
documents) delivered to the 'proper office'.[1]

---

[1]   See paras 2.49, 2.50 above for this, and the Land Registration (Proper Office) Order 2003,
SI 2003/2040 (set out in Appendix 2).

2.71   The importance of official copies is that a person using an official
copy is entitled to rely upon that copy. Where there is a mistake in the
official copy the person who relied upon the official copy is not liable
for loss suffered by another by reason of the mistake (LRA 2002,
s 67(2)) and any person who does suffer loss is entitled to an
indemnity (LRA 2002, Sch 8, para 1). The official copy is admissible
in evidence to the same extent as the original (LRA 2002, s 67(1)).

Electronic inspection/copies

2.72   In the future it will be possible to inspect the register electronically
from a remote terminal. Rules and limitations governing this access
will be set down in a notice issued under the LRR 2003, Sch 2.

Historical information

2.73 The register of title and the documents held by the registrar will provide only limited historical information in respect of the title. On occasions it is necessary to discover the historical position of a piece of land. It is possible to apply to the registrar for the last edition of the register for a specified day or every edition for a specified day of a specified registered title kept by the registrar in electronic form (LRR 2003, r 144). If the registrar is keeping the registered title as it existed at the date specified in the application in electronic form he must issue the copy applied for or, if part only is held, a copy of that part (LRR 2003, r 144(3)).

2.74 This ability, whilst apparently wide, is subject to significant limitations. First, the register has only recently been held in electronic form. Second, there is no requirement for the registrar to keep any historical information whatsoever, so it is entirely possible that the record will not exist.

Conclusiveness of filed copies

2.75 On occasions the registrar will have relied upon an abstract, copy or extract from a document but no longer retains (or never had) the original. In those circumstances it is important that the documents held by the registrar are conclusive and that the parties to the disposition cannot raise matters apparent from the original documents but not in the documents held by the registrar. The LRA 2002, s 120 provides therefore, that where:
- a disposition relates to land to which a registered estate relates; and
- an entry in the register relating to the registered estate refers to a document kept by the registrar which is not an original

as between the parties to the disposition, the document kept by the registrar is taken to be correct and to contain all the material parts of the original documents, no party to the disposition may require production of the original document and no party to the disposition is to be affected by any provision of the original document which is not contained in the document kept by the registrar. This applies not only to registered dispositions but to other dispositions related to registered land (eg the disposition of an interest which is then protected by a notice).

Exempt information

2.76 The exemption applies to an 'exempt information document' which, it is claimed, contains 'prejudicial information' (LRR 2003, r 136(1)).

It is necessary to apply to the registrar for a document to be designated as an exempt information document (see paras 2.79, 2.80). The application can only be made in respect of documents which are or will be referred to on the register, or which relate to an application and which are or will be kept by the registrar (LRR 2003, r 136(7)). Public access cannot be withheld in relation to information which is required to appear on the register, such as the name of the proprietor, the land, the date of and parties to a lease, adverse interests, or the price paid on the most recent disposition (rr 5–9). There is no utility in seeking to obtain exemption for such information.

2.77   Prejudicial information is defined (LRR 2003, r 131) as:
- information that relates to an individual who is the applicant for exempt information status and if disclosed to other persons (whether to the public generally or specific persons) would, or would be likely to, cause substantial unwarranted damage or substantial unwarranted distress to the applicant or another; or
- information that if disclosed to other persons (whether to the public generally or specific persons) would, or would be likely to, prejudice the commercial interests of the applicant for exempt information status. The wording of this category is derived from the Freedom of Information Act 2000.[1]

---

[1]   See Freedom of Information Act 2000 s 43(2).

2.78   The definition may extend to a number of documents, and will include those documents that are commercially sensitive. Nevertheless, there are substantial restrictions contained within the definition.
- First, the information must relate to *the applicant*. It does not include cases where the applicant wishes to prevent distress to another individual, such as a spouse, child or other relative of his, which might be caused by information about that other individual being disclosed (and where that individual may not be aware of the information or may be unable to apply).
- Second, the requirement of 'substantial unwarranted damage or substantial unwarranted distress' appears to rule out the exclusion of information on the pure basis of privacy—a person may not wish details of their financial life to be made widely available whilst at the same time if this were to happen the result might not be substantial damage or distress.

2.79   The application for designation of a document as an exempt information document is made in form EX1 and EX1A. It must be accompanied by a copy of the relevant document which excludes the prejudicial information and which is certified to be a true copy of the relevant document from which the prejudicial information has been excluded (r 136(2)). See Land Registry Practice Guide 57 *Exempting documents from the general right to inspect and copy.*

2.80 If the registrar is satisfied that the application is in order and that it is not groundless he must designate the document as an exempt information document unless he considers that doing so could adversely affect the keeping of the Register (LRR 2003, r 136(4)). At this stage there is no burden on the applicant to establish that the information is actually prejudicial information, other than the minimal requirement that the application not be groundless.

2.81 Once a document is designated as an exempt information document the general right of inspection does not apply, and the only document that may be inspected is the document with the exempt parts edited out which was provided with the application for exemption (LRR 2003, r 133).

2.82 The status may be removed in two ways. First, the person who obtained the designation may apply for its removal. Second, if another person successfully applies for an official copy of the document, on the basis that none of the information contained within the document is prejudicial information, the status will be removed.[1] Even if the status is not removed, it is possible for other persons to apply successfully for disclosure of it to them in full, as described below.

---

[1]   See the LRR 2003, rr 138 and 137(5) and below.

2.83 Any person may apply for an official copy of an exempt information document, using Form EX2 (LRR 2003, r 137(2)). This requires him to say why the available edited document is not sufficient for his purposes, and either why he considers the omitted information is not prejudicial information, or why he considers the public interest in disclosure is outweighed by the public interest in non-disclosure. It is for the registrar to decide whether to provide the copy. The registrar must give notice of the application to the person who obtained the exemption in the first place unless satisfied that this is unnecessary or impractical (r 137(3)). A copy is provided if the registrar decides that:
   •   none of the information excluded from the edited information document is prejudicial information; or
   •   although some of the information excluded is prejudicial information, the public interest in providing an official copy of the exempt information document to the applicant outweighs the public interest in not doing so (r 137(4)).[1]

If a copy of the document is provided following a decision by the registrar that none of the information is prejudicial information, the exempt information document designation will be removed (r 137(5)).

---

[1]   The wording of the second alternative derives from Freedom of Information Act 2000, s 2(1)(b) and (2)(b).

2.84   In the event of an objection being made to an application for disclosure of exempt information, the procedure for dealing with objections to applications set out in LRA 2002, s 73 would seem to apply. This procedure is expressed to be mandatory in relation to any objection to any application, subject to certain exceptions not relevant to exempt information, and the s 73 procedure requires a reference to the adjudicator unless the objection is groundless or can be resolved by agreement (s 73(7)).[1] This would apparently mean that in the event of an objection the adjudicator would make the decision as to whether the information is prejudicial, or whether there is a public interest in providing an official copy of it. However, we understand that the land registry take the view that the decision on disclosure of exempt information under LRR 2003, r 137(4) is exclusively a matter for the decision of the registrar, and cannot be referred to the adjudicator, presumably because r 137(4) states that the decision is that of the registrar.[2] There is a difficult question here as to whether the general provisions of LRA 2002, s 73 are displaced by LRR 2003, r 137(4) in this way.

---

[1]   For the objection and adjudication procedures see paras 15.4–15.8, 15.27 et seq.
[2]   *The LRR 2003—A Land Registry Consultation,* Chapter 9, paras 23, 24, and 30, make it clear that the rules on exempt information, as they appeared in draft in the Consultation, were intended to confer the decision-making power over these matters on the registrar to the exclusion of the adjudicator. Although the draft rules concerning exempt information in the Consultation were amended in various ways to produce the LRR 2003, none of the amendments relate to the procedure in the event of an objection to disclosure of it.

2.85   Overall, the procedure appears to be designed so that there is a relatively summary system of designating documents as being exempt information documents. This designation is only seriously challenged if a person applies to see the document. The key to the success of the system is likely to be the number of applications made for designation and the manner in which the definition of 'prejudicial information' is treated by the registrar (or the adjudicator if he has jurisdiction). If there are too many applications, or if the definition is treated as being too confined, it may be that the system will fail to cope and will lose the faith of conveyancers and the public. A concern is that commercial conveyancers will think it prudent to place the more sensitive information related to a transaction into a separate document or documents from that used to carry out the conveyancing. There is also a question whether Article 8 (or Article 1 of the First Protocol) of the European Convention for the Protection of Human Rights and Fundamental Freedoms is infringed by these provisions. For further discussion of these rules in relation to leases see paras 6.66 et seq.

Transitional provisions

2.86   For some considerable time the registrar will continue to hold documents provided under the old regime. The LRR 2003 provide that for the period of two years a person may only inspect and make copies of such documents[1] at the registrar's discretion (LRR 2003, r 139). This reflects the old rule under the LRA 1925, s 112.[2] After the expiry of this period all documents, whenever acquired by the registrar, will be open to inspection or copying unless classified as exempt information documents. In other words, conveyancers have two years in which to review their files and decide which documents should be so classified.

[1]   That is, documents kept by the registrar before the commencement date, or which relate to an application made before the commencement date, see LRR 2003, r 131.
[2]   Although there may be a legitimate fear that the registrar will exercise his discretion more generously in circumstances where the rest of the register and the related documents are open to inspection

Criminal proceedings, insolvency and tax liability

2.87   Certain persons, listed in the LRR 2003, Sch 5, and including senior police officers, DTI and Inland Revenue inspectors, trustees in bankruptcy and liquidators, may apply to inspect or obtain official copies of the original of any exempt commercial information document and of any document protected by the transitional provisions described above (LRR 2003, r 140).

3 E-Conveyancing

OVERVIEW

3.1 Electronic Conveyancing was seen by the Law Commission as being inevitable.[1] It is not only at the heart of many of the changes[2] brought about by the Land Registration Act 2002 (LRA 2002) but is also the justification for decisions to make no change.[3] Despite this, the exact nature of how such a system would work, along with the actual mechanics of the process, were only sketched out in the most limited manner. The LRA 2002 itself, as was intended, sets out only the most basic skeleton for an electronic system around which it will be necessary to develop a complex and largely new system of conveyancing.

[1]   See Law Com No 271), paras 1.2 and 1.4.
[2]   Eg the reduction of overriding interests, see Law Com No 271, para 1.8.
[3]   Eg priorities, see Law Com No 271, para 5.3.

3.2 The precise details of the system as it will be remain unknown. However, the Land Registry have embarked on a comprehensive exercise of devising a new system, consulting on that system[1] and educating conveyancing professionals on it.[2] This means that it is possible to predict, with some detail and with some confidence, both the nature and the mechanics of the scheme as it will operate.

[1]   E-Conveyancing; A Land Registry Consultation, May 2002 (referred to as 'E-Conveyancing').
[2]   A model has been created and will be demonstrated nationally.

3.3 The main features of the new electronic system of land registration will be:
- the conveyancing professionals will have a secure computer link direct to the Land Registry network;
- such a computer link will allow the professional to search the register. More ambitiously it is intended that the link will eventually form a 'one stop shop' allowing the professional to discover all relevant information about a property (eg including local authority searches) within a single search using the computer terminal;

- the conveyancer will have the ability, through the computer link, to alter the register. Thus on the completion of the sale of a property, the register will be altered to reflect the sale with no further intervention from Land Registry staff. It is central to the scheme that this will mean that sale and transfer of title will eventually be simultaneous and the registration gap will be eliminated;[1]
- in order to avoid the likelihood that registrations taking effect in the above manner would cause numerous errors in the register[2] the system will involve the Registry at a much earlier stage with a process whereby the information and documentation needed for the sale will be identified and built up prior to the registration itself. At the initial stages the Registry computer system will check the draft contract and ensure that the details provided are correct with requisitions raised in respect of inaccuracies. The contract will then be 'validated' by the system and a notional register created to show what the register will look like when sale is completed;
- the involvement of the Registry at this early stage will allow for a process of 'chain management' where transactions are linked. It will be possible for any interested party in the chain to deduce the stage at which each link in the chain is and from there to identify the causes of the delay. It is hoped that this will lead to a faster conveyancing process;
- at completion there will not only be the automatic transfer of title but also an automatic transfer of funds for that purchase and immediate payment of stamp duty and Land Registry fees.

---

[1] See the Law Com No 254, para 7.29; Law Com No 271, para 1.8; and E-Conveyancing, paras 3.4 and 3.5.
[2] At present around 50% of applications contain errors that result in the Land Registry raising requisitions (E-Conveyancing, para 3.4).

3.4 What is intended is a system of conveyancing that will involve all participants being linked and guided by a computer system and that will eventually lead to all the final steps of the process occurring automatically. Although the underlying mechanics of the system will inevitably be complex and involve some novel challenges for the professionals involved it can be seen that the process has the potential to be considerably simpler and operate significantly more smoothly than the present one.

IN CONTEXT

E-Commerce

3.5   The concept of e-conveyancing was not created in a vacuum. As computer technology and security has developed and business has become increasingly multinational, various individuals and organisations have begun to conduct commerce electronically. Most of these systems are based upon the internet and e-mail forms of communication. It is now rare for an office not to have such systems available to them and many rely upon them for internal and external communication and as a means to contact and serve their customers. It is common for consumer goods and services to be purchased over the internet, often with no or very little paper documentation being provided at any stage in the transaction.

3.6   What is probably less common is for larger value and more important contracts to be concluded and/or signed in a purely electronic manner. It remains the case that a final formal contract will normally be concluded on paper even if the draft has been developed and discussed purely 'electronically'. The reasons for this are probably both practical and legal. It remains the case that paper documents with a signature in ink are regarded (whether accurately or not) as a necessary formality to bind a person. This necessity is also reflected in a number of statutory requirements.[1] Nevertheless, within specific fields, electronic systems for trading securities on the stock exchange (CREST) and for trading gilt-edged securities have existed for some considerable period of time.

---

[1]   See the Law of Property Miscellaneous Provisions Act 1989, s 2 and the Law of Property Act 1925, s 53(1)(c) although see paras 3.11–3.13 below.

3.7   There have, however, been a number of steps taken to change both the perception and the reality. A European Directive[1] requires member states to ensure that their legal systems allow contracts to be concluded electronically. The UK has implemented this in the Electronic Communications Act 2000. Section 7 provides that an electronic signature and its certification shall be admissible in evidence. Section 8 includes wide powers to modify legislation in order to remove restrictions upon the use of electronic communication or storage.[2] In addition the Act contains numerous provisions for the regulation and approval of the authorities which will ensure that the system is secure and reliable. In this way it is hoped that industry and commerce will develop sufficient confidence to conduct and conclude important negotiations electronically.

¹   Council Directive (EC) 1999/93, OJ L13, 19.01.2000, p 12.
²   The first draft order under the Electronic Communications Act 2000 is discussed below, see para 3.11.

E-Conveyancing

3.8   At the same time, within the field of conveyancing itself there have been a number of steps towards a system of electronic conveyancing.¹ The Land Registry had, by the time of Law Com No. 254, already computerised all of the titles held by it and made it possible for searches of the register to be conducted electronically through direct access from a remote terminal.² In addition the Registry has developed a system allowing mortgage lenders to request the discharge of a mortgage charge (Electronic Notification of Discharges (END)), which is now 'live', and has completed the pilot of a system to allow such requests to be initiated automatically when a loan balance reaches zero and for the charge entry then to be automatically cancelled (Electronic Discharges (EDs)). The proposed system of electronic conveyancing has itself been developed into a model, which has been demonstrated to a large number of practitioners.

¹   The Law Commission described electronic conveyancing as 'the logical culmination of a process that has been going on for a number of years', Law Com No 271, para 2.41.
²   Law Com No 254, para 11.17.

3.9   In the field of conveyancing itself, there are now a number of systems on the market that allow conveyancers to conduct the system of conveyancing electronically. Such systems allow the conveyancer to manage all stages of the transaction by computer (allowing a much larger number of transactions to be handled), to communicate with other professionals involved in the transaction (eg the seller or buyer's solicitor, estate agents, surveyors) and will in some cases print out the necessary forms and documentation at the appropriate times.¹ Such systems could easily be developed into software capable of running or managing an electronic conveyancing system (the development of software in this way is the favoured option of the Land Registry).²

¹   See, for example, TM Property Service Ltd at www.territorium.co.uk which also lists a number of case management software companies on its website.
²   E-Conveyancing, para 5.5.

Timetable of change

3.10 Electronic conveyancing was not intended to come into being at the same time as the LRA 2002 came into force. The present timetable¹ provides for a working system to be built in 2004/5 and for pilot versions to be commenced in late 2005 or 2006 with the system being 'rolled out' thereafter. Although it is likely that the system will eventually be compulsory there is as yet no date for when this will happen and it is unlikely to be for some considerable time.[2]

---

[1]   See E-Conveyancing, para 2.4.
[2]   If the system is popular it ought to expand naturally. In addition there is likely to be a form of 'peer group pressure' amongst conveyancers since, for example, without all members of a chain using the system the advantages of chain management will not exist.

FORMAL REQUIREMENTS

Contract

3.11   The LRA 2002 does not apply to contracts for the sale or disposition of land or other interests in land. In order for such contracts not to fall foul of the requirements of the Law of Property (Miscellaneous Provisions) Act 1989, s 2 it is probably[1] necessary to amend that section. The Lord Chancellor has therefore proposed making an order under the Electronic Communications Act 2000, s 8.[2] A draft order has been produced which would insert a new section, s 2A, into the Law of Property (Miscellaneous Provisions) Act 1989. This will provide that where a document meets the requirements of s 2A it will be regarded for the purposes of s 2 and any other enactment as: (a) in writing; and (b) signed by each individual and sealed by each corporation whose electronic signature it has.

---

[1]   The Law Commission have argued that the requirement of 'writing' and 'signatures' are both fulfilled by the use of electronic documents and signatures, see Electronic Commerce: Formal Requirements in Commercial Transactions: Advice from the Law Commission, December 2001. This would mean that no amendment was necessary, although it might well be desirable in order to clarify the position and to impose additional requirements.
[2]   This authorises the appropriate Minister to modify the provisions of primary and secondary legislation as he thinks fit for the purpose of authorising or facilitating the use of electronic communications or electronic storage for the various purposes set out in the Electronic Communications Act 2000, s 8(2). If the amendment is not necessary (see the footnote above) there may be some doubt as to whether the power to make the order exists (but see s 8(4)(m) and the view of the Law Commission in Electronic Commerce: Formal Requirements In Commercial Transactions: Advice from the Law Commission).

3.12   The requirements of the draft s 2A of the Law of Property (Miscellaneous Provisions) Act 1989, and therefore the formalities that will be required for electronic contracts for the sale or disposition of land or interests in land, are that:

(a)   all the terms which the parties have expressly agreed are incorporated into the document;

(b)   the document makes provision for the time and date when the contract takes effect;

(c)   the document has the electronic signature of each person by whom it purports to be authenticated; and

(d)   each electronic signature is certified.[1]

---

[1]   Save for (a) these provisions mirror those of the LRA 2002, see para 3.15.

3.13   This amendment will apply to all contracts for the sale or other disposition of land. Therefore, even if the conveyance were proceeding outside the electronic system of conveyancing it would be possible, provided the above formalities were complied with, to exchange contracts electronically.

Dispositions

3.14   The LRA 2002, s 91 is the cornerstone of the new system. It provides that any document in electronic form that meets the requirements of the section is to be regarded in writing and signed by each individual and sealed by each corporation[1] whose signature it has. The document is also to be regarded for the purposes of any enactment as a deed. The effect is not to amend the formality requirements of the 'old' law but to sidestep them by ensuring that any document created according to the rules of the 'new' system will fulfil those requirements. It is in this way that the electronically created deed of transfer will be capable of transferring the title to the land (Law of Property Act 1925, s 52(1)) and the electronically created legal charge of mortgaging it (Law of Property Act 1925, s 85(1)).

---

[1]   A document signed electronically by a corporation (corporations are permitted to have their own signatures by s 91(4)(b)) will be presumed to be executed by the corporation as in the case of corporation seals, see s 91(9) amending the Companies Act 1985, s 36A(4).

3.15   In order to meet the requirements of the LRA 2002, s 91, the document must purport to effect a disposition which falls within s 91(2) and meet the conditions in s 91(3). The dispositions to which the section applies are, essentially, registered dispositions and dispositions of interests which are protected by notice on the register[1] (although they must also be specified by the LRR 2003). The conditions that the document must meet are that:

- the document makes provision of the time and date when it takes effect;

- the document has the electronic signature of each person by whom it purports to be authenticated;

- each electronic signature is certified; and
- such other conditions as the LRR 2003 may provide are met.[2]

---

[1]   It was a principal aim of the LRA 2002 that the register would be as accurate as possible. As a result it was proposed that not only registered interests but also those interests protected by notice on the register should be capable of being conveyed electronically. Thus, eventually their transfer or creation and protection by notice would be both simultaneous and one and the same thing. See Law Com No 254, para 7.29 and Law Com No 271, paras 13.81 and 13.82.
[2]   As yet there are no proposals.

3.16   The Law of Property Act 1925, s 75 entitles a purchaser to require that a conveyance is attested by some person appointed by him who may be his solicitor. As attestation is inappropriate to electronic conveyancing[1] this provision does not apply to documents to which the LRA 2002, s 91 applies.

---

[1]   See Law Com No 271, para 13.31.

THE SYSTEM

Computer system

3.17   It is expected that the system of electronic conveyancing will be supported by a single central computer system, which may or may not be run by the Land Registry. The system will perform a number of different functions. It will be the point of access for information held not only by the Land Registry but also by the Valuation Office Agency, the Inland Revenue and Companies House. It will allow the professional to communicate with other professionals involved in the conveyancing system. It will also be the point at which the conveyancer will enter the details of proposed and actual transfers or sales of land and interests in land.

3.18   Access to this system from the computer on a person's desk will probably be through varying types of 'channels' which will compete against one another. In other words the average high street conveyancer will probably be offered a choice of services offered by a number of commercial organisations who will have been granted access to the central system by the organisation in charge of that system. It is likely that different channels will be used by large conveyancing firms from those used by smaller firms with a smaller number of transactions and from those used by mortgage lenders. Access to the channels will be through computer software provided to the professional and through either a dedicated network link or along a phone line. The system is unlikely ever to be accessible via the internet.[1]

---

[1] See E-Conveyancing, para 4.1.5. It is conceivable that the Registry will allow some forms of information to be accessible via the internet and their existing Land Registry Direct service (which is internet based) will continue to run alongside.

Network access agreements

3.19 It will be vital to the conveyancing professional to be able to obtain access to the system. As the system becomes increasingly popular and eventually compulsory the refusal of access will mean that the conveyancing professional is barred from working. Equally important to the registrar will be the need to ensure that those who access the network do not prejudice the integrity and reliability of the system. A balance will be struck through the use of network access agreements. The LRA 2002, Sch 5, para 1(1) states that:

> 'A person who is not a member of the land registry may only have access to a land registry network under authority conferred by means of an agreement with the registrar.'

This agreement may authorise the user to communicate, post or retrieve information, make changes to the register and so forth. It is likely that there will be different forms of agreement offering varying levels of access to different types of user.

3.20 The registrar will be obliged to enter into a network access agreement with any applicant provided that the applicant meets criteria that will be set out in the rules. At present the Registry have not made any solid proposals for what criteria they will require. However, it can be expected that these criteria will attempt to ensure that any applicant will, amongst other things:

- ensure the confidentiality of private information kept on the network;
- be competent and proficient to use the network. Schedule 5 gives the registrar the power to arrange for the provision of education and training in relation to the use of the network. It is likely that participation in a process of continuing training and education will be a prerequisite for a network access agreement;
- be insured adequately for potential liabilities arising from the use of the network;[1]
- ensure the security of the network.[2]

It is possible (although this is only speculation) that the criteria will be met by membership of a professional body (eg the Law Society) along with the relevant qualification from that organisation.

---

[1]   These first three matters are those which the Lord Chancellor must have regard to in drawing up rules in relation to network access agreements, see LRA 2002, Sch 5, para 11(3).
[2]   See E-Conveyancing, para 5.6.2.

3.21 The network access agreement will allow access to the network upon certain terms (LRA 2002, Sch 5, para 2). The terms may vary from different types of user and may well specify the transactions for which the particular user is permitted to access the network. The terms may also specify that the user carry out specified transactions in no other way than electronically, so prohibiting the user from carrying them out in both a paper form and electronically. It will be possible for the registrar to charge for access. Rules will also make provision about 'how to go about network transactions' (LRA 2002, Sch 5, para 5), including provision about the procedures to be followed in dealing with the Registry and the supply of information. The ability to lay down terms enabling network transactions to be monitored will, amongst other things, allow the registrar to establish the system of 'chain management' described below.[1]

---

[1]   See paras 3.32, 3.48.

3.22 It is easy to envisage situations where the obligations owed under network access agreements will conflict with the professional's duty to the client. For example, the rules will require the conveyancer to provide information to the registrar and this may well include information that the client may not wish to reveal.[1] The LRA 2002 provides that to the extent that an obligation not owed under a network access agreement conflicts with a duty that is owed under such an agreement, the obligation not owed under the agreement is 'discharged'. This provision may well become controversial (although it awaits the draft rules on electronic conveyancing to see how controversial) since it has the potential to be extremely wide ranging and could override not only duties of confidentiality but also duties including the duty to act in the best interest of the client.

---

[1]   For example in 'chain management' the clients may wish the conveyancer to conceal the true position but the rules will almost certainly oblige the conveyancer to make disclosure (see E-Conveyancing, para 6.3).

3.23 The rules will allow the registrar to terminate a network access agreement and will set out the grounds for termination and the procedure to be followed. The registrar will use these powers to ensure that those persons with access to the network continue to comply with the terms of the agreement, the criteria imposed in order to obtain the agreement and any other conditions specified by the rules (LRA 2002, Sch 5, para 3(3)).

3.24 In the event that a person is aggrieved by a decision of the registrar with regard to entry into, or termination of, a network access agreement that person will be able to appeal to the adjudicator.[1] He will have power to give such directions as he feels appropriate to give effect to his determination (LRA 2002, Sch 5, para 4).

---

[1] See para 15.36.

Electronic signatures

3.25 In order for any document in electronic form to effect any disposition under the LRA 2002 it must have the electronic signature of each person by whom it purports to be authenticated and those signatures must be certified (LRA 2002, s 91).[1] Electronic signatures are the means by which documents in an electronic form are authenticated as having been sent and/or authorised by the person from whom they purport to have been sent and/or authorised and as not having been altered or otherwise tampered with by some third party.

---

[1] See para 3.15.

3.26 Although there are different systems of electronic signatures they all work along the same principal lines. A person who wishes to have an electronic signature will create two 'keys', a private key and a public key.[1] These are in fact complex algorithms used to encrypt documents into an unreadable mathematical code and then to decrypt them. The private key is used to 'sign' the document, which has the effect of encrypting the document. The encrypted document is sent to the recipient. The recipient will obtain the public key of the sender from a certification body which keeps it generally available and certifies its veracity. It is not possible to deduce the private key from the public key. The public key will decrypt the document. Any attempt to alter the document without thereafter signing it with the private key will mean that neither the public key nor the private key will decrypt the document. Thus, the fact that the public key successfully decrypted the document means that it must have come from the sender and has not been altered in transit. The role of the certification authority, by holding and publishing the public key and by identifying it as belonging to the sender, is crucial to the process.[2] The certification authorities are themselves overseen by a form of regulation (in the UK a voluntary system known as 'tScheme' exists).

---

[1] Due to the reliance on 'public keys' and the bodies that hold and certify these, the systems are frequently referred to as 'Public Key Infrastructures' (PKI).
[2] The Law Society is currently considering whether it would be appropriate for it to be a certification authority for its members, see *Law Society of England and Wales; Response to HM Land Registry's E-Conveyancing Consultation*, November 2002, para 6.6. The Law Society have also expressed concerns about what it is the certification authority is actually able to certify,

since it will be difficult for them to absolutely verify identities and to be sure that a private key has not been obtained by a third party, see 'Response of the Law Society to the Consultation Paper produced the Lord Chancellor's Department under Reference CP:5/2001'.

3.27 Although apparently complex (and involving some highly advanced mathematics) the system is based on relatively simple principles. In practice it works through the use of software and the simple click of the appropriate button with the mouse. It provides an extremely accurate means of verifying the authenticity of a document sent electronically and has the added advantage that the process also confirms that the document has not been altered.

Agency

3.28 It will be a necessary feature of electronic conveyancing that the conveyancing professional will have to sign documents electronically on behalf of the client. When the system first begins it is unlikely that electronic signatures will be so prevalent that the normal residential vendor or purchaser will have one. Even when such signatures are common it is likely that it will often prove more convenient for the professional to sign the document on his client's behalf.

3.29 The LRA 2002, Sch 5, para 8 states:

'Where—
- (a) a person who is authorised under a network access agreement to do so uses the network for the making of a disposition or contract, and
- (b) the document which purports to effect the disposition or to be the contract—
  - (i) purports to be authenticated by him as agent, and
  - (ii) contains a statement to the effect that he is acting under the authority of his principal,

he shall be deemed, in favour of any other party, to be so acting.'

The LRA 2002, s 91(6) states that:

> 'if a document is authenticated by a person as agent it is to be regarded for the purposes of any enactment as authenticated by him under the written authority of his principal.'

3.30 It follows that whenever the conveyancing professional purports to sign the document electronically, or otherwise holds out the document as 'authenticated by him as agent', he will be deemed to have been acting as an agent and (where required by statute) with written authority to do so. This will be so whether or not he had the authority to act as agent and whether or not that authority extended to executing that disposition. This is a significant departure from the present system where an agent acting outside of the scope of any actual or apparent authority is liable for a breach of the warranty of authority but is not able to bind the purported principal and so is unable to actually provide good title.

3.31 These provisions resolve any difficulty over the use of electronic signatures by professionals on behalf of their clients. However, they could lead to a whole new field of difficulties. Although it is intended that network access agreements will require the conveyancer to obtain the written authority of the client to sign any document on the client's behalf,[1] it can be expected that there will be numerous disputes between clients and their conveyancers over the extent of authority granted to the conveyancer. In addition there is a significant potential for fraud on the part of the dishonest professional, or someone with access to the honest professional's electronic signature and network access, who will not only be able to hold himself out as having authority that he does not have but will also be deemed to in fact have that authority.[2] This final set of difficulties will apparently have to be resolved through rectification and indemnity and through insurance.[3]

---

[1]   See Law Com No 271, para 13.62.
[2]   See M Dowden [2001] 41 EG 180.
[3]   See C Harpum [2001] 46 EG 175. As the article points out, the source of the fraud will be easily deduced so that in fact such frauds may be rare.

Chain management

3.32 The registrar is expected to include rules providing for the monitoring of network transactions (LRA 2002, Sch 5, paras 2(2)(c) and 5(2)). This information will be used to draw a picture of the position of linked transactions.[1] This will allow persons involved in a 'chain' of transactions to deduce where any delays in the chain are occurring. It is hoped that this in turn will cause 'chains' to move faster as the 'slowest link' can be easily identified and pressure brought to bear upon him. It is proposed that one aspect of the network access agreement will be an obligation on conveyancers to disclose progress.[2]

---

[1]   See the diagram on page 48 of E-Conveyancing.
[2]   This will override any duties, such as confidentiality, owed to the client, see para 3.22.

3.33 The Law Commission's proposals involved a more 'pro-active' approach than that described above. Under their scheme a chain manager would oversee the conduct of any chain and would himself manage the chain and 'push' the slowest link.[1] The Registry's proposals do not go this far, although they are consulting on whether 'there is an additional role for a chain manager to facilitate the progress of chain transactions'.[2] The Law Society do not favour the use of chain managers.[3]

[1]   See *Land Registration for the Twenty-First Century, A Conveyancing Revolution* (2001) (Law Com No 271), para 13.63.
[2]   E-Conveyancing, question 30, page 70.
[3]   *Law Society of England and Wales; Response to HM Land Registry's E-Conveyancing Consultation*, November 2002, para 7.15.

DIY conveyancing

3.34 When the Land Registry network becomes available, the LRA 2002 obliges the registrar to provide such assistance as 'he thinks appropriate' for the purpose of enabling persons who wish to do their own conveyancing to do so by means of the network. It is envisaged that such individuals will be able to use terminals at District Land Registries and that staff will be available to assist.[1] Terminals may also be provided at other locations.[2] It is apparent that careful checks will have to exist to ensure that the persons using the network in this way are who they say they are.

[1]   This does not include the provision of legal advice, see the LRA 2002, Sch 5, para 7(2).
[2]   So far unspecified. The Chancery Bar Association's response to E-Conveyancing suggested the possibility of terminals in local authority offices and in post offices.

Concerns

3.35 The proposed changes are radical and involve the use of a system that has no exact comparator. There are therefore legitimate concerns as to whether it will serve the function that it is being asked to serve. Sceptical professionals used to the current (relatively) efficient system hardly need reminding of the public services track record in commissioning and installing computer systems.[1] The concerns that have been expressed by all parties (including the Law Commission, the Registry and the Law Society) centre around three major issues: reliability, security and cost.

[1]   Eg the National Air Traffic Control System.

Reliability

3.36 In respect of reliability there are really two issues. The first is the reliability of the system itself. The Registry states that it is its aim to build a system that never fails. Nevertheless, it intends to create contingency measures and back up systems, possibly including the ability to revert to a paper based system. Only time will tell if the Registry's aims can be met. The second issue relates to the reliability of the information on the register. It is notable that the current system contains numerous scope for errors with documents submitted to the Registry having to be 'data transferred'.[1] The new system ought to reduce the scope for such errors because data will be inputted at an early stage and (it is hoped) thereafter be subject to a number of checks.[2] Nevertheless, the fact that the professionals rather than the Registry will be entering the data may itself create the opportunity for errors.

---

[1] There were around 9,000 such errors in 2000/2001, see E-Conveyancing page 83.
[2] A notional register will be created upon the drafting of contracts, at which time the Registry will be able to raise automatic requisitions on obvious errors (eg names and title numbers). In the ideal world this will be checked before exchange and again before completion.

Fraud

3.37 Conveyancing is an easy and, at times, profitable target for fraudsters. There is an inevitable fear that a new system will present new opportunities. The significant weak point of the new system will be the point at which it is accessed. The system of electronic signatures will not be able to verify that the individuals who instruct conveyancers are who they say they are. It will probably be unable to prevent the unauthorised use of a private key by an individual who has managed to obtain it by unlawful means and it is conceivable that such means could include 'hacking' into conveyancers' computers.[1]

---

[1] For more details see *Law Society of England and Wales; Response to HM Land Registry's E-Conveyancing Consultation*, November 2002.

3.38 The system will be designed to prevent such 'attacks' as much as possible. It is likely that a condition of access to the network will be a level of security around the terminal and its use. The fact that fraudulent transactions will be capable of being traced to their source may be a useful deterrent and may prevent repeat occurrences. The system will also have an audit function which means that unusual patterns of activity will be capable of detection. Nevertheless, it will probably never be possible to fully protect the system from fraud. Ultimately, the costs of such fraud will have to be met through rectification and indemnity, and through insurance.

Cost

3.39 The Registry estimates that the introduction of the system will reduce the unit costs of conveyancing transactions by something in the region of £16. This estimate has been criticised as being optimistic and some have suggested that there will be no savings.[1] For conveyancers the costs may well be high. There are likely to be increased burdens of installation, maintenance, audit and security. A particular issue is the costs occasioned by security breaches. There is also a concern that the professional will be made to insure against security breaches through an in-built assumption that if fraud occurs, the conveyancer must have been negligent.[2] The Law Society has stated that any system must take into account that breaches of security could occur without the solicitor being aware and that liability and responsibility for such breaches should rest with the Land Registry.[3]

---

[1]   See E-Conveyancing, page 85 and Raymond Perry Bricks and Mortar – The real cost of IT, Law Society's Gazette Vol 98 No 45 p 30 22/11/2001.
[2]   See Raymond Perry (above) and *Law Society of England and Wales; Response to HM Land Registry's E-Conveyancing Consultation*, November 2002.
[3]   *Law Society of England and Wales; Response to HM Land Registry's E-Conveyancing Consultation*, para 3.9, November 2002.

CONTRACT TO COMPLETION—THE SYSTEM IN OPERATION

Pre-contract

3.40   As at present, the initial purchase offer will not bind either party until contracts are exchanged. Once the offer is made, the conveyancer will take the client's instructions. The details will probably be entered on to case management software. It is likely that this software will have the capacity to link the conveyancer both to his opposite number in the sale transaction and to the other professionals involved in the process, including the estate agent and surveyor. They will be able to view information on those parts of the sale that are useful to them and to communicate with the conveyancer.

3.41   The computer terminal will be used, via the direct link to the network, to obtain details of the title of the property. This search will not only reveal the property's registered title but also information previously discovered by separate searches, such as the information held by local authorities in respect of the property.

3.42   The Government remains committed to the introduction of seller's packs. If these do become common then the information about the property will, using the system described above, be obtained at the beginning of the marketing of the property by the seller's conveyancer.

Contract and exchange

Draft contract

3.43   Once the transaction details have been entered on to the computer it will be possible for the seller's conveyancer to create a draft contract.[1] Once this has been checked by that conveyancer it can be entered onto the network. The system will check the draft contract to ensure that the registered title, number and address of the property do not conflict and (if necessary) automatic requisitions will be made. The submission of the draft contract will cause a notional register to be created. This will show what the register will look like after the proposed transaction has been completed. In this way it is hoped that all outstanding difficulties with the conveyance will be resolved before completion.

[1]   It is likely that the software itself will generate this.

3.44   Once this process of validation has been completed, the draft contract will be placed on the system to be viewed by the buyer's solicitor. Any searches and enquiries that are then necessary will be conducted electronically.

Exchange

3.45   Once the details of deposits, payment dates, mortgage offers[1] etc are finalised, the parties will be ready to exchange contracts. In fact there will be no exchange in the traditional sense. Instead the conveyancers will 'release' the contract electronically on behalf of their clients. Thereafter it will be treated as binding.

[1]   See para 3.47.

Notice and priority periods

3.46   The 'exchange' of contracts will be communicated automatically to the Registry. This will cause a notice to be placed on the register. The notice will serve two functions, first to ensure that the register describes (so far as possible) the existence of all interests in the land[1] and second to create a priority period similar to that now given by official searches. During this priority period (the duration has not been decided) it will not be possible to bring any other application onto the register, provided that the contract proceeds to completion.

---

[1]   The fundamental objective of the Bill as proposed by the Law Commission was to ensure that the register was a complete and accurate reflection of the state of the title of the land at any given time, see Law Com No 271, para 1.5.

Mortgage offer

3.47   There is no reason why mortgage offers cannot be made electronically and it is already reasonably common for 'in principle' offers to be made over the internet. It is likely that the mortgage offer will be incorporated into the system and that either the offer or the draft legal charge (or both) will generate an automatic entry on the notional register. It is not yet clear whether the practice of the purchaser's conveyancer creating the charge document will change.

Chain management

3.48   For residential transactions, which are frequently parts of a chain of other transactions, the Registry expect to create a 'linked transaction matrix'. This means that the parties to a chain will have access to a grid that shows the stage at which each part of the chain has reached. Therefore, whenever stages such as the issue of contracts, the requesting of searches, the completion of enquiries etc are passed by one link in the chain, this is recorded and can be seen by other links in the chain. It will therefore be possible to deduce who is holding up the chain (although not why) and so (it is hoped) pressure will be brought on that party causing the chain to move at a faster rate.[1]

---

[1]   See para 3.32 and note the overriding obligations owed under the network access agreements, para 3.22.

Completion

3.49   On the day and time agreed by the parties, provided that the system indicates that all documentation has been signed and that the finance is in order, completion will be automatic. The register will be updated to reflect the transfer of title from seller to buyer, the creation of a new charge and the discharge of old charges. Relevant information will be sent automatically to the Inland Revenue and Valuation Office Agency and (in relevant cases) details will be registered at Companies House.

Electronic Fund Transfer (EFT)

3.50 There is little purpose in allowing completion to take place automatically if the funds essential to that completion must be transferred manually. Accordingly, it is expected that a system of Electronic Fund Transfer (EFT) will be created. The details of this system are far from clear.[1] It is apparent that the system will be designed so that simultaneous with the transfer of legal title and the creation and discharge of legal charges will be the transfer of the funds upon which these transactions are based. Funds will flow from the buyer's mortgagee to the seller and on to his mortgagee. The funds necessary to pay stamp duty and land registration fees will also be automatically transferred.

---

[1] A further consultation on this aspect is expected at a later date (E-Conveyancing, para 7.1).

Stamp duty

3.51 The Finance Act 2003 fundamentally altered stamp duty in relation to land transactions. It introduced a new tax, stamp duty land tax ('SDLT') which replaces the old stamp duty.[1] The principal difference is that the new tax is, in essence, a tax upon transactions rather than upon the documents underlying or evidencing those transactions. The tax prevents a number of common avoidance measures and this is probably the main driving force behind the changes. However, if stamp duty is to remain in a world of electronic conveyancing, it is essential that it change from being a tax on paper documents and one of the objectives of the legislation was 'to create a regime that supports the Government's e-business agenda and in particular the introduction of electronic conveyancing'.[2]

---

[1] From 1 December 2003. See also paras 5.36 et seq, 6.72 et seq.

[2] See 'Modernising Stamp Duty on land and buildings in the UK, Inland Revenue Consultative Document, April 2002' in the Executive Summary.

3.52 SDLT is payable by the purchaser, who is liable to make a return to the Revenue and to pay the tax owing, within 30 days of the transaction.[1] Where transactions are completed electronically, it is envisaged that the tax will be paid as part and parcel of the electronic conveyance, using electronic fund transfer. The Revenue expect that in time the Registry system will be integrated with the Inland Revenue Stamp systems so that the use of the Registry system will satisfy all the notification and payment requirements that arise.[2] It is proposed that the 30-day period allowed for payment of the tax will be reduced so that the use of paper documents does not give a cash flow advantage.[3]

[1]   See Finance Act 2003, s 76.

[2]   See 'Modernising Stamp Duty on land and buildings in the UK, Inland Revenue Consultative Document, April 2002', para 7.10.

[3]   See 'Modernising Stamp Duty on land and buildings in the UK, Inland Revenue Consultative Document, April 2002', para 3.13, and Finance Act 2003 s 76(2), which confers power on the Inland Revenue to make regulations shortening the period for making a return or requiring it to be made on the same date as the transaction.

Other transactions

3.53   The above discussion relates only to the more common process of a sale of land. The new system will be designed to incorporate all dispositions of registered estate and charges including transfers of part[1] and more complex 'one-off' commercial transactions. Similarly, it will be possible for the system to deal with first registrations[2] and with the creation and disposition of leases. More unusual forms of sale, such as auctions or sales without the initial contract stage, will also be capable of being included.

[1]   The Registry hopes to have in place, before the introduction of electronic conveyancing, its vectorised Index Map so making transfers by reference to an electronic plan relatively straightforward.

[2]   First registration would lead to only a provisional registration without title being finally conferred. This registration would then be examined by the Registry staff and eventually approved.

3.54   Eventually the system will also include the creation and transfer of interests that are not entered on the register but are protected by the registration of a notice on the register. For example, the grant of an express easement will be carried out through the network and the act of granting it (by electronically signing the document) will also cause the interest to be protected by notice.

Storage and supply of information

3.55   Once the transaction has completed, the documents (whether electronic or not) supplied to the Registry will be stored. Under the LRA 2002, s 66, any person has the right to inspect and make copies of any document referred to in the register of title and any other document kept by him and which relates to an application by him. The only exception to this relates to exempt information documents, which are documents containing (or said to contain) prejudicial information. It is necessary to apply for a document to receive this status.[1]

[1]   See the LRR 2003, rr 136–138 and paras 2.65 et seq.

MAKING THE PROCESS COMPULSORY

3.56 The LRA 2002, s 93 contains the power to make the system of electronic conveyancing compulsory. Where either a disposition of a registered estate or charge or an interest which is the subject of a notice in the register[1] is of 'a description specified by the rules' s 93(2) means that that disposition will only have effect if:

  (a) it is made by means of a document in electronic form; and
  (b) when the document purports to take effect it is electronically communicated to the registrar and the relevant registration requirements (set out in Sch 2 for registrable dispositions and to be set out in the rules for other dispositions or contracts) are met.

---

[1] See paras 7.20 et seq.

3.57 LRA 2002, s 93 therefore has two effects on those dispositions specified by the rules[1] made under it. First, it will require all such dispositions to be made in electronic form. Second, the registration of a disposition must occur simultaneously with the making of that disposition. It is this second effect which is the ultimate goal of electronic conveyancing, because it is this which will ensure the total accuracy of the register at all times and eliminate the registration gap.[2]

---

[1] Disposition will include postponement (see the LRA 2002, s 93(6)) so that the provisions will apply (for example) to an agreement to postpone the priority of one charge to another (see Law Com No 271, para 13.83).
[2] See Law Com No 271, paras 13.76–13.79.

3.58 As is apparent, the power under the section need not be applied in 'blanket' fashion to all conveyances, but can be extended from one type of disposition to another. It will therefore be possible to 'roll out' compulsory electronic conveyancing in stages.

4 First registration

4.1 One of the policy objectives of the legislation is to register as much unregistered land as possible, as quickly as possible. The major changes for this purpose which were made by the Land Registration Act 1997 (LRA 1997) are carried forward, subject to minor alterations, by the Land Registration Act 2002 (LRA 2002). The LRA 2002 does not extend the kinds of transaction which give rise to compulsory registration—the LRA 1997 had already extended these considerably—but it greatly increases the kinds of interest capable of voluntary registration and subject to compulsory registration, by extending registration to various types of interest which were not previously registrable, most notably to leases of a duration of between 7 and 21 years.[1] It also encourages voluntary registration by making it no longer possible, after a transitional period of two years, to register a caution against first registration to protect an estate or interest which could be registered.[2] The adverse possession rules also encourage voluntary registration by estate owners who are vulnerable to adverse possession claims.[3]

---

[1] See Chapter 6.
[2] See para 4.4.
[3] See Chapter 13 below, and in particular para 13.6.

4.2 The types of interest in land capable of registration with their own separate registered title are: freeholds, leaseholds, rentcharges, franchises, and profits à prendre in gross (LRA 2002, ss 3(1), 4(1)), subject to the point that certain short leases are not registrable (LRA 2002, ss 3(3), (4), (7), 4(1)(b)–(g)). All other rights over or interests in land—eg charges, easements, appurtenant profits à prendre, restrictive covenants—can only be registered (if at all) by being entered on the register of one of these types of separately registrable interests. The freehold and leasehold interests capable of voluntary registration and subject to compulsory registration (and the circumstances in which compulsory registration arises) are set out in paras 5.2 and 5.9 (freeholds) and paras 6.3, 6.5 and 6.9 (leaseholds). First registration of a freehold or leasehold estate following a mortgage or charge of it is also discussed in paras 8.3–8.6. Adverse possession rights and first registration are discussed in para 13.31. This chapter deals with certain aspects of first registration common to all categories of estate or interest: cautions against first registration, failure to comply with the requirement of first registration, dealings after an event giving rise to compulsory registration but before registration, and applications for first registration.

CAUTIONS AGAINST FIRST REGISTRATION

4.3   In relation to land which is already registered, cautions are replaced by unilateral notices as a means of protecting interests in that land.[1] A unilateral notice gives priority for the interest protected by the notice, while a caution only gave a right to be informed of an application to register a dealing. In the case of land which is not registered, the LRA 2002 cannot regulate the priorities of interests, and a caution remains the appropriate way of protecting the interests of anyone with an unregistered estate or interest in land who might be adversely affected by some other person obtaining registration of an estate in that land. The LRA 2002 therefore continues to provide for cautions against first registration, which merely give a right to be informed of an application for registration. By virtue of the LRA 2002, s 15(1) a person may lodge a caution against the registration of title to an unregistered legal estate if he claims to be the owner of a 'qualifying estate' or entitled to an interest affecting a 'qualifying estate'. A 'qualifying estate' for this purpose is a legal estate which relates to the land to which the caution relates, and is an interest of any of the following kinds: an estate in land (ie the freehold or a lease), a rentcharge, a franchise, or a profit à prendre in gross (LRA 2002, s 15(2)). An interest affecting an estate is an adverse right affecting the title to it (LRA 2002, s 132(3)(b)). The application must be made in Form CT1 and contain sufficient details so that the extent of the land to which it relates can be identified (LRR 2003, r 42). Form CT1 requires the cautioner's interest in the land to be verified by a statutory declaration or a conveyancer's certificate. However, after a transitional period of two years, the categories of estate which can be protected by a caution against first registration are severely restricted: see para 4.4 below.

---

[1]   See paras 7.24, 7.35–7.39.

4.4   With effect from 13 October 2005,[1] a caution against first registration on the basis of a claim to be 'the owner of a qualifying estate' cannot be lodged (and a caution previously lodged under the LRA 2002 will cease to have effect on that date)[2] by virtue of ownership of a freehold estate in land or a leasehold estate in land granted for a term of which more than seven years are unexpired (LRA 2002, s 15(3)(a)). Also, with effect from the same date, no caution may be lodged on the basis of being 'entitled to an interest affecting a qualifying estate' (and a previously lodged one will cease to have effect on that date) by virtue of entitlement to a leasehold estate granted for a term of which more than seven years are unexpired (LRA 2002, s 15(3)(b) and Sch 12, para 14). The point of the latter exception is that such a lease is both itself a legal estate, and an interest in another legal estate, ie that out of which it was granted. Entitlement to a lease in this context almost certainly refers to being the lessee under, or being entitled to have vested in him, a currently subsisting lease. It corresponds to the reference to being entitled to an interest affecting a qualifying estate in the LRA 2002, s 15(1), and it also corresponds to the references to being entitled to a legal estate in the context of voluntary registration (LRA 2002, s 3(2)(b)). It is submitted that this latter exception does not include, for example, someone who has a tenancy agreement, taking effect in equity under the rule in *Walsh v Lonsdale*[3] and not effective at law, with more than seven years left to run, as this would not be a right capable of substantive registration. The reason for these restrictions on the right to lodge a caution against first registration, which are an innovation of the LRA 2002, is to encourage voluntary registration of the excluded estates by depriving owners of such estates in land of the alternative of using a caution against first registration as a way of protecting themselves against others trying to register themselves as proprietors of the estate in question.

---

[1]   The LRA 2002, Sch 12, para 14(1) defers this restriction for two years from the commencement of s 15.
[2]   See the LRA 2002, Sch 12, para 14(2), which also provides that a caution lodged before 13 October 2005 will still be effective in relation to an application for registration made before that date.
[3]   (1882) 21 ChD 9. See Halsbury's Laws of England, 4th ed reissue, vol 27(1), paras 53–55.

4.5   Where a caution against first registration has been lodged or applied for before 13 October 2003 the position is as follows. A caution lodged under the Land Registration Act 1925 (LRA 1925), s 53 is within the definition of caution against first registration for the purposes of the LRA 2002 (LRA 2002, Sch 12, para 16). This means that it has the same consequences as a caution against first registration lodged under the LRA 2002, s 15, and the provisions of the LRA 2002 and the Land Registration Rules 2003, SI 2003/1417 (LRR 2003) relating to cautions against first registration (see below) will apply, save that there does not seem to be anything which causes it to cease to have effect on and after 13 October 2005 if it is a caution lodged in respect of a freehold or a lease with more than seven years unexpired, as would be the case with such a caution lodged under the LRA 2002, s 15 before 13 October 2005 (LRA 2002, Sch 12, para 14).[1] The detailed provisions of the LRR 2003 as to the form of the register of these cautions are disapplied.[2] Liability under the LRA 1925, s 56(3), for lodging a caution without sufficient cause, is carried forward (LRA 2002, Sch 12, para 4). An application for a caution against first registration made before 13 October 2003, but still pending on that date, will continue to be governed by the LRA 1925, s 53(1) and (2) (LRA 2002, Sch 12, para 6), and so will count for the foregoing purposes as one lodged under the LRA 1925, s 53.

---

¹ See para 4.4.
² Land Registration Act 2002 (Transitional Provisions) Order 2003, SI 2003/1953, art 14(2) disapplying the LRR 2003, r 41(2)–(5). In other words the existing records of cautions against first registration will continue and will not be converted to the form prescribed by the LRR 2003.

4.6   The existence of a caution against first registration lodged under the LRA 2002 is recorded against the relevant land on the index map (LRA 2002, s 68(1)(c))¹ (as was done under the LRA 1925). The relevant details of any caution against first registration under the LRA 2002 are kept in a register which can be, and is intended to be, kept in electronic form (LRA 2002, s 19; LRR 2003, r 40(1)). There is an individual caution register for each caution, with its own 'caution title number', or more than one if the registrar decides to exercise his power to open separate caution registers for separate areas of land affected by the caution (LRR 2003, rr 40(2), (3), and 41(1)). Each caution register is in two parts: the caution property register, and a cautioner's register (LRR 2003, r 41(2)). The caution property register contains a description of the legal estate to which the caution relates and a description of the cautioner's interest (LRR 2003, r 41(3)). If the caution relates to an estate in land, a rentcharge, or an affecting franchise,² there will be a plan (LRR 2003, r 41(4)). The cautioner's register will contain the name of the cautioner, including its registered number if it is a registered company or a limited liability partnership, an address for service, and details of any person consenting to the lodging of the caution (LRR 2003, r 41(5)). There is public access to the register of cautions against first registration (LRA 2002, s 66(1)(d)).³

---

¹ For the index map see paras 2.20–2.23 above.
² Ie a franchise relating to a defined area of land and adversely affecting title: see the definition in the LRR 2003, r 217(1).
³ See also the LRR 2003, r 133 and para 2.66 above.

4.7   After the lodging of a caution against first registration, and before anyone attempts to register the land or any estate in the land to which the caution relates, there can be changes to, or cancellation of, the caution as follows:

(1)   The cautioner may withdraw it (LRA 2002, s 17; LRR 2003, r 43).¹

(2)   The owner of the legal estate to which the caution relates, or the owner of a legal estate deriving from it, may apply to have the caution cancelled (LRA 2002, s 18; LRR 2003, r 44),² subject as follows. He cannot do so if he, or a person from whom he derives title, confirmed to the registrar in writing his consent to the caution (LRA 2002, s 18(2); LRR 2003, r 47), unless the interest claimed by the cautioner has come to an end or the consent was obtained by fraud, misrepresentation, mistake, undue influence, or duress (LRA 2002, s 18(2); LRR 2003, r 46). These provisions for cancellation are an innovation of the

LRA 2002—previously a caution against first registration could only be challenged by applying for registration of the estate subject to the caution. The person for the time being shown as cautioner in the cautioner's register (LRA 2002, s 22; LRR 2003, r 52) is given until 12 noon on the fifteenth business day[3] from issue to him of notice of the application to cancel the caution to object (or such longer period up to 12 noon on the thirtieth business day after issue of the notice as the registrar may allow),[4] after which, in the absence of objection, the caution is cancelled (LRA 2002, s 18(3) and (4); LRR 2003, r 53(1)). If there is an objection, the standard procedure for dealing with objections is then followed (LRA 2002, s 73; LRR 2003, r 19).[5]

(3)   The registrar may alter the cautions register to correct a mistake or bring it up to date (LRA 2002, s 21).[6] He must do so if satisfied that the cautioner does not own the interest, or not all of it, or it did not exist or has come to an end, or where someone has succeeded to the relevant interest by operation of law (LRR 2003, rr 49 and 51).

(4)   The court may make an order for alteration of the cautions register to correct a mistake or bring it up to date (LRA 2002, s 20).[7] The court must do so if satisfied that the cautioner does not own the interest, or not all of it, or that the interest did not exist or has come to an end (LRR 2003, r 48(1)). An order of the court will impose a duty on the registrar, but only if an application for alteration of the cautions register pursuant to the court order is made to the registrar (LRA 2002, s 20(2); LRR 2003, r 48(3)).

The above provisions also apply to cautions against first registration lodged under LRA 1925.[8]

---

[1]   LRR 2003 r 43 requires Form WCT to be used and the land involved to be identified clearly if the withdrawal relates to only part of the land subject to the caution concerned.

[2]   LRR 2003 r 44 requires Form CCT to be used, and for evidence to be provided of entitlement to apply.

[3]   These are days when the registry is open to the public, ie at the moment days other than Saturdays, Sundays, and bank holidays, but this period will be extended if the registry starts opening on Saturdays: see the LRR 2003, r 216 and the definition of 'business days' in r 217(1). For service of notices see the LRR 2003, rr 197–199 and paras 2.25–2.33 above.

[4]   To get a longer period the cautioner must apply for it before 12 noon on the fifteenth business day from issue of the notice, giving reasons why a longer period should be allowed, and the registrar may consult the person who applied for cancellation, and may allow a longer period different from that requested: LRR 2003, r 53(2)–(4).

[5]   For the objection procedure see paras 15.4–15.8 below.

[6]   For applications for this to be done see the LRR 2003, r 50, under which the cautioner normally has to be informed of the application.

[7]   See also the LRR 2003, r 48(2) for the requirement that the order must state the relevant caution title number, describe the alteration to be made, and direct the registrar to make it.

[8]   This appears to be the combined effect of the LRA 2002, s 19(1), s 131(1) definitions of 'cautions against first registration' and 'cautions register', and Sch 12, para 16.

4.8   A caution against first registration is expressly something which does not by itself confer any validity or priority for the claimed right or interest in respect of which the caution is lodged (LRA 2002, s 16(3)). Its only effect is to give a right to receive notice of an application for registration of the estate to which the caution relates, and of the right to object to it, and a period in which to object before the application for registration is determined (LRA 2002, s 16(1) and (2)). Notice is given to the address entered in the cautions register (LRR 2003, rr 41(5)(b), 198), and it is important that the cautioner keep this entry up to date. The person for the time being shown as cautioner in the cautioner's register (LRA 2002, s 22; LRR 2003, r 52) is given until 12 noon on the fifteenth business day[1] from issue to him of notice of the application to register the relevant estate to object to the application (or such longer period up to 12 noon on the thirtieth business day after issue of the notice as the registrar may allow) (LRA 2002 s 16(2); LRR 2003, r 53(1)).[2] If there is an objection the standard procedure for dealing with objections is then followed (LRA 2002, s 73; LRR 2003, r 19).[3]

---

[1]   These are days when the registry is open to the public, ie at the moment days other than Saturdays, Sundays, and bank holidays, but this period will be extended if the registry starts opening on Saturdays: see the LRR 2003, r 216 and the definition of 'business day' in r 217(1). For service of notices see the LRR 2003, rr 197–199 and paras 2.25–2.33 above.

[2]   To get a longer period the cautioner must apply for it before 12 noon on the fifteenth business day from issue of the notice, giving reasons why a longer period should be allowed, and the registrar may consult the person who applied for registration, and may allow a longer period different from that requested: LRR 2003 r 53(2)–(4).

[3]   For the objection procedure see paras 15.4–15.8 below.

THE COMPULSORY REGISTRATION REQUIREMENT

4.9   The events which trigger compulsory registration, the legal estates in relation to which a triggering event can occur, and the persons who must apply for it, are discussed in paras 5.2–5.7 (freeholds) and 6.3–6.7 (leaseholds) below. The triggering events are all either transfers or grants of legal estates. If it is a transfer or grant by or to a charity, it must contain the appropriate prescribed statement.[1] Once an event triggering compulsory registration has occurred, the application for registration must be made within two months beginning with the day on which the triggering event occurred (LRA 2002, s 6(4)). This is subject to a power of the registrar by order to extend the time for doing so to such date as he may specify, which he may do after the two months period has expired (LRA 2002, s 6(5)), and the legislation does not set any upper limit on the extension of time which he may grant. However, there must be an application by a person interested in getting an extension of time, and the registrar must be satisfied that there is good reason for granting one (LRA 2002, s 6(5)).

---

[1]   See the Charities Act 1993, s 37(7), as substituted by the LRA 2002, Sch 11, para 29(2), and the LRR 2003, rr 179 and 180. See also paras 10.34–10.39 below.

4.10   If an application for registration is not made within the time limit discussed in para 4.9, including any extension of it ordered by the registrar, the disposition which triggered compulsory registration becomes void as regards the transfer, grant, or creation of a legal estate (LRA 2002, s 7(1)). If the event was a conveyance or assignment of a pre-existing freehold or leasehold estate the consequence of this is that the legal estate reverts to the person who conveyed or assigned the estate, and he holds it on a bare trust for the person to whom he conveyed or assigned it (LRA 2002, s 7(2)(a)).[1] If the event was the grant of a lease or the creation of a charge or mortgage, the consequence is that it has effect as a contract for valuable consideration to grant or create the lease, mortgage or charge in question (LRA 2002, s 7(2)(b)). There are two possible ways of remedying the situation if this has happened. One is to seek an order of the registrar extending the time for application for first registration to a future date (LRA 2002, s 6(5)).[2] If such an order were obtained, it would have the magic effect of shifting the legal estate back to the person in favour of whom it had been conveyed, assigned, granted, or created by the triggering event (LRA 2002, s 7(3)). The other is to obtain a fresh conveyance, assignment, grant, or creation of the estate concerned from the person who made the disposition which triggered compulsory registration, which he would be under an obligation to provide, but at the expense of the party obtaining it, who would also be liable to indemnify him against any other liability reasonably incurred by him as a result of the non-compliance with the registration requirement (LRA 2002, s 8). These provisions repeat the former LRA 1925, s 123A, added by the Land Registration Act 1997, with two differences of substance. One is that the LRA 2002 does not provide expressly that the compulsory registration provisions apply to a repeat conveyance, assignment, grant etc, whereas LRA 1925, s 123A(7) did make such a provision, a point discussed further in paras 5.4–5.6, 6.7 below, and the other is that LRA 2002 expressly provides that the possibility of reverter on failure to apply for registration in time is disregarded in determining whether a fee simple is a fee simple absolute (LRA 2002, s 7(4)), so as to counter any possibility of arguing that this possibility of reverter prevents a fee simple from being a legal estate.[3]

---

[1]   Note that a bare trust is a trust of land within the Trusts of Land and Appointment of Trustees Act 1996, s 1, and the trustee has all the powers of an absolute owner under s 6(1) of that Act.
[2]   See para 4.9 above.

4.11 The LRA 2002 applies to a dealing with an estate by someone who is already under an obligation to register that estate as if the dealing had taken place after the date of first registration of it (LRR 2003, r 38(1)).[1] If it is delivered for registration with the application for first registration it has effect from the time of making the latter application (LRR 2003, r 38(2)). As it will be dependent on the transaction giving rise to the registration requirement it will rank in priority after that transaction (LRR 2003, r 55(7)). The latter provision as to priority is needed because the effective date of first registration and of the registration of a registrable disposition is the date of delivery of the application rather than the date on which the registration is made (LRA 2002, s 74). Treating dealings with an estate by someone who is already under an obligation to register it as if the estate was already registered, which is much the same in substance as a provision of the former rules (LRR 1925, r 73), means, for example, that the use of the prescribed form of transfer is required if it is a transfer (LRR 2003, r 58),[2] that such a dealing only takes effect at law when the registration requirements have been met (but there is no time limit for doing so) (LRA 2002, s 27(1)),[3] that a mortgage by demise cannot be created (LRA 2002, s 23(1) and (2)),[4] and that it is interests which are within the LRA 2002, Sch 3, rather than ones within the LRA 2002, Sch 1, which will be overriding.[5] The Land Charges Act 1972 will not apply.[6] If the dealing is a transfer of a legal estate the transferee becomes the person who is under a duty to register the estate (LRA 2002 s 6(1)).[7] If the dealing is the grant of a lease or the creation of a charge, the lessee or chargee is not a successor in title within the LRA 2002, s 6(1),[8] and there does not seem to be any provision of the LRA 2002 or LRR 2003 which enables him to apply to the registrar to have the estate from which his estate derives registered.[9] Such a person should have a remedy under the covenants for title[10] against the lessor or chargor if the latter fails to register his estate, but it would be advisable to impose a special condition in any contract (or a covenant in the lease or charge) requiring him to apply for registration. The lessee in such a case can also protect his interest by registering a caution against first registration (paras 4.3 et seq) and registering his lease as an estate contract under the Land Charges Act 1972.

1 In exercise of the power in the LRA 2002, Sch 10, para 1.
2 See para 5.17.
3 See para 5.18.
4 See paras 8.1, 8.7.
5 See paras 7.62, 8.4.
6 Land Charges Act 1972, s 14(1).
7 See in particular the reference to the successor in title of the responsible estate owner.

[8]   This is clear from the fact that the obligation in the LRA 2002, s 6(1) is to apply to be registered as the proprietor of the registrable estate. Someone who has been granted a lease or charge out of or on the registrable estate is not someone who will be registered as proprietor of that estate.

[9]   Interestingly there used to be such a right under the LRR 1925, r 73(2), but this was removed with effect from 1 April 1998 by an amendment made to the LRR 1925, r 73 by the LRR 1997, SI 1997/3037, as part of the changes made to compulsory registration by and following LRA 1997.

[10]   See in particular the Law of Property (Miscellaneous Provisions) Act 1994, s 2(1). The case seems to fall between paras (a) and (b) of s 2(2) of that Act. The covenants for title may be incorporated in registered dispositions: LRR 2003, r 67(1) (pursuant to the LRA 2002, Sch 10, para 3). See para 9.34.

4.12   Where there has been a disposition before 13 October 2003 of unregistered land, which triggered compulsory registration under the LRA 1925, but was unfinished business as at 13 October 2003, the position is as follows. An application for first registration which has been made before 13 October 2003 but was still pending immediately before that date carries on as if the LRA 1925 was still in force (Land Registration Act 2002 (Transitional Provisions) Order 2003, SI 2003/1953 (LRA 2002 (TP) O 2003), art 3(1), (2)), save that (LRA 2002 (TP) O 2003, art 3(3)) the LRR 2003 will govern the giving of notices (LRA 2002 (TP) O 2003, art 5), disputes will be resolved under the LRA 2002 procedure (LRA 2002 (TP) O 2003, art 7), and land certificates cease to have a part to play (LRA 2002 (TP) O 2003, art 24). If no application has been made for first registration before 13 October 2003, the disposition is treated as if it were subject to the registration requirements of LRA 2002, both where it has become void for want of registration before 13 October 2003 (LRA 2002 (TP) O 2003, art 22), and where the time for applying for registration has not run out by that date (LRA 2002 (TP) O 2003, art 23), save that the period in which the compulsory registration requirement has to be fulfilled is the applicable period provided by the LRA 1925, s 123A(3), or such longer period as the registrar may allow under the LRA 2002, s 6(5) (LRA 2002 (TP) O 2003 art 23(2)). The basic period under the LRA 1925, s 123A(3) is two months, ie the same as under the LRA 2002, s 6(4), but the 'applicable period' under LRA 1925, s 123A(3) could be a greater period as a result of an extension of time having been already obtained from the registrar before 13 October 2003.

APPLICATIONS FOR FIRST REGISTRATION

4.13   An application for first registration must be in Form FR1 (LRR 2003, r 23(1)). It has to be accompanied by sufficient details to identify the land on the Ordnance Survey map (LRR 2003, r 24(1)(a)),[1] and the available documents of title (including the lease and a certified copy of it in the case of a leasehold estate) (LRR 2003, r 24(1)(b), (c)), and the documents submitted must be listed in duplicate on Form DL (LRR 2003, r 24(1)(d)). In the absence of the title deeds evidence must be provided to satisfy the registrar that the applicant is entitled to apply, and the absence of the documents of title must be accounted for 'where appropriate' (LRR 2003, r 27). If the person applying for registration is a company registered under the Companies Acts the application must state its registered number (LRR 2003, r 181(1)).[2] If the applicant is a non-exempt charity it must include in application for an appropriate restriction (LRR 2003, r 176),[3] and if it is an exempt charity it must submit its trust document (LRR 2003, r 182(1)).[4] In examining the title the registrar may have regard to any examination of title by a conveyancer prior to the application and to the nature of the property (LRR 2003, r 29), and may make searches and enquiries, give notices to other persons, direct the applicant to make searches and enquiries, or advertise the application (LRR 2003, r 30). If foreshore is involved the Crown Estate Commissioners, and in appropriate cases the Duchies of Lancaster or Cornwall or the Port of London Authority, must be notified and given time to object (LRR 2003, r 31). If the application is for first registration of a leasehold estate with absolute title,[5] and the lease was granted when either the reversion was not registered or it was but the grant of the lease was not required to be registered, and the immediate reversion on that lease is a registered estate which does not have the lease noted on its registered title,[6] the registrar must give notice of the application for first registration of the lease to the proprietor of that reversion unless it is clear that he consents to the registration of the lease (LRR 2003, r 37(1), (2), (4)). If the registrar does register the lease he is also required to note the lease on the reversioner's title (LRR 2003, r 37(3)).

---

[1] For the identification requirements for first registration of mines and minerals, cellars, flats, tunnels, etc see the LRR 2003, rr 25 and 26.
[2] See rr 181(2)–(4) and rr 182, 183, for the requirements regarding other types of corporate or unincorporated body.
[3] See paras 10.40–10.42.
[4] See paras 10.43–10.45 for exempt charities.
[5] See para 6.11.
[6] These preconditions principally relate to leases granted before 13 October 2003.

4.14 The policy of the LRA 2002 is to get the maximum in the way of interests in land recorded on the register, and an innovation of the LRA 2002[1] and the LRR 2003 is that they require disclosure of overriding interests to accompany an application for first registration, with a view to such interests being recorded on the register. The applicant is required by the LRR 2003, r 28(1) and (2) to provide the registrar, using Form DI, with information about any interests falling within the LRA 2002, Sch 1, ie interests which are overriding on first registration if they are not registered,[2] which affect his estate in the land and of which he has knowledge, with certain exceptions. The exceptions are the interests incapable of being noted on the register by virtue of the LRA 2002, ss 33 and 90(4),[3] and the express exceptions in the LRR 2003, r 28(2) for public rights, local land charges, and leases with a year or less to run. The combined effect of these provisions is set out in Appendix 1, Part A below. See also para 4.18.

---

[1]   See the LRA 2002 s 71(a), which is the power under which the LRR 2003, r 28 is made.

[2]   See para 7.5.

[3]   See para 7.23.

4.15 The registrar may enter a notice in the register in respect of any interest disclosed under the LRR 2003, r 28 (LRR 2003, r 28(4)),[1] and is under a duty to enter a notice in the register of the burden of any interest which appears from his examination of title to affect the registered estate, with the exception of any interest which is excluded from being protected by notice,[2] and also with the exception of any public right, any local land charge, any interest of a trivial or obvious character, and any interest the entry of a notice of which would be likely to cause confusion or inconvenience (LRR 2003, r 35). Also, the LRR 2003, r 9(a) requires the charges register of each registered estate to contain details of leases, charges, and any other interests which adversely affect the registered estate subsisting at the time of first registration of the estate or created thereafter. It is implicit in the LRR 2003, rr 9 and 35, and in the general structure of the legislation, that the registrar will note on the charges register any lease which has previously been registered, and on which the estate now being first registered is the immediate reversion. It seems to follow from this that the registrar will carry out an index map search as part of the process of examining the title. The registrar is required to note in the register that mines and minerals are excluded, if satisfied that they are (LRR 2003, r 32), and to enter legal mortgages or charges if satisfied of the entitlement of the mortgagee or chargee (LRR 2003, rr 22 and 34).[3] He may also make an entry in the property register if he finds that an agreement prevents the acquisition of rights of light or air for the benefit of the estate (LRR 2003, r 36).[4] If he notes on the register any interest which is an overriding interest within the LRA 2002, Sch 1,[5] it cannot be an overriding interest in relation to that registered title on any subsequent disposition (LRA 2002 s 29(3)), and it seems that the proprietor on first registration is subject to it by virtue of the entry in the register rather than Sch 1. The registrar must also enter restrictions in relation to various kinds of proprietor, such as joint proprietors or trustees, tenants for life under the Settled Land Act 1925, or non-exempt charities.[6]

1   See para 4.14 above for disclosure under the LRR 2003, r 28.

2   Ie any interest excluded under the LRA 2002, ss 33 or 90(4). See para 7.23. The most important categories of interests excluded from being protected by notice are beneficial interests under settlements or trusts, leases of three years or less, and restrictive covenants between lessor and lessee relating to the demised premises (LRA 2002, s 33(a)–(c)).

3   A charge created after a disposition which triggers the registration requirement will be subject to its own application for registration as if it were a disposition of registered land: LRR 2003 r 38 (see para 4.11).

4   See also the LRA 2002, s 37 and the LRR 2003, r 89.

5   See para 7.7.

6   See the LRA 2002, s 44; LRR 2003, rr 95 and 176, Sch 7, para 3, and paras 7.48 and 10.40–10.42.

4.16   As regards rights which benefit the estate being registered, the registrar must make a note that mines and minerals are included in it, if he is satisfied that they are (LRR 2003, r 32). It is possible to apply subsequently for a note to be added to a registered title that mines and minerals are included in the registered estate, but only on providing evidence that they were vested in the applicant for first registration of the estate at the time of first registration and in the same capacity as the remainder of the land was vested in him (LRR 2003, r 71). The registrar may enter the benefit of any appurtenant right if satisfied from examination of the title, or from evidence supplied with a specific written application for registration of the right, that the right subsists as a legal estate and benefits the estate being registered (LRR 2003, r 33(1)). If the registrar is not so satisfied he may enter details of the right claimed with such qualification as he thinks appropriate (LRR 2003, r 33(2)). If the right is claimed over an estate which is already registered, a decisive factor will of course be whether the right is binding on that estate, either by being overriding within the LRA 2003, Schs 1 or 3 (as the case may be), or by being noted on the charges register of the title concerned.[1]

1   See paras 7.4–7.7.

CONVEYANCING IMPLICATIONS

4.17   The interests in or rights adverse to unregistered land which do not need action to be taken by the persons entitled to them to protect them against registration of the land are those which fall within the LRA 2002, Sch 1,[1] although where a right or interest only falls within Sch 1 by virtue of actual occupation, the person entitled to it would be well advised not to rely on this but to seek other means of protecting the interest or right. The principal adverse interests or rights which are not within Sch 1 (other than by actual occupation), and which are capable of being protected by entries on the register if the land comes to be registered, are mortgages and charges,[2] certain leases,[3] and equitable rights such as equitable easements, the benefit of restrictive covenants,[4] tenancy agreements,[5] or options, rights of pre-emption or other contracts.[6] The available forms of protection are registration in the land charges register under the Land Charges Act 1972,[7] cautions against first registration, and, in the case of leases with more than seven years to run, applying for voluntary registration.[8] Where an interest registered under Land Charges Act 1972 is more than 15 years old, it will be a good idea to register a caution against first registration as well, because of the possibility that the name against which the land charge registration was made is in documents before the root of title, and so may not come to the notice of a disponee, and thus the registrar, under a disposition giving rise to compulsory registration the title. For the position as regards leases see para 6.47 et seq. Beneficial interests under trusts of land or in settled land may be protected by a caution against first registration, so as to ensure that an appropriate restriction is entered on the register when first registration takes place.[9]

---

[1]   See paras 7.7–7.16.
[2]   See para 8.6.
[3]   See para 6.49.
[4]   See paras 9.6–9.8, 9.29, 9.30.
[5]   See para 6.59.
[6]   See paras 11.3–11.10.
[7]   This is necessary in respect of various kinds of interest, so as to make them binding on the purchaser on any subsequent disposition which occurs before registration: see para 7.4.
[8]   See para 6.9. From 13 October 2005, registration of a caution against first registration will cease to be an available protection for leases with more than seven years to run (see para 4.4), and so voluntary registration is essential for such a lease which is not an overriding interest.
[9]   See paras 10.5, 10.9 for the protection of trust interests.

4.18   Turning to the position of an applicant for first registration, the LRR 2003, r 28 requirement of disclosure of rights or interests adverse to the estate being registered[1] relates only to rights which would be overriding interests, and therefore binding on the applicant, if they were not noted on the register. Where the existence and extent of such a right or interest is clear (eg it was expressly granted by a well-drafted deed), there is therefore no disadvantage to the applicant in disclosing it on first registration, unless he is planning fraudulent concealment of it on a future disposition. However, there will be cases where the existence of the right is arguable but not established, eg because more than one legal opinion may be entertained on whether it exists, or because proof of it depends on the assembly and interpretation of evidence. This is often the case with, for example, adverse possession rights, easements acquired by prescription, and easements which may have been granted by implication on the conveyance of a part of a holding of land. To disclose such a right to the registrar, with the possible consequence that it gets recorded on the register, is to give encouragement to the person who claims the adverse right which he would not have had if he was simply left to rely on the LRA 2002, Sch 1. Such cases will present a dilemma for the professional adviser. There seems to be no sanction for non-compliance. It seems unlikely that non-compliance is a criminal offence under LRA 2002, s 123,[2] particularly as failure to disclose an overriding interest does not cause it to lose its overriding status. The interests to be disclosed are those within the applicant's knowledge, and a conscientious professional adviser will ask his client if he knows of any interests of the relevant kind. The list of disclosable interests is quite complicated and technical (see Appendix 1), and the conscientous professional adviser may have considerable difficulty in explaining them to the applicant. The Lord Chancellor and rules committee would do well to replace the existing LRR 2003, rr 28 and 57 with simple lists of the more common types of overriding interest which are capable of being noted on the register. Where a person is in actual occupation of the land, it is important to bear in mind that it is only if that person has an interest of a kind which is overriding and is capable of being noted on the register that there is anything to disclose, and if he has, it is the interest and not the occupation which is to be disclosed. Two kinds of overriding interests commonly possessed by persons in actual occupation, namely periodic tenancies and beneficial interests under a trust of land, are not capable of being noted on the register (LRA 2002, s 33(a), (b)). There is no specific obligation on the applicant for first registration to disclose adverse rights or interests which fall outside the LRA 2002, Sch 1, and which therefore can only be protected by entries on the register, but failing to send the registrar a document which is in the possession of the applicant for first registration which discloses such a right or interest could be an offence.[3]

---

[1] See para 4.14.

[2] LRA 2002, s 123 makes suppressing information with the intention of concealing a person's right or claim an offence if done 'in the course of proceedings relating to registration under' LRA 2002. See paras 15.84, 15.85.

[3] Under the LRA 2002, s 123 (see the preceding footnote), and bearing in mind the obligation under the LRR 2003, r 24(1)(c) to submit to the registrar all documents relating to the title.

5 Freehold land

INTRODUCTION

5.1   Freeholds (this chapter) and leaseholds (Chapter 6) are the two main kinds of estate which are independently registrable with titles of their own, as opposed to the interests in registered land, such as easements, restrictive covenants, or charges, which can only be entered on the register in relation to a registered freehold or leasehold estate. Rentcharges, franchises, and profits à prendre in gross are the other independently registrable interests, and they are voluntarily but not compulsorily registrable (LRA 2002, s 3(1)(b)–(c)). On the other hand, lordships of the manor with no land attached to them cease to be registrable. The LRA 2002 makes only a few changes to the law concerning first registration of freehold land, and the effect of it, but makes considerable changes to the rules concerning dispositions of it and the interests to which it is subject. There is a new category of registered freehold land which became possible with effect from 27 September 2004,[1] namely commonhold under the Commonhold and Leasehold Reform Act 2002, Part 1. This is land which is divided into units in separate ownership which has shared common parts. The common parts are vested in a commonhold association, which is a company limited by guarantee of which the members are the unit holders. The mutual rights and obligations of the unit-holders and the commonhold association, which can include positive obligations, are defined in a commonhold community statement. Each unit will have its own registered title, as will the common parts, and commonhold land can only exist as registered land. The obligations of unit-holders to the commonhold association will be enforceable against successors in title to the units. The main purpose of commonhold is to provide a freehold alternative to the current methods, using long leases, of selling flats. For the details of commonhold see *Furber: the Commonhold and Leasehold Reform Act 2002* (Tottel) and *Commonhold: Law & Practice* (LexisNexis UK).

---

[1] For this commencement date see Commonhold and Leasehold Reform Act 2002 (Commencement No 4) Order 2004, SI 2004/1832.

COMPULSORY REGISTRATION

5.2 An unregistered freehold becomes compulsorily registrable if any of the following happens (LRA 2002, ss 4(1)(a), (b) and (g), (2)(a), (6), (7) and (8))—

- a transfer of it for valuable or other consideration (s 4(1)(a)(i));
- if it has a negative value, any transfer of it (s 4(1)(a)(i) and (6));
- a transfer of it by way of gift (s 4(1)(a)(i)), including, in relation to any trust where the settlor did not retain the entire beneficial interest when the trust was constituted, a transfer so as to constitute the trust, and a transfer uniting the bare legal title and the beneficial interest (s 4(7));
- a transfer of it in pursuance of an order of the court (s 4(1)(a)(i));
- an assent or vesting assent[1] in respect of it (s 4(1)(a)(ii));
- a transfer of it in circumstances where the Housing Act 1985, s 171A applies (a disposal by a landlord which leads to a person no longer being a secure tenant) (LRA 2002, s 4(1)(b));[2]
- the creation of a mortgage of it, where the mortgage has priority over any other mortgages of it, and is to be protected by deposit of title deeds (s 4(1)(g), (8)).[3]

The person who is required to apply for registration is the transferee, or (in the last-mentioned case) the mortgagor,[4] or the transferee's or mortgagor's successor in title (LRA 2002, s 6(1)–(3)) (for the grants of leases out of unregistered freeholds which are compulsorily registrable see para 6.5). 'Transfer' for this purpose does not include a transfer by operation of law (LRA 2002, s 4(3)), such as the devolution of property on death. There is no general definition of 'transfer' in the legislation, but it is clear from the context that it has a non-technical meaning and must, in relation to unregistered freehold land, include a conveyance. The time limits for registration and the consequences of failure to apply for it are as stated in paras 4.9 and 4.10. A grant by the Crown of a freehold out of demesne land also gives rise to a registration requirement (LRA 2002, s 80).[5] On the other hand, a transfer, assent, or mortgage of mines or minerals held apart from the surface is excluded from compulsory registration (LRA 2002, s 4(9)). As under the previous law, dealings before first registration, but after there has been a dealing which gives rise to a duty to apply for registration, are treated as if occurring after first registration (LRA 2002, Sch 10, para 1; LRR 2003, r 38).[6]

---

[1] Ie within the meaning of the term in the Settled Land Act 1925: LRA 2002, s 4(9). In practice the vesting assents to which this will apply are ones made after the death of a tenant for life where the land remains settled land, as it ceased to be possible to create new settlements under the Settled Land Act 1925 with effect from 1 January 1997 (Trusts of Land and Appointment of Trustees Act 1996, s 2(1)).

[2] Where such a transfer is of a freehold estate, it is also likely to fall within the LRA 2002, s 4(1)(a).

[3] See paras 8.3–8.4.

⁴ In the case of a mortgage which triggers registration, the mortgagee may apply if the mortgagor fails to: LRR 2003, r 21 made under the LRA 2002, s 6(6).
⁵ See para 12.21.
⁶ See para 4.11.

5.3   The main categories of transfer of a freehold which are not subject to compulsory registration are thus: transfers vesting freehold land in new trustees on a change of trustees of a trust of land; a vesting deed relating to settled land (within Settled Land Act 1925) on a change of tenant for life (or statutory owners) otherwise than on the death of a tenant for life;[1] a transfer to another or others to hold the freehold as nominee(s) or bare trustee(s) for the transferor, or by nominee(s) or bare trustee(s), who became such as a result of such a transfer, back to the person beneficially entitled; and a transfer of mines or minerals held separately from the surface. This is subject to the fact that all these events, apart from the transfer of mines or minerals held separately from the surface, will apparently be compulsorily registrable if the estate has a negative value.[2] The former express exclusions of incorporeal hereditaments, and corporeal hereditaments which are part of a manor and included in its sale, from compulsory registration, are not reproduced in the LRA 2002, s 4,[3] but this is because the narrower definition of 'land' in the LRA 2002, as compared with that in the LRA 1925,[4] means that an incorporeal hereditament by itself is outside the scope of compulsory registration, and that a corporeal hereditament will only be subject to it if it is a legal estate in land. Disregarding the special cases of land with a negative value (any disposition of which is compulsorily registrable) and mines and minerals held separately from the surface (not compulsorily registrable), broadly speaking the transfers falling outside the compulsory registration requirement are ones which neither give effect to a previous change in the beneficial ownership to a legal estate, nor bring about a change in the beneficial ownership. A change in beneficial entitlement to a legal estate without any change as to the person or persons holding the legal estate is also not an occasion of compulsory registration. The differences between these requirements and those of the previous law,[5] in relation to freeholds, are the omission of vesting deeds relating to settled land from compulsory registration,[6] and the LRA 2002, s 4(7), making it clear that transfers into or out of trusts, except where the current proprietor of land transfers it to a bare trustee for himself or such a bare trustee transfers it back to the beneficial owner, are subject to compulsory registration (see, further, paras 5.5 and 5.6 below).

¹ Registration is compulsory after the death of a tenant for life because a vesting assent is expressly included in the LRA 2002, s 4(1)(a)(ii). There might be an argument that a vesting instrument relating to settled land other than on the death of a tenant for life, is brought into compulsory registration by the LRA 2002, s 4(7)(b), but the wording of the latter provision does not really seem apt to cover the case of a limited owner who has a statutory right to have the freehold estate vested in him. The LRA 1925, s 123(1)(d) (as substituted by the LRA 1997, ss 1,

5(4)) expressly included vesting deeds among compulsorily registrable dispositions, but this feature has not been repeated in the corresponding provision of the LRA 2002, ie s 4(1).
[2] See the LRA 2002, s 4(6), which treats all transfers of land with a negative value as transferred for valuable or other consideration.
[3] See the LRA 1925, s 123(3) (as substituted by the LRA 1997, ss 1, 5(4)) for this former exclusion.
[4] Compare the definition of 'land' in the LRA 2002, s 132(1) with that in the LRA 1925, s 3(viii)—the latter includes incorporeal hereditaments while the former does not.
[5] Ie under the LRA 1925, s 123 as substituted by the LRA 1997, ss 1, 5(4), with effect from 1 April 1998.
[6] See footnote 1 above.

5.4   As described in para 4.10 above, when the transferee fails to register within the prescribed period an unregistered estate which has been the subject of a transfer which triggers compulsory registration, the legal estate reverts to the transferor, who holds that legal estate on a bare trust for the transferee (LRA 2002, s 7). As also mentioned in para 4.10 above, when this has happened and there is then a further remedial transfer of the legal estate by the transferor to the transferee, there is no express provision in LRA 2002, in contrast to that in LRA 1925 s 123(7A), that the further remedial transfer is subject to the compulsory registration requirement. This is presumably on the grounds that the general compulsory registration provisions in the LRA 2002, s 4[1] will apply to it anyway. However, there is an argument, set out in para 5.5 below, for saying that registration is not compulsory for a remedial transfer where what has happened is a *transfer* of a legal estate which triggered compulsory registration (there is much less of an argument in the case of a *grant* of a legal estate which triggers compulsory registration—see para 6.7 below).

[1] See para 5.2 above.

5.5   Consider the following. A sells the (unregistered) freehold of Blackacre to B. A conveys Blackacre to B on payment of the purchase money, but B fails to apply for registration within two months. B thus has the legal estate in Blackacre for two months, after which A then holds the legal estate in Blackacre on a bare trust for B (LRA 2002, s 7(2)(a)). A then conveys Blackacre to B again. If compulsory registration is to apply to this second conveyance it has to be either a transfer for a consideration or a transfer by way of gift (s 4(1)(a)). It is arguably not a transfer for a consideration because the consideration has already been given in return for the previous transfer which gave rise to the bare trust.[1] The reconveyance is not in return for a consideration, but in pursuance of B's beneficial interest and consequent right to require the legal estate to be vested in him, which is what he has acquired for the consideration already handed over. B is under a statutory obligation under s 8 to pay the costs of the remedial transfer and indemnify A, but that is a statutory obligation arising from B's failure, not the provision of consideration for the

73

remedial transfer. The remedial transfer is only a transfer by way of gift if it falls within s 4(7)(b), ie if it unites the bare legal title and the beneficial interest in property held under a trust under which the settlor did not, on constitution, retain the whole of the beneficial interest. Whether this last provision applies depends on whether the transferor or the transferee is the settlor for the purpose of this provision. It seems more likely that the transferee is the settlor, because it is his failure to register the transfer to him of the legal estate which became vested in him which has caused the trust to arise. If that is correct the settlor for this purpose did retain the beneficial interest on the constitution of the trust, and accordingly s 4(7)(b) does not apply. Looking at the overall policy of the legislation, such a remedial transfer is clearly intended fall within the compulsory registration requirement, and that may be sufficient for a court to find that a remedial transfer is subject to compulsory registration—probably on the basis that it is pursuant to a larger transaction for a consideration. On a narrow examination of the wording, however, there is the above argument for saying that the compulsory registration requirement does not apply to a remedial transfer.

---

[1]   If there was actual consideration in the conveyance, eg an indemnity against restrictive covenants, it clearly would trigger compulsory registration.

5.6   Does Land Registration Act 2002, s 4(7) prevent the compulsory registration requirement being avoided by the following method? The seller of an unregistered legal estate declares in writing (on being paid the purchase money) that he holds the legal estate on trust for the purchaser, then appoints as trustees of the estate persons nominated by the buyer, and then conveys the estate to them. It is arguable that the conveyance to the trustees would not be *for the purpose of constituting* a trust, within the meaning of s 4(7)(a), because the trust would have been constituted already by the declaration of trust. Section 4(7)(b) would, however, almost certainly be applicable if and when the legal estate was vested in the buyer, and so as a means of avoiding the compulsory registration requirement this is not an attractive option.

5.7   Where someone dies owning unregistered freehold land, the devolution of it on death or the grant of probate or letters of administration in relation to that person's estate are not events requiring registration, but when the personal representatives assent to the vesting of the land in a beneficiary, the latter is required to apply for registration (LRA 2002, s 4(1)(a)(ii)). The personal representatives can of course apply voluntarily to have it registered. Although grants of probate or letters of administration are orders of the court, they are not *transfers in pursuance of an order of a* court (within the LRA 2002, s 4(1)(a)(i)). In the case of a grant of probate it does not transfer title to the deceased's property, but it confirms it—strictly speaking the property devolves on the executors by virtue of the death and the will. Letters of administration do vest the deceased's property in the administrators, but the order is itself a transfer and so there is no transfer *pursuant* to a court order.

5.8 The Lord Chancellor has power by statutory instrument to extend the requirement of registration to events he may specify relating to unregistered estates in land, rentcharges, franchises, or profits à prendre in gross (LRA 2002, s 5(1)(a) and (2)). He may make consequential amendments of any legislation, but may not require an estate granted to a mortgagee to be registered (LRA 2002, s 5(1)(b) and (3)).

VOLUNTARY REGISTRATION

5.9 Any person may apply to be registered as proprietor of an unregistered freehold estate which is an estate in land, a rentcharge, a franchise, or a profit à prendre in gross, if he is the person in whom it is vested, or if he is entitled to require it to be vested in him (LRA 2002, s 3(1), (2)). However, a person cannot apply as a person entitled to require the estate to be vested in him where his entitlement is as a person who has contracted to buy (LRA 2002, s 3(6)).[1] A trustee of land, or a tenant for life under a Settled Land Act 1925 settlement, can thus apply to be registered, and so apparently can someone who is beneficially entitled to land under a bare trust. Where a mortgagor has become subject to the requirement to register as a result of creating a first mortgage protected by deposit of documents, the mortgagee will be able to apply to have the estate charged by the mortgage registered (LRA 2002, s 6(6); LRR 2003, r 21). The Crown is also able to register demesne land voluntarily by granting itself a freehold (LRA 2002, s 79),[2] and foreshore and UK internal waters are capable of registration (LRA 2002, s 130). Again, in relation to freehold land the differences from the previous law (LRA 1925, s 4)[3] are minor.[4]

---

[1] This is because the conveyance will be an occasion of compulsory registration, on which the fee is higher than for voluntary registration—see the Land Registration Fee Order 2004, SI 2004/595, Sch 1, Scale 1, set out in Appendix 2.

[2] See para 12.19.

[3] As amended by the Trusts of Land and Appointment of Trustees Act 1996, s 25, Sch 3, para 5.

[4] The main differences are the extension of registrability to franchises and profits à prendre in gross (LRA 2002, s 3(1)), and to demesne and territorial waters (LRA 2002, ss 79 and 130).

REGISTRATION AND CATEGORIES OF TITLE

5.10   For the details of applications for first registration, see paras 4.13–4.16. When someone applies to be registered as proprietor, he may be so registered with one of the following categories of freehold title.

Absolute title

5.11   A person may be registered with absolute title if the registrar is of the opinion that the person's title to the estate is such that a competent professional adviser would advise acceptance (LRA 2002, s 9(1), (2)). The registrar may disregard the fact that a person's title appears to him to be open to objection if he is of the opinion that the defect will not cause the holding under the title to be disturbed (LRA 2002, s 9(3)). First registration of a person as proprietor of a freehold estate with absolute title means that the estate is vested in him together with all interests subsisting for the benefit of the estate (LRA 2002, s 11(3)), and subject only to the interests entered on the register in relation to the estate (LRA 2002, s 11(4)(a)),[1] any unregistered interests which fall within any of the paragraphs of the LRA 2002, Sch 1 at time of registration (LRA 2002, s 11(4)(b)),[2] and any interests acquired under the Limitation Act 1980 of which the proprietor has notice (LRA 2002, s 11(4)(c)).[3] In relation to first registrations before 13 October 2006, such a person's registered estate will also be subject to any interests acquired under the Limitation Act 1980 of which the proprietor did *not* have notice (Sch 12, para 7). It should be noted that if an interest under the Limitation Act 1980 first comes to the notice of the proprietor after first registration, where the date of first registration is on or after 13 October 2006, it will not be binding under the LRA 2002, s 11(4)(c).[4] The estate is also subject to any beneficial interests in the estate of persons other than the proprietor of which the proprietor has notice (LRA 2002, s 11(5)).

---

[1]   See, further, paras 7.4, 7.5.

[2]   See, further, paras 7.7–7.16. The most important categories are short leases, interests of persons in actual occupation, and legal easements.

[3]   See, further, para 13.22.

[4]   See LRA 2002, s 11(1), and the opening words of s 11(4), which make it clear that the circumstances at the time of first registration are determinative. An interest under the Limitation Act 1980 could on or after 13 October 2006 still be overriding if the person entitled to it is in actual occupation (see para 7.9).

Qualified title

5.12   A person may be registered with qualified title if the registrar is of the opinion that the person's title to the estate has been established only for a limited period or subject to reservations which cannot be disregarded as something which will not cause the holding under the title to be disturbed (LRA 2002, s 9(1), (4)). Such registration has the same effect as registration with title absolute, except that it does not affect the enforcement of any estate, right or interest which appears from the register to be excepted from the effect of registration (LRA 2002, s 11(6)).

Possessory title

5.13 Possessory title is where, in the registrar's opinion, neither an absolute nor a qualified title may be registered but the applicant is in actual possession of the land in question or in receipt of the rents and profits of it (LRA 2002, s 9(1), (5)). Registration with possessory title has the same effect as registration with absolute title except that it does not affect the enforcement of any estate right or interest adverse to, or in derogation of the proprietor's title, subsisting at the time of registration or then capable of arising (LRA 2002, s 11(7)). So long as the title remains possessory, the name of the person first registered as proprietor will remain recorded on the proprietorship register of the title, despite subsequent dispositions of it (LRR 2003, r 8(1)(i)).

5.14 The position as regards categories of title is thus not very different from that under the previous law, the main difference being the narrowing of the categories of unregistered interest to which the registered proprietor's title is subject. It is possible for a qualified or possessory title to be upgraded subsequently: see para 5.15. For further provisions concerning the effect of registration as proprietor see paras 5.24–5.27. For possessory titles see also para 13.31.

Power to upgrade title

5.15 Where the title to a freehold (or leasehold) estate is entered in the register as possessory or qualified, it can be upgraded to absolute if the registrar is satisfied that the title is sufficiently robust (LRA 2002, s 62(1)). The registrar is to apply the same standards as when making a first registration with absolute title (LRA 2002, s 62(8)).[1] Alternatively, in the case of a possessory title, the registrar may upgrade it to absolute after 12 years of it being registered as possessory, if the registrar is satisfied that the registered proprietor is in possession of the land (LRA 2002, s 62(4)).[2] These are both subject to the qualification that such upgrading cannot occur if a claim adverse to the registered proprietor's title is outstanding where that claim is by virtue of a right or interest which is preserved by virtue of the existing entry about the class of title (LRA 2002, s 62(6)). The application for upgrading may only be made by the proprietor of the estate in question, a person entitled to be registered as proprietor of that estate, a proprietor of a registered charge affecting that estate, or a person interested in a registered estate which derives from that estate (LRA 2002, s 62(7)).[3] Once the title has been upgraded to absolute, the proprietor ceases to hold the estate subject to any estate, right or interest whose enforceability was preserved by virtue of the previous entry about the class of title (LRA 2002, s 63(1)).

---

[1]   For the standards in question see the LRA 2002, s 9(2) and (3), and para 5.11 above.

[2]   The Lord Chancellor may by order change the number of years registration as a possessory title which is required before this power is exercised: LRA 2002, s 62(9).

[3]   The application must be made in Form UT1 (LRR 2003, r 124(1)) and, except where 12 years' possessory title is relied on, must be accompanied by such documents as will satisfy the registrar as to the title (LRR 2003, r 124(2)). Where the applicant is not the registered proprietor he must provide evidence of his right to apply (LRR 2003, r 124(5), (6)).

DISPOSITIONS OF REGISTERED LAND

5.16   Once a legal estate in land is registered, a person who is the registered proprietor or is entitled to be registered as proprietor,[1] has power to make a disposition of any kind permitted by the general law in relation to it, other than a mortgage by demise, and also has power to charge the estate at law with the payment of money (LRA 2002, s 23(1)). The rules for dispositions of registered land also apply to dispositions of unregistered land by someone who has acquired the unregistered land under a disposition which gives rise to an obligation to register the title.[2] All dispositions transferring or creating a legal estate are required to be completed by registration, apart from leases for seven years or less, subject to there being certain special categories of lease which are registrable even though of seven years or less.[3] Thus a transfer of the estate, a grant out of it of a lease for more than seven years from the date of grant, or a grant of a lease of any other of the kinds set out in para 6.21, an express grant or reservation of a legal easement, right or privilege over land (other than one registrable under Commons Registration Act 1965),[4] an express grant or reservation of a legal rentcharge,[5] a grant of a right of entry annexed to a lease or rentcharge,[6] and the grant of a legal charge[7] are all dispositions which are required to be completed by registration (LRA 2002, s 27(2)). Until the registration requirements for these types of disposition are met, such dispositions do not operate at law (LRA 2002, s 27(1)),[8] and such dispositions are only effective if they comply with the requirements as to form and content provided by the rules (LRA 2002, s 25(1)).

---

[1]   Defined as a person entitled to exercise the owner's powers by the LRA 2002, s 24.

[2]   LRR 2003, r 38 (authorised by the LRA 2002, Sch 10, para 1) applies the LRA 2002 to dealings made by someone who is subject to an obligation under the LRA 2002, s 6 to register (see paras 5.2 et seq) as if the registration had taken place. See para 4.11.

[3]   For leases which are or are not registrable see para 6.21.

4   Ie an interest of a kind falling within the LPA 1925, s 1(2)(a), but not including a grant which arises from the operation of the LPA 1925, s 62 (general words implied in conveyances)—see the LRA 2002, s 27(7). See paras 9.11, 9.12. Where a profit à prendre is registered under the Commons Registration Act 1965 it will be an overriding interest under the LRA 2002, Sch 3, para 3(1).

5   Ie an interest of a kind falling within the LPA 1925, s 1(2)(b).

6   Ie an interest of a kind falling within the LPA 1925, s 1(2)(e).

7   See para 8.7.

8   For these requirements see para 5.18.

5.17   A transfer of a registered estate must be in Form TP1 (transfer of part of registered title(s)), TP2 (transfer of part of registered title(s) under a power of sale), TP3 (transfer of portfolio of titles), TR1 (transfer of whole of registered title(s)), TR2 (transfer of whole of registered title(s) under a power of sale), TR5 (transfer of portfolio of whole titles), AS1 (assent of whole of registered title(s)), or AS3 (assent of part of registered title(s) by personal representative), as appropriate (LRR 2003, r 58).[1] The covenants for title under the Law of Property (Miscellaneous Provisions) Act 1994—full title guarantee or limited title guarantee—may be included in the transfer (LRA 2002, Sch 10, para 3; LRR 2003, r 67(1)). If those covenants are limited or extended a prescribed form of words must be used in the transfer (LRR 2003, r 68).[2] There is no liability under the covenants for title for anything entered or noted in the register of title of the estate transferred.[3] A disposition by or to a charity, or into a Settled Land Act 1925 settlement, must contain the appropriate statements.[4] Execution of the transfer must be in accordance with the appropriate form of execution set out in the LRR 2003, Sch 9 (LRR 2003, r 206(3)). The requirements of Sch 9 are essentially the same as those for execution of a deed.[5] The requirement of registration also applies to dispositions by operation of law except for a transfer on the death or bankruptcy of an individual proprietor, a transfer on the dissolution of a corporate proprietor, or the creation of legal charge which is a local land charge (LRA 2002, s 27(5)). These exceptions do not leave many categories of disposition by operation of law to be ones required to be registered—vesting orders made by the court and vesting declarations in appointments of new trustees are the main and perhaps the only examples.[6] For dispositions by operation of law see, further, para 5.23.

1   In relation to an exchange of titles see the special requirement of the LRR 2003, r 59. As with all transfers there are detailed provisions relating to the forms and the execution of them in the LRR 2003, rr 206–212 and Sch 9. There is as yet no prescribed form for the grant of a lease, and a form of charge is provided, but it is not compulsory (LRR 2003, r 103—Form CH1). See also para 8.9.

2   For covenants for title see also para 9.34. For transfer of a registered estate subject to a rentcharge see the LRR 2003, r 69.

3   Law of Property (Miscellaneous Provisions) Act 1994, s 6(4), added by LRA 2002, s 133, Sch 11, para 31(2).

5.18 If a disposition is required to be registered, the requirements as to registration of it set out in the LRA 2002, Sch 2 have to be satisfied before it takes effect at law (LRA 2002, s 27(1) and (4), and Sch 2, paras 2 and 3). In the case of a transfer of a registered estate the transferee or his successor in title must be registered as proprietor (LRA 2002, Sch 2, para 2(1)). Where the transfer is of part only of the land in a title (which means that the transferred land will be put into a new register of title of its own), there must also be an entry, in the property register relating to the land which has not been transferred, referring to the removal of the estate comprised in the transfer, and entries in the register of the title to the retained part relating to any rights, covenants, provisions, and other matters created by the transfer which the registrar considers affect that part (LRA 2002, Sch 2, para 2(2) and LRR 2003, r 72).[1] In the case of a grant of a lease for more than seven years (or other lease of a kind which is required to be registered),[2] the grantee or his successor in title must be registered as the proprietor of the lease and a notice of the lease must be entered in 'the register' (LRA 2002, Sch 2, para 3)—this must refer to the register of the title out of which the lease has been granted. In the case of the grant of appurtenant legal interests which do not get their own title register—easements, rights or privileges over land, or appurtenant rent charges or rights of entry[3]—the requirement is entry of a notice in the register relating to the grantor's estate, and where the estate benefited by the interest is a registered estate, the registration of the proprietor of that estate as proprietor of the interest (LRA 2002, Sch 2, para 7).[4] The latter registration must be made in relation to the registered estate which benefits from the interest (LRA 2002, s 59(1)), and so the practical effect is that the interest is added to the property register of the estate benefited. In the case of a legal charge, the requirement of registration is fulfilled when the chargee or his successor in title is registered as proprietor (LRA 2002, Sch 2, para 8)—this registration is done in relation to the estate charged (LRA 2002, s 59(2)).[5] These requirements represent a change from the previous law in that they impose a double requirement in cases where two registered estates are involved, ie the transfer of part of an estate, the grant of a lease for more than seven years, or the grant of an easement, rentcharge, profit à prendre or right of entry, and explicitly makes the double registration requirement a pre-condition for becoming entitled to a legal estate: see further, paras 5.24 and 5.32 et seq. Under the LRA 1925 the registrar was required to enter such dispositions on the register of the estate out of which the transfer or grant was made, but doing so was not a pre-condition of the transferee or grantee becoming entitled to a legal estate.

[1] The registrar may as an alternative start a new title for the retained part: LRR 2003, r 72(3).
[2] See para 6.21.
[3] Ie any interest falling within the LPA 1925, s 1(2)(a), (b) or (e) which is not a legal rentcharge or profit à prendre in gross—the latter do qualify for their own register of title and there are registration requirements for them, similar to those for leases, in the LRA 2002, Sch 2, para 6.
[4] For easements see paras 9.11, 9.14.
[5] See para 8.7.

5.19 An application for registration of a registrable disposition of a registered estate must be made in Form AP1 (LRR 2003, r 13). If the transfer is executed by an attorney evidence of the power is required and certain supporting evidence may be required by the registrar (LRR 2003, rr 61–63). If the applicant is a registered company, its registered number must be stated (LRR 2003, r 181(1)).[1] There are some categories of applicant, eg non-exempt charities, or tenants for life under the Settled Land Act 1925 settlements, who must include an application for registration of an appropriate restriction.[2] An application to register a registrable disposition of a registered estate must be accompanied by disclosure on Form DI of the overriding interests within the LRA 2002, Sch 3[3] of which the applicant has knowledge, and which affect the registered estate, subject to a number of exceptions, (LRR 2003, r 57(1), (2), made under the LRA 2002, s 71). The exceptions are the interests incapable of being noted on the register by virtue of the LRA 2002, ss 33 and 90(4),[4] and the express exceptions in the LRR 2003, r 57(2) for public rights, local land charges, and leases with a year or less to run. The combined effect of these provisions is set out in Appendix 1, Part B, below. The application must be accompanied by any documents evidencing the disclosable overriding interests which are in the applicant's control (LRR 2003, r 57(4)). The comments on the first registration disclosure obligations in para 4.18 above apply also to these disclosure obligations on registering a registered disposition.

[1] See the LRR 2003, rr 181(2)–(4), and 182 and 183, for the requirements regarding other types of corporate or unincorporated body.
[2] For charities see the LRR 2003, r 176 and para 10.40, and for settled land see the LRR 2003, Sch 7 and paras 10.20–10.22.
[3] See paras 7.63.
[4] See para 7.23.

5.20 The effective date of registration of a disposition of a registered estate, which is a disposition of a kind required to be registered, is when the application is received by the land registry (LRA 2002, s 74).[1] If two or more applications, in respect of the same registered title, are treated as having been made at the same time, the position is as follows

(LRR 2003, r 55(1)). If one transaction is dependent on another the applications will be treated as being in the order which gives effect to them (LRR 2003, r 55(7)). In other cases the person, or the persons (if they are in agreement about this), making the applications may specify the relative priority of the applications. If they cannot agree on the priority the registrar will make a proposal as to it, but subject to any applicant's right to object and have the matter determined under the dispute resolution procedure (LRR 2003, r 55(2)–(6)).[2] When registering the effect of a disposition the registrar may enter a notice on the register of any of the interests falling within the LRA 2002, Sch 3 which have been disclosed under the LRR 2003, r 57 (LRR 2003, r 57(5)), and he has a general power to enter a notice on the register of any overriding interest to which an estate appears to be subject (LRA 2002, s 37).[3] Such registration will have the effect of depriving such interests of overriding status in relation to future dispositions (LRA 2002, s 29(3)). The registrar may also make entries in the register concerning positive covenants, or indemnity covenants in respect of positive or restrictive covenants, but must remove such entries if the covenants appear not to bind the current proprietor (LRR 2003, rr 64 and 65). He must also enter restrictions in relation to various kinds of proprietor, such as joint proprietors or trustees, tenants for life under the Settled Land Act 1925, or non-exempt charities (LRA 2002, s 44; LRR 2003, rr 95 and 176, Sch 7 para 3).[4]

---

[1]   For the time at which applications are made see the LRR 2003, r 15 and paras 2.44–2.46.
[2]   For the dispute procedure see para 15.4 et seq.
[3]   If he exercises this power he must give notice to interested parties under the LRR 2003, r 89.
[4]   See also paras 7.48, 7.53, 10.10–10.22, 10.40, 10.41.

5.21   If the disposition is for valuable consideration,[1] it will be subject to interests in the land which subsisted before the disposition was made only if they fall into one of the following categories—

    (1)   registered charges which have been registered, and interests which have been noted on the register, before the earlier of the registration of the disposition[2] or the beginning of any relevant priority period during which it was registered (LRA 2002, ss 29(2)(a)(i) and 72);[3]

    (2)   any overriding interest falling within the LRA 2002, Sch 3[4] which has never been the subject of a notice on the register (LRA 2002, s 29(2)(a)(ii) and (3)),[5] and

    (3)   any interest excepted from the effect of registration (s 29(2)(a)(iii)).[6]

A grant of a lease for valuable consideration, where the term of it is seven years or less and it is not a registrable disposition,[7] is treated as if it were a registrable disposition which is registered at the time of the grant (s 29(4)), so that it also will have priority over interests not on the register and not overriding at the time of the grant. A disposition which is not for valuable consideration will be subject to any interest to which the proprietor making the disposition is subject (eg a beneficial interest under a trust).[8]

For priorities of interests see further paras 7.17, 7.18.

---

[1] Valuable consideration does not include marriage consideration or a nominal consideration in money: LRA 2002, s 132(1). It did include marriage for the purposes of the LRA 1925—see s 3(xxxi) of that Act.
[2] The effective date of registration is the date of the application for registration: LRA 2002, s 74.
[3] The reason for registered charges being mentioned separately is that they are substantively registered (on the register relating to the estate subject to the charge) rather than noted (LRA 2002, s 59(2) and Sch 2, para 8). For priority periods see paras 7.82–7.84.
[4] For the categories of overriding interest within Sch 3 see paras 7.62, 7.66–7.81.
[5] LRA 2002, s 29(3) has the effect that once such an interest has been noted on the register it can only be protected by notice on the register and cannot again be overriding if it ceases to be noted on the register. The LRR 2003, rr 28 and 57, pursuant to the LRA 2002, s 71, require many kinds of overriding interest to be disclosed to the registrar, and the LRA 2002, s 37 and the LRR 2003, r 35 empower the registrar to note many kinds of them on the register. See paras 5.19, 5.20, 7.25, 7.26 and Appendix 1.
[6] Ie where the registration is with qualified or possessory title. See para 5.12 and 5.13.
[7] Some special kinds of lease are registrable despite being for seven years or less: see para 6.21.
[8] This follows from the LRA, s 23(1) (power of owner to make any disposition permitted by the general law other than a mortgage by demise) and s 28 which provides that except as provided by s 29 the priority of any interest affecting (inter alia) a registered freehold is not affected by a disposition.

5.22 Interests in or dispositions of registered estates, which do not take effect at law under dispositions for valuable consideration as described in paras 5.16–5.21, take their priority among themselves in the order in which they have come into existence or been made (LRA 2002, s 28). They will lose priority to a disposition for valuable consideration which takes effect at law (either by being a registrable disposition which has been registered, or by being a non-registrable lease for a term of seven years or less) unless protected by a notice on the register or by being an overriding interest within the LRA 2002, Sch 3.[1] It would seem that a disposition by the proprietor of a registered estate which is required to be completed by registration, but has not been, should be so protected by entry of a notice in the register relating to the disponor's estate,[2] although it is possible for it to be protected without the protection of a notice or other entry in the register where the disponee is in actual occupation and satisfies the conditions for it to be an overriding interest within the LRA 2002, Sch 3, para 2.[3] An exception to all this is that beneficial interests under trusts or settlements, cannot be protected by notice because they are interests which can be overreached by a sale, or other disposition of the land, if the correct procedure is followed.[4] They can be protected from a disposition in breach of the statutory overreaching procedure, or in breach of any restrictions on sale, leasing or other disposition imposed by the trust instrument (eg a requirement of consent of a beneficiary), by entry of an appropriate restriction on the register.[5] In the case of a trust of land,[6] if a beneficiary is in actual occupation, that can provide a measure of protection against a disposition in breach of the statutory overreaching rules.[7]

[1]   For the interests capable of being overriding, those which may be protected by notice, and those which can be protected in either fashion, see paras 7.20, 7.62.

[2]   Such a disposition is an effective disposition, and the lack of registration means only that it does not take effect at law (LRA 2002 ss 23(1) and 27(1)). It is presumably at least as substantial an interest as that under a contract of sale.

[3]   See paras 7.67–7.73.

[4]   See the LRA 2002, s 33(a) for the exclusion of trust interests from being capable of protection by notice. See also para 7.23(1).

[5]   See paras 7.45(1), 7.48, 7.53.

[6]   See para 10.2 for this term.

[7]   Under the LRA 2002, Sch 3, para 2. See para 7.67. Interests under a settlement under the Settled Land Act 1925 are specifically excluded from this paragraph, but beneficial interests under trusts of land can fall within it.

SUCCESSION TO REGISTERED LAND OTHER THAN BY DISPOSITION

5.23   A vesting order or vesting declaration relating to registered land is treated as a disposition, and takes effect only when registered (LRA 2002, s 27(5)).[1] It is produced to the registrar for registration, and in the case of a vesting declaration he needs to be satisfied that the persons making it were entitled to do so (LRR 2003, r 161). On the death of a registered proprietor the legal estate devolves on the personal representatives and they are not required to be registered as proprietors (LRA 2002, s 27(5)),[2] but they may be registered.[3] A transfer by them to a beneficiary or a purchaser on a sale by them is a registrable disposition, and if the personal representatives have not been registered as proprietors, the disponee must when applying for registration produce the original grant of probate or letters of administration (LRR 2003, r 162). In the event of a bankruptcy petition or a subsequent adjudication bankrupt of a registered proprietor, the interests of the creditors can only be protected by registration in the proprietorship register of a notice of the petition (LRA 2002, s 86(2), (3); LRR 2003, r 165), and then, in the event of adjudication, a bankruptcy restriction to the effect that no disposition may be registered unless the trustee in bankruptcy is first registered as proprietor (LRA 2002, s 86(4); LRR 2003, r 166).[4] The bankruptcy petition or order is not protected by any other means as an 'interest' affecting the estate (LRA 2002, s 86(1)). The trustee in bankruptcy is not under a positive requirement to be registered as proprietor (LRA 2002, s 27(5)(a)). In the absence of such a notice or restriction the bankrupt can make a valid transfer of the estate to a purchaser acting in good faith and without notice of the bankruptcy petition or adjudication (LRA 2002, s 86(5)).[5] If a company which is a registered proprietor of land is the subject of an administration order or goes into liquidation, there is provision for this to be entered on the register (LRR 2003, r 184). If a company is dissolved there is no requirement that this be registered (LRA 2002, s 27(5)(b)), but the fact of the dissolution may be noted by the registrar in the register (LRR 2003, r 185).

---

[1]   See also the Trustee Act 1925, ss 40 (vesting declarations) and 44–50 (vesting orders).
[2]   The personal representative thus takes the land subject to whatever interests it was subject to in the ownership of the deceased: LRA 2002, s 28.
[3]   See the LRR 2003, r 163 for the requirements, principally production of the grant of probate or letters of administration.
[4]   For registration of the trustee as proprietor see the LRR 2003, r 168.
[5]   The purchaser is not required to make a search under the Land Charges Act 1972 (LRA 2002, s 86(7)).

CONCLUSIVENESS OF REGISTER AND PROTECTION OF DISPONEES

5.24   The LRA 2002, s 58(1) provides that if, on the entry of a person on the register as proprietor of a legal estate, that estate would not otherwise be vested in him, it is deemed to be vested in him as a result of the registration.[1] This is subject to the qualification in the LRA 2002, s 58(2) that s 58(1) does not apply where the entry is made in pursuance of a registrable disposition in relation to which some other registration requirement remains to be met. This latter qualification relates particularly to cases where there is a double registration requirement:[2] the transfer of part of an estate, the grant of a lease for more than seven years, or the grant of an easement, rentcharge, profit à prendre or right of entry (LRA 2002, Sch 2, paras 2(2), 3, 6, and 7).[3] In all these cases there is a requirement that a notice or other entry be entered or made on the register relating to the estate from which the estate or interest is derived, as well as registration of the disponee as proprietor of the estate or interest, before the disposition takes effect at law (LRA 2002, s 27(1), (4), Sch 2). The LRA 2002, s 58(2) apparently only applies to qualify the effect of being registered as proprietor where there is an unfulfilled double requirement in relation to the disposition pursuant to which the registration is made. This raises the question as to whether the LRA 2002, s 58(1) would have the effect of vesting a legal estate in a successor in title of the original transferee or grantee under a double registration requirement disposition (ie a transfer of part of an estate, or the grant of a lease for more than seven years, or the grant of an easement, rentcharge, profit à prendre or right of entry) where the double registration requirement was not fulfilled in relation to the original transfer or grant and still remains unfulfilled at the time of the sale to a successor in title. It is submitted that it does not, because s 58(1) only applies to the entry of someone in the register as the proprietor *of a legal estate* (emphasis supplied), and in the situation under discussion the original transferee or grantee under the double registration requirement disposition does not become registered as the proprietor of a legal estate. It is also relevant that the powers of disposition and priority rules depend on the ownership or acquisition (respectively) of a legal estate (LRA 2002, ss 23 and 24 (powers of disposition), 29(1) (priorities)).[4]

---

[1] This restates in a more succinct and logical form the effect of the LRA 1925, s 69(1).

[2] See para 5.18 and the LRA 2002, Sch 2.

[3] See para 5.18.

[4] See also, in both cases, the definition of 'registered estate' in the LRA 2002, s 132(1) to the effect that it means a registered legal estate. See also paras 7.17, 7.18.

5.25 On the other hand, if the LRA 2002, s 58(1) does not have the effect of vesting a legal estate in the circumstances discussed in para 5.24 above, the LRA 2002, s 58(2) appears to be redundant, because the LRA 2002, s 27(1) already provides that no legal estate is acquired under a registrable disposition until all registration requirements have been met. The explanation may be that s 58(2) is there to clarify rather than make matters different from what they would be without it. The practical position is that a conflict between different entries on the register which has been brought about by some failure to fulfil a registration requirement is likely to be resolved in proceedings for rectification and indemnity.[1] The outcome of these will depend to a considerable extent on who made any relevant mistakes, and who is in possession of the relevant land, though it should also be noted that the protection for a proprietor in possession only applies to the proprietor of a legal estate (LRA 2002, Sch 4, para 3(2) and the definition of 'registered estate' in the LRA 2002, s 132(1)). The double registration requirement raises questions as to whether the titles to both relevant estates need to be checked on behalf of a purchaser of an estate or interest which is, or has been, the subject of a registrable disposition of this kind: see paras 5.32 et seq.

---

[1] See paras 14.17 et seq, 14.32 et seq.

5.26 The LRA 2002, s 26(1) provides that a person's right to exercise the owner's powers of disposition[1] in relation to a registered estate is to be taken to be free from any limitation affecting the validity of a disposition, unless it is a limitation reflected by an entry on the register or imposed by or under the LRA 2002 (LRA 2002, s 26(1) and

(2)). Any limitation on a proprietor's powers of disposition—eg the inability of the survivor of two trustees of land to give a good receipt for the purchase money in the event of a sale of the land—needs therefore to be the subject of a restriction on the register[2] if he is to be prevented from being able to make an effective disposition in breach of the limitation. Although the LRA 2002, s 26(1) enables a disponee to obtain a good title where the disposition is in breach of a limitation on the disponor's powers which is not reflected by an entry in the register, it does not affect the lawfulness of such a disposition (LRA 2002, s 26(3))—in other words the disponor's liability for making the disposition is not affected by this provision.

---

[1] See the LRA 2002, ss 23, 24 and para 5.16.
[2] See paras 7.40–7.42 for restrictions.

5.27 There are other aspects to the strength of a registered title: the categories of title (see paras 5.10 et seq); the priority rules (for which see paras 7.17, 7.18); the powers of disposition (for which see para 5.16); and the possibility of rectification, and of indemnity if rectification occurs (for which see paras 14.17 et seq, 14.32 et seq).

IMPLICATIONS FOR CONVEYANCING

5.28 As regards the events giving rise to first registration of freehold land, major changes were made by the LRA 1997, and the LRA 2002 carries forward these provisions in relation to freeholds, subject to very little alteration.[1] As regards dispositions of registered freehold land, the LRA 2002 redefines the basic rules in a more succinct and logical form, and changes the conceptual structure somewhat. The practical consequences are not very different from those of the LRA 1925, but there are some differences noted below, and the new double registration requirement for certain transactions is discussed separately in paras 5.32–5.35. An important procedural change is the requirement that applications for first registration and registration of dispositions should be accompanied by disclosure to the registrar of overriding interests known to the applicant, with a view to them being noted on the register: see paras 4.14, 4.18, and 5.19, and Appendix 1. There are, however, major changes relating to leases, easements, and overriding interests, discussed at paras 6.21, 7.62–7.81, 9.11, 9.13. One minor change is that the power to exclude souvenir land from registration is abolished and such land is henceforth within the system of registration.[2]

1   See paras 5.3 and para 5.9, n 5.

2   For the transitional provisions relating to this, see the LRA 2002 (Transitional Provisions) Order 2003, SI 2003/1953, arts 10–13. See also the Land Registry's Practice Guide no 17.

5.29   The LRA 1925 was ambiguous as to whether a transfer or lease of registered land conferred any proprietary interest before it was registered. However, the LRA 2002 makes a change to the way in which the basic rules for dispositions of registered estates are expressed. The LRA 2002 makes it clear that a transfer, lease, etc is a disposition (LRA 2002, s 23(1)), but one which does not take effect to transfer or grant a *legal estate* until the registration requirements are met (LRA 2002, s 27(1)). It is not stated explicitly in the LRA 2002 that this means that such a disposition confers an immediate equitable interest, but this is a strong inference. In the LRA 1925 it was felt necessary to provide expressly that the LPA 1925, s 62 (general words implied in conveyances) applied (LRA 1925, ss 19(3), 20(1)), presumably in case a transfer or lease of registered land was not a 'conveyance' within the meaning of the LPA 1925, s 205(1)(ii). Under the LRA 2002 a disposition is more obviously a 'conveyance' within this definition, and it was not felt necessary to provide expressly for the LPA 1925, s 62 to apply, although there is a clear indication that it is thought to apply to dispositions of registered estates (LRA 2002, s 27(7)). As under the previous law, express provision is made permitting incorporation of the covenants for title in registered dispositions (LRA 2002, Sch 10, para 3; LRR 2003, rr 67 and 68—and see para 9.34).

5.30   The LRA 2002 confers power to make rules for the obligations of the seller of a registered estate as to proof or perfection of title (LRA 2002, Sch 10, para 2). This power has not been exercised, and of course the former provisions on this topic in the LRA 1925, s 110 are repealed. One particular point about this is as follows. The references to successors in title in the LRA 2002, Sch 2, and the definition of 'person entitled to exercise the owner's powers' (LRA 2002, s 24), make it clear that there can be a series of dispositions off the register relating to a registered or registrable estate, ending with the last person in the series (a successor in title of the first transferee or grantee) then being registered as proprietor of the estate in question. However, it is no longer the case that a purchaser of an estate from someone who is not currently the registered proprietor can insist on the seller either becoming registered as proprietor, or procuring a direct transfer from the person who is currently the registered proprietor.[1] What sets a limit on the period during which off-register dealings in the right to be registered as the proprietor of a registered estate, or as the proprietor of a registrable estate granted out of a registered estate, is the priority period system (LRA 2002, s 72),[2] and the risk that if such dealings continue beyond the end of a relevant priority period without being completed by registration, the estate may become subject to rights created under some other disposition. Another part of the registered conveyancing scene which disappears is land certificates (and also charge certificates).[3]

---

[1]   As was the case under the LRA 1925, s 110(5). This provision is not reproduced in the LRA 2002 or the LRR 2003.

[2]   See also paras 7.82–7.87.

[3]   See paras 2.57–2.64.

5.31   The increase in public access to information is an important change. Before the LRA 2002 came into force there was public access to the register itself, and to documents referred to in the register with the important exception of leases and charges (Land Registration (Open Register) Rules 1991, SI 1991/122, r 3(1)). Under the LRA 2002 the latter exceptions cease, but subject to a right for interested parties to apply for exemption from public access to a document on the grounds that it would cause substantial unwarranted damage or distress, or prejudice the commercial interests of the applicant (LRA 2002, s 66(1); LRR 2003, r 131 et seq).[1] The compulsory recording of the price paid when there is first registration or a change of proprietor of a registered title (LRR 2003, r 8(2)) continues the rule which commenced about three and a half years before LRA 2002 came into force (LRR 1925, r 247, as substituted by SI 1999/3412, r 2 with effect from 1 April 2000), and which represents a return to the rule which prevailed before 1976.[2]

---

[1]   See para 2.65 et seq.

[2]   Under LRR 1925, r 247 in its original form. Between 1976 and 1 April 2000 this information was only recorded in the register if it was requested by the proprietor.

Implications for conveyancing—the double registration requirement

5.32   A subtle change made by the LRA 2002 with significant practical consequences for conveyancing is the double registration requirement in cases of the transfer of part of a registered estate, the grant of a lease for more than seven years (or other registrable lease) out of a registered estate, or the grant of an easement, rentcharge, profit à prendre or right of entry out of a registered estate (the transfer or grant taking place on or after 13 October 2003).[1] The double requirement also applies to any such transfer or grant made (on or after 13 October 2003) out of unregistered land by someone who has acquired the unregistered land under a disposition which gives rise to an obligation to register the title.[2] The practical questions which arise are:

(a)   whether a conveyancer, acting for someone who is the original acquirer of an estate or interest which is subject to a double registration requirement, should check that the disposition has been registered correctly in both the relevant places; and

(b)   whether a conveyancer, acting for someone acquiring a registered estate or interest of a kind which was subject to a double registration requirement when transferred or granted, should investigate the registered titles of both the estates in relation to which there was the double registration requirement.

Since there is public access to the register, there is no difficulty about access to the registered title of the relevant estate, and investigating it is therefore a practicable precaution to take, subject to the point that in the case of a title which has its origin in a transfer of part of a title, it will not always be apparent from the title entries that it has such an origin. The land registry is under a duty to register a disposition which is subject to a double registration requirement against the transferor's or grantor's title in accordance with the LRA 2002 (LRA 2002, s 38—leases, easements, etc—notice to be registered; and LRR 2003, r 72—transfers of part—entry in property register referring to the removal of the transferred part and entries relating to any easements, covenants etc), but error is not impossible, and could in particular cases be wholly or partly brought about by errors of sellers or buyers of registered land or conveyancers acting for them. The registry is perhaps unlikely to fail to make the second registration altogether, and the most likely thing to go wrong is a mix-up over plans, so that, for example, an easement granted across several servient titles does not get noted against all of them, or a transfer of part of a title or a grant of a lease gets entered or noted against the wrong title.

---

[1]   See paras 5.18 and 5.24. For other kinds of registrable lease, see para 6.21.

[2]   LRR 2003, r 38 (authorised by the LRA 2002, Sch 10, para 1) applies the LRA 2002 to dealings made by someone who is subject to an obligation under the LRA 2002, s 6 to register (see paras 5.2 et seq) as if the registration had taken place. See also para 4.11.

5.33   The position of someone who is the transferee or grantee under a transfer of part of a title, a grant of a registrable lease, or an express grant of an easement[1] (the transfer or grant taking place on or after 13 October 2003), who becomes registered as proprietor of the estate transferred or granted but the transfer or grant does not get entered or noted on the transferor's or grantor's title, is, it is suggested, as follows.

(1)   A legal estate is not obtained (LRA 2002, ss 27(1) and 58(2)).[2] Where an easement or lease is involved, the grantee is registered as proprietor, but only of an equitable interest. In the case of a transfer of part, there is a legal estate in relation to which the transferee is entitled to be registered as proprietor, but it presumably remains vested in the transferor unless and until the registration requirements, including an entry on the

transferor's title of the removal of the transferred part, are completed. The transferee's or grantee's lack of a legal estate has a number of other implications, mentioned below.

(2) In the case of a lease or easement, the grantee has an equitable interest capable of assignment, but none of the provisions of the LRA 2002 concerning powers of disposition (LRA 2002, ss 23 and 24)[3] and priorities (LRA 2002, s 29)[4] will apply, because of the lack of a legal estate. In the case of a transfer of part of a title, the transferee will have a right to be registered as proprietor of the legal estate and therefore a power of disposition over it (LRA 2002, ss 23 and 24),[5] but the legal estate apparently remains vested in the transferor and the right to be registered as proprietor will be at risk of being lost (under the priority rules in the LRA 2002, s 29)[6] to a subsequent purchaser of the legal estate from the transferor, unless the transferee is in actual occupation.

(3) The priority rules in the LRA 2002, s 29[6] will not apply in favour of the transferee or grantee, because a legal estate has not been acquired. As a result, the rights of the transferee or grantee would not obtain priority over rights acquired by someone else under a previous disposition where the latter rights are not protected on the register, and are not overriding ones within the LRA 2002, Sch 3. Further, the rights of the transferee or grantee might also become lost or deferred to rights under any subsequent disposition of the title out of which the transfer or grant is made, although in the case of a transfer of part of a title or a grant of a lease the transferee or grantee will retain priority over subsequent dispositions if he remains in actual occupation of all the land transferred or granted (and otherwise satisfies the LRA 2002, Sch 3, para 2).[7] An expressly granted easement[8] which has not been noted on the grantor's title is not capable of being actually occupied and, not being a legal estate, is not overriding under the LRA 2002, Sch 3, para 3.[9]

(4) The transferee or grantee will probably have a good claim for rectification, or payment of an indemnity in the event of rectification not being obtained,[10] so as to be put in the position he would have been in if the registration requirements had been satisfied on registration of the disposition. This will be particularly so if the mistake which caused the registration requirements not to be met is wholly that of the registry, or of someone other than himself and those acting for him, and, in the case of a transfer of part of a title or the grant a lease, if he is in possession of the land.[11] However, this is not the same as not having to make the claim in the first place.

We therefore recommend that a check is made, after registration of a disposition with a double registration requirement, that the double requirement has been satisfied.

---

[1]   Easements granted by the operation of the LPA 1925, s 62 are not subject to the double registration requirement to be legal easements: see the LRA 2002, s 27(7) and para 9.12. Similar points to those made in this and the next paragraph can be made about the grant of a rentcharge, profit à prendre or right of entry, or a lease of a franchise or manor (see the LRA 2002, Sch 2, paras 4–7), but the more usual transactions with a double registration requirement are concentrated on here.

[2]   See also paras 5.18 and 5.24.

[3]   See para 5.16.

[4]   See para 5.21 and paras 7.17, 7.18.

[5]   See para 5.16.

[6]   See para 5.21 and paras 7.17, 7.18.

[7]   See paras 7.67–7.73.

[8]   But not one granted by the operation of the LPA 1925, s 62: see the LRA 2002, s 27(7) and para 9.12.

[9]   See paras 9.11, 9.20.

[10]   See paras 14.17 et seq, 14.32 et seq for rectification and indemnity.

[11]   The restrictions on rectification against a proprietor in possession of the land (LRA 2002, Sch 3, para 3(2)) only apply to a proprietor who has a *legal estate* (see the definition of registered estate in the LRA 2002, s 132(1)) which in this case, for reasons given above, the transferee or grantee will not have. However, if he is in possession, it is unlikely that any rival claimant to the land will be in possession.

5.34   Where someone is purchasing, from a registered proprietor, land which was transferred to the latter out of a larger registered title, or a lease which was granted to him out of registered land, or land which includes the benefit of an easement which was expressly granted out of registered land (the transfer or grant taking place on or after 13 October 2003), such a purchaser will probably not obtain a legal estate after completion of the disposition to him, if the registration requirement that entry or notice be made on the title out of which the transfer of part, lease, or easement was made or granted, has not been fulfilled.[1] This is on the assumption that the LRA 2002, s 58(1) will not apply in this situation: see para 5.24. His position will therefore be no better than that of the original transferee or grantee, and accordingly it is recommended that the title out of which the transfer or grant was made is checked to see that the double registration requirement was fulfilled. Where the purchase is land acquired by the seller under a transfer of part of a registered title, the seller could still have the power of disposition over the legal estate,[2] but since that legal estate is still vested in his transferor, a disposition by the seller will probably still count as a transfer of part which still needs to be entered on his transferor's title.

---

[1]   See para 5.18.

[2]   See para 5.33, sub-paras (1) and (2).

5.35   Where a transfer of part of a title, a grant of a registrable lease, or a grant of an easement was made out of a registered estate before the coming into force of the LRA 2002, there was no double registration requirement and the transferee or grantee became entitled to a legal estate on being registered as proprietor (LRA 1925, s 19(1) and (2)).

These estates will continue as legal estates after the LRA 2002 is in force, irrespective of whether they are entered or noted on the titles out of which they were transferred or granted.

STAMP DUTY AND STAMP DUTY LAND TAX

5.36   Not long after the commencement of the LRA 2002 on 13 October 2003 stamp duty on transactions involving land was replaced by stamp duty land tax (SDLT) (Finance Act 2003 (FA 2003), Pts 4 and 5, and Schs 3–20). SDLT applies to any land transaction of which the effective date is on or after the 'implementation date' (FA 2003, Sch 19, para 2), which was 1 December 2003.[1] The effective date of a transaction is in most cases the date of completion (FA 2003, s 119(1)),[2] but if the contract was made before 11 July 2003 completion on or after 1 December 2003 is not subject to SDLT but to stamp duty (FA 2003, Sch 19, para 3(1), (2)), unless the contract was varied or assigned on or after 11 July 2003, or was an option, right of pre-emption, etc, exercised on or after that date, or there was a sub-sale on or after that date, and the contract was not substantially performed before that date (FA 2003, Sch 19, paras 3(3) and 4). Although there are many differences between the two taxes, the change from stamp duty to SDLT makes few differences to the tax payable or the necessity for paying it in relation to sales of freehold land where the land is already registered or where the sale triggers compulsory registration.[3] In particular the rates of SDLT and the threshold below which it is not charged remain the same as under stamp duty, save that, under SDLT, in the case of land which is not exclusively residential property, the tax threshold is £150,000 instead of £60,000 (it is, as under stamp duty, £60,000 for exclusively residential property) (FA 2003, s 55(2)).[4]

---

[1]   Stamp Duty Land Tax (Appointment of the Implementation Date) Regulations 2003, SI 2003/2837, reg 2.

[2]   The exceptions are contracts substantially performed without being completed, and options and rights of pre-emption: see the FA 2003, ss 44(4) and 46(3).

[3]   Although stamp duty was not compulsory, registration of a transaction at the land registry could not be obtained without paying it.

[4]   The rates continue to be 1 per cent for consideration which exceeds the threshold but does not exceed £250,000, 3 per cent for consideration which exceeds £250,000 but not £500,000, and 4 per cent for consideration exceeding £500,000 (FA 2003, s 55).

5.37   A major structural difference between SDLT and stamp duty is that SDLT is a compulsory tax where the purchaser is under a legal obligation, backed by a penalty regime, to make a return of a chargeable transaction and pay the tax, whereas under stamp duty the sanction was that a stampable document is not receivable in evidence or, in the case of a disposition of registered land, registrable, without being properly stamped. However, under SDLT there is one vestige of the former enforcement regime in the preconditions imposed on registration of land transactions. A land transaction subject to SDLT shall not be registered, recorded, or otherwise reflected in an entry made by the registrar, unless there is produced to him either a certificate of the Inland Revenue that a land transaction return has been delivered, or a self-certificate that no return is required (FA 2003, s 79(1), (3)). It should be noted that the latter does not correspond with stamp duty certificates that the consideration was below the stamp duty threshold. Any transfer of a registered freehold estate will require an SDLT return, even if the consideration is below the tax threshold, unless it is exempt under the FA 2003, Sch 3 (FA 2003, ss 77(3), 117). Self-certification will thus be confined to cases where the transaction is exempt under the FA 2003, Sch 3, eg where it is a gift or other transaction for no consideration (eg an appointment of new trustees), or is pursuant to a divorce, annulment, etc, or is a variation of the dispositions of a deceased person within two years of his death (FA 2003, Sch 3).[1] The registrar is required to allow the Inland Revenue to inspect certificates and self-certificates produced to the registrar (FA 2003, s 79(6)). The certification requirement does not apply to a contract, even where the contract has been substantially performed[2] (FA 2003, s 79(2), as amended by FA 2004, s 296, Sch 39, para 7). This means, for example, that the registrar may enter a notice to protect the priority of a contract,[3] without the purchaser under the contract being required to comply with the certification requirement or prove to the satisfaction of the registrar that the requirement does not apply.

---

[1]   Note that there is power by regulation for the Treasury to add to the transactions which are exempt in the FA 2003, Sch 3, para 5.

[2]   See para 5.38 for this term.

[3]   See paras 11.3, 11.4.

5.38   A further important difference between SDLT and stamp duty is that SDLT applies to sales of land or interests in land which are 'substantially performed', by the purchaser taking possession or most of the consideration being paid (FA 2003, s 44), as well as to such disposals as are completed by conveyance or transfer (stamp duty usually only applied to sales of land if there was a conveyance or transfer of the land). Under stamp duty, it was possible on a sale of land (eg between members of the same family) to avoid paying the duty by performing the contract in all respects other than the conveyance or transfer of the legal estate. This is not an available option under SDLT.

6 Leases and tenancies

INTRODUCTORY

6.1 One of the biggest changes made by the LRA 2002, in particular ss 3(3), 4(1) and (2), and 27(2), is that it makes all leases of more than seven years duration registrable (while under the LRA 1925 leases were only registrable if of more than 21 years duration).[1] It also makes registrable various specialised kinds of leasehold estate of seven years or less duration. Thus a lease of unregistered land (granted before 13 October 2003) with at least seven years to run may be registered voluntarily and must be registered if assigned for valuable consideration or by way of gift; a lease granted (after 12 October 2003) for more than seven years out of unregistered land is compulsorily registrable; and a grant of a lease for more than seven years out of an estate which is already registered must take effect by registering the lease. The resulting pattern is quite a complex one, because the transitional provisions have to cater for interests which were granted before 13 October 2003 and were not then registrable, but which still subsist and are of a kind now subject to registration: see further, paras 6.47 et seq. The government intend to extend registration to all leases of more than three years at some suitable time in the future, and the LRA 2002, s 118 confers a power to do this by statutory instrument after appropriate consultation.

---

[1] See para 6.49, footnote 1, for further details of what leases were and were not registrable under the LRA 1925.

6.2 The extension of registration to leases of more than seven years makes a great change to much leasehold conveyancing work, particularly in relation to commercial leases, and increases significantly the amount of work for the land registry, and it is to be hoped that the system is managing to cope. In the course of the debates on the Bill which became the LRA 2002 a government spokesman stated that the expected number of extra leases for registration would be between 20,000 and 30,000,[1] but this was based on figures from the stamp office of leases submitted for stamping, and it is probable that the number of leases of between 7 and 20 years duration which were granted but left unstamped in the relevant period was much more than these estimates assumed. However, the registry may be helped by a decrease in the number of grants of leases exceeding seven years, partly caused by a desire to avoid the requirement of registration and the consequent public access to leases and other documents once they have been registered,[2] partly to avoid or keep to a minimum the amount of stamp duty land tax (SDLT)—the tax on land transactions which replaced stamp duty with effect from 1 December 2003—which may be payable on the grant of any lease (see para 6.72 et seq), and partly, in the case of commercial leases, because the market was shifting in favour of shorter leases anyway.

---

[1]   HC Official Report, SC D, 11 December 2001, col 12.
[2]   See para 6.66 et seq.

COMPULSORY REGISTRATION

6.3   An unregistered leasehold estate in land becomes compulsorily registrable if, at a time when it has more than seven years to run, any of the following happens (LRA 2002, ss 4(1)(a), (g), (2)(b), (6), (7) and (8))—

- a transfer of it for valuable or other consideration (s 4(1)(a)(i));
- if it has a negative value, any transfer of it (s 4(1)(a)(i) and (6))—this provision is more likely to apply to transfers of existing leaseholds than to grants of leases or transfers of freeholds, since, for example, a rack rent lease where the rent is fixed for a period of years can come to have a negative value after a fall in rental values;
- a transfer of it by way of gift (s s 4(1)(a)(i)), including, in relation to any trust where the settlor did not retain the entire beneficial interest when the trust was constituted, a transfer so as to constitute the trust, and a transfer uniting the bare legal title and the beneficial interest (s 4(7));
- a transfer of it in pursuance of an order of the court (s 4(1)(a)(i));
- an assent or vesting assent[1] in respect of it (s 4(1)(a)(ii));
- the creation of a mortgage of it, where the mortgage has priority over any other mortgages of it, and is to be protected by deposit of title deeds (s 4(1)(g), (8)).[2]

A leasehold estate in land also becomes compulsorily registrable if it is transferred in circumstances where the Housing Act 1985, s 171A applies (a disposal by a landlord which leads to a person no longer being a secure tenant where the right to buy is preserved), and even if it has seven years or less to run at the time of the transfer (s 4(1)(b)).

The events which trigger compulsory registration of a leasehold estate, set out above, are subject to the exceptions from compulsory registration for the assignment of a mortgage term (in the rare case of a mortgage by demise) (s 4(4)(a)), the assignment or surrender of a lease to the owner of the immediate reversion where the term is to merge in that reversion (LRA 2002, s 4(4)(b)), a transfer of a lease of mines or minerals held apart from the surface (s 4(9)), and an assignment of a PPP lease (LRA 2002, s 90(2)).[3]

---

[1] Ie within the meaning of the term in the Settled Land Act 1925: LRA 2002, s 4(9). See also footnote 1 to para 5.2.
[2] See paras 8.3–8.5.
[3] For PPP leases see paras 12.26, 12.27.

6.4   If an event of any of the kinds set out in para 6.3 occurs, triggering compulsory registration of an existing leasehold estate, the person who is required to apply for registration is the transferee, or (in the case of a mortgage) the mortgagor, or the transferee's or mortgagor's successor in title ((LRA 2002, s 6(1)–(3)).[1] Whether the lease has sufficient duration remaining to be subject to the registration requirement is determined as at the time of the transfer,[2] and so the registration requirement does not lapse if the lease subsequently comes to have seven years or less remaining before any registration application is made. The expression 'transfer' is not the subject of a general definition in the legislation—the only statutory provision concerning its meaning is a provision that it does not include a transfer by operation of law (LRA 2002, s 4(3))—and it must, from its context, include an assignment of a lease. For the time limits for registration and the consequences of failure to apply for it see paras 4.9–4.12, and for the rules surrounding applications for first registration, see para 4.13 et seq. The summary of what are the transactions giving rise to compulsory registration in relation to freeholds in para 5.3 is applicable also to transactions relating to existing leaseholds with more than seven years to run. Where someone dies owning unregistered leasehold land, the devolution of it on death or the grant of probate or letters of administration in relation to that person's estate are not events requiring registration, but when the personal representatives assent to the vesting of the lease in a beneficiary the latter is required to apply for registration if there are more than seven years of it left to run at the time of the assent (LRA 2002, s 4(1)(a) and (2)).[3] Where a lease is transferred at a time when it is not registered but is already—as a result of a previous transfer or the grant of it—subject to an obligation to register under LRA 2002 s 4, the rules for dispositions of registered land apply.[4]

---

[1] In the case of a mortgage which triggers registration, the mortgagee may apply if the mortgagor fails to: LRR 2003, r 21 made under LRA 2002, s 6(6).
[2] This is clear from the wording of the LRA 2002, s 4(2)(b).
[3] See, further, para 5.7.

6.5   The grant of a leasehold estate in land for a term of more than seven years from the date of grant, which is a grant out of an unregistered legal estate,[1] and is not a grant to a person as mortgagee,[2] causes the lease so granted (but not the estate from which it is granted) to be subject to compulsory registration if the grant is in any of the following categories (LRA 2002, s 4(1)(c), (5), (6), (7), s 6(3)(a))—

- a grant for valuable or other consideration (s 4(1)(c)—into which category the great majority of grants of leases fall, because leases almost invariably contain covenants on the part of the lessee;
- if the lease has a negative value, the grant of it whether or not for a consideration (s 4(6));
- a grant by way of gift (s 4(1)(c)), including, in relation to any trust where the settlor did not retain the entire beneficial interest when the trust was constituted, a grant so as to constitute the trust, and a grant uniting the bare legal title and the beneficial interest (s 4(7));
- a grant pursuant to an order of the court s (4(1)(c)).

Also compulsorily registrable is a grant of a lease, of whatever duration, which is to take effect in possession more than three months after the date of grant (the date of grant being counted as the first day of the three months), if it is granted out of an unregistered freehold or an unregistered leasehold with more than seven years left to run, irrespective of whether it is granted for a consideration, by way of gift, or on some other basis (LRA 2002, s 4(1)(d)). Such a lease cannot commence more than 21 years after the date of grant if it is at a rent or in consideration of a premium (Law of Property Act 1925, s 149(3)).

The following are compulsorily registrable if they are granted out of an unregistered legal estate (even if that estate is a lease with seven years or less to run)—

- a grant in pursuance of the Housing Act 1985, Pt V (the right to buy) (LRA 2002, s 4(1)(e));
- a grant in circumstances where the Housing Act 1985, s 171A applies (a disposal by a landlord which leads to a person no longer being a secure tenant where the right to buy is preserved) (LRA 2002, s 4(1)(f)).

The grants of leases which are subject to compulsory registration, set out above, are subject to exceptions from compulsory registration for grants of leases of mines or minerals held apart from the surface (LRA 2002, s 4(9)), and for PPP leases (LRA 2002, s 90).[3] A grant by the Crown of a lease for more than seven years out of demesne land, for consideration or by way of gift or pursuant to a court order, also gives rise to a registration requirement (LRA 2002, s 80).[4]

---

[1]   LRA 2002, s 4(1)(c) and (2) also impose the express precondition that the grant must be out of a freehold estate or an unregistered leasehold with more than seven years left to run, but this adds nothing in cases where there is a precondition that the lease granted be longer than seven years.
[2]   The grant of a term of years to a person as mortgagee (ie where there is a mortgage by demise or sub-demise) is not subject to compulsory registration as a lease (LRA 2002, s 4(5)), but it can give rise to compulsory registration of the estate mortgaged (and thus to registration of the mortgage itself) if it is a protected first legal mortgage (LRA 2002, s 4(1)(g)). See paras 5.2, 6.3.
[3]   For mines and minerals see para 7.13. For PPP leases see paras 12.26, 12.27.
[4]   See para 12.21.

6.6   The person who is required to apply for registration of a newly granted lease, which is required to be registered as set out in para 6.5, is the grantee or his successor in title (s 6(1), (3)). For the time limits for registration and the consequences of failure to apply for it, see paras 4.9–4.12, and for the rules surrounding applications for first registration see paras 4.13 et seq. Leases are almost invariably granted for a consideration, in the form of tenant's covenants even if there is no premium or rent, and so the main question when a lease is granted out of unregistered land is whether the characteristics of the lease are such as to make it compulsorily registrable, rather than whether the transaction is such as to make it so. A grant out of an unregistered estate of an easement or other incorporeal hereditament which is appurtenant to land will not be subject to compulsory registration.[1] Where a lease is granted out of an estate which is for the time being not registered but is already—as a result of a previous disposition—subject to an obligation to register, the rules for dispositions of registered land apply.[2]

---

[1]   Because it is not a leasehold estate in land within the meaning of the LRA 2002, s 4(2), bearing in mind the definition of 'land' in the LRA 2002, s 132 (see also para 5.3).
[2]   LRR 2003, r 38 (authorised by the LRA 2002, Sch 10, para 1) applies the LRA 2002 to dealings made by someone who is subject to an obligation under the LRA 2002, s 6 to register (for which see paras 5.2, 6.3–6.5) as if the registration had taken place. For some consequences of this for grants of leases see para 4.11, and for grants of leases of registered land see para 6.19 et seq.

6.7   If the transferee or his successor in title fails to apply in time for registration of an unregistered legal estate which has become compulsorily registrable as a result of a transfer of it, the estate reverts to the transferor, and he holds it on bare trust for the transferee (LRA 2002, s 7, and see para 4.10). As set out in paras 5.4 and 5.5 above, there is an argument that a remedial transfer made after such reverter had occurred might not be subject to the compulsory registration requirement. This argument could theoretically be applicable where the estate in question is a leasehold, as well as where it is a freehold, but in the case of a leasehold there is the practical point that transfers of leases very often contain indemnity or other covenants by the transferee, which would be sufficient to cause such remedial transfer to be compulsorily registrable on the ground that it is a transfer for consideration within s 4(1)(a). Where the event triggering compulsory registration is the grant of a lease, and the grantee fails to apply for registration in time, any remedial grant of a replacement lease will be subject to the compulsory registration requirement. This is because leases almost invariably contain covenants on the part of the lessee which mean that they are grants for consideration within s 4(1)(c), and also because failure to apply for registration in time means that the grant of the lease has effect as a contract for valuable consideration to make the grant (s 7(2)(b)), with the probable consequence that a grant pursuant to such a deemed contract would be deemed to be for consideration if it was not actually for consideration.

6.8   The Lord Chancellor has the same power to extend compulsory registration to other events in relation to leaseholds as he has in relation to freeholds (for which see para 5.8 and the LRA 2002, s 4). He also has power under the LRA 2002, s 118 to shorten the term of lease which is subject to registration, ie required to be a registered estate and not per se an overriding interest. Although there is no limit set on which legal estates he can exercise the s 4 power in relation to, in practice he would need to use the s 118 power if he wanted to impose the requirement of registration on unregistered leases of seven years or less, because it would be inconsistent to impose a registration requirement on unregistered leases of a particular length without making leases of that length registrable in other respects. The intention is that the s 118 power will be eventually exercised to bring all leases of more than three years into the registration system.[1]

---

[1]   Law Com No 271, para 3.17.

VOLUNTARY REGISTRATION

6.9   An application may be made for registration of an unregistered leasehold estate which is an estate in land, a rentcharge, a franchise, or a profit à prendre in gross, if more than seven years of it are left unexpired (LRA 2002, s 3(1), (3)), or if the right to possession under it is discontinuous (LRA 2002, s 3(4)), except that application may not be made in respect of a leasehold estate held as mortgagee where there is a subsisting right of redemption (LRA 2002, s 3(5)). If a person holds in the same right a lease in possession and a lease to take effect on or within a month of the end of the lease in possession, the leases are for the purposes of the right to voluntary registration treated as one continuous term to the extent that the leases relate to the same land (LRA 2002, s 3(7)), so that if the total remaining duration of both leases is more than seven years, application for registration may be made. The application may only be made by the person in whom the estate is vested, or who is entitled to require it to be vested in him (LRA 2002, s 3(2)). However, a person cannot apply as a person entitled to require the estate to be vested in him where his entitlement is as a person who has contracted to buy (LRA 2002, s 3(6)).[1] A trustee of land, or a tenant for life under a Settled Land Act 1925 settlement, can thus apply to be registered, and so apparently can someone who is beneficially entitled to land under a bare trust but does not actually hold the legal estate.

---

[1]   The completion of the contract will be an occasion of compulsory registration, for which the fee is higher than for voluntary registration. See the Land Registration Fee Order 2004, SI 2004/595, Sch 1, Scale 1, set out in Appendix 2.

REGISTRATION AND CATEGORIES OF TITLE

6.10   For the details of applications for first registration, see paras 4.13 et seq. A practical problem for an application to register a lease can be identifying the demised premises on a plan to the satisfaction of the land registry. The requirement of LRR 2003, r 24(1)(a) is that there should be sufficient details, by plan or otherwise, so that the land to be registered can be identified clearly on the Ordnance Survey map. Many pre 13 October 2003 leases granted for 21 years or less, and with no thought of them ever having to be registered, will have no plan or an inadequate one attached. Also, where a new lease is being granted of part of the land in a particular title (whether the grantor's title is registered or unregistered), this identification requirement will in some cases require more extensive and detailed plan provision than would previously have been customary. Where someone applies to be registered as proprietor of an unregistered leasehold estate, he may be so registered with one of the following categories of leasehold title, depending on the strength of the evidence of his title.

Absolute title

6.11   A person may be registered with absolute title if the registrar is of the opinion that the person's title to the estate is such that a competent professional adviser would advise acceptance, and the registrar approves the lessor's title to grant the lease (LRA 2002, s 10(1), (2)). The registrar may disregard the fact that a person's title appears to him to be open to objection if he is of the opinion that the defect will not cause the holding under the title to be disturbed (LRA 2002, s 10(4)). Registration of a person as proprietor of a leasehold estate with absolute title means that the estate is vested in him together with all interests subsisting for the benefit of the estate (LRA 2002, s 12(3)), and subject only to the implied and express covenants, obligations, and liabilities incident to the leasehold estate (LRA 2002, s 12(4)(a)),[1] the interests entered on the register in relation to the estate (LRA 2002, s 12(4)(b)),[2] any unregistered interests which fall within any of the paragraphs of the LRA 2002, Sch 1 (LRA 2002, s 12(4)(c)),[3] and any interests acquired under the Limitation Act 1980 of which the proprietor has notice (LRA 2002, s 12(4)(d)).[4] In relation to first registrations before 13 October 2006, such a person's registered estate will also be subject to any interests acquired under the Limitation Act 1980 of which the proprietor did *not* have notice (LRA 2002, Sch 12, para 7). It should be noted that if an interest under the Limitation Act 1980 first comes to the notice of the proprietor after first registration, where the date of first registration is on or after 13 October 2006, it will not be binding under the LRA 2002, s 12(4)(d).[5] The estate is also subject to any beneficial interests in the estate of persons other than himself of which the proprietor has notice (LRA 2002, s 12(5)).

---

[1]   See further, para 6.34, 6.35.
[2]   See further, para 7.4, 7.5.
[3]   See further, paras 7.7–7.16. The most important categories are short leases, interests of persons in actual occupation, and legal easements.
[4]   See further, para 13.22.
[5]   See LRA 2002, s 12(1) and the opening words of s 12(4), which make it clear that the circumstances at the time of first registration are determinative. An interest under the Limitation Act 1980 could on or after 13 October 2006 still be overriding if the person entitled to it is in actual occupation (see para 7.15).

Good leasehold title

6.12   A person may be registered with this if the registrar does not approve the lessor's title to grant the lease, but otherwise the title is of the same quality as for an absolute title (LRA 2002, s 10(3)). Registration with this has the same effect as registration with absolute title, except that it does not affect the enforcement of any estate, right or interest affecting, or in derogation of, the title of the lessor to grant the lease (LRA 2002, s 12(6)).

Qualified title

6.13 A person may be registered with this if the registrar is of the opinion that the person's title to the estate, or the lessor's title to the reversion, has been established only for a limited period or subject to reservations which cannot be disregarded as something which will not cause the holding under the title to be disturbed (LRA 2002, s 10(5)). Such registration has the same effect as registration with absolute title, except that it does not affect the enforcement of any estate, right or interest which appears from the register to be excepted from the effect of registration (LRA 2002, s 12(7)).

Possessory title

6.14 This is where in the registrar's opinion neither an absolute nor a qualified title may be registered but the applicant is in actual possession of the land in question or in receipt of the rents and profits of it (LRA 2002, s 10(6)). Registration with possessory title has the same effect as registration with absolute title except that it does not affect the enforcement of any estate right or interest adverse to, or in derogation of the proprietor's title, subsisting at the time of registration or then capable of arising (LRA 2002, s 12(8)). First registration of leasehold estates with possessory title is unusual—in most cases the registrar will not register such titles because they are vulnerable to being terminated at any time by the owner of the paper title to the lease surrendering it to the owner of the estate superior to his.[1] A leasehold registration with such a title might perhaps be made where there was good evidence that the first registered proprietor is the owner of the paper title to the lease, but because of, eg, lost deeds, the registry is not prepared to register him with a better title than possessory.

---

[1]   See Land Registry Practice Guide 5, para 7.1, *Fairweather v St Marylebone Property Co Ltd* [1963] AC 510, and para 13.31.

Other aspects

6.15 The categories of leasehold title are thus the same as under the LRA 1925, but with the qualifying criteria and the consequences of registration reworded. It is possible for a good leasehold, qualified or possessory title to be upgraded subsequently: see para 6.18. The registrar will register appurtenant rights over other land which is not registered if an adequate title to it is proved, and he is satisfied that it is a legal estate which benefits the registered estate—if he is not so satisfied he can enter the details of the right claimed with an appropriate qualification (LRA 2002, s 13; LRR 2003, r 3). As regards the effect of registration as proprietor see further paras 5.24 et seq and paras 7.4, 7.5.

6.16   A policy objective behind the LRA 2002 is to encourage leasehold estates to be registered with absolute title. If there is an application for first registration of a lease with absolute title where the estate in reversion upon it is already registered with absolute title, there is clearly no difficulty about the lease being registered with absolute title. However, the registrar, before completing the application for registration of the lease with absolute title, must give notice of the application to the proprietor of the reversion where at the time of the grant of the lease the reversion was not registered, or where the reversion was registered but the grant of the lease was not required to be completed by registration (LRR 2003, r 37(1), (2)(a)). The registrar need not give notice to the reversioner if the lease is already noted on the register of the registered reversion, or it is apparent that the proprietor of the registered reversion consents to the application (LRR 2003, r 37(1), (2)(b), (c)). The registrar is required on completion of registration of the leasehold estate to enter notice of the lease in the register of the registered reversion (LRR 2003, r 37(3)), and so no specific application to the registrar to do this is necessary (but it will be prudent to check that it has been done). Noting on the register of the reversion is a mandatory requirement, but it is not actually a precondition of the leaseholder having a registered legal estate, as it is in the case of a grant of a registrable lease out of an estate that is already registered.[1] If an application for first registration of a lease is for a title less than absolute, and the title to the reversion is registered, the lessee must specifically apply to have the lease noted on the title to the reversion if he wants that done.[2]

---

[1]   See the LRA 2002, s 27(1) and Sch 2, para 3, and paras 5.18, 5.32 et seq, and 6.27 for this requirement in relation to leases granted out of registered estates.
[2]   The Land Registry's Practice Guide 25 *Leases—when to register*, para 6.2.

6.17   Where the reversion is not registered, providing evidence of the title to the reversion may not be practicable in the case of the voluntary registration of an existing lease, or the compulsory registration of one following an assignment of it, if, as would normally be the case, on the grant of the lease the title to the reversion was not deduced to the original lessee.[1] An owner of a lease granted before 13 October 2003 for more than seven years but for 21 years or less, where the estate in reversion on the lease is not registered and he does not have evidence of the title to the reversion, is at a commercial disadvantage if he wants to sell the lease, because a purchaser will be obliged to register it, and may well want to be able to register it with title absolute, particularly if it is to be used as security for a loan. By contrast, where a prospective lessee is negotiating to be granted a lease the grant of which will trigger compulsory registration of it, he may well be in a position (depending on the strength of his bargaining position) to insist on deduction of the title to the reversion. Further, the LRA 2002 has amended the Law of Property Act 1925, s 44 so that, contrary to the usual rule, a prospective lessee is entitled (in the absence of provision in the contract to the contrary) to call for the title to the freehold, or the title to any leasehold estate reversionary upon the grantor's estate (where the grantor is an underlessee), if the grant of the lease will be an event triggering compulsory registration of the lease.[2]

---

[1] Law of Property Act 1925, s 44(2) and (4).
[2] LRA 2002, Sch 11, para 2(2) adding a new sub-s (4A) to the Law of Property Act 1925, s 44.

6.18   Where the title to a leasehold estate has been entered in the register as good leasehold, the registrar may subsequently upgrade it to absolute if he is satisfied as to the superior title (LRA 2002, s 62(2)) (eg because the superior title becomes registered). Where the title to a leasehold estate is entered in the register as possessory or qualified, it may be upgraded to good if the registrar is satisfied as to the title to the estate, and to absolute if the registrar is satisfied as to the title to the estate and the superior estate (LRA 2002, s 62(3)). The registrar is to apply the same standards as when making a first registration with absolute or good leasehold title, as the case may be (LRA 2002, s 62(8)).[1] Alternatively, in the case of a possessory title, the registrar may upgrade it to absolute after 12 years of it being registered as possessory, if the registrar is satisfied that the registered proprietor is in possession of the land (LRA 2002, s 62(5)).[2] These are both subject to the qualification that such upgrading cannot occur if a claim adverse to the registered proprietor's title is outstanding where that claim is by virtue of a right or interest which is preserved by virtue of the existing entry about the class of title (LRA 2002, s 62(6)). The application for upgrading may only be made by the proprietor of the estate in question, a person entitled to be registered as proprietor of that estate, a proprietor of a registered charge affecting that estate, or a person interested in a registered estate which derives from that estate (LRA 2002, s 62(7)). Once the title has been upgraded to absolute the proprietor ceases to hold the estate subject to any estate, right or interest whose enforceability was preserved by virtue of the previous entry about the class of title (LRA 2002, s 63(1)). After an upgrade to good leasehold, the proprietor ceases to hold the estate subject to any estate, right or interest whose enforceability was preserved by virtue of the previous entry about the class of title, except that it does not affect or prejudice the enforcement of any estate, right, or interest affecting, or in derogation of, the title of the lessor to grant the lease (LRA 2002, s 63(2)). An application to upgrade the title must be made in Form UT1 (LRR 2003, r 124(1)) and, except where 12 years' possessory title is relied on, must be accompanied by such documents as will satisfy the registrar as to the title, and, where absolute title is sought, as to the lessor's title to grant the lease (LRR 2003, r 124(2)–(4)). Where the applicant is not the registered proprietor he must provide evidence of his right to apply (LRR 2003, r 124(5), (6)).

---

1   For the standards in question see the LRA 2002, s 10(2)–(4), and paras 6.11, 6.12.
2   The Lord Chancellor may by order change the number of years registration as a possessory title which is required before this power is exercised: LRA 2002, s 62(9).

THE GRANT OF A LEASE OUT OF A REGISTERED ESTATE

6.19   The general rules as to dispositions of registered estates, summarised in paras 5.16–5.22, apply to the grant of a lease, whether out of a registered freehold estate or out of a registered leasehold estate. This and the following paragraphs concentrate on matters particularly relevant to grants of leasehold estates out of registered estates. It will be recalled that a person who is the registered proprietor, or is entitled to be registered as proprietor,[1] of a registered estate, has power to make a disposition of any kind permitted by the general law (other than a mortgage by demise) (LRA 2002, s 23(1)). The grant of a lease out of a registered estate is thus governed by the general law of leases, subject to any requirements as to form and content imposed by rules made under the LRA 2002, s 25(1), of which there are very few so far,[2] subject to any restrictions on the power to grant leases which are expressed or implied by a restriction entered in the register of the grantor's title,[3] and subject to the requirements of the LRA 2002 as to the completion of the grant by registration where it is a lease of a kind required to be so completed.[4] The LRA 2002 also determines to a considerable extent the adverse rights or interests to which the grant of a lease is subject.[5] The rules for dispositions of registered land also apply to a disposition of unregistered land which is made by a person who has acquired the unregistered land under a disposition which gives rise to an obligation to register the title, and accordingly those rules will apply to the grant of a lease by someone already under an obligation to register his title.[6]

---

1   Defined as a person entitled to exercise the owner's powers by the LRA 2002, s 24.
2   See LRR 2003, r 212(2), (3) and para 6.24 for such as there are.
3   LRA 2002, s 41(1), and see paras 7.40–7.42. There will often be such a restriction affecting the power to lease if the land is subject to a charge (see para 8.13) or is vested in a tenant for life or statutory owner under the Settled Land Act 1925 (see paras 10.20–10.22). If the powers of the proprietor to grant a lease are limited or excluded, but there is no restriction on the register of title to give effect to the limit or exclusion, a lease in breach of it will be valid: see the LRA 2002, s 26 and para 5.26.
4   See the LRA 2002, s 27 and paras 5.18, 5.24, 5.32 et seq, and 6.27.

5   See the LRA 2002, s 29 and para 6.33 et seq.
6   The LRR 2003, r 38 (authorised by the LRA 2002, Sch 10, para 1) applies the LRA 2002 to dealings made by someone who is subject to an obligation under the LRA 2002, s 6 to register (see paras 5.2 et seq and 6.3 et seq) as if the registration had taken place. For some consequences of this for grants of leases see para 4.11.

6.20   The grant of a lease out of a registered estate is required to be completed by registration, ie to be registered with a title of its own, and also to be noted on the grantor's title, before it takes effect as the grant of a legal estate,[1] if it falls within one of the categories set out in para 6.21. It must be emphasised that to fall within one of the following categories a grant must be of a legal estate, ie a lease granted by deed[2] (for tenancy agreements, taking effect in equity only, see para 6.58 et seq). It is important to be clear in borderline cases whether a lease granted out of a registered estate is a lease which is required to be registered or not—and see para 6.23 for further discussion of the borderline. A lease granted out of a registered estate which is required to be registered but has not been registered is a precarious interest which can only maintain full priority over subsequent dispositions of the land so long as the lessee is in actual and obvious occupation of the whole of the demised premises (and if it is a lease granted more than three months before its commencement which has not yet commenced, even occupation by the lessee will not protect it),[3] whereas a lease which is not required to be registered is an overriding interest which is binding on all subsequent disponees.[4]

[1]   LRA 2002, s 27(1), (4), Sch 2, para 3. See paras 5.18, 5.24, and 5.32 et seq for this double registration requirement and its consequences.
[2]   Law of Property Act 1925, s 52(1). That it is only legal estates which are registrable is made clear by the reference to the grant of a term of years absolute in the LRA 2002, s 27(2)(b), and by the definitions of registered estate and registered land in the LRA 2002, s 132(1).
[3]   See the LRA 2002, Sch 3, para 2, and paras 6.60, 6.61 and 7.72 below.
[4]   See the LRA 2002, Sch 3, para 1, in particular the exclusion from it of leases which are registrable dispositions.

6.21   The categories of lease which are required to be registered (when granted out of a registered freehold or leasehold estate) are:
   (1)   a grant of a term of more than seven years from the date of the grant.[1] A lease which is granted for more than seven years as at the date of grant does not cease to be registrable when it comes to have seven years or less to run by the time of the application for registration;[2]
   (2)   a grant of a lease which is to take effect in possession more than three months after the date of grant (the date of grant being counted as the first day of the three months) (LRA 2002, s 27(2)(b)(ii)). Such a lease is required to be registered, irrespective of its length or the circumstances of its grant, provided that it is granted out of a registered freehold or

leasehold estate, but note that it cannot commence more than 21 years after the date of grant if it is at a rent or in consideration of a premium (Law of Property Act 1925, s 149(3)). Note also that it is particularly important to register a lease in this category, because it cannot be an overriding interest by virtue of the lessee's actual occupation so long as it has not fallen into possession.[3] Where the current lessee of land under a registered lease is granted a new lease to commence when his current one expires, the registrar could add the new lease to the same title;[4]

(3)   a grant of a lease under which the right to possession is discontinuous (LRA 2002, s 27(2)(b)(iii)), eg a timeshare lease (but many timeshare arrangements are licences rather than leases). This is the only category of lease which, irrespective of its length, must on its grant be registered if granted out of a registered estate, but which, if the total of the discontinuous periods does not exceed seven years,[5] is not compulsorily registrable (though voluntarily registrable) if granted out of an unregistered estate;[6]

(4)   a grant in pursuance of the Housing Act 1985, Pt V (the right to buy) (LRA 2002, s 27(2)(b)(iv));

(5)   a grant in circumstances where the Housing Act 1985, s 171A applies (a disposal by a landlord which leads to a person no longer being a secure tenant) (LRA 2002, s 27(2)(b)(v)).

Where the registered estate is a franchise or manor, any lease of it is required to be registered (LRA 2002, s 27(2)(c)).

---

[1]   LRA 2002, s 27(2)(b)(i). The Lord Chancellor has power to reduce the length of term in excess of which a lease is a registrable lease: LRA 2002, s 118.
[2]   This follows from the fact that this category of registrable lease is defined wholly by reference to the period of the lease from the date of grant.
[3]   See the LRA 2002, Sch 3, para 2(d) and 7.72. There is an argument that para 2(d) is ineffective: see paras 6.60, 61.
[4]   Under his powers in the LRR 2003, r 3(1).
[5]   It is reasonably clear that in deciding whether a discontinuous lease is a term of more than seven years it is a matter of adding together the periods granted, so that a grant of one week a year for 80 years is a grant of 80 weeks—compare the VAT case of *Cottage Holiday Associates Ltd v Customs and Excise Comrs* [1983] STC 278, where it was held that such a lease was not a tenancy for a term certain exceeding 21 years.
[6]   See the LRA 2002, s 3(4) for the right to register this type of lease voluntarily, and note that such leases are not included in the list of the compulsorily registrable types of lease in the LRA 2002, s 4(1).

6.22   Accordingly, a lease of seven years or less, which runs continuously and commences three months or less from the date of grant (and is not pursuant to the Housing Act 1985, Pt V or within the Housing Act 1985, s 171A) is not registrable, and is protected by being an overriding interest which is binding on the registered proprietor from time to time of the estate from which it was granted without any registration or noting on the register of the grantor's title (LRA 2002,

Sch 3, para 1). However, within this category there is a difference of treatment between a lease for three years or less and a lease for seven years or less but for more than three years. The latter kind of lease may be noted on the title to the reversion, even though it does not get a registered title of its own,[1] and the LRR 2003 require such a lease to be disclosed to the registrar when there is a registrable disposition of the estate out of which it was granted, with a view to such lease being noted on the register.[2] Once so noted it is protected by being noted on the register (LRA 2002, s 29(2)(a)(i)) and ceases to be an overriding interest (LRA 2002, s 29(3)). A lease of three years or less, which can, if it is a rack rent lease taking immediate effect, be created orally or by writing other than a deed (Law of Property Act 1925, ss 52(2)(d); 54(2)), may not be noted on the register (LRA 2002, s 33(b)). A weekly, monthly, quarterly or annual periodic tenancy will fall into this category. The intermediate category of a lease which is not registrable but which may be noted on the register of the superior title will disappear if and when all leases for more than three years become registrable, as is the intention behind LRA 2002.[3]

---

[1]   This follows from the wide meaning of 'interest' in the LRA 2002, s 32, and see the LRA 2002, s 132(3)(b) (references to an interest affecting an estate are to an adverse right affecting the title to that estate).
[2]   LRR 2003, r 57, made under the LRA 2002, s 71.
[3]   The power for this purpose is in the LRA 2002, s 118. For the intention to do this see Law Com No 271, para 3.17.

6.23   A grant of exactly seven years is not registrable, a grant of seven years and one day is. The reason for the definition of the term of a registrable lease being more than seven years *from the date of grant* (LRA 2002, s 27(2)(b)(i)) is to make clear that in the common case of a lease expressed to be for a specified period of years from a date earlier than the date of grant, the part of that period before the date of grant is disregarded in deciding whether the lease is registrable. It seems reasonably clear, however, that where a lease is for a term which commences after the date of grant, but no more than three months after the date of grant,[1] the period between date of grant and the commencement of the lease is not counted when determining whether the lease is registrable. Thus a lease for a term of seven years from 25 March 2004 where the date of grant is 3 February 2004 is not a registrable lease. A lease for a term of seven years 'from' the date on which it is granted may or may not include the date of grant (it is a question of construction of the lease),[2] but, whether or not it includes that day, it is still only a lease for seven years and is not registrable. A lease granted on 25 March 2004 expressed to be for a term 'commencing on the date hereof and ending on 25 March 2011' is a grant of seven years and one day and is registrable. A lease granted on 25 March 2004 for a term of seven years and three months from 25 December 2003 is registrable if 25 December 2003 is not included in the term and is not registrable if it is. Where it is desired to grant a lease of seven years, it should be decided whether or not it is desired to register it, and a few days should be added or subtracted according to what is desired (or if a non-registrable lease is desired the grant of the lease can be put off until a few days after the commencement of the term). If a lease is preceded by a contract, what it says in the contract makes no difference to the registrability of the lease. Thus if a contract is made on 11 November 2003 to grant a term of seven years and one month from 1 December 2003, and the tenant takes up occupation on 1 December 2003 but the lease is only executed on 2 January 2004, the lease is not required to be registered.

---

[1]   If the period was more than three months the lease would be registrable even if of a duration of seven years or less (LRA 2002, s 27(2)(b)(ii)). See para 6.21.

[2]   See 27(1) *Halsbury's Laws* (4th edn reissue) para 206.

6.24   There is no prescribed form for the grant of a lease of registered land, and at the time of writing this the only formal requirements are that the title number of the title out of which it is granted should be referred to (LRR 2003, r 212(3)), and that it should not bear the number of a form in the LRR 2003, Sch 1 (LRR 2003, r 212(2)). The land registry proposed in the consultation draft of the LRR 2003 to introduce a standard form of lease,[1] but decided not to proceed with it as a result of the responses to the consultation. In September 2004 the land registry issued a consultation paper[2] which proposed two alternative possibilities for prescribing the presentation of the salient features of a registrable lease, without proposing a standard form for the entire lease. The choice between these possibilities will depend on the outcome of the consultation. The first alternative possibility is a new Form L1 (Lease Front Sheet), which would be required by the amended LRR 2003 to be attached to the front of the lease and on which prescribed information about the lease would be entered (some information compulsory, some optional).[3] The second alternative would be to require specified clauses to appear at the beginning of the lease. In relation to the formal requirements for grants of subleases the following trap lurks in the legal undergrowth. Where a sublease is granted for the whole of the remainder of the term of the grantor's lease it operates as an assignment of that lease, not as the grant of a sublease.[4] If by mischance what is intended to be a sublease (and is in form a sublease) in fact operates as an assignment of a registered leasehold estate, the application for registration of it might be rejected by the land registry, because an assignment of a registered estate is required to be made in the prescribed form of transfer (LRR 2003, r 58).[5]

---

[1]   See *Report on responses to Land Registration Rules 2003 — a Land Registry Consultation*, p 10 para 17. For the proposed standard form which was not proceeded with see *Land Registration Rules 2003, A Land Registry Consultation*, proposed rule 59 and proposed Form L1 in Sch 1 to the proposed rules.

2   *Land Registry Consultation Paper September 2004, Presentation of prescribed information in registrable leases.* The closing date for responses was 10 December 2004.
3   The proposed required information is landlord's title number, the title numbers of any other titles affected, the parties, the property, any legislation affecting the lease, term, any premium, initial rent, restrictions on alienation, any restrictions required on the register, a declaration of trust if there are co-owners, easements, options and rights of pre-emption, frustration clauses and restrictive covenants affecting premises other than those comprised in the lease.
4   27(1) *Halsbury's Laws* (4th edn reissue) para 84.
5   See paras 5.17, 6.29. The Land Registry's Practice Guide 49 *Rejection of applications for registration* states that applications will be rejected where there is a prescribed form for a registered disposition and it has not been used.

6.25   It is necessary for the lease to be valid as a matter of general law for the land registry to accept it for registration. If, for example, it does not satisfy the requirements for execution as a deed,[1] or does not specify the date of commencement and length of the term with sufficient certainty,[2] or commences more than 21 years after the date of grant and is at a premium or reserves a rent,[3] or is a grant by the lessor to himself,[4] registration will be refused on the grounds that it is not an effective grant of a legal estate or is completely void and of no effect.[5]

1   See the Law of Property Act 1925, s 52(1) for the necessity of a deed if a legal estate is to be granted (unless it is an immediate rack rent lease for a term not exceeding three years—Law of Property Act 1925, ss 52(2)(d) and 54(2)). See the Law of Property (Miscellaneous Provisions) Act 1989, s 1 (individuals) and the Companies Act 1985, s 36A (inserted by the Companies Act 1989, s 130) (companies) for the requirements for execution as a deed.
2   See 27(1) *Halsbury's Laws* (4th edn reissue) para 205 et seq.
3   And thus void by virtue of the Law of Property Act 1925, s 149(3).
4   And thus void: *Rye v Rye* [1962] AC 496.
5   See the Land Registry's Practice Guide 25 *Leases—when to register*, para 5.

6.26   The covenants for title under the Law of Property (Miscellaneous Provisions) Act 1994 may be incorporated,[1] but they are subject to the qualification that the transferor is not liable for anything entered on the register of title.[2] Where a disposition is made pursuant to a contract or option created before 1 July 1995 the covenants for title implied by the Law of Property Act 1925, s 76 can apply (Law of Property (Miscellaneous Provisions) Act 1994, ss 11 and 13), subject to the qualification that there is no liability in respect of an overriding interest falling within the LRA 2002, Sch 3 of which the purchaser has notice (LRR 2003, r 67(2)).[3] One situation in which the pre-1 July 1995 covenants for title may still be relevant is the grant of a lease pursuant to an option (typically an option to renew a lease) granted before 1 July 1995.

1   Authorised for registered land by the LRA 2002, Sch 10, para 3(a) and the LRR 2003, r 67. See para 9.34
2   Law of Property (Miscellaneous Provisions) Act 1994, s 6(4), added by the LRA 2002, Sch 11, para 31(2). The covenants for title are thus principally important where there are undisclosed overriding interests constituting a breach of the covenant, or where the grantor is himself holding under a lease (which might, for example, be liable to forfeiture).

³ This continues the former LRR 1925, r 77(1). In relation to post 30 June 1995 covenants the differently worded Law of Property (Miscellaneous Provisions) Act 1994, s 6(2) has much the same effect.

6.27 Applications for registration of a registrable lease granted out of a registered estate (ie a lease which must be registered if the lessee is to have a legal estate—see para 6.21) must be on form AP1 (LRR 2003, r 13(1)), and accompanied by the appropriate fee. The lease, obviously, must be submitted to the registry with the application, and also a certified copy of it if the applicant wants the lease to be returned by the registrar (LRR 2003, r 203(3)).¹ The lease or the certified copy will be retained by the registrar and will be a document open to public inspection unless there is an application for it to be designated an exempt information document (LRR 2003, rr 133 and 136–138).² The application must be accompanied by disclosure of overriding interests in the manner and to the extent required by the LRR 2003, r 57.³ Any restrictions which the applicant wants registered or is under a duty to have registered must be applied for on Form RX1, and cannot be applied for in the lease.⁴ Registration of the lease will involve a new title being opened. The property register will contain sufficient particulars to identify the lease but no more information about its contents, save that if the lease contains a provision prohibiting or restricting dispositions of the leasehold estate an entry will be made stating that all estates, rights, interests, powers and remedies arising on or by reason of a disposition made in breach of that prohibition or restriction are excepted from the effect of registration (LRR 2003, r 6).⁵ Where a right of re-entry is contained in the lease the registrar need not make any entry regarding such right in the registered title of the reversionary estate.⁶ Any premium paid or value declared will apparently be recorded in the register until there is a change of proprietor (when any premium or value declared on transfer to a new proprietor will be substituted) (LRR 2003, r 8(2)).⁷ It will be recalled that registration of a newly granted lease of registered land is only effective to vest a legal estate in the lessee if the lease is noted on the grantor's title as well as being registered in a leasehold title of its own.⁸ There is no need to apply specifically for noting of the lease on the grantor's title because the land registry is under an obligation to do this (LRA 2002, s 38). For reasons given in paras 5.32 and 5.33 it will be a sensible precaution for any conveyancer acting for the original grantee of such a lease to check that this double registration requirement has been properly and correctly carried out once the land registry has notified the grantee or conveyancer that the registration process is complete. For the interests which are binding on the original lessee of a lease see para 6.34.

---

¹ For the requirements for certifying, and as to who may certify, a certified copy see the LRR 2003, r 217(1), definitions of 'certified copy' and 'conveyancer'.
² See paras 2.76 et seq, 6.66 et seq.
³ See, further, paras 5.19, 7.26, 7.63 and Appendix 1.
⁴ LRR 2003, r 92(1), none of the exceptions in r 92(7) being applicable.

5   It is possible that this rule is ultra vires if and in so far as it purports to make non-registrable a disposition which the LRA 2002 requires or permits to be registered, as the power relied on seems to be the power to prescribe how the register is kept (LRA 2002, s 1(2)), although r 6 might be justified under the LRA 2002, Sch 10, para 8. LRR 2003, r 6 repeats the former LRR 1925, r 45, but LRA 1925 contained a specific provision relating to it (LRA 1925, s 8(2)) which is not re-enacted in the LRA 2002.
6   LRR 2003, r 77, and see also the LRA 2002, Sch 2, para 7(3).
7   See also Land Registry Practice Guide 7 *Entry of price paid or value stated on the register.*
8   LRA 2002, s 27(1) and Sch 2, para 3. See para 5.18.

6.28   Where the registrar retains a copy of a lease, the LRA 2002, s 120 provides protection against copying errors for persons acquiring any interest in the land subject to that lease. Section 120(1) and (2) provides that where a copy of a document is retained by the registrar and is referred to by an entry in the register relating to a registered estate, that copy kept by the registrar is taken to be correct as between the parties to any disposition relating to the land to which that registered estate relates. It is also as between those parties to be taken to contain all material parts of the original document, and no such party may require production of the original document, or is to be affected by a provision of the original document not contained in the copy (s 120(2)–(4)). There is also a right to indemnity against loss by reason of a mistake in a copy document retained by the registrar and referred to in the register (LRA 2002, Sch 8, para 1(1)(e)).

TRANSFERS OF REGISTERED LEASEHOLD LAND

6.29   In relation to transfers of registered leases the rules for transfers of registered estates discussed in the previous chapter on freeholds at para 5.16 et seq apply. In particular, it should be noted that the prescribed forms of transfer must be used.[1] If a transfer is of part of a registered leasehold estate and it contains a legal apportionment of or exoneration from the rent reserved by the lease, the transfer must include a statement in the additional provisions panel, with any necessary alterations and additions, stating how the rent is apportioned between the part of the land transferred and the part retained, using the wording prescribed by the rules.[2] Legal apportionment in this context presumably means an apportionment which is binding on the landlord, as a result of his agreement to it, or as a result going through one of the procedures for binding the landlord.[3]

1   LRR 2003, r 58. See para 5.17.
2   LRR 2003, r 60(1), where the relevant wording is set out.
3   Either apportionment by the Secretary of State for Rural Affairs under the Landlord and Tenant Act 1927, s 20, or, if it is a lease granted after 31 December 1995, the procedure laid down in the Landlord and Tenants (Covenants) Act 1995, s 10.

6.30   As with freehold land the covenants for title under the Law of Property (Miscellaneous Provisions) Act 1994[1] are subject to the qualification that the transferor is not liable for anything entered on the register of title.[2] Where a disposition is made pursuant to a contract or option created before 1 July 1995 the covenants for title implied by the Law of Property Act 1925, s 76 can apply (Law of Property (Miscellaneous Provisions) Act 1994, ss 11 and 13), subject to the qualification that there is no liability in respect of an overriding interest falling within the LRA 2002, Sch 3 of which the purchaser has notice (LRR 2003, r 67(2)).[3] In the case of a transfer of a leasehold estate the covenants for title have a more important part to play than in the case of a transfer of a freehold, because of the implied covenant that the lease is still subsisting and that there is no subsisting breach of condition or tenant's obligation and nothing which would render the lease liable to forfeiture (Law of Property (Miscellaneous Provisions) Act 1994, s 4). These are not matters which will necessarily be apparent from entries on the register of title.

---

[1]   Authorised for registered land by the LRA 2002, Sch 10, para 3(a) and the LRR 2003, r 67.
[2]   Law of Property (Miscellaneous Provisions) Act 1994, s 6(4), added by the LRA 2002, Sch 11, para 31(2).
[3]   See para 6.26, footnote 3.

6.31   Where the lease was granted before 1 January 1996 there is (in the absence of agreement to the contrary) implied in any transfer of it a covenant by the transferee to indemnify the transferor against payment of the rent and compliance with the covenants and conditions contained in the lease (LRA 2002, Sch 12, para 20(1), (2)). In the case of a transfer of part of the land comprised in a lease granted before 1 January 1996 there is (in the absence of agreement to the contrary) an implied indemnity covenant by the transferee in favour of the transferor in respect of the rent apportioned to the transferred part (where the rent reserved by the lease has been apportioned) and in respect of compliance with the covenants and conditions in the lease which affect the part transferred (LRA 2002, Sch 12, para 20(3)). There is also an implied covenant by the transferor in favour of the transferee to indemnify the transferee in respect of the same matters so far as they relate to the land retained by him (LRA 2002, Sch 12, para 20(4)). These implied covenants will extend to the entire rent in a case where, without the consent of the landlord, the entire rent is agreed to be payable out of the transferred part or out of the retained part (LRR 2003, r 60(2) and (3)). If these implied covenants are modified or negatived by the provisions of the transfer then an entry to that effect must be made in register (LRR 2003, r 66).

6.32   For the interests which are binding on the assignee of a lease see para 6.35. Where the leasehold estate is one which was granted out of a registered estate (including an unregistered estate which was subject to a requirement of compulsory registration at the time of the grant—see paras, 4.11, 6.6), there are a number of reasons for a purchaser or his conveyancer looking at the title to the reversion on the lease before purchasing:

(1) to check that the lease has been noted against the superior title. If the lease was granted out of a registered estate (or one already subject to a requirement of compulsory registration) the lease is not a legal estate if it is not noted against the superior title (see paras 5.18, 5.32, 5.33);

(2) to see if there are any rights, in particular easements, noted against the superior title, which are not noted on the leasehold title but which could affect the latter (see para 6.44);

(3) where the superior title is leasehold, to examine the lease for, eg, restrictive covenants which are binding on subleases (see paras 6.41, 6.42).

THE INTERESTS TO WHICH LEASEHOLD ESTATES ARE SUBJECT

6.33 The general rules as to priorities mentioned in para 5.21 and described in Chapter 7 below apply to registered leasehold estates, but there are some particular points to note about priorities and leases, arising from the following factors:

(1) when a registrable lease is granted out of a registered estate, a new registered title is created (see paras 6.34, 6.38–6.40);

(2) a leasehold estate may be burdened with interests or obligations contained in the lease or a superior lease which are not entered in the register of title (see para 6.34);

(3) there are leases, granted out of registered estates, which are not capable of registration because they are of seven years or less (and not in one of the special registrable categories)—see paras 6.36, 6.37.

The discussion below focuses on leases granted out of estates which are already registered by the time of the grant (or are already under an obligation to be registered and so treated as if already registered by the LRR 2003, r 38). Leases which were granted by dispositions out of unregistered estates which subsequently become registered will be subject to burdens incident to the estate as in (2) above, but the other points are not directly relevant.

6.34 It is a very unusual lease which is not granted for valuable consideration—even if there is no rent or premium the lessee usually enters into some covenants—and so the adverse interests (of persons other than the parties to the lease) to which the grant of a lease of registered land is subject will almost invariably be governed by the LRA 2002, s 29.[1] Where s 29 applies, a registered leasehold estate granted out of a registered estate will when granted and registered be subject to the following:

(1)   interests created before the grant of the lease which are protected by the time of its registration[2] by being the subject of a notice in the register or (in the case of a charge) by being registered (s 29(2)(a)(i)). It should be emphasised that when a lease is granted out of a registered estate, the interests which maintain their priority over the original lessee by virtue of being noted or entered in the register are those which are noted or entered in the *lessor's* title;

(2)   overriding interests falling within any of the paragraphs of the LRA 2002, Sch 3 at the time of the grant of the lease which are not and have not been noted on the register (s 29(2)(a)(ii) and (3)). See further paras 7.17, 7.18, 7.62–7.81;

(3)   interests which appear from the register to be excepted from the effect of registration (s 29(2)(a)(iii)): see further para 6.40. Again this refers to matters appearing from the *lessor's* title to be so excepted;

(4)   where the lessor's estate is leasehold, interests of which the burden is incident to that estate (s 29(2)(b)). Therefore, where what has been granted is an underlease, the burden of an interest incident to the grantor's lease will be binding on the underlessee. Examples of such interests are restrictive covenants contained in the grantor's lease,[3] or a right to enter the premises to inspect or carry out repairs. Section 29(2)(b) is not relevant to the burden on the original lessee of the terms of his own lease, which are binding on him because he personally has agreed to accept them.

---

[1]   If it is not granted for valuable consideration, it is subject to all interests previously created: LRA 2002, s 28.

[2]   The date of registration is the date of applying for registration, and so if the application is not rejected and is made within a priority period there is no opportunity to obtain priority for an interest not protected when the lease is granted: see paras 7.82–7.87.

[3]   See paras 6.41, 6.42.

6.35   Where a registered leasehold estate is transferred to a new proprietor, and the transfer is for valuable consideration,[1] the list of interests to which the new proprietor will be subject is as in para 6.34 subject to the following differences:

(a)   the interests whose priority over the lease are preserved under the LRA 2002, s 29(2)(a)(i) by virtue of an entry in the register are those which are so entered on the title of the lease itself;

(b)   the interests whose priority is preserved under s 29(2)(a)(iii) by appearing from the register to be excepted from the effect of registration are those so excepted from the register of title of the lease itself;

(c)   the burdens of interests incident to the leasehold estate which has been transferred are what are binding on of the transferee by virtue of s 29(2)(b). It is possible, however, that these would include interests which are incident to the lessor's estate where the lessor is himself a lessee: see para 6.34. Section 29(2)(b) means that the register does not attempt to record the lessor's rights as against the lessee conferred by the lease (or any variation of it), and any purchaser of the estate must study the lease (and any variation of it) for these. The only exception is that the LRR 2003, r 6 provides that if the lease contains a provision prohibiting or restricting dispositions of the leasehold estate an entry will be made stating that all estates, rights, interests, powers and remedies arising on or by reason of a disposition made in breach of that prohibition or restriction are excepted from the effect of registration.[2]

---

[1]   As in the case of the grant of a lease, if it is not granted for valuable consideration, it is subject to all interests previously created: LRA 2002, s 28.

[2]   See para 6.27.

6.36   Where a lease is granted out of a registered estate and is a lease which is not required to be completed by registration (eg it is for seven years or less),[1] the LRA 2002, s 29(4) provides that s 29 has effect as if the grant was a registrable disposition which was registered at the time of the grant.[2] Accordingly, the relevant law of priorities in relation to the grant of such a lease is that of registered rather than unregistered land. Once granted, however, such a lease is an unregistered estate and subject to the law of unregistered land. Legal estates or interests to which such a lease is subject when granted will be binding on successors in title to the lease, but equitable interests such as estate contracts or restrictive covenants, even though they are noted on the grantor's title and thus are binding on the original lessee under the lease, will only be binding on successors in title to the lease if they are registered in the land charges registry under the Land Charges Act 1972. This is unfortunate, though less so than under the LRA 1925 because the possible duration of an unregistered lease of registered land is so much less.

---

[1]   See para 6.21 for the types of lease which are registrable, and those which are not registrable.

[2]   This was also the case under the LRA 1925: see the final paragraphs of the LRA 1925, ss 19(2) and 22(2).

6.37   However, leases for seven years or less (and not required to be registered)[1] are within the registration system to some extent.

Although such a lease is an overriding interest within the LRA 2002, Sch 3, para 1, if it is granted for more than three years it may be noted on the lessor's title on the application of the lessee (LRA 2002, ss 33(b) and 34(1)), the registrar has power to note it on the lessor's title if it comes to the registrar's notice (s 37), and on any subsequent registrable disposition of the lessor's estate the applicant for registration of that disposition is required to notify the registrar of the existence of such an unregistered lease (LRR 2003, r 57). The LRA 2002, s 29(3) has the effect that once such a lease is noted on the lessor's title, it can maintain its priority over subsequent dispositions of the lessor's estate only by virtue of continuing to be noted on the title to that estate. See, further, paras 7.17(2), 7.62. Another respect in which a non-registrable lease falls partly within the system of land registration is that if the grant of the lease includes the express grant of an appurtenant legal easement, that easement must be noted against the title of the servient tenement if the grant of the easement is to take effect as a legal easement (LRA 2002, s 27(1), (2)(d), and (4), and Sch 2, para 7(2)). See also paras 6.43, 6.44. There is the further point that if the lessee of a lease which is not registered, because its duration is seven years or less, is then granted a further lease of the same land commencing on or within one month after the expiry of his current lease, he may voluntarily register his current lease if the total period unexpired of the combination of both leases is more than seven years (LRA 2002, s 3(1), (3), (7)), in addition to being required to register the reversionary lease if it commences more than three months after the date of the grant (LRA 2002, s 27(2)(b)(ii)).

---

[1]   See para 6.21 for the types of lease which are registrable, and those which are not registrable.

6.38   Returning to the case of a lease granted out of a registered estate which is of seven years or more duration (or otherwise required to be registered),[1] it follows from what is said in para 6.35 that it is of considerable importance that the land registrar should enter on the registered title of the new lease any adverse interests noted on the lessor's title, at the time of the registration of the new lease, which are also adverse to the lessee's title. This is especially so of interests which are not overriding ones within the LRA 2002, Sch 3, such as estate contracts, restrictive covenants or equitable easements, because without being noted on the title to the lease they will not be binding on any transferee for value of it, unless 'the register' in the LRA 2002, s 29(2)(a)(i) means the whole register of all land kept by the registrar (as opposed to referring only to the registered title of the lease itself). It seems most unlikely that 'the register' has this wider meaning in the context of s 29, as it would defeat much of the purpose of the registered conveyancing system for a purchaser of a registered estate to be bound by interests which are not entered on the register of the title he is purchasing and not within the LRA 2002, Sch 3, as a result of them being entered on some other registered title.

---

¹ See para 6.21 for the types of lease which are registrable, and those which are not registrable.

6.39 Interestingly, there is no provision of the LRA 2002 or the LRR 2003 which specifically requires the registrar to enter, on the registered of title of a registered lease granted out of a registered estate, interests noted on the lessor's title which are also adverse to the lessee's. However, the LRR 2003, r 9(a) requires the charges register of a registered estate, where appropriate, to contain details of interests which adversely affect it at the time of first registration of the estate, and accordingly this rule imposes such an obligation if 'first registration' in this rule includes first registration of a lease granted out of a registered estate. Although the expression 'first registration' is generally used in the legislation to refer to first registration of an existing unregistered legal estate, there is no definition or similar provision which expressly confines it to that meaning, and it is strongly arguable in relation to r 9(a) that the expression does have this wider meaning in this rule. It is also possible that the LRR 2003, r 35 also imposes such an obligation, but the context and wording of r 35 make it more likely that 'first registration' in that rule is confined to first registration of an existing unregistered legal estate. The general duty under the LRR 2003, r 57 of an applicant for registration of a registrable disposition to disclose adverse interests, and the general powers of the registrar under the LRR 2003, r 57 and the LRA 2002, s 37 to note such interests on the register, apply in relation to the grant of a lease of registered land, but these provisions only apply in respect of interests which are overriding interests within the LRA 2002, Sch 3. For further discussion of leases and easements see paras 6.43 and 6.44, and of leases and restrictive covenants see paras 6.41 and 6.42.

6.40 Further to what is said in paras 6.33 and 6.38, the LRA 2002 and LRR 2003 do not make express provision as to the title to be conferred when a lease granted out of registered land is first registered. The important provision here is the LRA 2002, s 29(2)(iii), which provides that a disposition for value is subject to any interest which appears from the register to be excepted from the effect of registration. By the LRA 2002, s 28 a disposition not for value is also subject to any such interest.¹ The other relevant provisions are the LRA 2002, Sch 4, para 2(1)(c) and 5(c) which provide that the court or the registrar may make an order for alteration of the register for the purpose of giving effect to any estate, right or interest excepted from the effect of registration, and the fact that the definition of 'rectification' and the indemnity provisions in the LRA 2002, Sch 4, para 1 and Sch 8, para 1(1) do not include or relate to alteration of the register to give effect to interests etc excepted from the effect of registration. This means that where the registered title of the grantor of a lease is less than absolute, the lessee gets no better title. Where the grantor's title is a qualified title[2] the registered title of the lessee will be qualified in the same way. Where the grantor's title is possessory or good leasehold,[3] the appropriate title of the lessee will presumably be a qualified title. Under the LRA 1925, interests excepted from the effect of registration relating to a leasehold title which was less than an absolute title were overriding interests (LRA 1925, s 70(1)(h)). Such interests are not made overriding interests by LRA 2002 because it was thought sufficient that s 29(2)(a)(iii) provides that dispositions of a registered estate are subject to interests excepted from the effect of registration.[4]

---

[1]   See paras 7.17, 7.18.
[2]   See the LRA 2002, ss 9(4), 10(5), 11(6) and 12(7), and paras 5.12, 6.13.
[3]   See the LRA 2002, ss 9(5), 10(3) and (6), 11(7) and 12(6) and (8), and paras 5.13, 6.12, 6.14.
[4]   See Law Com No 254, para 5.79 and Law Com No 271, paras 8.79 and 8.80 for more details of the reasoning behind this change.

LEASES AND OTHER TYPES OF INTEREST

Restrictive covenants

6.41   The proprietor of a registered leasehold estate, where his lease was granted out of a registered estate, may be subject to or have the benefit of restrictive covenants[1] as follows:

(1)   his own lease may contain covenants restrictive of his activities in the demised premises. These are binding on the original lessee as a matter of contract, and on his successors in title as an interest of which the burden is 'incident to the estate' and therefore binding under the LRA 2002, s 29(2)(b) without being noted on the registered title to the lease;

(2)   he may have the benefit of a restrictive covenant given by the lessor in respect of other land of the lessor which is not included in the demise. This is binding on the lessor as a matter of contract, and on successors in title to the lessor if the lessee has had it noted on the title to the land subject to the covenant. Restrictive covenants between lessor and lessee relating to land other than the demised premises may under the LRA 2002, contrary to the position under the LRA 1925, be protected by notice, because the exclusion from such

protection in the LRA 2002, s 33(c) is confined to covenants relating to the demised premises (while the corresponding provision of LRA 1925, s 50(1), applied to any covenant between lessor and lessee).[2] The benefit of the covenant should also be entered in the property register of the lessee's own title (LRR 2003, r 5(b)(ii)) but this does not seem to be essential to its enforceability (and see also para 9.30);

(3)   he may be subject to a restrictive covenant in favour of adjacent or nearby land which was binding on the lessor's estate and noted on the title to that estate immediately before the lease was granted. This will be binding on the original lessee by virtue of the notice of the covenant on the lessor's title at the time of grant of the lease (LRA 2002, s 29(2)(a)(i)), and binding on successors in title to the lease if a corresponding notice of the restrictive covenant is entered on the leasehold title: see para 6.38;

(4)   where the lease is an underlease the lessee may be subject to a restrictive covenant relating to the demised premises made between a superior lessor and a superior lessee—the latter may be his own lessor or an intermediate lessee higher up the chain of title. This is discussed in para 6.42.

---

[1]   On restrictive covenants and land registration see para 9.29 et seq.
[2]   *Oceanic Village Ltd v United Attractions Ltd* [2000] Ch 234.

6.42   Under the general law relating to unregistered land, a restrictive covenant entered into by a lessee in favour of the lessor and relating to the demised premises is binding on underlessees of the premises who have notice of the covenant,[1] and it is not required to be registered under the Land Charges Act 1972 in order to be binding on successors in title (see the Land Charges Act 1972, s 2(5)(ii)). Where a restrictive covenant relating to the demised premises is contained in a lease granted after 31 December 1995 it is binding on underlessees of those premises whether or not they have notice of it (Landlord and Tenant (Covenants) Act 1995, s 3(5)). The LRA 2002, s 33(c) excludes a restrictive covenant between lessor and lessee relating to the demised premises from being noted on the register, and presumably such a covenant is within the LRA 2002, s 29(2)(b) as an interest of which the burden is 'incident to the estate'. However, it may be that in relation to such a covenant in a lease granted before 1 January 1996 an underlessee must have notice of it for it to be binding on him. In practice underleases often repeat any restrictive covenants contained in superior leases, and where they do so the effect of the covenants contained in a superior lease is less likely to be an important issue.

---

[1]   27(1) *Halsbury's Laws* (4th edn reissue) para 475.

Easements

6.43   The position as regards easements is similar to that regarding restrictive covenants, but with the important difference that an easement can be a legal and overriding interest, whereas restrictive covenants are equitable interests only. The lessee under a lease which was granted out of a registered estate, may be subject to or have the benefit of easements as follows (where all relevant events are after 12 October 2003).

(1)   The lessee's own lease may be subject to an easement reserved to the lessor by the lease in favour of other land of the lessor. This is binding on the original lessee as a matter of contract, and it might be thought to be binding on his successors in title as an interest of which the burden is 'incident to the estate' and therefore binding under the LRA 2002, s 29(2)(b) without being noted on the registered title to the lease. However, the better view, and the cautious advice, is that such an easement is a reservation out of the estate rather than an incident of it, so that to be a legal easement it must satisfy the requirements of the LRA 2002, s 27(2)(d) and Sch 2, para 7 and be noted on the charges register of the title to the lease and entered on the title to the lessor's estate.[1] If it is correct that such an easement is not an interest which is incident to the legal estate, it will only be binding on transferees of the lease for valuable consideration if it is noted on the registered title to the lease. Where the reservation is out of a leasehold estate which is not registrable (ie where the lease is of seven years or less duration and not in a special category of registrable lease),[2] the better view is that the registration requirements of the LRA 2002, s 27(2)(d) and Sch 2, para 7 do not apply, because it is not a reservation out of a registered estate.[3]

(2)   The lessee may have the benefit of an easement granted, by the lease, over other land of the lessor which is not included in the demise. This is binding on the lessor as a matter of contract. If it is expressly granted, it will be binding on transferees for valuable consideration of the servient land only if the lessee has had it noted on the title to that land, and the benefit of the easement must be entered in the property register of the lessee's own title, if it is to be a legal easement (LRA 2002, s 27(2)(d) and Sch 2, para 7).[4] If it is entered only on the title to the servient land, it will still apparently be binding on the successors in title to that land, but as an equitable rather than a legal interest. Where such an easement is expressly granted as an appurtenance to a lease which is not registrable (ie where the lease is of seven years or less duration and not in a special category of registrable lease)[5] it must be noted on the lessor's title to the servient land if it is to take effect at law and binding on successors in title to the servient land (LRA 2002, Sch 2,

para 7).[6] The application to register a notice against the title to the servient land where an easement is created for the benefit of an unregistered estate must be made in Form AP1 (LRR 2003, r 90). However, if the easement arises as a matter of implied grant under the LPA 1925, s 62, it will be a legal easement without being registered (LRA 2002, s 27(7)) and thus binding on successors in title by virtue of the LRA 2002, s 29(2)(a)(ii) and Sch 3, para 3 (subject to the exceptions in para 3).[7]

(3)　The lessee may be subject to an easement which was binding on the lessor's estate immediately before the lease was granted. Such an easement may have been binding because it was a legal easement which was an overriding interest within Sch 3 (and not noted on the lessor's title), or because it was noted on the lessor's title. In either case it will be binding on the lessee and his successor in successors in title, subject to the point that if it was binding on the original lessee by virtue of being noted against the lessor's title, there is a question whether it needs to be noted against the lessee's title to be binding on his successors in title, discussed further in para 6.44. Such noting on the lessee's title should happen automatically: see paras 6.38, 6.39.

(4)　The demised premises may include an easement appurtenant to the demised premises which the lessor already enjoyed over land in other ownership before the lease was granted. If this was sufficiently protected so as to bind transferees for value of the servient land before the lease was granted, it should continue to be so protected for the lessee. The benefit of it should be entered in the property register of the title to the lease, but if it is by some oversight omitted from the leasehold title it should remain enforceable by the lessee, provided it was included (expressly or by implication) in the premises demised by the lease.

---

[1]　See paras 9.11, 9.15.
[2]　See para 6.21 for the categories of registrable lease.
[3]　See further, para 9.11.
[4]　See paras 9.11, 9.15.
[5]　See para 6.21 for the categories of registrable lease.
[6]　See also para 9.20.
[7]　See paras 9.12, 9.15, 9.16.

6.44　On the effect of an easement to which the lessor's estate was subject before the grant of a lease, consider the following example. A grants to B a ten-year lease at a time when the demised premises are subject to a right of way over them in favour of adjoining land in the ownership of C. The right of way is one which was expressly granted by A to C after 12 October 2003 when the land of both was already registered, and the right is noted on A's title and entered on C's title and thus constitutes a legal easement. By an oversight the registered title of the lease granted to B does not have noted on it that it is subject to C's right of way. B then transfers his leasehold estate to D. Does D take the lease subject to C's right of way? As it is a legal easement it is an overriding interest within the LRA 2002, Sch 3, para 3 (assuming that it is sufficiently obvious, in use, or known for Sch 3, para 3 to apply). The only doubt as to whether it is binding on D in this example arises from the LRA 2002, s 29(3) which provides that interests falling within Sch 3 do not have their priority protected by virtue of that fact if they have been the subject of a notice in the register at any time since 13 October 2003. The crucial question is, therefore, whether the reference to 'the register' in s 29(3) refers only to the register of title of the lease itself, in which case the easement will be binding on D, or would include the register of title to A's estate, in which case it will not be binding on D. The first of these possibilities seems more likely as a matter of principle, though if the second is correct C should be entitled to an indemnity. If the right of way had been an equitable rather than a legal right at the time when B's lease was granted, eg because the benefit of it was not entered on C's title (as required by the LRA 2002, Sch 2, para 7), it would only be binding on D if it was noted on the leasehold title when it was transferred to D.

Charges

6.45   The statutory power of leasing in the Law of Property Act 1925, s 99 of a mortgagor in possession (which applies unless restricted or excluded by the mortgage) applies to registered charges by virtue of the LRA 2002, s 51. A lease within the terms of that power would, it seems, be binding on the chargee even if it was in contravention of a restriction or exclusion of the statutory power of leasing which was contained the charge, unless there was an appropriate restriction on the register of title (LRA 2002, s 26(1), (2)). Where such a restriction is lacking, it might be argued that the exclusion or restriction is 'reflected by an entry in the register' within the LRA 2002, s 26(2), on the grounds that the charge is referred to and identified in the register, and contains the restriction or exclusion, but it is suggested that 'reflected by an entry' means that there must be an entry which draws specific attention to the existence of such restriction or exclusion, and that a reference to a document which might or might not contain it would not be sufficient.

Leaseholders' contractual and statutory rights to a new lease, or purchase of the reversion

6.46   If the lessee under a lease of which the immediate reversion is registered has an option or other contractual right to an extension of the lease, or to the acquisition of the freehold or other estate in reversion, the only safe way of protecting priority for the rights under such a contract is by a notice entered on the title to the reversion subject to the right.[1] However, if no such notice is entered, it will be possible for the right to be protected as an overriding interest under the LRA 2002, Sch 3, para 2 if the lessee is in actual occupation of the premises and none of the para 2 exceptions apply.[2] Sch 3, para 2 will only protect such a right so far as it relates to the land in which the lessee is in occupation. The treatment of rights under the Leasehold Reform Act 1967 and the Leasehold Reform, Housing and Urban Development Act 1993, Pt I, Chs I and II is the same as under the Land Registration Act 1925. In particular, once a tenant has served notice under either Act of his desire to have the freehold or an extended lease he must register the notice as if it were an estate contract, and his rights under the notice will not be overriding ones within the LRA 2002, Sch 1, para 2 or Sch 3, para 2 (interests of persons in actual occupation): see the Leasehold Reform Act 1967, s 5(5) as amended by the LRA 2002, Sch 11, para 8, and the Leasehold Reform, Housing and Urban Development Act 1993, s 97(1) as amended by the LRA 2002, Sch 11, para 30. The treatment of the right to buy under Housing Act 1985, Part 5 carries forward what was the position under LRA 1925: after a disposal, within Housing Act 1985, s 171A, of the landlord's interest under which the right is preserved, the right can only be preserved against subsequent dispositions of the reversion by being noted on the title to it, and cannot be an overriding interest (Housing Act 1985, Sch 9A, para 6(1), as substituted by LRA 2002, Sch 11, para 18). An application to the court for a new lease of registered land under the Landlord and Tenant Act 1954, Pt II must be protected by a notice as a pending land action, and cannot be an overriding interest under the LRA 2002, Sch 1, para 2 or Sch 3, para 2 (interests of persons in actual occupation): LRA 2002, s 87(1) and (3). There are various other statutory rights excluded from being overriding interests: see para 7.81.

---

[1]   For notices see paras 7.20 et seq.

[2]   For the LRA 2002, Sch 3, para 2 see paras 7.67–7.73. Actual occupation will not protect such a right where the reversion is not a registered estate: see para 6.59.

THE DIFFERENT CATEGORIES OF LEASE OR TENANCY AND THEIR PROTECTION AGAINST SUBSEQUENT DISPOSITIONS OF THE ESTATE IN REVERSION

6.47   In the case of wholly unregistered land a lease is a legal estate binding on any successor in title to the estate in reversion on it, whether or not the successor has notice of the lease, and whether or not he acquired the estate in reversion for valuable consideration. However, a lease which was granted out of unregistered land where the estate in reversion later becomes registered, or a lease which was granted out of an estate which was already registered, is capable of losing its priority to a successor in title to the estate in reversion if it is not properly protected against subsequent dispositions of the reversion. The available means of protection before the estate in reversion becomes registered are cautions against first registration (see paras 4.3 et seq) and substantive first registration where the lease gets its own registered title and title number (see para 6.9). The available forms of protection after registration of the estate in reversion are noting on the registered title to the reversion (paras 7.20 et seq), being overriding within Sch 1, para 1 or Sch 3, para 1 to the LRA 2002 (paras 6.22, 6.36, 6.37), and being overriding within para 2 of either of those Schedules (see paras 7.9, 7.67–7.73). Paras 6.48 to 6.61 discuss the various kinds of lessee's or tenant's interests, and the protection which is available to them respectively against dispositions of the immediate reversion. Para 6.62 discusses the position of sub-tenants as against the owners of titles superior to that of the owner of the immediate reversion.

Leases granted before 13 October 2003 for more than 21 years from the date of grant which are now registered

6.48   If the estate in reversion on the lease is unregistered, such a lease has priority over any subsequent disposition of that reversionary estate by virtue of being a legal estate. If the estate in reversion has been or comes to be registered, such a lease will have priority over any subsequent disposition of the estate in reversion if either it is noted on the title to the reversion (see paras 5.21, 6.34, 6.35, 7.17, 7.18 and 7.20 et seq) or the lessee is in actual and obvious occupation of the whole of the demised premises (see paras 7.17, 7.18, 7.67–7.73). If the reversion was registered before the grant of the lease then the grant will have been a registered disposition which the registrar should have noted on the title to the reversion when registering the grant of the lease. If the reversion became first registered after the grant of the lease, the lease should have been noted on the title to the reversion at first registration of the reversion—if first registration was after 12 October 2003 the relevant provision for this is the LRR 2003, r 35 (see also r 9(a)).

Leases granted before 13 October 2003 for more than 21 years from the date of grant which remain unregistered

6.49   Leases of such a duration which are still unregistered will be ones which have not been the subject of an event which has triggered compulsory registration, and which were either:
   (i)   granted out of an unregistered estate in land before December 1990 in an area of England or Wales which was not subject to compulsory registration at the time of the grant; or
   (ii)   were granted before 1 January 1987 out of an unregistered estate in land in an area of compulsory registration, but were of less than 40 years' duration.[1]

A lease granted before 1 January 1987 out of registered or unregistered land for more than 21 years but with an absolute prohibition on assignment could also still remain unregistered.[2] A lease granted for more than 21 years is not an overriding interest within either Sch 1, para 1 or Sch 3, para 1 of LRA 2002. If the lessee is in actual occupation of the whole of the demised premises, it will be an overriding interest within either Sch 1, para 2 or Sch 3, para 2 of LRA 2002, provided, where Sch 3, para 2 is the relevant provision, that none of the exceptions in that para apply.[3] If the immediate reversion was a registered estate on 13 October 2003, and the lessee was in receipt of rents and profits of the demised premises immediately before 13 October 2003, the lease will continue as an overriding interest by virtue of such receipt by virtue of the LRA 2002, Sch 12, para 8 until there is some interruption in the flow of rents and profits.[4] The narrowing of the rights protected by occupation under Sch 1, para 2 and Sch 3, para 2 of the LRA 2002 (as compared with the LRA 1925, s 70(1)(g)) means that this type of protection is precarious, or non-existent where the property is let to sub tenants and the LRA 2002, Sch 12, para 8 does not apply, and anyone entitled to an unregistered lease of more than 21 years should seek the protection of an appropriate entry on the register. Where the immediate reversion is not registered it will be possible to obtain a measure of protection against the reversion becoming registered and the lease not being noted on its title by registering a caution against first registration, but if there are more than seven years unexpired at the time of lodging the caution, it will only have effect until 12 October 2005 (LRA 2002, s 15 and Sch 12, para 14).[5] Because of the way in which the LRA 2002, s 15(3) and Sch 12, para 14(2) are worded, if there are more than seven years unexpired at the date of lodging the caution, but seven years or less unexpired on 12 October 2005, the caution will still lapse on the latter date, but it will then be possible to register a new caution against first registration. On the other hand, if a caution against first registration was lodged before 13 October 2003 under the LRA 1925, s 53, it seems that it will not be subject to lapse on 12 October 2005 (see the LRA 2002, Sch 12, para 16). If there will be more than seven years left to run on 12 October 2005, the only enduring method of protection is voluntary registration,[6] and the sensible course of action would be to proceed to apply for it now, though a caution against first registration should be lodged as an interim measure while the registration application is put together. If the reversion on the lease is already registered, the primary concern is to check that the lease is noted on the register of title to the reversion, and to apply for a such a notice to be entered there if this turns out not to have been done.[7] A transfer of such a lease by way of sale or gift will trigger compulsory registration of it if it still has more than seven years to run at the time of the transfer.[8]

---

[1]   Under the LRA 1925, s 123(1) as originally enacted leases granted out of *unregistered* land were only subject to compulsory registration if they were for 40 years or more, although unregistered leases with more than 21 years to run could be voluntarily registered, and an assignable lease for more than 21 years granted out of a *registered* estate had to be registered. All leases of more than 21 years were made compulsorily registrable (if in areas of compulsory registration) with effect from 1 January 1987 by virtue of the Land Registration Act 1986, s 2 (amending the LRA 1925, s 123(1)), and the commencement order SI 1986/2117. From December 1990 compulsory registration applied to the whole of England and Wales.

[2]   Under the LRA 1925, s 8(2) as originally enacted leases subject to an absolute prohibition on assignment could not be registered, but with effect from 1 January 1987 by virtue of the Land Registration Act 1986, s 3, amending the LRA 1925, s 8(2), and the commencement order SI 1986/2117, they became registrable.

[3]   See paras 7.69–7.71.

[4]   See paras 7.74–7.76.

[5]   See para 4.4.

[6]   See para 6.9.

[7]   See paras 7.20 et seq for the notice procedure.

[8]   See paras 6.3, 6.4 for compulsory first registration of leases.

Leases granted (whether out of registered or unregistered land) before 13 October 2003 for more than seven years but for 21 years or less (from date of grant)

6.50   These were not registrable and were overriding interests before 13 October 2003, and they continue under the transitional provision in the LRA 2002, Sch 12, para 12 to be overriding interests[1] on and after that date, unless they are leases pursuant to the Housing Act 1985, Pt 5 or to which s 171A of that Act applied.[2] What the LRA 2002, Sch 12, para 12 provides is that LRA 2002, Sch 1, para 1 and Sch 3, para 1 (leases which are overriding interests)[3] are taken to include an interest which immediately before 13 October 2003 was an overriding interest under the LRA 1925, s 70(1)(k). The wording of the latter provision was 'Leases granted for a term not exceeding twenty-one years', but it was subject to exclusion from overriding status for leases pursuant to the Housing Act 1985, Pt 5 or to which the Housing Act 1985, s 171A applied.[4] Strictly, an interest of a kind listed in the LRA 1925, s 70(1) was only an overriding interest when the estate which was subject to it was registered (see the opening words of s 70(1)). However, the reference in the LRA 2002, Sch 12, para 12 to the LRA 2002, Sch 1, para 1 implies that the Sch 12, para 12 includes leases which would have been overriding interests if the immediate reversion had been registered immediately before 13 October 2003 (but in fact was not registered), since Sch 1 is only relevant to first registration of an estate after 12 October 2003.[5] It is important to bear in mind, however, that a sale or gift of an unregistered lease of more than seven years which is an overriding interest will still trigger compulsory registration of it if there are more than seven years left to run of the lease at the time of the sale or gift.[6] The editors of Ruoff and Roper, *Registered Conveyancing*, post Release 25 (January 2004), para 17.006, express the view that once such a lease becomes subject to compulsory registration, it ceases to be an overriding interest within LRA 2002, Sch 1, para 1 and Sch 3, para 1. There are strong objections to this view, as follows. LRA 2002, Sch 12, para 12 is not qualified in this way, and the rest of the legislation is completely lacking in a provision to this effect. What the editors of Ruoff and Roper refer to in support of this proposition is that the policy of the Act is to bring as much as possible onto the register of title. However, such a general statement of policy has no necessary implication of this particular result. The sanctions against failure to apply for registration of such a lease after an event triggering compulsory registration seem quite strong enough[7] without also depriving the lessee of priority for the lease as well, and such a lease will anyway cease to have overriding status if it comes to be noted against the title to the reversion (LRA 2002, s 29(3)), whether or not it itself becomes registered.

---

[1]   See para 7.89(9).
[2]   Ie leases pursuant to the right to buy, or to a private sector landlord preserving the right to buy, which were registrable before 13 October 2003 and continue to be registrable as from that date under the LRA 2002, s 4 (see paras 6.5, 6.21).
[3]   See paras 6.51, 6.56, 6.57.
[4]   Housing Act 1985, s 154(7) and Sch 9A, para 3, before repeal by the LRA 2002, Sch 13 as from 13 October 2003.
[5]   See para 7.7.
[6]   See para 6.3.
[7]   See para 4.10.

Leases of seven years or less granted before 13 October 2003 out of an unregistered or a registered estate

6.51   This category includes, in addition to leases granted by deed for the relevant duration, leases created in writing other than by deed, or orally, for a term of three years or less, taking effect in possession and at the best rent which can be reasonably obtained without taking a premium, as these also constitute legal estates (Law of Property Act 1925, ss 52(1), (2)(d), 54(2)). Leases in this category, other than ones granted pursuant to the Housing Act 1985, Pt 5 or to which the Housing Act 1985, s 171A applied, are overriding interests within LRA 2002, Sch 1, para 1 and Sch 3, para 1,[1] and are not capable of substantive registration in their own right, except voluntarily in some circumstances (for which see below). Leases granted before 13 October 2003 pursuant to the Housing Act 1985, Pt 5 (right to buy) or to which the Housing Act 1985, s 171A (preservation of right to buy) applied were required to be registered when granted,[2] whatever their length, and were excluded from being overriding interests,[3] and so they will either be registered estates, or, if they have not been registered within the period for doing so, equitable interests only.[4] Where the reversion is a registered estate, a lease which was granted for seven years or less but for more than three years may be noted on the register of the reversion (LRA 2002, ss 32 and 33(b)), and if that happens it ceases to override a registered disposition of the reversion and maintains priority over such a disposition by virtue of the notice (s 29(3)). There are two ways in which a lease of seven years or less may be voluntarily registrable. One is where the right to possession is discontinuous (LRA 2002, s 3(4)), and the other is where the lessee has a reversionary lease of the same property which takes effect in possession on or within a month of the end of the current lease, and the two leases taken together add up to more than seven years unexpired (s 3(7)). For reversionary leases, see also paras 6.60 and 6.61.

---

[1]   Either because LRA 2002, Sch 1, para 1 and Sch 3, para 1 refer to leases of seven years or less granted before 12 October 2003, or because LRA 2002, Sch 12, para 12 adds them to it.

[2]   Housing Act 1985 ss 154(1), (6), and 171G, and Sch 9A, paras 2 and 3, before they were amended or repealed by LRA 2002, Sch 11, para 18, and Sch 13.

[3]   Housing Act 1985 ss 154(7), and 171G, and Sch 9A, paras 3 and 6(1)(b) before they were amended or repealed by LRA 2002, Sch 11, para 18, and Sch 13.

[4]   Housing Act 1985 ss 154(1), (6), and 171G, and Sch 9A, paras 2 and 6 before they were amended or repealed by LRA 2002, Sch 11, para 18, and Sch 13; LRA 1925, ss 8, 20, 22, 23, and 123 (grants before 1 April 1998) or 123A (grants on or after 1 April 1998).

Leases of more than seven years granted out of a registered estate after 12 October 2003

6.52   Such a lease[1] is required to be substantively registered, by having its own registered title, and also to be noted on the title to the estate out of which it was granted, before it takes effect as a legal estate (see paras 6.20, 6.21). If neither or only one of these requirements is fulfilled, it is presumably an equitable interest only. If it is noted on the title to the estate out of which it was granted, but is not substantively registered, it has the same protection as it would have if it took effect at law. This is an example of the registration system cutting across the traditional distinctions of legal and equitable interests. If such a lease is substantively registered with its own title, but by some oversight does not get noted on the title of the lessor, it seems that (where the lessee is not in actual occupation) the priority of the lease is not preserved against a subsequent disposition of the lessor's estate: LRA 2002, s 29(2)(i) makes it clear that a notice on the lessor's title is required to preserve the lease's priority by means of the register. If the registration requirements have not been fulfilled, such a lease can be protected against a subsequent disposition of the lessor's estate to the extent that the demised premises are in the actual occupation of the lessee: see paras 7.67–7.73.

---

[1]   Including one granted out of an unregistered estate which is already subject to the compulsory registration requirement: see para 4.11, and note the difficulties for the lessee there discussed which this could involve.

Special category leases granted out of a registered estate after 12 October 2003

6.53   By special category leases is meant the types of lease which when granted are required be registered even though they may be for seven years or less. They are set out in more detail in para 6.21. They are Housing Act 1985 right to buy and preservation of right to buy leases, leases with a discontinuous right to possession, and leases to take effect in possession after the end of the period of three months beginning with the date of the grant (LRA 2002, s 27(2)(b)(ii)–(v)). What is said in para 6.52 and its footnote about leases granted for more than seven years applies equally here with one qualification. This is that a lease granted to take effect in possession after the end of the period of three months beginning with the date of the grant, which has not yet taken effect in possession, is expressed to be excluded from the LRA 2002, Sch 3, para 2 (see para 2(d)) and so is not an interest protected by the actual occupation of the person entitled to it. For further discussion of this see paras 6.60 and 6.61.

Leases of more than seven years granted out of an unregistered estate after 12 October 2003

6.54   It is a very unusual lease that is not granted for some consideration, and so almost certainly such a lease will have been a compulsorily registrable lease (see para 6.5). If the lessee has duly applied to register the lease, and the application is successful, the position will then be the same as that described in para 6.48. If not, the lease will have been converted into a contract to grant the lease (LRA 2002, s 7(2)(b)), and become an equitable interest the consequences of which are as described in para 6.58.

Special category leases granted out of an unregistered estate after 12 October 2003

6.55 These special category leases are the types of lease which when granted out of an unregistered estate are subject to compulsory registration even though they may be for seven years or less. They are set out in more detail in para 6.5. They are the Housing Act 1985 right to buy and preservation of right to buy leases, and leases to take effect in possession after the end of the period of three months beginning with the date of the grant (LRA 2002, s 4(1)(d), (e), and (f)). There are two differences between the list in the LRA 2002 s 4 of special categories of lease required to be registered if granted out of an unregistered estate, and the list of special categories in s 27 required to be completed by registration when granted out a registered estate (see para 6.53). These are, first, that a lease under which possession is discontinuous is not subject to compulsory registration when granted out of an unregistered estate, but must be completed by registration when granted out of a registered estate, and, second, that the grant out of an unregistered estate of a lease for a term of years to take effect in possession after the end of three months beginning with the date of grant is only compulsorily registrable if it is granted out of an estate which has more than seven years to run at the date of the grant. What is said above in para 6.54 about leases granted for more than seven years applies equally here, subject to the qualification mentioned in para 6.53, and discussed further in paras 6.60, 6.61, that a lease granted to take effect more than three months after the date of grant is apparently not capable being an overriding interest by virtue of the lessee's actual occupation (under the LRA 2002, Sch 3, para 2) on the occasion of a disposition of the estate in reversion after the latter estate has become registered.

Leases of seven years or less (other than special category leases referred to in para 6.53) granted out of a registered estate after 12 October 2003

6.56 This category can include, in addition to leases granted by deed for the relevant duration, tenancies created in writing other than by deed, or orally, for a term of three years or less, taking effect in possession and at the best rent which can be reasonably obtained without taking a premium, as these also constitute legal estates (Law of Property Act 1925, ss 52(1), (2)(d), 54(2)). Leases in this category are protected as overriding interests under the LRA 2002, Sch 3, para 1. As already mentioned, if they are for more than three years they may come to be noted on the title to the estate in reversion, at which point they cease to have a overriding status (LRA 2002, s 29(3)).

Leases of seven years or less (other than special category leases referred to in para 6.55) granted out of an unregistered estate after 12 October 2003

6.57 As in the case of the leases referred to in para 6.56, this category can include, in addition to leases granted by deed for the relevant duration, rack rent tenancies of three years or less created informally and falling within Law of Property Act 1925, s 54(2). Leases in this category have the security of being legal estates so long as the reversion is not registered, and of being overriding interests within the LRA 2002, Sch 1, para 1 and Sch 3, para 1 if the reversion becomes registered, but again subject to ceasing to be overriding if they are for more than three years and come to be noted on the title to the reversion (LRA 2002, s 29(3)).

Tenancy agreements and other tenancies taking effect as equitable interests

6.58 The LRA 2002 only makes terms of years of more than seven years registrable if they are legal estates, and only protects terms of years of seven years or less as per se overriding interests within the LRA 2002, Sch 1, para 1 and Sch 3, para 1 if they are legal estates. Equitable leases, falling short of being legal estates, are not capable of having a registered title, nor of being per se overriding interests within Sch 1, para 1 and Sch 3, para 1. They include the following—

(i) a tenancy agreement which is neither a grant by deed (Law of Property Act 1925, s 52(1)) nor an informal tenancy for a term of three years or less which constitutes a grant of a legal estate (Law of Property Act 1925, ss 52(2)(d), 54(2));[1]

(ii) an intended grant of a lease by deed which is defective in some way as a grant of a legal estate;[2]

(iii) a grant of a lease out of a unregistered estate which was such as to trigger compulsory registration of the lease, where the lessee has failed to apply to have the lease registered and the period for doing so has expired (see paras 4.10, 6.5);

(iv) a grant of a lease out of a registered estate such that the lease so granted is required to be registered, but it has not been (see para 6.20).

Someone who is negotiating to take a lease of more than seven years can avoid the requirement that a lease of such length be registered by entering into a tenancy agreement, but the stamp duty land tax liability, if any, will be exactly the same as it would be for a grant of a lease (see para 6.76), and the agreement needs to be protected against subsequent dispositions (see para 6.59).

---

1   See Halsbury's Laws of England, 4th ed, vol 27(1) reissue, paras 52–54.
2   See Halsbury's Laws of England, 4th ed, vol 27(1) reissue, para 94.

6.59   Where the estate in land subject to a tenancy agreement or other equitable tenancy is registered, the tenancy can be protected by being noted on the title to the estate out of which it was granted (LRA 2002, s 32),[1] or by the tenant being in actual occupation of all the land comprised in the tenancy.[2] Where the estate in reversion is not registered, it is essential for the tenancy to be registered as an estate contract under the Land Charges Act 1972, even if the tenant is in occupation of the whole of the premises subject to the tenancy, because actual occupation by the tenant will not provide protection against a disposition of the estate in reversion for money or money's worth (Land Charges Act 1972, s 4(6)). This will be so even though any disposition of the reversion for money or money's worth will be one which triggers compulsory registration. In such a case the tenancy will not be an overriding interest binding on the reversion under LRA 2002, s 11(4)(b) (if it is freehold) or s 12(4)(c) (if it is leasehold), when the reversion comes to be first registered, because the tenancy will not then be an interest 'affecting the estate [ie the reversion] at the time of registration' (see the opening words of ss 11(4) and 12(4)).[3] The tenancy will have become void under Land Charges Act 1972 s 4(6) on the completion of the disposition which gave rise to the obligation to register, before the application to register the estate in reversion was made. If, on the other hand, compulsory registration of the reversion is triggered by a gift of it, occupation by a tenant under a tenancy agreement will preserve priority for the agreement even if there is a disposition for money or money's worth of the reversion by the donee of it before registration is applied for. This is because the gift would not affect the priority of the tenancy agreement, and the subsequent sale would be subject to the priority rules for registered land (LRR 2003, r 38). Where the estate in reversion is not registered, it will be a sensible precaution for the tenant under a tenancy agreement to protect it by registering a caution against first registration[4] as well as registering it as a land charge under Land Charges Act 1972.

---

1   See paras 7.17, 7.18, 7.20 et seq.
2   LRA 2002, Sch 3, para 2 would then make it an overriding interest. See paras 7.17, 7.18, 7.67–7.71.
3   See paras 7.4, 7.9(d).
4   See paras 4.3 et seq.

Future leases, and agreements and options to grant them

6.60   A lease, granted after 12 October 2003, to take effect in possession after the end of the period of three months beginning with the date of the grant is an estate which is required to be registered, even if it is for a term of seven years or less (LRA 2002, ss 4(1)(d) and 27(2)(b)(ii)).[1] Accordingly, such a lease is not an overriding interest within LRA 2002, Sch 1, para 1 or Sch 3, para 1. In addition, so long as it has not yet taken effect in possession, such a lease is excluded from the LRA 2002, Sch 3, para 2 by para 2(d), and so is not an interest protected by the actual occupation of the person entitled to it against a disposition of the estate in reversion on it, where the estate in reversion is a registered estate.[2] However, there is an inconsistency in the legislative drafting here, which provides an argument that such a lease which has not fallen into possession and has not been registered would still be protected under Sch 3, para 2 where the lessee was in actual occupation, despite para 2(d). This is because if such a lease was granted out of a registered estate (after 12 October 2003) and not registered, it would be an equitable interest not a legal one, because compliance with the registration requirements of the LRA 2002, s 27 and Sch 2 are a pre-requisite of the grant taking effect at law. If it is to take effect at law, it is essential that it be noted against the title to the reversion (Sch 2, para 3(2)(b)), and once so noted it cannot have overriding status (s 29(3)). If such a lease is granted out of an unregistered freehold estate, or an unregistered leasehold estate with more than seven years to run, it ceases to be a grant of a legal estate after two months if there is no application to register it, and it becomes a contract to grant a lease (ss 6(4) and 7(1) and (2)).[3] Therefore, on a strict interpretation, the LRA 2002, Sch 3, para 2(d) does not apply to any post 12 October 2003 grants, as it is very definitely worded so as to refer to a grant of a legal estate—it begins with the words 'a leasehold estate in land granted ...'. Sch 3, para 2(d) hardly has any function in relation to reversionary leases granted before 13 October 2003 which have not yet taken effect in possession, because these are either for a term of more than 21 years, and as such are likely to have been subject to compulsory registration, in which case they are not legal estates if they have not been registered, or they are for a term of 21 years or less, in which case they will apparently be overriding interests within Sch 1, para 1 and Sch 3, para 1, even if they commence after 12 October 2003 (LRA 2002, Sch 12, para 12). This argument leaves Sch 3, para 2(d) as applying only to a reversionary lease granted before December 1990 in an area not subject to compulsory registration, which has still not taken effect in possession, and where the estate in reversion upon it is now registered.[4]

---

[1]   Except where granted out of an unregistered lease with seven years or less to run: LRA 2002, s 4(1)(d) and (2)(b). See para 6.5.

[2]   Such an interest is not excluded from Sch 1, para 2, and so can be binding on first registration of the lessor's estate where the lessee is in actual occupation. In practice this will not often happen: see para 6.61.

[3]   And as such unlikely to survive first registration of the reversion: see para 6.61.

[4]   A reversionary sub-lease granted out of a lease with less than seven years to run would be a legal estate, but the estate out of which it was granted is unlikely to become registered.

6.61 The trouble with the argument in para 6.60 is that it would render the exception in LRA 2002, Sch 3, para 2(d) almost completely redundant, and construing para 2(d) according to its intention and purpose the court would almost certainly hold that this exception applies to a leasehold interest granted (after 12 October 2003) out of a registered estate so as to commence more than three months after the date of grant which would be a legal estate but for the failure to register it.[1] It is less clear whether the same would apply to such a lease which has not been registered which was granted (after 12 October 2003) out of an unregistered estate which has later become registered—because s 7(2)(b) provides expressly that such lease has become a contract to grant it as a result of the failure to register it—but the point is unlikely to arise in practice. This is because if the conversion under s 7(2)(b) of the reversionary lease to a contract to grant it has occurred before any disposition of the reversion, and such contract was not registered as an estate contract under Land Charges Act 1972, and the disposition of the reversion was for money or money's worth, it will have become void against the purchaser of the reversion even if the prospective lessee was in actual occupation of the demised premises (see para 6.59).[2] The exception from LRA 2002, Sch 3, para 2, in para 2(d) does not appear to apply to a contract to grant a lease more than three months in the future, even though the policy reasons for excluding a reversionary lease from para 2 seem to apply equally strongly to a contract to grant a reversionary lease.[3] However, if a grant which is an equitable interest as a result of a failure to register the estate can fall within para 2(d), the possibility that an agreement to grant such an estate might fall within it cannot be completely ruled out. Accordingly, a contract to be granted a reversionary lease out of a registered estate, even where the prospective grantee is in actual occupation under an existing lease, should always be protected by applying to have it noted on the title to the reversion. Options to renew a lease are clearly outside para 2(d), but it is still advisable to have these noted on the register of the reversion because reliance on occupation does not protect the right in all circumstances (eg after subletting).[4] If an option to renew is contained in a lease which is submitted for registration, the land registry will usually note the option on the lessor's title without any specific request for them to do so, but where the option is exercised and becomes a contract, or a contract to renew is entered into after the lease has been granted and registered, it will be up to the prospective grantee to apply to have it noted on the prospective grantor's title.

---

[1]   Law Com No 271 para 8.63 makes it clear that this was the intention, and would be a relevant aid to the interpretation of para 2(d).

[2]   If the disposition of the reversion was a gift, and possibly also where it was for a consideration but was made during the two-month period for applying to register the lease (ie when it was still a legal estate), then the reversionary lease or the right to the reversionary lease would be binding on the purchaser of the reversion upon it if the lessee was in occupation of

the demised premises (a reversionary lease is not excluded from LRA 2002, Sch 1, para 2). The question would then arise on a subsequent disposition of the reversion upon it for a consideration whether such lease lost priority because of Sch 3, para 2(d).

[3] These are essentially that occupation under a current lease, by a tenant who has a further lease starting at a future date, provides no indication that he has the further interest. See Law Com No 271 paras 3.32, 8.63.

[4] See, further, para 7.9.

Sub-tenancies

6.62 In general, and apart from statutory intervention,[1] a sub-tenant does not have a better title than that of the owner of the estate in reversion out of which the sub-tenancy was granted.[2] The LRA 2002 does not alter this fundamental principle of land law. Where a sub-lease is a registered estate with title absolute the chain of title back to the freehold is sound, and if it is registered with a good, qualified or possessory title there are or may be weak links in the chain but the register draws attention to the fact and at least in some cases indicates what the weak links are. The priority given to a non-registrable lease of seven years or less by LRA 2002, Sch 3, para 1, or given to any other kind of lease or tenancy by Sch 3, para 2 where the tenant is in actual occupation, is priority in relation to the estate which such lease or tenancy affects, ie the estate out of which it was granted. A sub-tenancy is only good against estates superior to the estate out of which it was granted if each link in the chain of title from that superior estate to the sub-tenant is sufficiently protected against dispositions of the estate in reversion upon it. The fact that under LRA 2002, Sch 1, para 2 and Sch 3, para 2, in contrast to the position under LRA 1925 s 70(1)(g), a person in receipt of rents and profits of land does not have an overriding interest (apart from a limited transitional provision in LRA 2002, Sch 12, para 8),[3] renders more precarious the position of subtenants, even those in actual occupation, where there are weak links in the chain of title. This is illustrated by the following example. A is registered freehold owner of Blackacre. After 12 October 2003, A grants to B a 14 year lease of it. B fails to register the lease and it is not noted on the register of A's title. B then lets Blackacre to C for 6 years. C goes into actual occupation of the land. A then sells the freehold to X. X takes free of B's lease, and also free of C's subtenancy. Although C is in actual occupation of the land, and has a tenancy of six years or less, his interest does not affect A's estate.[4] Under LRA 1925, on the other hand, C's tenancy would have been secure because B's interest would have been an overriding interest (LRA 1925 s 70(1)(g)). A cautious conveyancer acting for someone taking a subtenancy of registered land should make sure that there is a good chain of title back to the freehold, even where the subtenancy is of seven years or less. Note, however, that where a lease is a registered estate, and the estate in reversion on it is registered with less than an absolute title, the lessee may apply to have the title to the reversion upgraded, as he is a person interested in a registered estate which derives from it (LRA 2002, s 62(7)(d)—see para 6.18).

---

[1]   Eg Landlord and Tenant Act 1954 Part II, especially ss 24 and 65, Rent Act 1977 s 137.
[2]   27(1) *Halsbury's Laws* (4th edn reissue) para 84, footnote 1.
[3]   See para 7.74–7.76.
[4]   Law Com No 254, para 5.66(1), in discussing whether an interest of a person in receipt of rents and profits should cease to be an overriding interest, has an example which is similar, though involving an unregistered disposition of the freehold rather than an unregistered intermediate lease.

VARIATION AND TERMINATION OF REGISTERED LEASES

6.63   An application to register the variation of a lease (or of any other disposition of a registered estate or a registered charge which has been completed by registration) must be accompanied by the instrument (if any) effecting the variation and evidence to satisfy the registrar that the variation has effect at law (LRR 2003, r 78). The application is on Form AP1 (r 13), and the deed of variation and a certified copy should be submitted with it. If the variation extends the term of the existing lease or adds to the demised premises it constitutes a surrender of the existing lease and the grant of a new one, and will be so treated by the land registry.[1] This will mean that the application is treated as being for closure of the existing leasehold title and registration of a new lease, and that evidence will be required of the consent of any superior lessor or chargee of the lessor's estate whose consent is required, and of the release of any charge which there may be on the current lease. If instead of a surrender and grant of a new lease there is a grant of a further lease to commence more than three months from the date of its grant and when the current one terminates, it will in most cases be a registrable disposition even if the new lease is for seven years or less (LRA 2002, ss 4(1)(d) and 27(2)(b)(ii) and see paras 6.5, 6.21), save where it is granted out of an unregistered leasehold estate of which seven years or less have still to run (s 4(1)(d) and (2)).

---

[1]   See Land Registry Practice Guide No 28, para 2.1.

6.64   On the expiry of the term of a registered lease, or its termination by forfeiture or exercise of a right to terminate it early, or its surrender or merger, the owner of the estate which was in immediate reversion on it will wish to have the registered title to the lease closed and, where the reversion was itself a registered estate, have any notice of the former lease on his own title deleted. It is not an automatic process and the owner of the estate will have to apply. An application to record in the register the determination of a registered estate must be accompanied by evidence to satisfy the registrar that the estate has determined, and if the registrar is satisfied that the estate has determined, he must close the registered title to the estate and cancel any notice in any other registered title relating to it (LRR 2003, r 79). In most case the land registry want the original lease to be submitted, or an explanation of why it is not available.[1] If the application is based on expiry of the term of the lease, it is necessary to provide evidence either that the Landlord and Tenant Act 1954, Pt II does not apply, or else that the lease has been duly terminated in accordance with it.[2] If a lease is of land which becomes comprised in a registration of land as commonhold land, such lease will terminate automatically on the commonhold registration taking effect and the leasehold title closed (Commonhold and Leasehold Reform Act 2002, ss 7(3)(d) and 9(3)(d)).[3]

---

[1]   See Land Registry Practice Guide No 26.

[2]   See Land Registry Practice Guide No 26, para 3.7.

[3]   In force from 27 September 2004 (SI 2004/1832). For registration of land as commonhold see Commonhold (Land Registration) Rules 2004 (SI 2004/1830) and Land Registry Practice Guide No 60.

6.65   If it appears to the registrar that a right to determine a registered estate in land is exercisable, he may enter the fact in the register (LRA 2002, s 64(1)). Such entries are to be made in the property register, and the application for such an entry must be supported by evidence to satisfy the registrar that the applicant has the right to determine the registered estate and that the right is exercisable (LRR 2003, r 125(1), (2)). Before making an entry under r 125 the registrar must give notice of the application to the proprietor of the registered estate and the proprietor of a registered charge on that estate (r 125(4)). The person entitled to determine the registered estate, the proprietor of the registered estate, a person entitled to be registered as proprietor of it, or any other person whom the registrar is satisfied has an interest in the removal of the entry can apply to have it removed (r 125(5)). This must be supported by evidence to satisfy the registrar that the right to determine the registered estate is not exercisable (r 125(6)), though this seems an unnecessary requirement in the case of an application by the person entitled to determine the estate. The principal purpose of these provisions is in relation to rights of termination arising on non-payment of a rentcharge, but it seems to be sufficiently generally worded to be an available procedure where a right to forfeit a registered lease has become exercisable (and has not been waived), and the lessor wishes to make life difficult for the lessee without enforcing the forfeiture. It remains to be seen whether the registrar will allow the r 125 procedure to be used in this way—he is only obliged to register an exercisable right of termination in relation to rentcharges (r 125(3)), and in other cases retains a discretion as to whether to do so.

PUBLIC ACCESS TO INFORMATION ABOUT LEASES

6.66 The register of title is in the public domain, and has been since 3 December 1990. The registered title to a lease will identify the demised premises and contain information about rights benefiting or burdening the lease, and about the price paid (if any), and will identify the lease, including date, parties, and length of term, but not, where the lease is granted or first registered after 12 October 2003, the rent payable.[1] This information (apart from the rent) cannot be exempted, under the exempt information rules discussed below, from being publicly available. The registrar holds copies of all substantively registered leases, but not of all of the leases which are not themselves registered estates but which have been noted on the register of title to the estates in reversion upon them (on this aspect see para 6.70). Anyone trying to find out what is in a lease of which a copy is held by the registrar must apply under the rules concerning public availability of documents, which are discussed in detail at paras 2.66 et seq. An important aspect of these rules is that, under the LRA 2002, s 66 and the LRR 2003, r 135, leases (and charges) referred to in the register of title, and of which the registrar holds a copy, become for the first time publicly available documents, as from the commencement of the LRA 2002 on 13 October 2003. This is subject to:

(1)   r 139 under which the registrar for two years beginning with 13 October 2003 has a discretion to refuse public access to a document where the entry on the register referring to it was made before 13 October 2003; and

(2)   to the procedure under r 136 whereby a document can be designated as an exempt information document of which some or all of it is not open to public scrutiny unless someone successfully applies under r 137 for access to it.

In the debates on the Bill which became the LRA 2002 it was stated on behalf of the government that the extension of public access to leases was because users of the land registration system (presumably tenants rather than landlords) were keen to see an extension of the information provided about the state of the property market and changes in it. It was further stated that this would shed light on commercial property transactions and foster a free and competitive market.[2]

1   See Land Registry Practice Guide No 25, para 7.2. This is a change of practice from that which prevailed before 13 October 2003, because there is now public access to registered leases.
2   See 627 HL Official Reports (5th series) (30 October 2001) col 1362, and also HC Official Reports, SC D, 11 December 2001, col 35.

6.67   The grounds for seeking exemption from public disclosure of all or part of a document of which a copy is held by the registrar are: (a) the certainty or likelihood of substantial unwarranted damage or substantial unwarranted distress to the applicant (being an individual) or another; or (b) the certainty or likelihood of prejudice to the commercial interests of the applicant (see the definition of 'prejudicial information' in the LRR 2003, r 131). The procedure is that on an application for designation of a document as an exempt information document the registrar must so designate it if satisfied that the claim is 'not groundless' (r 136(4)). The registrar may, and presumably in practice will, make an appropriate entry in the register of any affected title (r 136(5)). Serious challenge to the exempt status of the information only arises where someone applies under r 137 to see the exempt document or exempt parts of it. Notice of the application is normally given to the person who applied for the document be made exempt (r 137(3)). The exempt information is to be disclosed by the registrar if he decides that none of the excluded information is prejudicial, or that the public interest in providing a copy of the exempt information document to the applicant outweighs the public interest in not doing so (r 137(4)). The wording of the definition of category (b) prejudicial information, and of the circumstances in which disclosure of it may be ordered, derive from the Freedom of Information Act 2000.[1]

1   See the Freedom of Information Act 2000, ss 2(1)(b) and 43(2).

6.68   A type of application for exemption of information which is likely to arise in practice is an application by a lessor who has just granted a lease of commercial premises in a location where he owns a number of other similar lettable units in the same location—in, eg an office block, an industrial estate, or a shopping centre—and who claims prejudice to his commercial interests if the lessees or prospective lessees of the other units know what sort of deal this particular lessee has managed to negotiate. Exemption is only available for the parts of a document which are prejudicial, not for the whole of a document which contains some prejudicial information, and an application for exemption has to be accompanied by a copy of the document with the allegedly prejudicial information edited out (LRR 2003, r 136(2)(b)). If an application for exemption is made in respect of a lease, an application should also be made in respect of the counterpart, as the land registry apparently regard them as separate documents for this purpose. The application for exemption would relate to the amount of the initial rent, and such matters as rent review provisions, initial rent-free or concessionary rent periods, service charge provisions, or covenants by lessor or lessee to spend money on improving or altering the demised premises. There will often be sufficient of the lease in the public domain for any person looking for comparables to be able to tell whether the particular lease is likely to be a suitable comparable, and therefore one in relation to which he should apply to see the exempt information. If a person who is negotiating to take a lease of similar premises, or who is already a lessee of such premises and is involved in a rent review or a business lease renewal under the Landlord and Tenant Act 1954, Pt II, does the balance of public interest lie in a disclosure of the exempt information or in its withholding? In an ordinary case, it will be difficult to resist such an application for access to the exempt information. There is a clear public interest in openness and competitiveness in the lettings market, as it should help to keep down the cost to the public of goods and services. It is not easy to think of any obvious *public* interest in the withholding of the information—the exercise required by LRR 2003, r 137(4) is not one of balancing public interest in disclosure against private interest in withholding information, but public interest in disclosure as against *public* interest in withholding it. There is a question whether enforced disclosure under these rules could be a breach of the European Convention for the Protection of Human Rights and Fundamental Freedoms, Article 8.

6.69   Accordingly, landlords who wish to avoid disclosure of this kind of information, can where practicable insist on only granting leases of seven years or less (but see, further, para 6.70). Landlords who need to grant leases of more than seven years duration, and wish to avoid public access to them, could try insisting on the rent provisions etc being put into a collateral document which is not submitted to the registrar and not referred to on the register when the lease is registered. It would seem that a collateral deed fixing the rent and any other consideration for the lease would, at any rate in a lease granted after 31 December 1995,[1] be binding on successors in title to both lessor and lessee whether or not it is referred to on the register. However, there would still be the delicate problem of what rent provisions to have in the lease itself. Some subtlety would be required to devise rent provisions which do not betray the fact that the real rent provisions are in some other document. If an interested party knows that a collateral document exists it will not be exempt from disclosure if litigation or arbitration to which it is relevant should take place—see para 6.71. If the lease which is in the public domain contains rent provisions which are at variance with the amount of SDLT paid, the unwelcome attention of the Inland Revenue might be attracted. Another possibility would be a tenancy agreement, ie an equitable lease only,[2] which is not registrable, but which is not an overriding interest unless the tenant is in obvious actual occupation of the demised premises, and which would therefore have to be noted on the title out of which it was granted for the tenant to be sure of maintaining priority over subsequent dispositions. If the unilateral notice procedure was used to protect it, providing a copy to the registrar would be avoided (see para 6.70).

---

[1]   Ie where the transmission of the benefit and burden of landlord and tenant is governed by the Landlord and Tenant (Covenants) Act 1995.
[2]   See paras 6.58, 6.59.

6.70   It is possible to keep a lease out of the public domain where it is granted for seven years or less, but even that is not entirely straightforward where the lease is for a term exceeding three years. If it is for three years or less (and not in one of the special categories which is registrable)[1] it is prohibited from being noted on the register (LRA 2002, s 33 (b)). If it is for more than three years and for seven years or less (and not in one of the special categories which is a registrable) it will be an overriding interest and need not be noted on the register so long as there is no registrable disposition of the estate out of which it was granted. Once there is such a disposition, however, the applicant for registration of the disposition will be under an obligation to disclose the lease to the registrar and provide a copy of it unless it has one year or less to run (see the LRR 2003, rr 28 and 57).[2] Where the lessor's title is a registered title, providing a copy of the lease to the registrar on a disposition of the lessor's title is apparently avoided if, before the disposition, the lessee has successfully applied to have a unilateral notice of it entered on the lessor's title. An application for the entry of a unilateral notice does not require submission of the lease, whereas an application to enter an agreed notice of the lease would require submission of it or a copy of it (see the LRR 2003, rr 81 and 214).[3] A prospective lessor whose estate is not registered would have to have his title voluntarily registered before granting the lease if he wished to take advantage of the privacy afforded by the unilateral notice procedure. Use of the unilateral notice procedure depends on the initiative of the lessee, but a covenant to apply for a unilateral notice without submitting a copy of the lease to the registrar could be made one of the terms of the tenancy. The same point about the relative merits of agreed and unilateral notices for preserving privacy apply where what has been granted is a tenancy agreement,[4] not taking effect at law, the only difference between the two cases being that such an interest is not per se an overriding interest, whereas a lease for seven years or less is (a tenancy agreement can of course be an overriding interest by virtue of the tenant's actual occupation).[5]

---

[1]　See paras 6.5, 6.21 for these.
[2]　See para 5.19.
[3]　See paras 7.30, 7.32, 7.35. The registrar's power to retain it (so that it becomes open to public inspection) is in LRR 2003, r 203.
[4]　See paras 6.58, 6.59, 6.69.
[5]　See para 7.9.

6.71　If a rent review arbitration, or a court application for a new tenancy under the Landlord and Tenant Act 1954, Pt 2, is under way, and a party wishes to obtain a copy of a lease of other premises which it is thought could be a comparable for the purpose of determining the rent, it is possible to apply for an order for disclosure of such lease where the other party to the arbitration or application was a party to the lease (under Civil Procedure Rules, r 31.12), or, where neither party to the lease of which disclosure is sought is a party to the arbitration or application, an order for disclosure against a non-party or a witness summons to produce such lease (under Civil Procedure Rules, rr 31.17 or 34.2). An important difference between the effect of the court procedure for disclosure and the land registration procedure for disclosure is that in the case of disclosure by court order the person to whom it is disclosed may only use it or disclose its contents for the purpose of the proceedings, whereas once a document is disclosed under the land registration procedure the LRA 2002 and the LRR 2003 contain no restriction on the use to which the information may be put or the person or persons or the public at large to whom it might be disclosed.

STAMP DUTY LAND TAX

6.72　Grantees of leases granted after 30 November 2003 for a term exceeding seven years are hit by the double whammy of being required both to register the lease and to pay Stamp Duty Land Tax (SDLT) (replacing stamp duty). The principal SDLT legislation is in the Finance Act 2003 (FA 2003), Pt 4. It commenced on 1 December 2003 by virtue of the Stamp duty Land Tax (Appointment of the Implementation Date) Order 2003 (SI 2003/2899). Shortly before the implementation date, the SDLT provisions of FA 2003 concerning leases were substantially amended, and a long and detailed new Sch 17A concerning SDLT on leases was introduced, by the Stamp Duty and Stamp Duty Land Tax (Variation of the Finance Act 2003) (No 2) Regulations 2003 (SI 2003/2816)[1] and the Stamp Duty Land Tax (Amendment of Schedule 5 to the Finance Act 2003) Regulations 2003 (SI 2003/2914). FA 2003 was further amended by FA 2004, and also the changes made by SI 2003/2816 were amended to some extent by FA 2004 with effect from 18 March 2004. All the changes made by SI 2003/2816, as amended by FA 2004, were then re-enacted by FA 2004, Sch 39, Part 2 with effect from 22 July 2004, subject to some further changes (SI 2003/2816 being revoked by FA 2004, Sch 39, para 14). The reason for replacing SI 2003/2816 by statute, but not SI 2003/2914, is that the latter instrument was made under the power in FA 2003, s 112 to make permanent amendments to FA 2003, Sch 5, while the former was made under the power in s 109 to make general amendments where the power was limited to making amendments effective for a maximum of 18 months. The references to FA 2003 below are to it as amended by SI 2003/2914 and FA 2004 in relation to events on or after 22 July 2004. SDLT, as compared with stamp duty, does not make any substantial difference to what tax is paid on sales of registered estates which are completed by registration, although procedurally it is quite different (see paras 5.36–5.38), but it does make a considerable difference to the tax on grants of leases, in two main respects. One is that it imposes a tax on rent calculated on a new basis which very much increases the amount of tax payable at higher rent levels and/or on longer leases, although it also raises the value threshold at which tax becomes chargeable, and the other is that it is a compulsory tax which becomes payable if a transaction is substantially performed, whether or not any documents are involved (see para 6.76). The purpose of the following paragraphs is to give an overview rather than a detailed account of how SDLT affects leases and their registration.

---

[1]   These regulations were a reissue, with errors corrected, of the Stamp Duty and Stamp Duty Land Tax (Variation of the Finance Act 2003) Regulations 2003 (SI 2003/2760).

6.73   In the days of stamp duty it was a common practice not to stamp leases of 21 years or less, which of course had the status of overriding interests under the LRA 1925, s 70(1)(k) whether they were stamped or not, and which were not registrable and so were not subject to the need for stamping in order to be registered. The introduction by the LRA 2002 of compulsory registration for leases of more than seven years would have had the practical effect of bringing many more leases within the stamp duty net without the introduction of SDLT, but SDLT carries that one stage further by being compulsorily payable in all cases. By being compulsory, SDLT has the consequence that grantees of post-30 November 2003 leases for more than seven years are saved from the dilemma of whether to abstain from submitting their lease for registration, and hope to rely on their own occupation to preserve their rights, so as not to pay stamp duty. The owner of an unregistered and unstamped lease for a term of more than seven years granted before 13 October 2003, of which there are more than seven years left of the term, has the problem that if he wishes to assign it he (or his assignee) will have to pay the stamp duty interest and penalties in order to be able to comply with the compulsory registration requirement which will arise on any assignment.[1] He has the alternative of granting an underlease if the covenants in his own lease permit it, if the SDLT liability on granting the underlease would be less than the cost of stamping the lease, and if an underlease of seven years or less will be sufficient for the purposes of the prospective underlessee. The reason for it having to be an underlease of seven years or less is that if it were to be for more than seven years it would itself be registrable,[2] and it might not then be practicable to register it without producing the lease out of which it is granted to the land registry.[3] For this purpose the lease would need to be stamped (Stamp Act 1891 ss 14(4) and 17).

---

[1] See para 6.3.

[2] See para 6.5.

[3] See paras 4.13, 6.5. Although it would be possible to apply for a good leasehold title only (so that the lessor's title would not be examined), it would still seem to be necessary to produce the lessor's lease to the land registry to show that the grant was out of a lease with more than seven years to run (LRA 2002, s 4(2)(b)).

6.74   The grant or assignment of a lease in return for a premium is chargeable to SDLT on the premium in the same way as any other chargeable consideration given in return for the acquisition of an interest in land (see para 5.36), save that if the average annual rent is more than £600 there is no nil rate, ie the premium is subject to SDLT at 1 per cent even if it does not exceed the relevant (business or residential property) tax threshold (FA 2003, Sch 5, para 9). Where the chargeable consideration for the grant of a lease consists wholly or partly of rent, however, special rules apply. The rent is first capitalised in accordance with a statutory formula which appears in the FA 2003, Sch 5, para 3. What this requires is for the total rent payable throughout the term of the lease to be aggregated, but with the rent for each year discounted by 3.5 per cent[1] for every year it was in the future at the time of grant of the lease. The formula has the effect that the discount is calculated by dividing the rent for any given year of the lease by (1+0.35) multiplied by itself the same number of times as the number of the year of lease. Thus the rent for the third year of a lease will be divided by 1.035 multiplied by itself three times (ie 1.035 to the power of 3). A calculator for SDLT on rent is available on the Inland Revenue website, and the Inland Revenue have provided a useful guide to calculating the SDLT on a lease in their SDLT Information Bulletin No 6, with a table of capitalisation factors.

---

[1] The Treasury has power to vary the rate of discount: FA 2003, Sch 5, para 8.

6.75   Where the lease is for more than five years, and the rent is not constant throughout the term, and some or all future rent is of an uncertain amount, the capitalisation calculation must be based on the actual rent for the first five years, but on the assumption that the highest annual rent payable during a continuous period of twelve months during the first five years is the rent for the sixth and subsequent years (see the FA 2003, Sch 17A, para 7), subject to the anti-avoidance provisions in Sch 17A, paras 13–15 (see para 6.78). If the rent during any of the first five years is uncertain at the outset an estimate of what it might be is made in the initial return, and a further return, adjusting the liability to the correct one, has to be made when the uncertain rent becomes certain (see the FA 2003, Sch 17A, para 8). The SDLT on the rent is 1 per cent of the capitalised value in excess of the threshold (FA 2003, Sch 5, para 2).[1] The threshold is £60,000 in the case of wholly residential property, and £150,000 in the case of non residential or mixed residential and non-residential property. If the demised premises are in a disadvantaged area a residential lease will not pay tax on the capitalised rental value if it does not exceed £150,000, and a business lease will be wholly relieved from paying SDLT (FA 2003, Sch 6, para 5). There are various other reliefs: see FA 2003, ss 57–75.

---

[1]   FA 2003, Sch 5, para 2 as enacted provided for SDLT at 1 per cent to be chargeable on the entire capitalised value if it exceeded the threshold, but SI 2003/2914 amended it so that SDLT is only on the excess of the capitalised value over the threshold.

6.76   The SDLT legislation incorporates a great many anti-avoidance provisions, and because leases and tenancy agreements take many forms and are highly flexible, the Inland Revenue and the Treasury have been working particularly hard on devising anti-avoidance provisions for them—as mentioned in para 6.72, a major product of this great effort is the Sch 17A introduced by statutory instrument very shortly before SDLT commenced. There is the general point, relevant to all land transactions, that SDLT cannot be avoided by avoiding the use of documents or using informal documents—if the transaction is substantially performed, then SDLT is payable if the consideration exceeds the tax threshold (FA 2003, s 44), and in the case of an agreement for a lease which is substantially performed without a formal lease being granted it is treated as the grant of a lease starting at the time of substantial performance (FA 2003, Sch 17A, para 12A).[1] Substantial performance, in the case of a lease, means the lessee taking up occupation or receiving the rents and profits of the land, or making the first payment of rent under the lease (FA 2003, s 44(5)–(7)). If a lease is subsequently granted pursuant to such a contract the transaction is treated as a surrender and regrant (Sch 17A, para 12A(3)—and see para 6.82 for surrender and regrant). Many of the anti-avoidance provisions for leases are aimed at preventing rent coming to be fixed at a date subsequent to the grant of the lease and thus falling out of charge, and preventing transactions such as a lease followed by renewal or variation of the lease being assessed separately with two nil rate bands rather than being treated as a single transaction with only one.

---

[1]   FA 2003, Sch 17A was originally inserted by SI 2003/2816 without para 12A, with effect from 1 December 2003. Para 12A was inserted by FA 2004, Sch 39, para 11(4) from 18 March 2004 until 21 July 2004, and by FA 2004, Sch 39, para 22 with effect from 22 July 2004.

6.77   The scope of some of the anti-avoidance and other provisions can be illustrated by the following example. A grants B a lease of a wholly residential property for seven years less three days under which the rent is £9,000 per year for the first five years to be followed by a rent review. The lease gives B a right to terminate the lease on notice after three years, contains a forfeiture clause, and is stated to continue after the end of the term until either party serves a notice to terminate it. These factors are ignored at the outset, and it is a term of seven years less three days for SDLT purposes (FA 2003, Sch 17A, paras 2 and 3). Because the lease is for less than seven years and the capitalised value of the rent, which is £54,972.75, is below the £60,000 threshold, no SDLT return is required at the outset (FA 2003, s 77). In working out the value of the rent, B's obligations to repair and pay service charges are ignored as chargeable consideration (FA 2003, Sch 17A, para 10), although if the rent is expressed as a single sum inclusive of a service element the entire rent will be chargeable unless there is apportionment between the two in the lease (FA 2003, Sch 4, para 4 and Sch 17A, para 6).

6.78   Continuing the example in the previous paragraph, if the rent review provisions were deliberately weighted to raise the rent very significantly for the last two years of the term, or for any other reason the rent so fixed was an abnormal increase applying the formula in the FA 2003, Sch 17A, para 15, then this would be treated as the grant of a new lease in consideration of the difference between the rent fixed under the rent review and the previous rent (Sch 17A, para 14), and an agreed increase in rent outside the provisions of the rent review would also be treated as grant of a new lease by Sch 17A, para 13. In either case this would or might be a 'linked' transaction (see para 6.80). However, continuing this example on the assumption that neither of these things happens, neither A nor B serves notice to terminate the lease at the end of the term, and the lease as soon as it has run beyond the original term is treated for Sch 17A purposes as having another year added to its term (Sch 17A, para 3(2)(a), (b)). If it runs beyond the end of the first year from the end of the original term the original term is then deemed to have a further year added, and so on (Sch 17A, para 3(2)(c)). This means that the capitalised value of the rent has to be recalculated for each additional year at the beginning of it, and if the calculation gives rise to an SDLT liability, or an additional one, a return must be put in and the tax paid within 30 days (Sch 17A, para 3(3)). In this example, on the day following the end of the original term, the effect is that another year's rent is added into the capitalisation calculation, at the original rate of £9,000 (Sch 17A, para 7(3)), and the lease would be deemed to be a term of eight years less three days with a capital value of £61,809.42 on which SDLT of £18 would then be payable. Interest on it would run from the expiry of 30 days after the first day after the end of the original term (s 87(1), (3)(ab)). Further, at the beginning of every further year in which B remained the tenant under the lease he would have to render a further return and pay some more SDLT. These rules would also apply where the lease was, for example, a business lease continued beyond its original term under Landlord and Tenant Act 1954, Part II, or was continued by some other similar statutory provision (Sch 17A, para 3(1)(b)).

6.79 However, it is important to note that although an SDLT return is required for a lease originally granted for a rent or a premium (or other consideration in money or money's worth—see Sch 4, para 1) for a term of seven years or more, whether or not there is a liability for SDLT on its grant (s 77(2)(a)), the treatment of B's lease in the above example as being for more than seven years does not give rise to an obligation to put in an SDLT return unless and until the chargeable consideration exceeds the SDLT threshold (see FA 2003, Sch 17A, paras 3(2) and (5) excluding para 3 from applying for the purposes of s 77). The same is true of a periodic tenancy, which is initially treated for SDLT charging purposes as being for one year when granted, then for two years if it continues for more than one year, and so on (Sch 17A, para 4(1), (5)(a)), but which continues to be treated for the purposes of s 77 as being a term of less than seven years (Sch 17A, para 4(4A)), so that a return is only required if an SDLT liability arises. Without this exclusion in relation to s 77,[1] all periodic tenants, however low the rent they were paying, would have been under an obligation to put in an SDLT return once they had continued as tenants under the same tenancy for seven years.

---

[1] The exclusion of s 77 from the effect of these rules first appeared in the substituted FA 2003, Sch 17A, paras 3 and 4, inserted by FA 2004 Sch 39, para 22, with effect from 22 July 2004. As the exclusion relates to events occurring at least seven years after 1 December 2003, its enactment was not an urgent priority.

6.80 The treatment of transactions such as the grant of a new lease to an existing tenant, or an agreed variation in the rent payable, depends importantly on whether it is a transaction which is 'linked' with the original grant of the lease. Transactions are 'linked' for SDLT purposes if they form part of a single scheme, arrangement or series of transactions between the same vendor and purchaser or, in either case, persons connected with them (FA 2003, s 108(1)). Whether the grant of a new lease to an existing tenant is a transaction which is 'linked' with the original lease is a question of fact. In the case of an ordinary arm's length negotiation of a new lease when the existing lease is coming to an end, they will normally not be linked transactions.[1] If, on the other hand, the landlord and tenant had sought to avoid SDLT by granting a short lease initially coupled with an understanding that a renewal would later be granted, the two leases probably would be linked. They would also be linked if the renewal was pursuant to an option to renew in the first lease,[2] at any rate if the landlord and tenant are still the same persons as under the original lease or are successors in title connected[3] to the original parties. An increase in rent falling within FA 2003, Sch 17A, para 15 as 'abnormal' is treated as a grant of a lease linked with the original one (Sch 17A, para 14(5)), but an increase in rent by agreement within Sch 17A, para 13 is treated as the grant of a new lease but not necessarily as a grant linked with the existing lease.

---

[1]   This is the view so far taken by the Revenue in their SDLT Manual, draft chapter on Leases, para 13100.
[2]   This is the view so far taken by the Revenue in their SDLT Manual, draft chapter on Leases, para 10810a, Example 3.
[3]   Ie within the definition of connected persons in Income and Corporation Taxes Act 1988, s 839 (see FA 2003, s 108(1)).

6.81   Where an actual new lease, or a deemed one under FA 2003, Sch 17A, paras 13 or 14, is 'linked' to the original lease (and any other linked leases or deemed leases), the linked leases are treated as if there was a single lease for the aggregate term and rent under all the relevant leases (Sch 17A, para 5), so that when a subsequent linked lease or deemed linked lease is granted or deemed to be granted a fresh return has to be put in under FA 2003, s 81A and any tax or additional tax paid. There will be only one nil-rate band for the combined linked leases, but on the other hand the rent in later years which comes to be added on as a result of the later linked transactions will be brought into the calculations of the rental value of the combined linked leases at a greater temporal discount than would be the case if the rental value of the later lease was calculated on its own (see para 6.74 for the temporal discount). The amount of the overall rental value of the linked leases is then apportioned to the new linked lease under a formula which will give it some but not all the benefit of this greater temporal discount (FA 2003, Sch 5, para 2(6)).[1] Where the new lease is not linked, the SDLT is calculated on the new lease taken by itself, with its own nil-rate band and the temporal discount factor related to the date of grant of the new lease rather than that of the original lease. Where the original lease and any other apparently linked lease was granted before 1 December 2003 it or they are left out of account in applying these rules (FA 2003, Sch 19, para 7(4)).

---

[1]   Assuming that FA 2003, Sch 5, para 2(5), (6), are not excluded from operating by Sch 17A, para 5.

6.82 Where a new lease is granted to take effect in possession before the expiry of the previous one, so that the earlier lease is surrendered, the transaction is excluded by FA 2003, Sch 17A, para 16 from the SDLT provision (FA 2003, Sch 4, para 5) which taxes exchanges of interests. The new lease is charged to SDLT on its rental value and/or premium, on its own, or in combination with earlier dispositions where it is a linked transaction. Also, in calculating the taxable value of the rent under such new lease, there is an offset against the rent payable under the new lease for the rent which would have been payable under the old lease in the period of overlap between the two (FA 2003, Sch 17A, para 9). The offset is in respect of the rent on the basis of which the SDLT had been paid under the old lease (Sch 17A, para 9(4)). Thus if the overlap period includes a period of years after the end of the first five years of the original lease, and the original lease contained five-yearly rent reviews, what is offset in respect of that period will be the rent payable during the 12 month period of highest rent during the first five years of the original lease (see Sch 17A, para 7 and para 6.75 above), which may be less than the rent which would actually have been paid under the original lease in the period in question. This overlap relief provision, ie Sch 17A, para 9, is, however, disregarded in applying in relation to the new lease the rule in Sch 17A, para 7 that the rent after the first five years of a lease is assumed to be the rent payable in the 12 months of highest rent in the first five years (Sch 17A, para 7(3)). Sch 17A, para 9 apparently applies whether or not the surrendered and the new leases are linked transactions.

6.83 For the SDLT procedural provisions, and in particular the need, when applying to the registrar to register a disposition, to send with the application a Revenue certificate that an SDLT return has been made in respect of the disposition, or to submit a self-certificate that no such return is required, see para 5.37. These rules also apply to the registration of a grant of a lease (see the FA 2003, s 79(2)). Such a certificate is not required in order to have a tenancy agreement which is not a grant of a legal estate noted on the title to the estate in reversion, even if it has been substantially performed (FA 2003, s 79(2)(c)).[1] Where a lease which is a grant of a legal estate is not registrable because it is granted for seven years or less (and is not in one of the special categories which is a registrable),[2] the certification requirement will still have to be complied with if the lessee applies to the registrar to have the lease noted on the title to the reversion (see the FA 2003, s 79(1)). However, where a lease is for a term of less than seven years, and the chargeable consideration is not great enough to incur an SDLT liability (disregarding the effect of any available relief), the lessee is not required to render an SDLT return (FA 2003, s 77(2)(b)) and can self-certify that none is required, if he applies to have his lease noted against the reversioner's title, or, in the case of a lease which is required to be registered, applies to register it.

[1]   This exception is by way of an amendment made to s 79 by FA 2004, s 297 with effect from 17 March 2004.
[2]   See para 6.21.

6.84   The certification requirement in FA 2003, s 79 will not apply in relation to a lease of seven years or less which is not registrable,[1] where there is a disposition of the estate in reversion upon it, and the transferee of the reversion, when applying to the land registry to register the disposition of the reversion, discloses the existence of such lease to the registrar in compliance with the obligation to do so under the LRR 2003, r 57[2] and it is duly noted on the title: this follows from the closing words of the FA 2003, s 79(1). Where a lease has been granted for exactly seven years for a consideration, an SDLT return is required but the lease is not registrable—compare the wording of the FA 2003, s 77(2) with the LRA 2002, s 27(2)(b)(i). A return has to be sent to the Revenue if the reason why no tax is payable is because of an applicable relief (as distinct from an *exemption* under the FA 2003, Sch 3). Although, for reasons given in paras 6.77–6.81, there may be a subsequent liability or liabilities to render further SDLT returns in respect of a lease or a tenancy agreement which has been registered or noted on the register, there will be no further interaction between the SDLT provisions and land registration unless the event giving rise to a further liability is also something in respect of which there is an application to the registrar to make an entry or amend an entry in the register, and it is not excluded from FA 2003, s 79(1) by s 79(2) or (2A). Thus a surrender and new grant of a lease can only be registered by the registrar if accompanied by the appropriate SDLT certificate, but the entry of a notice of a variation of a lease entered under LRA 2002, s 34[3] can be applied for without such certification (FA 2003, s 79(2A)). A transfer of a registered lease will of course require Inland Revenue certification or self-certification, as appropriate.

[1]   See para 6.21 for these.
[2]   See para 5.19 for this.
[3]   See paras 6.63, 7.2 et seq.

6.85   On the assignment of a lease, the assumption by the assignee of the obligation to pay rent or perform some other covenant is not treated as chargeable consideration (FA 2003, Sch 17A, para 17). Accordingly the SDLT on the assignment of a lease, including the transfer of a registered lease, will only be on any premium paid by the assignee (a reverse premium is not taxable: Sch 17A, para 18). Where, for example, the lease is transferred as part of the sale of the business and the transferee pays for the lease and the other assets of the business in a single transaction, or what is in substance a single transaction, the consideration has to be apportioned between the lease and the other assets on a just and reasonable basis, and what is the correct basis is in no way determined by any apportionment made by agreement between the parties (FA 2003, Sch 4, para 4). There is one situation were there can be SDLT on the assignment of a lease as if it were the grant of that lease, namely where there was a relief on the original grant of the lease in any of the categories of sale and leaseback, group relief or reconstruction or acquisition relief, transfers involving public bodies, charities relief, or any relief carried forward from stamp duty by regulations under the FA 2003, s 123, and the assignment is the first one after the grant of the lease which does not attract relief under any of those provisions: see the FA 2003, Sch 17A, para 11.

7 Protection and priority of interests in registered land

INTRODUCTION

7.1 An issue of priority, in the most general sense, arises whenever there is a question (a) whether an estate in land is subject to or free from a proprietary interest of someone other than the owner, or (b) as to which of two or more such interests prevails if it is not possible for all of them to take effect (or to take effect to their full extent). This chapter describes the principles applicable generally to the protection of proprietary interests and the related priority issues. Further rules applicable to particular interests are considered at the appropriate points elsewhere in this book.

7.2 The principal distinctions relevant to the priority of interests in registered land are
  (a) that between
      (i) the first registration of land, where the question is, what interests have arisen, and are binding on the person who will be first registered proprietor, under the rules applicable to unregistered land before registration is effected, and
      (ii) dispositions of registered land, where priority is entirely governed by the Land Registration Act 2002 ('LRA 2002') and Land Registration Rules 2003 ('LRR 2003'); and
  (b) that between
      (i) interests which bind the registered proprietor, and disponees from him, without being the subject of an entry on the register, and
      (ii) interests which have to be protected by such an entry.

Interests in unregistered and registered land are not created or transferred in the same way, (specifically, under the LRA 2002, s 27, almost all *legal*, as opposed to equitable, estates and interests in registered land can only be created or transferred by entry on the register,) and under the LRA 2002 the class of unregistered interests which override first registration is wider than the class of unregistered interests which override registered dispositions for value.[1] This chapter is therefore arranged as follows:
  • Protection of interests on first registration by entry on the register (paras 7.4–7.6);

- Unregistered interests binding on the first registered proprietor (paras 7.7–7.16);
- General rules of priority of interests in registered land (paras 7.17–7.19);
- Protection by entry of notice on the register (paras 7.20–7.39);
- Protection by entry of restriction on the register (paras 7.40–7.61);
- Unregistered interests binding on registered disponees for value (paras 7.62–7.81);
- The 'priority search' procedure for fixing the priority of an intended registered disposition (paras 7.82–7.87);
- A summary of the transitional provisions applicable to priority issues (paras 7.88–7.89).

---

[1] LRA 2002, Sch 1, paras 1, 2 and 3, and Sch 3, paras 1, 2 and 3. See also Law Com no 271, para 8.3.

7.3 Further priority rules are considered elsewhere, as follows:
- Cautions against first registration: Chapter 4, paras 4.3–4.8;
- Registration with a title which is less than an absolute title: Chapter 5, paras 5.12–5.15 (freehold), and Chapter 6, paras 6.12–6.15, 6.18 and 6.40 (leasehold);
- Mortgages and charges: Chapter 8, paras 8.14–8.21, in particular the rules as to the priority of further advances, paras 8.16–8.20;
- Easements: Chapter 9, paras 9.17–9.26;
- Restrictive covenants: Chapter 9, paras 9.29–9.31;
- Beneficial interests under trusts of land and Settled Land Act settlements: Chapter 10, paras 10.4–10.5 (general principles); 10.9–10.14 (co-ownership and other trusts of land); 10.19–10.22 (Settled Land Act settlements); 10.39–10.44 (charities); and 10.51–10.60 (beneficiary occupying trust land);
- Rights of pre-emption: Chapter 11, paras 11.6–11.10;
- Equities by estoppel and 'mere equities': Chapter 11, paras 11.14 and 11.18;
- Franchises, manorial rights and Crown rents: Chapter 12, paras 12.12, 12.15 and 12.17;
- Rights under the Limitation Acts accrued before first registration: Chapter 13, para 13.30;
- Rights under the Limitation Acts accrued over registered land before the LRA 2002 came into force: Chapter 13, para 13.31.

FIRST REGISTRATION – PROTECTION OF INTERESTS BY ENTRY ON THE REGISTER

7.4   The LRA 2002 provides, by ss 11(4)(a), (freehold land,) and 12(4)(b), (leasehold land,)[1] that on first registration, the registered estate is vested in the proprietor subject to specified classes of interest affecting it at the time of registration,[2] including *'interests which are the subject of an entry in the register in relation to the estate'*. The application for first registration is required to be accompanied by *'all deeds and documents relating to the title that are in the control of the applicant'* (LRR 2003, r 24(1)(c), corresponding with the LRR 1925, r 20(i) and (ii)). The register of title is prepared with entries of charges, and notices or restrictions[3] in respect of other interests, appearing from the title documents to be binding on the registered estate in the hands of the first registered proprietor (LRR 2003, r 35(1)).[4] Where registration is effected voluntarily (LRA 2002, s 3),[5] all interests disclosed which bind the applicant are entered on the register, including any land charges previously created by him even if they are not registered under the Land Charges Act 1972 and would therefore be void against a purchaser of the land from him.[6] Where the registration is compulsory because of a disposition of the land (LRA 2002, s 4),[7] the interests to be registered include any which arise under that disposition. In either case, if a caution against first registration is registered at the time of the application (LRA 2002, s 15),[8] the cautioner's interest is entered on the register if he establishes (LRA 2002, ss 16(1) and (2) and 73(1) and (5)), or the applicant accepts, that it exists and is binding on the applicant.

---

[1]   Corresponding with the LRA 1925, ss 5(a) and 9(b) respectively.
[2]   The registration has effect from the time of the making of the application for registration: LRA 2002, s 74(a). For the time when an application is taken to be made, see the LRR 2003, r 15, considered in para 7.87.
[3]   Paras 7.20–7.39 and 7.40–7.61 respectively.
[4]   By the LRR 2003, r 35(2), the rule does not apply to interests which cannot be protected by notice, public rights, local land charges, and trivial or obvious interests.
[5]   See Chapter 4, para 4.2; Chapter 5, para 5.9; Chapter 6, para 6.9.
[6]   Land Charges Act 1972, s 4(5) and (6), avoids unregistered land charges against purchasers of the land affected, but not against the landowner who created them.
[7]   See Chapter 5, paras 5.2, 5.3 (freeholds); Chapter 6, paras 6.3–6.5 (leaseholds).
[8]   See Chapter 4, paras 4.3–4.8.

7.5   The LRA 2002, s 71(a),[1] also authorises the making of rules requiring an applicant for first registration to provide information to the registrar about any interest which (a) affects the estate to be registered, (b) would be binding on it although unregistered,[2] and (c) is of a description specified by the rules. This power has been exercised (LRR 2003, r 28,) to require the applicant to provide information about any such interests within his actual knowledge[3] and affecting the estate to be registered (other than local land charges), unless they cannot be protected by entry of a notice on the register (LRR 2003, r 28(2)(a)),[4] or are apparent from the documents of title accompanying the application (LRR 2003, r 28(2)(b)). The prescribed form of application for first registration requires the applicant to list any such interests.[5] These requirements are designed to promote the objective of making the register as nearly conclusive as possible.[6] The effect is to make third-party rights, if clearly shown to exist,[7] binding as registered interests (rather than as overriding interests), and apparent on any subsequent search of the register. It is thought that the interests most frequently registered under this procedure will be leases for more than three and less than seven years (LRA 2002, s 33(b) and Sch 1, para 1), and prescriptive easements (LRA 2002, Sch 1, para 3).[8] At the time of writing there is no effective sanction for failure to give the information required by the LRR 2003, r 28: there is no provision preventing an interest which should have been disclosed, but has not, continuing to be binding on the registered estate. It is contemplated that when electronic conveyancing is introduced, network transaction rules will require conveyancers who enter into network access agreements[9] to comply with this rule.[10]

---

[1] This provision develops the principle of the LRR 1925, r 19 (as substituted by LRR 1997, r 2(1) and Sch 1 para 3). See Law Com no 254, paras 5.104–5.107; Chapter 4, paras 4.14 and 4.18; and Appendix 1, Part A.

[2] Ie under the LRA 2002, Sch 1: see paras 7.7–7.16.

[3] There is no obligation on the applicant or his conveyancer to make further searches for any such interests not actually revealed by such investigations of the title as were undertaken in preparation for the transaction triggering the requirement of registration.

[4] As to interests which cannot be protected by notice, see the LRA 2002, ss 33 and 90(4), and para 7.23.

[5] See Form FR1 (prescribed by the LRR 2003, r 23), panel 12, and Form DI (prescribed by r 28).

[6] See paras 1.9–1.10.

[7] By the LRR 2003, r 35, the registrar is to enter a notice of *'the burden of any interest which appears from his examination of the title to affect the registered estate'*. See also Law Com no 271, para 8.91.

[8] Easements created by grant will normally appear from the documents of title.

[9] See Chapter 3, paras 3.19–3.24.

[10] See Law Com no 271, para 8.91.

7.6 Where a disposition of an estate in unregistered land creates a land charge affecting that estate,[1] the Land Charges Act 1972 does not apply to the land charge if the requirement of registration (LRA 2002, ss 4, 6 and 7,)[2] applies to the estate because of the disposition.[3] In the absence of any provision to that effect, such a land charge would have to be registered under the Land Charges Act 1972 against the name of the disponee, to protect its priority against any further dealing by him before making an application for first registration. The LRA 2002 applies to such a further dealing as if it took place after registration.[4]

---

[1] Such as a restrictive covenant, within the Land Charges Act 1972, s 2(5)(ii), class D, by the purchaser in favour of the vendor.

2   See Chapter 4, para 4.9; Chapter 5, paras 5.2, 5.3; Chapter 6, paras 6.3–6.5.
3   Land Charges Act 1972, s 14(3), as amended by the LRA 2002, Sch 11, para 10.
4   LRR 2003, r 38, made under the LRA 2002, Sch 10, para 1.

UNREGISTERED INTERESTS BINDING ON FIRST REGISTERED PROPRIETOR

7.7   On first registration, the registered estate is vested in the proprietor subject to *'unregistered interests which fall within any of the paragraphs of Schedule 1'* to the LRA 2002 (see ss 11(4)(b) and 12(4)(c)).[1] Those interests are as follows:

- A lease which is not required to be substantively registered (Sch 1, para 1);[2]
- A 'PPP lease' (LRA 2002, s 90; Greater London Authority Act 1999, s 218),[3] ie a lease created for 'public-private partnerships relating to transport in London';
- An interest of a person in actual occupation, so far as relating to the land he occupies, other than an interest under a Settled Land Act settlement (Sch 1, para 2);[4]
- A legal easement or profit à prendre (Sch 1, para 3);[5]
- A customary or public right (Sch 1, paras 4 and 5);[6]
- A local land charge (Sch 1, para 6);[7]
- Coal and certain other mineral rights (Sch 1, paras 7, 8 and 9);[8]
- For ten years from the coming into force of the LRA 2002 (see s 117(1)), a franchise, manorial right, Crown rent, non-statutory right as to an embankment or sea or river wall, and a right to payment in lieu of tithe (Sch 1, paras 10–14);[9]
- For three years from the coming into force of the LRA 2002, a right acquired before that date under the Limitation Act 1980 (Sch 1, para 15);[10]
- For ten years from the coming into force of the LRA 2002, a right in respect of the repair of a church chancel (Sch 1, para 16).[11]

Schedule 1 does not apply, however, to a sub-sale or other subsequent disposition which is completed before an application is made to register a disposition giving rise to the requirement of registration. The LRA 2002 applies to such a sub-sale or other disposition as if it had taken place after first registration (LRR 2003, r 38[12]); it is therefore subject to the overriding interests specified in Sch 3.[13]

1   If such an interest is in fact protected by an entry on the register (eg under the procedure described in para 7.5), these provisions do not apply, but the interest is binding under s 11(4)(a) or s 12(4)(b).
2   Ie any lease granted after the commencement of the LRA 2002 for a term not exceeding seven years (and not required by s 4(1)(d), (e) or (f) to be registered); this adapts the principle of

the LRA 1925, s 70(1)(k), to the provisions of the LRA 2002 for compulsory registration of leases. By the LRA 2002, Sch 12, para 12, this paragraph also includes a lease granted before the commencement of the LRA 2002 for a term not exceeding 21 years, which was an overriding interest under the LRA 1925, s 70(1)(k).

³   LRA 2002, s 90(5), provides that Sch 1 has effect as if it included a paragraph referring to a PPP lease; this preserves the effect of the LRA 1925, s 70(1)(kk), inserted by the Greater London Authority Act 1999, s 219(7).

⁴   See para 7.9.

⁵   See para 7.10, and Chapter 9, para 9.4.

⁶   See para 7.11.

⁷   See para 7.12.

⁸   See para 7.13.

⁹   See para 7.14, and Chapter 12, paras 12.12, 12.15 and 12.17. The interests in Sch 1, paras 10–14, were all overriding interests under LRA 1925, s 70(1): paras (b), (d), (e) and (j).

¹⁰   Temporarily inserted by the LRA 2002, Sch 12, para 7; see Chapter 13, para 13.31.

¹¹   Temporarily inserted by the Land Registration Act 2002 (Transitional Provisions) (No 2) Order 2003, SI 2003/2431; see para 7.14.

¹²   Made under the LRA 2002, Sch 10, para 1.

¹³   See paras 7.62 et seq.

Leasehold estates in land

7.8   Leases which are not registrable because the term granted is less than that which triggers the requirement of compulsory registration,[1] and PPP leases,[2] are considered further elsewhere in this book.

¹   See the discussion in Chapter 6, paras 6.47–6.62, of the protection of leases and tenancies on dispositions of the reversionary interest.

²   Chapter 12, paras 12.26–12.27.

Interests of persons in actual occupation

7.9   The LRA 2002, Sch 1, para 2, by which an interest belonging to a person in 'actual occupation' of the land is binding on the first registered proprietor (under LRA 2002, ss 11(4)(b) and 12(4)(c)), is similar but not identical in effect to the equivalent provisions of the previous legislation (LRA 1925, s 70(1)(g)). The main features of Sch 1, para 2, are as follows.

   (a)   The caselaw on the meaning of the expression '*actual occupation*' in the previous legislation continues to be applicable.[1] In particular, occupation concurrently with the owner of the 'paper title' is capable of being '*actual occupation*' within the ordinary meaning of those words;[2] there must be some degree of permanence and continuity (rather than mere fleeting presence), although the acts of an agent may suffice.[3]

   (b)   Paragraph 2 protects all the proprietary rights of an occupier which bind the first registered proprietor under the general law, and is not confined to the interest which confers the right to occupy the land.[4] This corresponds with the previous law.[5]

(c) The occupier's rights are protected only *'so far as relating to'* the land he or she occupies; if that occupation extends to part only of the land in the registered title, but the occupier has some additional right applicable to all or part of the remainder, para 2[6] does not apply. This alters the previous law.[7]

(d) Paragraph 2 protects interests affecting the estate *'at the time of registration'* (LRA 2002, ss 11(4) and 12(4)), and where first registration is required in consequence of a disposition of the land (LRA 2002, s 4(1)), the legal estate passes to the disponee by virtue of the disposition, and before registration is effected.[8] When registered as first proprietor, the disponee therefore takes free from any registrable but unregistered land charge if the effect of the disposition is to make it void against him under the LCA 1972,[9] even if the person entitled to the benefit of the land charge is in actual occupation of the land affected. The most important consequence, it is thought, is that an unregistered estate contract, including an unregistered option to purchase granted to a tenant of the land (or to anyone else), remains binding on the first registered proprietor if the purchaser or option-holder is in occupation and either the registration is effected voluntarily by the vendor or grantor of the option (LRA 2002, s 3(2)(a)),[10] or it is required in consequence of a gratuitous disposition (LRA 2002, s 4(1)),[11] but the contract or option is avoided, despite the purchaser or option-holder being in occupation, if the trigger for registration is a disposition for money or money's worth.

(e) An occupier's protection under paragraph 2 against a first registered proprietor is not affected by whether any inquiries are addressed to the occupier or how such inquiries are answered. This is a change in the law, though it appears to be unlikely to have significant practical consequences.[12]

(f) Paragraph 2 does not protect the interest of someone who is not in occupation, but is receiving the rents and profits of the land, at the time of first registration. This is also a change in the law.[13]

(g) An occupier entitled to a beneficial interest under a trust of land is protected by para 2,[14] but not an occupier entitled to an interest under a 'strict settlement' under the Settled Land Act 1925.[15] On both these points the effect of the previous law is reproduced.[16]

---

[1] The Law Commission's draft Bill contained a partial definition of 'actual occupation' in terms of the owner of the interest, or his agent or employee, being physically present on the land; that provision was removed at Report stage in the House of Lords, on the basis that the Bill was not intended to change the established meaning of 'actual occupation', but the inclusion of such a partial definition would be capable of creating uncertainty on the point: 627 HL Official Report (5th Series) col 1326 (Report Stage, 30 October 2001).

[2]   *Hodgson v Marks* [1971] Ch 892, CA; *Williams & Glyn's Bank Ltd v Boland* [1981] AC 487, HL.

[3]   *Abbey National Building Society v Cann* [1991] 1 AC 56 at 93F–H.

[4]   LRA 2002, ss 11(4) and 12(4), provide for the first registered proprietor to be subject to *'interests affecting the estate'* which fall within (inter alia) para 2; and by s 132(3)(b) an *'interest affecting an estate'* includes any *'adverse right affecting the title to the estate'*.

[5]   LRA 1925, s 70(1)(g); *Webb v Pollmount Ltd* [1966] Ch 584.

[6]   If the additional right falls within any other paragraph of Sch 1, for example as a legal easement, it will be protected accordingly.

[7]   The effect of *Ferrishurst Ltd v Wallcite Ltd* [1999] Ch 355 is reversed. See Law Com no 271, paras 8.19 and 8.55–8.58.

[8]   LRA 2002, s 27(1), does not apply, because the land is not registered at the time of the disposition; by s 7(1) the disposition *becomes* void as regards the legal estate if no application for registration is made in due time. See also Chapter 4, para 4.10.

[9]   Land Charges Act 1972, s 4(5) and (6): an unregistered puisne mortgage, limited owner's charge or general equitable charge is void against any disponee, whether gratuitous or for value; an unregistered estate contract, restrictive covenant or equitable easement is void against a disponee for money or money's worth.

[10]   See Chapter 5, para 5.9; Chapter 6, para 6.9. Failure to register a land charge under Land Charges Act 1972 does not avoid it as against the person who created it.

[11]   See Chapter 5, para 5.3; Chapter 6, paras 6.3, 6.4.

[12]   See Law Com no 271, para 8.21.

[13]   See Law Com no 271, para 8.18.

[14]   An interest under a trust of land (including a trust for sale), within the Trusts of Land and Appointment of Trustees Act 1996, is an *'adverse right affecting the title'* within the LRA 2002, s 132(3)(b). See Chapter 10, paras 10.53–10.54.

[15]   The words of para 2 specifically so provide. See further Chapter 10, para 10.55.

[16]   See *Williams & Glyn's Bank Ltd v Boland* [1981] AC 487, and *City of London Building Society v Flegg* [1988] AC 54, as to trusts for sale; the same considerations apply to trusts of land under Trusts of Land and Appointment of Trustees Act 1996. The LRA 1925, s 86(2), provided that interests under Settled Land Act settlements took effect as minor interests *'and not otherwise'*.

Easements and profits à prendre

7.10   The effect of first registration on existing easements is considered in the chapter on easements.[1] It appears to be sufficient at this point to note that under the LRA 2002, Sch 1, para 3, only *legal*, as opposed to equitable, easements (and profits à prendre) are capable of overriding first registration of the servient land;[2] and legal easements created by express grant, or otherwise appearing from the documents of title, will in practice be protected by a notice on the register of the title of the servient land and will take effect as registered, not as overriding, interests.[3]

[1]   Chapter 9; see paras 9.3–9.9.

[2]   If *Celsteel Ltd v Alton House Holdings Ltd* [1985] 1 WLR 204 had the effect in any circumstances of making an equitable easement binding, as an overriding interest, against the first registered proprietor of the servient land, the LRA 2002, Sch 1, para 3, changes the law. There is no saving for any equitable easements in existence at the coming into force of the LRA 2002 and having (or potentially having) that effect; contrast the LRA 2002, Sch 12, para 9, (Chapter 9, para 9.27) relating to easements affecting registered land at the commencement of the LRA 2002.

[3]   See LRA 2002, ss 11(4)(a), (b), and 12(4)(b), (c), and para 7.4.

Customary and public rights

7.11   'Customary' rights, which override first registration under the LRA 2002, Sch 1, para 4, are ancient, certain, reasonable and continuous rights enjoyed by some or all of the inhabitants of a particular locality as such (and not as appurtenant to any interest in land);[1] the range of activities which may be authorised by customary rights is extensive.[2] 'Public' rights, within the LRA 2002, Sch 1, para 5, are presently existing (but not potential future) rights '*exercisable by anyone, whether he owns land or not, merely by virtue of the general law*'.[3] The commonest of such rights is the public's entitlement to use the highway. The LRA 2002 continues the previous status, under the LRA 1925, s 70(1)(a), of customary and public rights as overriding interests binding on a first registered proprietor.

---

[1]   See *Megarry and Wade on Real Property* (6th edn) para 18–078; Law Com no 271, para 8.27.
[2]   The inhabitants of a parish may be entitled (for example) to a customary right to use a path leading to the parish church; to use a common for recreation; or to water cattle at a pond. See *Megarry and Wade*, paras 18-059 and 18-078.
[3]   *Overseas Investment Services Ltd v Simcobuild Construction Ltd* (1995) 70 P&CR 322, CA; see Law Com no 271, para 8.28.

Local land charges

7.12   By the LRA 2002, Sch 1, para 6, local land charges are excluded from registration under that Act because they are subject to a separate system, under the Local Land Charges Act 1975, regulating their registration and priority.[1] Local land charges are a miscellaneous category of obligations enforceable by public authorities, and may either regulate the use of land in specie, or secure the repayment of money expended under statutory powers by the authority concerned.[2] A local land charge securing the payment of money must be registered under the LRA 2002 before it can be realised (LRA 2002, s 55).[3] These provisions are to the same effect as the previous law (LRA 1925, ss 70(1)(i) and 59(2) proviso).

---

[1]   See Law Com no 271, para 8.29. Any matter which was registered as a local land charge before the commencement of the Local Land Charges Act 1975 also retains overriding status even if it is not a land charge within the meaning of that Act: LRA 2002, Sch 12, para 13, preserving the effect of the Local Land Charges Act 1975, s 19(3).
[2]   See the definition in the Local Land Charges Act 1975, s 1(1).
[3]   See Chapter 8, para 8.27.

Mines and minerals

7.13   The LRA 2002, Sch 1, paras 7, 8 and 9, which are to the same effect as the previous law,[1] make it unnecessary to register interests in coal and coal mines; mineral rights created before 1898 in relation to land registered before 1898; and mineral rights created before the first registration of the land affected, where that registration took place between 1898 and 1925 inclusive. It would not be practicable to register these rights.[2]

---

[1]   LRA 1925, s 70(1)(l) and (m), the latter paragraph inserted by the Coal Industry Act 1994, Sch 9.
[2]   See Law Com no 271, paras 8.32–8.34.

Miscellaneous

7.14   By the LRA 2002, Sch 1, paras 10–14, franchises, manorial rights, Crown rents, non-statutory rights as to embankments or sea or river walls, and rights to payments in lieu of tithe, are overriding interests as against the first registered proprietor of the land affected. These interests, and the liability of 'rectorial property' for chancel repairs, were overriding interests under the previous law (LRA 1925, s 70(1)(b), (d), (e) and (j)).[1] The Court of Appeal held in 2001 that chancel repair liability was unenforceable,[2] and it was therefore omitted from the LRA 2002.[3] However, the House of Lords reversed the Court of Appeal's decision in 2003,[4] and *'a right in respect of the repair of a church chancel'* has therefore been inserted in the LRA 2002 as Sch 1, para 16.[5] All the interests mentioned in Sch 1, paras 10–14 and 16, will cease to override first registration ten years after Sch 1 comes into force;[6] during that period, no fee may be charged for an application by the owner of an interest within paras 10–14 to lodge a caution against first registration of the land affected (LRA 2002, s 117(2)(a)).[7] The purpose of these provisions is (a) to ensure that in due course all such interests will only bind registered land if they are protected on the register, and (b) to give their owners a sufficient opportunity to obtain that protection.[8]

---

[1]   Various other rights within those paragraphs are obsolete, and are not mentioned in Sch 1; see para 7.15.
[2]   *Aston Cantlow Parochial Church Council v Wallbank* [2001] EWCA Civ 713, [2002] Ch 51, applying the Human Rights Act 1998, s 6, and the European Convention on Human Rights, First Protocol, Art 1.
[3]   See Law Com no 271, para 8.75.
[4]   *Aston Cantlow Parochial Church Council v Wallbank* [2003] UKHL 37, [2004] 1 AC 546.
[5]   Inserted by Land Registration Act 2002 (Transitional Provisions) (No 2) Order 2003, SI 2003/2431, art 2(1).
[6]   LRA 2002, s 117(1), as to paras 10–14; Land Registration Act 2002 (Transitional Provisions) (No 2) Order 2003, SI 2003/2431, art 2(1), as to para 16.
[7]   For cautions against first registration, see Chapter 4, paras 4.3–4.8. The announcement by the Department of Constitutional Affairs of the provision being made for chancel repair rights, Press Release 360/03 of 24 September 2003, indicates that the Land Registry intends to waive the fee for entries in respect of such rights.
[8]   See Law Com no 271, paras 8.35–8.46 and 8.81–8.89.

7.15 The LRA 2002 does not preserve the overriding status, as against the first registered proprietor, of various other interests which had that status under the LRA 1925, s 70(1). Customary and other rights originating in tenure (other than Crown rents) are obsolete.[1] Where the rights of the 'paper title' owner of unregistered land were barred by adverse possession (LRA 1925, s 70(1)(f),) before the commencement of the LRA 2002, the adverse possessor's 'title by limitation' remains an overriding interest indefinitely if he remains in occupation (LRA 2002, Sch 1, para 2), but will retain that status for three years, only, from the commencement of the LRA 2002 if he has ceased, or subsequently ceases, to occupy the land (LRA 2002, Sch 12, para 7).[2] The rights of a person in receipt of the rents and profits of the land are omitted from Sch 1, para 2.[3] Where land is registered with qualified, possessory or good leasehold title,[4] the priority of the estates and interests excepted from the effect of registration[5] is protected by the sections regulating those categories of title.[6]

---

[1]   Such interests were among those listed in the LRA 1925, s 70(1)(a) and (b). See Law Com no 254, paras 5.26 and 5.32–5.36.
[2]   See Chapter 13, para 13.31.
[3]   Compare the LRA 1925, s 70(1)(g); and see Law Com no 271, para 8.18, and Chapter 6, para 6.62.
[4]   See Chapter 5, paras 5.12–5.15, and Chapter 6, paras 6.12–6.15 and 6.18.
[5]   Formerly overriding interests under the LRA 1925, s 70(1)(h).
[6]   LRA 2002, s 11(6) and (7), freeholds, and s 12(6), (7) and (8), leaseholds.

7.16 Rights arising from a tenant's notice to acquire the freehold or an extended lease of a house, under the Leasehold Reform Act 1967, do not fall within LRA 2002, Sch 1, but must be protected by registering an estate contract (Leasehold Reform Act 1967, s 5(5)).[1] Similar provisions exclude from Sch 1, para 2 an access order under the Access to Neighbouring Land Act 1992;[2] a notice claiming collective enfranchisement or a new lease under the Leasehold Reform, Housing and Urban Development Act 1993;[3] a request for an overriding lease under the Landlord and Tenant (Covenants) Act 1995;[4] and a spouse's matrimonial home rights under the Family Law Act 1996;[5] LRA 2002 has not made any substantive change to the law affecting these rights. Schedule 1, para 2 is also inapplicable to pending land actions, writs and orders affecting land, orders appointing a receiver or sequestrator, and deeds of arrangement.[6]

---

[1]   Amended by LRA 2002, Sch 11, para 8(2).
[2]   S 5(5), substituted by LRA 2002, Sch 11, para 26(6).
[3]   S 97(1), amended by LRA 2002, Sch 11, para 30(3).
[4]   S 20(6), amended by LRA 2002, Sch 11, para 33(4).
[5]   S 31(10), amended by LRA 2002, Sch 11, para 34(2).
[6]   LRA 2002, s 87(3). A person entitled to such an interest in unregistered land can enter a caution against first registration: LRA 2002, ss 87(1) and 15(1). For cautions against first registration, see Chapter 4, paras 4.3–4.8.

GENERAL RULES OF PRIORITY OF INTERESTS IN REGISTERED LAND

7.17 The LRA 2002, ss 28–30, introduce a comprehensive code of rules governing the effect of a disposition of a registered estate or charge on the priority of an interest[1] affecting that estate or charge. By s 28(1), the basic rule is that the priority of the interest is not affected by the disposition, whether or not the interest or the disposition is registered (s 28(2)), unless a statutory exception applies. The most important exception, under ss 29 and 30, is that if a registrable disposition (within LRA 2002, s 27,) of a registered estate or charge is made for valuable consideration[2] and is completed by registration, the interest of the disponee takes priority over any other interest affecting the estate or charge immediately before the disposition, unless the priority of that other interest is *'protected'* at the time of registration: see s 29(1), as to registered dispositions of registered estates, and s 30(1), as to registered dispositions of registered charges. An interest is *'protected'* for this purpose if:

(1)   it is a registered charge or the subject of a notice in the register[3] (LRA 2002, ss 29(2)(a)(i)[4] and 30(2)(a)(i)); or

(2)   it falls within any of the paragraphs of the LRA 2002, Sch 3 (LRA 2002, ss 29(2)(a)(ii) and 30(2)(a)(ii)),[5] unless it has been the subject of a notice in the register at any time since the LRA 2002 came into force (see ss 29(3) and 30(3)); or

(3)   it appears from the register to be excepted from the effect of registration[6] (LRA 2002, ss 29(2)(a)(iii)[7] and 30(2)(a)(iii)); or

(4)   in the case of a disposition of, or of a charge relating to, a leasehold estate, the burden of the interest is incident to the estate[8] (LRA 2002, ss 29(2)(b)[9] and 30(2)(b)).

The grant of a lease which is not required to be registered has effect, for the purpose of priority under s 29, as if it involved a registered disposition which was registered at the time of the grant (see s 29(4)).[10] 'Equities by estoppel' and 'mere equities' affecting registered land are expressly declared to be interests capable, subject to the priority rules, of binding successors in title.[11]

---

[1]   Ie any adverse right affecting the title to the estate or charge: LRA 2002, s 132(3)(b).

[2]   Not including either 'marriage consideration' or a nominal consideration in money: LRA 2002, s 132(1). The exclusion of 'marriage consideration' is a change in the law; compare the LRA 1925, s 3(xxxi), and Law Com no 271, para 5.8.

[3]   For registered charges, see the LRA 2002, ss 27(2)(f) and 48 and Chapter 8, paras 8.7–8.10; and for notices see the LRA 2002, ss 32–39 and paras 7.20–7.39.

[4]   Corresponding with the LRA 1925, ss 20(1)(a) and 23(1)(b).

[5]   Corresponding (with modifications) with the LRA 1925, s 70(1); see paras 7.62–7.81.

[6]   The effect is that where the estate or charge is registered with possessory, qualified or good leasehold title, all the adverse rights which remained enforceable against the first registered proprietor, because the title was not registered as absolute, continue to be enforceable against subsequent registered proprietors even though they take under dispositions for valuable consideration. (See Chapter 5, paras 5.12–5.15, and Chapter 6, paras 6.12–6.14.)

7   Corresponding with the LRA 1925, ss 20(2) and (3) and 23(2)–(4).
8   'Tenant covenants' in 'new tenancies', within the Landlord and Tenant (Covenants) Act 1995
are by s 3(1) of that Act *'annexed and incident to'* the demised premises. The existence of such
interests will be apparent to the disponee from the lease; compare Law Com no 271, para 5.13.
9   Corresponding with the LRA 1925, s 23(1)(a).
10   Corresponding with the LRA 1925, ss 19(2) and 22(2).
11   LRA 2002, s 116, considered in Chapter 11, paras 11.11–11.18.

7.18   Certain features of the priority rules under the LRA 2002, ss 28–30, warrant more detailed consideration.

(1)   The effect of the 'basic rule' under LRA 2002, s 28(1) and (2), that the priority of an interest affecting a registered estate is not affected by a disposition of that estate, is that if no statutory exception applies (LRA 2002, ss 29–31), priorities are governed simply by the order in which interests are created, and it is not possible for an incumbrancer interested in registered land to lose priority by 'gross negligence' or 'inequitable conduct' through the (uncertain and unpredictable) operation of the maxim of the general law that *'where the equities are equal'* the first in time prevails, and its corollary that where the equities are unequal, a later interest may gain priority.[1] Where those principles would deprive a negligent incumbrancer of priority, they would do so in favour of a person taking under a subsequent disposition by the owner of the estate; but the 'basic rule' under LRA 2002 is that a disposition does not affect the priority of an interest affecting a registered estate, and therefore if no statutory exception to the basic rule is applicable, even a negligent incumbrancer retains against a subsequent disponee the priority he enjoyed against the disponor.

(2)   Because the LRA 2002, s 28, establishes a general rule that a disposition does not affect priority, to which ss 29 and 30 create an *exception* (LRA 2002, s 28(1), *'Except as provided by sections 29 and 30, ...'*) by which an 'unprotected' interest is postponed to an interest under a registered disposition for valuable consideration, a person who claims to have obtained priority over an 'unprotected' interest bears the onus of proving[2] not only that the disposition relied on was registrable and registered, which will appear from the register, but also that it was made for valuable consideration, which may not be apparent. It is thought that if the register does refer to valuable consideration having been given, or if a document which relates to the disposition, and is mentioned in the register and kept by the registrar,[3] contains such a reference, that will be sufficient to discharge the onus if no evidence to the contrary is tendered.

(3)   The LRA 2002, s 28(1), specifically provides that ss 28–30 regulate the effect on priority of a disposition of a *registered* estate or charge, and ss 28–30 therefore do not apply to the

priority as between themselves of successive dealings with *unregistered* equitable interests in registered land (or a registered charge) which is held in trust; the relative priorities of dealings with such interests therefore continue to be governed by the order in which notice of the dealings is received by the trustees.[4]

(4)   By the LRA 2002, ss 29(1) and 30(1), a registered disposition for valuable consideration takes priority over an existing interest which affected the registered estate (or charge) *immediately before the disposition* and is not protected *at the time of registration*. This has two consequences:

(a)   an interest arising simultaneously with the disposition, (for example a restrictive covenant by the purchaser in favour of the vendor,) or created thereafter but before the effective date of registration, (for example a lease granted by the purchaser after completing the purchase but before applying for registration,)[5] retains priority over the interest of the disponee, if it is entitled to such priority under the general law,[6] even if it is not protected at the time of registration. This principle does not apply to an unpaid vendor's lien, which arises on exchange of contracts for sale[7] and is already in existence *immediately before* completion of the transfer to the purchaser; it must therefore be protected by a notice on the register if it is to remain enforceable;[8]

(b)   an interest which is in existence but not protected at the time of the disposition will nevertheless retain its priority if it can be protected before the date as of which the disposition is registered. However, it will rarely, if ever, be practicable for a person with an unprotected interest to take advantage of this principle: if the disponee makes use of the 'priority search' procedure (LRA 2002, s 72, and LRR 2003, rr 147–154),[9] any notice entered on the register during the priority period, whether before or after completion of the disposition, will be postponed to the disposition when it is registered (LRA 2002, s 72(2)); and a person who is not in occupation of the land at the time of a disposition cannot preserve the priority of an unregistered interest by going into occupation before the date as of which the disposition is registered.[10]

---

[1]   Compare *Taylor v Russell* [1892] AC 244 at 262; and see *Snell's Equity* (30th edn, 2000) paras 4-33 to 4-40; Law Com no 271, paras 5.2 and 5.5; Law Com no 254, para 7.17.

[2]   Compare the principle of unregistered conveyancing that a party who claims to take free of a prior equitable interest as a *'purchaser of a legal estate for value and without notice'* bears the onus of proof on all elements of that claim; *Re Nisbet and Potts Contract* [1906] 1 Ch 386 at 404.

[3]   Any person may inspect such a document, and an official copy is admissible in evidence to the same extent as the original: LRA 2002, ss 66(1)(b) and 67(1)(b).

4   Under the rule in *Dearle v Hall* (1828) 3 Russ 1, as applied to equitable interests in land by the Law of Property Act 1925, s 137 (as amended).

5   By the LRA 2002, s 74, an entry in the register has effect from the time of the application for that entry to be made.

6   It is entitled to such priority if it is created by the disponee; compare the restrictive covenant and lease mentioned in the text, and Law Com no 271, para 5.10.

7   *Barclays Bank plc v Estates & Commercial Ltd* [1997] 1 WLR 415.

8   See Law Com no 271, para 5.10.

9   See paras 7.82–7.87.

10   The LRA 2002, Sch 3, para 2, protects an interest belonging *'at the time of the disposition'* to a person in actual occupation; see paras 7.64–7.65.

7.19   There is a further statutory exception to the 'basic rule' of priority in relation to an Inland Revenue charge (ie a charge under the Inheritance Tax Act 1984, s 237, for unpaid inheritance tax and interest on it): the priority of such a charge is determined[1] in accordance with the Inheritance Tax Act 1984, ss 237(6) and 238(1)(a), by which the charge ceases to affect any registered land which is disposed of to a purchaser in good faith for consideration in money or money's worth,[2] if the charge is not protected by notice on the register at the time of registration of the disposition (Inheritance Tax Act 1984, s 238(3)(a)). If that happens, the charge continues to apply to the price or other property representing the land in the hands of the disponor (Inheritance Tax Act 1984, s 238(1)), and it is therefore thought that a purchaser who actually knows of the existence of an Inland Revenue charge, and also (necessarily) knows that it is not protected on the register, may still act *'in good faith'*, unless in addition he knows (or is aware of facts which clearly indicate[3]) that the disponor intends to evade making payment of the sums secured by the charge.

1   Under the LRA 2002, s 31, continuing the effect of the LRA 1925, s 73 (as amended).

2   See the Inheritance Tax Act 1984, s 272; the definition includes a lessee, mortgagee or other person who acquires an interest in the land, but does not include a nominal consideration.

3   It is thought that such a purchaser would be prudent not to accept a request to remit the purchase price directly to a bank account in an overseas jurisdiction.

PROTECTION BY ENTRY OF NOTICE ON THE REGISTER

7.20   A notice is an entry in the register in respect of the burden of an interest affecting a registered estate or charge (LRA 2002, s 32(1)),[1] made in relation to that estate or charge (LRA 2002, s 32(2)).[2] A notice does not guarantee the validity of the interest to which it relates; but if that interest is valid, the notice protects its priority if the estate or charge affected is the subject of a registered disposition for valuable consideration (LRA 2002, ss 32(3), 29(2)(a)(i) and 30(2)(a)(i)). Notices registered under the LRA 1925 before the commencement of the LRA 2002 continue to have effect.[3] An interest within any paragraph of the LRA 2002, Sch 3, overrides registered dispositions for value of the land affected, even though it is not itself registered (LRA 2002, ss 29(2)(a)(ii) and 30(2)(a)(ii)),[4] unless it has been the subject of a notice on the register since the commencement of the LRA 2002 (see ss 29(3) and 30(3)); once such an interest has been entered on the register, it can only be protected by remaining registered.

---

[1]   By s 132(3)(b) an *'interest affecting'* a registered estate means an adverse right affecting the title to that estate.

[2]   Under the LRR 2003, r 84(1), the entry is made in the charges register, except that under the LRA 2002, s 86(2), and the LRR 2003, r 165(1), a bankruptcy notice in respect of a bankruptcy petition against the proprietor of registered land is entered in the proprietorship register.

[3]   LRA 2002, Sch 12, para 2(1), to the effect that such notices operate as if they were 'agreed', rather than 'unilateral', notices; see para 7.24.

[4]   See paras 7.17 and 7.62–7.81.

7.21   The right to apply for the entry of a notice, and the right to object to such an application, must not be exercised without reasonable cause: LRA 2002, s 77(1)(b) and (c). Any person who suffers damage from a breach of this duty has a statutory cause of action against the party in breach: LRA 2002, s 77(2).[1]

---

[1]   See Law Com no 271, para 6.28.

7.22   If, before the commencement of the LRA 2002, a person lodged a caution under the LRA 1925, s 54, in respect of any estate, right, interest or claim, he may only apply to register a notice in respect of that matter if he also applies to withdraw the caution: LRA 2002, Sch 12, para 17.

7.23   A notice may not be entered in respect of:
    (1)   an interest under a trust of land or a settlement under the Settled Land Act 1925 (LRA 2002, s 33(a));[1]
    (2)   a lease granted for a term of not more than three years from when it is granted and which is not required to be registered (LRA 2002, s 33(b));[2]
    (3)   a restrictive covenant made between lessor and lessee, so far as it relates to the demised premises (LRA 2002, s 33(c));[3]
    (4)   an interest capable of registration under the Commons Registration Act 1965 (LRA 2002, s 33(d));
    (5)   interests in coal and coal mines (LRA 2002, s 33(e));[4]
    (6)   a 'PPP lease' created for a public-private partnership relating to transport in London (LRA 2002, s 90(4) and (6)),[5] or

(7)   an order appointing a receiver or sequestrator, or a deed of arrangement (LRA 2002, s 87(2)).[6]

---

[1]   The appropriate entry to protect such interests is a restriction; see paras 7.40–7.61.
[2]   Under Sch 3, para 1, such a lease overrides registered dispositions of the reversionary interest.
[3]   Such a covenant by a lessee in favour of the lessor is binding on assignees of the lease under the LRA 2002, s 29(2)(b).
[4]   Under Sch 3, para 7, such interests override registered dispositions of the surface of the land.
[5]   Under s 90(5) such a lease overrides registered dispositions of the reversionary interest.
[6]   The appropriate entry is a restriction: see the LRR 2003, r 93(s) and (t); r 93 is considered further in para 7.51.

Classes of notice

7.24   There are three main classes of notice:
(a)   notices that the registrar may or must enter in specified circumstances (LRR 2003, rr 35 and 37, and LRA 2002, ss 37 and 38);[1]
(b)   'agreed' notices, entered on application (LRA 2002, s 34);[2] and
(c)   'unilateral' notices, also entered on application (LRA 2002, ss 34(2)(b) and 35–36).[3]

The principal difference between these classes is that notices entered by the registrar without application, and agreed notices, remain on the register until removed on the protected interest coming to an end or, in case of dispute between the registered proprietor of the land and the person claiming the benefit of that interest, on an order for rectification or alteration of the register (under LRA 2002, s 65 and Sch 4,)[4] being made; but where a unilateral notice is entered, the registrar must give notice of it to the registered proprietor of the land (LRA 2002, s 35(1)), who can apply, then or subsequently, to have the notice cancelled (LRA 2002, s 36(1)), requiring the beneficiary of the notice to defend his claim (LRA 2002, ss 36(2) and (3) and 73). In this respect a unilateral notice resembles a caution against dealings under the LRA 1925 ss 54–55, but unlike a caution, such a notice is not automatically 'warned' on an application being made to register a disposition of the land, and if the proprietor, or the applicant for registration of the disposition, does not actively seek to have the notice cancelled, it remains on the register, and protects the priority of the beneficiary's interest if that interest is valid (LRA 2002, s 32(3)).[5]

---

[1]   See paras 7.25–7.27.
[2]   See paras 7.28–7.34.
[3]   See paras 7.35–7.39.
[4]   See Chapter 14 and 626 HL Official Report (5th series) Col 1440 (Committee Stage, 17 July 2001).
[5]   See Law Com no 271, paras 6.26–6.31.

Notices that the registrar may or must enter

7.25 On completion of a first registration, the registrar is required to enter in the register a notice of the burden of any interest, capable of being protected by a notice and not being a public right or a local land charge, which appears from his examination of the title to affect the registered estate (LRR 2003, r 35(1) and (2)). This will include any such interests disclosed by the applicant under the obligation to give information about interests within the LRA 2002, Sch 1, which, to his knowledge, affect the estate (LRA 2002, s 71(a), and LRR 2003, r 28). On first registration of a lease, if the immediate reversionary interest was not registered when the lease was granted but has since been registered, or the grant of the lease was not required to be completed by registration, the registrar must enter notice of the lease in the register of the reversion, if it is not already noted (LRR 2003, r 37).

7.26 If it appears to the registrar that a registered estate is subject to an unregistered interest which falls within any paragraph of the LRA 2002, Sch 1, and is capable of being protected by a notice, he may (but is not required to) enter a notice in respect of that interest (LRA 2002, s 37(1)). This will include any such interests disclosed, by a person applying to register a disposition, under the obligation to give information about interests within the LRA 2002, Sch 3, (capable of being protected by a notice,) which, to his knowledge, affect the estate (LRA 2002, s 71(b), and LRR 2003, r 57).[1] When the registrar makes such an entry, he must give notice of it:

(a) to the registered proprietor of the title affected, except that he is not obliged to do so if the proprietor applied, or consented to an application, for the entry (LRA 2002, s 37(2), and LRR 2003, r 89(1)(a) and (2)); and

(b) to any person who appears to be entitled to the interest protected by the notice, except that he is not obliged to give notice to any such person who applied for or consented to the entry, or whose name and address for service are not set out in the individual register of the title (LRR 2003, r 89(1)(b) and (3)).[2]

---

[1]   See Chapter 5, para 5.19, and Appendix 1, Part B.
[2]   It is doubted whether such a person's address *for service* will normally appear in the individual register if the registrar makes the entry as a result of information provided by someone else, for example under the LRR 2003, r 57.

7.27 Where the grant of a lease of, or of a legal easement over, registered land is completed by registration (LRA 2002, s 27(2)(b) and (d) respectively), the registrar must enter a notice in respect of that interest in the register of the reversionary or servient title.[1] The procedures for varying and cancelling a notice entered by the registrar without application are the same as those applicable to an agreed notice: see LRR 2003, rr 84(4) and 87.[2]

---

[1]   LRA 2002, s 38, and Sch 2, paras 3(2)(b), lease, and 7(2)(a), easement.
[2]   Considered in paras 7.33–7.34.

'Agreed' notices

7.28   An 'agreed' notice may be entered if the registered proprietor of the estate or charge affected, or a person entitled to be registered as proprietor,[1] applies for the entry or consents to it (LRA 2002, s 34(3)(a) and (b) and (4)), or if the registrar is satisfied as to the validity of the applicant's claim (LRA 2002, s 34(3)(c)). In the latter case, the applicant can obtain protection for an interest such as, for example, an estate contract with (or an option to purchase from) the registered proprietor, if he can satisfy the registrar that the interest is valid, even if a dispute has arisen and the registered proprietor is not willing to consent to the notice being entered. The registrar is not obliged to give notice to the registered proprietor before, or after, entering an 'agreed' notice without his consent,[2] but in practice the proprietor will be notified when such an entry has been made.[3] Any dispute between the applicant and the proprietor can be resolved on an application to the registrar and (if necessary) a reference to the adjudicator (LRA 2002, Sch 4, paras 5 and 6, and s 73), or by an application directly to the court (LRA 2002, Sch 4, para 2(1)(a) and (b)). It is considered that on an interim application in such proceedings, the court has jurisdiction, in appropriate circumstances, to require the party claiming the benefit of the notice to give a cross-undertaking in damages for the benefit of the registered proprietor, as a condition of the notice being allowed to remain on the register until final resolution of the dispute.[4]

---

[1]   Where a registrable transfer creates an interest in the transferred land which can be protected by a notice, or the transferee creates such an interest between completion and registration of the transfer, the transferee can apply for or consent to the entry of a notice, and the transferor need not be concerned with it.
[2]   LRA 2002, s 35(1), applies only to unilateral notices, and the LRR 2003, r 89, applies only to notices entered by the registrar under s 37 of the LRA 2002.
[3]   See Land Registry Practice Guide 19, para 3.3.2.
[4]   See *Tiverton Estates Ltd v Wearwell Ltd* [1975] Ch 146 at 161 and 172. It is considered that the LRA 2002, s 77(1)(b), may not provide the registered proprietor with a sufficient remedy if, for example, a notice is correctly registered to protect a sale contract which subsequently 'goes off': compare *Clearbrook Property Holdings Ltd v Verrier* [1974] 1 WLR 243 at 246.

7.29   By LRA 2002, s 34(2), and LRR 2003, r 80, an agreed notice, and not a unilateral notice, must be used to protect:

   (1)   matrimonial home rights under the Family Law Act 1996 or the Matrimonial Homes Act 1983 or 1967 (LRR 2003, r 217(1), defining a 'matrimonial home rights notice');

   (2)   an Inland Revenue charge for unpaid inheritance tax (LRR 2003, r 217(1), defining an 'inheritance tax notice');

(3)   an order under the Access to Neighbouring Land Act 1992;

(4)   a variation of a lease by or under an order under the Landlord and Tenant Act 1987, ss 38 or 39; and

(5)   a public or customary right.

In relation to interests in classes (1) to (4) this rule reproduces, in substance, the position under the LRA 1925, where applicants were able to register notices (as opposed to cautions against dealings) without the production of the registered proprietor's land certificate.[1]

---

[1]   See Law Com no 271, para 6.25.

Application for an agreed notice

7.30   An application for an agreed notice must be made in Form AN1 (LRR 2003, r 81(1)(a)), unless it is an application for a matrimonial home rights notice (LRR 2003, r 81(2); definition in r 217(1)), and must be accompanied by the order or instrument (if any) giving rise to the interest claimed, or such other details as satisfy the registrar of the nature of that interest (LRR 2003, r 81(1)(b)),[1] and accompanied also, where appropriate, by *either* the consent of the registered proprietor of the land or charge affected, or of a person entitled to be registered as proprietor, and evidence of such a person's entitlement to registration, *or alternatively* evidence to satisfy the registrar that the applicant's claim is valid (LRR 2003, r 81(1)(c)). Any necessary consents can be included in the form (see Form AN1, panels 11 and 14); and if the application for a notice accompanies an application for registration of a new proprietor, the latter's entitlement to be registered can be established by reference to that application (see Form AN1, panel 12).

---

[1]   It is necessary to show that the interest is not one of those excluded by the LRA 2002, s 33; see para 7.23 and Land Registry Practice Guide 19, para 3.6.4.

Application for a matrimonial home rights notice

7.31   An application to enter a matrimonial home rights notice must be made in Form MH1 (LRR 2002, r 82(1)), and an application to renew such a notice or a matrimonial home rights caution must be made in Form MH2 (LRR 2002, r 82(2)), accompanied in either case by an office copy, or a conveyancer's[1] certificate that he holds an office copy, of any order made under the Family Law Act 1996, s 33(5), in relation to the property (LRR 2003, r 82(3)).[2]

---

[1]   Ie a solicitor, a licensed conveyancer or a Fellow of the Institute of Legal Executives: LRR 2003, r 217(1).

[2]   A conveyancer's certificate can be included in Form MH1, panel 10, or Form MH2, panel 8.

Entry, variation and removal of an agreed notice

7.32   An agreed notice must be entered in the charges register of the registered title affected (LRR 2003, r 84(1)), and must identify the estate or charge affected, with sufficient details, if the protected interest affects only part of the estate in the title, to identify clearly that part (LRR 2003, r 84(2)); where only part of the title is affected, that part will normally be shown on the title plan. The entry must also give details of the interest protected (LRR 2003, r 84(3)). The entry, and the documents supplied in support of the application, are open to public inspection (LRA 2002, s 66(1)), unless the procedure for making a document an 'exempt information document' has been followed (LRA 2002, s 66(2), and LRR 2003, rr 133(2) and 136).[1] A unilateral notice can be registered even if the registered proprietor is not in dispute with the person entitled to the protected interest, and discloses fewer details of that interest than appear from an agreed notice (LRR 2003, r 84(5));[2] so registration of a unilateral notice is a possible alternative method (which the Land Registry recognises[3]) of protecting the confidentiality of sensitive personal or commercial information.

---

[1]   See Chapter 2, paras 2.76–2.85.
[2]   See para 7.35.
[3]   See Land Registry Practice Guide 19, para 3.4.2.

7.33   If an interest protected by a notice is varied, an agreed notice can be entered on the register in respect of the variation, in accordance with the procedure already considered (LRR 2003, r 81(1)).[1] The register entry must give details of the variation (LRR 2003, r 84(4)). Where an interest protected by a notice is varied, the registrar will not usually alter the original notice, but will require a separate notice to be entered in respect of the variation.[2]

---

[1]   See para 7.30.
[2]   See Land Registry Practice Guide 19, para 3.9.1.

7.34   An application to cancel a notice (other than a unilateral notice or matrimonial home rights notice) must be made in Form CN1, and must be accompanied by evidence to satisfy the registrar of the determination of the interest (LRR 2003, r 87(1)). The registrar must cancel the notice, or make an entry in the register that the protected interest has come to an end, if he is satisfied of that fact (LRR 2003, r 87(2)). If the interest has only come to an end in part, the registrar must make an appropriate entry (LRR 2003, r 87(3)). There is no requirement to notify the person entitled to the protected interest of an application, by (for example) the registered proprietor of the land, for cancellation of an agreed notice, and therefore if there is in fact a dispute, that person may not become aware of the application, or exercise his right to object to it (under LRA 2002, s 73, and LRR 2003, r 19), before the notice is cancelled; but if the registered proprietor makes such an application knowing that there is a dispute as to whether the protected interest has determined, he is likely to commit the offence of suppressing information with the intention of substantiating a false claim (LRA 2002, s 123).[1]

---

[1]   However, the duty under the LRA 2002, s 77, to act reasonably, which gives a remedy to any person who suffers damage from its breach, does not apply to making (as opposed to objecting to) an application to the registrar.

'Unilateral' notices

7.35   An application to register a unilateral notice (under LRA 2002, s 34(2)(b),) must be in Form UN1 (LRR 2003, r 83), which must set out the nature of the interest protected, in a statutory declaration or certificate;[1] but it is not essential *either* to procure the consent of the registered proprietor or of a person entitled to be registered as proprietor, *or* to satisfy the registrar that the interest is valid, *or* to provide a copy of any documentation creating that interest, and a unilateral notice can therefore be used to secure 'holding' protection for a disputed claim (LRA 2002, s 32(3)), or to protect the priority of an interest whilst maintaining the confidentiality of information in the instrument creating it.[2] The notice must be entered in the charges register of the title affected (LRR 2003, r 84(1)), and the entry must identify the estate or charge affected, with sufficient details, if the protected interest affects only part of the estate in the title, to identify that part (LRR 2003, r 84(2)). The entry must also indicate that the notice is a unilateral notice (LRA 2002, s 35(2)(a)), identify the beneficiary of the notice (LRA 2002, s 35(2)(b)), and give *'such details of the interest protected as the registrar considers appropriate'* (LRR 2003, r 84(5)); in practice these details will normally be brief and not particularly informative.[3]

---

[1]   Form UN1, panels 11 and 12. This information must show that the interest is not excluded by the LRA 2002, s 33, (para 7.23,) from protection by entry of a notice.
[2]   See Law Com no 271, para 6.26.
[3]   Anyone proposing to deal with the registered proprietor can ask him what interest the notice protects, and if appropriate can insist that he clears it off the register by applying for it to be cancelled (para 7.36).

7.36   If the registrar enters a unilateral notice, he must give notice of the entry to the registered proprietor of the estate or charge to which it relates (LRA 2002, s 35(1)(a)).[1] The proprietor, or a person entitled to be registered as proprietor, may apply at any time for the notice to be cancelled (LRA 2002, s 36(1)), but no-one else can do so.[2] The application must be in Form UN4 (LRR 2003, r 86(1)), and in the case of an application by a person entitled to be registered as proprietor, it must be accompanied by evidence of that person's entitlement, or by a conveyancer's certificate that he is satisfied that the applicant is so entitled (LRR 2003, r 86(2); the certificate can be given in Form UN4, panel 11). The registrar must notify the beneficiary of the notice that the application has been made, and indicate the consequences of failing to object to it (LRA 2002, s 36(2)). If the beneficiary does not, before 12 noon on the fifteenth business day after the date of issue of the registrar's notice (LRR 2003, r 86(3)),[3] exercise his right to object to the application for cancellation of the unilateral notice (under the LRA 2002, s 73(1)), the registrar must cancel the notice (LRA 2002, s 36(3)).[4] A person entitled to be registered as beneficiary of the notice (LRA 2002, s 36(4), and LRR 2003, r 88,) may also object to the application for cancellation (LRR 2003, r 86(7)), but no-one else can do so (LRA 2002, s 73(3)).

[1]   The power under the LRA 2002, s 35(1)(b), to make rules requiring other persons also to be given such notice, has not been exercised.
[2]   It is considered that a chargee of registered land may in practice be able (if necessary) to require the chargor to apply for cancellation of a unilateral notice entered in the register against the land, if the secured debt is payable on demand, or if repayment can be required on the happening of any event which puts the security in jeopardy.
[3]   The LRR 2003, r 86(4)–(6), enable the registrar to extend that period, if the beneficiary makes a request (with reasons) for an extension of the period before it expires. The period runs from the date of issue of the registrar's notice, not the date of deemed service under r 199, and the risk of non-delivery is on the recipient beneficiary, who should therefore ensure that his addresses for service are kept up-to-date.
[4]   The effect is similar to that of the procedure for 'warning off' a caution against dealings under the LRA 1925, ss 54–55, and the LRR 1925, rr 218–221.

7.37   If the beneficiary of a unilateral notice, or a person entitled to be registered as beneficiary, exercises his right to object to an application for the notice to be cancelled,[1] the ordinary procedure for resolving an objection to an application is followed:[2] the registrar must give notice of the objection to the applicant, and if it cannot be disposed of by agreement and the registrar is not satisfied that it is groundless, the matter must be referred to the adjudicator (LRA 2002, s 73(5)–(7)). It is considered that court proceedings must be taken if the registered proprietor seeks an undertaking in damages[3] from the beneficiary of the notice, or either party wishes to apply for any other form of interim relief.[4] When the dispute has been resolved, an entry will be made in the register, if appropriate, to give effect to the decision reached.[5]

[1]   Para 7.36.
[2]   See Chapter 15, paras 15.6–15.7, 15.27–15.28 and 15.37 et seq.
[3]   See *Tiverton Estates Ltd v Wearwell Ltd* [1975] Ch 146, and para 7.28.
[4]   The LRA 2002, ss 107–114, and the Adjudicator to HM Land Registry (Practice and Procedure) Rules 2003, SI 2003/2171, do not authorise the adjudicator to grant an injunction or other relief in lieu of an injunction.
[5]   See, in relation to a decision of the adjudicator, the Adjudicator to HM Land Registry (Practice and Procedure) Rules 2003, SI 2003/2171, r 41.

7.38   A person entitled to the benefit of an interest protected by a unilateral notice may apply to be entered in the register in place of, or in addition to, the registered beneficiary (LRR 2003, r 88(1)). The procedure can be used to add, or to substitute, either someone who has been entitled to the benefit of the interest since it arose, or someone to whom it has been transferred or has devolved. The application must be in Form UN3, and accompanied by evidence to satisfy the registrar of the applicant's entitlement (LRR 2003, r 88(2)).[1] The registrar must serve notice of the application on the registered beneficiary (LRR 2003, r 88(4)), unless either he or she has signed the Form UN3 or otherwise consents to the application, or the applicant is the registered beneficiary's personal representative and evidence of his title to act accompanies the application (LRR 2003, r 88(5)).[2] If the registered beneficiary does not object to the application, (LRA 2002, s 73, applies if the registered beneficiary does object,) and the registrar is satisfied of the applicant's entitlement, he must enter the applicant in the register in place of, or in addition to, the registered beneficiary, as appropriate (LRR 2003, r 88(3)).

---

[1]   The nature of the evidence depends on the reason why the applicant claims to be entitled. The validity of the protected interest itself does not have to be established.
[2]   The usual evidence of a personal representative's entitlement to act is an office copy of the grant of representation, but it is thought that in case of urgency, other evidence, such as a copy of the will, the registered beneficiary's death certificate, and evidence that the applicant is the person named as executor, may be sufficient.

7.39   The registered beneficiary of a unilateral notice may apply for it to be removed from the register (LRA 2002, s 36(3)), as may his personal representative or trustee in bankruptcy, who must provide evidence to satisfy the registrar as to his appointment (LRR 2003, r 85(2)). The application must be in Form UN2 (LRR 2003, r 85(1)), which makes provision for the notice to be removed as to part only of the land in the registered title affected (panel 7). If the registrar is satisfied that the application is in order, he must remove the notice (LRR 2003, r 85(3)).

PROTECTION BY ENTRY OF RESTRICTION ON THE REGISTER

7.40   A restriction is a register entry regulating the making of entries in the register in respect of a disposition of the registered estate or charge (LRA 2002, s 40(1)). It does so by prohibiting entries, either generally or in respect of specified classes of disposition (LRA 2002, s 40(2)(a)), and the prohibition may be either for an indefinite period, for a specified period, or until the occurrence of a specified event

(LRA 2002, s 40(2)(b)). The events which may be specified include, but are not limited to, the giving of notice to or the obtaining of consent from a person named or otherwise identified in the restriction, or the making of an order by the court or the registrar (LRA 2002, s 40(3)). The terms in which restrictions may be framed are considered further below.[1] Where a restriction is entered in the register, no subsequent entry may be made, in respect of a disposition to which it applies, except in accordance with its terms (LRA 2002, s 41(1)), unless the registrar makes an order disapplying or modifying it (LRA 2002, s 41(2)).[2] The operation of a restriction is in principle the same as that of an equivalent entry under the LRA 1925, and the LRA 2002 applies to restrictions and inhibitions[3] entered under the earlier Act in the same way that it applies to restrictions entered after its commencement (LRA 2002, Sch 12, para 2(2)).

---

[1] Paras 7.43–7.45.
[2] See paras 7.57–7.58.
[3] Under the LRA 1925, s 57, an inhibition was an entry entirely prohibiting the registration of any dealing with the land; it was in substance a draconian type of restriction, and is not retained as a separate form of entry. Compare the prescribed form of bankruptcy restriction under the LRA 2002, s 86(4), and the LRR 2003, r 166(1).

7.41 A restriction protects an interest of a person other than the registered proprietor by preventing the making of an entry on the register which adversely affects that interest; it does not confer continuing priority protection on such an interest as against a subsequent registered disponee of the land, which is the function of a notice (LRA 2002, ss 29(2)(a)(i) and 30(2)(a)(i)),[1] and the entry of a restriction to protect the priority of an interest which is or could be the subject of a notice is prohibited (LRA 2002, s 42(2)).[2] Further, a restriction only operates to prevent or control the making of an *entry on the register* in respect of a disposition (LRA 2002, s 40(1)), and therefore does not confer any protection against the creation of an interest which does not have to be registered (eg a short lease within the LRA 2002, Sch 3, para 1);[3] and the registrar will not register a restriction which attempts to prevent or control the entry of a notice[4] (as opposed to the registration of a registrable disposition). However, the function of a restriction is wider in one important respect than that of a notice, in that a restriction can and must (LRA 2002, s 26(2)(a),) be entered if there is to be an effective sanction against dispositions which contravene any limitations on the registered proprietor's power of dealing with the land, even if those limitations are not related to any proprietary rights of a third party (eg a restriction against registration of an *ultra vires* disposition by a local authority which is registered as proprietor of the land).

---

[1] See paras 7.17, 7.20 and 7.23.
[2] See Law Com no 271, para 6.44.
[3] See Chapter 6, paras 6.21–6.23.
[4] See Land Registry Practice Guide 19, para 4.1.4.

Grounds for entering a restriction

7.42   There are three grounds on which the registrar can enter a restriction if it appears to him to be 'necessary or desirable' to do so.

(1)   A restriction can be used for *'preventing invalidity or unlawfulness in relation to dispositions'* of the land (LRA 2002, s 42(1)(a)). This permits (for example) a restriction against registration of dispositions which are contrary to the provisions of a corporate proprietor's constitution, or are not authorised under the powers of proprietors who are trustees (compare LRR 2003, Sch 4, Form B), or which would constitute a breach of a contract made by the proprietor in relation to the land (eg a right of pre-emption).

(2)   A restriction can be used to secure that interests under a trust of land (or a strict settlement) are effectively overreached (LRA 2002, s 42(1)(b)), and transferred to the proceeds of sale when the land is sold; this is the function of the restriction frequently entered against registration of a disposition by a sole proprietor under which capital money arises (LRR 2003, Sch 4, Form A).[1]

(3)   A restriction can also be used to *'protect a right or claim'* in relation to the land (LRA 2002, s 42(1)(c)), subject to the prohibition on entering a restriction to protect the priority of an interest which is or could be protected by a notice (LRA 2002, s 42(2)).[2] The court can make an order for a restriction to be entered for this purpose (LRA 2002, s 46(1), (2)).[3] This enables, for example, a charging order over an interest in proceeds of sale of land,[4] or an application for a freezing order,[5] to be protected.

---

[1]   See paras 7.45(1) and 7.48.
[2]   Considered in para 7.41.
[3]   See para 7.55.
[4]   LRA 2002, s 42(4); see the LRR 2003, Sch 4, Form K.
[5]   CPR 25.1(1)(f); see the LRR 2003, Sch 4, Form CC.

Standard forms of restriction

7.43   Standard forms of restriction are prescribed (LRA 2002, s 43(2)(d), and LRR 2003, r 91(1) and Sch 4), and should be used in the situations to which they apply.[1] Where there is no appropriate standard form of restriction, the registrar is authorised to approve an application for a restriction in terms drafted for the circumstances of the particular case, but may only do so if it appears to him that the terms of the proposed restriction are reasonable, and applying it would be straightforward and would not place an unreasonable burden on him (LRA 2002, s 43(3)). A non-standard restriction will therefore not be accepted if applying it would require the registry to decide any factual question to which the answer might not be clear.[2] It is considered that where a restriction is needed to reinforce a contractual obligation under an agreement between the registered proprietor and a third party, for example an obligation of the proprietor to ensure that a disponee of the land enters into a novation of the agreement with the third party,[3] the appropriate restriction will not be one specially worded to refer directly to performance of the proprietor's obligation, but one of the standard forms, requiring either the third party's certificate that the obligation has been complied with (LRR 2003, Sch 4, Form L), or simply the third party's consent (LRR 2003, Sch 4, Form N).[4] There are no standard forms of restriction to prevent *ultra vires* dispositions by local authorities, NHS trusts and other corporate bodies with limited capacity;[5] it is suggested[6] that the appropriate restriction in such cases will normally be one requiring any disposition to comply with the corporate body's constitution '*as evidenced by a certificate signed by its [proper officer eg] head of legal services*'.

---

[1]   See Land Registry Practice Guide 19, para 4.3.2.

[2]   Law Com no 271, para 6.50, refers to a restriction precluding any disposition until certain building works have been completed as an example of a form which will not be accepted because of the potential difficulty of applying it.

[3]   Such a provision may be used to protect a right to contributions to the upkeep of common parts of an estate, or a right to payment of 'overage' on a resale which realises development value.

[4]   It is suggested that the third party should not readily accept a restriction requiring only that the registered proprietor is to give him notice of any proposed disposition; compare para 7.45(6).

[5]   See the LRA 2002, s 26, by which 'owner's powers' are to be taken to be free from any limitation not reflected by an entry in the register or imposed by or under the LRA 2002; a limitation under any other statutory provision must be reflected by entering a restriction.

[6]   On the analogy of the LRR 2003, Sch 4, Form R, compliance with club rules.

7.44   The standard forms of restriction (LRR 2003, r 91(1) and Sch 4,) follow the principle that they only refer to an actual fact, or actual compliance with a legal requirement, if it will be clear from the terms of a disposition and the general law whether the fact exists or the requirement is satisfied. For example, in overreaching cases, Form A (applicable to trusts of land) in effect requires any capital money to be paid to two trustees or a trust corporation, and where the Settled Land Act 1925 applies, Forms G, H and I prevent registration of dispositions under which capital money arises unless it is paid to the trustees of the settlement. Similarly, the prescribed form of bankruptcy restriction (under the LRR 2003, r 166(1),) prohibits the registration of any disposition until the trustee in bankruptcy is registered as proprietor; and in freezing order and restraint order cases, Forms AA, BB, EE and FF require a further court order. Where the propriety of a disposition controlled by a restriction will depend on factual matters extraneous to the registration process, which the registry cannot itself verify, for the system to be workable the restriction has to be framed as requiring a *statement as to* the existence of the relevant fact or compliance with the relevant requirement. For example Form B requires a certificate by trustee proprietors as to compliance with specific limitations on their statutory powers, and Forms U to Y require a certificate by, or consent from, the Secretary of State, or other relevant authority, as to compliance with the provisions of the Housing Acts.

7.45 The standard forms can be classified as follows.

(1) Restrictions to ensure that overreaching procedures are followed: Form A, relating to a trust of land and preventing registration of a disposition by a sole trustee (not being a trust corporation) under which capital money arises; Forms G, H and I, relating to settled land.

(2) Restrictions requiring actual compliance with a specified enactment: Form D, relating to dispositions of parsonage, church or churchyard land; Form E, requiring dispositions of charity land to contain the necessary certificate under the Charities Act 1993, ss 36–39; Forms G, H and I, requiring compliance with the Settled Land Act 1925. A bankruptcy restriction (LRR 2003, r 166(1),) falls into this category, in that it requires the trustee in bankruptcy to be registered as proprietor of the bankrupt's land, as required by insolvency law.

(3) Restrictions requiring a third party's certificate as to compliance with, or consent under, a specified enactment: Forms U, V, W, X and Y require a certificate, or consent, from the relevant local authority, the Secretary of State, or the relevant housing association or registered social landlord, under various provisions of the Housing Acts.

(4) Restrictions requiring a statutory declaration or a certificate, by or on behalf of the disponor, of compliance with the terms of a private instrument: Forms B and C require declarations or conveyancers' certificates as to compliance with any limitations on the powers of trustees or personal representatives; Form R requires a certificate or other evidence of compliance with club rules. In these cases the certificate or declaration is made by or on behalf of a party interested in completing the disposition regulated by the restriction; there are criminal sanctions for making false statements (LRA 2002, ss 123–124).[1]

(5) Restrictions requiring a certificate of a third party as to compliance with the terms of a private instrument, or simply the third party's consent: Forms L, M, N, O, P, Q, S and T. If the third party refuses to give a required consent or certificate, and the proprietor contends that it should be given under whatever substantive legal relationship exists between them, that dispute will have to be resolved *either* in ordinary litigation between them, *or* on a reference to the adjudicator.[2]

(6)   Restrictions requiring the applicant's certificate that notice of the disposition has been given to a specified person: Form J requires a certificate that notice has been given to the trustee in bankruptcy of a party having a beneficial interest in the land; Form K requires a certificate that notice has been given to a party with the benefit of a charging order over a beneficial interest in the land.[3] The protection given by this form of restriction is similar to the effect of a caution against dealings under the LRA 1925, ss 54–55,[4] in that the party interested is given notice of the proposed dealing and has to take action to protect his interest. The notice is given by the applicant, not by the registry; there are criminal sanctions against deliberate misstatement in the certificate (LRA 2002, ss 123(1) and 124(1)), but the risk of the notice being lost in the post appears to be on the intended recipient.

(7)   Restrictions requiring a court order or the consent of the party applying for such an order: Forms AA to HH, relating to freezing orders, restraint orders, interim receiving orders, and applications for such orders.

It will always be necessary to consider whether the precise terms of a particular standard form of restriction will provide the protection needed in a particular case.

---

[1]   Offences of suppression of information with intent to conceal a claim or substantiate a false claim, and dishonestly inducing another to change or authorise a change in the register.

[2]   The likely course of events is that the proprietor will apply under the LRA 2002, s 41(2), and the LRR 2003, r 96, for an order disapplying the restriction; the third party will object under s 73(1), and if the objection is not groundless and the dispute cannot be resolved by agreement, the matter will be referred to the adjudicator under s 73(7). See para 7.57, and Chapter 15, paras 15.6–15.7, 15.27–15.28 and 15.37 et seq.

[3]   By the LRA 2002, s 42(4), a person who has the benefit of a charging order over an interest under a trust of land is treated as having a right or claim in relation to the land, which can be protected by a restriction under s 42(1)(c).

[4]   Prospectively repealed; see para 7.88.

Entering a restriction

7.46   A restriction may be entered in the register:[1]

(1)   by the registrar without any application for the entry having been made (LRA 2002, ss 42(1) and 44);[2]

(2)   on an application made by or with the consent of the registered proprietor or a person entitled to be registered as proprietor (LRA 2002, s 43(1)(a) and (b));[3]

(3)   on an application by any other person with a sufficient interest in the making of the entry (LRA 2002, s 43(1)(c), and LRR 2003, r 93);[4] or

(4)   pursuant to a court order (LRA 2002, s 46).[5]

¹   In the proprietorship register if it relates to the registered estate: LRR 2003, r 8(1)(d). If a restriction regulates dispositions of a registered charge, it is entered in the charges register in relation to that charge: LRR 2003, r 9(f). See also the LRA 2002, s 40(4).

²   Paras 7.47–7.48.

³   Para 7.50.

⁴   Para 7.51.

⁵   Paras 7.55–7.56.

7.47   The registrar may enter a restriction, if it appears to him to be appropriate for any of the specified statutory purposes (LRA 2002, s 42(1)), even if no application for the entry has been made; he must give the registered proprietor notice of any restriction which is entered without an application (LRA 2002, s 42(3)). If the proprietor does not accept that the entry should have been made, the matter cannot be referred to the adjudicator.[1] The Joint Report suggests[2] that the proprietor's remedy is by way of judicial review; but it is respectfully suggested that if the proprietor correctly contends that the entry should not have been made, removal of the entry from the register amounts to *'correcting a mistake'*,[3] and the proprietor can therefore bring an ordinary action in the Chancery Division of the High Court, or in the county court (LRA 2002, s 132(3)(a)), as an alternative to judicial review proceedings in the Administrative Court of the Queen's Bench Division.[4]

¹   The proprietor in such a case is not objecting to an *application to* the registrar, so the LRA 2002, s 73, does not apply.

²   Law Com no 271, para 6.45.

³   Within the LRA 2002, Sch 4, para 2(1)(a); see Chapter 14.

⁴   By the CPR rr 54.4 and 54.5, judicial review proceedings can only be brought with the court's permission, and must normally be begun within three months of the ground for the claim arising: it is submitted that these limitations are not necessarily appropriate to a claim brought, in substance, to protect a landowner's ability to deal freely with his property, particularly if the restriction in question was entered in the register on private law rather than public law grounds.

7.48   Certain restrictions are obligatory. If two or more persons are registered as joint proprietors of registered land, the registrar must enter a restriction in Form A[1] to ensure that overreachable interests will be overreached. As soon as practicable after registration of a bankruptcy order (under the Land Charges Act 1972), the registrar must enter a bankruptcy restriction[2] in relation to any registered estate or charge which appears to him to be affected by the order. Where any other enactment requires a restriction to be entered, it must be in the form specified in the LRR 2003 or in the relevant enactment, or if none is specified then in such form as the registrar directs (LRR 2003, r 95(1)). Forms U to Y (LRR 2003, Sch 4) are specified (LRR 2003, r 95(2)(b)–(h),) as the forms of restriction to be used under the Housing Acts 1985, 1988 and 1996 and the Local Government and Housing Act 1989.

---

1   LRA 2002, s 44(1), and LRR 2003, rr 91(1) and 95(2)(a) and Sch 4. It appears that no such restriction will be entered if the material available to the registrar shows that the proprietors are beneficial joint tenants and the survivor will be beneficially entitled to the entire interest and able to give a good receipt for the proceeds of any sale: see Land Registry Practice Guide 19, para 4.2.2.
2   LRA 2002, s 86(4), and LRR 2003, r 166(1). By r 166(2), the registrar must give notice to the registered proprietor of the making of the entry.

Application for a restriction

7.49   An application for a restriction must be made in Form RX1 (LRR 2003, r 92(1)), *except* that an application may be made for a standard form of restriction in the 'additional provisions' panel of any of the prescribed forms of 'transfer of whole', 'transfer of part' or assent (LRR 2003, r 92(7)(a)), in panel 7 of Form CH1 (LRR 2003, r 92(7)(b)), or in an 'approved charge' (LRR 2003, r 92(7)(c)).[1] Form RX1 also does not have to be used for an application to give effect to a court order for the entry of a restriction (LRA 2002, s 46, and LRR 2003, r 92(8)).

---

1   An 'approved charge' is one the form of which, including the application for the restriction, has first been approved by the registrar: r 92(10). See Chapter 8, para 8.13.

7.50   The application must contain full details of the required restriction (LRR 2003, r 92(2)(a)), and an address for service (LRR 2003, r 198,) of any person to whom the restriction requires notice to be given or whose consent or certificate is required, or who is named in the restriction if it is in a standard form (LRR 2003, r 92(2)(b)). A registered proprietor, or a person who is entitled to be registered as proprietor, can give his consent to the application in Form RX1 (panel 15). If he does not do so, either his consent (LRR 2003, r 92(2)(c)), or a conveyancer's certificate that the conveyancer holds such consent, must accompany the application (LRR 2003, r 92(6)); such a certificate can be given in Form RX1, panel 11. An application by or with the consent of a person entitled to be registered as proprietor must be accompanied by evidence to satisfy the registrar of that entitlement (LRR 2003, r 92(2)(d)), which can take the form of a conveyancer's certificate that he is satisfied of that person's entitlement, and that *either* he holds the originals of the documents evidencing that entitlement, *or* an application is pending at the land registry for that person to be registered as proprietor (LRR 2003, r 92(5)); the certificate can be given in Form RX1, panel 12. An application by a person claiming a *'sufficient interest'* (LRA 2002, s 43(1)(c),)[1] in the making of the entry must be supported by a statement identifying that interest (LRR 2003, r 92(2)(e), (3)); the statement can be made in Form RX1, panel 13.

---

1   See para 7.51.

7.51 Certain classes of person are taken, by LRR 2003, r 93,[1] to have a sufficient interest to apply for particular restrictions; the rule is framed on the principle that a person who has an entitlement to restrain or control dispositions, or particular classes of disposition, has a sufficient interest to apply for the restriction appropriate to that entitlement. Thus a beneficiary of a trust of land, and a person interested in the administration of the estate of a deceased person where that estate includes land, has a sufficient interest to apply for a restriction reflecting the inability of a sole trustee (not being a trust corporation) to give a valid receipt for capital money, or reflecting any other limitation on the trustees' or personal representatives' powers of disposition (LRR 2003, r 93(a)–(d)). Similarly, anyone who has obtained or is applying for a freezing order (LRR 2003, r 93(h), (i) and (r)), a restraint order (LRR 2003, r 93(l) and (m)), or an interim receiving order (LRR 2003, r 93(u) and (v)), or who is interested in a beneficial interest under a trust of land as trustee in bankruptcy of the original beneficiary, or as a judgment creditor with a charging order (LRR 2003, r 93(j) and (k)), has a sufficient interest to apply for the appropriate restriction. The precise terms of the rule will have to be considered in every case in which any paragraph of it may be applicable, but it is not exhaustive, and a person who can demonstrate an entitlement to control any or all dispositions by the registered proprietor can apply for an appropriate restriction without having to demonstrate that he falls within one of the specifically prescribed classes of applicant.[2]

---

[1] Made under the LRA 2002, s 43(2)(c).

[2] A person entitled to a right of pre-emption is not within any paragraph of the LRR 2003, r 93, but his right to apply for a restriction is clear. It is thought that r 93 may have been framed to remove doubts in relation to rights arising from non-consensual relationships, or in situations in which a consensual relationship has become hostile, where there may be a particularly high probability of the registered proprietor not consenting to an application for a restriction.

7.52 The right to apply for the entry of a restriction, and the right to object to such an application, must not be exercised without reasonable cause (LRA 2002, s 77(1)(b) and (c)). Any person who suffers damage from a breach of this duty has a statutory cause of action against the party in breach (LRA 2002, s 77(2)). If, before the commencement of the LRA 2002, a person lodged a caution (under the LRA 1925, s 54,) in respect of any estate, right, interest or claim, he may only apply to enter a restriction in respect of that matter if he also applies to withdraw the caution (LRA 2002, Sch 12, para 17).

When an application for a restriction must be made

7.53 There are certain situations in which the making of an application for a restriction is mandatory (LRR 2003, r 94, made under the LRA 2002, s 43(2)(a)); their common feature is that an application must be made when an event happens in consequence of which the registered proprietor ceases to be entitled to the land beneficially, or becomes subject to limitations on his powers to dispose of it, but there is no disposition of the land to be registered or, although there is such a disposition, the need for a restriction does not automatically appear from the documents necessary to secure its registration. This principle applies to the following cases.

(1)   The proprietor must apply for a restriction in Form A where land becomes subject to a trust of land, otherwise than on a registrable disposition, or there is a change in the trusts on which it is held, and the survivor of joint proprietors will not be able to give a good receipt for capital money (LRR 2003, r 94(1)(a) and (b)); a severance of a beneficial joint tenancy is a change in the trusts which has that effect.

(2)   Similarly a sole or last surviving trustee of a trust of land must apply for a Form A restriction if he acquires land by a registrable disposition or by a transaction which triggers first registration (LRR 2003, r 94(2)).

(3)   When a personal representative of a deceased proprietor applies to be registered, he must apply for a restriction in Form C if his powers in relation to the land have been limited by the deceased's will or by a variation, by the parties entitled to the estate, of the intestacy rules (LRR 2003, r 94(3)).

(4)   The proprietor, or a person applying to be registered as first proprietor, of land, including in each case the personal representatives of a deceased sole or last surviving trustee (LRR 2003, r 94(7)), must apply for a restriction in Form B if, on the making of a declaration of trust, or on a change in the trusts affecting the land, or on its acquisition by trustees as first proprietors, the trustees' powers are limited (LRR 2003, r 94(4), (5)).

(5)   The provisions of the LRR 2003, r 94, requiring applications for restrictions in relation to limitations on trustees' powers, do not apply to land held on charitable, ecclesiastical or public trusts (LRR 2003, r 94(6), disapplying sub-rules (3), (4) and (5)). However, an application must be made to register a restriction in Form E if land is transferred to a non-exempt charity by a disposition triggering first registration, a registrable disposition or a vesting order, unless the restriction is already registered or the documents effecting the disposition show that the land belongs to such a charity (LRR 2003, rr 94(8) and 176(2), (4)), or if registered land is held by or in trust for a corporation which becomes a non-exempt charity (LRR 2003, rr 94(8) and 176(3), (4)).

(6)   Similarly where land is vested in the official custodian by virtue of an order under the Charities Act 1993, s 18, an application to register him as proprietor, either on first

registration or following a registrable disposition, must be accompanied by an application for a restriction in Form F (LRR 2003, rr 94(8) and 178(2)).

Notifiable applications

7.54 The registrar must give notice of any *'notifiable'* application for a restriction, and of the right to object to it, to the registered proprietor of the estate, or charge, to which the application relates (LRA 2002, s 45(1)(a)).[1] A *'notifiable'* application is defined by LRA 2002, s 45(3), as one which is not made by or with the consent of the registered proprietor or a person entitled to be registered as proprietor, is not one which rules require to be made, (ie an application under the LRR 2003, r 94,[2] is not notifiable,) and does not relate to a restriction reflecting a limitation on dispositions imposed by an order or undertaking: the result is that the proprietor must be told of any application for a restriction which is neither consensual nor mandatory, and is therefore potentially contentious. The registrar may not determine such an application before the end of the period prescribed for this purpose, unless the proprietor has either exercised his right to object to it (under the LRA 2002, s 73), or given the registrar notice that he does not intend to do so (LRA 2002, s 45(2)). The prescribed period is the period ending at 12 noon on the fifteenth business day after the *issue* of the notice (LRR 2003, r 92(9)).[3] If the proprietor objects to the application, the matter must be referred to the adjudicator if the objection does not appear to the registrar to be groundless and cannot be disposed of by agreement after notice of it has been given to the applicant (LRA 2002, s 73(5)–(7)).[4]

---

[1] Para (b) of that subsection allows rules to provide for the notice also to be given to other persons, but the power has not been exercised.
[2] Para 7.53.
[3] The time is computed from the date on which the registry sends the notice, and not from when it is taken under r 199(4) to be served.
[4] See Chapter 15.

Court order for entry of restriction

7.55 The court can make an order requiring the registrar to enter a restriction, if it appears to be necessary or desirable to do so for the purpose of protecting a right or claim relating to registered land (LRA 2002, s 46(1)).[1] This does not permit a restriction to protect the priority of an interest protected or capable of being protected by a notice (LRA 2002, s 46(2)).[2] The court can direct that a restriction ordered by the court is to have *'overriding priority'*, which means (LRA 2002, ss 46(3) and 72(4),) that it overrides the protection conferred on (for example) an estate contract by a priority search

(LRA 2002, s 72(1), (2), and LRR 2003, rr 147–154).[3] The application to enter the restriction on the register should be made in Form AP1 (LRR 2003, rr 13(1) and 92(8), disapplying the requirement in r 92(1) to use Form RX1). The registrar must make such entry as will ensure that the register shows the priority of the restriction ordered (LRA 2002, s 46(4), and LRR 2003, r 100(1)), and must give notice to any person with the benefit of an official search of which the priority period has not expired when the entry is made, unless he is satisfied that such notice is not necessary (LRR 2003, r 100(2)).

---

[1]   Forms AA to HH in the LRR 2003, Sch 4, are standard forms relating to court orders and applications for orders, but other forms may be used in appropriate cases if they comply with the LRA 2002, s 43(3); see Land Registry Practice Guide 19, para 4.6.1.
[2]   Compare the LRA 2002, s 42(2), and para 7.41.
[3]   See paras 7.82–7.87.

7.56   The court can impose terms and conditions on an order for *'overriding priority'* (LRA 2003, s 46(5)). It is suggested that if *'overriding priority'* is ordered in order to prevent (for example) a freezing order being stultified by completion of a contract for sale, but the applicant for the order does not have a *proprietary* interest competing with that of the contracting purchaser, and the latter has acted throughout in good faith, it will not be appropriate to defeat the contract entirely. It is therefore submitted that in addition to requiring a cross-undertaking in damages from the applicant,[1] the court should include provisions in its order to allow the contract to be completed on terms ensuring that the proceeds of sale are safeguarded (if necessary by payment into court).

---

[1]   See CPR Pt 25, PD 25, para 5.1(1), and Sch B, para (1) in the annexed form of freezing order, and compare Law Com no 271, para 6.53.

Disapplying or modifying restrictions

7.57   The registrar has power to make an order disapplying, or making specified modifications to, a restriction, in relation either to a specified disposition or to dispositions of a specified kind (LRA 2002, s 41(2)). Such an order can only be made on an application by a person who appears to the registrar to have a sufficient interest in the restriction (LRA 2002, s 41(3)). It is considered

   (1)   that the registered proprietor of the land has such an interest if he wishes to enter into a disposition which is unobjectionable in principle but circumstances have arisen in which it is not possible to comply with the restriction, for example because it requires a consent to the disposition from a named individual who has disappeared or a company which has been dissolved,[1] and

(2) that the power to disapply or modify a restriction will be used to preserve, so far as is practicable and appropriate in altered circumstances, the protection the entry was made to secure.

The statutory duty to act reasonably does not apply to an application to disapply or modify a restriction (LRA 2002, s 77(1)(b), refers only to applying for the *entry* of a restriction), but it is considered that someone who makes such an application which is disputed, and ultimately fails, can at least be made liable for the costs of proceedings in court or before the adjudicator.[2]

---

[1] Compare Law Com no 271, para 6.37.

[2] Compare the Adjudicator to HM Land Registry (Practice and Procedure) Rules 2003, SI 2003/2171, r 42.

7.58 An application for an order disapplying or modifying a restriction must be made in Form RX2 (LRR 2003, r 96(1)), which must give details of the order sought, the applicant's interest in the restriction, the disposition or kinds of disposition affected, and the reasons why the applicant considers the order should be made (LRR 2003, r 96(2)). The registrar may require further evidence from the applicant, and may make such further enquiries and serve such notices as he thinks fit in order to determine the application (LRR 2003, r 96(3), (4)). A note of the terms of any order made must be entered in the register (LRR 2003, r 96(5)).

Removal of restrictions from the register

7.59 The registrar can remove a restriction from the register if it has become superfluous (LRA 2002, Sch 4, para 5(d)), for example if the restriction relates only to dispositions during a specified period which has expired, or if the entire interest in the registered estate has been transferred (in accordance with the terms of the restriction if applicable) to a new proprietor whose ability to deal with it is not subject to the limitations applicable to the former proprietor. The registrar is also required to cancel any restriction protecting an interest under a trust of land if, on registering a disposition of the land, he is satisfied that it is no longer subject to that trust (LRR 2003, r 99).

7.60 A restriction may also be cancelled on an application made for the purpose and accompanied by evidence that the restriction is no longer required (LRR 2003, r 97(1), (2), requiring Form RX3 to be used). The registrar is entitled to require further documents or evidence to be supplied, or to require notice of the application to be given to other persons appearing to be interested (LRR 2003, r 17), but is not required to do so. If he is satisfied that the restriction is no longer required, he must cancel it (LRR 2003, r 97(3)). An application for cancellation is the only way of obtaining the removal of a mandatory restriction.[1]

---

[1]   A mandatory restriction cannot be withdrawn by consent: see para 7.61.

7.61   A restriction can be withdrawn on an application made by or with the consent of all the persons appearing to the registrar to have an interest in it (LRA 2002, s 47, and LRR 2003, r 98(1), (2), prescribing Form RX4), including in particular any person specified in the restriction whose consent to a disposition it requires, or to whom it requires notice to be given, or from whom it requires a certificate (LRR 2003, r 98(3)–(5)). The registrar may accept a conveyancer's certificate that the conveyancer holds any of the necessary consents to the application (LRR 2003, r 98(7)). Any such consents, or a conveyancer's certificate, can be given in the application form (Form RX4, panels 13 and 11 respectively). An application for withdrawal by consent cannot be made, however, in respect of:

(1)   a restriction reflecting a limitation on the proprietor's powers of disposition imposed by statute or by the general law;

(2)   a restriction entered on an application the making of which was mandatory;

(3)   a restriction which the registrar was obliged to enter;

(4)   a restriction reflecting a limitation on the registered proprietor's powers under an order or undertaking; or

(5)   a restriction ordered by the court to be entered.

See LRR 2003, r 98(6)(a)–(e). If it is desired to remove a restriction within any of these categories, an application must be made to cancel it, on evidence to satisfy the registrar that it is no longer required (LRR 2003, r 97).[1]

---

[1]   Considered in para 7.60.

UNREGISTERED INTERESTS BINDING ON REGISTERED DISPONEES FOR VALUE

7.62   When a registrable disposition for valuable consideration is completed by registration, the priority of any interest affecting the estate or charge disposed of is protected, and the disponee takes subject to it, if it falls within any of the paragraphs of the LRA 2002, Sch 3, at the time of registration,[1] unless it has been the subject of a notice in the register at any time since the commencement of the LRA 2002 (see ss 29(3) and 30(3)).[2] The list of interests in Sch 3 is similar, but not identical, to the list in Sch 1 of unregistered interests which bind the first registered proprietor.[3] Schedule 3 includes:

(1)   a lease granted for a term not exceeding seven years from the date of the grant, unless it falls within one of the categories of shorter leases which are required to be registered (Sch 3, para 1);[4]

(2)   a 'PPP lease' (LRA 2002, s 90; Greater London Authority Act 1999, s 218),[5] ie a lease created for 'public-private partnerships relating to transport in London';

(3)   an interest belonging at the time of the disposition to a person in actual occupation, so far as relating to the land he occupies (Sch 3, para 2), but not including:[6]

    (a)   an interest under a Settled Land Act settlement;

    (b)   an interest not disclosed on inquiry, when the person entitled to it could reasonably have been expected to disclose it;

    (c)   an interest not actually known to the disponee, if it would not have been obvious, on a reasonably careful inspection of the land at the time of the disposition, that the person entitled to the interest was in occupation; and

    (d)   a reversionary lease which has not yet taken effect in possession;

(4)   an interest of a person who has been continuously in receipt of the rents and profits of the land since before the commencement of the LRA 2002, unless that person did not disclose it in answer to an inquiry when he could reasonably have been expected to do so (Sch 3, para 2A);[7]

(5)   a legal easement or profit à prendre which is known to the disponee, or is obvious on inspection, or has been exercised in the year ending with the day of the disposition, or was an overriding interest under LRA 1925 immediately before the commencement of LRA 2002 (Sch 3, para 3);[8]

(6)   a customary or public right (Sch 3, paras 4 and 5);[9]

(7)   a local land charge (Sch 3, para 6);[10]

(8)   coal and certain other mineral rights (Sch 3, paras 7, 8 and 9);[11]

(9)   for ten years from the coming into force of the LRA 2002 (see s 117(1)), a franchise, manorial right, Crown rent, non-statutory right as to an embankment or sea or river wall, and a right to payment in lieu of tithe (Sch 3, paras 10–14);[12]

(10) for three years from the coming into force of the LRA 2002, a right to the land arising before that date by virtue of the Limitation Act 1980 and the LRA 1925, s 75(1) (Sch 3, para 15);[13]

(11) for ten years from the coming into force of the LRA 2002, a right in respect of the repair of a church chancel (Sch 3, para 16).[14]

A disposition which triggers the requirement of compulsory registration (LRA 2002, s 4,)[15] may be followed by a further dealing with the land before it has actually been registered. The LRA 2002 applies to such a further dealing as if it had taken place after the date of first registration (LRR 2003, r 38),[16] and if that dealing is itself a registrable disposition, it therefore takes effect subject to any unregistered interests within Sch 3; Sch 1 does not apply.

---

[1]   LRA 2002, s 29(1), (2)(a)(ii), registered estate, and s 30(1), (2)(a)(ii), registered charge. If such an interest is in fact protected by a notice on the register (for example under the LRA 2002, s 37(1), and the LRR 2003, r 57, considered in paras 7.25–7.26), these provisions do not apply, but the interest is binding under s 29(2)(a)(i) or s 30(2)(a)(i).

[2]   Such an interest, once registered, cannot regain overriding status if it is removed from the register.

[3]   See paras 7.7–7.16.

[4]   See Chapter 6, paras 6.21–6.23. LRA 2002, Sch 12, para 12, provides that Sch 3, para 1, is to be taken to include a lease granted before the commencement of the LRA 2002 for a term not exceeding 21 years, which was an overriding interest under the LRA 1925, s 70(1)(k).

[5]   LRA 2002, s 90(5), provides that Sch 3 has effect as if it included a paragraph referring to a PPP lease; this preserves the effect of the LRA 1925, s 70(1)(kk), inserted by the Greater London Authority Act 1999, s 219(7).

[6]   The test to be satisfied if an interest is to fall within this paragraph is stricter than that under Sch 1, para 2. See paras 7.67–7.73.

[7]   Inserted by the LRA 2002, Sch 12, para 8; see paras 7.74–7.76. There is no equivalent provision in Sch 1.

[8]   The test is stricter than that under Sch 1, para 3. See Chapter 9, paras 9.19–9.25 and 9.27–9.28.

[9]   See paras 7.11 and 7.78.

[10]   See paras 7.12 and 7.78 and Chapter 8, paras 8.21 and 8.27.

[11]   See paras 7.13 and 7.78.

[12]   See paras 7.14 and 7.79, and Chapter 12, paras 12.12, 12.15 and 12.17. The interests in Sch 1, paras 10–14, were all overriding interests under the LRA 1925, s 70(1): paras (b), (d), (e) and (j).

[13]   Temporarily inserted by the LRA 2002, Sch 12, para 11; see Chapter 13, para 13.30.

[14]   Temporarily inserted by the Land Registration Act 2002 (Transitional Provisions) (No 2) Order 2003, SI 2003/2431; see paras 7.14 and 7.79.

[15]   See Chapter 4.

[16]   Made under the LRA 2002, Sch 10, para 1.

7.63   The policy of the LRA 2002 is to make the register, so far as possible, a comprehensive record of the title,[1] and for that purpose to reduce the unregistered interests which are binding on successive proprietors to those which it is not reasonably practicable to protect by registration.[2] Several specific provisions contribute to achieving this objective:

   (1)   certain categories of interest will cease to have overriding effect ten years after the commencement of the LRA 2002 (see s 117(1) and Schs 1 and 3, paras 10–14 and 16);[3]

   (2)   expressly granted easements can only be effective as legal easements if they are registered (LRA 2002, s 27(2)(d)),[4] and therefore cannot have overriding effect; the introduction of electronic conveyancing[5] will make this principle applicable to all interests which are simultaneously created and registered on-line;

   (3)   a person applying to register a registrable disposition is required to inform the registrar of all interests within the LRA 2002, Sch 3, which are within his actual knowledge, affect the estate to which the application relates, and are

capable of being protected by a notice,[6] and the registrar may enter a notice in the register in respect of any interest so disclosed (LRA 2002, s 71(b), and LRR 2003, r 57(1), (5)), which will thereafter be protected by the notice;

(4)   the registrar is authorised to enter a notice in respect of any unregistered interest within the LRA 2002, Sch 1, which appears to him to affect a registered estate and is capable of being protected by a notice (LRA 2002, s 37);[7]

(5)   an interest which has been protected by a notice at any time since the commencement of the LRA 2002 cannot subsequently have overriding effect under Sch 3 if the notice is removed from the register (LRA 2002, ss 29(3) and 30(3)).

---

[1]   See Law Com no 271, paras 1.5 and 8.1.
[2]   See Law Com no 271, paras 8.6 and 8.53; a requirement to register an interest in land is more likely to be recognised (and complied with) if the interest is created by a deliberate, documented transaction than if it arises informally.
[3]   See paras 7.14 and 7.79.
[4]   See Chapter 9, paras 9.11 and 9.20.
[5]   See Chapter 3.
[6]   See Chapter 5, para 5.19, and Appendix 1, Part B.
[7]   See paras 7.25–7.26.

7.64   The LRA 2002, ss 28–30 and Sch 3, do not raise the technical difficulties which existed under the LRA 1925, ss 20, 23 and 70, in relation to adverse interests coming into existence in the 'registration gap' (in 'paper' conveyancing) between completion of a registrable disposition for value and the effective date of its registration.[1] The position under the LRA 2002 is that:

(1)   every adverse interest affecting the land (or charge) immediately before completion and falling within any paragraph of Sch 3 is binding on the disponee if it still exists when the disposition is registered (LRA 2002, ss 29(1) and (2)(a)(ii) and 30(1) and (2)(a)(ii));[2]

(2)   an adverse interest existing at completion, and not falling within any other paragraph of Sch 3, is not protected by para 2, so as to bind the disponee, if the person to whom it belongs is not in occupation of the land at the date of the disposition, even if he or she goes into occupation during the 'registration gap' and stays there until the effective date of registration;[3] and

(3)   any adverse interest which arises or is created after completion of the disposition but before the effective date of registration takes priority over the disponee's interest if, but only if, it is entitled to that priority under the general law.[4]

---

[1]   *Abbey National Building Society v Cann* [1991] 1 AC 56.
[2]   Subsection (1) of each section postpones an adverse interest which affects the estate immediately before the disposition unless it is 'protected' within sub-s (2) 'at the time of registration'.

[3]   In those circumstances the adverse interest is not one *'belonging **at the time of the disposition** to a person in actual occupation'* (emphasis added) within Sch 3, para 2.
[4]   The LRA 2002, ss 29(1) and 30(1), are not engaged, because they apply only to interests existing *'immediately before'* the disposition; the priority of an interest arising after that time is therefore governed by s 28, and is not affected by the disposition, whether or not the disposition or the interest is registered; see paras 7.17–7.18.

7.65   It is considered that where interests are created by, or arise against, the registered proprietor between completion and registration of a registrable charge or lease, they will normally not be entitled to priority as against the chargee or tenant, but will take effect against the proprietor's equity of redemption or reversion. However, some local land charges are capable of taking priority over all other interests in the land affected;[1] and if the statutory power of leasing is not excluded (Law of Property Act 1925, s 99(1), (13)), a chargor can grant certain leases which are binding on the chargee.

A question may arise as to the priority of an interest of a third party ('X') who is not in occupation when the registered proprietor ('O') completes a transfer on sale to a purchaser ('P'), if X contrives to enter into occupation before P completes a transfer on sub-sale[2] to a sub-purchaser ('S'), (without having previously applied to register O's transfer, or taken possession,) and S then applies to register both transfers, with X still in occupation. It may be contended that X has priority over S because he is in occupation at completion (and at registration[3]) of the disposition by P to S. However, it is submitted that the better view is that the registration of S as proprietor satisfies the registration requirements in relation to the transfer by O to P (LRA 2002, Sch 2, para 2(1)),[4] so that X's interest is postponed to that of P because X was not in occupation at the date of that transfer (LRA 2002, s 29(1)),[5] and therefore S, as P's successor in title, also has priority over X.

[1]   Compare Chapter 8, para 8.21.
[2]   Relying on the LRA 2002, s 24(b), allowing a person entitled to be registered as proprietor to exercise 'owner's powers'.
[3]   See para 7.68.
[4]   The registration requirements in the case of a transfer are satisfied by entering the transferee 'or his successor in title' in the register as proprietor.
[5]   See para 7.64, point (2).

Leases of registered land

7.66   Leases which are not registrable dispositions,[1] and PPP leases,[2] are considered further elsewhere in this work.

[1]   Chapter 6, paras 6.21–6.23.
[2]   Chapter 12, paras 12.26–12.27.

Interests of persons in actual occupation

7.67   The LRA 2002, Sch 3, para 2, specifies the conditions which must be satisfied if an interest belonging to a person in actual occupation of registered land is to be binding, by reason of that occupation, on a registered disponee of that land for value. Some of these conditions are the same as those applicable on first registration, under Sch 1, para 2, but others are significantly different and more stringent. The common features of the two versions of para 2 are that:[1]

  (1)   the case-law under the LRA 1925 on the meaning of *'actual occupation'* continues to be applicable;

  (2)   the protection extends to all of an occupier's proprietary rights and not merely the interest conferring the right to occupy;

  (3)   only rights relating to the actual land occupied, and not any rights over other land in the same registered title, are protected by occupation; and

  (4)   an interest under a trust of land, but not an interest under a 'strict settlement' within the Settled Land Act 1925, can be so protected.

---

[1]   These features, and the main relevant authorities under the LRA 1925, are considered above, in para 7.9(a), (b), (c) and (g).

7.68   An interest falls within the LRA 2002, Sch 3, para 2, if it belongs to the occupier *'at the time of the disposition'* in relation to which an issue of priority arises; the significance of this requirement, in relation to the 'registration gap', has already been considered.[1] It is submitted that the occupier must be in occupation both

  (1)   at the time of the disposition, to comply with the words of Sch 3, para 2, and

  (2)   at the effective date of registration, to comply with the requirement of the LRA 2002, s 29(1) and (2)(a)(ii), that the interest must be *'protected'* by falling within one of the paragraphs of Sch 3 *'at the time of registration'*,

if his interest is to retain priority against the disponee.

---

[1]   Paragraphs 7.64–7.65.

When occupiers' rights are not protected

7.69   A right of a person in actual occupation is not protected under the LRA 2002, Sch 3, para 2, if inquiry is made of him before the disposition and he does not disclose that right when he could reasonably have been expected to do so (LRA 2002, Sch 3, para 2(b)). This is similar to the rule under the LRA 1925, s 70(1)(g), protecting an occupier's rights *'save where enquiry is made of such person and the rights are not disclosed'*; but the protection of a right which is not disclosed in answer to an inquiry, if the occupier *'could not reasonably have been expected'* to disclose it, is a change in the law. It is suggested that whether an occupier could *'reasonably have been expected'* to disclose a particular right must depend at least in part on the terms of the inquiry made, and that the safe course for an intending disponee is to ask the occupier not only *'By what right are you in occupation of this land?'*, but also *'Do you have any other rights in relation to this land?'*, and possibly even *'Does any relevant document accurately record what you agreed with the proprietor?'*.[1] Nevertheless, it is also thought that the safe course for the occupier is to make full disclosure of all his rights, even if an inquiry is made in restricted terms.[2]

---

[1]   Compare *Blacklocks v JB Developments (Godalming) Ltd* [1982] Ch 183: a right to rectification of a conveyance was held to be an overriding interest within the LRA 1925, s 70(1)(g).
[2]   It appears to be in both the disponee's and the occupier's interest to minimise the risk of dispute over questions such as whether an occupier who is in occupation as a tenant *'could reasonably have been expected'* to disclose a right of pre-emption, or a rectification claim, as well as his tenancy agreement.

7.70   An occupier's interest is excluded from protection under the LRA 2002, Sch 3, para 2 if his occupation *'would not have been obvious on a reasonably careful inspection of the land at the time of the disposition'* (LRA 2002, Sch 3, para 2(c)(i)), unless the disponee actually knows of that interest at that time (LRA 2002, Sch 3, para 2(c)(ii)). The purpose of this exclusion is to restrict para 2 to interests which amount to 'patent' defects in title, and are therefore not subject to a vendor of land's contractual obligation to disclose 'latent' defects.[1] Under the general law a 'patent' defect is one which *'arises either to the eye, or by necessary implication from something which is visible to the eye'*.[2] The effect of the requirement that the occupation must be *'obvious'* is thus to make constructive notice to the disponee insufficient to protect the occupier's interest.

---

[1]   See Law Com no 271, para 8.62.
[2]   *Yandle & Sons v Sutton* [1922] 2 Ch 199 at 210.

7.71   It is considered that the occupation of someone other than the proprietor, such as the proprietor's spouse, is *'obvious'* if a person attentively viewing the whole of the property would or should realise that the proprietor is not the only person using it.[1] If a person's occupation is not *'obvious on a reasonably careful inspection'*, the fact that the disponee nevertheless knows of that occupation is not, without more, enough to protect the occupier's interest:[2] the disponee must actually know of the interest itself (LRA 2002, Sch 3, para 2(c)(ii)). It is suggested, however, that an intending disponee who actually knows the land is occupied by someone other than, or in addition to, the registered proprietor, but does not know what right (if any) the occupier has, will be unwise to rely on being able to establish that such occupation is not *'obvious'*, and the safe course in such circumstances is to ask both the proprietor and the occupier to clarify the latter's status. Any interests which either of them may disclose will bind the disponee because he knows of them, and will normally be entered on the register when the disposition is registered (LRA 2002, ss 37 and 71(b), and LRR 2003, r 57),[3] so that they will bind subsequent registered proprietors as registered rather than as overriding interests.

[1] Occupation concurrently with the proprietor is capable of being *'actual occupation'*: see *Hodgson v Marks* [1971] Ch 892, and para 7.9(a).
[2] It is respectfully submitted that the contrary statement in Law Com no 271, para 8.62, is erroneous.
[3] See paras 7.26 and 7.63(3).

7.72 The LRA 2002, Sch 3, para 2, does not protect a lease granted to take effect in possession more than three months after the date of the grant, if it has not taken effect in possession at the time of the disposition of the superior interest which raises an issue of priority (LRA 2002, Sch 3, para 2(d)). This reflects the requirement that such a lease must be completed by registration, even if it grants a term of less than seven years, in order to operate at law (LRA 2002, s 27(2)(b)(ii)).[1]

[1] See Chapter 6, paras 6.21, 6.60 and 6.61.

7.73 The LRA 2002 does not alter the principle that an interest is not automatically binding on a registered disponee by reason only of the fact that the person entitled to it is actually (and obviously) in occupation of the land affected. Such an interest will be overreached, for example, by a disposition which is effective for that purpose under the general law,[1] or may be postponed to a charge securing a loan made to fund the proprietor's purchase of the property, if to the occupier's knowledge the property could not have been acquired without that finance.[2]

[1] *City of London Building Society v Flegg* [1988] AC 54, HL.
[2] See *Bristol and West Building Society v Henning* [1985] 2 All ER 606.

Receipt of rents and profits

7.74 The LRA 2002, Sch 3, para 2A,[1] applies to an interest which was an overriding interest immediately before the commencement of the LRA 2002 by virtue of a person's receipt of rents and profits, unless inquiry is made of that person before the disposition and he fails to disclose that interest when he could reasonably have been expected to do so (LRA 2002, Sch 3, para 2A(1)). This preserves the status of such interests under the LRA 1925, s 70(1)(g), but only for so long as any such interest would have continued, under the previous law, to be an overriding interest by virtue of receipt of rents and profits (LRA 2002, Sch 3, para 2A(2)). The protection of a right which is not disclosed in answer to an inquiry, if the person in receipt of rents could not *'reasonably have been expected'* to disclose it, is a change in the law, corresponding with that made in relation to occupiers' rights (LRA 2002, Sch 3, para 2(b)). It is thought that considerations similar to those discussed above[2] apply to the question of what a person in receipt of rents can reasonably be expected to disclose.

---

[1]   Inserted in Sch 3 by the LRA 2002, Sch 12, para 8, as a transitional provision.
[2]   See para 7.69.

7.75   It is thought that interests for which 'receipt of rents and profits' is the only available protection will be comparatively rare. Paragraph 2A can only apply to an unregistered interest belonging to someone who is not himself in occupation of the land, but is receiving the income; and it is only relevant to a question of the priority of that interest on a disposition of a superior registered[1] estate. If the interest of such a person at the commencement of the LRA 2002 is a lease granted for a term of less than 21 years, that will override registered dispositions independently of para 2A; see LRA 2002, Sch 12, para 12, preserving the effect of the LRA 1925, s 70(1)(k), in relation to leases in existence at the commencement of the LRA 2002. An unregistered lease for more than 21 years will probably have been granted before first registration of the superior interest,[2] and is likely to have been noted on the title to that interest when it was registered. It is possible that an agreement for a lease was left uncompleted, and was not protected by any registered entry, before the commencement of the LRA 2002, with the contracting tenant receiving the rents under sublettings continuously from that time until registration of a disposition of the superior interest, or that a sole trustee of a trust of land was registered as proprietor, without an appropriate restriction, before that time, with a beneficiary under the trust receiving the rents from then until registration of a disposition by the trustee; but such situations are believed to be uncommon.

---

[1]   The LRA 2002, Sch 1, does not contain any equivalent provision applicable on first registration of a superior unregistered estate.
[2]   Unless it is a lease for less than 40 years granted out of a registered estate before the commencement of the LRA 1986, s 2: see the LRA 1925, s 123, as originally enacted, and Chapter 6, para 6.49.

7.76   The LRA 2002, Sch 3, para 2A(2), permanently terminates the protection of an interest under that paragraph if the person entitled to it ceases to receive rents and profits. This will occur if an occupational lease expires and the tenant vacates, so that there is a void period;[1] or (it is thought) if the tenant does not vacate but a renewed lease is not granted until after the expiration of the original term, unless in fact rent continues to be paid pending the renewal. If a new occupational lease is granted to a new tenant without any intervening void period, it is thought that protection continues, provided at least a nominal rent is reserved (and paid) for any concessionary 'fitting-out' period allowed to the new tenant.[2]

---

[1]   Even if the 'landlord' goes into actual occupation of the property, within Sch 3, para 2, para 2A does not revive on a re-letting.
[2]   It is thought that if a concessionary period is entirely rent-free, protection under para 2A will cease: compare *Strand Securities Ltd v Caswell* [1965] Ch 958.

Easements and profits à prendre

7.77   The extent to which easements can override registered dispositions for value, under the LRA 2002, Sch 3, para 3, is considered in the chapter on easements.[1] For present purposes the most important consideration relating to easements is that they should be registered, if it is practicable to do so, against both the dominant and the servient land.

---

[1]   Chapter 9, paras 9.19–9.25 and 9.27–9.28.

Customary and public rights, local land charges, mines and minerals

7.78   Customary and public rights, local land charges, coal rights, and certain other mineral rights, are overriding interests in relation to registered dispositions of the land affected, under the LRA 2002, Sch 3, paras 4–9, as well as on first registration of such land, and are considered above in the latter context.[1]

---

[1]   Paras 7.11–7.13.

Miscellaneous

7.79   Franchises, manorial rights, Crown rents, non-statutory rights as to embankments or sea or river walls, rights to payment in lieu of tithe, and rights in respect of chancel repairs,[1] will override registered dispositions, under the LRA 2002, Sch 3, paras 10–14 and 16, for ten years from the commencement of the LRA 2002 (see s 117(1)); during that period, no fee may be charged for an application by the owner of an interest within paras 10–14 for entry of a notice in respect of that interest (LRA 2002, s 117(2)(b)).[2] The purpose of these provisions is to phase out the overriding status of these interests, whilst giving their owners a sufficient opportunity to protect them on the register.[3]

---

[1]   Chancel repair rights are inserted as the LRA 2002, Sch 3, para 16, by the Land Registration Act 2002 (Transitional Provisions) (No 2) Order 2003, SI 2003/2431, art 2(2). The reasons for this separate treatment of chancel repairs are outlined in para 7.14.

[2]   It has been indicated (see para 7.14) that the registry will also waive the fee for entering a notice in respect of chancel repairs.

[3]   Compare Law Com no 271, paras 8.88 and 8.89.

Adverse possession

7.80   A person who was in adverse possession of registered land, before the commencement of the LRA 2002, for a sufficient period to cause the registered estate to be held in trust for him (LRA 1925, s 75(1)), is entitled to be registered as proprietor of that estate (LRA 2002, Sch 12, para 18(1)), and that right is protected as against registered disponees of the estate for value, by the LRA 2002, Sch 3, para 2, for so long as that person remains in actual occupation of the whole of the land adversely possessed. If he goes out of occupation, either before or after the commencement of the LRA 2002, his right to be registered as proprietor continues to be binding on such disponees, for the period of three years only from such commencement, under Sch 3, para 15 (inserted by the LRA 2002, Sch 12, para 11).

Interests which do not override registered dispositions

7.81   The LRA 2002, Sch 3, does not preserve the overriding status of customary and other rights originating in tenure (formerly among those listed in the LRA 1925, s 70(1)(a) and (b)), which (except for Crown rents) are obsolete.[1] Where land is registered with qualified, possessory or good leasehold title,[2] the priority of the estates and interests excepted from the effect of registration, which were formerly overriding interests (under the LRA 1925, s 70(1)(h)), is protected by the sections regulating those categories of title (LRA 2002, s 11(6) and (7), freeholds, and s 12(6), (7) and (8), leaseholds). Sch 3, para 2, is inapplicable to pending land actions, writs and orders affecting land, orders appointing a receiver or sequestrator, and deeds of arrangement (LRA 2002, s 87(3)). Various statutory rights are specifically excluded either from protection under any provision of Sch 3, or from Sch 3, para 2, but the LRA 2002 has not made any substantive change to the law affecting these rights.

(1)   Rights arising from a tenant's notice to acquire the freehold or an extended lease of a house, under the Leasehold Reform Act 1967, do not fall within the LRA 2002, Sch 3, but must be

protected by registering a notice (Leasehold Reform Act 1967, s 5(5), amended by the LRA 2002, Sch 11, para 8(2)).[3]

(2)   The 'preserved right to buy' under the Housing Act 1985, ss 71A–H, is also excluded from Sch 3 and liable to be postponed if not protected by a notice (Housing Act 1985, Sch 9A, para 6(1), substituted by the LRA 2002, Sch 11, para 18(10)).[4]

(3)   An access order under the Access to Neighbouring Land Act 1992 is excluded from Sch 3, para 2 (Access to Neighbouring Land Act 1992, s 5(5), substituted by the LRA 2002, Sch 11, para 26(4)).

(4)   A notice claiming collective enfranchisement, or a new lease, under the Leasehold Reform, Housing and Urban Development Act 1993 is excluded from Sch 3, para 2 (Leasehold Reform, Housing and Urban Development Act 1993, s 97(1), amended by the LRA 2002, Sch 11, para 30(3)).

(5)   A request for an overriding lease under the Landlord and Tenant (Covenants) Act 1995 is excluded from Sch 3, para 2 (Landlord and Tenant (Covenants) Act 1995, s 20(6), amended by the LRA 2002, Sch 11, para 33(4)).

(6)   A spouse's matrimonial home rights under the Family Law Act 1996 are also excluded from Sch 3, para 2 (Family Law Act 1996, s 31(10), amended by the LRA 2002, Sch 11, para 34(2)).

---

[1]   See Law Com no 254, paras 5.26 and 5.32–5.36.
[2]   See Chapter 5, paras 5.12–5.15, and Chapter 6, paras 6.12–6.15.
[3]   As to protection by notice, see paras 7.20–7.39.
[4]   Unlike the other statutory rights mentioned in the text, the 'preserved right to buy' can only exist in relation to registered land (because it arises as a result of a transaction which triggers first registration if the land is not already registered), and there is therefore no equivalent provision in relation to the LRA 2002, Sch 1.

'PRIORITY SEARCH' PROCEDURE FIXING PRIORITY OF INTENDED REGISTERED DISPOSITIONS

7.82   A proposing disponee for value is always concerned to know what interests will be protected on the register at the time as of which the disposition in his favour is registered,[1] so as to be binding on him (LRA 2002, s 29(2)(a)(i)).[2] The LRA 2002, s 72, and the LRR 2003, rr 147–154, reproducing the effect of the previous law,[3] enable a disponee to apply for an official search of the register in advance of completion of the disposition, showing the state of the register at the time of the search application, and provide that if an application is subsequently made, within a specified priority period, to register the disposition, any new entries made in the register during the priority period are postponed to the entry made in respect of that disposition. These provisions are described in more detail in the following paragraphs. They do not protect a disponee against any interests coming into being after the time of the search application which are binding on the disponee without being registered (ie under the LRA 2002, Sch 3),[4] and cannot be used to protect the grant of a lease which is not a registrable disposition.[5] The LRA 2002 also confers a power to make rules creating a similar priority period when a contract for the making of a registrable disposition is noted on the register (LRA 2002, s 72(6)(a)(ii)), but this power has not yet been exercised.[6]

---

[1] Ie the time when it is entered in the 'day list' kept under the LRR 2003, r 12, or, if earlier, the time specified in r 15(1)(b) or (2)(b): LRA 2002, s 74(b).

[2] See paras 7.17–7.18.

[3] Land Registration (Official Searches) Rules 1993, SI 1993/3276, as amended.

[4] See paras 7.62–7.81.

[5] Ie a lease not falling within the LRA 2002, s 27(2)(b); see Chapter 6, paras 6.21–6.23. The LRA 2002, s 72(1) and (2), give priority to an *entry in the register* pursuant to a 'protected application', and for 'priority search' purposes there is no provision equivalent to the LRA 2002, s 29(4), treating such a lease as if it were registrable and registered.

[6] It is contemplated that when 'electronic conveyancing' is applied to the making of contracts for registrable dispositions, so that a contract only comes into being when an appropriate register entry is made, rules under this power will create a priority period from the time of the contract, enabling the disposition to be completed subject only to the register entries subsisting when the contract was made and registered. See Law Com no 271, para 9.69.

7.83   An intending disponee of registered land (LRR 2003, r 147(1), read with the definition of 'purchaser' in r 131,) may apply for an 'official search with priority' of the individual register of the registered title which is to be the subject of a registered disposition for valuable consideration (LRR 2003, r 147(1), read with the definition of 'protectable disposition' in r 131). Where the land to which the disposition relates is the subject of a pending application for first registration,[1] an intending disponee may apply for such a search in relation to that pending application (LRR 2003, r 147(2)). The application must be in Form OS1 if it relates to the whole of the land in the title or first registration application, or Form OS2 if it relates to part only (LRR 2003, r 147(3)). It must specify (panel 9 of Form OS1 and of Form OS2) whether the applicant intends to purchase the property, to take a lease or to take a registrable charge, and must be delivered to the 'proper office',[2] unless it is made electronically or under special written arrangements (Land Registration (Proper Office) Order 2003, art 2). The search application is taken to be made on the date and at the time it is entered in the day list (LRR 2003, r 148(1)). If that application is in order and is not withdrawn (LRR 2003, rr 148(2) and 150(1)),[3] the day list entry has the effect that any subsequent entry in the register is postponed to an application to register the disposition to which the search relates (LRA 2002, s 72(1) and (2), and

LRR 2003, r 148(3)), if the application for registration is made before the end of the thirtieth business day after the search was entered in the day list (LRR 2003, r 131, definition of *'priority period'*, para (a)),[4] unless *either* the subsequent entry is protected by the priority period of an earlier-ranking official search (LRA 2002, s 72(3)), *or* it is a restriction with *'overriding priority'* under a court order (LRA 2002, ss 72(4) and 46(3)).[5]

---

[1]   In such a case the LRA 2002 applies to the disposition as if the land were already registered: LRR 2003, r 38.

[2]   LRA 2002, s 100(3), and Land Registration (Proper Office) Order 2003, SI 2003/2040, art 3.

[3]   By r 150(2), a search cannot be withdrawn after the application it protects has been made and completed.

[4]   Para (b) of the definition ensures that the priority period will not be altered by the introduction of Saturday opening of the registry under r 216(2)–(4).

[5]   See paras 7.55–7.56.

7.84   If an application for an official search with priority is in order, the registry must issue an *'official search certificate with priority'*, showing, most importantly, the entries made in the register from the *'search from date'*[1] down to the date and time that the search application was entered in the day list (LRR 2003, r 149(1)). The effect of the procedure is to update the applicant's knowledge of the register and to 'freeze' it in its updated form, as against him, for the duration of the priority period. The search certificate may be issued in paper form, or electronically if an appropriate registry notice is in force (LRR 2003, rr 149(2) and 132(2), referring to the LRR 2003, Sch 2),[2] and must show[3]

(1)   the title number or pending application number (as appropriate);

(2)   the date and time of the certificate;

(3)   information to identify the property affected if that is only part of the land in the relevant title or first registration application;

(4)   details of the applicant;

(5)   where the search relates to a registered title, details of any adverse entries made since the end of the *'search from date'*, and where it relates to a first registration application, the name of the applicant for such registration and the date and time when that application was entered on the day list; and (in either case)

(6)   notice of any relevant pending application,

(7)   notice of any relevant official search the priority of which has not expired, and

(8)   the date and time of expiration of the priority of the search to which the certificate relates.

Information as to pending applications and unexpired priority searches is necessary, in addition to updated register entries, to enable the applicant to verify that registration of the intended disposition in his favour will not be subject to any registered matter which, as against the disponor, he is not obliged to accept.

---

[1]   The date specified as such in the official copy of the register entries already held by the applicant, being the date to which that copy relates: see the definition in the LRR 2003, r 131.

[2]   If the search is made against the whole of a registered title, there have been no adverse entries since the 'search from date', and the day list contains no pending applications or unexpired priority searches, the result of the search can be given orally or on-line through the Land Registry Telephone Service, Land Registry Direct, National Land Information Service or a Land Registry Customer Information Centre: see Land Registry Practice Guide 12, para 4.1.

[3]   LRR 2003, r 149(3) and Sch 6, Pts 3 (registered title) and 4 (pending first registration application).

7.85   It frequently happens that a registrable disposition of registered land, or of land subject to a pending first registration application,[1] is dependent on a prior registrable disposition affecting the same land: the commonest example of such a sequence of transactions is a sale intended to be financed by a secured loan, where a registrable charge is dependent on, and is completed simultaneously with, a registrable transfer.[2] In such a case, a priority search in respect of the dependent transaction (ie, in the example given, the charge,) also protects the priority of the prior disposition,[3] (ie the transfer,) provided the application to register the prior disposition is made within the priority period of the search relating to the dependent disposition (LRR 2003, rr 151(3) and (4)(a) and 152(3) and (5)(a)), and both dispositions and, where they are subject to a pending first registration application, that application, are in due course completed by registration (LRR 2003, rr 151(4)(b) and 152(4), (5)(b)).

---

[1]   By the LRR 2003, r 38, the LRA 2002 applies to dealings with such land as if they took place after completion of the application for first registration.

[2]   A similar situation might arise in connection with a sale and an immediate lease-back for a term exceeding seven years.

[3]   LRR 2003, r 151(1) and (2), registered title, and r 152(1) and (2), dealings with land subject to a pending first registration application.

7.86   Where two (or more) official search certificates with priority are in operation at the same time, they operate to confer priority on the related applications for registration of dispositions in the order in which the disponees' respective applications for official searches with priority were entered in the day list, unless the disponees agree otherwise (LRR 2003, r 153(1); see also the LRA 2002, s 72(3)). However, where one of those transactions is dependent on another the registrar must assume, unless the contrary appears, that the disponees have agreed to their applications having priority in the order necessary to give effect to the sequence of the documents carrying out those transactions (LRR 2003, r 153(2)). Thus, if an

intending purchaser and his intending mortgagee both apply for
official searches with priority, the order of those applications does not
affect the relative priority of their interests when registered.

Time at which applications are taken to be made

7.87 A registered disposition made in pursuance of an official search
with priority ranks ahead of entries and applications made after the
date of the search if the application to register the disposition is
made *'before the end of'* (LRA 2002, s 72(1)(b),) the priority period
conferred by the search. That period expires at midnight at the end
of the thirtieth business day after the application for the search is
entered on the day list;[1] the date and time of its expiration are
shown on the search certificate.[2] The application to register the
disposition is also taken to be made at midnight at the end of the
thirtieth day of the period if it is received by the registry[3] after 12
noon on the twenty-ninth business day, or before 12 noon on the
thirtieth business day (LRR 2003, r 15(1)(b)), or at any time on a day
between those days which is not a business day (LRR 2003,
r 15(2)(b)), unless it is in fact entered in the day list before midnight
on the thirtieth business day, in which event it is taken to be made at
the time when it is so entered (LRR 2003, r 15(1)(a), (2)(a)). If an
application to register a disposition is taken to have been made at
the same time as the expiry of a priority period under an application
for an official search, the application in respect of the disposition is
to be taken to be within the priority period.[4] The effect is that an
application pursuant to an official search with priority is treated as
made within the priority period, and other entries (including any
entry made pursuant to another application treated as made at the
same time) are postponed accordingly, if it is delivered to the
registry before 12 noon on the last day of that period, even if it is not
in fact entered in the day list before the end of that day.

---

[1]   LRR 2003, rr 131, definition of 'priority period', para (a), and 148(3).
[2]   LRR 2003, r 149(3) and Sch 6, Pt 3, para I (registered title) and Pt 4, para J (application for
first registration). See para 7.84(8).
[3]   By the LRR 2003, r 15(3), such an application is received when it is delivered: (a) to the
'proper office' designated under the LRA 2002, s 100(3), and Land Registration (Proper Office)
Order 2003, SI 2003/2040, art 3 and Schedule; or (b) in accordance with a written arrangement
between the registry and the applicant or his conveyancer; or (c) in accordance with a notice
under the LRR 2003, Sch 2, as to electronic delivery of applications.
[4]   LRR 2003, r 154(1), application relating to a dealing with a registered title; and r 154(2),
application relating to a dealing with land subject to a first registration application.

SUMMARY OF TRANSITIONAL PROVISIONS APPLICABLE TO PRIORITY ISSUES

7.88   No cautions against dealings with registered estates or charges can be registered after the commencement of the LRA 2002, which contains no provisions authorising the making of such entries.[1] However, all such cautions entered on the register under the LRA 1925, s 54, before the commencement of the LRA 2002 continue to have effect, as do the LRA 1925, ss 55 and 56, in relation to such cautions.[2] A notice 'warning' a caution must be served on the cautioner (LRR 2003, r 220, makes r 199 applicable to such notices,) following an application to register a dealing with the land (LRA 1925 s 55(1)), or if the proprietor, or a person entitled (but for the existence of the caution) to be registered as proprietor, applies (in Form CCD: LRR 2003, r 223(2),) for the caution to be cancelled (LRR 2003, r 223(1), (3)). The cautioner may show cause why the caution should not be cancelled; the period allowed for this purpose is that expiring at 12 noon on the fifteenth business day after the registrar issues the warning-off notice, or later if the registrar so permits: LRR 2003, rr 218 and 221(2); the time is computed from the issue, rather than the service, of the notice. If the cautioner delivers a written statement which satisfies the registrar that there is a fairly arguable case that effect should not be given to the application which led to the service of the notice, the registrar must make an order that the caution is to continue until withdrawn or otherwise disposed of (LRR 2003, r 221(3), (4)), and must give notice of that order to the applicant and the cautioner, whereupon the latter is treated as having objected under the LRA 2002, s 73, to the former's application, and the matter is referred to the adjudicator if not disposed of by agreement (LRR 2003, r 221(5), applying the LRA 2002, s 73(5), (7)).[3] If the original application does not proceed, the caution continues to have effect (LRR 2003, r 221(6)); if the cautioner does not show cause, the caution is cancelled.[4] A cautioner may apply to withdraw his caution (LRR 2003, r 222, prescribing Form WCT), and must do so if he applies to register a notice or restriction in respect of the estate, right, interest or claim to which the caution relates (LRA 2002, Sch 12, para 17).

---

[1]   See Law Com no 254, paras 6.10–6.23 and 6.43–6.54, and Law Com no 271, paras 6.2–6.4, for the reasons for the abolition of cautions against dealings.

[2]   LRA 2002, Sch 12, para 2(3), as modified by the Land Registration Act 2002 (Transitional Provisions) Order 2003, SI 2003/1953, art 17.

[3]   Where a notice warning a caution was issued before the commencement of the LRA 2002, any dispute proceeds under the LRA 1925 and the LRR 1925 as amended, and cannot be referred to the adjudicator: Land Registration Act 2002 (Transitional Provisions) Order 2003, SI 2003/1953, art 6.

[4]   LRA 1925, s 55(1), as modified by the LRA 2002, Sch 12, para 2(3), and Land Registration Act 2002 (Transitional Provisions) Order 2003, SI 2003/1953, art 17.

7.89 The validity of entries in the register made before the commencement of the LRA 2002 is not affected by the repeals made by the LRA 2002: see Sch 12, para 1. Further specific transitional provisions applicable to priority issues are as follows.

(1) An unregistered franchise, manorial right, Crown rent, non-statutory right in respect of an embankment or sea or river wall, right to payment in lieu of tithe, or right in respect of chancel repairs, will not be binding either on the first registered proprietor (when unregistered land subject to any such right becomes registered), or on a registered disponee for value of registered land subject to any such right, if the first registration or disposition takes place more than ten years after the commencement of the LRA 2002: s 117(1) and Land Registration Act 2002 (Transitional Provisions) (No 2) Order 2003, SI 2003/2431, art 2.[1]

(2) The LRA 2002 applies to notices entered under the LRA 1925 as it applies to agreed notices under s 34(2)(a): LRA 2002, Sch 12, para 2(1).[2]

(3) The LRA 2002 applies to restrictions and inhibitions entered under the LRA 1925 as it applies to restrictions entered under the LRA 2002: Sch 12, para 2(2).[3]

(4) Any still subsisting notice of deposit of a Land Certificate continues to operate as a caution against dealings under the LRA 1925, s 54: LRA 2002, Sch 12, para 3.[4]

(5) If a person acquired a 'title by limitation', to unregistered or registered land, before the commencement of the LRA 2002, but he is not in actual occupation of the relevant land, his rights as adverse possessor will only be binding on the first registered proprietor, on the 'paper title' to unregistered land being registered, or on a registered disponee for value of registered land, if the first registration or disposition takes place within three years from the commencement of the LRA 2002: Sch 12, paras 7 and 11.[5]

(6) An interest in registered land which was an overriding interest immediately before the commencement of the LRA 2002 because the person entitled to it was in receipt of the rents and profits of the land, within the LRA 1925, s 70(1)(g), continues (subject to qualifications) to be binding on a registered disponee for value of the land: LRA 2002, Sch 12, para 8.[6]

(7) An easement (or a profit à prendre) which was an overriding interest in relation to registered servient land immediately before the commencement of the LRA 2002 continues to be binding on a registered disponee for value of that land, whether it is a legal or an equitable interest, and whether or not it is known or obvious to the disponee or was exercised in the year before the relevant disposition: LRA 2002, Sch 12, para 9.[7]

(8)   A legal easement (or profit à prendre) is binding on a registered disponee for value of registered servient land, whether or not it is known or obvious to the disponee, if the disposition takes place within three years of the commencement of the LRA 2002: Sch 12, para 10.[8]

(9)   An unregistered lease granted before the commencement of the LRA 2002 for a term not exceeding 21 years continues to be binding on a first registered proprietor of the reversionary interest, if it is unregistered, and on a registered disponee for value of that interest if it is registered: LRA 2002, Sch 12, para 12.[9]

(10)   Where an application is made to register a charge in a form which was approved before the commencement of the LRA 2002 and includes an application for a restriction, and the registrar considers that there is a standard form of restriction with equivalent effect, he must enter that standard form of restriction in the register: Land Registration Act 2002 (Transitional Provisions) Order 2003, SI 2003/1953, art 8.[10]

(11)   An obligation of a chargee to make a further advance which was noted on the register before the commencement of the LRA 2002 is effective to safeguard the priority of a further advance made, in accordance with that obligation, after such commencement: Land Registration Act 2002 (Transitional Provisions) Order 2003, SI 2003/1953, art 25.[11]

---

[1]   See paras 7.14 and 7.79.
[2]   See para 7.20.
[3]   See para 7.40.
[4]   See Chapter 8, para 8.12.
[5]   See paras 7.15 and 7.80 and Chapter 13, paras 13.30 and 13.31.
[6]   See paras 7.74–7.78.
[7]   See Chapter 9, para 9.27.
[8]   See Chapter 9, para 9.28.
[9]   See paras 7.7 and 7.62 and Chapter 6, para 6.50.
[10]   See Chapter 8, para 8.13.
[11]   See Chapter 8, para 8.18.

8 Mortgages and charges

INTRODUCTION

8.1 The principal changes made by the Land Registration Act 2002 ('LRA 2002') to the law relating to mortgages and charges of registered land are that:

- the mortgage by demise or sub-demise is abolished, and the charge by way of legal mortgage becomes the only form of security operating at law (LRA 2002, s 23);
- the rules governing the making of further advances are revised and modernised (LRA 2002, s 49);
- the registrar is required to give existing chargees notice of the registration of any statutory charge which takes priority over securities already protected on the register (LRA 2002, s 50);
- there is no longer any implied personal covenant by the registered proprietor of the land to pay the sums secured by the charge,[1] which removes a trap formerly existing for landowners granting third party security.

---

[1] LRA 1925, s 28, is repealed (with the remainder of that Act, by LRA 2002, s 135 and Sch 13,) and is not replaced.

8.2 The discussion of mortgages and charges in this chapter is arranged as follows:

(1) mortgages and charges over unregistered land and first registration—paras 8.3–8.6;

(2) creation and protection of charges over registered land—paras 8.7–8.13;

(3) priority of charges over registered land and of further advances on such securities—paras 8.14–8.21;

(4) chargees' powers—paras 8.22–8.28;

(5) discharge and transfer of charges—paras 8.29–8.33;

(6) sub-charges—paras 8.34–8.37.

(1) MORTGAGES AND CHARGES OVER UNREGISTERED LAND AND FIRST REGISTRATION

8.3 A freehold estate in land, or a lease which has more than seven years to run (LRA 2002, s 4(2),) must be registered on the grant of a *'protected first legal mortgage'* over it (LRA 2002, ss 4(1)(g) and 6(2)(a));[1] for this purpose a legal mortgage is *'protected'* if it takes effect on its creation as a mortgage to be protected by the deposit of documents relating to the mortgaged estate, and a *'first'* legal mortgage is one which, on its creation, ranks in priority ahead of any other mortgages then subsisting: LRA 2002, s 4(8).[2]

The primary duty to apply for registration is imposed on the owner of the estate mortgaged (LRA 2002, s 6(2)(b),) but the mortgagee may make an application, in the name of the mortgagor, for that estate to be registered, whether or not the mortgagor consents: LRR 2003, r 21, made under LRA 2002, s 6(6).[3] When the estate is registered, the registrar must also enter the mortgagee as the proprietor of the charge if he is satisfied of the mortgagee's entitlement (LRR 2003, r 22); the entry is made in the charges register (LRR 2003, r 9).

If no application for registration is made within two months of the creation of the mortgage, or any extension of that period permitted by the registrar (LRA 2002, s 6(4) and (5),)[4] the mortgage becomes void as regards the creation of a legal estate, and has effect as a contract for valuable consideration to create an appropriate legal security (LRA 2002, s 7(1) and (2)(b)); the mortgagor is liable to pay any costs incurred in re-granting the mortgage, and to indemnify the mortgagee in respect of any other liability reasonably incurred because of the failure to register: LRA 2002, s 8.

---

[1] Form CH1 may be used.

[2] The requirement of registration therefore does not apply on the creation of a first legal mortgage not protected by a deposit of documents, (which should be registered under the Land Charges Act 1972, s 2(4)(i) as a Class C(i) land charge,) or on the creation of a second or subsequent mortgage.

[3] In either case the application must be made in Form FR1, prescribed by LRR 2003, r 23.

[4] See also Chapter 4, paras 4.9 and 4.10.

8.4 It is considered that where an estate is registered as a result of the grant of a protected first legal mortgage, the mortgagee as well as the registered proprietor takes subject to the overriding interests specified in LRA 2002, Sch 1.[1] However, if the trigger for first registration is a sale of the land, financed by a loan secured by a mortgage created by the purchaser at completion of the purchase, it is submitted that although the purchaser is registered as proprietor subject to the overriding interests in Sch 1, the mortgage is a dealing with the registrable estate undertaken whilst the purchaser is under a duty to apply for first registration,[2] with the consequence that LRA 2002 applies to the mortgage as if it had taken place after the date of first registration of the purchaser's estate,[3] so that the interests which override the mortgage are those specified in LRA 2002, Sch 3: see LRA 2002, s 29(1) and (2)(a)(ii). It appears to follow:

(a) that in such a case the purchaser takes subject to any unregistered legal easement over the land which subsists at the time of registration (LRA 2002, ss 11(4)(b) and 12(4)(c), and Sch 1, para 3),[4] but the mortgagee is not bound by such an easement unless he actually knows of it, or it would have been obvious on a reasonably careful inspection of the land, or it has been exercised in the previous year (LRA 2002, Sch 3, para 3);[5] and

(b) if there is in fact someone in occupation of the land who has and retains a beneficial interest in it,[6] the purchaser is automatically subject to the occupier's interest (LRA 2002, Sch 1, para 2),[7] but the mortgagee is only bound by it if he made inquiry of the occupier and the interest was not disclosed when that might reasonably have been expected, or if the occupier's occupation would have been obvious on a reasonably careful inspection of the land, or if the mortgagee actually knew of the interest (LRA 2002, Sch 3, para 2).[8]

---

[1]   This is not expressly stated in LRA 2002. Sections 11(4)(b) and 12(4)(c) make Sch 1 applicable on first registration, but by ss 11(1) and 12(1) those provisions in terms apply only to the registration of a person as the proprietor of a freehold or leasehold estate, with no reference to registration as proprietor of a mortgage or charge. It is submitted, however, that under the general law a legal mortgagee takes subject to all existing interests which are binding on the mortgagor, unless statute makes express provision to some other effect (or the defence of 'purchaser for value without notice' is available), and that on first registration LRA 2002, s 29, is not such a provision and Sch 3 therefore does not apply, because the grant of a mortgage within s 4(1)(g) is not a disposition *'of a registered estate'*.

[2]   Within LRR 2003, r 38(1), made under LRA 2002, Sch 10, para 1.

[3]   Ibid.

[4]   See Chapter 9, para 9.4.

[5]   See Chapter 9, para 9.19.

[6]   As may happen if the owner of residential property sells it to a relative, on terms that the vendor is to be entitled to continue to live in the property, and the purchaser raises the price on mortgage.

[7]   See Chapter 7, para 7.9

[8]   See Chapter 7, paras 7.67–7.73. In the example given above of an occupier who receives a payment funded by the mortgage loan, it is submitted that the stricter test under Sch 3 is appropriate. Compare also *Paddington Building Society v Mendelsohn* (1985) 50 P&CR 244, CA.

8.5   There is nothing to prohibit the grant of a mortgage of unregistered land by demise or sub-demise, even if the grant triggers the requirement of registration,[1] but it is doubted whether there will ever be any reason to do so. A mortgage term cannot be registered as a lease, either voluntarily (LRA 2002, s 3(5),) or on the grant (LRA 2002, s 4(5),) or an assignment (LRA 2002, s 4(4)(a),) of the security.

---

¹   LRA 2002, s 23, considered further in para 8.7 below, defines an owner's powers of disposition in terms precluding the grant of such a mortgage, but *'in relation to a registered estate'* only.

8.6   If at the time of first registration the land is subject to a legal mortgage which did not itself trigger the requirement of registration, and was not created after the event which triggered that requirement, the registrar must enter the mortgagee as proprietor of that charge if he is satisfied of the mortgagee's entitlement.[1] If at that time it appears from the registrar's examination of the title that the land is subject to an equitable charge, he must enter a notice of the burden of that interest (LRR 2003, r 35). An equitable charge will bind the first registered proprietor if it is secured by a deposit of documents relating to the legal estate or registered as a land charge of class C(iii), (see Land Charges Act 1972, s 2(4)(a)(iii),) or if the landowner himself created it before applying for voluntary first registration.[2] Any legal or equitable mortgagee of unregistered land is entitled to lodge a caution against first registration (LRA 2002, s 15(1)(b) and (2),)[3] to ensure that his security is duly protected when the land is registered.

---

¹   LRR 2003, r 34, made under LRA 2002, s 13(b); the entry is made in the charges register under r 9.
²   If the requirement of registration is triggered under LRA 2002, s 4(1)(a), by a gratuitous transfer, any equitable charge which should be but is not registered as a class C(iii) land charge will be void as against the transferee under Land Charges Act 1972, s 4(5).   Voluntary registration, not involving any transfer, does not avoid any unregistered land charges created by and binding on the proprietor.
³   See Chapter 4, paras 4.3–4.8.

---

(2) CREATION AND PROTECTION OF CHARGES OVER REGISTERED LAND

8.7   The proprietor, or a person entitled to be registered as proprietor, of registered land (LRA 2002, s 24,) has power to make a disposition of that land of any kind permitted by the general law, *other than* a mortgage by demise or sub-demise (LRA 2002, s 23(1)(a),) but including power to create a charge by deed by way of legal mortgage,[1] and also *'power to charge the land at law with the payment of money'*: LRA 2002, s 23(1)(b).[2]

A *'charge'* is widely defined (LRA 2002, s 132(1),) as *'any mortgage, charge or lien for securing money or money's worth'*, and therefore includes not only a security for repayment of money lent, plus interest, but also a charge created by or under a statute,[3] a security for future indebtedness,[4] or for contingent indebtedness which may never arise at all,[5] and a security supporting any other form of obligation by providing a means for discharging a financial liability arising from a breach of that obligation.[6]

A charge does not operate at law until it is completed by registration (LRA 2002, s 27(1) and (2)(f),)[7] which is effected by entering the chargee, or his successor in title, as proprietor of the charge (LRA 2002, Sch 2, para 8,) in the charges register (LRR 2003, r 9,) of the title to the land affected: LRA 2002, s 59(2). On completion of the registration requirements, the charge takes effect as a charge by deed by way of legal mortgage (LRA 2002, s 51), in accordance with Law of Property Act 1925, s 87.[8]

---

[1]   Such a charge, under Law of Property Act 1925, s 87, is a disposition *'permitted by the general law'* and therefore authorised in relation to registered land by LRA 2002, s 23(1)(a).
[2]   There is no practical difference between the effects of the two forms of charge which can operate at law: see Law Com no 271, para 7.3.
[3]   See also LRA 2002, s 50, and para 8.21 below, as to the priority of such charges.
[4]   For example a charge securing the debit balance from time to time on an overdraft or other running account. See LRA 2002, s 49, and paras 8.16–8.20 below, in relation to 'further advances'.
[5]   For example a charge supporting a guarantor's obligation to pay someone else's debt if called upon to do so.
[6]   See Law Com no 254, paras 9.2–9.3, and Law Com no 271, para 7.5. It is considered that since the practical effect of a charge in support of a non-financial obligation is to provide a monetary remedy for any default, such a charge is one for the *'payment of money'* and can be created under LRA 2002, s 23(1)(b), as well as under Law of Property Act 1925, s 87.
[7]   By LRA 2002, s 27(5)(c), this does not apply to a legal charge which is a local land charge created by operation of law.
[8]   LRA 2002, s 132(1), provides that *'legal mortgage'* has the same meaning as in Law of Property Act 1925 ('LPA 1925'), which includes, by LPA 1925, s 205(1)(xvi), a charge by way of legal mortgage; LPA 1925, s 87(1), confers on the chargee under such a charge the same *'protection powers and remedies'* as a mortgage by demise; and LRA 2002, s 133 and Sch 11, para 2(8), insert a new sub-s (4) in s 87, to the effect that s 87(1) is not affected by the abolition of the power to mortgage registered land by demise or sub-demise.

8.8   An applicant for registration of a charge created by a company registered under the Companies Acts, by a limited liability partnership, or by a Northern Ireland company, must produce to the registrar a certificate from the appropriate Companies Registry that the charge has been registered under the applicable legislation relating to company charges (LRR 2003, r 111(1)).[1] If the necessary certificate is not produced, the registrar must enter a note in the register that the charge is subject to the provisions of the relevant section (LRR 2003, r 111(2)). In such a case the security is void against any liquidator or administrator of the company or LLP (see Companies Act 1985, s 395(1)).

An application to register a body corporate as proprietor of a charge must state that body's registered number if it is a company registered under the Companies Acts in any part of the United Kingdom (LRR 2003, r 181(1),) or a LLP under the Limited Liability Partnerships

Act 2000 (LRR 2003, r 181(4)); in the case of an overseas company, evidence must be provided of its constitution and of its powers to deal with land and to lend money on mortgage (LRR 2003, r 183(1) and (2)).[2]

---

[1]   The most important of such provisions is Companies Act 1985, s 395, applying to English companies and, by Limited Liability Partnerships Regulations 2001 (SI 2001/1090), reg 4(1) and Sch 2, Pt 1, to English LLPs.

[2]   LRR 2003, r 183(2), also authorises the registrar to require further evidence, and a translation of the constitutional documentation will be required if it is not in English or Welsh: see Land Registry Practice Guide 29, para 9.

8.9   Rules are authorised to be made (LRA 2002, s 25,) prescribing requirements as to the form and contents of registrable dispositions. A legal charge may be made in Form CH1; the use of that form is optional and not mandatory (LRR 2003, r 103), but it has the advantage that a standard form restriction (LRR 2003, r 91(1),)[1] can be applied for[2] without requiring a separate application: LRR 2003, r 92(7)(b).[3]

Land Registration Act 1925 provided (by s 28) for a personal covenant by the mortgagor to pay the mortgage money (and interest) to be implied, if not expressly excluded, in any registered mortgage. This provision could have the effect of inserting in a 'third party mortgage', granted by an owner of land as security for someone else's indebtedness, a personal obligation of the mortgagor to pay the whole debt, enforceable by an ordinary action for a money judgment as well as by enforcement of the security, and not restricted to the value of the land.[4] This risk does not exist in relation to legal charges registered under LRA 2002.[5] Nevertheless it is suggested that the safer course is to include in any third party charge an express statement that the chargor's liability is enforceable only by realisation of the security and is restricted in amount to the sum realised,[6] if that is what the parties intend.

---

[1]   See Chapter 7, paras 7.43–7.45.

[2]   In panel 7 of Form CH1.

[3]   Disapplying the requirement under r 92(1) to use Form RX1.

[4]   Compare *Re Stonewood Investments' Mortgage* (15 July 1981, unreported,) and *Fairmile Portfolio Management v Davies Arnold Cooper* [1998] EGCS 149.

[5]   LRA 1925, s 28, is repealed by LRA 2002, s 135 and Sch 13, and is not replaced. If Form CH1 is used to create a legal charge, a personal covenant by the chargor for the payment of the sum secured can be inserted in panel 8, but is not mandatory.

[6]   The chargor's liability and the chargee's remedies can validly be restricted, but any attempt to exclude liability completely is liable to fail as being inconsistent with the fundamental nature of the transaction: compare *Williams v Hathaway* (1877) 6 Ch D 544.

8.10   When a charge has been granted for valuable consideration[1] and registered so as to operate at law (LRA 2002, ss 27(1) and (2)(f), 51, 59(2), and Sch 2, para 8),[2] it takes priority over any other subsisting interests in the land unless they are registered or protected on the register, or are overriding interests within LRA 2002, Sch 3: see s 29(1) and (2),[3] under which such a charge also retains its priority on the occasion of any subsequent registered disposition of the land for value.

---

[1] Defined by LRA 2002, s 132(1), as excluding marriage consideration and a nominal consideration in money. It is rare for a legal charge to be created gratuitously.
[2] See para 8.7 above.
[3] See Chapter 7, paras 7.17–7.18.

8.11 An application to register an instrument varying the terms of a registered charge must be made by, or with the consent of, the proprietor of the charge and the proprietor of the estate charged, (LRR 2003, r 113(1)(a),) and with the consent of the proprietor, or a person entitled to be registered as the proprietor, of any charge of equal or inferior priority which is prejudicially affected by the variation (LRR 2003, r 113(1)(b),)[1] except that no separate consent is required from a person who has executed the instrument of variation: LRR 2003, r 113(1). The registrar may accept a certificate from a conveyancer[2] confirming that the conveyancer holds any necessary consents: LRR 2003, r 113(2). If the registrar is satisfied that the proprietor of any other charge prejudicially affected by the variation is bound by it, he must make a note of the variation in the register (LRR 2003, r 113(3)); if he is not so satisfied, he may make an entry that an instrument *'expressed'* to vary the terms of the charge has been entered into: LRR 2003, r 113(4).

---

[1] The Land Registry considers that a reduction in the interest rate or in the capital debt does not adversely affect other securities, but that an increase in the interest rate or the capital debt, an extension of the repayment period, or the creation of an obligation to make further advances, may do so: see Land Registry Practice Guide 29, para 12.
[2] Ie a solicitor, a licensed conveyancer or a Fellow of the Institute of Legal Executives: LRR 2003, r 217(1).

8.12 A registered proprietor can create equitable security over registered land in any manner permitted by the general law: LRA 2002, s 23(1)(a). That does not include security constituted by a deposit of documents of title (Law of Property (Miscellaneous Provisions) Act 1989, s 2),[1] and LRA 2002 does not contain any provision as to that form of security.[2] An equitable charge should be protected by entering a notice on the register in order to protect its priority against subsequent registered dispositions for value (LRA 2002, ss 28, 29(1) and (2), and 32).[3] The realisation of equitable security is considered below.[4]

---

[1] See *United Bank of Kuwait plc v Sahib* [1997] Ch 107.
[2] LRA 1925, s 66, is repealed and not replaced. See Law Com no 271, para 7.10. But any notice of deposit of a Land Certificate registered before 3 April 1995, (LRR 1925, r 239, as substituted by LRR 1995, r 4(1),) and still subsisting, continues to operate as a caution against dealings: LRA 2002, Sch 12, para 3.

8.13 A security may impose an obligation on the chargor not to make any specified dispositions of the land whilst the security continues in force.[1] A restriction can be entered to ensure that no registered disposition is made contrary to such an obligation;[2] such an entry protects the particular contractual obligation, and therefore does not contravene the principle (under LRA 2002, s 42(2),)[3] that a restriction may not be entered to protect the priority of an interest which is or could be the subject of a notice. An application for a standard form of restriction (LRR 2003, r 91(1) and Sch 4,) may be made in panel 7 of Form CH1, or in a form of charge which (including the application for the restriction) has first been approved by the registrar: LRR 2003, r 92(7)(b) and (c) and (10).[4] It is thought that where such a restriction is needed, Form P (LRR 2003, Sch 4), prohibiting the registration of any, or of specified, dispositions without a written consent signed by the proprietor of a specified charge, or by his conveyancer, will often be appropriate.

Where a form of charge approved before the commencement of LRA 2002 (and remaining approved) is used after such commencement and contains an application for a restriction, and the registrar considers that there is a standard form of restriction to like or similar effect to the restriction applied for, he must enter that standard form of restriction in the register (Land Registration Act 2002 (Transitional Provisions) Order 2003, SI 2003/1953, art 18).

[1] For example not to grant a lease, or not to create a further charge, or not to do so without the (first) chargee's consent.
[2] Compare Law Com no 271, para 6.40(2).
[3] See Chapter 7, para 7.41.
[4] Disapplying in relation to such applications the requirement under subrule (1) to use Form RX1 to apply for the entry of a restriction. Applications for approval of forms of charge are handled by the Land Registry Head Office, Commercial Arrangements Section: see Land Registry Practice Guide 30.

(3) PRIORITY OF CHARGES OVER REGISTERED LAND AND OF FURTHER ADVANCES ON SUCH CHARGES

8.14 If there are two or more legal charges registered against the same title, they rank as between themselves in the order shown in the register (LRA 2002, s 48(1)). Unless an entry in the register provides for some other order of priority, the order *'shown in the register'* is the order in which the charges are entered in the individual register of the title: LRR 2003, r 101, made under LRA 2002, s 48(2)(a). An application to change the order of priority[1] must be made by or with the consent of the proprietor, or a person entitled to be registered as the proprietor, of any charge whose priority is adversely affected by the alteration, except that no separate consent is required from a person who has executed the instrument altering the priority of the charges: LRR 2003, r 102(1), made under LRA 2002, s 48(2)(b). The registrar may accept a certificate from a conveyancer[2] confirming that the conveyancer holds any necessary consents (LRR 2003, r 102(2),) and must make an entry in the register in such terms as he considers appropriate: LRR 2003, r 102(3). Although the chargor is usually party to any agreement between chargees altering the relative priority of their securities, his concurrence is not essential to its validity,[3] and he is not required to make or consent to an application to register an alteration of the priority of registered charges as between themselves.

---

[1]   To give effect (for example) to an agreement that a later charge is to take priority over an earlier one, or that an earlier charge is to have priority only up to a specified figure and to rank after a later charge as to any balance of the amount secured.

[2]   Ie a solicitor, a licensed conveyancer or a Fellow of the Institute of Legal Executives: LRR 2003 r 217(1).

[3]   *Cheah Theem Swee v Equiticorp Finance Group Ltd* [1992] 1 AC 472.

8.15   The priority of equitable charges is governed by the general principle (LRA 2002, ss 28 and 29,)[1] that the priority of an interest affecting a registered estate is not affected by a disposition of that estate, whether or not the interest or the disposition is registered, except that a registrable disposition for valuable consideration takes priority, when completed by registration, over any interest affecting the estate which is not protected on the register and is not an overriding interest within LRA 2002, Sch 3. An equitable charge should be protected by a notice (under LRA 2002, ss 32 and 34,)[2] on the register, to safeguard its priority against subsequent registered dispositions. As against another similar charge, and also as against any other estate or interest not taking priority as a registered disposition,[3] an equitable charge takes priority according to the date on which it is created. It is considered that if such a security confers on the chargee a power of attorney to execute a legal charge on behalf of the chargor, and the chargee creates and registers a legal charge accordingly, that charge retains the priority of the original equitable charge as against any registered, noted or overriding interest which may have arisen after the date of the equitable, but before that of the legal, charge.[4] Thus, if the sequence of events is:

   (1)   the registered proprietor creates an equitable charge containing such a power of attorney;

   (2)   the registered proprietor contracts to sell the charged land for less than the amount secured by the charge; and

   (3)   the chargee creates and registers a legal charge,

it is considered that the chargee retains priority over the purchaser, even if the sale contract is the subject of a notice on the register or the purchaser is in actual occupation of the land at the date of the legal charge.

---

[1]   See Law Com no 271, para 7.17, and Chapter 7 paras 7.17–7.18.
[2]   See Chapter 7, paras 7.20–7.39.
[3]   A short lease, not required to be registered, also operates for priority purposes as if it were a registered disposition: LRA 2002, s 29(4).
[4]   Any such intervening interest came into being subject to all the rights conferred by the equitable charge, including the right to create a legal charge; and LRA 2002, s 29, postpones unprotected interests to registered dispositions for value, but does *not* provide affirmatively that protected interests always have priority over such dispositions: protected interests take priority if, but only if, they are entitled to it under s 28 and the general law.

8.16   LRA 2002, s 49, contains an exhaustive (subsection (6))[1] catalogue of the situations in which a lender can 'tack' further advances, ie lend further money on the security of a charge of registered land with priority to a subsequent charge created before the further advance is made. There are four such situations, which can be shortly described as:

   (1)   advances made without notice of the subsequent charge (LRA 2002, s 49(1) and (2));[2]

   (2)   advances made under an obligation, entered on the register, to make them (LRA 2002, s 49(3));[3]

   (3)   advances up to an agreed maximum amount entered on the register (LRA 2002, s 49(4));[4] and

   (4)   advances made with the agreement of the subsequent chargee (LRA 2002, s 49(6)).[5]

The first, second and third of these forms of tacking are only available to registered legal chargees; all four are effective against all subsequent charges, whether legal or equitable.[6] Security should therefore always be taken by way of legal charge, and registered as such, if it is contemplated that further advances will or may be made. The detailed considerations applicable to the four permitted forms of tacking are as follows.

---

[1]   By Law of Property Act 1925, s 94(4), as originally enacted, that section did not apply to charges 'registered under' LRA 1925, ie charges substantively registered as legal charges; equitable charges of registered land were therefore subject to s 94. LRA 2002, s 133 and Sch 11, para 2(9), amend s 94(4) to exclude 'charges on registered land' from that section, so that tacking in relation to equitable as well as legal charges of registered land is now governed exclusively by LRA 2002, s 49.
[2]   See para 8.17.
[3]   See para 8.18.
[4]   See para 8.19.
[5]   See para 8.20.
[6]   LRA 2002, s 49(1), (3) and (4), enable 'the proprietor of a registered charge' to make further advances with priority to 'a subsequent charge'; s 49(6) authorises tacking in relation to 'a charge over registered land' by agreement with 'the subsequent chargee'.

8.17 *Tacking without notice of subsequent charge.* The registered proprietor of a prior charge may make a further advance with priority to a subsequent charge if he has not received notice of its creation *from the subsequent chargee*: LRA 2002, s 49(1). The former provision (LRA 1925, s 30(1),) for the registrar to give notice of a proposed register entry prejudicial to the priority of further advances is repealed and not replaced; the new enactment is intended to give statutory effect to the established practice of subsequent chargees giving prior chargees notice of their securities, which is effective at common law to prevent tacking.[1] However, LRA 2002 also provides (by s 49(2)) that such a notice is to be treated as received at the time when, in accordance with rules, (see LRR 2003, r 107,[2]) it ought to have been received; it is thought that the effect is to deem a subsequent chargee's notice to have been received at the specified time even if it is delayed or fails to arrive at all, so that if the sending of the notice is proved, the first lender loses priority for advances made after the time when it ought to have been received, even if he does not actually have any reason to be aware of the subsequent charge's existence. If this be correct, it is a change in the law: before the enactment of s 49(2), a subsequent chargee's notice only prevented tacking if it was successful in putting the prior chargee on notice of the subsequent charge. No indemnity is payable to a prior chargee who loses priority for a further advance because a subsequent chargee's notice is delayed or fails to arrive.[3] It is therefore suggested that the safe course for a lender who intends to make further advances is not to rely on s 49(1) at all, but to use the new statutory facility (under LRA 2002, s 49(4),)[4] to agree and register a maximum amount for which the charge is security.[5]

LRA 2002, s 49(1), does not require the prior charge to be expressed to secure further advances, and it is therefore suggested that a second chargee should always give notice of his security to the first chargee; it is also suggested that the risk of dispute over whether or when notice was given will be reduced if the notice can be sent by a means which generates a record of the fact and time of delivery.[6]

A notice under LRA 2002, s 49(1), can be sent by post to (LRR 2003, r 107(2)(a),)[7] or be left at (LRR 2003, r 107(2)(b),) the prior chargee's address for service as entered in the register, or sent to a document exchange box number (LRR 2003, r 107(2)(c),) or electronic address (LRR 2003, r 107(2)(d),) registered as an additional address for service of the prior chargee; or it may be sent by post, document exchange, fax or electronic transmission to an address or number provided by the prior chargee to the subsequent chargee for the purpose of notices under s 49(1): LRR 2003, r 107(2)(e) and (3).[8] Such a notice is to be treated as received:[9]

(1)   if posted to an address in the United Kingdom, on the second working day after posting;

(2)   if left at a postal address, on the working day after it is left;

(3)   if posted to an address outside the United Kingdom, on the seventh working day after posting;

(4)   if sent through a document exchange, on the second working day after being left at the sender's exchange;

(5)   if sent by fax, on the working day after transmission;

(6)   if transmitted to an electronic address, on the second working day after transmission.

A *'working day'* is any day from Monday to Friday, other than Christmas Day, Good Friday or a bank holiday (LRR 2003, r 107(6)); and a notice posted or transmitted after 5 pm on a working day, or on a day which is not a working day, is treated as posted or transmitted on the next working day: LRR 2003, r 107(5). These provisions identify a day, but not in express terms a time on that day, when a notice is treated as received, and it is unclear whether the relevant time is the first moment of the day, the beginning of ordinary business hours, or some other time.[10] It appears, further, to be arguable that a s 49(1) notice is not effective until the time specified in LRR 2003, r 107, even if it is shown actually to have been received before then.[11] It is suggested that until these issues have been resolved, the safe course (in the absence of agreement between the lenders) will be:

- for a prior chargee not to rely on further advances having priority after a s 49(1) notice has actually been received; and

- for a subsequent chargee not to permit drawdown of the facility secured by the new charge until the day after that on which the s 49(1) notice is treated as received.

---

[1]   See Law Com no 271, paras 7.19 and 7.30.

[2]   Discussed in detail in the later sections of this paragraph.

[3]   Such a loss does not fall within any of the categories in LRA 2002, Sch 8, para 1. See also Law Com no 271, para 7.30.

[4]   See para 8.19.

[5]   There is no transitional provision to stop LRA 2002, s 49(2), operating as described in the text in relation to further advances on a charge registered before the commencement of LRA 2002. (The Land Registration Act 2002 (Transitional Provisions) Order 2003, SI 2003/1953, art 3, preserves the effect of LRA 1925, s 30(1) and (2), in relation only to applications for registration of subsequent charges which were pending at the commencement of LRA 2002.) However, unless the first chargee is under an obligation to make further advances, (in which case his priority will be maintained by LRA 2002, s 49(3), if that obligation is registered,) he can refuse to lend further until a maximum amount has been agreed and registered as a variation of the security.

[6]   For instance by recorded delivery post, or (when permissible) by fax on equipment which produces a timed report of successful transmission.

[7]   The effect of the definition of *'post'* in LRR 2003, r 107(6), is that first class post must be used for a notice sent to an address within the United Kingdom.

[8]   This will enable institutional lenders to give one another addresses which can be used for s 49(1) notices relating to all their charges. However, a notice sent to the prior chargee's registered address for service is always effective, even if an alternative has been provided under LRR 2003, r 107(3), and if more than one address for service is registered, it is considered that notice sent to any of them is effective, and that if notices are sent to more than one such address, the prior chargee is to be taken to have received notice of the subsequent charge at the earliest time at which any one of those notices is treated as received under the provisions of LRR 2003, r 107.

[9]   See the Table in LRR 2003 r 107(4).

[10] A question might arise as to the priority of indebtedness created by a withdrawal from a cash machine between midnight and the start of business hours.

[11] Compare the words *'shall be treated as received at the time ...'* in LRA 2002, s 49(2), with *'shall be deemed to be served on the day ...'* in CPR r 6.7(1); the latter expression was construed in *Anderton v Clwyd County Council (No 2)* [2002] 3 All ER 813, [2002] 1 WLR 3174, [2002] EWCA Civ 933, paras 25–36, as deeming service of proceedings to take place on, and not before, the specified date, even if the relevant documents were proved or admitted to have been received on an earlier day.

8.18 *Tacking in pursuance of an obligation entered on the register.* The registered proprietor of a prior charge may also make a further advance with priority to a subsequent charge if that advance is made in pursuance of an obligation to make it (LRA 2002, s 49(3)(a),) and the obligation was entered in the register when the subsequent charge was created: LRA 2002, s 49(3)(b). This reproduces the previous law as between obligatory further advances and registered charges subsequent to that creating the obligation,[1] and also gives obligatory further advances priority over equitable charges created before such advances are made.[2] If the proprietor, or a person applying to be registered as proprietor, of a registered charge is under an obligation to make further advances on the security of the charge, he may apply for the obligation to be entered in the register: LRR 2003, r 108(1). The application must be made in Form CH2 (LRR 2003, r 108(2),) unless it is contained in panel 7 of Form CH1 or in a charge the form of which has been approved by the registrar: LRR 2003, r 108(3). The registrar must make an appropriate entry in the register: LRR 2003, r 108(4). A note of an obligation to make further advances made in the register before the commencement of LRA 2002 (under LRA 1925, s 30(3),) continues to be effective for the purposes of LRA 2002 and LRR 2003: Land Registration Act 2002 (Transitional Provisions) Order 2003, SI 2003/1953, art 25.

[1] LRA 1925, s 30(3), which provided that *'a subsequent registered charge'* was postponed to further advances that the first mortgagee was obliged to make, if the obligation was noted on the register.

[2] See Law Com no 271, paras 7.22 and 7.31.

8.19 *Tacking where an agreed maximum amount is entered on the register.* The registered proprietor of a prior charge may also make a further advance with priority to a subsequent charge if the parties to the prior charge have agreed a maximum amount for which that charge is security (LRA 2002, s 49(4)(a),) the agreement is entered in the register (LRA 2002, s 49(4)(b),) and the aggregate of the further advance and the other money secured does not exceed the agreed maximum.[1] The agreement is not required to be contained in or made at the same time as the charge, and the parties to a registered charge which was in existence at the commencement of LRA 2002 can therefore enter into such an agreement, and register it, if they wish.[2] It is considered that if the maximum is exceeded, priority is lost as to the excess only, but that in the absence of any agreement between the borrower and the prior chargee as to the application of subsequent repayments,[3] there is a possibility of such repayments being appropriated to the earlier lending and reducing the amount for which the prior chargee has priority;[4] it is therefore suggested that it will be to the latter's advantage to include, in any agreement as to the maximum amount secured, a provision that if the sum owing ever exceeds the agreed maximum amount, subsequent repayments are to be treated as appropriated to the excess until the borrowing is reduced below that amount.

The agreed maximum amount is inclusive of any unpaid interest and costs (other than costs of realising the security),[5] so it appears probable that lenders adopting this procedure will seek to agree a maximum amount significantly in excess of what they actually expect to advance; and the prior lenders' safety margin will reduce the residual value of the property on which subsequent lenders will be prepared to rely as security.

Where the parties to a registered or registrable charge have agreed a maximum amount for which the charge is security, the proprietor, or a person applying to be registered as proprietor, of the charge may apply for the agreement to be entered in the register: LRR 2003, r 109(1). The application must be in Form CH3 in all cases (even if the agreement is contained in a charge in Form CH1 or in a charge in a form approved by the registrar): LRR 2003, r 109(2). The registrar must make an entry in the register in such terms as he considers appropriate to give effect to the application: LRR 2003, r 109(3).

There is power (LRA 2002, s 49(5),) to make rules disapplying the facility to tack further advances up to a limit, or making such tacking subject to compliance with specified conditions, in relation to charges of a description specified in such rules; the power has not been exercised.

---

[1]   This is not stated in terms in LRA 2002, s 49(4), but is implicit in the scheme and objective of the subsection. See Law Com no 271, paras 7.32–7.35.

[2]   LRA 2002, s 49(4)(a), requires only that the agreement must be made between the parties to the prior charge. See also Land Registry Practice Guide 29, para 7, indicating that the registry will accept an application (in Form CH3) to register such an agreement contained in a deed of variation.

[3]   For example credits to an overdrawn current account in the ordinary course of business.

[4]   See *Devaynes v Noble, Clayton's Case* (1816) 1 Mer 529, appropriating debits and credits to a running account against one another in date order.

[5]   The parties have to agree a maximum *'amount'*, and not (for example) a maximum *'advance'*, for which the charge is security. See Law Com no 271, para 7.34.

8.20   *Tacking by agreement with subsequent chargee.* Tacking otherwise than in accordance with the rules described above is only possible with the agreement of the subsequent chargee: LRA 2002, s 49(6). Tacking by agreement is permitted whether the prior charge is legal or equitable.[1] It is thought that the most frequent form of such agreement will be a priority agreement between incumbrancers regulating the priority of future as well as immediate advances. If such an agreement gives one incumbrancer priority up to a specified limit, but the limit is not entered on the register (LRA 2002, s 49(4),) it will be effective as between the parties to it, but not as against any subsequent chargee.

---

[1]   LRA 2002, s 49(6), applies to tacking *in relation to a charge over registered land*, and is not confined to advances on the security of a registered charge.

8.21   Some charges created or arising under statutes and securing the payment of money have priority over all interests in the land affected, including earlier charges.[1] A significant proportion of such charges are in favour of local authorities and operate as local land charges,[2] so that they remain binding on registered disponees of the land for value even if they are not registered under LRA 2002 (see ss 28(1), 29(1) and (2)(a)(ii), and Sch 3, para 6),[3] but the title to such a charge must nevertheless be registered before it is enforced (LRA 2002, s 55).[4]

A person applying, either on the creation of the charge or when enforcement is imminent, to register a statutory charge which has the effect of postponing existing securities, must lodge Form SC with the application (LRR 2003, r 105(1)); the form requires the applicant to identify the provision which confers priority and the charges over which priority is claimed.[5] If the registrar is satisfied that the charge has the priority claimed, he must make an entry showing that priority in the charges register of the title affected (LRR 2003, r 105(2)); if he is not so satisfied but considers that the applicant has an arguable case, he may make an entry in the charges register that the applicant claims such priority: LRR 2003, r 105(3). On making an entry in either form, the registrar must give notice of it[6] to the registered proprietor of every registered charge entered in the charges register at the time the statutory charge is registered, (LRR 2003, r 106(1)(a),) and also to any person who appears to be entitled to a charge protected by a notice on the charges register at that time, (LRR 2003, r 106(1)(b),) unless, in the case of a charge protected by a notice, the name and address for service of the person entitled are not set out in the individual register in which the notice is entered: LRR 2003, r 106(2).

If an entry is made indicating that the statutory charge has priority, any person who suffers loss because of a failure by the registrar to give notice of that entry, is entitled to be indemnified: LRA 2002, s 103 and Sch 8, para 1(1)(h).[7] A person who wishes to dispute the priority indicated by such an entry can either apply for the register to be rectified (under LRA 2002, s 65 and Sch 4,)[8] by removing the relevant entry, or defer taking action, (though it may be thought advisable to notify the statutory chargee that the priority will be challenged if it becomes material,) until the security is realised, and then litigate the issue against the statutory chargee if the proceeds of realisation are not enough to discharge all sums owing but not paid by the proprietor of the land.[9]

If the registrar makes an entry of a claim that the statutory charge has priority, the proprietor of that charge, or the proprietor of a charge registered against the title which, subject to that claim for priority, would rank ahead of, or with equal priority to, the statutory charge,[10] may apply for the entry to be removed, or to be replaced by an entry that the statutory charge has the priority claimed: LRR 2003, r 105(5).[11] Any such application must be supported by evidence (LRR 2003, r 105(7),) and before it is determined, the registrar must give notice of it to the proprietors of any other registered charges affected by the claim to priority: LRR 2003, r 105(8), referring to r 105(5). If any of such proprietors object to the application, and the objection is not groundless and cannot be disposed of by agreement, it must be referred to the adjudicator (LRA 2002, s 73).[12] It is considered that the proprietor of a charge which would be adversely affected by a claim to statutory priority, if established, is not obliged to make an immediate application to remove the entry, if he prefers to leave the issue to be decided only if it actually becomes significant. It is also submitted that if a dispute over statutory priority is referred to the adjudicator, and the sum for which priority is claimed is comparatively small and amply covered by the value of the land affected after allowing for the amount secured by the earlier charge, then unless the dispute depends on oral evidence which may become 'stale', the appropriate course may be to stay the matter indefinitely and only decide it if a decision becomes essential.[13]

---

[1] For example a charge under Housing Act 1985, s 193 and Sch 10, para 7(1), for recovery of the expenses of works required by a repairs notice, which are *'a charge on the premises'*; the equivalent provision in Housing Act 1925, s 3(3), was held in *Paddington Borough Council v Finucane* [1928] Ch 567 to create a charge on the whole of the proprietary interests in the premises.

[2] See for example Highways Act 1980, s 212(3), by which a sum apportioned to any premises in respect of the expenses of street works is *'a charge on the premises and all estates and interests therein'*, and Local Land Charges Act 1975, s 1(1)(a), as amended.

[3] See Chapter 7, paras 7.12 and 7.78.

[4] See para 8.27.

[5] Form SC panels 10 and 11 respectively. The form can also be used to make a claim for statutory priority for a charge which has already been registered: see panel 9 and LRR 2003, r 105(6).

[6] LRA 2002, s 50, entry that the charge has priority, and LRR 2003, r 105(4), entry of claim to priority.

[7] For indemnity generally see Chapter 14. The proprietor of an earlier charge might suffer loss because of a failure to give such a notice if he lent further money in ignorance of the existence of the statutory charge and the security proved to be insufficient.

[8] See Chapter 14.

[9] Compare Law Com no 271, para 7.41, to the effect that the issues raised are difficult, and often do not actually need to be decided.

[10] Including another statutory chargee claiming priority: LRR 2003, r 105(6).

[11] A person entitled to a charge which is not registered, but is only protected by a notice, cannot make an application under this rule.

(4) CHARGEES' POWERS

8.22 A registered charge has effect as a charge by deed by way of legal mortgage (LRA 2002, s 51), and subject to any entry in the register to the contrary, the proprietor of such a charge is to be taken to have all the powers of disposition over the charged property conferred on a legal mortgagee by the general law: LRA 2002, s 52(1).[1] If, therefore, the charge provides (for example) that the chargee's power of sale is not to arise until a future date,[2] or that his power of leasing (under Law of Property Act 1925, s 99(2),) is to be restricted, a sale or lease contrary to those provisions will be effective to confer title on the purchaser or tenant (LRA 2002, s 52(2),)[3] unless the limitations on the chargee's powers are reinforced by an entry on the register; the appropriate entry will normally be a restriction.[4] The effect of the presumption that, in the absence of a contrary register entry, the chargee's powers are unrestricted, is only to prevent a disponee's title being questioned, and does not affect the lawfulness of a disposition: LRA 2002, s 52(2). It therefore does not affect any remedy of the chargor against the chargee in respect of a misuse of the latter's apparent powers,[5] or any remedy there may be against the disponee personally[6] if he has actually participated in wrongdoing by the chargee.

1 See para 8.23.
2 The statutory power of sale under Law of Property Act 1925, s 101(1)(i), arises *'when the mortgage money has become due'*, and is therefore postponed to the extent that the date for repayment of the loan is deferred.
3 Compare the similar rules in LRA 2002, s 26, as to the exercise of 'owners' powers' under s 23.
4 See Chapter 7, paras 7.40–7.45; Form S or Form T in LRR 2003, Sch 4, should be used if it is practicable to do so.
5 Compare Law Com no 271, para 7.7, referring to a possible right to damages. The amount of the chargor's loss will have to be assessed by reference to the fact that the disposition is unchallengeable and the land irrecoverable, but the question arises whether the chargor's omission to register an appropriate restriction is a failure to mitigate, justifying a reduction in the damages awarded; the analogy of a sale of unregistered land in breach of an unregistered estate contract, where the disappointed purchaser can recover full damages, (see *Wright v Dean* [1948] Ch 686,) suggests that non-registration of a restriction does not have this effect.
6 For inducing breach of contract or as a constructive trustee.

8.23   Subject to restrictions on enforcing security over the property of a company in administration (Insolvency Act 1986, Sch B1, para 43(2),)[1] the general law empowers a mortgagee under a mortgage made by deed, most importantly, to sell (Law of Property Act 1925 ('LPA 1925'), ss 101(1)(i) and (2) and 103–107,) or let (LPA 1925, ss 99(2) and 100,)[2] the mortgaged land, to insure it (LPA 1925, ss 101(1)(ii) and 108), and to appoint a receiver of its income (LPA 1925, ss 101(1)(iii) and 109), subject to compliance with the conditions and limitations applicable to those powers respectively. A full treatment of a mortgagee's powers would be outside the scope of this book; the following paragraphs deal only with the provisions of LRA 2002 and LRR 2003 which relate to the exercise of those powers.

---

[1]   Inserted by Enterprise Act 2002, s 248 and Sch 16, with effect from 15 September 2003 (Enterprise Act 2002 (Commencement No 4 &c) Order 2003, SI 2003/2093, art 2(1) and Sch 1).
[2]   LPA 1925 s 100 confers power to accept a surrender of a lease to enable an authorised lease to be granted.

8.24   A sale under the chargee's statutory power transfers the charged property to the purchaser free from the charge and from all estates, interests and rights to which the charge has priority, but subject to any charges or other interests which have priority to it (LPA 1925, ss 88(1), 89(1) and 104(1),) and therefore overrides any charges, leases or other proprietary rights created or arising after the date of the charge under which the property is sold,[1] even if they are entered on the register or fall within one of the paragraphs of LRA 2002, Sch 3.[2]

A chargee of a dwelling house who brings an action to enforce the security must give notice of the action to any person who has registered matrimonial home rights against the property (Family Law Act 1996, ss 30–31 and 56);[3] notice is not required if an official search reveals no such rights and the action is brought within 15 working days after the date of the search certificate (Family Law Act 1996, s 56(3) and (5).[4]

A sale under the chargee's power of the whole of the land in a registered title must be completed by a transfer in Form TR2, and a sale of part by a transfer in Form TP2 (LRR 2003, r 58).

If the proceeds of sale are more than enough to discharge the principal, interest and costs due to the selling chargee, he holds the surplus in trust for the chargee next in priority of whose interest he has notice, or for the chargor (LPA 1925, s 105).[5] He is taken for this purpose to have notice of all entries in the register immediately before the disposition on sale (LRA 2002, s 54), and should therefore search the register as close to the time of completion as is possible.

---

[1]   Provided such interests have not acquired priority by agreement or by statute: compare para 8.21. If LPA 1925, s 99(1), is not excluded by the terms of the charge, it enables the chargor (whilst in possession of the land) to grant certain leases which will be binding on the chargee.

[2] LRA 2002 postpones any unprotected right to a registered disposition for valuable consideration, but does not enable a protected interest to avoid the distinct overriding effect of LPA 1925, s 104(1), as applied to registered land by LRA 2002, ss 51–52.

[3] A person having matrimonial home rights is entitled under Family Law Act 1996, ss 30(3) and 55, to make payments in respect of the charge, and to be joined in the action in order to invoke the court's jurisdiction to adjourn possession proceedings or to suspend the operation of a possession order.

[4] Applying the priority period in Land Charges Act 1972, s 11(5), (6)(a). By LRR 2003, r 158, an application for such a search must be in Form MH3.

[5] See also Law Com no 271, para 7.43.

8.25 A chargee who is entitled to consolidate two or more registered charges on different properties[1] may apply to the registrar for an entry to be made in respect of that right in the individual register in which any of those charges is registered (LRR 2003, r 110(1), made under LRA 2002, s 57). The application must be made in Form CC (LRR 2003, r 110(2),) and the registrar must make an entry in the individual register in such terms as he considers appropriate to give effect to it: LRR 2003, r 110(3).

A right to consolidate several charges may exist if any one of them reserves it, (LPA 1925, s 93(1),) provided all other necessary conditions are satisfied; but it is considered that where a purchaser for valuable consideration of land acquires it subject to a registered charge which is not discharged, but continues to be binding, he nevertheless takes free from any right of the chargee to consolidate any other security, unless that right is either entered on the individual register of the title to that land, or reserved by the charge registered against it.[2]

[1] Ie to insist that they are all redeemed together; for the detailed rules see 32 *Halsbury's Laws* (4th edn reissue) paras 698–713. Questions of consolidation arise comparatively infrequently in practice.

[2] It is submitted that the right to consolidate is an *'interest affecting the estate'* within LRA 2002, s 29(1), and overridden by a registered disposition for valuable consideration if not protected on the register. (It is unlikely that land will ever be sold, subject to a continuing charge, at a time when a chargee with a right to consolidate another security is in occupation of it, enabling that right to fall within LRA 2002, Sch 3, para 2.) Any other result would derogate from the principle that so far as possible the register should be a complete and accurate reflection of the state of the title: Law Com no 271, para 1.5.

8.26 Where a chargee has obtained an order for foreclosure absolute,[1] he can make an application[2] to be registered as proprietor of the registered estate affected; the application must be accompanied by the order (LRR 2003, r 112(1),) or by a conveyancer's certificate confirming that he holds the order or an office copy of it: LRR 2003, r 112(3). The registrar must cancel the registration of the charge in respect of which the order was made, and all entries in respect of interests over which the charge has priority, and enter the applicant as proprietor of the registered estate: LRR 2003, r 112(2). This corresponds with the effect of the foreclosure order under the general law.

---

1   Ie a court order extinguishing the rights of the registered proprietor of the land and making the chargee sole owner of it; see 32 *Halsbury's Laws* (4th edn reissue) paras 767–815. Foreclosure orders are rarely made.
2   Form AP1, under LRR 2003 r 13(1); no other form is prescribed.

8.27   A local land charge affecting registered land and securing the payment of money[1] is not required to be registered under LRA 2002 in order to take effect as a legal charge, (LRA 2002, s 27(5)(c),) and is not overridden by a registered disposition for valuable consideration of the land charged (LRA 2002, s 29(1) and (2)(a)(ii) and Sch 3, para 6). However, it may only be realised if the title to it is registered (LRA 2002, s 55);[2] and the application for registration must be supported by evidence of the charge (LRR 2003, r 104).

---

1   See the Local Land Charges Act 1975, ss 1(1)(a) (as amended) and 7; a local land charge registered as such takes effect as a charge by way of legal mortgage.
2   The purpose of this provision is to ensure that the register shows what powers exist to dispose of any registered land: see Law Com no 271, para 7.42.

8.28   An equitable chargee whose security is capable of registration as a legal charge can register it, with priority as of the date of its creation if in the meantime it has been protected by a notice on the register, (LRA 2002, s 29(1) and (2)(a)(i),) and when registered it can be enforced as a legal charge as described above.[1]

If an equitable security includes a power for the chargee to create a legal charge as the chargor's attorney, and he exercises the power and applies to register the legal charge, it will be necessary to produce to the registrar either the original, or evidence in one of the prescribed forms, of the equitable security containing the power of attorney, (LRR 2003, r 61(1)(a)–(d),) and if more than 12 months have elapsed since the power was created, a statutory declaration or certificate that it has not been revoked will also be required (LRR 2003, r 62 and Sch 3, Form 2).[2] It is considered that such a legal charge, when registered, has the same priority as the original equitable charge.[3] If an equitable charge by deed contains a power of sale and a power of attorney for the chargee to complete the sale by transferring the property, there is nothing in LRA 2002 to affect the principle that the transfer may[4] have to be treated for priority purposes as made by the chargor, and ineffective to clear off other charges unless they are specifically released[5] by the chargees entitled to them.

The court has power to enforce an equitable charge by making an order for sale, and to make a vesting order, or an order appointing a person to convey the land, in order to carry out the sale (LPA 1925, ss 90(1) and 91(2) and (7)); but it is submitted that the powers under those provisions to vest a mortgage term in the chargee, although not expressly repealed, cannot now be effectively exercised in relation to registered land.[6]

[1]   See paras 8.22–8.24.

[2]   A power of attorney supporting an equitable charge will normally be expressed to be given by way of security, under Powers of Attorney Act 1971, s 4, and Form 2 will confirm that the chargee had no knowledge, when the power was exercised, that it was not in fact given by way of security, or of any revocation with the attorney's consent, or of any other event having the effect of revoking it.

[3]   See para 8.15.

[4]   Compare *Re White Rose Cottage* [1965] Ch 940. It appears to be arguable that LRA 2002, s 51, prevents a sale under a charge from clearing off subsequent incumbrances if the charge is not itself registered; but the better view, it is submitted, is that LRA 2002, s 23(1)(a), enables a registered proprietor to create equitable security in the same way and with the same effect as was possible before the commencement of LRA 2002.

[5]   See para 8.29.

[6]   LPA 1925, ss 90 and 91, enable the court to create a mortgage term 'as if' that term had been created under that Act; it is submitted that those sections must now be interpreted consistently with the effect of LRA 2002, s 23(1)(a), which makes it impossible to mortgage registered land by demise under LPA 1925 (or otherwise).

(5) DISCHARGE, RELEASE AND TRANSFER OF CHARGES

8.29 Unless the procedure for electronic notification of the discharge of a registered charge is used (LRR 2003, r 115),[1] the discharge of the whole of the land in a registered title must be in Form DS1 (LRR 2003, r 114(1),) and executed by the chargee as a deed or authenticated in such other manner as the registrar may approve: LRR 2003, r 114(3). In the case of building society charges, the registry will accept a discharge executed by the society as a deed,[2] or sealed with its seal countersigned by a person authorised by the board, or signed by a person so authorised;[3] and institutional lenders which execute numerous discharges in a manner authorised by special provisions of their respective constitutions (rather than under the general law) can make arrangements with Land Registry Headquarters to obviate the need to provide evidence of their ability to do so with every application to register a discharge.[4] The application to register a discharge in Form DS1 must be made in Form AP1 or DS2: LRR 2003, r 114(5).

A release of part of the land in a registered title must be in Form DS3, (LRR 2003, r 114(2),) executed or authenticated in the same way as a discharge of the whole (LRR 2003, r 114(3), considered above); the application to register it must be in Form AP1: LRR 2003, r 114(5).[5]

Where a charge is registered in the name of two or more proprietors jointly, a receipt for the money secured can be given by them or the survivors or survivor of them, or by the personal representative of the last survivor (LRA 2002, s 56). It is thought that an application to register a discharge or release by the survivors or survivor of joint chargees should be accompanied by an application (under LRR 2003, r 164,)[6] to remove the name of the deceased chargee; a discharge or release by the personal representative of the last survivor should be accompanied by the original grant of representation: LRR 2003, r 162(1).[7] The prescribed forms of discharge and of release are acknowledgements by the lender that the property specified *'is no longer charged as security for the payment of the sums due under the charge'*,[8] and do not affect the lender's right to recover from the borrower any part of the debt which has not been repaid.

The registrar is also entitled to accept and act upon any other proof of satisfaction of a charge that he may regard as sufficient: LRR 2003, r 114(4).[9]

---

[1]   See para 8.30.

[2]   In accordance with LPA 1925, s 74(1), or in any other way permitted by the society's constitution and rules.

[3]   Building Societies (Prescribed Form of Receipt) Rules 1997, SI 1997/2869; see Land Registry Practice Guide 31, para 3.4.

[4]   Practice Guide 31, para 3.7; see paras 3.2–3.6 of that Guide for a fuller list of the forms of authentication of discharges which the registry will accept.

[5]   Form DS2 cannot be used to apply for registration of a release of part of the land in a title from a charge.

[6]   The application must be supported by evidence of the death, which may be a death certificate, a conveyancer's written confirmation of the fact of the death, the original grant of representation, or a certificate by a conveyancer that he holds the original grant or an office copy; see Land Registry Practice Guide 6, para 3.

[7]   Land Registry Practice Guide 6, para 2.3, indicates that a conveyancer's certificate will be accepted.

[8]   Panel 6 of Form DS1 and of Form DS3.

[9]   It is considered that if litigation as to the sum required to redeem results in an order that the property is to be discharged on payment of a specified sum into court, this provision will enable the entry of the charge to be removed on an application supported by the order and payment schedule, without the need to obtain a Form DS1 from a recalcitrant or untraceable chargee.

8.30   Lenders authorised by the registry to do so[1] can send an electronic notification of the discharge of a registered charge ('END') to the registry in substitution for an executed paper Form DS1: LRR 2003, r 115(1) and (2). A paper application in Form AP1, DS2 or DS2E is also required; the entry of the charge will be removed when the registry has received the application and a matching END.[2] There is power to make arrangements for electronic notification of the release of part of the land in a title from a registered charge (LRR 2003, r 115(1)(b),) but at the time of writing no such arrangements are in force.

---

[1]   The Land Registry website maintains an up-to-date list of such lenders.

[2]   See Land Registry Practice Guide 31, para 6.

8.31   If an equitable charge protected by a notice on the register is discharged, or released as to part of the land, the ordinary procedure for removal or modification of the notice must be used. If it is an agreed notice (LRA 2002, s 34(2)(a),)[1] a notice entered by the registrar (LRA 2002, s 37),[2] or a notice entered before the commencement of LRA 2002, (LRA 1925, s 49, and LRA 2002, Sch 12 para 2(1),)[3] an application for its cancellation should be made in Form CN1 and accompanied by evidence to satisfy the registrar of its discharge or release: LRR 2003, r 87(1).[4] In relation to a fixed equitable charge, the registry will accept as sufficient evidence a Form DS1 or DS3 executed by the chargee, a receipt endorsed on the charge, or a letter from the chargee confirming that the charge has not been assigned and has been discharged.[5] In relation to a floating charge, the evidence may be a copy declaration of satisfaction stamped as registered by the Companies Registry, a letter from the Registrar of Companies, a letter from the chargee, or, if a transfer of the land on sale has been lodged for registration, a certificate signed by the solicitor, licensed conveyancer or secretary of the chargor that no event which would crystallise the charge occurred before the date of the transfer.[6]

If the charge is protected by a unilateral notice, (LRA 2002, s 34(2)(b),)[7] the beneficiary of the notice (ie the chargee) can apply for it to be removed (LRA 2002, s 35(3), and LRR 2003, r 85, requiring Form UN2 to be used).[8] If the chargee does not make such an application after the amount owing has been repaid, the registered proprietor of the land can apply for the notice to be cancelled, (LRA 2002, s 36(1), and LRR 2003, r 86, requiring Form UN4 to be used,)[9] and the entry will be removed if the chargee does not object when the registrar gives him notice of the application.[10] If the chargee does object and the objection cannot be resolved by agreement, the dispute will be referred to the adjudicator (LRA 2002, s 73(7)).[11]

---

[1]   See Chapter 7, paras 7.24 and 7.28.
[2]   See Chapter 7, paras 7.25–7.26.
[3]   For notices of deposit of a land certificate, see para 8.32.
[4]   See Chapter 7, para 7.34.
[5]   See Land Registry Practice Guide 31, para 4.2.1.
[6]   See Land Registry Practice Guide 31, para 4.2.2.
[7]   See Chapter 7, paras 7.24 and 7.35.
[8]   See Chapter 7, para 7.39.
[9]   See Chapter 7, para 7.36.
[10]   See LRA 2002, s 36(2) and (3), and LRR 2003, r 86(3)–(6), specifying 15 business days from issue of the notice (subject to possible extension) as the time within which an objection must be made; see Chapter 7, para 7.36.
[11]   See Chapter 15.

8.32   An equitable charge may be protected by a caution against dealings (LRA 1925, s 54,) registered before the commencement of LRA 2002, or by a notice of deposit of the land certificate of the charged land, operating as a caution (LRR 1925, r 239),[1] if the notice was registered before 3 April 1995 (LRR 1995, r 4). Such entries continue to have effect after the commencement of LRA 2002 (LRA 2002, Sch 12, paras 1, 2(3) and (4), and 3). When a charge protected by a caution is discharged, or released in part, the chargee can apply to withdraw the caution (LRR 2003, r 222(1), requiring Form WCT to be used,) as to the whole or part[2] of the registered title; if he does not do so, the proprietor of the land can 'warn off' the caution (LRR 2003, rr 223, requiring Form CCD to be used, and 221).[3]

---

[1]   See LRR 1925, r 239(4), as originally in force, and r 239(1) as amended by LRR 1995, r 4.
[2]   See panel 7 of Form WCT.
[3]   See Chapter 7, para 7.88.

8.33   A registered charge can be transferred: LRA 2002, s 23(2). A transfer of a single charge must be in Form TR3, or Form AS2 if the transfer is by the personal representative of an individual chargee who has died to a beneficiary of the estate; and two or more charges can be transferred, by the same transferor to the same transferee, by a transfer in Form TR4 (LRR 2003, r 116). The transfer does not operate at law until it is completed by registration: LRA 2002, s 27(3)(a).[1] Registration has the effect, if the transfer is made for valuable consideration, of giving it priority over any interest affecting the charge immediately before execution of the transfer which is neither protected on the register, nor an interest within LRA 2002, Sch 3, at the time of registration (LRA 2002, s 30).[2]

An equitable charge can be assigned by any means which is effective under the general law. If it is protected by a unilateral notice, the assignee can apply to be registered as the beneficiary of that notice (LRR 2003, r 88, requiring Form UN3 to be used).[3] If the charge is protected by an agreed notice, it is considered that the assignee acquires title to it, and that the charge retains its original priority, even if no alteration is made to the register (LRA 2002, s 32(3)); but it is suggested that the safer course is to apply for a further notice, showing the assignee's entitlement, by way of variation of the original notice, (LRR 2003, rr 81 and 84(4),)[4] to ensure that neither the registered proprietor nor a prior chargee (see LRA 2002, s 54,)[5] makes payment to the assignor.

---

[1]   By Sch 2, para 10, the transferee must be entered in the register as the proprietor of the charge.
[2]   Compare LRA 2002, s 29, considered in Chapter 7, paras 7.17–7.18; LRA 2002, Sch 3, is considered in paras 7.62–7.81.
[3]   Form UN3 must be supported by evidence of the applicant's entitlement; the assignor should sign the form or consent to the application in some other way. See Chapter 7, para 7.38.
[4]   LRR 2003 r 81 requires Form AN1 to be used and supported by appropriate evidence. See Chapter 7, para 7.33.
[5]   See para 8.24.

(6) SUB-CHARGES

8.34 The proprietor of a registered charge has power to charge at law with the payment of money the indebtedness secured by the registered charge (LRA 2002, s 23(2)(b)); no other form of legal sub-charge is possible: LRA 2002, s 23(2)(a) and (3).[1] No form of sub-charge is specifically prescribed; Form CH1 is applicable to a *'registered estate'* (LRR 2003, r 103), which does not include a registered charge, (LRA 2002, s 132(1),)[2] but (it is thought) the form can be adapted for use as a sub-charge. A sub-charge only operates at law when it is completed by registration, (LRA 2002, s 27(3)(b),) which is effected by entering the sub-chargee in the register as proprietor of the sub-charge (LRA 2002, Sch 2, para 11).[3] Registration of the sub-charge has the effect, if it is made for valuable consideration, of giving it priority over any interest affecting the charge immediately before the execution of the sub-charge which is neither protected on the register, nor an interest within LRA 2002, Sch 3, at the time of registration (LRA 2002, s 30).[4]

The priority of registered sub-charges as between themselves is governed by the order in which they are shown on the register, (LRA 2002, s 48(1),) which is the order in which they are entered in the individual register of the title affected (LRR 2003, r 101), subject to any agreement to the contrary made between all the sub-chargees affected and entered in the register (LRR 2003, r 102).[5]

---

[1] Excluding from a registered chargee's 'owner's powers' the ability to create a legal sub-mortgage.
[2] Applicable to LRR 2003 by virtue of the Interpretation Act 1978, s 11.
[3] Under LRR 2003, r 9(b), the entry is made in the charges register.
[4] Compare LRA 2002, ss 29, considered in Chapter 7, paras 7.17–7.18; LRA 2002, Sch 3, is considered in paras 7.62–7.81.
[5] See para 8.14.

8.35 It is considered that a registered sub-charge is a *'registered charge'*[1] for the purpose of the statutory provisions as to tacking further advances (LRA 2002, s 49; LRR 2003, rr 107–109),[2] and for the purpose of the rules governing the discharge and transfer of charges (LRR 2003, rr 114–116).[3]

---

[1] See the definitions of *'charge'* and *'registered charge'* in LRA 2002, s 132(1), which are not restricted to charges over a *'registered estate'*.
[2] See paras 8.16–8.20.
[3] See paras 8.29 and 8.33.

8.36 The registered proprietor of a sub-charge has the same powers as the sub-chargor[1] in relation to the property subject to the principal charge (LRA 2002, s 53). If those powers have become exercisable as against the proprietor of the land charged, and the sub-chargee is also entitled to enforce his security as against the proprietor of the charge, he can therefore sell the land (under LPA 1925, ss 101(1)(i) and 103–107); he may retain the amount owing on his sub-charge, up to the amount owing on the principal charge, and must then account to the principal chargee for any balance of the sum owing on the principal charge, and to the person next entitled, subject to discharge of that charge,[2] for any amount by which the proceeds of sale exceed that sum. If the sub-chargor defaults but the principal chargor does not, so that only the sub-charge is realisable, the sub-chargee can require the interest and other sums accruing due under the principal charge to be paid to him, or can realise his security by selling (if a purchaser can be found) the secured debt owing from the chargor to the principal chargee.

---

[1]   See paras 8.22–8.24.
[2]   See para 8.24.

8.37 A registered chargee can create an equitable sub-charge in any way permitted by the general law (LRA 2002, s 23(2)(a)); such a sub-charge can be protected by entering a notice[1] in relation to the principal charge. An equitable sub-charge can be enforced in the same way as an equitable charge.[2]

---

[1]   See Chapter 7, paras 7.20–7.39.
[2]   See para 8.28.

---

9 Easements and covenants

EASEMENTS: INTRODUCTORY

9.1   The law of land registration as relating to easements is inevitably complex, because of the range of characteristics (and the number of possible combinations of characteristics) of easements under the general law. An easement:

- always affects two titles, being exercisable over servient land for the benefit of dominant land;
- may exist at law for an interest equivalent to a legal estate, or only as an equitable interest;
- may arise by express grant or reservation, by implied grant or reservation, or by prescription;
- may come into existence before or on first registration of the servient or the dominant land, or by prescription against registered land, or by a disposition of registered land;
- may or may not itself be entered in the registered title of the servient or of the dominant land;
- may be affected by a disposition of the servient land.

The discussion of easements in this chapter is arranged as follows:
(1)   first registration—paras 9.3–9.9;
(2)   the creation of easements over and for the benefit of registered land—paras 9.10–9.16;
(3)   the effect on easements of dispositions of registered land—paras 9.17–9.26;
(4)   transitional provisions—paras 9.27–9.28.

Within each section, the servient and the dominant land will be considered separately, and the distinctions between legal and equitable easements, between express grant, implied grant and prescription, and between registered and unregistered easements, will be mentioned where they are relevant.

9.2   It is appropriate, before embarking on a consideration of the detailed rules, to emphasise one important practical consideration.

> *If an easement of any description affects registered land, the safest course, if practicable, is always to enter it on the registered title to both the servient and the dominant land.*

EASEMENTS: (1) FIRST REGISTRATION (A) OF SERVIENT LAND

9.3   Where unregistered land is subject either to a legal or to an equitable easement, however arising, the dominant owner[1] is entitled to lodge a caution against first registration (LRA 2002, ss 15(1)(b) and 132(3)(b),)[2] and it is suggested that doing so is a worthwhile precaution, particularly as regards an implied or prescriptive easement,[3] since that will ensure that any purchaser of the servient land actually becomes aware of its existence, and eliminates the risk of a dispute arising on the purchaser only discovering after completion that the easement impedes his proposed use of the land. In relation to an equitable easement, however, lodging a caution against first registration does not obviate the need also to register a Class D(iii) land charge, (Land Charges Act 1972, s 2(5)(iii),) because what the cautioner receives is notice of an application for first registration which has actually been made: LRA 2002, s 16(1). If the application is based on a sale or other disposition for money or money's worth,[4] any unregistered land charge will have become void against the cautioner on completion of that disposition, and therefore before the notice is given: Land Charges Act 1972, s 4(6).[5]

---

[1]   Or a tenant of the dominant land who is entitled to make use of the easement: such a tenant has an 'interest affecting' the servient land within LRA 2002, s 15(1)(b).
[2]   See Chapter 4, paras 4.3–4.8.
[3]   Such easements may not be readily apparent from the documents of title, and the servient owner may not in fact remember their existence and disclose them to a prospective buyer.
[4]   It is thought that such dispositions are likely to continue to be the most frequent occasions for first registration.
[5]   See para 9.7.

9.4   Every legal easement, however arising, which exists at the time of first registration of the servient land,[1] is binding on the first registered proprietor, whether it is entered on the register (LRA 2002, ss 11(4)(a) and 12(4)(b),)[2] or remains unregistered (LRA 2002, ss 11(4)(b) and 12(4)(c) and Sch 1, para 3). In the latter case it is immaterial whether the easement is within the proprietor's knowledge or obvious on inspection, or has been exercised in the previous year.[3] A legal easement granted by a disposition of the servient land giving rise to the requirement of registration (under LRA 2002, s 4(1),)[4] is within these rules: such a disposition operates immediately on its execution to create the easement as a legal interest (LRA 2002, ss 4(1) and 7(1),)[5] which therefore already exists 'at the time of' first registration. An easement expressly granted by such a disposition will normally be made the subject of a notice in the register;[6] an easement arising by implication[7] will not necessarily be dealt with in that way, but it will nevertheless remain binding (LRA 2002, ss 11(4)(b) and 12(4)(c) and Sch 1, para 3).

¹   The registration is effective from the time the application for registration is made: LRA 2002, s 74(a) and LRR 2003, r 15. See Chapter 7, para 7.87.

²   See para 9.5.

³   Contrast LRA 2002, Sch 1, para 3, with Sch 3, para 3 (considered further in paras 9.19–9.25).

⁴   See Chapter 5, paras 5.2 and 5.3, and Chapter 6, paras 6.3–6.5.

⁵   See Chapter 4, para 4.10.

⁶   See para 9.5.

⁷   Such as an easement under Law of Property Act 1925, s 62(1) and (2), or a 'continuous and apparent' easement within the principle of *Wheeldon v Burrows* (1879) 12 Ch D 31.

9.5   If the documents relating to the title which are submitted to the Land Registry with the application for first registration (LRR 2003, r 24(1)(c),)¹ show the existence of an easement, or if it is within the actual knowledge² of the applicant and disclosed in the application (LRA 2002, s 71(a), and LRR 2003, r 28),³ the registrar must enter a notice (LRA 2002, s 32,) of the burden of the easement in the register (LRR 2003, r 35). If the notice is subsequently removed, the easement will not be capable of overriding later registered dispositions for value: LRA 2002, s 29(3).

¹   See Chapter 4, paras 4.13 and 4.14.

²   An easement arising by prescription may (though it will not necessarily) be present to the mind of the applicant, even if it is not mentioned in the documents relating to the title.

³   Form FR1, panel 12, and Form DI. See Chapter 7, paras 7.4 and 7.5.

9.6   An equitable easement¹ is less securely protected than a legal easement on first registration of the servient land, because it does not automatically bind the first registered proprietor if it is not protected by a notice on the register.² It is convenient to consider separately the effect of:

(1)   first registration which follows a disposition of the servient land for money or money's worth; and

(2)   first registration which follows a gratuitous disposition or is effected voluntarily.

¹   Equitable easements are not particularly common. When such a right does arise, it is normally because an instrument which in terms creates an easement is not executed as a deed and therefore, by Law of Property Act 1925, s 52(1), does not grant any legal, as opposed to equitable, estate or interest. It is thought that the rules governing the creation and protection of equitable easements are principally relevant where the parties to an agreement for a lease do not actually complete it by the grant of a lease, but allow it to operate for an extended period 'in equity' only, and the agreement includes rights of access, use of service media, &c, over other property of the landlord. See Chapter 6, para 6.43(2).

²   LRA 2002, Sch 1, para 3, applies only to *legal* easements, and there is no transitional provision for unregistered land equivalent to Sch 12, para 9, (see para 9.27,) preserving the overriding status of any easement which was an overriding interest *in relation to a registered estate* immediately before the coming into force of Sch 3. LRA 2002 reverses, in relation to equitable easements over unregistered land existing at the commencement of the Act as well as such easements created thereafter, the effect of the decision in *Celsteel Ltd v Alton House*

Holdings Ltd [1985] 1 WLR 204, that equitable easements were overriding interests for the purpose of LRA 1925 if they were *'openly exercised and enjoyed'*: see Law Com no 254, paras 5.7–5.9 and 5.18; Law Com no 271, para 8.25.

9.7   Where the requirement of registration arises because of a disposition of the servient land for money or money's worth,[1] an equitable easement is binding on the disponee if (but only if) it is either registered as a Class D(iii) land charge before completion of the disposition (Land Charges Act 1972, ss 2(5)(iii) and 4(6),) or created by the instrument which gives rise to the requirement of registration.[2] In either case the easement will be revealed by the documents relating to the title which are lodged with the application for registration, (LRR 2003, r 24(1)(c),) and its efficacy will be maintained by entering a notice in the register of title (LRA 2002, ss 11(4)(a) and 12(4)(b); LRR 2003, r 35). If it is not binding on the disponee, no such notice will be entered.

[1]   LRA 2002, s 4(1), as referring to transactions for money or equivalent consideration.
[2]   Land Charges Act 1972, s 14(3), as amended by LRA 2002, Sch 11, para 10(3).

9.8   Where the requirement of registration arises because of a gratuitous disposition,[1] or registration is effected voluntarily, (LRA 2002, s 3(2),) and the land is subject to an equitable easement which is binding on the owner who disposes of the land or applies for voluntary registration, that easement remains valid, even if it is not registered as a land charge.[2] If in fact it is so registered (or is created by the instrument triggering registration), it will appear from the documentary title and will be protected by a notice. If the easement is not registered as a land charge and no notice is entered on the registered title, it is considered that the first registered proprietor will nevertheless continue to be bound (LRA 2002, ss 11(5) and 12(5));[3] but if the proprietor subsequently makes a disposition of the land for valuable consideration, and there is still no notice registered in respect of the easement, it will lose priority to the interest under that disposition: LRA 2002, s 29(1) and (2)(a).[4] If the dominant owner does not attempt to protect the easement before the disposition is made, the fact that the land was registered before that time will make no difference to the eventual outcome. However, if the dominant owner registers a Class D(iii) land charge after (and not knowing that) the title has been registered, but before the subsequent disposition, the land charge registration will be ineffective,[5] and the result will be that a gratuitous disposition, or a voluntary registration, has deprived the owner of the benefit of an easement which would otherwise have remained valid.[6]

[1]   LRA 2002, s 4(1), as referring to gratuitous transactions.
[2]   Land Charges Act 1972, s 4(6), only avoids an unregistered land charge against a purchaser of a legal estate *'for money or money's worth'*.

[3]   It is submitted that if the applicant for first registration is bound by the easement immediately before the application is made, to that extent he is *'not entitled [to the registered estate] solely for his own benefit'* for the purpose of ss 11(5) and 12(5).

[4]   See Chapter 7, paras 7.17 and 7.18.

[5]   Land Charges Act 1972, s 14(1), as amended by LRA 2002, Sch 11, para 10(2).

[6]   The combination of events which produces this result is unlikely to occur frequently; but it is thought that the possibility serves to emphasise the desirability of registering a Class D(iii) land charge whenever appropriate, and of using the 'priority notice' procedure (Land Charges Act 1972, s 11,) when doing so.

EASEMENTS: (1) FIRST REGISTRATION (B) OF DOMINANT LAND

9.9   The benefit of all subsisting easements appurtenant to dominant land vests automatically in the first registered proprietor, (LRA 2002, ss 11(3) and 12(3),) whether those easements are legal or equitable, and whether they were created by express or implied grant or arose by prescription. An entry may be made in the register of title[1] showing the benefit of a legal easement, if the registrar is satisfied, either from examination of the title, or from a written application providing details of the easement and evidence of its existence, that it subsists as a legal interest and benefits the registered estate: LRR 2003, r 33(1). If the registrar is not so satisfied, he may enter details of the right claimed with such qualification as he considers appropriate: LRR 2003, r 33(2). There is no provision for making an entry on the register of the benefit of an easement which is equitable rather than legal.[2]

[1]   In the property register: LRR 2003, r 5(b)(ii).

[2]   Similarly LRR 1925, rr 252 and 257, authorised the entry of the benefit of an appurtenant right only if it was capable of subsisting as a legal estate.

EASEMENTS: (2) CREATION (A) OVER REGISTERED SERVIENT LAND

9.10   The proprietor, or a person entitled to be registered as proprietor, of registered land has power to grant easements over it in accordance with the general law (LRA 2002, ss 23(1)(a) and 24). LRA 2002 authorises the making of rules prescribing requirements as to the form and content of a registrable disposition, (LRA 2002, s 25,) but no rules have been made which significantly affect the way in which easements can be created,[1] and it is thought that LRA 2002 and LRR 2003 do not make it necessary to modify the conveyancing forms previously used for that purpose.

---

[1]   The prescribed forms of transfer specified in LRR 2003, r 58, allow for the inclusion of grants and reservations of easements and other rights, but do not make any specific provision as to the form or content of such transactions. See for example Form TP1, panel 13; Form TR1, panel 12.

9.11   An easement over registered land which is expressly granted or reserved does not take effect as a legal easement until the grant is completed by registration.[1] An express grant for this purpose does not include a grant as a result of the operation of the 'word-saving' provisions of Law of Property Act 1925, s 62 (LRA 2002, s 27(7));[2] but every legal easement created by express words must be registered. For an expressly granted easement to be effective as a legal interest, a notice in respect of it must always be entered in the register of the servient land: LRA 2002, s 27(4) and Sch 2, para 7(2)(a).[3] If the dominant land is registered, its proprietor must also be entered as proprietor of the easement (LRA 2002, Sch 2, para 7(2)(b),)[4] on the title to the dominant land: LRA 2002, s 59(1).[5] The necessity for an express grant to be completed by registration applies even where the easement is appurtenant to a lease for seven years or less (LRA 2002, ss 4(1)(c)–(f) and 27(2)(b),)[6] which is not itself required to be registered.[7] It is thought, however, that if a short lease, not itself registrable, is granted subject to an express reservation of easements for the benefit of other property of the landlord,[8] the reservation does not have to be completed by registration in order to take effect as a legal easement.[9]

---

[1]   LRA 2002, s 27(1) and (2)(d), fundamentally changing the principles applicable to express legal easements under LRA 1925.

[2]   See Law Com no 271, para 4.25. It is considered that s 27(2) is a sufficient indication that LPA 1925, s 62, does apply to a transfer of registered land, even though: (a) the latter section in terms applies to a *'conveyance'*, defined by LPA 1925, s 205(1)(ii), as including any *'assurance of property or of any interest therein by any instrument'*; (b) by LRA 2002, s 27(1), the legal estate vests in the transferee on registration of the disposition, not its execution; and (c) LRA 2002 does not reproduce the provisions of LRA 1925, ss 20(1), and 23(1), vesting in the transferee *'the appropriate rights and interests which would, under Law of Property Act 1925, have been transferred if the land had not been registered'*.

[3]   By LRR 2003, rr 9(a) and 84(1), the notice is entered in the charges register. Where the dominant land is unregistered, r 90(b) requires the application to be made on Form AP1 if the easement is to operate at law; it will be equitable only, but its priority will still be protected by the entry made, if the application is on Form AN1 or Form UN1.

[4]   The requirements of paras 7(2)(a) and (b) of LRA 2002 Sch 2 are cumulative, and registration of the dominant owner as proprietor of the easement under para 7(2)(b) does not vest it in him as a legal interest unless notice is also entered on the servient title as required by para 7(2)(a): see LRA 2002, ss 38 and 58(2).

[5]   By LRR 2003, r 5(b)(ii), the entry is made in the property register.

[6]   There is power under LRA 2002 s 118(1) to require even shorter leases to be registered. See Chapter 6, paras 6.1 and 6.8.

[7] See Law Com no 271, para 6.11. The proposal in Law Com no 254, para 5.19, that easements appurtenant to an overriding interest should themselves be overriding interests, (ie should not be *required* to be registered,) was not adopted in LRA 2002 as enacted. See further para 9.20.

[8] For example a five-year lease of a floor of an office block with a reservation of rights, for the benefit of the rest of the block, to use pipes, drains and cables passing through the area comprised in the lease.

[9] There is (ex hypothesi) no registered servient estate against which the burden of such reserved easements can be entered. It is submitted that LRA 2002, s 27(2)(d), is to be interpreted as requiring registration of any express grant or reservation of an easement over or out of the registered estate.

9.12　An easement over registered land created by implied grant or reservation,[1] or arising by prescription, takes effect as a legal easement without being registered.[2] The dominant owner can apply, however, for a notice of such an easement to be entered in the registered title of the servient land: LRA 2002, ss 32 and 34(1).[3] If the proprietor of that land consents to the entry, it will be an 'agreed' notice, with permanent effect: LRA 2002, s 34(3)(b).[4] Alternatively the dominant owner can apply, without the servient proprietor's consent, for entry of a 'unilateral' notice; the servient proprietor is notified of the entry and has the right to apply for cancellation of the notice (LRA 2002, ss 35 and 36),[5] but unless and until it is actually cancelled, a unilateral notice protects the easement's priority on any subsequent disposition of the servient land for valuable consideration: LRA 2002, ss 29(2) and 32(3).[6] The registrar may also enter notice of any unregistered easement which falls within LRA 2002, Sch 1, para 3,[7] and appears to affect registered land: LRA 2002, s 37(1).[8] This power can be used to enter a notice of a pre-existing unregistered easement disclosed on an application for first registration, or for registration of a disposition, of the servient land (LRA 2002, s 71, and LRR 2003, rr 28 and 57).

[1] Either through the operation of Law of Property Act 1925, s 62, or as a 'continuous and apparent' easement under the principle of *Wheeldon v Burrows* (1879) 12 Ch D 31.

[2] LRA 2002, s 27(2)(d), applies only to easements *expressly* granted or reserved, and there is no other provision of LRA 2002 or of LRR 2003 altering in relation to registered land the effect of the general law as to the creation of legal easements.

[3] As to notices generally, see Chapter 7, paras 7.20–7.27.

[4] Chapter 7, para 7.28.

[5] Chapter 7, paras 7.35–7.37.

[6] Chapter 7, paras 7.17, 7.18 and 7.24.

[7] Ie any legal easement, whether or not known to the servient owner or obvious on inspection, or exercised in the previous year, and including an easement granted or arising before LRA 2002 came into force.

[8] If the registrar enters such a notice, by LRR 2003, r 89, he must give notice of it to the registered proprietor of the servient land and to the dominant owner, unless (in either case) that person makes or consents to an application to enter the notice, or (in the case of the dominant owner) his name and address for service are not set out in the register of the title of the servient land.

9.13 The power of the registered proprietor (or a person entitled to be registered as the proprietor) to grant easements, in accordance with the general law (LRA 2002, ss 23(1)(a) and 24), includes power to create equitable easements.[1] An easement expressed to be granted as a legal easement takes effect in equity[2] until the grant is completed by registration.[3] An equitable easement, however it arises (after the commencement of LRA 2002[4]), loses priority to a registrable disposition of the servient land for valuable consideration unless it is protected by a notice in the registered title to that land when the disposition is registered: LRA 2002, s 29(1) and (2)(a).[5]

---

[1]   LRA 2002, s 23(1)(a), authorises *'a disposition of any kind permitted by the general law ...'.*
[2]   By LRA 2002, s 27(1), a registrable disposition *'does not operate at law'* until it has been registered.
[3]   See para 9.12.
[4]   See the transitional provision in LRA 2002, Sch 12, para 9, considered in para 9.27.
[5]   LRA 2002, Sch 3, para 3 applies only to legal easements. See para 9.20.

EASEMENTS: (2) CREATION (B) IN FAVOUR OF REGISTERED DOMINANT LAND

9.14 Except that expressly granted easements over registered land must themselves be registered, in relation to the servient land and also, if it is registered, the dominant land, in order to have effect at law,[1] easements for the benefit of registered land can be created or arise in any way permitted by the general law.[2] Although the registration of the benefit of such easements is not essential,[3] it is possible and will in many cases be convenient.

---

[1]   See para 9.11.
[2]   See LRA 2002, s 23(1)(a), in relation to registered servient land. Section 27(2) does not make registration necessary in order to create equitable easements, or legal easements arising by implication or prescription.
[3]   If the burden but not the benefit of an expressly granted easement is registered, it takes effect in equity and not at law; but the benefit of the equitable interest is appurtenant to the dominant land under the general law, and the registration of the burden is sufficient to ensure that it binds a registered disponee of the servient land for valuable consideration: see para 9.18.

9.15 The registered proprietor of dominant land may apply for the registration, as appurtenant to his estate, of the benefit of a legal easement which has been expressly granted over unregistered servient land (LRR 2003, r 73(1)); the grant, and evidence of the grantor's title to the unregistered (servient) estate, must be submitted to the registry with the application: LRR 2003, r 73(2). The entry is made in the property register of the dominant land: LRR 2003, r 5(b)(ii). 'Express grant' for this purpose does not include a grant through the operation of Law of Property Act 1925, s 62: LRR 2003, r 73(3). An express easement over unregistered land can nevertheless operate as a legal easement without being registered in this way.[1] It is thought that in practice a freestanding grant of an easement over unregistered land, not forming part of a larger transaction, will most commonly relate to a freehold or long leasehold title which was not registered at the commencement of LRA 2002 and has not become registered. However, if it is correct that an easement expressly reserved on the grant of a short (unregistrable) lease of registered land does not itself have to be registered in order to operate as a legal easement,[2] it is thought that such a right can be treated as 'expressly granted'[3] for the benefit of the landlord's estate, and registered as appurtenant to it.

---

[1] LRA 2002, s 27(2)(d), applies to dispositions of a registered estate, and LRR 2003, r 73(1), is permissive, not mandatory.
[2] See para 9.11.
[3] Within LRR 2003, r 73(1).

9.16 The registered proprietor of dominant land may also apply, whether the servient land is registered or unregistered, for the registration as appurtenant to his estate of the benefit of a legal easement acquired otherwise than by express grant, (LRR 2003, r 74(1),) ie acquired through the operation of Law of Property Act 1925, s 62, (LRR 2003, r 74(3),) under the principle of *Wheeldon v Burrows*[1] (or otherwise by implication) or by prescription. The application must be accompanied by sufficient evidence to satisfy the registrar that the easement is a subsisting legal easement and benefits the applicant's registered estate: LRR 2003, r 74(2). However, the right to an implied or prescriptive easement, or its exact scope, may not be completely clear; if the registrar is not satisfied that the applicant's claim is correct, he is not bound to reject the application, or to require the applicant to prove the claim by agreement with or court proceedings against the servient owner, but may enter *'details of the right claimed ... with such qualification as he considers appropriate'*.[2] The entry is made in the property register: LRR 2003, rr 5(b)(ii) and 75(2).

---

[1] (1879) 12 Ch D 31.
[2] LRR 2003, r 75, which also applies to applications under r 73, and is similar in effect to LRR 1925, r 254(2).

EASEMENTS: (3) EFFECT OF DISPOSITIONS (A) OF REGISTERED SERVIENT LAND

9.17   A registered gratuitous disposition of registered land, and any unregistered disposition of such land either gratuitously or for consideration, (other than the grant for valuable consideration of a legal lease which is not required to be registered,[1]) has effect subject to all easements, whether legal or equitable, affecting the land.[2]

---

[1]   LRA 2002, s 29(4); see Chapter 6, para 6.36, and Chapter 7, para 7.17.
[2]   LRA 2002, ss 28 and 29(1); see Chapter 7, para 7.17.

9.18   A registered disposition of registered land for valuable consideration has effect subject to all easements which are protected by notice on the register: LRA 2002, s 29(1) and (2)(a)(i).[1] An easement which has been so protected at any time since the commencement of LRA 2002 cannot override registered dispositions[2] if the notice is removed from the register: LRA 2002, s 29(3). The same principles apply on the grant, for valuable consideration, of a lease which is not required to be registered: LRA 2002, s 29(4).[3]

---

[1]   See Chapter 7, paras 7.17 and 7.18.
[2]   Under LRA 2002, Sch 3, para 3; see paras 9.19–9.23.
[3]   See Chapter 6, para 6.36, and Chapter 7, para 7.17.

9.19   A registered disposition of registered land for valuable consideration[1] also has effect subject to any easement falling within LRA 2002, Sch 3, para 3 (LRA 2002, s 29(2)(a)(ii),) which applies to:

'(1) A legal easement ..., except for an easement ... which at the time of the disposition—

(a)   is not within the actual knowledge of the person to whom the disposition is made, and

(b)   would not have been obvious on a reasonably careful inspection of the land over which the easement ... is exercisable.

(2) The exception in sub-paragraph (1) does not apply if the person entitled to the easement ... proves that it has been exercised in the period of one year ending with the day of the disposition.'

Transitional provisions ensure that all easements which were overriding interests in relation to registered land, under LRA 1925, s 70(1)(a), and LRR 1925, r 258, at the commencement of LRA 2002, continue to be overriding interests under Sch 3, para 3, even if they would not fall within that paragraph if they had been created after it came into force (LRA 2002, Sch 12, para 9),[2] and further disapply the exception in para 3(1)(a) and (b) for three years from the commencement of LRA 2002

(LRA 2002, Sch 12, para 10).[3] In practice, therefore, many of the issues raised by para 3, and considered below, will only affect easements created by implied grant, or arising on the completion of a period of prescription, *after* the commencement of LRA 2002 (on 13 October 2003), and only in relation to dispositions of the servient land made after 12 October 2006.

The effect of the somewhat complex provisions of LRA 2002, Sch 3, para 3, is that an unregistered easement over registered land, created or arising after the commencement of LRA 2002, overrides registered dispositions of the servient land for valuable consideration if:

(1) It is a legal and not merely an equitable easement; *and*

(2) *either*:
   (a)   the disponee actually knew of it at the time of the disposition, the onus of proof being on the disponee to show that he did not have such knowledge; *or*
   (b)   it would have been obvious on a reasonably careful inspection of the servient land at the time of the disposition, the onus of proving that it would not have been obvious being, again, on the disponee; *or*
   (c)   it was exercised in the year ending with the day of the disposition, the onus of proof being on the dominant owner to show that it was so exercised.

Various issues appear to arise on these elements of Sch 3, para 3, and are considered in more detail below.[4] It is thought, however, that most of these issues will only rarely arise in practice, because a dominant owner will usually be able to establish that an unregistered legal easement binds a disponee of the servient land by showing that the right was exercised in the year before the disposition, in which case it will be irrelevant whether the disponee knew of it or it would have been obvious on inspection.[5]

---

[1]   And the grant for such consideration of a lease which is not required to be registered: LRA 2002, s 29(4).

[2]   See para 9.27.

[3]   See para 9.28.

[4]   See paras 9.20–9.23.

[5]   The analysis in Law Com no 271, paras 8.65–8.72, has a rather different emphasis: the general proposition is advanced that an easement should only be an overriding interest if a disponee of the servient land can readily discover it; and the inclusion of rights which have recently been exercised, as a separate category in addition to 'known' and 'obvious' rights, is directed particularly to 'invisible' easements, for example rights to use underground drains.

Legal easements

9.20   Since, in relation to easements created or arising after the date of commencement of LRA 2002, Sch 3, para 3, applies only to *legal* easements, and easements expressly granted after that date cannot take effect as legal easements unless they are registered, (LRA 2002, s 27(2)(d),)[1] the only post-commencement unregistered easements capable of binding a registered disponee for value are those created by implied grant or arising by prescription. For this purpose easements arising under the deeming provisions of Law of Property Act 1925, s 62, are not created by express grant, (LRA 2002, s 27(7),)[2] and can therefore subsist as legal easements without being registered.[3] The other main categories of easements created by implied grant are easements required to enable the land to be used for the purpose contemplated by the parties to the grant;[4] 'continuous and apparent' easements within the principle of *Wheeldon v Burrows*;[5] and 'easements of necessity' without which the dominant land would be unusable.[6] All of these classes of implied easements, if not registered, will be capable of falling within Sch 3, para 3, so as to bind a registered disponee for value of the servient land. Easements arising by prescription are also legal easements capable of falling within that paragraph.[7]

The requirement to register an expressly granted easement includes an easement contained in a short lease which is not itself required to be registered.[8] It is thought that where such a lease grants the tenant an express easement over other registered land belonging to the landlord, who later sells both the reversionary interest in the demised premises, and the servient land, to the same purchaser, the landlord's covenant for quiet enjoyment and his obligation not to derogate from his grant will be binding on the purchaser and will require him not to interfere with the tenant's use of the easement, even if it has not been registered. However, if the landlord retains the reversionary interest in the demised premises but sells the servient land, or sells the two parcels to different purchasers, there appears to be no escape from the conclusion that the tenant's easement is not binding on the new proprietor of the servient land, unless it is registered. In this respect the position of a tenant with an express easement is weaker than that of a tenant with an equivalent right arising by implication in any of the ways described above.[9] It therefore appears to be advisable for a landlord who grants a short lease containing express easements to take steps to protect himself against potential liability to the tenant in respect of an interference with the easement by a purchaser of the servient land, either by ensuring that the easement is registered, or by requiring the purchaser to contract, for the tenant's benefit,[10] to permit its continued use.

If a lease not required to be registered expressly grants the tenant the right to make use of an easement which is already appurtenant to the demised premises in the landlord's hands, and exercisable over land belonging to a third party, it is thought that the tenant will still be entitled to use the easement, after a registered disposition of the servient land, if it continues to be binding on the disponee in favour of the landlord, even if the tenant's own right is not registered.[11]

¹ See para 9.11.
² For the effect of s 62 see 14 *Halsbury's Laws* (4th edn) para 55.
³ See para 9.11.
⁴ See 14 *Halsbury's Laws* (4th edn) para 70; *Sovmots Investments Ltd v Secretary of State for the Environment* [1977] QB 411.
⁵ (1879) 12 Ch D 31; 14 *Halsbury's Laws* (4th edn) paras 60–69.
⁶ *Nickerson v Barraclough* [1981] Ch 426; 14 *Halsbury's Laws* (4th edn) para 66.
⁷ See further para 9.24 as to easements acquired or in the course of acquisition by prescription.
⁸ See Law Com no 271, para 6.11, suggesting that this may in practice encourage the entry of notices in the register, where this is permissible under LRA 2002, s 33(b), in respect of leases not required to be registered. (See also Chapter 6, para 6.43; s 33 is considered in Chapter 7, para 7.23.)
⁹ In the debate on the Land Registration Bill at Report stage in the House of Lords, the Parliamentary Secretary, Lord Chancellor's Department, indicated that to exempt express easements appurtenant to short leases from the requirement of registration would be inconsistent with the objective of making the register a comprehensive record of all matters affecting the title: 627 HL Official Report (5th series) cols 1354–1355.
¹⁰ Under Contracts (Rights of Third Parties) Act 1999.
¹¹ The new servient owner is not entitled to prevent continued use by the landlord or anyone properly authorised by him; and the landlord is bound to continue to provide the tenant with the benefit of the grant in the lease. Compare 14 *Halsbury's Laws* (4th edn) para 161.

Disponee's actual knowledge

9.21   An unregistered easement does not override a registered disposition of the servient land for value if *'at the time of the disposition'* it is not within the *'actual knowledge'* of the disponee (and none of the other conditions of LRA 2002, Sch 3, para 3, is satisfied).¹ It is thought that the time of the disposition, for this purpose, is the date on which the transfer is executed and delivered, so that knowledge acquired by the disponee at any time before that date, whether before or after exchange of contracts, will preserve the easement's overriding status, but knowledge acquired subsequently, even before the effective date of registration of the disposition,² does not have that effect. It does not matter whether the disponee's knowledge derives from information supplied by the disponor, from inspection of the land, or from any other source. One objective of the legislation, however, is to encourage a purchaser to make and the vendor to answer an inquiry (before contract) as to easements known to the vendor;³ the latter's incentive to answer fully is that if he does not do so, and there is in fact a legal easement over the land which is neither obvious on inspection nor otherwise known to the purchaser, but which binds the purchaser because it has been exercised in the previous year, (LRA 2002, Sch 3, para 3(2),)⁴ the vendor will be liable to the purchaser in damages for breach of his duty to disclose irremovable latent defects in title,⁵ or, if he knows of the easement and transfers 'with full title guarantee', for breach of the implied covenant that the property is free from third party rights known to him: Law of Property (Miscellaneous Provisions) Act 1994, s 3(1).

It is thought that unregistered easements which are known to the disponee's conveyancer[6] are to be treated as also being within the knowledge of the disponee for the purpose of LRA 2002, Sch 3, para 3(1)(a), since it is the conveyancer's duty to inform his or her client of their existence.[7]

---

[1]   LRA 2002, ss 28(1) and 29(1) and (2)(a)(ii), (discussed in Chapter 7, paras 7.17 and 7.18,) and Sch 3, para 3(1)(a).

[2]   Ie, in 'paper' conveyancing, during the 'registration gap' between completion of the transfer and delivery to the Land Registry of the application to register it: LRA 2002, s 74(b). The issue will not arise under electronic conveyancing, with simultaneous completion and registration of transactions; see Chapter 3, para 3.49.

[3]   See Law Com no 271, para 8.71.

[4]   See para 9.23.

[5]   Compare *Megarry and Wade on Real Property* (6th edn) para 12-068.

[6]   Defined in LRR 2003, r 217.

[7]   Under the ordinary law of principal and agent applicable to conveyancing transactions. It is submitted that LRA 2002, Sch 3, para 3(1)(a), should not be construed in such a way as to enable the disponee to benefit from a breach of that duty, by taking free from an easement actually known to the conveyancer, in the (admittedly uncommon) situation in which the conveyancer finds out about an unregistered easement which would not otherwise be binding because it is not obvious on inspection and has not been exercised in the past year.

Obvious on reasonably careful inspection

9.22   The purpose of this provision is to ensure that a disponee for value (LRA 2002, ss 28(1) and 29(1) and (2)(a)(ii), and Sch 3, para 3(1)(b),) takes subject to any legal easement which is of such a character as to be a 'patent', as opposed to a 'latent', defect in title as between a vendor and a purchaser of the servient land; it is not sufficient that the disponee would have 'constructive notice' of the easement in an equivalent transaction relating to unregistered land.[1] If the inquiries described above[2] are made and fully answered as a matter of routine, obvious easements as well as 'latent' ones will normally become known to the disponee and will be binding on him accordingly: LRA 2002, Sch 3, para 3(1)(a). They will also be required to be notified to the Registry when the disponee applies to be registered as proprietor of the land, (LRA 2002, s 71(b); LRR 2003, r 57(1),) and will then be entered on the register (LRR 2003, r 57(5),) so as to be binding as registered interests,[3] not as overriding interests, on subsequent dispositions for value.

In cases (which it is thought will be rare) in which an easement is not within the disponee's knowledge and has not been exercised during the previous year, the words *'obvious on a reasonably careful inspection of the land over which the easement ... is exercisable'* will determine whether the disponee is bound by the easement, and may raise several questions of interpretation.

   (1)   The word *'obvious'* is emphatic, and may possibly impose a more stringent test than would have applied under (for

example) a requirement that the easement 'would have been discovered' on an appropriate inspection.

(2) Strictly speaking the statutory words require the existence of the dominant owner's legal right by way of easement, and not merely the acts done or advantages enjoyed by him, to be *'obvious'*, but it is submitted that the language should not be construed as requiring the inspection to show that those acts were done or advantages enjoyed under a legal right: inspection alone cannot exclude the possibility of those matters being merely permissive, and it would be wrong to adopt an interpretation which meant that no easement could ever satisfy the statutory test.

(3) The statutory words do not state in terms, but it is submitted that the implication should be made, that the *'reasonably careful inspection'* is assumed to be undertaken by the disponee or his conveyancer, with the benefit of any knowledge he has acquired from other investigations of the title. For example, if the register shows that the dominant land used to be part of the same title as the land the subject of the current transaction, that will suggest that access observed to be obtained to the land previously sold, over the retained land, is enjoyed under an implied grant.

(4) The statutory words refer to an inspection of the *servient* land: circumstances could occur in which the only visible clue to the existence of an easement was a feature on the dominant land, (for example a door in a wall situated entirely on the dominant land might be an indication of the existence of a right of way over a paved yard showing no other sign of that right,) but it is submitted that a *'reasonably careful inspection'* of the servient land should be taken to include an inspection of that land's relationship to its surroundings.

The intention of the framers of the legislation was that such issues should be resolved by applying the rules for identifying 'patent' defects in title as between vendor and purchaser.[4]

---

[1]   See Law Com no 271, para 5.21.
[2]   See para 9.21.
[3]   See para 9.18.
[4]   See 626 HL Official Report (5th Series) cols 1432–1436; 627 HL Official Report (5th Series) cols 1325–1328; HC Official Report, SC D, 13 December 2001, cols 67–70.

Exercised in the year ending with the day of the disposition

9.23   A right to use a pipe, drain or other underground apparatus frequently exists without any visible sign on the surface of the servient land; LRA 2002 deals with this situation by providing that a legal easement is binding on a disponee of that land for value if the dominant owner proves that the easement has been exercised in the period of one year ending with the day of the disposition.[1] The purpose of this provision[2] is to create an exception to the general principle that only easements which are known or readily discoverable should bind a purchaser without being registered, but LRA 2002, Sch 3, para 3(2), is not confined to rights to use concealed apparatus, and it is thought that in practice, if an easement is actually important for the enjoyment of the dominant land, the dominant owner will usually be able to discharge the onus of proving that it has been exercised within the year before a disposition of the servient land.[3] If that is proved, it will not be necessary to resolve any question of whether a conveyancer's knowledge is to be taken to be that of his client,[4] or of whether a right is *'obvious'* in particular circumstances.[5]

It is considered that the exercise of an easement on a single occasion within the year is sufficient: the dominant owner has to prove that the right has been exercised *'in'*, not *'throughout'*, or even *'during'*, the period specified. It is also considered that *'the day of the disposition'* is the date of completion of the transfer (or lease) of the servient land, and not (in 'paper' conveyancing) the later date as of which the disposition is registered.[6]

The word *'exercised'* applies most naturally, it is thought, to a positive act, such as walking or driving along a right of way, or running water or gas through a pipe, and it is not clear whether easements not involving specific actions on the servient land by the dominant owner, such as the right to the passage of light to a window, or the right to support for a building, can be *'exercised'* for the purpose of LRA 2002, Sch 3, para 3(2);[7] it is submitted that no distinction should be drawn between different types of easement, and that any right which has in fact been used, in whatever manner is appropriate to the nature of that right, should be taken to have been *'exercised'*.

It is thought that a registered proprietor may incur liability under the implied covenants for title (Law of Property (Miscellaneous Provisions) Act 1994, s 3(1) or (3),) to the disponee under a subsequent disposition of the servient land (or to that disponee's successors in title), if he allows an 'invisible' easement to come into being and it is not disclosed or otherwise known to that disponee or obvious on inspection, but binds him because it has been exercised in the year ending with the disposition.[8]

---

[1] LRA 2002, Sch 3, para 3(2), disapplying para 3(1)(a) and (b) where such exercise is established.

[2] See Law Com no 271, paras 8.69 and 8.70.

[3] This may not be so in relation (for example) to a fire-escape, a seasonal access for specific agricultural purposes, (such as access once a year by a combine-harvester, where there is a more convenient route available for smaller machines used for other operations,) or a logging-track used for carting felled timber at intervals of several decades.

[4] For the purpose of LRA 2002, Sch 3, para 3(1)(a); see para 9.21.

[5] For the purpose of LRA 2002, Sch 3, para 3(1)(b); see para 9.22.

[6] Compare the discussion of *'the time of the disposition'* in para 9.21. If exercise on a single occasion suffices, then unless *'ending with'* in LRA 2002, Sch 3, para 3(2), can be read as meaning *'ending immediately before'*, it appears that the exercise of an easement on the same day as, but after, actual completion of a disposition of the servient land, is enough to make the easement binding on the disponee.

[7] The only specific examples considered in Law Com no 271, paras 8.69–8.72, are rights of drainage and rights to use a water-supply pipe.

[8] See para 9.34.

9.24 LRA 2002 makes no specific provision for cases in which land is disposed of whilst a third party is making use of it in a manner capable of giving rise to a prescriptive easement, but has not yet actually acquired such a right because the use has not continued for a long enough period: no special provision for such cases is required, because no actual property right exists until the prescription period is complete, but if use sufficient to create a prescriptive right has begun, a disposition of the 'servient' land normally does not interrupt the running of that period.[1] However, it is thought that a dominant owner will never, or only in most unusual circumstances, be able to overcome a failure to satisfy the requirements of LRA 2002, Sch 3, para 3, by claiming that the prescriptive period was incomplete and still running at the date of the relevant disposition, and was only completed between that date and the time when a dispute arose: if at the date of the disposition the alleged right was not known or obvious to the disponee, and had not been exercised in the previous year, it is unlikely that the dominant owner will be able to prove the continuous, open use which is required for the establishment of a prescriptive easement.

[1] See Law Com no 271, paras 5.37 and 5.38.

9.25 A wide variety of questions may arise in connection with the application of the principles in paras 9.19–9.23 to particular easements affecting registered land which is the subject of a disposition. The following general considerations apply where an easement is not disclosed by the disponor (who may not realise that it exists) and is not otherwise actually known to the disponee.

(1) Discontinuous easements conferring rights to go onto the servient land for a particular purpose, such as rights of way, rights of parking or recreation, and rights of access to repair and maintain buildings on the dominant land, will always bind a disponee of the servient land for value if they can be shown to have been used in the year ending with the disposition. They may also be binding as *'obvious on a reasonably careful inspection'* if there are relevant physical features on the servient land, such as a made-up track or pathway leading to the dominant land.

(2)   A right of access to repair may not be obvious, and may not be exercised every year; but if a disponee of the servient land therefore takes free of it, the right to apply for an access order under the Access to Neighbouring Land Act 1992 will still be available.

(3)   Easements to use services, such as pipes, drains and cables in, on or over the servient land, will normally be binding on a disponee because it will be possible to show that they were used in the year ending with the disposition. Open watercourses and overhead cables are likely also to be *'obvious'*.

(4)   Negative easements, such as rights of light and support, which merely entitle the dominant owner to prevent certain acts on the servient land to the detriment of a building on the dominant land, raise the questions whether such rights are obvious on inspection of the *servient* land, and whether they can be *'exercised'*. If either or both of those conditions can be satisfied whilst the relevant building remains on the dominant land, it is thought that such easements may be lost if that building is demolished, even with a view to redevelopment to a design which would continue to be entitled to the easements, and the servient land changes hands more than a year after the demolition but before the building is rebuilt.

(5)   Easements to use rights of way and conducting media carry with them the right for the dominant owner to enter the servient land and carry out works of repair and maintenance to the access-way, pipes, cables, &c, which he uses. It is submitted that for the purpose of LRA 2002, Sch 3, para 3, such ancillary rights are to be treated as part of the relevant substantive easement, so as to continue to be exercisable if that substantive easement is binding on a disponee, and it is not necessary for the ancillary rights considered separately to satisfy one or more of the conditions in para 3: such rights do not in fact have any independent existence and do not, it is submitted, impose any significant extra burden on the servient land.

EASEMENTS: (3) EFFECT OF DISPOSITIONS (B) OF REGISTERED DOMINANT LAND

9.26   A disposition of registered dominant land carries with it the benefit of all easements subsisting for the benefit of that land, (whether those easements are legal or equitable, and whether or not they are recorded on the individual register for that land,) in accordance with the general law, (LRA 2002, s 23(1)(a); Law of Property Act 1925, s 62(1) and (2),) unless the instrument effecting the disposition expresses a contrary intention: Law of Property Act 1925, s 62(4). An easement which is expressly granted over registered land does not have effect as a *legal* easement unless the benefit of it is registered, (LRA 2002, s 27(2)(d) and Sch 2, para 7(2),)[1] but it is effective, and transferable, as an equitable easement even if not so registered. Registration of the benefit of express easements over unregistered land, and of the benefit of implied and prescriptive easements, is optional and not mandatory (LRR 2003, rr 73 and 74).[2]

---

[1]   See para 9.11.

[2]   See paras 9.15 and 9.16.

EASEMENTS: (4) TRANSITIONAL PROVISIONS

9.27   Where an estate in land was registered before LRA 2002, Sch 3, came into force (on 13 October 2003), all easements which were then overriding interests in relation to that registered estate continue to be overriding interests indefinitely, even if they do not satisfy the conditions of Sch 3, para 3: LRA 2002, Sch 12, para 9(1) and (2). This provision applies to equitable easements which were overriding interests in relation to registered land before the commencement of LRA 2002,[1] but does not extend the class of easements affecting unregistered land which will override first registration,[2] and does not affect the principle that if the burden of an easement is registered against the servient land and the entry is later removed from the register, the easement cannot thereafter be an overriding interest.[3]

---

[1]   LRA 2002, Sch 12, para 9, provides that in relation to pre-commencement easements *'which would not fall within'* Sch 3, para 3, that Schedule has effect as if such easements *'were not excluded'* from para 3, and thus disapplies the restriction of that paragraph to legal easements. See Law Com no 271, para 8.73(2), referring to the need to register equitable easements created after LRA 2002 came into force, and contrast LRA 2002, Sch 12, para 10 (see para 9.28), which refers to the *'exception'* from para 3.

[2]   LRA 2002, Sch 12, para 9, applies only to an easement which was an overriding interest *'in relation to a registered estate'* immediately before Sch 3 came into force. See paras 9.6–9.8.

[3]   LRA 2002, Sch 12, para 9, does not affect the operation of LRA 2002, s 29(3); see Chapter 7, para 7.17.

9.28   For the period of three years beginning with the date of commencement of LRA 2002, Sch 3, ie until 12 October 2006, para 3(1) of that Schedule has effect *'with the omission of the exception'* (LRA 2002, Sch 12, para 10), so that a legal[1] easement which is neither known to the disponee, nor obvious on a reasonably careful inspection, is nevertheless binding on a registered disponee for value. Since the status of easements which were overriding interests at the commencement of LRA 2002 is separately preserved,[2] the practical effect of this further provision is restricted to cases in which a legal easement is created by implied grant, or arises on the completion of a period of prescription, and thereafter the servient land is the subject of a registered disposition for valuable consideration, and both those events occur on or after 13 October 2003 and before or on 12 October 2006.

---

[1]   LRA 2002, Sch 3, para 3(1) applies to *'a legal easement ... except'* one which is not known and not obvious; so disapplying the *'exception'* does not affect the requirement that only a legal easement can have overriding effect.
[2]   LRA 2002, Sch 12, para 9, considered in para 9.27.

COVENANTS: (1) RESTRICTIVE COVENANTS

9.29   Restrictive covenants under the principle of *Tulk v Moxhay*,[1] limiting for the benefit of one parcel of land the use which may be made of another, can subsist and can be created (LRA 2002, s 23(1)(a),) over and for the benefit of registered land, but they cannot operate as overriding interests in relation to the burdened land, either on first registration or on a registered disposition for value,[2] and therefore must always be protected by a notice[3] on the charges register (LRR 2003, r 84(1),) of the title to that land.

---

[1]   (1848) 2 Ph 774.
[2]   Restrictive covenants are not included in any of the paragraphs of LRA 2002, Sch 1 or Sch 3.
[3]   A notice is appropriate, rather than a restriction, because a restrictive covenant is intended to be enforceable against the burdened land whoever may become the proprietor; see Chapter 7, para 7.20 and Law Com no 271, para 6.9.

9.30   A restrictive covenant entered into before the burdened land is registered is binding on the first registered proprietor if:

(1)   it was entered into before 1 January 1926 and the first proprietor has notice of it; or

(2)   it was entered into after 31 December 1925 and is registered as a Class D(ii) land charge (Land Charges Act 1972, ss 2(5)(ii) and 4(6)); or

(3)   it is created by the instrument giving rise to the requirement of registration;[1] or

(4)   it is not registered as a land charge but the first proprietor is the original covenantor or a voluntary disponee from the original covenantor.[2]

Such a covenant will normally be disclosed by the documents delivered with the application for first registration, (LRR 2003, r 24(1)(c),)[3] and the registrar will enter a notice in respect of it: LRR 2003, r 35(1).

A restrictive covenant *'between a lessor and a lessee'* in respect of unregistered land cannot be registered as a land charge, (Land Charges Act 1925, s 2(5)(ii),) and a covenant with a tenant restricting the use of unregistered land which belongs to the landlord but is not demised by the lease[4] is therefore binding on a subsequent buyer (or tenant) of that land from the landlord who has notice of it.[5] However, the scope of the equivalent provision in LRA 2002, s 33(c), is narrower, forbidding only the entry of a notice in the register in respect of a restrictive covenant between a lessor and a lessee *'so far as relating to the demised premises'*. To ensure complete protection of a restrictive covenant in a lease in respect of unregistered land of the landlord which is not comprised in the tenancy, the tenant should therefore register a caution against first registration (LRA 2002, s 15(1)(b),)[6] of the land subject to the covenant, and require a notice of the covenant to be entered when the title to that land is registered.

---

[1]   Land Charges Act 1972, s 14(3), as amended by LRA 2002, Sch 11, para 10(3).
[2]   See the discussion in para 9.8 of the similar considerations applying to an equitable easement.
[3]   Even if a pre-1926 covenant is before the root of title, subsequent transactions are routinely expressed to be subject to it.
[4]   Such as a density covenant in respect of retained land in a leasehold residential development.
[5]   See *Megarry and Wade on Real Property* (6th edn) para 5-103.
[6]   See Chapter 4, paras 4.3–4.8, and Chapter 6, paras 6.41 and 6.42.

9.31   The proprietor, or a person entitled to be registered as proprietor,[1] of registered land can enter into a restrictive covenant in exercise of his power to make a disposition *'of any kind permitted by the general law'*: LRA 2002, s 23(1)(a). There is power to make rules providing for the form and contents of registrable dispositions (LRA 2002, s 25(1)); the prescribed forms of transfer[2] allow for the inclusion of restrictive covenants.[3] The covenantee should apply, as soon as is practicable after completion of the instrument containing the covenant, for the entry of a notice in respect of it,[4] in order to preserve its priority against a subsequent registered disposition of that land for value.[5] A covenant in a lease by which the landlord restricts the use of other (registered) land, not included in the demise, can[6] and therefore should be protected by registration of a notice against the land affected by the covenant.

¹   A purchaser who covenants, in the transfer to him, with the vendor for the benefit of the latter's retained land, does so as a person entitled to be registered.

²   Under LRR 2003, r 58.

³   See for example Form TP1, panel 13; Form TR1, panel 12.

⁴   It is thought that this will normally be an application in Form AN1, (LRR 2003, r 81(1)(a),) for an agreed notice under LRA 2002, s 34(3); even if for some reason the covenantor's consent to the application is not forthcoming, a certified copy of the instrument containing the covenant will be powerful evidence, for the purpose of s 34(3)(c), of the validity of the covenantee's claim. As to notices generally, see Chapter 7, paras 7.20–7.24.

⁵   LRA 2002, ss 28 and 29, in particular s 29(2); see Chapter 7, paras 7.17 and 7.18.

⁶   LRA 2002, s 33(c), forbids entry of a notice in respect of a restrictive covenant between a lessor and a lessee only *'so far as relating to the demised premises'*.

9.32   On first registration of land entitled to the benefit of a restrictive covenant, the benefit vests automatically in the first registered proprietor: LRA 2002, ss 11(3) and 12(3). Where such a covenant is entered into for the benefit of registered land, it takes effect as a *'disposition of a kind permitted by the general law',* (LRA 2002, s 23(1)(a),) and the benefit therefore vests in the proprietor and his successors in accordance with the ordinary rules governing entitlement to enforce restrictive covenants.¹ There is no provision of LRA 2002 or of LRR 2003 adversely affecting the validity of a restrictive covenant if the benefit of it is not entered on the registered title to the covenantee's land, but details of *'covenants benefiting the registered estate'* can be entered in the proprietorship register, (LRR 2003, r 5(b)(ii),) and it is suggested that the risk of subsequent disputes will be reduced if, whenever practicable, the land intended to have the benefit of a restrictive covenant is accurately defined and an appropriate entry is made on the title.

¹   The details of those rules are outside the scope of this book.

COVENANTS: (2) POSITIVE AND INDEMNITY COVENANTS

9.33   Entries may be made in the proprietorship register in respect of positive covenants relating to a registered estate and given by the proprietor or any previous proprietor, (LRR 2003, rr 8(1)(f) and 64(1),) and of indemnity covenants by the proprietor in respect of restrictive covenants and other matters affecting the estate and of positive covenants relating to the estate: LRR 2003, r 65(1). Such an entry must, where practicable, refer to the instrument containing the covenant, (LRR 2003, rr 64(2) and 65(2),) and must be removed if it appears to the registrar that the covenant does not bind the current registered proprietor: LRR 2003, rr 64(3) and 65(3). A positive or indemnity covenant is usually binding only on the covenantor and not on his or her successors in title, but there are exceptions to this principle, for example where an easement to use shared roads or drains is made conditional on the dominant owner observing a covenant to contribute to their upkeep,[1] and in such a situation an entry in respect of the covenant will remain on the register when the covenantor disposes of the land.

[1] *Halsall v Brizell* [1957] Ch 169; *Rhone v Stephens* [1994] 2 AC 310. Positive obligations enforceable against successors in title of the covenantor can also be created as 'planning obligations' under the Town and Country Planning Act 1990, s 106, which are registrable as local land charges: see s 106(1)(b) and (d), (3)(b) and (11).

COVENANTS: (3) COVENANTS FOR TITLE

9.34   A registrable disposition may be made with 'full title guarantee' or with 'limited title guarantee' under Law of Property (Miscellaneous Provisions) Act 1994 ('LP(MP)A 1994'), ss 2–5,[1] and the effect of such covenants may be limited or extended: LP(MP)A 1.[2] The benefit of a covenant for title is annexed to and goes with the estate or interest of the covenantee and can be enforced by every person in whom that estate or interest (or any part of it) is for the time being vested (LP(MP)A 1994, s 7), but no references to covenants for title are to be made on the register, (LRR 2003, r 67(5),) except where a registrable disposition of leasehold land limits or extends the statutory covenants that the lease is subsisting and that there is neither any subsisting breach of a condition or tenant's obligation nor any subsisting ground for forfeiture.[3] Unless a transfer containing a covenant for title (or a copy of it) is preserved and handed over on each subsequent dealing, a successor in title of the covenantee may therefore not actually know of the existence of a claim on that covenant against a previous proprietor of the land; but it is thought that claims under covenants for title will in practice be comparatively infrequent, because those covenants do not impose any liability for matters to which the disposition containing them is expressly made subject, (LP(MP)A 1994, s 6(1),) or for anything which, at the time of that disposition, is actually known, or is a necessary consequence of facts actually known, to the disponee: LP(MP)A 1994, s 6(2). Where the disposition is of an interest the title to which is registered under LRA 2002, the covenants for title do not impose any liability for anything which, at the time of the disposition, is entered in the register in relation to that interest: LP(MP)A 1994, s 6(4), inserted by LRA 2002, Sch 11, para 31(2). However, it appears that a registered proprietor who disposes of part of his land, in such a way as to create by implication a legal easement over the land he retains, may incur liability under an implied covenant for freedom from incumbrances, (LP(MP)A 1994, s 3(1)(b) and (3)(a),) in a subsequent disposition of the retained land, if that easement is not disclosed or otherwise known to the later disponee or such as to be obvious on a reasonably careful inspection of the land, but is binding on that disponee because it has been exercised in the year ending on the day of the disposition (LRA 2002, Sch 3, para 3);[4] and it seems that such a liability can even arise in respect of an easement which binds a disponee of the servient land because it would have been obvious on inspection of that land,[5] if the disponee does not actually make an inspection and the disponor does not disclose that the easement exists.

---

[1]   Applied to registered land by LRR 2003, r 67(1).
[2]   LRR 2003, r 68, requires any such limitation or modification to be in specified terms referring to the relevant section of LP(MP)A 1994.
[3]   LRR 2003, r 67(6), referring to LP(MP)A 1994, s 4.
[4]   See paras 9.19 and 9.23.
[5]   See paras 9.19 and 9.22.

10 Trusts and charities

INTRODUCTION

10.1 As was previously the case under the LRA 1925, the treatment of equitable interests is the result of two policy desires. The first, the so called 'curtain principle', is to ensure that all equitable interests are kept 'off the register'. The second is for all interests existing in or over registered land to be stated on the register. The result is a system where only legal estates can exist as registered estates (see the definition in the LRA 2002, s 132) and equitable interests depend upon protection through registration of notices or restrictions.[1] The potential harshness of this is mitigated somewhat by the fact that some equitable interests can be overriding interests, which are protected without registration, where a person entitled to such an interest is in actual occupation of the land.[2]

---

[1] See paras 7.20–7.61.
[2] See para 7.9.

10.2 Probably the most common form of equitable interest is an interest in or arising out of a trust. In relation to land there are two distinct forms of trusts, trusts of land and settlements under the Settled Land Act 1925 (SLA 1925). Any trust consisting of or including land is a trust of land unless it was an existing settlement under the SLA 1925 on 31 December 1996.[1] Trusts of land include co-ownership of land by joint tenants or tenants in common as well as trusts for persons in succession or discretionary trusts. A settlement under the SLA 1925 is one made before 1 January 1997 where land is held on trust for persons in succession, or on certain other kinds of trust, where no trust for sale of the land was imposed.[2] Since January 1997 it has not been possible to create new SLA 1925 settlements.[3] As a result, by far the most common form of trust involving land is the trust of land.

---

[1] See the Trusts of Land and Appointment of Trustees Act 1996 (TLATA 1996), s 1. The definition includes charitable trusts which consist of or include land (although these are dealt with as a separate topic below). There exists an additional category of land to which the Universities and College Estates Act 1925 applies.
[2] For a more comprehensive discussion of settlements see Megarry and Wade, *The Law of Real Property* (6th edn) Chapter 8.

3   There are two exceptions to this, see the TLATA 1996, s 2(1). These are where a settlement created on the occasion of an alteration in any interest in, or of a person becoming entitled under, a settlement which: (1) was in existence on 1 January 1997; or (2) derives from a settlement created before 1 January 1997. For an explanation of these exceptions see Megarry and Wade, *The Law of Real Property* (6th edn), para 8-070.

10.3   All interests in trusts are capable of being overreached by a conveyance of the legal estate. Overreaching will only occur where the disposition is within the powers of the trustees and where the requirements in the Law of Property Act 1925, s 2(1) are complied with. In the case of a trust of land the requirement is for the capital monies arising from the transaction to be paid to two trustees or to a trust corporation (Law of Property Act 1925, ss 2(1)(ii) and 27).[1] The result of the interest being overreached is that it ceases to exist in or over the land and instead becomes an interest in the purchase money.[2]

1   In addition a sole personal representative, acting as such, may give a valid capital receipt for capital money (s 27(2)).
2   For a comprehensive explanation of overreaching in the context of the 1925 legislation see Charles Harpum [1990] CLJ 277.

PROTECTION OF TRUST INTERESTS

10.4   The registrar is not affected with notice of a trust (LRA 2002, s 78). It is not possible to protect either a trust of land or a settlement using a notice (LRA 2002, s 33(a)). This is because notices are intended for those interests that will, provided the interest is protected, bind any person who acquires the land. This is not the case in respect of an interest under a trust of land or a settlement because such interests are capable of being overreached provided the disposition is one within the powers of the trustees and that the capital monies are paid to two trustees or to a trust corporation.[1] Trust interests are protected against the trustees making disposals which are outside the powers of the trustees, or which fail to satisfy the requirement of payment of capital money to two trustees or a trust corporation, by registration of an appropriate restriction or restrictions.

1   See para 10.3 and Law Com no 271, para 6.9.

10.5   The use of a restriction, provided the appropriate wording is used, ensures:
   (1)   that the purchaser is aware of the steps necessary to overreach that interest;

(2) that steps short of those capable of overreaching and which would, without the restriction, defeat the interest, cannot be taken by the registered proprietor;

(3) that the details of the beneficial interest are kept off the register in accordance with the 'curtain principle';

(4) that restrictions on the owner's powers of disposition are reflected by the register.

10.6 If a trust interest is not protected by a restriction on the register, and there is a registered disposition where the procedure for overreaching the beneficial interests has not been followed or the disposition is not within the trustees' powers, the transferee under that disposition will take free of that interest, unless it is an overriding interest as discussed below (LRA 2002, ss 11(4), 12(4), 26, 29(2) and 30(2)).[1] If a beneficiary finds that the appropriate restriction has not been entered in the register of title to registered land in which he is beneficially interested, he may apply to the registrar for registration of such a restriction (LRA 2002, s 43(1)(c); LRR 2003, r 93(a)–(e) (trusts of land), and Sch 7, para 3(2) (land in a Settled Land Act 1925 settlement)).[2] The registered proprietor will be notified of the application (LRA 2002, s 45), and the dispute procedure will be invoked if the application is opposed.[3] Where the appropriate restrictions are in place but a beneficiary has grounds for having the trustees replaced,[4] he should start court proceedings for removal of the trustee and register a notice of the proceedings as a pending land action (LRA 2002, s 87(1); LRR 2003, r 172).[5] If he does not obtain registration of a notice (or a restriction)[6] to protect the priority of such proceedings against a disposition by the registered proprietor, the claim will not be an overriding interest even if he is in actual occupation of the land (LRA 2002, s 87(3)).

---

[1] See paras 10.51ff for trust interests as overriding interests.

[2] Note also the LRR 2003, r 93(f)—the Charity Commissioners may apply for a restriction in relation to registered land held on charitable trusts. For applications for restrictions see para xx above.

[3] LRR 2003, r 92(9) prescribes the period for objecting, and LRA 2002 and the LRR 2003, r 19 make provision for objections. See also paras 15.4 and 15.27.

[4] See Underhill and Hayton, *Law Relating to Trusts and Trustees* (16th edn) pp 743–750 and Chapter 15.

[5] These provisions also permit a pending action to be the subject of a restriction, but a notice seems more appropriate to a claim of this kind.

[6] See preceding n 5.

FIRST REGISTRATION

10.7 The effect of a first registration is to register the proprietor with the freehold or leasehold estate in the land subject only to: interests which are the subject of entry in the register; interests which are overriding; and interests which have been acquired under the Limitation Act 1980 (LRA 2002, ss 11(4) and 12(4)).[1]

---
[1]   See Chapter 4.

10.8   Where, however, a proprietor does not own the land for his own benefit, or solely for his own benefit, the estate will be vested in him subject to such of the interests of which he has notice (LRA 2002, ss 11(5) and 12(5)). Accordingly, it will not be possible to defeat a trust interest of which a proprietor is aware, or of which a purchaser has notice, merely by registering the transaction. Nevertheless, failure to protect the interests after first registration of the estate will lead to them being defeated by a subsequent sale unless they are overriding.

10.9   Where the land is unregistered it will not be possible to protect the interest by the use of a restriction. It will therefore be necessary to register a caution against first registration in order to ensure that the interest is protected on the title when the land is first registered.[1]

---
[1]   See paras 4.3 et seq.

JOINT PROPRIETORS

10.10 On an application for first registration of land held by joint proprietors the prescribed application form (Form FR1) contains a section where the proprietors must indicate, by placing an 'x' in the appropriate box, whether the land is held in the form of a joint tenancy or a tenancy in common or on some other terms. On the transfer of a registered estate to joint proprietors the prescribed form of transfer[1] contains a similar section. Ticking the appropriate box acts as a declaration of trust and, in the absence of fraud or reasons for rectification, it is binding on those parties to the application or transfer who assent to its terms.[2]

---
[1]   See the LRR 2003, r 58.
[2]   *Goodman v Gallant* [1986] 1 FLR 513; *Re Gorman* [1990] 1 WLR 616; *Roy v Roy* [1996] 1 FLR 541; and Megarry and Wade, *The Law of Real Property* (6th edn) para 9-026.

10.11 Where the proprietors indicate that they hold the land as joint tenants there is no reason for the entry of a restriction. A sale of the land can only take place where all the legal proprietors consent. In the event of the death of one of more of them the survivors will be able to give a receipt for the capital money since the other's interest will have been acquired by survivorship.

10.12 Where the proprietors hold the land as tenants in common this will not be the case. In the event of one of two proprietors dying, a sale by the survivor will not overreach the interests in the land without a new trustee being appointed. Therefore, the registrar is required to enter a restriction in the register indicating that a sale to the survivor will not overreach the interests in the land (LRA 2002, s 44(1); LRR 2003, r 95(2)(a)). Similarly, in the event that the interests become those of tenants in common the proprietors are required to apply for the registration of a restriction (LRR 2003, r 94(1)).

10.13 The form of restriction is Form A (LRR 2003, Sch 4). This states:

> 'No disposition by a sole proprietor of the registered estate (except a trust corporation) under which capital money arises is to be registered unless authorised by an order of the court.'

It is substantially identical to the restriction under the old rules in Form 62.

TRUSTS OF LAND

10.14 Form A is also the appropriate restriction where the land is held by trustee or trustees of an express trust of land. The transfer form, or the application for first registration ought to indicate that the land is held upon the terms of an express trust.[1] The registrar will then be required to enter the restriction. In addition wherever:

   (1)   the land becomes subject to a trust of land where the survivor of the proprietors will not be able to give a valid receipt for capital monies;
   (2)   the trusts in which the land is held change so that the survivor of the proprietors will not be able to give a valid receipt for capital monies;
   (3)   a sole or last surviving trustee of land applies to register a disposition of a registered estate in his favour or to be registered as proprietor of an unregistered estate,

the proprietor or trustee must apply for a restriction to be entered (LRR 2003, r 94(1), (2)).[2]

---

[1]   See para 10.10.

[2]   A restriction which a proprietor is required to apply for is not a notifiable application (LRA 2002, s 45(3)) so that the restriction can be entered without giving notice to persons interested in its registration. See para 7.54.

10.15 Under the Trusts of Land and Appointment of Trustees Act 1996 (TLATA 1996), s 8 it is possible for the powers of the trustee(s) to be limited by the express terms of the disposition creating the trust. Possible limitations include requirements for the consent of a third party for the exercise of any of the powers set out in the TLATA 1996, ss 6 and 7, including the power to sell or charge the land. Where such limitations exist, or are created, the proprietor must apply for a restriction in Form B requiring a statutory declaration, or a certificate by the conveyancer, stating that a disposition is in accordance with the relevant limitation (LRR 2003, r 94(4) and (5)). The restriction may, where appropriate, be in addition to the restriction in Form A.

SETTLED LAND

Introduction

10.16 Settlements under the Settled Land Act 1925 (SLA 1925) are not dealt with in the LRA 2002 at all, instead being confined to a schedule to the LRR 2003 (LRA 2002, s 89; LRR 2003, Sch 7).

10.17 In any settlement there usually exists a set of trustees and a tenant for life (or statutory owner).[1] The land that is the subject of the settlement must be vested in the tenant for life who has the power to sell it (SLA 1925, s 4; LRR 2003, Sch 7, para 1). The principal function of the trustees is to receive the capital monies, such as monies from the receipt of a sale of land (SLA 1925, ss 18(1) and 75(1)).[2]

---

[1]   There will be a statutory owner where the tenant for life is a minor (in which case the statutory owner will be the trustees of the settlement or the personal representatives in whom the land is vested) or where there is no tenant for life (in which case the statutory owner will be the person in whose favour the powers of a tenant for life are conferred by the settlement or else the trustees of the settlement). Although the trustees of the settlement may be the same person as the statutory owner the two functions are very different.

[2]   For further examples see Megarry and Wade, *The Law of Real Property* (6th edn), para 8-094.

10.18 A settlement will consist of two documents:
   (1)   the trust instrument – this will set out the terms of the settlement, contain the appointment of trustees and the power to appoint new trustees and set out any powers in addition to those contained in the SLA 1925 (SLA 1925, s 4(3)). In the event that the settlement was created by will the trust instrument will be the will (SLA 1925, s 6);

(2) the vesting instrument – this will set out a description of the settled land, whom the land is vested in, the names of the trustees of the settlement, any powers other than those conferred by the SLA 1925 which relate to the land and the name of any person entitled to appoint new trustees of the settlement (SLA 1925, s 5).

10.19 The purpose in separating the terms of the trust (contained in the trust instrument) from the ownership of the trust land (set out in the vesting instrument) is that a purchaser, who is concerned only to ensure that the purchase overreaches the settlement, need only consider the matters set out in the vesting instrument and need give no thought to the terms of the settlement itself.[1] Indeed, the purchaser is not usually entitled to see the trust instrument (SLA 1925, s 110(2)). If there is no vesting deed any disposition by the tenant for life does not take effect in favour of a purchaser of the legal estate but operates only as a contract for valuable consideration to carry out the transaction after the requisite vesting instrument has been executed or made (SLA 1925, s 13). This is a significant incentive for the tenant for life to ensure that a vesting deed does exist.[2]

---

[1] Megarry and Wade, *The Law of Real Property* (6th edn), para 8-028.
[2] Megarry and Wade, *The Law of Real Property* (6th edn), para 8-023.

Protection by restriction

10.20 There are, under the provisions of the 1925 legislation, two requirements for a disposition of the settled land to overreach the settlement (SLA 1925, s 18; Law of Property Act 1925, s 2(1)(i)). These are that:
(1) the disposition takes place in accordance with the powers conferred on the tenant for life;[1]
(2) the capital monies arising out of the disposition are paid to or on the direction of the trustees of the settlement (not being less than two in number unless a trust corporation).

---

[1] A disposition that is not authorised by the statute is void except insofar as it is capable of binding the interest of the tenant for life, SLA 1925, s 18(1).

10.21 Accordingly it is necessary to protect a settlement with the use of a restriction preventing dispositions otherwise than in accordance with the above.[1] LRR 2003 prescribe three different forms of restriction, Forms G, H, and I (LRR 2003, Sch 4 and Sch 7, paras 3(1), 4(1)). The wording of the restrictions varies according to whether there is a tenant for life and trustees (G), statutory owners as trustees of the settlement and registered proprietor (H), or a tenant for life but no trustees (I).

10.22 Where registered land has been settled and the registered proprietor is the tenant for life under the settlement the registered proprietor must make a declaration in Form 6 (LRR 2003, Sch 3, Form 6 and Sch 7, para 5). (equivalent in its contents to a vesting deed) and apply for the entry of a restriction in Form G (LRR 2003, Sch 7, para 5). Similar obligations are placed upon first registrations of settled land (LRR 2003, Sch 7, para 2)[1] and where registered land is purchased with capital money of a settlement (and therefore becomes part of the settlement) (LRR 2003, Sch 7, para 6).[2]

---

1   A first registration will be 'triggered' by an assent of the land subject to the settlement: see the LRA 2002, s 4 and paras 5.2–5.5 and 6.3–6.6. Thus, where a tenant for life in whom the (unregistered) settled land has been vested dies, the resulting assent will give rise to an obligation to register the land.

2   The transfer must also include a declaration, prescribed by para 6, which is in the terms of a vesting deed.

Sale of the land

10.23 Provided the terms of the registered restriction are complied with the purchaser will take free of any of the interests arising under the settlement. The interests of the settlement will transfer to the capital monies paid to the trustees.

Tenant for life ceases to be tenant for life

10.24 A tenant for life may cease to be a tenant for life in his own lifetime, without becoming absolutely interested in the property of the settlement. This might occur, for example, where the tenant for life's interest is one which comes to an end when some specified event occurs (eg a will which gives the testator's widow an interest for life or until remarriage) and it does occur, or is subject to a power of appointment which is exercised.[1]

---

1   See Megarry and Wade, *The Law of Real Property* (6th edn), para 8-032.

10.25 The tenant for life, on the termination of his interest as tenant for life, is obliged to transfer the land to his successor in title or to the statutory owner (SLA 1925, s 7(4); LRR 2003, Sch 7, para 8). If the settlement continues after the transfer the trustees of the settlement must, in relation to registered land subject to the settlement, apply for any necessary restrictions as may be required to protect the beneficial interests and powers under the settlement (LRR 2003, Sch 7, para 8(b)).[1] If the settlement is at an end (because the new proprietor is absolutely entitled under the terms of the trust) the trustees should execute a deed of discharge and apply for the removal of the restriction in Form RX3 (LRR 2003, r 97).[2]

---

[1]   For example, if the tenant for life conveys to the trustees as statutory owners it will be necessary to change the registered restrictions from Form G to Form H.
[2]   See para 10.30.

Death of tenant for life

10.26 On the death of the tenant for life there are two possibilities:[1]
- (1)   the land ceases to be settled because either the remainderman is absolutely entitled or because the land becomes subject to a trust of land;
- (2)   the land remains settled because the terms of the settlement provide for a further tenant for life or other continuing trusts.

---

[1]   Megarry and Wade, *The Law of Real Property* (6th edn), para 8-033 to 8-035.

10.27 In the first scenario the land vests in the personal representatives of the tenant for life. They must transfer the land to the remainderman or the trustees of the trust of land using a normal conveyance or assent.[1] The application to register the transfer must be accompanied by the grant of probate or letters of administration to the personal representative (if the personal representative is not already registered as proprietor) and Form RX3 for the cancellation of the restrictions entered on the register relating to the settlement (LRR 2003, Sch 7, para 12(2)).

---

[1]   *Re Bridgett and Hayes' Contract* [1928] Ch 163.

10.28 In the second scenario special personal representatives, usually the trustees of the settlement, may apply for a grant in respect of the land (Administration of Estates Act 1925, s 22(1)).[1] They take out a grant of letters of administration[2] limited to the settled land and execute a vesting assent, in form AS1 or AS2 as appropriate, in favour of the new tenant for life. The application to register the vesting assent in favour of the tenant for life must be accompanied by the grant of letters of administration (if the personal representative is not already registered as proprietor),[3] the vesting assent and an application in Form RX1 for entry of a restriction on Form G or H as appropriate (LRR 2003, Sch 7, para 12(1)(a)). The vesting assent must contain the prescribed declaration (LRR 2003, Sch 7, para 12(1)(b)).

---

[1]   In the case of an intestacy no statutory title is prescribed, see Megarry and Wade, *The Law of Real Property* (6th edn), para 8-035 and nn 58 and 59.

² The LRR 2003, Sch 7, para 11(2) and (3) contemplate that there might be a grant of probate, but in fact special personal representatives in relation to settled land have, since 14 October 1991, been granted letters of administration, not probate: see the Non-contentious Probate Rules 1987, SI 1987/2024, r 29, as substituted by SI 1991/1876.

³ The special personal representatives are entitled to apply to be registered as proprietors under the terms of the LRR 2003, Sch 7, para 11.

10.29 The responsibility for ensuring that the transfer is to the person entitled and in accordance with the terms of the settlement lies with the personal representatives. The registrar is under no duty and is not entitled either to investigate the reasons why any transfer is made by the personal representative nor to consider the terms of the will and, provided the terms of any restriction are complied with, will be entitled to assume, whether he knows of the terms of the will or not, that the personal representative is acting correctly and within his powers (LRR 2003, Sch 7, para 12(3)).

The settlement ends

10.30 The principal reasons for a settlement coming to an end are:
- the tenant for life becomes absolutely entitled under the terms of the settlement;
- the tenant for life dies or ceases to be tenant for life,[1] and the persons thereafter entitled are entitled absolutely or on the terms of a trust of land.

¹ See para 10.24.

10.31 Where the settlement comes to an end the trustees of the settlement are required to execute a deed declaring that they are discharged from their duties (SLA 1925, s 17). A purchaser of the land is entitled to assume that the land to which the deed relates has ceased to be settled land and (unless the deed provides otherwise) is not subject to a trust of land (SLA 1925, s 17(3)).

10.32 Once the deed of discharge is executed it is necessary for it to be registered in order for the relevant restrictions to be removed. An application to do so is made on Form RX3 (LRR 2003, Sch 7, para 14).

Protection of proprietors/personal representatives

10.33 Provided the proprietor or personal representatives in good faith comply with the requirements of the LRR 2003 in executing a transfer of settled land or discharge of trustees, and in applying for the appropriate restrictions that may be required for the protection of the beneficial interests and powers under a settlement, the proprietor or personal representative:

- is absolutely discharged from all liability in respect of the equitable interests and powers taking effect under the settlement;
- is entitled to be kept indemnified at the cost of the trust estate from all liabilities affecting the settled land (LRR 2003, Sch 7, para 15).[1]

---

[1] Note that to the extent that this provision conflicts with the SLA 1925 it is likely that it overrides such provision, see the LRA 2002, s 89(2). However, it is arguable that the LRA 2002, s 89 gave the rules power to only expressly modify the SLA 1925, not to override its provisions by implication.

CHARITIES

General

10.34 A charity is an institution which is established for charitable purposes and is subject to the control of the court's jurisdiction with respect to charities.[1] 'Charitable purposes' are purposes which are exclusively charitable according to the law of England and Wales (Charities Act 1993 (CA 1993), s 97(1)). In order to determine what purposes are charitable it is necessary to refer to the preamble to the Charitable Uses Act 1601, which along with the authorities, establish that charity, in its legal sense, consists of four principal divisions: the relief of poverty; the advancement of education; the advancement of religion and other purposes beneficial to the community not falling within the other three divisions.[2]

---

[1] See the CA 1993, s 96(1) and Halsbury's Laws of England, 4th ed reissue, vol 5(2), para 1.
[2] See Halsbury's Laws of England, 4th ed reissue, vol 5(2), paras 1–49.

10.35 A charity may or may not be incorporated (under the CA 1993, Pt VII). It will usually be administered and run by trustees who are responsible for the charity's property and its proper administration (CA 1993, s 54). The Charity Commissioners maintain a register of charities, with particulars of their trusts and any other information which the Commissioners may consider desirable (CA 1993, s 3). Any charity entered on the register is, for all purposes, deemed to be charitable (CA 1993, s 4(1)).

Restrictions on dispositions

10.36 Charities hold land on a trust of land (Trusts of Land and Appointment of Trustees Act 1996 (TLATA 1996), ss 1(1) and 2(5)).[1] As such, in relation to the land and for the purposes of exercising their functions as trustees, they have all the powers of disposition of an absolute owner (TLATA 1996, s 6(1)).[1]

---

[1]   Prior to January 1997 the trustees were given the powers conferred upon a life tenant and the trustees of a settlement by the SLA 1925 (s 29(1)). This was repealed by the TLATA 1996, s 25(2), Sch 4.

10.37 These powers are restricted by CA 1993, ss 36–40 which, in essence, lay down a procedure through which a charity (not being an exempt charity)[1] must go before disposing of its land.

    (1)   There is an absolute prohibition on any sale, lease or other disposition to a person connected to the charity or to a trustee or nominee for a connected person without an order of the court or of the Charities Commissioners (CA 1993, s 36(1) and (2)).[2]

    (2)   For other transactions the trustees may obtain an order of the court or the Charities Commission. Alternatively they may comply with requirements, contained in the CA 1993, ss 36 and 39 (the form of which varies according to the transaction), to obtain, consider and implement advice about the proposed transaction as well comply with requirements to give public notice of the proposed disposition, invite representations and take into consideration those representations.

    (3)   A contract for sale, lease or other disposition as well as the conveyance, transfer, lease or other instrument itself must contain a statement that the land is held by or in trust for a charity, whether the charity is an exempt charity, whether the disposition falls within certain exceptions contained in the CA 1993, s 36(9) and whether, if the charity is not exempt and the disposition is not exempt under those requirements, the land is land to which the restrictions on disposition imposed by the CA 1993, s 36 or s 39 apply (CA 1993, ss 37(1) and 39(1)). In the case of the disposition or mortgage itself the statement is in a form prescribed by the LRR 2003 (LRR 2003, r 180).

    (4)   Where the land is sold, leased, or otherwise disposed of, the trustees must certify in the instrument by which the disposition is effected that the requirements of the CA 1993, s 36 have been complied with (CA 1993, s 37(2)). Similarly where the land is mortgaged the charity must certify that the requirements of the CA 1993, s 38 have been complied with (CA 1993, s 39(2)).

¹ See para 10.43.

² A 'connected person' is defined in the CA 1993, Sch 5 and includes the trustees of the charity, donors of the land to the charity, certain defined relations of those persons, an officer, agent or employee of the charity.

10.38 The consequences of a failure by the charity to take the relevant steps depends upon the nature of the transaction. Where the charity enters into a contract for the sale, leasing or otherwise disposing of land, but has not obtained or considered the requisite advice, the contract will be void. This is irrespective of whether the purchaser acted in good faith.¹

¹ *Bayoumi v Women's Total Abstinence Union Ltd* [2003] EWHC 212 (Ch), [2003] Ch 283.

10.39 Where the charity actually disposes of the land by sale, lease, or otherwise and the disposition does contain the required certificate of compliance, then in favour of any person who acquires an interest in the land for money or money's worth it shall be conclusively presumed that the facts were as stated in the certificate (CA 1993, s 37(3)). Therefore, any failure to comply with the relevant procedure will make no difference to the purchaser provided the correct certificate is provided. Where the certificate is not provided and where the relevant procedure has not been followed, the disposition will only be valid if the purchaser acquires an interest in the land for money or money's worth and acts in good faith (CA 1993, s 37(4)).

Protection by restriction

10.40 The registrar is required to reflect the limitations on the charities' powers of disposition by entry of a restriction on the register (CA 1993, s 37(7)). The obligation arises wherever the disposition or other instrument effecting the disposition contains the statement required by the CA 1993.¹ Similarly any application for:

- first registration of an unregistered estate;
- to register a transfer of a registered estate to the official custodian;²
- to register the vesting by operation of law of the registered estate in a person other than the proprietor of that estate,

must, if related to a registered or unregistered estate held by or in trust for a non-exempt charity, be accompanied by an application for entry of an appropriate restriction (unless that restriction is already on the register) (LRR 2003, r 176(2)).

¹ See para 10.37.
² See para 10.49.

10.41 The restriction appropriate to charities is Form E (LRR 2003, r 176 and Sch 4)[1] as follows:

> 'No disposition by the proprietor of the registered estate to which section 36 or section 38 of the Charities Act 1993 applies is to be registered unless the instrument contains a certificate complying with section 37(2) or section 39(2) of that Act as appropriate.'

Since such a certificate will prevent the disposition to a purchaser for money or money's worth from being void, whether or not the purchaser acts in good faith,[2] this restriction will normally ensure that the purchaser is properly protected.

---

[1]   There is also Form F for where the official custodian is registered as proprietor: see the LRR 2003, r 178 and Sch 4.
[2]   See above para 10.39.

10.42 It may also be necessary for the registrar to enter other restrictions appropriate to the charities' ownership of the land, such as a restriction preventing the sale of the land to the survivor of two or more joint proprietors.

Exempt charities

10.43 Exempt charities are those charities listed in the CA 1993, Sch 2. They are generally free from the restrictions of the CA 1993. The restrictions on dispositions of land do not apply to them (CA 1993, s 36(10)) although the requirement to include a statement within a contract for the sale, lease, mortgage or other disposition of land as well as within the conveyance, transfer, lease, mortgage or other disposition contained within the CA 1993, s 37 does.

10.44 Since there is no restriction on an exempt charities' powers of disposition there is no requirement to register a restriction in respect of land held by that charity. However, the registrar may need to register a restriction reflecting restrictions on dispositions contained within the trusts of the charity or any legislation governing the charity.

10.45 In the event that a registered estate is held by or in trust for a corporation, and the corporation becomes a non-exempt charity, the charity trustees must apply for the entry of the appropriate restriction, reflecting the fact that s 36 of the Charities Act 1993 now limits their powers of disposition (LRR 2003, r 176(3)).

Dispositions to a charity

10.46 Any contract for sale, lease or other disposition of land which will result in the land being held by or in trust for a charity must contain a statement (CA 1993, s 37(5)):

- that the land will, as a result of the disposition, be held by or in trust for a charity;
- whether the charity is an exempt charity; and
- if it is not an exempt charity, that the restrictions on dispositions imposed on non-exempt charities[1] will apply to the land.

---

[1] See para 10.37.

10.47 The conveyance, transfer or other instrument effecting the disposition itself must contain the same statement (CA 1993, s 37(5)(b)). Where the disposition is a registrable disposition or triggers the requirement of first registration the statement must be in the form prescribed by the LRR 2003, r 179 (CA 1993, s 37(7)), namely either:

> 'The land transferred (*or as the case may be*) will, as a result of this transfer (*or as the case may be*) be held by (or in trust for) (*charity*), an exempt charity.'

or

> 'The land transferred (*or as the case may be*) will, as a result of this transfer (*or as the case may be*) be held by (*or in trust for*) (*charity*), a non-exempt charity, and the restrictions on disposition imposed by section 36 of the Charities Act 1993 will apply to the land (subject to section 36(9) of that Act).'

Miscellaneous

10.48 Where a registered disposition of a registered estate or registered charge is made in favour of charity trustees incorporated under the CA 1993, Pt VII the registered disposition must describe the charity as 'a body corporate under Part VII of the Charities Act 1993'. The application to register the disposition must be accompanied by the certificate granted by the Charity Commissioners, under the CA 1993, s 50, permitting the trustees to incorporate (LRR 2003, r 177).

10.49 Where an application is made to register the official custodian as proprietor of a registered estate or registered charge the application must be accompanied by the court order, under the CA 1993, s 21(1), or the order of the Charities Commissioners under the CA 1993, ss 16 or 18. The address for service remains that of the charity trustees or (where incorporated) the charity unless the order is made under the CA 1993, s 18 (LRR 2003, r 178).

TRANSITIONAL PROVISIONS— EXPRESS PROTECTION

10.50 Under the LRA 1925 interests under trusts could be protected by restrictions or by cautions against dealing. Nothing in the LRA 2002 affects the validity of these entries so they will continue to have effect as under the previous system until the interest is extinguished or the registration is amended in line with the new system (LRA 2002, Sch 12, para 1).[1]

---

[1]   See the LRR 2003, rr 218–223 for the operation of cautions against dealing in the new system. See para 7.88.

TRUST INTERESTS AS OVERRIDING INTERESTS

10.51 As discussed above, interests under trusts are protected by the entry of a restriction on the register.[1] If such an interest is not so protected, the transferee under a registered disposition will take the land free of such interest where the procedure for overreaching the beneficial interests has not been followed, unless it is an overriding interest as discussed below (LRA 2002, ss 11(4), 12(4), 26, 29(2), and 30(2)).[2]

---

[1]   See paras 10.4 et seq.
[2]   See para 10.33.

10.52 In addition to being capable of protection by registration, interests under trusts of land can be overriding interests. Such a trust interest is not an overriding interest in its own right, but it can be one as an interest belonging to a person in actual occupation of the land (LRA 2002, Sch 1, para 2 (first registrations); LRA 2002, Sch 3, para 2 (registered dispositions)).[1] Interests under settlements within the SLA 1925 are expressly excluded from being overriding interests (LRA 2002, Sch 1, para 2 and Sch 3, para 2).

---

[1]   See para 7.9.

Requirements

10.53 In respect of a first registration of land the interest under a trust will be protected as an overriding interest provided, at the time of the disposition:

- it is not an interest under a settlement under the SLA 1925;
- it is an interest of a person who is in actual occupation of the land (LRA 2002, Sch 1, para 2).

In respect of a registration of a registered disposition, the interest under a trust will be protected as an overriding interest provided, at the time of the disposition:

- it is not an interest under a settlement under the SLA 1925;
- it is an interest of a person who is in actual occupation of the land;
- it is not an interest of a person of whom inquiry was made before the disposition and who failed to disclose the right when he could reasonably have been expected to do so;
- it is not an interest of a person whose occupation would not have been obvious on a reasonably careful inspection of the land at the time of the disposition and of which the person to whom the disposition is made does not have actual knowledge at that time (LRA 2002, Sch 3, para 2).

10.54 It makes no difference whether or not the trust interest is express or implied, nor whether it ought to have been protected by restriction on its creation.

10.55 The exception for interests under settlements under the SLA 1925 is a continuation of an exception under the old regime (LRA 1925, s 86(2)). The Law Commission had proposed abolishing this exception but this proposal was rejected on consultation.[1]

---

[1]   See Law Com no 271, para 8.17.

Part only

10.56 Where the beneficiary occupies only part of the land in which the trust interest exists, the interest will only be overriding in respect of that part which is occupied by the beneficiary.[1] It is therefore possible for a registered proprietor to discover that he is obliged to hold one half of a registered title for A, whilst the remaining half is free of A's interests altogether.[2]

---

[1]   See para 7.9.
[2]   Contrast the result, under the old system, in *Ferrishurst v Wallcite Ltd* [1999] Ch 355.

Overreaching v overriding

10.57 In order for an interest to be overriding it must continue to exist after the registered disposition or first registration. It follows that, where the interest is overreached by the disposition it will not bind the purchaser irrespective of the fact it would, were it not being overreached, have been an overriding interest.[1]

---

[1]   See *City of London Building Society v Flegg* [1988] AC 54.

Example

10.58 Under the LRA 1925, overriding interests arising under trusts of persons in actual occupation most commonly arose where the sole registered proprietor mortgaged, or re-mortgaged, the land without disclosing an interest of an occupant (commonly a cohabitant or spouse) who had an interest in the land. These interests most commonly arose under an implied trust arising either from contributions towards the purchase price, or from contributions towards a mortgage or household expenses, coupled with a common intention that that person should have an interest in the land.[1]

---

[1]   See *William and Glyn's Bank v Boland* [1981] AC 487 and *Lloyds Bank v Rosett* [1991] 1 AC 107.

10.59 The LRA 2002 has changed little. A typical example of overriding interests protecting the priority of an unprotected interest under a trust will be as follows.

(1)   A and B are married. A was registered as the sole proprietor although B paid half of the original deposit and has contributed towards the mortgage. B was assured by A that B would have an interest in the land.[1]

(2)   A obtains a re-mortgage from the C bank for an amount significantly higher than the existing mortgage. C is not made aware of B's occupation although that occupation would have been obvious on a reasonable inspection of the land (LRA 2002, Sch 3, para 2(c)).

(3)   As the C bank is unaware of B, no inquiry is made of B and so B does not fail to disclose the interest, even if B could reasonably have been expected to (LRA 2002, Sch 3, para 2(b)).

(4)   The purchase monies are paid to A alone and so do not overreach B's interest.

Under this example the C bank's interest will be subject to B's equitable interest save insofar as the C bank is able to rely on its right of subrogation in discharging the old mortgage.

---

[1]   A contribution towards the purchase price and/or the mortgage payments may give rise to a resulting trust. Such payments, or in some circumstances, payments towards household expenses coupled with a stated intention that B would have a beneficial interest upon which B relies may give rise to a constructive trust. See *Lloyds Bank v Rossett* [1991] 1 AC 107.

10.60 In practice, this scenario will commonly be avoided by the bank by ensuring that it is aware of all persons over the age of 18 who occupy the land and requiring them to disclose all interests they might have in the land, after taking independent advice.[1]

---

[1]   See *Royal Bank of Scotland v Etridge* [2001] UKHL 44, [2002] 2 AC 773.

Transitional provisions

10.61 Under the LRA 1925 an interest might be overriding by virtue of the person, whose interest it was, being in receipt of rent and profits of the land (LRA 1925, s 70(1)(g)). Where an interest was overriding as a result of this provision immediately before 13 October 2003, then it shall remain so until such time as it would have ceased to be overriding under the LRA 1925, by virtue of receipt of rents and profits (LRA 2002, Sch 12, para 8).[1] This could obviously be relevant to someone with a life or absolute interest in let or partly let property under a trust of land. It is quite narrowly drawn, so that any interruption in the flow of rent after 13 October 2003 will apparently terminate the overriding status of the beneficiary's rights, and if the property is again let to a tenant, the beneficiary will not be in actual occupation.

---

[1]   See paras 7.74–7.78.

CHARGING ORDERS ON BENEFICIAL INTERESTS

10.62 A charging order over a beneficiary's interest in registered land arises where a creditor obtains a charging order to enforce a money judgment against A where A and B jointly own the land. The order will charge A's interest but not B's and so exists only as a charge on the equitable interest (Charging Orders Act 1979, s 2(1)(a)). The order has the same effect as an equitable charge created by the debtor and so prevents the sale of the land without the discharge of the charge.[1]

---

[1]   The chargee is additionally entitled to apply for an order for sale of the land: see the TLATA 1996, s 14(1) and CPR r 73.10.

10.63 Although the interest exists only in the equitable interest and not in the registered estate, the LRA 2002 expressly states that the owner of the charging order shall be treated as having a right or claim in relation to the registered land (LRA 2002, s 42(4) and 42(1)(c)). The correct form of protection is a restriction.[1] The form of restriction is Form K (LRR 2003, r 93(k)).

---

[1]   Under the LRA 1925 they were protected by a caution against dealing. Interests protected in this manner continue to be protected: see the LRA 2002, Sch 12, para 1. See para 7.88.

ADVERSE POSSESSION

10.64 The new system abandons the device of the trust that was employed in the LRA 1925, s 75(1). Accordingly, a squatter who successfully acquires title under the new regime will be registered as the 'new proprietor of the estate' and before such registration will have a fee simple absolute in possession (LRA 2002, Sch 6, paras 4, 5 and 7).[1]

---

[1]   See also Law Com no 271, para 14.71 and para 13.22.

10.65 Where land is held on trust by the registered proprietor with one or more of the beneficiaries having an interest in reversion or remainder, the squatter will not be regarded as being in adverse possession for so long as there as such successive interests. Only when all the interests of the beneficiaries are interests in possession can a squatter be treated as being in adverse possession (LRA 2002, Sch 6, para 12).[1]

---

[1]   See para 13.19.

10.66 The registration of the squatter as the new proprietor of the estate will not affect the priority of any interest affecting the estate. As a result the squatter will take the land subject to the same estates, rights and interests that bound the previous proprietor (LRA 2002, Sch 6, para 9).[1]

---

[1]   See para 13.20.

10.67 It is not clear from this whether the squatter will obtain the land free of those trust interests that bound the owner. For example if, A was the registered proprietor and held the land on trust for himself and B, it is reasonably clear that the squatter, S, will take the land free of A's interest. But, what of B's? The fact that the priority of B's interest is not affected by the registration of S suggests that he is bound by the interest. However, this would appear to make the registration of S almost futile (what if B is entitled to 95% of the beneficial interest?). It also brings into question the purpose of providing that adverse possession can only take place where all interests in the land are interests in possession.[1]

1   See paras 13.17–13.19.

11 Contracts; including contracts for the sale of land, options, rights of pre-emption, estoppel and mere equities

INTRODUCTION

11.1 This chapter is concerned with the manner in which the following rights and interests in registered land are protected:
- contracts for the sale or other disposition of land;
- options over land;
- rights of pre-emption in relation to land;
- rights or interests arising under proprietary estoppel;
- mere equities.

11.2 In respect of the last three interests, the Land Registration Act 2002 (LRA 2002) made significant changes. Under the old regime it was either impossible (in the case of rights of pre-emption and mere equities) or arguable (in the case of proprietary estoppel) whether the interests could be protected by the entry of a notice on the affected land. The Law Commission proposed that the position should be changed[1] and as a result all such entries may be protected by the entry of a notice. However, the changes also make some subtle but distinct changes to the nature and effect of these interests. In addition these changes will only take effect in relation to registered land so that these interests will differ according to whether or not the land is registered.

---

[1] See Law Com No 271, paras 5.26–5.36.

CONTRACTS

11.3 A contract for the sale or other disposition of land gives the purchaser an equitable interest in the land. As such it is a burden affecting a registered estate and can be protected by the registration of a notice in relation to the registered estate affected by it (LRA 2002, s 32(1)).

11.4 In the event that the purchaser is in occupation of the land, the interest will exist as an overriding interest in respect of the land that is occupied, and provided none of the exceptions apply (LRA 2002, Sch 1, para 2 and Sch 3, para 2).

OPTIONS

11.5 Similarly, an option gives the holder an equitable right in that land. That right is capable of being protected by the registration of a notice and can exist as an overriding interest in the event that the grantee of the option is in actual occupation.

RIGHTS OF PRE-EMPTION

11.6 A right of pre-emption imposes an obligation on the owner of land to offer the land for sale to the owner of the right before offering it to any third party. Following the decision of the Court of Appeal in *Pritchard v Briggs*[1] such interests do not exist as interests in land until the obligation to offer the land for sale arises. As a result, under the old system they were capable of registration as minor interests but this did not affect their priority until the land owner demonstrated an animus to sell the land.

---
[1]   [1980] Ch 338, CA.

11.7 This was heavily criticised as being inconsistent with the law regarding options and contrary to the principles of the legislation.[1] The Law Commission proposed reversing the effect of *Pritchard v Briggs* in respect of registered land and this proposal was strongly supported on consultation.[2]

---
[1]   See eg HWR Wade, 'Rights of Pre-Emption: Interests in Land' (1980) 96 LQR 488.
[2]   See Law Com No 271, paras 5.26–5.28.

11.8 The LRA 2002, s 115 provides that a right of pre-emption in relation to registered land has effect from the time of creation as an interest capable of binding successors in title. As a result it is capable of protection by the use of a notice and can exist as an overriding interest if the grantee of the right is in actual occupation of the land.

11.9   The LRA 2002, s 115 relates only to those interests created after 13 October 2003. In respect of interests created before that day it will be necessary to apply *Pritchard v Briggs* unless and until that decision is reversed.

11.10 The LRA 2002, s 115 also only relates to rights of pre-emption 'in relation to registered land'. The rule in *Pritchard v Briggs* will continue to apply in respect of rights of pre-emption over unregistered land. It is not clear whether the first registration of land in circumstances which did not trigger the right of pre-emption (perhaps by voluntary registration) would lead to the section applying. If it did it would apply retrospectively to the time of creation of the interest.

PROPRIETARY ESTOPPEL

11.11 An estoppel in relation to land (commonly known as a proprietary estoppel) arises where the owner of land induces, encourages or allows a person to believe that he has, or will have, some right or benefit in respect of the land, that person acts to his detriment in reliance on the belief or representation and the owner then acts contrary to the representation or belief in an unconscionable manner.[1]

---

[1]   Megarry and Wade, *The Law of Real Property* (6th edn), para 13-001.

11.12 It was previously unclear whether such interests were capable of being protected by registration or as overriding interests because of doubts as to when the equity arose.[1] It was the practice of the Land Registry to treat the interest as one that could be protected by a notice or a caution and it was accepted by the authorities that the equity arising by the estoppel could be an overriding interest.[2] The issue was not, however, fully certain.[3]

---

[1]   See Megarry and Wade, *The Law of Real Property* (6th edn), paras 13-028 to 13-032.
[2]   See Megarry and Wade, *The Law of Real Property* (6th edn), para 13-032 for the cases cited there (n 22).
[3]   See *Lee-Parker v Izzett (No 2)* [1972] 1 WLR 775 and *Haberman v Koehler* (1996) 73 P&CR 515.

11.13 The Law Commission recommended that the proprietary status of the equity arising by estoppel should be confirmed in relation to registered land.[1] This recommendation was broadly supported.[2]

1   See the Law Com No 254, para 3.36 and Law Com No 271, para 5.30.
2   See Law Com No 271, para 5.30.

11.14 The LRA 2002, s 116 declares 'for the avoidance of doubt' that in relation to registered land an equity by estoppel has effect from the time the equity arises as an interest capable of binding successors in title. As a result such interests are capable of protection by notice and can exist as an overriding interest if the grantee of the right is in actual occupation of the land. The section applies to all equities by estoppel in relation to registered land whenever created.

MERE EQUITIES

11.15 A mere equity is not a right of property but a right, usually of a procedural nature, which is ancillary to some right of property and which limits or qualifies it in some way.[1] The rights include the right to have a transaction set aside or to have a document rectified for mistake.

1   John McGhee *Snell's Equity* (13th edn), para 2-05.

11.16 The priority of mere equities in land has always been unclear. It appears that they are capable of being defeated both by the disposition of the legal title to the land and by a sale of the equitable interest on which they are dependant to a bona fide purchaser for value without notice.

11.17 The Law Commission criticised both the uncertainty in respect of mere equities and the likely imputation of the doctrine of notice into registered land.[1] They recommended that the uncertainty be resolved and that the general principles of priority applicable to registered land be applied to interests that were mere equities.[2]

1   See Law Com No 271, paras 5.34 and 5.35.
2   See Law Com No 271, para 5.36.

11.18 The LRA 2002, s 116 declares 'for the avoidance of doubt' that in relation to registered land a mere equity has effect from the time the equity arises as an interest capable of binding successors in title. As a result such interests are capable of protection by notice and can exist as an overriding interest if the grantee of the right is in actual occupation of the land. The section applies to all mere equities in relation to registered land whenever created.

12 Miscellaneous interests and the rights of the Crown

RENTCHARGES

12.1 Rentcharges are incorporeal hereditaments. They secure the payment of rent by an estate holder of land. Rentcharges may be legal or equitable. Since 1925 a rentcharge can be legal only if it is an interest in possession and either perpetual or for a term of years absolute (Law of Property Act 1925, s 1(2)(b)). To create new legal rentcharges, it is generally necessary to do so by deed, unless the interest is reserved by the disponee of land or created under statutory powers. The Rentcharges Act 1977 made provision to abolish many rentcharges and to limit the creation of new ones. Nevertheless, a large number still exist and they will have importance for some time to come.[1]

---

[1] For a full explanation of rentcharges, see Megarry and Wade, *The Law of Real Property* (6th edn), paras 18-014–18-039.

12.2 A legal estate in a rentcharge is capable of registration with its own title provided that it is perpetual, or that more than seven years are unexpired (LRA 2002, s 3(1)(a) and (3)). Rentcharges are not subject to compulsory registration, although there is power for the Lord Chancellor to extend the compulsory registration requirements to include them (LRA 2002, s 5(2)(b)). It is possible to register a caution against the first registration of a legal rentcharge (LRA 2002, s 15).

12.3 In order to protect the priority of a rentcharge (whether legal or equitable) it will be necessary to protect it by the entry of a notice on the register of the title of the estate affected (LRA 2002, s 29). Where the estate affected by the rentcharge is unregistered, the proprietor of a rentcharge is able to register a caution against first registration of that estate (LRA 2002, s 15(1), (2)).

12.4 Where a legal rentcharge is created by a disposition out of a registered estate (and that rentcharge is for a term exceeding seven years) the grantee, or his successor in title, must be entered in the register as the proprietor of the interest created and a notice in respect of the interest created must also be entered in the register (LRA 2002, Sch 2, para 6). Until these requirements are met the disposition will not operate at law and the proprietor will not be deemed to be vested with a legal estate (LRA 2002, ss 27(1) and 58).

12.5 It is possible to obtain a title to a rentcharge by adverse possession. The reforms introduced in respect of adverse possession against registered land are extended to include adverse possession against registered rentcharges (LRR 2003, Sch 8 introduced under the power in the LRA 2002, s 88). This may well be a major incentive to voluntarily register legal rentcharges.

PROFITS À PRENDRE IN GROSS

12.6 Most profits à prendre exist for the benefit of some land. However, certain profits benefit the owner independently of his or her ownership of land. These are said to exist 'in gross'.[1]

---

[1] See Megarry and Wade, *The Law of Real Property* (6th edn), para 18-085.

12.7 Under the old system such interests were not capable of being registered and could only be protected by the registration of a notice or caution against the title of the estate affected. The suggestion that such interests should be capable of being registered was supported on consultation. As a result, such interests may now be registered with their own registered title (LRA 2002, s 3(1)(d)). They are not subject to compulsory registration (although there is power to extend these requirements). It is also possible to register a caution against first registration of a profit à prendre in gross.

12.8 The provisions regarding overriding interests in respect of profits à prendre apply in the same way to profits à prendre in gross.[1] Thus all legal profits à prendre in gross will be overriding interests on first registration and all will be overriding on a disposition unless at the time of the disposition: (a) they are not within the knowledge of the person to whom the disposition is made; and (b) they would not have been obvious on a reasonably careful inspection of the land, unless exercised within one year of the disposition (LRA 2002, Sch 1, para 3 and Sch 3, para 3).

---

[1] See para 7.10.

12.9 Where a profit à prendre in gross is created by a disposition (and that profit à prendre in gross is for a term exceeding seven years) the grantee, or his successor in title, must be entered in the register as the proprietor of the interest created and a notice in respect of the interest created must also be entered in the register (LRA 2002, Sch 2, para 6). Until these requirements are met the disposition will not operate at law and the proprietor will not be deemed to be vested with a legal estate (LRA 2002, ss 27(1) and 58).[1]

---

[1]   See para 2.3.

FRANCHISES

12.10 Franchises, which are incorporeal hereditaments, arise by royal grant. They are described as 'a royal privilege or branch of the royal prerogative subsisting in the hands of a subject, by grant from the King'.[1] As well as being capable of creation by express grant they can also arise by prescription. Whilst the types of interests that may exist as franchises is quite varied, the most important franchise today is the right to hold a market.[2]

---

[1]   *Spook Erection Ltd v Secretary of State for the Environment* [1989] QB 300.
[2]   See Megarry and Wade, *The Law of Real Property* (6th edn), para 18-013.

12.11 Under the old system it was not possible to register a franchise. It could be protected by the entry of a notice or caution but also existed as an overriding interest. The Law Commission proposed that it should be possible to register the right with its own title. Accordingly, they are now capable of registration with their own title. They are not subject to compulsory registration (although there is power to extend these requirements). It is also possible to register a caution against first registration of a franchise.

12.12 Whilst it is possible to protect a franchise by the registration of a notice or caution against the title of the estate affected, they do continue to exist as overriding interests. However, they will cease to be overriding after 13 October 2013 (LRA 2002, s 117), so it will be necessary to slowly bring all such interests on to the register before that date.[1]

---

[1]   See Law Com No 271, para 8.40.

12.13 Where a grant is made out of a franchise of a term of years of more than seven years, the grantee, or his successor in title, must be entered in the register as proprietor of the lease and a notice in respect of the lease must also be entered in the register (LRA 2002, Sch 2, para 4). Until these requirements are met the disposition will not operate at law and the proprietor will not be deemed to be vested with a legal estate (LRA 2002, ss 27(1) and 58).[1]

---

[1]   See para 2.3.

MANORS AND MANORIAL RIGHTS

12.14 Manors, which are wholly incorporeal and impose no burden on the land within the manor, were formally capable of being registered with their own title. Under the LRA 2002 such rights will no longer be capable of registration. Furthermore, on the application of any proprietor of a manor that is registered, the registrar may remove the title to the manor from the register (LRA 2002, s 119).

12.15 Seignorial and manorial rights are certain rights of the lord (or, in some cases, of the tenant). A precise list of those rights which exist can be found in the Law of Property Act 1922 (Sch 12, paras 5 and 6). They have not been capable of creation since 1925. Such rights will exist as overriding interests until 13 October 2013 (LRA 2002, Sch 1, para 11, Sch 3 and s 117).

RIGHTS OF THE CROWN

Crown rents

12.16 There is some confusion over what the term 'Crown rents' means. In the consultative document the Law Commission stated that it believed that it probably referred to the rents payable on land that belonged to the Crown at the time of the Norman Conquest and which were then granted by the Crown to a subject in return for the payment of rent (ancient demesne).[1] In Law Com No 271, however, it was stated that the Crown Estate had explained that the term might refer to rent payable to the Crown for freehold land in a manor or ancient demesne or the rent reserved to the Crown under the grant of a freehold estate.[2] There were examples of the latter types of rights in conveyances up to 1949, although in some cases the Crown had sold on and was no longer the recipient of the rents.

---

[1]   Law Com No 254 Para 5.35.
[2]   Law Com No 271 Para 8.43.

12.17 With some reluctance, the Law Commission proposed that such interests should continue to be overriding.[1] They will therefore remain overriding until 13 October 2013 (LRA 2002, Sch 1, para 12, Sch 3 and s 117).

---

[1]   See Law Com No 271, para 8.44.

Demesne

12.18 Demesne lands are those lands held by the Crown as sovereign or lord paramount. Land held on a fee simple has been granted by the Crown to the subject. Where land is held in demesne, no estate (and so no fee simple) in the land exists. The land that is held in demesne includes the foreshore around England and Wales (where not granted to or vested in a private owner), land that has escheated to the Crown (see below) and the ancient lands that have never been granted away in fee.[1] The amount of land that is held in demesne is therefore substantial.

---

[1]   See Law Com No 271, para 11.7.

12.19 Under the LRA 1925 it was not possible to register land held in demesne because only estates in land could be registered and, as explained above, the Crown held no such estate. This remains the case in the new LRA 2002. However, the LRA 2002 provides for the voluntary registration of demesne land by providing that Her Majesty may grant an estate in fee simple in possession to Herself (LRA 2002, s 79(1)).[1] This grant is not to be regarded as having been made unless an application to register the estate is made within the period of two months beginning with the date of the grant (LRA 2002, s 79(3)).[2] It follows that the power to make such a grant in fee simple is only available where the land is registered shortly afterwards. Foreshore and other internal waters, which are mostly owned by the Crown, are capable of registration, and this can be extended to other territorial waters by order made by the Lord Chancellor (LRA 2002, s 130), though no such order has yet been made. An important consequence of these powers is that the Crown can by registering land make it much more difficult for others to obtain a title to it by adverse possession (see Chapter 13), especially in relation to foreshore (see paras 13.28 and 13.29).

---

[1] Although the Crown may hold a fee simple it is doubtful whether it could, prior to this provision, make a grant in fee simple to itself.

[2] However, the period may be extended on the application of Her Majesty if the registrar is satisfied that there is a good reason for doing so, see LRA 2002, s 79(4) and (5).

12.20 It is also made possible to register cautions against the first registration of demesne land, by stating that the relevant section applies as if the demesne land were held by Her Majesty 'for an unregistered estate in fee simple absolute in possession' (LRA 2002, s 81).

12.21 The provisions of compulsory registration are extended to grants of estates out of demesne land to include grants (LRA 2002, s 80):
- of an estate in fee simple absolute in possession (other than to Her Majesty under s 79);
- of a term of years absolute of more than seven years from the date of the grant;
- of an estate in land for valuable or other consideration by way of gift or in pursuance of an order of any court. The reference to grants by gift includes any grant for the purpose of constituting a trust under which Her Majesty does not retain the whole beneficial ownership.

This does not include the grant of an estate in mines or minerals.

Escheat and bona vacantia

12.22 Escheat occurs when a freehold estate determines. The Crown, as the sovereign or lord paramount becomes entitled to the land in its own right. In the cases where the land is held of a mesne lord (such as the Royal Duchies) the lord will hold by virtue of that lord's own estate in fee simple. Where the land is held directly of the Crown, it will be held by the Crown in demesne. Whomever holds the land on an escheat, subordinate rights and interests created out of the freehold survive the termination of the interest.[1]

---

[1] *Scmalla Properties v Gesso Properties (BVI) Ltd* [1995] BCC 793.

12.23 The Law Commission believed that something like 500 freehold estates escheat every year.[1] The principal circumstance in which an escheat arises is the disclaimer of a freehold estate under the provisions of insolvency.[2]

12.24 Under the previous system, where an estate escheated it ceased to be held as an estate in land and so its registered title came to an end and was closed. Under the LRR 2003, rr 79 and 173 the registrar may enter a note of the determination of the freehold in the property register of the estate and in the property register of an inferior affected registered title (and where there is doubt as to the determination the entry must record this doubt). He need not close the registered title to the estate until a freehold estate in land in respect of the land in which the former estate subsisted has been registered. The wider powers, which include, for example, power for the rules to provide for determination to be dependant upon the meeting of certain requirements, have not been exercised.

12.25 Bona vacantia occurs where land vests in the Crown or the Royal Duchies for lack of an owner but the estate continues to exist. This occurs, for example, under the Companies Act 1985, s 654[1] and under the rules of intestacy where there are no persons falling within the relevant classes of beneficiaries (Administration of Estates Act 1925, s 46(1)(vi)). This operation is unaffected by the LRA 2002, and such transfers can simply be registered with the Crown or the Duchy as the registered proprietor. However, rules may make provision about how the passing of a registered estate in this manner is to be dealt with and the LRR 2003, r 185 states that where a company is dissolved a notice of that dissolution may be entered on the registers of the estates of that company.

---

1   Where the Crown may then choose to disclaim so causing the land to vest in itself as having escheated. For an explanation of this see Law Com No 271, para 11.25.

PPP LEASES

12.26 Public-Private Partnership (PPP) leases will arise out of the arrangements for the future running of the London Underground.[1] The legislation concerning such leases is complex and the disposition of such leases is severely restricted. There would be serious practical difficulties with registering such leases, arising mainly out of the difficulties of mapping and identifying the land concerned. As a result the Law Commission proposed[2] that the provisions of the LRA 2002 should generally be disapplied to these leases.

1   See the Greater London Authority Act 1999, ss 210–219.
2   They indicated a degree of reluctance (see para 13 of Law Com No 271) and it may be speculated that they were under some pressure to include this exception since Law Com No 271 and the Bill were drawn up around the time that Government was giving very active consideration to these leases.

12.27 As a result:

- no application for a first registration of a PPP lease[1] may be made;
- the requirement of registration does not apply to the grant or transfer of a PPP lease;
- the grant of a term of years absolute under a PPP lease and the express grant of a legal interest for the benefit of a PPP lease is not required to be completed by registration;
- no notice may be entered in the register in respect of an interest under a PPP lease;
- such leases will exist as overriding interests.

1   A PPP lease is given the same meaning as in the Greater London Authority Act 1999, s 218, see the LRA 2002, s 90(6).

13 Adverse possession

THE POLICY AIMS

13.1 One of the statistics which emerged at the Report Stage of the Land Registration Act 2002 (LRA 2002) in the House of Lords was that each year the Land Registry received over 20,000 applications for registration based in whole or in part on adverse possession. In about three quarters (15,000) of those cases, the applicant had been successful in barring the previous owner. Around three quarters of Land Registry hearings had involved squatting, and in approximately 60% of cases the squatter had succeeded in whole or in part.

13.2 The Parliamentary Secretary, Lord Chancellor's Department, expressly stated that one of the aims of the relevant provisions, in so far as they affected adverse possession, was to eradicate the time, money and anxiety which adverse possession disputes will previously have cost the former owner.[1]

---

[1]   HL, Report Stage, 30 October 2001, col 1332.

13.3 The Law Commission in its Report *Land Registration for the 21st Century, A Conveyancing Revolution* (Law Com no 271) observed[1] that there appeared to be considerable public disquiet with the way that the law on adverse possession operated. The basic thrust behind the adverse possession provisions of the LRA 2002 is to strengthen the position of registered owners. The Law Commission expressly endorsed[2] the sentiments of Mr Justice Neuberger at first instance in *J A Pye (Oxford) Holdings Ltd v Graham,*[3] at least insofar as they related to registered land, to the effect that the law was illogical and disproportionate:

> 'illogical because the only reason the owner can be said to have sat on his rights is because of the existence of the 12 year limitation period in the first place; if no limitation period existed, he would be entitled to claim possession whenever he wanted the land ... disproportionate, because ... it does seem draconian to the owner and a windfall for the squatter that, just because the owner has taken no steps to evict the squatter for 12 years, the owner should lose ... land to the squatter with no compensation whatsoever'.[4]

292

1   Law Com no 271, para 14.4.
2   Law Com no 271, para 14.2.
3   [2000] Ch 676.
4   [2000] Ch 676, 709, 710.

13.4   As it was put by Lord Hope in the House of Lords in *JA Pye (Oxford) Holdings Ltd v Graham*:

> 'a much more rigorous regime has been enacted in Schedule 6 to the Land Registration Act 2002. Its effect will make it much harder for a squatter who is in possession of registered land to obtain a title to it against the wishes of the registered proprietor. The unfairness in the old regime ... lies not in the absence of compensation, although that is an important factor, but in the lack of safeguards against oversight or inadvertence on the part of the registered proprietor'.[1]

To similar effect was the view of Lord Bingham:

> 'in the case of unregistered land, and in the days before registration became the norm, such a result could no doubt be justified as avoiding protracted uncertainty as to where the title to land lay. But where land is registered it is difficult to see any justification for a legal rule which compels such an apparently unjust result, and even harder to see why the party gaining a title should not be required to pay some compensation at least to the party losing it ...'.[2]

Lord Bingham therefore described the new regime as 'reassuring'.

1   [2003] 1 AC 419 at 446–447.
2   [2003] 1 AC 419 at 426.

13.5   The aim of the adverse possession provisions of the LRA 2002 is therefore severely to attenuate the circumstances where, in registered land, an adverse possessor can claim a title.

THE SCHEME

13.6   The scheme of the adverse possession provisions of the LRA 2002[1] is as follows.

   (1)   Adverse possession of itself, for however long, will not bar the owner's title to a registered estate.

(2)   A squatter will be entitled to apply to be registered as proprietor after ten years' adverse possession (LRA 2002, Sch 6, para 1(1)),[2] and the registered proprietor, any registered chargee, and certain other persons interested in the land, will be notified of the application (LRA 2002, Sch 6, para 2(1)).

(3)   If the application is not opposed by any of those notified, the squatter will be registered as proprietor of the estate (LRA 2002, Sch 6, para 4).

(4)   If any of those notified oppose the application it will be refused, unless the adverse possessor can bring him or herself within one of three limited exceptions (LRA 2002, Sch 6, para 5(1)).[3]

(5)   If there is a dispute as to whether the squatter is entitled to be registered then, unless it can be disposed of by agreement, the matter will be referred by the registrar to the adjudicator for resolution (LRA 2002, s 73(1) and (7), s 108(1)(a)).[4]

(6)   If the application for registration is refused but the squatter remains in adverse possession for a further two years, he or she will be entitled to apply once again to be registered and will this time be registered as proprietor, whether or not the registered proprietor objects (LRA 2002, Sch 6, para 6(1)). The purpose of this provision is to give the registered proprietor one, and only one, opportunity to secure his position. In other words, if the application for registration is refused but the squatter remains in adverse possession, it will be incumbent upon the registered proprietor to take proceedings to recover possession.

(7)   Where the registered proprietor brings proceedings to recover possession from a squatter, the action will succeed unless the squatter can establish that he or she falls within one of the three limited exceptions (LRA 2002, s 98(1)).[5] Thus, provision is made for the situation not only where the adverse possessor applies to be registered, but also the situation where the registered proprietor brings possession proceedings. The three limited exceptions apply in both instances.

(8)   If the registered proprietor or chargee does commence possession proceedings against the squatter within two years of the rejection of the squatter's application, but then fails to take any steps to enforce the judgment within two years of obtaining it, then the squatter will be entitled to be registered (LRA 2002, s 98(4)), the intention being that the onus should be on the registered proprietor or chargee to enforce a judgment for possession once obtained.

(9)   If the registered proprietor of the estate or charge commences proceedings against the squatter within two years of the rejection of the squatter's application for registration, but they are discontinued or struck out after that 2 year period has elapsed, then, provided that the squatter has remained in

adverse possession since he applied to be registered as proprietor, he will be entitled to apply once again to be registered.[6]

(10) If the squatter does eventually succeed in his application, he is registered as proprietor of the estate against which he would have acquired title under the Limitation Act 1980, s 15 if the land had not been registered (LRA 2002, Sch 6, paras 1(1) and 11(1)).[7] Thus, if there is and has been throughout the ten years possession a (registered) leasehold estate as well as a (registered) freehold one, it is the leasehold which he will be registered as proprietor of.

---

[1]   Law Com no 271, para 14.5. See also a helpful article in the [2003] 20 Sep EG 140.
[2]   For the meaning of adverse possession in this context see paras 13.18 and 13.23.
[3]   For the time limit for opposing the application see para 13.16, and for the three limited exceptions see para 13.9.
[4]   The role of the adjudicator is dealt with in Chapter 15.
[5]   For the exceptions see para 13.9.
[6]   This being the consequence of the LRA 2002, Sch 6, para 6(2).
[7]   For the meaning of adverse possession in this context see paras 13.18 and 13.23.

13.7   The scheme has been introduced by disapplying the provisions of the Limitation Act 1980, ss 15 and 17, with the result that no period of limitation will now run against a person other than a chargee in relation to registered land and title will not now be extinguished on the expiry of the time limit contained in s 15 (LRA 2002, s 96(1)), and by bringing into operation the new regime contained in the LRA 2002, Schedule 6 (LRA 2002, s 97). As it is put in Law Com no 271 (at para 14.6) the scheme is intended to 'produce a decisive result. Either the squatter is evicted or otherwise ceases to be in *adverse* possession, or he or she is registered as proprietor of the land'.

13.8   The position as regards a charge on registered land is that the rights of a chargee can still become barred under the Limitation Act 1980, eg as a result of the chargor continuing in possession and there being no payment or acknowledgment of the debt for 12 years after it became due.[1] The rights of the chargor of registered land against the chargee, on the other hand, are subject neither to the Limitation Act 1980[2] nor to the LRA 2002, Sch 6 procedure.[3] Thus, if the chargee is in possession of the land, the chargor's right of redemption is never barred by limitation, and the chargee cannot after ten years apply to be registered as proprietor under the LRA 2002, Sch 6, para 1. If the chargee has been in possession of the land for a long time and thinks that the chargor has disappeared, he will have to bring an action for foreclosure if he wants to establish title to the land free of the chargor's rights.

---

¹   LRA 2002, s 96(1) preserves the effect of the Limitation Act 1980, s 15 as to time running against a chargee, and the Limitation Act 1980, s 20 (time limit for recovery of mortgage money) is not displaced or restricted by the LRA 2002.
²   LRA 2002, s 96(2) disapplies the Limitation Act 1980, s 16 so that there is no limitation period for redemption of a charge.
³   The definition of adverse possession for the purposes of the LRA 2002, Sch 6, para 11, refers only to possession which would be adverse possession under the Limitation Act 1980, s 15, and not to possession which would be adverse under s 16 (right of redemption). On the meaning of adverse possession in the LRA 2002, Sch 6 see also para 13.23.

13.9   The three limited exceptions, within one of which a squatter must fall if he is to succeed in being registered as proprietor or resist possession proceedings in the circumstances outlined in para 13.6, are as follows.

(1)   The first is where there is an equitable estoppel. That is, where it would be unconscionable because of an equity by estoppel for the registered proprietor to dispossess the applicant, and the circumstances are such that the applicant ought to be registered as proprietor (LRA 2002, Sch 6, para 5(2)).

(2)   The second exception is where the applicant is for some other reason entitled to be registered as the proprietor of the estate (LRA 2002, Sch 6, para 5(3)). This is intended to cover situations where, for example, the claimant is entitled to the land under the will or intestacy of the deceased proprietor, or where the claimant has contracted to buy land and pay the purchase price, but the legal estate has never been transferred to him or her.¹

(3)   The third exception is where the land to which the application relates is adjacent to land belonging to the applicant, the exact line of the boundary between the two has never been fixed, and for at least ten years of the period of adverse possession on the date of the application the applicant (or any predecessor in title) reasonably believes that the land to which the application relates belongs to him; and the estate to which the application relates was registered more than one year prior to the date of the application (LRA 2002, Sch 6, para 5(4)). There is a one-year delay in the introduction of this third exception: see para 13.31.

---

¹   Law Com no 271, para 14.43.

13.10 It may be said that the first and second exceptions are not really exceptions at all, but rather reflect the existing general law. It is therefore really the third exception which is a departure from the general law. The sort of case intended to fall within this exception is:

(1)   where the boundaries as they appear on the ground and as they are according to the register do not coincide because the physical features (trees or other landmarks) suggest that the

boundaries are in one place but where in fact, according to the registered plan they are in another; or

(2) when an estate was laid down, the dividing fences and walls were erected in the wrong place and not in accordance with the Registry plan.[1]

---

[1] Law Com no 271, para 14.46.

13.11 The first exception or condition was originally in terms that it would be established where 'it would be unconscionable for the registered proprietor to seek to dispossess the applicant' and the circumstances are such that the applicant ought to be registered as the proprietor. The Law Commission's intention by use of the expression 'unconscionable' was to catch cases of proprietary estoppel. Where, for example, the squatter had entered into possession of the land pursuant to some informal and legally ineffective transaction and, say, had paid valuable consideration under an agreement which was in effect a void contract because it did not comply with necessary formal requirements, the Law Commission thought that to deny registration in those circumstances would be unjust.[1] There were concerns, however, that 'unconscionability' might be a significantly wider concept than proprietary estoppel. It might, for example, embrace laches. In other words, simply sitting on one's rights for many years could lead to one losing one's title. That was not the intention of the Law Commission. The provisions were therefore amended so that the first exceptional condition will only be satisfied where:

'it would be unconscionable *because of an equity by estoppel for the registered proprietor to seek to dispossess the applicant*, and … the circumstances are such that the applicant ought to be registered as the proprietor' (emphasis added) (LRA 2002, Sch 6, para 5(2)).

---

[1] See the consultative report which preceded Law Com no 271, *Land Registration for the 21st Century* (Law Com no 254), para 14.39.

THE NOTICE PROCEDURE

13.12 The notice procedure is fundamental.[1] The idea is that once an application is made by a squatter to the registrar, the registrar must serve notice of that application on, in effect, those who would be prejudiced if the squatter's application were successful (LRA 2002, Sch 6, para 2). If no counter-notice is served, the registrar must enter the applicant as the new proprietor (LRA 2002, Sch 6, para 4). In Ruoff & Roper's *Registered Conveyancing* it has been stated that: 'the returns of official notices through the dead letter office bear witness to the fact that many proprietors fail to supply the Land Registry with a current address for service'.[2] Given the importance of the notice procedure, and the fact that if no counter-notice is served by the registered proprietor, the adverse possessor will be registered, it is going to be of critical importance for a person to ensure that he keeps his or her address up to date in the register. A person may have no more than three addresses for service (LRR 2003, r 198(4)).

[1]   Land Registry Practice Guide 4 explains the Land Registry's approach to applications involving adverse possession of registered land made after 13 October 2003. Land Registry Practice Guide 5 explains the Land Registry's approach to applications involving adverse possession of unregistered land and the procedures for making such applications.
[2]   See Ruoff & Roper's *Registered Conveyancing*, 1991 issue, para 3.10.

13.13   Under the LRR 2003 r 188 an application by a squatter for registration as the proprietor of a registered estate in land or a registered rentcharge must be on a specific form (Form ADV 1) and accompanied by:
   (1)   a statutory declaration:
      (a)   made by the applicant;
      (b)   which is not more than one month old; and
      (c)   which provides evidence of adverse possession for the period required by the LRA 2002;
   (2)   any supporting statutory declarations;
   (3)   a plan enabling the extent of the land or area affected by the rentcharge to be fully identified on the Ordnance Map;
   (4)   any additional evidence that the applicant considers necessary to support his claim (LRR 2003, r 188).

The hope is that by making provision in some detail as to what is to be included within the statutory declaration, the application will contain all of the information required by the LRA 2002 at the outset, and result in the Land Registry being able to deal with applications more quickly. In turn, the registrar will be able to include the details of the claim in the notice which he must serve on interested parties, and this should allow the recipient to make a more informed decision over whether or not to contest the application.

13.14   The registrar must give notice to any person able to satisfy him that he has an interest in a registered estate or a registered rentcharge which would be prejudiced if the squatter's application was successful (LRA 2002, Sch 6, para 2). A person with such an interest in the registered estate or rentcharge can apply to the registrar to enter his details as a person entitled to be notified in the register (LRR 2003, r 194(1), (2)), using Form ADV 2. If he satisfies the registrar that he is interested in the registered estate or rentcharge so that the registration of a squatter will prejudice his interest, the registrar must enter his name in the proprietorship register as a person entitled to be notified under the LRA 2002, Sch 6, para 2 (LRR 2003, r 194(3)).

13.15 The LRR 2003, r 194 is intended to introduce flexibility in the categories of persons who should be entitled to receive notice. It is sufficiently widely drawn that it should allow those with a general supervisory interest in the registered estate, for example, in the case of land held on charitable trust, the Charity Commissioners, to register their interest. It will therefore be of importance for all those who believe that they have an interest in a registered estate or rentcharge to register their interest, and to ensure that an address for service is readily available.[1]

---

[1]   For notices and addresses for service, see the LRR 2003, rr 198 and 199, and paras 2.29–2.35.

13.16 The period allowed for someone who receives notice of a squatter's application for registration as proprietor of a registered estate or rentcharge, to insist that the squatter makes out his case under one of the three conditions, is the period ending at 12 noon on the 65th business day after the date of issue of the notice of such an application (LRR 2003, r 189). It will therefore be of critical importance for the person who receives such a notice to deal with it promptly. The notice to the registrar insisting that the squatter makes out his case must be in Form NAP (LRR 2003, r 190(1)).

LAND HELD ON TRUST: FUTURE INTERESTS

13.17 Under the general law, if adverse possession begins before a reversion or remainder interest under a trust falls into possession, the 12-year period runs against the reversioner or remainderman from the beginning of the adverse possession. However, the reversioner or remainderman has an alternative period of six years from the falling into possession of his interest. Accordingly, he has to sue within 12 years of the previous owner's dispossession, or within six years of his own interest vesting in possession, whichever is the longer period. Where there are successive interests it is therefore difficult, or at least more difficult, to obtain a title by way of adverse possession.

13.18 Under the LRA 2002, the squatter is not be regarded as being in adverse possession, for the purposes of an application under the LRA 2002, Sch 6,[1] at any time when a registered estate is held in trust, as long as there are successive interests in the land. It is only where the interest of each of the beneficiaries in the estate is an interest in possession that a squatter can commence adverse possession (LRA 2002, Sch 6, para 12).[2] As the Law Commission recognised,[3] the approach adopted will make it very difficult for a squatter to acquire title to land which is held on trust by way of successive interests.

---

[1]   See para 13.6.
[2]   See Law Com no 271, para 14.93.
[3]   Law Com no 271, para 14.94.

13.19 This approach did not receive unqualified approval in the House of Lords when considering the Bill which became the LRA 2002.[1] The new system set out in the LRA 2002, Sch 6 requires a notice to be given to the proprietor, (it will be the trustees in this scenario), before registration of an adverse possessor can take place, and at that point, the trustees will have notice of the adverse possession and it will not be too late for them to act. Therefore, it should be entirely irrelevant whether a beneficiary has an interest in possession in the estate or not. This is in a context where the policy behind property legislation since 1925 has been to keep equitable interests away from the investigation of title. The Government was not, however, persuaded by these arguments. The whole thrust of the policy behind the LRA 2002, Sch 6 is to make it significantly more difficult for an adverse possessor to obtain title, and so there was thought to be insufficient reason to make the provisions more tender towards an adverse possessor simply because there are limited interests.

---

[1]   See Lord Goodhart, HL, Third Reading, 8 November 2001, cols 319–321 and Lord Thomas, HL, Report Stage, 30 October 2001, col 1380.

PRIORITIES

13.20 The general principle will be that the registration of the squatter as proprietor will not affect the priorities of any interests affecting the registered estate (LRA 2002, Sch 6, para 9 (2)), and he or she will take the land subject to the same estates, rights and interests that bound the previous proprietor. This general principle is, however, subject to an exception in the case of a registered chargee. A registered chargee will be one of the classes which will have the opportunity to object, or to bring possession proceedings against the squatter. Given the ability to object, the policy behind the LRA 2002, Sch 6 is that the registered chargee should object, and if he does not object, and the squatter is registered then that squatter will take free from the interest of the registered chargee (LRA 2002, Sch 6, para 9(3)).[1] However, this is where the squatter succeeds because his application to be registered as proprietor is not opposed. Where the squatter succeeds by being within one of the limited exceptions described in para 13.9, he will be subject to any registered charges to which the estate is subject (LRA 2002 Sch 6 para 9(4)).[2]

---

[1]   See Law Com no 271, para 14.74.
[2]   For apportionment where the charge affects other land as well see the LRA 2002, Sch 6, para 10 and para 13.27.

TRUST DEVICE ABANDONED

13.21 Under the Land Registration Act 1925, s 75(1) the trust was used as a means of a giving effect to the rights of squatters. The registered proprietor's estate was not extinguished but was deemed to be held by the registered proprietor for the time being on trust for the person who had acquired title by adverse possession. This concept gave rise to serious difficulties.[1] For example, it was not clear whether the statutory trust involved all the usual incidents of a trust. The result of the LRA 2002 is that when an adverse possessor is registered, the registrar will register him or her as the new proprietor of the relevant estate, and the squatter will be the successor in title to the previous registered proprietor (LRA 2002, Sch 6, paras 1(1) and 9).

---

[1]   See, for example, *Fairweather v St Marylebone Property Co Ltd* [1963] AC 510; *Spectrum Investment Co v Holmes* [1981] 1 WLR 221; *Central London Commercial Estates Ltd v Kato Kagaku* [1998] 4 All ER 948; *Spectrum Investment Co v Holmes* [1981] 1 All ER 6; and E Cooke 'Adverse Possession—Problems of Title in Registered Land' (1994) 14 LS 1.

THE PROTECTION OF SQUATTERS' RIGHTS ON REGISTRATION OR DISPOSITION OF THE LAND

13.22 The category of overriding interest comprised within the Land Registration Act 1925, s 70(1)(f), namely 'rights acquired or in course of being acquired under the Limitation Acts' is abolished. The Law Commission was particularly concerned with the situation where:

(1)   a squatter ceases to occupy registered land after he or she had become entitled to be registered as proprietor;

(2)   the registered proprietor then resumes possession and sells it to a buyer before the squatter's right to be registered is itself barred by the registered proprietor's own adverse possession.

The Law Commission thought it inequitable in those circumstances that the buyer would then be bound by the squatter's overriding interest if the buyer did not have any notice of it.[1] On the other hand, they wanted to ensure that on first registration of land with the owner of the paper title or his successor as first registered proprietor, in circumstances where a squatter has already acquired title by adverse possession before first registration of the land and then gone out of possession, the registered proprietor should be subject to the squatter's rights if he does have notice of them (LRA 2002, s 11(4)(c)).[2] However, so long as a squatter with a title to land acquired by adverse possession, either before first registration of the land or after first registration of the land but before 13 October 2002, remains in actual and obvious occupation of that land, his interest will be an overriding interest to which any registered proprietor will be subject, and which will be protected against any dealings by the registered proprietor (LRA 2002, Sch 1, para 2 and Sch 3, para 2).[3] There is also a transitional period of three years, ending with 12 October 2006, during which any title acquired by adverse possession over registered land before 13 October 2003 is an overriding interest (LRA 2002, Sch 12 para 11),[4] and during which any title acquired by adverse possession over unregistered land before 13 October 2003 is an overriding interest on first registration of the land (LRA 2002, Sch 12, para 7),[5] even if the person entitled to it is out of occupation and the first registered proprietor has no notice of his rights.

---

[1]   See Law Com no 271, paras 8.77–8.78.
[2]   See Law Com no 271, paras 3.46–3.47, and see para 13.30 below.
[3]   See para 13.30 below.
[4]   See para 13.30 below.
[5]   But not on a subsequent disposition of the land. See para 13.31 below.

MEANING OF ADVERSE POSSESSION AND SUCCESSIVE SQUATTERS

13.23   The limited rights under the LRA 2002, Sch 6 for a squatter to apply to be registered as proprietor of a registered estate, described in para 13.6, arise after ten years, or ten years plus a further two years, of 'adverse possession' (LRA 2002, Sch 6, paras 1(1) and 6(1)) of that estate. For this purpose a person is in adverse possession of an estate in land if a period of limitation under the Limitation Act 1980, s 15 would run in his favour in relation to the estate if it were not prevented from doing so by the LRA 2002, s 96 (LRA 2002, Sch 6, para 11(1)),[1] subject to three differences noted below. A period of adverse possession before the estate was registered may count towards the ten years (LRA 2002, Sch 6, para 1(4)). The first of the three differences from the general law is as follows. Under the general law, if a squatter has himself dispossessed another squatter he can add the former period of occupation to his own,[2] but this principle is not retained by the LRA 2002. Accordingly, where a squatter has evicted a prior squatter, the subsequent squatter cannot add the prior squatter's period of adverse possession to his own in order to make up the necessary ten-year period. However, it will be sufficient if:

- X is the successor in title of an earlier squatter Y from whom he acquired the land, and added together, the two periods of adverse possession amount to ten years; or
- X has been in adverse possession, has been dispossessed by a second squatter Y, and then has recovered the land from Y.

In either case X can add Y's period of possession to make up the necessary ten-year period (LRA 2002, Sch 6, para 11(2)).[3] The second difference is that the commencement of legal proceedings is disregarded (LRA 2002, Sch 6, para 11(3)(a)), although if proceedings for possession have been started or there has been a judgment for possession within the preceding two years it is a bar on a squatter applying to be registered as proprietor (LRA 2002, Sch 6, para 1(3)). The third difference from the general law is that the Limitation Act 1980, Sch 1, para 6 is disapplied (LRA 2002, Sch 6, para 11(3)(b)), and so there is no adverse possession for the LRA 2002, Sch 6 purposes where a tenant pays rent to a person wrongly claiming to be the owner.

---

[1]   For the relevant general law see Megarry & Wade, *The Law of Real Property* (6th edn), paras 21-013 to 21-025.
[2]   See Megarry & Wade, *The Law of Real Property* (6th edn), paras 21-021 to 21-022.
[3]   See Law Com no 271, para 14.20.

13.24   As also mentioned in para 13.18, there is no adverse possession against land for the LRA 2002, Sch 6 purposes so long as it is held in trust for persons in succession. The LRA 2002, Sch 6 thus depends importantly on the general law of adverse possession,[1] although where a squatter's application to be registered as proprietor is opposed and he does not come within any of the three exceptions described in para 13.9, it will be unnecessary to decide whether he really has been in adverse possession, because his application will fail regardless of that fact. It should also be noted that there is nothing in the LRA 2002, Sch 6 to displace the rules of the general law of adverse possession concerning leases, so that, for example, if a squatter has been in adverse possession for ten years of land of which the freehold is registered and which has been subject to a registered lease throughout the ten years, and the lease is then surrendered to the freeholder by the registered proprietor of the lease before the squatter applies under the LRA 2002, Sch 6, para 1, the squatter will then have to possess the land for another ten years before he can so apply.[2]

---

[1]   See Megarry & Wade, *The Law of Real Property* (6th edn) paras 21-013 to 21-025.
[2]   *Fairweather v St Marylebone Property Co Ltd* [1963] AC 510. Interestingly, this did not apply to land registered under the LRA 1925: *Spectrum Investment Co v Holmes* [1981] 1 WLR 221.

MENTAL DISABILITY OR PHYSICAL IMPAIRMENT

13.25 Special protection is given to those suffering from a mental disability or physical impairment. No application can be made by a squatter to be registered as proprietor during any period in which the existing registered proprietor is unable, because of mental disability, to make decisions about issues of the kind to which an application for registration would give rise, or unable to communicate such decisions because of mental disability or physical impairment (LRA 2002, Sch 6, paras 8(2) and (3)). Given that the service of notices is fundamental to the new regime, it was thought to be unfair that an adverse possessor might acquire a title simply because there was no one who might have the capacity to serve a counter-notice.[1]

---

[1]   Law Com no 271, para 14.29. See also the similar exception for an enemy or a prisoner of war: LRA 2002, Sch 6, para 8(1).

APPORTIONMENT

13.26 The general principle, endorsed most recently in *Carroll v Manek*,[1] was that if a squatter had adversely possessed land part of which was burdened by a charge, not only did the squatter take subject to the charge, but if he wished to sell the land, he also had to pay the full amount of the debt covered by the charge. The Law Commission were concerned that if, say, a squatter has obtained title to a small portion of a large estate, the whole of which is encumbered, under pre-existing principles the squatter would be discouraged from making an application to register, and this would run contrary to the policy to keep land in commerce.[2]

¹   (1999) 79 P & CR 173 at 178.
²   Law Com no 271, para 14.78.

13.27 Accordingly, under the LRA 2002, where a squatter is registered as proprietor, but the land is subject to a binding charge,¹ the squatter may require the chargee to apportion the charge (LRA 2002, Sch 6, para 10(1)). That apportionment will be on the basis of the respective values of the parcels of land subject to the charge, and the amount of the mortgage debt at the time when the squatter required the chargee to make the apportionment (LRA 2002, Sch 6, para 10(1)). The Land Registry have not yet drafted any rules to deal with the operation of these provisions, albeit that the requirements of such rules have been the subject of consultation.²

¹   See the LRA 2002, Sch 6, para 9(3) and (4) for the circumstances in which a charge is binding on a squatter, and para 13.20.
²   Land Registry, *New rules consultation*, Chapter 11, para 25.

CROWN FORESHORE

13.28 Most foreshore is held by the Crown in demesne, that is, in its capacity as paramount feudal lord, and not for an estate in fee simple. The LRA 2002 makes provision for the Crown to grant to itself a fee simple out of land held in demesne in order to register it (LRA 2002, s 79(1)).¹ Under the Limitation Act 1980, the limitation period for the recovery of foreshore by the Crown is 60 years, or where land has ceased to be foreshore but remains in the ownership of the Crown, either 60 years from the date of accrual of the cause of action, or 30 years from the date on which land ceased to be foreshore, whichever period expired first (Limitation Act 1980, Sch 1, Part 2, para 11).

¹   See paras 12.18 and 12.19.

13.29 As a result of the difficulty which the Crown might have in monitoring the substantial areas comprised within the foreshore, the LRA 2002 provides for a special period in relation to adverse possession of the foreshore: a squatter must be in adverse possession for 60 years instead of ten years before the squatter can invoke the provisions of the scheme contained within the LRA 2002, Sch 6 (LRA 2002, Sch 6, para 13). The combined effect of the Crown being able to grant itself an estate and then register it, and the new law of adverse possession of registered land under LRA 2002 described in this chapter, is that for the future it will be possible for the Crown to make it far more difficult for adverse possession rights to arise in relation to foreshore.

VESTED RIGHTS AND TRANSITIONAL PROVISIONS

13.30 The LRA 2002 will not deprive an adverse possessor of rights to which he became entitled before 13 October 2003, or rights acquired after that date under the general law in relation to unregistered land. Accordingly, any squatter who had become entitled to a registered estate under the LRA 1925, s 75, but who had not been registered as proprietor of it by 13 October 2003, will continue to have an entitlement to be registered as proprietor of the estate to which he was deemed to be beneficially entitled under the LRA 1925, s 75(1) at midnight on 12 October 2003 (LRA 2002, Sch 12, para 18(1)).[1] This entitlement will constitute a defence to any possession proceedings (LRA 2002, Sch 12, para 18(2)).[2] It will also be a proprietary right, so that it will be protected against third parties as an overriding interest, provided that the squatter is in actual and obvious occupation (LRA 2002, Sch 3, para 2).[3] Under a transitional provision it will also be an overriding interest on any disposition before 13 October 2006 of the estate to which the squatter is entitled, irrespective of whether the squatter is in occupation (LRA 2002, Sch 12, para 11). A squatter who is entitled to be registered as proprietor as a consequence of having become entitled under the LRA 1925, s 75, should apply using Form AP1 (LRR 2003, r 13)[4] supported by evidence of adverse possession for at least 12 years before 13 October 2003.

---

[1]   See also Land Registry Practice Guide 5 *Adverse possession of unregistered land and transitional provisions for registered land in the Land Registration Act 2002.*
[2]   If the defence is made out in a possession action, the court must order the registrar to register the defendant as proprietor: LRA 2002, Sch 12, para 18(3).
[3]   See para 7.67.
[4]   See also Land Registry Practice Guide 5, para 10.2.

13.31 Where a squatter acquires title to unregistered land by adverse possession, if the estate in the land to which the possession was adverse is subsequently registered by the owner of the paper title or his successor in title, the squatter's rights will be an overriding interest so long as the squatter is in actual and obvious occupation of the land (LRA 2002, Sch 1 para 2 and Sch 3, para 2).[1] If such a squatter is not in occupation of the land, his rights will be an overriding interest on first registration of the estate in question if the first registered proprietor has notice of those rights before applying for registration

(LRA 2002, ss 11(4)(c) and 74), and if the squatter acquired his rights by adverse possession before 13 October 2003 his rights will, during a transitional period ending on 12 October 2006, be an overriding interest on first registration even if the first proprietor has no notice of them (LRA 2002, Sch 12, para 7). However, the rights of such a squatter who is not in actual occupation of the land are not overriding on any subsequent disposition (including one made after compulsory registration has been triggered but before registration—LRR 2003, r 38)[2] by the registered proprietor, even where he acquired his rights before 13 October 2003 and the disposition is during the transitional period. Accordingly, anyone with a squatter's title to unregistered land should apply to have the land registered with the squatter as proprietor. There is also the transitional alternative that such a person may, until 13 October 2005, lodge a caution against first registration in respect of a right of this kind, but it must be remembered that such a caution will cease to be effective from 13 October 2005 (LRA 2002, s 15 and Sch 12, para 14).[3] The application for registration should be made on Form FR1 and be supported by evidence of adverse possession, usually statutory declarations.[4] If the application is successful the registrar will usually register the squatter with possessory title[5]—the proprietor can then apply to upgrade the title after 12 years.[6] Where unregistered land has been subject to a lease during the period of adverse possession, the registrar will reject any application by the squatter for registration[7] because of the precariousness of the possessory title, it being capable of being destroyed, eg by a surrender by the lessee under the lease to the owner of the immediate reversion.[8]

---

[1]   See para 7.67.
[2]   See para 4.11.
[3]   See para 4.4.
[4]   See the LRR 2003, r 23 and Land Registry Practice Guide 5, part 5. See also paras 2.36–2.42.
[5]   See Land Registry Practice Guide 5, para 6.4.
[6]   See para 5.15.
[7]   See Land Registry Practice Guide 5, para 7.1.
[8]   *Fairweather v St Marylebone Property Co Ltd* [1963] AC 510. This did not apply to land registered under the LRA 1925 (*Spectrum Investment Co v Holmes* [1981] 1 WLR 221), and so a squatter who acquired title by adverse possession to registered land before 13 October 2003, while the land was subject to a lease, may obtain registration as proprietor of that lease. See para 13.30.

13.32   In respect of the first and second exceptions dealt with in para 13.9 the registered proprietor is in the same position as he or she is under the present general law, thus no transitional provision has been made in relation to these two exceptions. The third exception (concerning land at or near an inexact boundary) does, however, represent a change in the law. The Law Commission were concerned that a squatter might find that he is entitled to be registered as proprietor on the basis of the third exception on the day that the legislation was bought into force, even though he or she had only been in adverse possession for ten years and, the day before, the registered proprietor could have successfully brought possession proceedings against him. There was therefore a transitional provision to cover this one limited exception. The third limited exception came into force one year after the rest of the LRA 2002, Sch 6, ie on 13 October 2004 (Land Registration Act 2002 (Commencement No 4) Order 2003, SI 2003/1725, art 2(2), deferring the commencement of the LRA, s 98(1) and Sch 1, para 5(4) and (5) until 13 October 2004), so that registered proprietors had one year from 13 October 2003 to take proceedings against any squatter who might fall within the third limited exception.

PRACTICAL CONSEQUENCES OF THE CHANGE IN THE LAW

13.33 The most obvious practical consequence of the change in the law is that in the case of registered land it will now be much more difficult to acquire a title by adverse possession.

13.34 The Law Commission took a deliberate policy decision to restrict its proposals to registered land. It expressly recognised that this might lead to an anomalous result where, for example, a squatter adversely possesses against a number of titles, some of which are registered and some unregistered in which event the provisions could lead to the situation where the adverse possessor will acquire title to the unregistered land but not the registered land.[1] Having a different system for registered and unregistered land has not filled all commentators with enthusiasm.[2] The Law Commission in its Third Report on Land Registration[3] did take a different view, and did not then report upon adverse possession because it considered that any substantive reform of the topic should be undertaken separately, and ought not to be conditioned purely by registered conveyancing considerations.

---

[1]   (1998) Law Com no 254, para 10.18.
[2]   See, for example, J E Adams, (1998) 62 Conv 438 at 441.
[3]   (1977) Law Com no 158, para 2.36.

13.35 The Law Commission does still see some utility for adverse possession in the context of unregistered land. In registered land, of course, title derives from the registered title, whilst in unregistered land it derives from possession, and the Law Commission has taken the view that retention of adverse possession for unregistered land, and the fact that it extinguishes an earlier right to possess, may facilitate and cheapen the investigation of title to unregistered land.[1] It may help to keep land in commerce.

---

[1] (1998) Law Com no 254, para 10.9.

13.36 The obvious consequence of drawing a distinction between registered and unregistered land is that, where it is practicable to do so a landowner holding unregistered land might now be well advised to register his title if there is any concern that adverse possession might, sometime in the future, pose a problem. Indeed, the Law Commission in an entirely separate report, on Limitation of Actions made that very observation,[1] namely that if an owner of unregistered land wishes to benefit from the same protection as a registered proprietor, he or she can apply for registration of his or her land. It is a particularly attractive option for landowners, such as local authorities or land dealers, in relation to land for which they do not have any current use, but of which they have hope for the future. There is also an incentive to anyone who has acquired title by adverse possession to unregistered land to apply for registration of the land with him as proprietor, because his title could be defeated if the owner of the paper title or his successor became the registered proprietor: see para 13.31.

---

[1] (2001) Law Com no 270, para 4.132.

14 Alteration of the register and indemnity

INTRODUCTION

14.1 In any system there is the scope for errors and frauds. These lead to inaccuracies and inconsistencies which require correction. The need to alter the register in order to correct these inaccuracies and inconsistencies exists in tension with the underlying purpose of registration: to provide certainty of title to owners and purchasers of land and interests in land. This tension has traditionally been resolved by imposing strict requirements for rectification of the register and by providing indemnities to those who suffer loss from errors in the register or from rectifications of the register.

14.2 The changes made by the Land Registration Act 2002 (LRA 2002) centre upon a distinction between alterations that involve correcting mistakes in the register to the prejudice of the registered proprietor and other alterations. The former are described as rectifications whereas the latter fall within the more general description of 'alterations'. In contrast to mere alterations, the availability of rectification is restricted in cases where the proprietor is in possession. Indemnity in respect of mistakes in the register is available only in cases where the register is rectified or would have been had it not been for the restrictions placed on rectification.

ALTERATION AND RECTIFICATION

14.3 Rectifications of the register are a particular kind of alteration of the register, where the alteration: (a) involves the correction of a mistake; and (b) prejudicially affects the title of a registered proprietor (LRA 2002, Sch 4, para 1). It should be noted that the term rectification is not used in the same sense as the power exercised by courts of equity in rectifying mistakes in documents.[1]

---

[1] See eg John McGhee *Snell's Equity* (13th edn), para 43-01. For a case involving rectification of a document leading to rectification of the register see *James Hay Pension Trustees Ltd v Cooper Estates Ltd* [2005] EWHC 36.

Alteration of the register

14.4 Alteration may be carried out either pursuant to a court order, or by the registrar.

14.5 The court[1] may make an order for alteration of the register for the purpose of:
- correcting a mistake;
- bringing the register up to date;
- giving effect to any estate, right or interest excepted from the effect of registration (LRA 2002, Sch 4, para 2(1)).

---

[1] Court' means both the High Court and the county court, LRA 2002, s 132(3).

14.6 Whilst the LRA 2002, Sch 4 states that the court 'may' make an order to alter the register, the rules limit this discretion,[1] so that the court 'must' make an order if, in any proceedings it decides that:
- (a) there is a mistake in the register;
- (b) the register is not up to date; and
- (c) there is an estate, right or interest excepted from the effect of registration that should be given effect to (LRR 2003, r 126(1)).[2]

The court will not be obliged to make such an order if 'there are exceptional circumstances that justify not doing so' (LRR 2003, r 126(2)). It remains to be seen what will be required to establish such exceptional circumstances. The court retains an additional discretion to alter the register where it discovers, in the course of proceedings, that any of the grounds are made out but does not decide within those proceedings that this is so.[3] It is, however, doubtful that a court would make an order for alteration where it had not specifically determined that the grounds for doing so had arisen.

---

[1] Under the LRA 2002, Sch 4, para 4(a), which states that the rules may make provision about the circumstances in which there is a duty to exercise the power of alteration.
[2] It is suggested that the reference to 'mistakes in the register' is an error, since as explained below at para 14.11, it is difficult to describe the register itself as mistaken and this does not appear to be consistent with the legislation.
[3] See Law Com No 271, para 10.12.

14.7 Since it is not the court that will alter the register, but the registrar once in receipt of the order, it is provided that the order has effect, when served on the registrar, to impose a duty on him to give effect to it.[1] The order is required to state the title number of the title affected by the alteration and must direct the registrar to make the alteration.[2] Service on the registrar is effected by making an application to the registrar, accompanied by the order, for the registrar to give effect to the order.[3]

---

[1] It is presumed that in the unlikely event that the registrar failed to give effect to the order, the failure could be the subject of judicial review. It may also be the case that the section gives rise to a statutory duty for which damages can be recovered.
[2] LRR 2003 127(1).
[3] LRR 2003 127(2).

14.8 The registrar has the same powers as the court and is, in addition, able to alter the register for the purpose of removing a superfluous entry (LRA 2002, Sch 4, para 5). The registrar's discretion to make the alteration is general (he 'may' alter the register). It is not restricted by the rules and there is no duty imposed on him to make the alteration.[1]

---

[1] Despite there being power to do so, see the LRA 2002, Sch 4, para 7(a). Law Com No 271 stated that this was an 'important power' and that it was likely to be used to impose a duty of the registrar to make an alteration, whenever grounds for doing so were discovered, regardless of the circumstances under which the grounds came to light (para 10.20).

14.9 The alteration may arise by reason of an application being made to the registrar or the registrar may himself decide that it is necessary.[1] The registrar is obliged to give notice of the proposed alteration to the registered proprietor of any registered estate or charge and any person who appears to him to be entitled to an interest protected by a notice wherever that estate charge or interest would be affected by the proposed alteration (LRR 2003, r 128).[2] He may also make such enquiries as he thinks fit.

---

[1] Law Com No 271 expected that the registrar would make regular audits of the register to discover inaccuracies and superfluous entries, see paras 10.19 and 10.20.
[2] This does not apply where the person's name and address for service under the LRR 2003, r 198 are not set out in the individual register in which the notice is entered.

14.10 If the proposed alteration arises out of an application to which the registered proprietor objects the matter must either be determined by agreement, or referred to the adjudicator. The matter may then be determined by the adjudicator or by reference to the court.[1]

---

[1] See Chapter 15.

Mistakes

14.11 The register is the source of title and is conclusive as to the title of the person registered. It follows that it is not logically possible to describe the register itself as mistaken. Thus, in exercising powers to correct a mistake the court or the registrar is not, it is suggested, searching for a mistake in the register, but instead seeking to correct some mistake which led to the entry itself.

14.12 Mistakes which were common under the old system, and are likely to remain so under the new, include:

- the mistaken inclusion of land on the first registration of title. This can arise as a result of defective plans and is common in cases of developments where registration of individual titles is often made pursuant to the original plans, but where the development itself may not have proceeded consistently with those plans;

- double conveyances where land, or more commonly strips of land, were sold twice to two purchasers. Again, this was often due to defective plans and was common in cases of developments. The error may be detected on the registration of the second conveyance but this is not always the case.

14.13 An interesting issue arises in circumstances where it is alleged that the registrar was wrong in making, or not making, an entry in the register. In many such cases the only means of challenging the registrar's decision is to apply for judicial review.[1] However, it would also seem possible to apply to the court, or even to the registrar, for an alteration of the register on the grounds that the entry in it (or the decision leading to the entry) was mistaken. This would avoid the strict procedural rules involved in judicial review as well as the relatively high standards required to make out the grounds for review.[2]

---

[1] Eg the entry of a restriction on the register against the wishes of the proprietor (see para xx) or where an objection to an application is determined as being groundless (see para xx) or the entry.

[2] See also para 15.8.

Bringing the register up to date

14.14 This is a relatively wide class of alterations. It will include cases where parties rights or interests have altered without a registrable disposition having taken place, such as the termination of a lease. It also includes cases where the court concludes that a party is entitled to a right or interest, such as an easement over registered land, or where the court concludes that a right or interest has come to an end, such as the forfeiture of a lease.

Estates, rights or interests excepted from the effect of registration

14.15 Where a proprietor is registered with good leasehold, qualified or possessory title, that title is expressly subject to certain estates, rights or interests, which are said to be excepted from the effect of registration (LRA 2002, ss 11(6) and (7), 12(6), (7) and (8)). The

LRA 2002 gives express power to the court and to the registrar to rectify the register to bring those estates, rights or interests on to the register, or to give effect to them.

Superfluous entries

14.16 This power, which is given solely to the registrar, is intended to allow for the 'tidying up' of the register. It will frequently be the case that entries have been made on the register to protect some right or interest and have remained where that right or interest has ceased to exist, or where the need for protection in this form has ceased. This power allows the registrar to remove such entries.

Rectification of the register

14.17 Rectification only occurs where the proposed alteration of the register: (a) involves the correction of a mistake; and (b) prejudicially affects the title of a registered proprietor.

14.18 The restrictions on rectification apply only in relation to that land which is in the possession of the proprietor. Land is in the possession of a proprietor where the land is physically in his possession[1] or in that of a person who is entitled to be registered as proprietor of the registered estate (not including a person entitled to be registered by virtue of rights accruing under adverse possession). In relationships of:
- landlord and tenant;
- mortgagor and mortgagee;
- licensor and licensee;
- trustee and beneficiary,

the landlord, mortgagor, licensor or trustee is treated as being in possession of the land (LRA 2002, s 131).

---

[1]   It is assumed that this is a reference to the proprietor being himself in occupation of the land.

14.19 In respect of such land, no rectification of the register may take place without the proprietor's consent. The exceptions to this are:
- where the proprietor has by fraud or lack of proper care caused or substantially contributed to the mistake;
- where it would for any reason be unjust for the alteration not to be made (LRA 2002, Sch 4, paras 3 and 6).

14.20 Where the court or the registrar do have the power to make the rectification they must do so unless there are exceptional circumstances which justify its not doing so (LRA 2002 Sch 4, paras 3(3) and 6(3)).

14.21 The restrictions on rectification reflect the policy, found in the previous system,[1] that a registered proprietor who is in possession of land should be protected from the effect of alterations correcting mistakes which are not the fault of that proprietor. The restrictions do not apply to cases of alterations to bring the register up to date, to remove superfluous entries, or to give effect to an alteration of estates, rights or interests excepted from the effect of registration because such alterations either involve no prejudice to the proprietor, or involve giving effect to rights to which the land was already subject to.

---

[1]   See the Land Registration Act 1925, s 82(3), as amended by the Administration of Justice Act 1977, s 24.

14.22 Where a person suffers loss by reason of the rectification of the register, he is entitled to an indemnity for that loss, subject to the restrictions that apply where the mistake arose out of fraud or lack of proper care. Similarly, where an alteration would have been made but was not because of the restrictions on the availability of rectification, indemnity is available for the loss suffered by reason of the mistake.[1]

---

[1]   See para 14.36.

The cautions register

14.23 The register of cautions against first registration (referred to as the cautions register) may be altered either pursuant to a court order, or by the registrar. The power to do so arises, in both cases, where the proposed alteration is for the purpose of:
- correcting a mistake;
- bringing the register up to date.

14.24 Where in any proceedings the court determines that the cautioner does not own the relevant interest, or only owns part, or that the interest either wholly or in part did not exist or has come to an end, it must make an order for the alteration of the cautions register (LRR 2003, r 48(1)). Similarly, where the registrar is satisfied of those matters he must, on application, alter the cautions register (LRR 2003, r 49). Before making any alteration to the cautions register the registrar must serve a notice on the cautioner giving details of the application, unless satisfied that service of the notice is unnecessary (LRR 2003, r 50(2)).

14.25 A court order must state the caution title number of the individual caution register affected, describe the alteration that is to be made and direct the registrar to make the alteration (LRR 2003, r 48(2)). The order is served on the registrar by making an application to him to give effect to it (LRR 2003, r 48(3)).

14.26 Where a person claims that the whole of an interest described in an individual cautions register is vested in him by operation of law as successor to the cautioner, he may apply to be registered in place of the cautioner. The application will be given effect to unless (if the registrar decided it was necessary to serve notice on the cautioner) the cautioner objects in time (LRR 2003, r 51).

The correction of mistakes in documents

14.27 The registrar is given power to correct mistakes in applications made to him or in accompanying documents (LRA 2002, Sch 10, para 6(e)).

14.28 In the case of a mistake of a clerical or like nature, the alteration will have effect as if made by the applicant or other interested party or parties, in all circumstances (LRR 2003, r 130(2)(a)). This gives the registrar a useful power to correct simple mistakes without requiring the mistake to be corrected by the parties and the application re-submitted.

14.29 In the case of any other mistake, that is mistakes of a more fundamental nature, the applicant and every other interested party must either request or consent to the alteration. Thereafter, the alteration will take effect as if made by them (LRR 2003, r 130(2)(b)).

E-Conveyancing

14.30 Since in a system of e-conveyancing the conveyancers will themselves be entering rights and interests on the register, it follows that in many cases they will also be empowered to make alterations to the register, for example removing interests or restrictions that no longer exist or are no longer required. These powers will be regulated by network access agreements.[1]

---
[1]   See generally Chapter 3.

Transitional

14.31 The powers to alter the register and the restrictions on rectification will apply from 13 October 2003. This will be the case irrespective of the date of the entry to be altered, or when the mistake giving rise to the alteration, was made. However, where proceedings have been instituted before 13 October 2003 they will continue until concluded as if the LRA 2002 had not been passed.[1] As a result, the rules in the LRA 1925 regarding rectification, will continue to apply to existing proceedings until those proceedings are determined. For these purposes proceedings are not determined until the register has been rectified or altered pursuant to any final order made in the proceedings.[2]

---

[1]   See the Land Registration Act 2002 (Transitional Provisions) Order 2003, SI 2003/1953, para 9.
[2]   See the Land Registration Act 2002 (Transitional Provisions) Order 2003, SI 2003/1953, para 9(3).

INDEMNITY

Grounds

14.32 A person is entitled to be indemnified by the registrar if he suffers loss by reason of (LRA 2002, Sch 8, para 1(1)):
- rectification of the register;
- a mistake whose correction would involve rectification of the register;
- a mistake in an official search;
- a mistake in an official copy;
- a mistake in a document kept by the Registrar which is not an original and is referred to in the register;
- the loss or destruction of a document lodged at the registry for inspection or safe custody;
- a mistake in the cautions register;
- a failure by the registrar to perform his duty, under s 50, to give notice of the creation of a statutory charge.[1]

---

[1]   See the LRR 2003, r 106(1) for those persons who are entitled to such notification.

14.33 No indemnity is payable on account of any mines or minerals, or the existence of the right to work or get mines or minerals, unless it is noted in the register that the title to the registered estate concerned includes the mines or minerals.

Rectification

14.34 Indemnity is not available wherever the register is altered, but only where the alteration involves a rectification of the register, that is an alteration which involves the correction of a mistake and prejudicially affects the title of a registered proprietor. It follows from the definition that the person most likely to apply for the indemnity is the registered proprietor whose title is affected. Nevertheless, the provisions do not restrict indemnity to this person alone.

14.35 In order to widen the availability of indemnity it is provided that:
- where loss is suffered by reason of a change of title, that loss is to be regarded as having been suffered by reason of the rectification of the register. Thus, where a person with a right to defeat the title of an adverse possessor loses those rights, because title is upgraded from possessory to absolute title, that person is entitled to claim loss as if the register had been rectified;
- where a proprietor relies in good faith on a disposition that was forged and the register is rectified, the proprietor is entitled to be regarded as having suffered loss by reason of the rectification as if the disposition had not been forged. Thus, where a person is registered as proprietor of land and mortgages that title to a mortgagor who is acting in good faith, if the register is subsequently corrected to reverse the effect of the forgery, the mortgagor will nevertheless be entitled to claim an indemnity on the basis that the proprietor had good title. This reverses the effect of *A-G v Odell*.[1]

---

[1]   [1906] 2 Ch 47. See Law Com No 271, para 10.31(2).

14.36 Indemnity is also payable for 'a mistake whose correction would involve rectification of the register'. This means that indemnity is available wherever a mistake exists in the register which prejudicially affects the title of a registered proprietor. The indemnity may be used to compensate where rectification is refused due to restrictions placed on the availability of rectification. It is further available where rectification is granted but the person in whose favour rectification is granted has suffered loss by reason of the mistake.[1]

---

[1]   See Law Com No 271, para 10.32.

14.37 Indemnity for the correction of a mistake whose correction would involve rectification, is not available until a decision as to rectification has been made, and the loss suffered by reason of the mistake must be determined in the light of the decision (LRA 2002, Sch 8, para 1(3)). This means that a claimant must always apply for rectification before being able to obtain indemnity for the loss suffered by reason of the mistake.

Fraud or lack of care

14.38 It is unsurprising that no indemnity is payable to a claimant on account of any loss that is suffered wholly or partly as a result of his own fraud (LRA 2002, Sch 8, para 5(1)). Although this provision was intended as an absolute bar to indemnity in cases of fraud,[1] it is possible that cases will arise where there is fraud, but some loss is not suffered either wholly or partly as a result of the fraud. In these cases it would seem that indemnity is payable for that loss.

---

[1]   See Law Com No 271, para 10.47(2).

14.39 In cases of lack of proper care the claimant is not entitled to any loss suffered wholly as a result of his own lack of proper care (LRA 2002, Sch 8, para 5(1)). Where the loss is suffered by a claimant only partly as a result of his own lack of proper care the indemnity payable will be reduced to such extent as is fair having regard to the claimant's share in the responsibility for the loss (LRA 2002, Sch 8, para 5(2)). This is analogous to the reduction of damages in tort for contributory negligence.

14.40 Fraud or lack of care on the part of a person from whom the claimant derives title (otherwise than under a disposition for valuable consideration or protected by an entry in the register) is to be treated as if it were fraud or lack of proper care on the part of the claimant (LRA 2002, Sch 8, para 5(3)).

14.41 These provisions have an important overlap with rectification of the register. The register may be rectified contrary to the interests of a proprietor in possession where the proprietor 'has by fraud or lack of proper care caused or substantially contributed to the mistake' (LRA 2002, Sch 4, para 3(2)(a)). In cases of fraud the proprietor will additionally be prevented from seeking any indemnity. In cases of a lack of proper care, since the lack of proper care must have either caused or substantially contributed to the mistake, there will either be no indemnity payable or the indemnity will be very small.

Assessment of loss

14.42 The indemnity payable is an indemnity for the loss suffered by reason of the mistake, rectification, or loss or destruction of documents. The indemnity is for all loss suffered and so includes both direct and consequential loss.

14.43 In one respect the LRA 2002 places a cap on the amount of indemnity. Where an indemnity is payable in respect of the loss of an estate, interest or charge, the value of the estate, interest or charge for the purposes of the indemnity is to be regarded as not exceeding:

- in the case of an indemnity for rectification, its value immediately before the rectification of the register (but as if there were to be no rectification); and
- in the case of an indemnity for a mistake whose correction would involve rectification of the register, its value at the time when the mistake which caused the loss was made (LRA 2002, Sch 8, para 6).

This replicates the provisions in the Land Registration Act 1925, s 83(5).

Costs and expenses

14.44 In respect of loss consisting of costs or expenses incurred in relation to the loss being claimed for, such costs and expenses are only payable in respect of costs and expenses incurred by the claimant with the consent of the registrar (LRA 2002, Sch 8, para 3(1)). It is possible for this approval to be given after the costs and expenses are incurred (LRA 2002, Sch 8, para 3(3)).

14.45 The requirement of consent does not apply where the costs and expenses must be incurred urgently and it is not reasonably practicable to apply for the registrar's consent (LRA 2002, Sch 8, para 3(2)).

14.46 Where an indemnity has been applied for, but is not payable, the registrar may pay such amount as he thinks fit in respect of any costs and expenses reasonably incurred by the claimant in connection with the claim which have been incurred with the consent of the registrar. Such costs and expenses may also be met where the registrar considers that the costs and expenses had to be incurred urgently and that it was not reasonably practicable to apply for his consent, or where the registrar has subsequently approved the incurring of the costs and expenses (LRA 2002, Sch 8, para 4(1), (2)).

14.47 Similarly, where the register is altered in a case not involving rectification, the registrar may pay such amount as he thinks fit in respect of any costs and expenses reasonably incurred by a person in connection with the alteration which have been incurred with the consent of the registrar. Consent may be waived in cases of sufficient urgency, or where the registrar subsequently approves the incurring of the costs (LRA 2002, Sch 4, para 9).

Interest

14.48 Interest on an amount payable by way of indemnity is payable as follows (LRR 2003, r 195).

- Where the register is rectified, interest is payable from the date of rectification to the date of payment.
- In all other cases of indemnity interest is payable from the date the loss is suffered by reason of the relevant mistake, loss, destruction or failure to the date of payment.
- Periods where the registrar or the court is satisfied that the claimant has not taken reasonable steps to pursue with due diligence the claim for indemnity or the application for rectification, are excluded.
- Interest on costs and expenses is payable from the date when the claimant pays them to the date of payment.

14.49 The rate is the rate or rates set for court judgment debts (currently 8%).

Time limit

14.50 The right to claim an indemnity is treated as if it were a simple contract debt under the Limitation Act 1980. The claimant therefore normally has six years from the date the cause of action arises to bring his claim, although this will be subject to the exceptions, such as cases where the claimant is under a disability. The cause of action is treated as arising at the time when the claimant knew, or but for his own default might have known, of the existence of his claim (LRA 2002, Sch 8, para 8).

Determination and enforcement

14.51 A person claiming an indemnity is entitled to apply to the court for the determination of any question as to whether he is entitled to an indemnity and the amount of such indemnity (LRA 2002, Sch 8, para 7(1)). Similarly, since the LRA 2002 gives the claimant an entitlement to the indemnity itself, in the event that the registrar refused to pay such an indemnity the claimant would be entitled to apply to the court for an order that the registrar do so.

14.52 The provisions in respect of costs and expenses do not apply to costs and expenses incurred in such applications to court (LRA 2002, Sch 8, para 7(2)), so that the claimant must rely upon the rules of court in order to recover his costs.

Recovery by the registrar

14.53 The registrar is expressly given rights to recover any indemnity payable under the LRA 2002 (including any interest so paid):

- the registrar is entitled to recover the amount paid from any person who caused or substantially contributed to the loss by his fraud;
- the registrar may enforce any right of action (of whatever nature and however arising) which the claimant would have been entitled to enforce had the indemnity not been paid;
- the registrar may enforce any right of action (of whatever nature and however arising) which the person in whose favour the register has been rectified would have been entitled to enforce had it not been rectified.

The second right is in the nature of a statutory right of subrogation. However, the third right goes beyond a typical insurer's right of subrogation. The Report stated that it was intended to cover cases where the register had been rectified in X's favour where X's solicitor was the cause of the mistake by reason of his negligence. In these circumstances loss incurred by Y by reason of the rectification is met by the registrar. The registrar may then recover that loss from X's solicitor even though Y would have had no cause of action against the solicitor because the solicitor owed him no duty (and X would have no right because he has suffered no loss).[1]

---

[1]   See Law Com No 271, para 10.52.

Transitional

14.54 The provisions will apply to any claims made after 13 October 2003. They will also apply to any claims begun but not concluded by settlement or final determination on that date (LRA 2002, Sch 12, para 9). On an appeal heard after 13 October 2003 in relation to a decision made before that date, at least where the appeal is a true appeal and not a re-hearing, the old provisions will apply.

14.55 The provisions in respect of payment of costs and expenses[1] will not apply in relation to costs and expenses incurred in proceedings, negotiations or other matters begun before 27 April 1997.

---

[1]   See paras 14.44–14.47.

15 Resolution of disputes: registrar, courts and adjudicator

OVERVIEW

15.1 Under the Land Registration Act 1925 (LRA 1925), where a dispute arose that could not be disposed of by agreement, the Chief Land Registrar was obliged to hold a hearing to determine the questions in dispute (LRR 1925, r 299(1)),[1] unless it was decided that one of the parties should be directed to issue proceedings within a specified time (LRR 1925, r 299(3)). The jurisdiction of the Chief Land Registrar was delegated to the Solicitor to HM Land Registry, which title included District Registrars.[2] There was a right of appeal to the Chancery Division of the High Court (LRR 1925, r 300(1)).

---

[1] It was possible for the matter to be determined without agreement where the parties were informed of this intention and made no objection (LRR 1925, r 299(2)).
[2] Under the Land Registration (Conduct of Business) Regulations 2000, SI 2000/2212.

15.2 It was feared that there could be a perception that the Solicitor to HM Land Registry was not sufficiently independent, particularly where disputes involved the decisions of officials of the registry. For this reason a new independent office of the adjudicator was created to deal with disputes in the new system.[1]

---

[1] Law Com no 271, para 16.1.

15.3 The adjudicator forms one 'tier' of a three tier system, consisting of the registrar, the adjudicator and the courts:
- the registrar acts as the first port of call for all registration matters. Some matters begin and end with the registrar, who is given certain powers to require the production of documents and to make costs orders;
- other matters are referred to the adjudicator by the registrar. Only in one area, that of applications for rectification or setting aside of a document, is the application commenced in front of the adjudicator;

- the courts' role continues to be extensive. They have an overlapping jurisdiction, since for many disputes it is possible for the matter to be determined either by the court, by the registrar or by the adjudicator. They also determine disputes that the adjudicator decides should be referred to them and hear challenges to both the registrar and the adjudicator by way of appeal and by way of judicial review. Furthermore, the Land Registration Act 2002 (LRA 2002) creates certain rights enforceable only by the courts as well as creating criminal offences.

THE REGISTRAR

Jurisdiction

Objections to applications

15.4   Most matters will come before the registrar by way of an application. For example, it is necessary to apply to register a disposition or a unilateral notice or to register a squatter as proprietor. Any application which is made is recorded in the day list (LRR 2003, r 12) and will remain recorded there while any dispute concerning the application is resolved. If an official search is made of the title to which the application relates, the day list entry for the application will be disclosed (LRR 2003, r 149(3) and Sch 6, Pts 3 and 4). If the application is ultimately successful, it will take priority with effect from the date on which the application was made (LRA 2002, s 74; LRR 2003, r 20). Accordingly, any application is protected against dealings in the land after it was made, and anyone acquiring or attempting to acquire an interest in the land, should have notice of the application.

15.5   Subject to two exceptions, any person may object to an application (LRA 2002, s 73). The exceptions exist in respect of applications for the cancellation of cautions against first registration and unilateral notices where only the person who lodged the caution, or is shown as the beneficiary of the unilateral notice, may object (LRA 2002, s 73(2), (3)).[1]

---

[1]   These subsections confer power to extend by rules the classes of persons who may object, but this power has not been exercised.

15.6 An objection is made by delivering to the registrar at the appropriate office, a written statement, signed by the objector or his conveyancer. The objection must state that the objector objects to the application, the grounds for the objection and give the full name of the objector along with the address to which communications must be sent (LRR 2003, r 19).

15.7 Where an objection is made the registrar must, unless he considers the objection to be groundless, give notice of the objection to the applicant and may not determine the application until the objection has been disposed of. The registrar has no power to impose a decision upon either the applicant or the objector. Instead he will attempt to obtain the parties' agreement. If the matter cannot be determined by agreement the registrar must refer the matter to the adjudicator (LRA 2002, s 73(7)).

15.8 If the registrar considers the objection to be groundless he will proceed to determine the application and is not prevented from doing so by the objection (LRA 2002, s 73(6)). There is no appeal from a decision by the registrar that the objection is groundless. The only means of challenge may be by way of judicial review, although it may be arguable that the aggrieved objector can apply after the application is granted, for the register to be altered on the grounds that it is mistaken.[1]

---
[1]   See para 14.13.

Other matters

15.9 Disputes may arise in circumstances where no objection is made to an application. For example:
 - the registrar might consider that an applicant for registration cannot show that he is entitled to be registered, or that the title ought be registered with a lower quality title than that applied for (LRA 2002, ss 9, 10),[1] or otherwise subject to a defect (LRA 2002, s 64);
 - the registrar might consider that a restriction ought to be registered on a title (LRA 2002, s 42(1));
 - the registrar might exercise his powers to alter the register (LRA 2002, Sch 4, para 5);
 - the registrar is empowered to decide whether documents should be designated as exempt information document and whether copies of such documents should be provided to persons applying for such copies (LRR 2003, rr 136–138).[2]

---
[1]   See paras 5.10–5.15 and 6.10–6.18.
[2]   See paras 2.65 et seq.

15.10 Disputes arising in these circumstances will be decided by the registrar without reference to the adjudicator. There is no right of appeal from such a decision. The only means of challenge may be by way of judicial review although it may be arguable that the aggrieved objector can apply, after the application is granted, for the register to be altered on the grounds that it is mistaken.[1]

---

[1]   See para 14.13.

Land registry network

15.11 When e-conveyancing is introduced,[1] conveyancers will need to be able to access the land registry network. In order to do so they will have to have a network access agreement with the registrar (LRA 2002, Sch 5, para 1(1)).[2] The registrar will have the power to determine whether an applicant for such an agreement meets the necessary criteria and will also be able to terminate a network access agreement (LRA 2002, Sch 5, paras 1–3).[3] A person who is aggrieved by a decision of the registrar with respect to the entry into or termination of a network access agreement may appeal against the decision to the adjudicator (LRA 2002, Sch 5, para 4).

---

[1]   See para 3.10. No date has yet been set for this.
[2]   See para 3.19.
[3]   See paras 3.20 and 3.23.

Documents and costs

Documents

15.12 The registrar has power to require a person to produce a document 'for the purposes of proceedings before him' (LRA 2002, s 75(1)).[1] The power can only be exercised where the registrar receives a request from a person who is a party to the proceedings that he should require a document holder[2] to produce a document for the purpose of those proceedings (LRR 2003, r 201). The request is made in Form PRD1. Notice of the request must be given to the document holder who must be given 20 business days (or such other period as the registrar thinks appropriate) to deliver a written response to the registrar. The response should state whether the document holder opposes the request and, if so, the grounds for the opposition (LRR 2003, r 201(6)).[3]

---

[1]   See para 15.19 for a discussion of the meaning of 'proceedings'.
[2]   A document holder is 'the person who is alleged to have control of a document which is the subject of a request' for its production, LRR 2003, r 201(9).

3   It must also give an address to which communications may be sent and be signed by the document holder or his conveyancer ('conveyancer' includes a solicitor whether or not acting as a conveyancer, see the LRR 2003, r 217(1)).

15.13 The registrar must determine the matter on the basis of the request and any response received. If satisfied that:
- the document is in the control of the document holder;
- the document is relevant to the proceedings; and
- disclosure of the document is necessary in order to dispose fairly of the proceedings, or to save costs,

the registrar may require the production of the document if he is not aware of any valid ground entitling the document holder to withhold the document (LRR 2003, r 201(7)).[1] It is apparent that the registrar retains a residual discretion to refuse to require the document to be produced even where the grounds for doing so are made out.[2] The registrar may, as a condition of making the requirement, provide that the person who has made the request pay the reasonable costs incurred in complying with the requirement by the document holder (LRR 2003, r 201(8)).

1   'Any valid ground' will plainly include legal professional privilege.
2   The registrar 'may' make the requirement: see the LRR 2003, r 201(7).

15.14 Once made, the requirement to produce a document shall be enforceable as an order of the court, so that a breach of it may be enforced as a contempt of court (LRA 2002, s 75(4)).

Costs

15.15 The registrar has power where a party who has incurred costs in relation to proceedings before the registrar to make an order that another party to those proceedings pay the whole or part of the costs (LRA 2002, s 76(1); LRR 2003, r 202(1)). The power is exercisable only upon a request by the party seeking the order. The registrar may only make the order where the costs have been occasioned 'by the unreasonable conduct of that party in relation to the proceedings' (LRR 2003, r 202(2)).

15.16 A request that the other party pay the costs of the proceedings is made by delivering to the registrar a written statement by 12 noon on the 20th business day after the completion of the proceedings to which the request relates (LRR 2003, r 202(3)). The statement must identify the party against whom the order is sought, state in full the grounds for the request, give an address for communications, and be signed by the person making the request of his conveyancer (LRR 2003, r 202(4)). Notice of the request must then be given to the party against whom the order is sought and that party must be given 20 business days, or such other period as the registrar thinks appropriate, to deliver a written response the registrar (LRR 2003, r 202(8)). The response must state whether or not the recipient opposes the request and, if so, on what grounds.[1]

---

[1]   The response must also state the address to which communications may be sent and be signed by the recipient or his conveyancer: LRR 2003, r 202(9).

15.17 The registrar must then determine the matter on the basis of the request and any response made, all the circumstances including the conduct of the parties and the result of any enquiries he considers it necessary to make (LRR 2003, r 202(10)). The order may require a party to pay the whole of such part of the costs incurred in the proceedings by the requesting payment as the registrar thinks fit, and may either specify the sum to be paid, or require the costs to be assessed by the court (LRR 2003, r 202(12)). If the order requires the costs to be assessed by the court it may specify the basis of assessment to be used by the court (LRR 2003, r 202(12)(b)).[1]

---

[1]   The court may assess costs on either the standard or the indemnity basis. On the standard basis the court must, in deciding how much to award, consider whether the costs were proportionately and reasonably incurred or were proportionately and reasonable in amount. On the indemnity basis the court must decide whether the costs were unreasonably incurred or unreasonable in amount. In other words, on the standard basis the burden is on the receiving party to establish what costs should be paid, whereas the burden is reversed on the indemnity basis. See CPR r 44.5.

15.18 The order made is enforceable as an order of the court (LRA 2002, s 76(4)). The registrar must send to all parties his written reasons for any order he makes (LRR 2003, r 202(11)).

Meaning of 'proceedings'

15.19 The powers to require the production of documents and to order costs against parties exist in respect of 'proceedings' before the registrar (LRA 2002, ss 75(1) and 76(1)). It is not defined by the LRA 2002 and there is no other reference to 'proceedings' before the registrar. It is far from certain what amounts to proceedings before the registrar in order for these powers to arise.
- The manner in which the LRR 2003 are drafted means that the powers are only exercisable on the request of one party against another (LRR 2003, rr 201(1) and 202(1), (2)). As a result the powers have no application in disputes arising between the registrar and an individual. For example, they would not apply where the registrar wishes to refuse an application for registration and is opposed by the applicant himself.
- The powers would therefore appear to exist only in circumstances where an application is met with an objection

by another party. However, such cases must be referred to the adjudicator unless it is possible to dispose of them by agreement (LRA 2002, s 73(7)). It is difficult to see how an attempt by the registrar to seek the agreement of the two parties can be described as 'proceedings' and it appears that the Law Commission did not think the word included such cases.[1]

If this reasoning is correct it may well follow that the combination of the LRA 2002 and the LRR 2003 has led to a situation where the powers are not exercisable at all. There is also a reference to 'proceedings' in the LRA 2002, s 123 (offence of suppression of information).[2]

---

[1] See Law Com no 271, paras 16.11–16.14 which suggest that the Law Commission believed the powers would apply to proceedings other than those that had to be referred to the adjudicator.

[2] See para 15.84.

Appeal

15.20 A person aggrieved by a requirement to produce a document or to pay costs may appeal to a county court. The county court may make any order which it thinks appropriate (LRA 2002, ss 75(4) and 76(5)).

Use of a specialist

15.21 The registrar may refer to a specialist:

- The examination of the whole or part of any title lodged with an application for first registration; or
- any question or other matter which arises in the course of any proceedings before the registrar and which, in his opinion, requires the advice of an appropriate specialist;

The registrar may then act upon that advice or opinion. A specialist means a person whom the registrar considers has the appropriate knowledge, experience, and expertise to advise on the matter referred to him (LRR 2003, r 200).

Challenging the registrar

15.22 Save for the powers to require the production of documents or to order a party to pay costs (where there is a right of appeal to the county court) there is no right of appeal from the registrar. The only means of challenging a decision of the registrar is therefore by way of judicial review.

15.23 However, where the decision of the registrar led to an entry in the register, it may be possible for the aggrieved party to make an application to the court (or even to the registrar) for alteration of the register on the ground that it is mistaken.[1] The use of this mechanism to air such disputes was probably not intended,[2] however, it seems difficult to see why the provisions would not apply. Utilising this route would avoid the strict procedural rules involved in judicial review (including time limits) as well as the relatively high standards required to make out the grounds for review.

---

[1]   See para 14.13.

[2]   See eg Law Com No 271, para 6.45.

THE ADJUDICATOR

The office of adjudicator

15.24 The Lord Chancellor is empowered to appoint a person to be the adjudicator to HM Land Registry. To be qualified the person must hold a ten year general qualification within the meaning of the Courts and Legal Services Act 1990, s 71.[1] The Lord Chancellor has general powers in respect of the length the appointment, the remuneration and compensation for loss of office. The Adjudicator can be removed on the grounds of incapacity and misbehaviour and may resign his office at any time (LRA 2002, Sch 9, paras 1 and 2).

---

[1]   Under the Courts and Legal Services Act 1990, s 71(3)(c) a person has a general qualification if 'he has a right of audience in relation to any class of proceedings in any part of the Supreme Court, or all proceedings in county courts or magistrates courts'.

15.25 The adjudicator will not be able to carry out all the functions of the office without assistance. He is empowered to appoint such staff as he thinks fit and may delegate any of his functions to them (LRA 2002, Sch 9, paras 3 and 4). This includes the power to delegate his judicial functions, although any non-administrative functions may only be delegated to persons with a ten year general qualification within the meaning of the Courts and Legal Services Act 1990, s 71. The adjudicator to Her Majesty's Land Registry (Practice and Procedure) Rules 2003, SI 2003/2171 (AHMLR(PP)R 2003) provide that, when exercising any non-administrative function of the adjudicator, the member of the adjudicator's staff is not subject to the direction of the Lord Chancellor or any other person or body (AHMLR(PP)R 2003, r 61).

Jurisdiction

15.26 The adjudicator has no general powers in respect of land registration and will not exercise any supervisory function over HM Land Registry or the registrar. The adjudicator's jurisdiction is confined to:

- determining disputes arising from objections to applications referred by the registrar;[1]
- making any order for the rectification or setting aside of a document related to registration which the High Court could make (LRA 2002, s 108(2));[2]
- determining any appeal from the registrar in respect of a decision as to the entry into, or termination of, a network access agreement.[3]

---

[1]   See paras 2.55 and 15.27 et seq.

[2]   See also para 15.30 for a more precise explanation of the documents over which this jurisdiction exists.

[3]   See paras 3.24 and 15.36.

Objections to applications

15.27 Where the registrar is unable to dispose by agreement of an objection to an application, he must refer the matter to the adjudicator (LRA 2002, s 73(7)).[1] The referral may relate to the whole of the objection or, where the parties are able to agree in part, to only that part of the objection that is disputed.

---

[1]   See also paras 15.4–15.8.

15.28 The procedure for referring the dispute to the adjudicator is set out in the Land Registration (Referral to the Adjudicator to HM Land Registry) Rules 2003, SI 2003/2114 (LR(RAHMLR)R 2003). Once the registrar is obliged to make a reference he must prepare a case summary outlining the nature of the dispute, the identity of the parties and the documents that will be sent to the adjudicator (see the LR(RAHMLR)R 2003, r 3(2) for the required contents of the case summary). The parties are given an opportunity to comment on the case summary, which may then be amended as the registrar thinks appropriate in the light of those comments. The case summary is then sent to the registrar along with the documents listed in it and a written notice informing the adjudicator that the matter is referred under the LRA 2002, s 73(7). The parties are informed that the matter has been referred to the adjudicator and are sent a copy of the case summary in the form sent to the adjudicator (see the LR(RAHMLR)R 2003, r 5). At this stage the registrar's involvement with the dispute ends.

15.29 In cases involving adverse possession, where the adjudicator is asked to decide whether the squatter should be registered with title and it is decided that it would be unconscionable for the registered proprietor to dispossess the squatter but that the circumstances are not such that the applicant ought to be registered as proprietor (LRA 2002, Sch 6, paras 1 and 5(2)), the adjudicator must determine how the equity due to the applicant is to be satisfied. In order to allow the adjudicator to make an order that will satisfy the equity, the adjudicator is given the power to make any order that the High Court could make in the exercise of its equitable jurisdiction. This means that hearings considering an application for a squatter to be registered will not only consider that issue, but also what relief he should be granted in the event that the squatter is not so registered.

Applications to rectify or set aside documents

15.30 The adjudicator has the power to make any order which the High Court could make for the rectification or setting aside of a document which:
- effects a qualifying disposition of a registered charge or estate;
- is a contract to make a qualifying disposition; or
- effects a transfer of an interest which is the subject of a notice in the register (LRA 2002, s 108(2)).

A qualifying disposition is a registrable disposition, or a disposition which creates an interest which may be the subject of a notice in the register (LRA 2002, s 108(3)).

15.31 This jurisdiction concerns rectification of documents in the true sense, as opposed to rectification of the register.[1] The High Court's jurisdiction to rectify documents is an equitable one and based upon the court's power to amend a document to reflect the parties' true intentions. It depends upon clear and unambiguous evidence that the instrument either does not accurately represent the agreement of the parties at the time that it was executed, or at least that it is doubtful whether it does.[2] Where the mistake is that of only one party to the instrument, there may still be rectification if the other party was fraudulent, or knew of the mistake but did not correct it because it was to his advantage.[3]

---

[1]   See para 14.11.
[2]   See John McGhee *Snell's Equity* (13th edn), para 43-09.
[3]   See John McGhee *Snell's Equity* (13th edn), paras 43-11 to 43-14.

15.32 Strictly speaking, the High Court's jurisdiction to set aside a document is a jurisdiction to set aside the transaction, as opposed to the document that represents the transaction (it is not thought that this technical point affects the nature or extent of the adjudicator's jurisdiction). It may be exercised, for example, where a contract was entered into under a fundamental mistake, where a party was unduly influenced, or where the transaction is unconscionable.

15.33 The application is made to the adjudicator directly. It should be in writing and should set out the matters specified in the AHMLR(PP)R 2003, r 16. If the adjudicator considers that the application is groundless he must reject the rectification application (AHMLR(PP)R 2003, r 16(3)). If not rejected the adjudicator must serve notice of the application on a person against whom the order is sought and any other person who, in the opinion of the adjudicator, should be a party to the proceedings (AHMLR(PP)R 2003, r 17(2)). Any objection to the application must be lodged within 28 days of service of the notice (AHMLR(PP)R 2003, r 17(3)). The objection must set out the grounds of the objection and set out the matters specified in AHMLR(PP)R 2003 (AHMLR(PP)R 2003, r 18).

15.34 The general law about the effect of an order of the High Court for the rectification or setting aside of a document applies to any order of the adjudicator (LRA 2002, s 108(4)). Thus, where the adjudicator rectifies a document that rectification has retrospective effect and does not require a new document to be executed.[1]

---

[1]   See John McGhee *Snell's Equity* (13th edn), para 43–23.

15.35 It is notable that the adjudicator has no power to refer these types of applications to the court. Therefore, it is possible that the adjudicator will be required to determine cases, such as applications alleging undue influence, where the facts will be seriously disputed and where there are serious allegations of impropriety. It remains to be seen whether parties will choose to have such matters determined before the adjudicator.

Network access agreements

15.36 As yet there are no published criteria for obtaining or keeping a network access agreement, and no rules have yet been made governing this jurisdiction.

Procedure

Overriding objective

15.37 When exercising any power given to the adjudicator by the AHMLR(PP)R 2003 or in interpreting those rules the adjudicator must seek to give effect to the overriding objective. The parties are required to help the adjudicator to further the overriding objective (AHMLR(PP)R 2003, r 3(3), (4)).

15.38 The overriding objective is to deal with matters justly (AHMLR(PP)R 2003, r 3(1)). Dealing with matters justly includes, so far as practicable (AHMLR(PP)R 2003, r 3(2)):

'(a)   ensuring that the parties are on an equal footing;

(b)   saving expense;

(c)   dealing with the matter in ways that are proportionate—

(i)   to the value of the land or other interests involved;

(ii)   to the importance of the matter;

(iii)   to the complexity of the issues in the matter; and

(iv)   to the financial position of each party; and

(d)   ensuring that the matter is dealt with expeditiously and fairly.'

15.39 The device of the overriding objective is now familiar to anyone who has had experience of the Civil Procedure Rules (CPR r 1) and it is probably not surprising that the device has been used in these rules. It is not easy to see what practical application the objective will have, other than a reminder to the parties (and their representatives) that the objective of any judicial process is to resolve the dispute with as little fuss and expense as is possible.

Direction to commence court proceedings

15.40 At any time following the receipt of a reference from the registrar the adjudicator may, instead of deciding the matter himself, direct a party to commence proceedings in court for the purpose of obtaining the court's decision on the matter (LRA 2002, s 110(1)). This power does not apply to applications to rectify or set aside a document, nor does it apply to appeals from a decision of the registrar in respect of network access agreements. The direction will specify a time within which proceedings must be commenced. The direction may be for proceedings to be issued related to only part of the issues before the adjudicator.

15.41 Where the adjudicator is considering making such a direction, he will inform the parties in writing and give them an opportunity to make written representations to him. If he considers it appropriate he will hold a hearing. Representations can concern not only whether there should be a direction, but also which party should be directed to commence the court proceedings, the time within which they should be commenced and the questions which the court should determine (AHMLR(PP)R 2003, r 6).

15.42 Once such a direction is made the proceedings will be adjourned pending the outcome of the court's decision and, once the court has made its decision, will be closed unless the court directs otherwise (AHMLR(PP)R 2003, r 8). If the proceedings relate only to part of the issues before the adjudicator, the adjudicator will adjourn the part that is to be brought before the court and has a discretion as to whether or not to adjourn any part of the remaining dispute before him. For so long as the court proceedings are ongoing the party who was directed to commence proceedings must notify the court of any substantive decision of the adjudicator within 14 days of service on that party of the decision (AHMLR(PP)R 2003, r 9).

15.43 A party who is directed to commence proceedings by the adjudicator must, within 14 days of their commencement, inform the adjudicator that the proceedings have been commenced. Where that party receives the court's decision on any application for an extension of time or the final decision of the court he must serve it on the adjudicator within 14 days (AHMLR(PP)R 2003, r 7).

15.44 A party who fails to comply with the direction to commence proceedings may well find that the adjudicator will cancel the objection or application (AHMLR(PP)R 2003, r 55).

15.45 It is also possible that proceedings will be issued by one of the parties without a direction being given by the adjudicator. In these circumstances, provided the proceedings concern or relate to the proceedings before the adjudicator, the party who commenced the proceedings is obliged to inform the adjudicator of the proceedings and of their relationship to the dispute before the adjudicator (AHMLR(PP)R 2003, r 10). The adjudicator may then adjourn the whole or part of the proceedings pending the outcome of the court proceedings (AHMLR(PP)R 2003, r 11).

Case summaries and statements of case

15.46 A reference from the registrar will be commenced with a case summary from the registrar.[1] Once the reference is received the adjudicator will decide which party will be treated as the applicant and which the respondent.

---

[1] See para 15.28.

15.47 The applicant must send to the Adjudicator and the other parties, within 28 days of service of notification of the receipt of the reference, a statement of case and a copy of all the documents contained in his statement of case (AHMLR(PP)R 2003, r 12). The respondent must send his own statement of case and documents within 28 days of the receipt of the applicant's (AHMLR(PP)R 2003, r 13).

15.48 The statement of case will only partially resemble a statement of case in court proceedings. It must be in writing and must include:
- confirmation of the party's address for service;
- the party's reasons for supporting or objecting to the original application;
- the facts on which the party intends to rely in the proceedings;
- a list of the documents on which the party intends to rely;
- a list of the witnesses that the party intends to call to give evidence in support of his case (AHMLR(PP)R 2003, r 14).

15.49 Applications for rectification or setting aside of a document take a slightly different form. The application must be addressed to the adjudicator and include the following information:
- the name and address of the person or persons against whom the order is sought;
- details of the remedy being sought;
- the grounds on which the application is based;
- a list of documents on which the party intends to rely;
- a list of the witnesses that the party intends to call to give evidence in support of the rectification application;
- the applicant's name and address for service.

It must also include a copy of the documents listed as wells as a copy of the document to which the rectification application relates (AHMLR(PP)R 2003, r 16).

15.50 In order to serve an objection to a rectification application the objector must serve on the adjudicator and the other parties:
- a written statement setting out the grounds of the objection;
- a list and a copy of documents on which the party intends to rely;
- a list of the witnesses that the party intends to call to give evidence in support of his case;
- confirmation of his name and address for service (AHMLR(PP)R 2003, r 18).

Directions

15.51 The AHMLR(PP)R 2003 contain detailed provisions to allow the dispute to be dealt with, many of which are very similar to the Civil Procedure Rules. The adjudicator may at any time, on the application of one party or otherwise, make directions to enable the parties to prepare for the hearing of the dispute or to assist the adjudicator to conduct the proceedings or to determine all or part of the dispute without a hearing (AHMLR(PP)R 2003, r 20).

15.52 The directions that the adjudicator may make are not confined to those set out in the AHMLR(PP)R 2003 (AHMLR(PP)R 2003, r 20). Those that are set out in the AHMLR(PP)R 2003 include:

- consolidating proceedings (AHMLR(PP)R 2003, r 22);
- requiring a party to state whether he will attend or be represented at a hearing and call witnesses (AHMLR(PP)R 2003, r 28);
- adding or substituting parties (AHMLR(PP)R 2003, r 24);
- requiring a party to provide further information, or other statements or summaries of his case (AHMLR(PP)R 2003, r 25);
- requiring a party to allow the adjudicator to make a site inspection (AHMLR(PP)R 2003, r 30);
- requiring the provision of witness statements (AHMLR(PP)R 2003, r 26);
- requirements for the disclosure and inspection of documents (AHMLR(PP)R 2003, r 27);
- requirements for any person to give evidence or produce a document or other material (AHMLR(PP)R 2003, r 28);
- requiring the parties to provide an estimate of the length of the hearing (AHMLR(PP)R 2003, r 29);
- holding a hearing, or making a decision, on a preliminary issue (AHMLR(PP)R 2003, r 31).

15.53 Where a party has failed to comply with a direction, the adjudicator has general powers to impose a sanction, either on the application of the other party or on his own motion. The sanction may include the cancellation of the application or any objection to the application (AHMLR(PP)R 2003, r 55). He has a general power to extend any time limit, whether in the AHMLR(PP)R 2003 or set by the adjudicator, and to change the date time or location for any hearing (AHMLR(PP)R 2003, r 58).

Applications, notifications and objections

15.54 Applications must be made in writing, addressed to the adjudicator, state the nature of the application, the reasons for it and be signed by the party or parties making the application or consenting to it (AHMLR(PP)R 2003, r 51(2)). These requirements (either all or part) may be dispensed with by the adjudicator if the application is made at a time when all persons are before the adjudicator (normally at a hearing) or if the adjudicator considers it appropriate or practical to do so (AHMLR(PP)R 2003, r 51(3)). If the application does not have the consent of all the parties the adjudicator must serve notice of it on the persons who would be affected by it, giving details of the application and stating that the party has a right to make written objections to the application and the period within which such objections must be lodged (AHMLR(PP)R 2003, r 51(5), (6)).

15.55 The adjudicator may act of his own motion on the application, but if he intends to do so must serve notice of his intention on all parties who will be affected (AHMLR(PP)R 2003, r 51(7)), unless he does not consider it to be appropriate or practicable to do so (AHMLR(PP)R 2003, r 51(10)). The notice must set out the adjudicator's intention and state that a party has a right to make written objections and the time within which such objections must be lodged (AHMLR(PP)R 2003, r 51(8)).

15.56 Unless an application, representation or objection is frivolous or vexatious, or made after the expiry of a time limit specified for making it, the adjudicator is obliged to consider it (AHMLR(PP)R 2003, r 52(1)). If it is received after the expiry of a time limit the adjudicator may consider it, but is not obliged to do so (AHMLR(PP)R 2003, r 52(2)). In considering any application, representation or objection the adjudicator must make all enquiries he thinks necessary and must, if he considers it necessary, give the person making it and the other parties the opportunity to appear before him or to make written submissions (AHMLR(PP)R 2003, r 52(3)).

Hearings

15.57 Where the adjudicator is to hold a hearing he must, no later than 28 days before the hearing unless agreed otherwise by the parties, serve notice of his intention on such parties as he considers necessary, specifying the date, time and location of the hearing (AHMLR(PP)R 2003, r 34). The hearing must be published at the office of the adjudicator and, if different, the venue where the hearing will take place (AHMLR(PP)R 2003, r 36).

15.58 There is no presumption that hearing will be in public or in private. It is expected that most hearings will be in public unless there is some reason for them to be held in private.

15.59 At the hearing a party may either conduct the case himself or be represented or assisted. The representation or assistance may or may not be provided by a legally qualified person. The adjudicator has the power to refuse to permit a person to represent or assist a person at the hearing but only where he is satisfied that there is sufficient reason for doing so (AHMLR(PP)R 2003, r 35).

15.60 If a party does not attend and is not represented, provided that party has been served with notice of the proceedings, the adjudicator may hear and reach a substantive decision in the party's absence if:

    (1)   he is not satisfied that any reasons given for the absence are justified; or

    (2)   the absent party consents; or

    (3)   it would be unjust to adjourn the hearing.

Otherwise he must adjourn the hearing (AHMLR(PP)R 2003, r 38).

Substantive decisions

15.61 The AHMLR(PP)R 2003 distinguish between substantive decisions and other decisions. A substantive decision is a decision of the adjudicator on the matter or on any substantive issue that arises in it. It does not include any direction in interim parts of the proceedings (AHMLR(PP)R 2003, r 2).

15.62 There is a presumption that a substantive decision is to be made following a hearing (AHMLR(PP)R 2003, r 33(1)). The presumption does not apply to other decisions. In order to make a substantive decision without a hearing the adjudicator must first:

    (1)   satisfy himself that there is no important public interest consideration that requires a public hearing; and

    (2)   serve notice of his intentions on the parties (AHMLR(PP)R 2003, r 33(2)).

Notice is not required if the adjudicator does not consider it appropriate or practicable to serve notice of if the parties have requested the decision to be taken without a hearing (AHMLR(PP)R 2003, r 33(3)). The notice will indicate the intention to make the decision without a hearing and give a period within which written objections may be made. The adjudicator may then only decide the matter without a hearing if the parties agree or make no objections within the specified period (AHMLR(PP)R 2003, r 33(2)(b)). If any party makes an objection he must hold a hearing of the substantive decision.

15.63 A substantive decision may be made at the end of a hearing or reserved (AHMLR(PP)R 2003, r 39(1)). It must be recorded in a substantive order (AHMLR(PP)R 2003, r 39(2))[1] which must be served on every party to the proceedings and, if it requires the registrar to take action, on the registrar (AHMLR(PP)R 2003, r 40(2)). The order and decision should be publicly available (AHMLR(PP)R 2003, r 46(1) (2)) and the adjudicator may provide copies of it to the public on request (AHMLR(PP)R 2003, r 40(5)). Reasons must be given for the decision and any steps that need to be taken to give effect to the decision, in writing (AHMLR(PP)R 2003, r 40(6)).

---

[1]   The order must be in writing, dated, signed, state the substantive decision reached, state any requirements that give effect to the decision and state the possible consequences of a party's failure to comply with any time limits in the order. See the AHMLR(PP)R 2003, r 40(1).

15.64 The adjudicator has no power to vary or set aside a substantive decision once made (AHMLR(PP)R 2003, r 39(3)).

Costs

15.65 The adjudicator has power to make a costs order and may do so either on the application of a party or of his own motion (AHMLR(PP)R 2003, r 42(2)). In deciding whether and what costs order to make he must have regard to all the circumstances of the proceedings (AHMLR(PP)R 2003, r 42(3) and (1)(a)). This includes the conduct of the parties during (but not prior to) the proceedings, whether a party has succeeded on part of the case even if not wholly successful, and any representations made to the adjudicator by the parties (AHMLR(PP)R 2003, r 42(1)(a)). Conduct of the parties includes whether it was reasonable for a party to raise, pursue or contest a particular allegation or issue, the manner in which a party has pursued or defended his case and whether a party who has succeeded has exaggerated his case either in whole or in part (AHMLR(PP)R 2003, r 42(1)(b)).

15.66 The costs order may require a party to pay the whole or part of the costs of the other party, specify a fixed sum or proportion, specify that the costs are to be assessed by the adjudicator if not agreed; and may specify the time within which the costs must be paid (AHMLR(PP)R 2003, r 42(4)). If the costs are to be assessed they may be assessed on either the standard or the indemnity basis (AHMLR(PP)R 2003, r 42(7)).[1]

---

[1]   Where costs are to be assessed on the standard basis the adjudicator must only allow costs which are proportionate to the matters in issue and must resolve any doubts that he may have as to whether costs were reasonably incurred or reasonable and proportionate in favour of the paying party. Where costs are to be assessed on the indemnity basis the adjudicator must resolve any doubt that he may have as to whether costs were reasonably incurred or were reasonable in amount in favour of the paying party. In either case the adjudicator will not allow costs that have been unreasonably incurred or are unreasonable in amount.

15.67 The adjudicator has an additional power to make a 'costs thrown away order'. This is, in effect, a wasted costs order and will be an order requiring a party's legal representative to pay costs resulting from any neglect or delay of the legal representative (AHMLR(PP)R 2003, r 43). The order may be made where the adjudicator is satisfied that a party has incurred the costs unnecessarily as a result of the neglect or delay of the legal representative and that it is just in all the circumstances for the legal representative to compensate the party who has incurred or paid the costs thrown away (AHMLR(PP)R 2003, r 43(2)).

Appeals

15.68 Any person aggrieved by a decision of the adjudicator may appeal to the High Court (LRA 2002, s 111(1)). There is no limit on the nature of the decision, so it may or may not be a substantive decision. The exception to the general rule is that an appeal from a decision by the adjudicator about the entry into, or termination of, a network access agreement where the appeal can only be made on a point of law (LRA 2002, s 111(2)).[1]

---

[1]   It should be noted that the appeal to the court will be a second appeal since the decision of the adjudicator will have been made on an appeal against the registrar's decision.

15.69 In order to appeal, it is necessary to seek permission to appeal, either from the adjudicator or the High Court. An application to the adjudicator is made in the same way as any other application. Where an application is made to the High Court[1] the court's decision must be served on the adjudicator as soon as reasonably practicable and in any event within 14 days of receipt by the appellant of the decision.[2]

---

[1]   See CPR r 52.
[2]   See CPR 52 Practice Direction para 23.8B(2).

15.70 The appeal will be heard in the Chancery Division.[1] The normal provisions of the Civil Procedure Rules concerning appeals will apply and the appeal will be a review of the original decision.

---

[1]   CPR 52 Practice Direction para 23.2(17).

15.71 The party may need a stay of the implementation of the order pending the outcome of the appeal. The adjudicator may grant such a stay of his own motion. Alternatively, the person may apply for a stay at the same time as applying for permission to appeal (where applying for permission from the adjudicator) providing reasons for the application (AHMLR(PP)R 2003, r 45). Where a stay is sought and obtained from the court a copy of the order must be served on the adjudicator and the Chief Land Registrar as soon as reasonably practicable and in any event within 14 days of receipt by the appellant of the appeal court's order to stay.[1]

---

[1]   CPR 52 Practice Direction para 23.8B(3).

COURTS

15.72 The courts[1] will continue to have an extensive role in determining disputes involving registered land and issues arising out of the system of land registration. This role arises in a number of ways. First, the LRA 2002 does nothing to restrict the court's general ability to hear disputes, so that many actions will simply be heard in court in the normal way. Second, disputes that begin before the registrar and are referred to the adjudicator may themselves be referred to the court. Third, the LRA 2002 confers jurisdiction on the courts in two specific areas. Fourth, the courts are empowered to hear appeals from the registrar and the adjudicator. Finally, there is the possibility of the actions of either the registrar or the adjudicator being challenged by judicial review.

---

[1] References to 'the court' in the LRA 2002 are to the High Court or a county court (LRA 2002, s 132(3)) although, as will be seen, in some cases the LRA 2002 specifically refers to the High Court or to county courts.

The courts' existing jurisdiction

15.73 As under the old system many disputes that involve registered land, or raise specific issues of land registration, will begin and end in the courts with little or no reference to the registrar. By way of example, the disputes with which the courts will continue to be engaged will include:

- actions for possession of registered land, including actions where the defendant alleges that he has title, or ought to be registered with title, by reason of adverse possession;[1]
- actions involving allegations of express or implied rights, such as easements, over registered land;[2]
- actions involving trusts over or including registered land;[3]
- actions for declarations as to the meaning and effect of documents dealing with and disposing of registered land whether or not those documents were themselves registrable.

---

[1] See para 13.6.
[2] See, for example, para 9.1.
[3] See paras 10.58–10.60.

15.74 In many such cases it may be necessary for the register to be altered to reflect the outcome of the proceedings. Thus, the LRA 2002 contains a number of powers which the court can exercise:

(1) the court has power to make an order for alteration of the register for the purpose of correcting a mistake, bringing the register up to date, or giving effect to any estate, right or

interest excepted from the effect of registration (LRA 2002, Sch 4, para 2);[1]

(2) the court may make an order for the alteration of the cautions register for the purpose of correcting a mistake or bringing the register up to date (LRA 2002, s 20)[2] and must make such an order if it decides that the cautioner does not own the relevant interest, or only owns part, or if the interest either wholly or in part did not exist or has come to an end (LRR 2003, r 48);

(3) the court may, if it considers it necessary or desirable to do so for the purpose of protecting a right or claim in relation to a registered estate or charge, make an order requiring the registrar to enter a restriction on the register and such an order may include a direction that the entry is to have an overriding priority (LRA 2002, s 46; LRR 2003, r 100);[3]

(4) where a squatter successfully defends a possession action on the basis of his adverse possession the court must order the registrar to register him as the proprietor of the estate over which his entitlement extends (LRA 2002, s 98(5)).[4]

---

[1] See also para 14.6. Note the difference in the court's powers where the alteration is by way of rectification or otherwise: see para 14.19.
[2] See also para 14.6.
[3] See also para 7.55.
[4] See also para 13.6.

The LRA 2002 and litigation

15.75 There are a number of features of the LRA 2002 and the LRR 2003 to keep in mind when conducting litigation concerning registered land. These are as follows.

(1) The public availability of documents and title entries can be an important source of information at the stage of preparation of proceedings and assessing whether there is a claim and how strong it is (LRA 2002, s 66; LRR 2003, rr 134 and 135).[1] The main innovation of the LRA 2002 is that leases and charges, and any documents in the possession of the registrar which relate to an application to him which are not referred to in the register, are open to inspection (in addition to the register of title and documents other than leases and charges referred to in it).[2] This is subject to these newly available categories being only available at the registrar's discretion until 12 October 2005 where they came into the registrar's possession before 13 October 2003, and also subject to interested parties' rights to apply for confidentiality (LRR 2003, rr 136 and 139).[3]

(2) Where there is an insolvent administration or a criminal investigation, a trustee in bankruptcy or other public official listed in the LRR 2003, Sch 5 may apply under the LRR 2003, r 140 to see documents otherwise withheld from public view.

(3)   Another innovation as a matter of law, although it regularises and publicises a previous practice, is the right to apply for historical information as to the state of a particular registered title at a past date, if the registrar has retained it (LRA 2002, s 69; LRR 2003, r 144).

(4)   Title to registered land should now be proved by production of official copies of the register of title, as land certificates have now ceased to be documents of title.[4]

(5)   Some disputes will be capable of being tried either by the courts, or by the adjudicator, and in such cases there will be a choice between starting court proceedings or making an application to the registrar in the expectation that it will be opposed and thus lead to a reference to the adjudicator. It is too soon to say whether adjudication by the adjudicator will be cheaper than court proceedings, but it is to be hoped that it will be. Possible disadvantages might be that, when the adjudication alternative is pursued, it may take some time to get to the stage of a reference to the adjudicator by the registrar, and there is the risk that the adjudicator might decide that the matter has to be decided by the courts, in which case it would have been better to have started off with court proceedings.

(6)   When court proceedings have been started, claiming some right or relief relating to registered land, it may be important to register a notice of the proceedings as a pending land action to maintain priority for what is being claimed (LRA 2002, s 87(1)).[5] This will be particularly so where the claim is one which has no existence independently of the proceedings, such as an application for a new business tenancy under the Landlord and Tenant Act 1954, Pt II or an application to remove a trustee, because a pending land action cannot be an overriding interest even if the claimant is in actual occupation of the land (LRA 2002, s 87(3)). Where the claim is in respect of a right with an independent existence, such as a beneficial interest under a trust or an equitable easement, registration of the proceedings will be important if the right is not protected in some other way, eg as an overriding interest[6] or by a notice on the register.[7]

---

[1]   See paras 2.65 et seq.

[2]   See para 2.66.

[3]   See para 2.76.

[4]   For admission of official copies of the register in evidence see the LRA 2002, s 67 and para 2.64, and for abolition of land certificates see para 2.61.

[5]   See also para 7.20.

[6]   See para 7.20.

[7]   See para 7.20.

References from the adjudicator

15.76 Where the adjudicator decides that a matter is better dealt with by way of court proceedings, he is able to direct a party to commence proceedings within a specified time (LRA 2002, s 110(1)).[1] Proceedings will then be begun in the normal way. The party who has been directed to commence the proceedings is under an obligation to inform the adjudicator of the commencement of the proceedings and of their outcome. The proceedings in front of the adjudicator will be adjourned pending the decision of the court.[2]

[1] See para 15.40.
[2] See para 15.42.

Rights arising from the LRA 2002

Duty to act reasonably

15.77 Under the LRA 2002, s 77 a person owes a duty not to lodge a caution against first registration, apply for the entry of a notice or restriction, or object to an application to the registrar without reasonable cause. The duty is owed to any person who suffers damage in consequence of its breach.[1] The duty that the section gives rise to is a statutory duty that is enforceable by proceedings in court.

[1] See para 2.56.

Indemnity

15.78 The rights to an indemnity from the registrar, arising in the LRA 2002, Sch 8, are enforceable by the courts and a person is given the authority to apply to court to obtain a determination of any question as to whether he is entitled to an indemnity or the amount of such an indemnity (LRA 2002, Sch 8, para 7).[1] Furthermore, the registrar's right to recover from third parties monies paid by way of an indemnity under the LRA 2002, Sch 8 is enforceable by court proceedings (LRA 2002, Sch 8, para 10).[2]

[1] See para 14.51.
[2] See also para 14.53.

Appeals

15.79 The only right of appeal from the registrar exists in respect of a decision to require the production of documents or the payment of costs (LRA 2002, ss 75(4) and 76(5)). The appeal is to the county court.

15.80 There is a general right to appeal from any decision of the adjudicator. The appeal is to the High Court and will be heard in the Chancery Division.[1]

___
[1]   See CPR 52 Practice Direction para 23.2(17).

15.81 The AHMLR(PP)R 2003 include some provisions for the provision or refusal of permission to appeal a decision of the adjudicator. There are no such provisions in respect of appeals from the registrar. However, all appeals require permission to appeal.[1] It follows that where the appeal is from the adjudicator, it will be possible to obtain permission either from the adjudicator, or from the court. However, where the appeal is from the registrar it will only be possible to obtain permission from the court.

___
[1]   CPR r 52.3.

15.82 Part 52 of the Civil Procedure Rules states that 'every appeal will be limited to a review of the decision of the lower courts'.[1] These provisions apply to appeals both from the registrar and the adjudicator. As a result it will not be possible, unless the court considers that in the circumstances of the individual case it would be in the interests of justice, to obtain a re-hearing on an appeal.

___
[1]   CPR r 52.11.

Judicial review

15.83 The court's ability to consider by way of judicial review, the decisions of both the registrar and the adjudicator are in no way limited by the LRA 2002. In many circumstances judicial review is the only means of challenging a decision of the registrar. The existence of a general right of appeal from the adjudicator may mean that few challenges from the adjudicator's decisions are made in this way.

Offences

15.84 The LRA 2002 creates three offences. These are:
   (1)   suppressing information with the intention of concealing a person's right or claim, or substantiating a false claim, in the course of proceedings relating to registration (LRA 2002, s 123);
   (2)   dishonestly inducing another to change the register of title or the cautions register, or to authorise the making of such a change (LRA 2002, s 124(1));

(3) intentionally or recklessly making an unauthorised change in the register of title or the cautions register (LRA 2002, s 124(2)).

All three offences are triable either way. On indictment the maximum sentence is two years imprisonment or a fine (on which no limit is placed). On summary conviction the maximum sentence is six months imprisonment or a fine not exceeding the statutory maximum or to both.

15.85 The first of these offences again (LRA 2002, ss 75(1) and 76(1))[1] raises the question of what 'proceedings' relating to registration are. Is an application for first registration of land, or for registration of a disposition of registered land, within the meaning of the term? It probably is, although the term is perhaps more usually understood as referring to dispute resolution of some sort rather than an application for an administrative act to be carried out. The Law Commission thought that the term covered 'any procedure in connection with an application to the registrar'[2]—presumably including the application itself, which is surely the point at which any suppression of the kind prohibited is most likely to take place. The second and third offences, concerning alteration of the register, will take on particular significance when the move to electronic conveyancing is made.[3] This is because a large number of individuals will have the power to alter the register or to authorise such alterations. In those circumstances it was believed necessary to create specific offences related to dishonestly causing a change in the register or to intentionally or recklessly making an unauthorised change.

---

[1] See also para 15.19 for another example, where, however, the meaning of the term is restricted by context and the provisions of the LRR 2003 more than is the case in the LRA 2002, s 123.
[2] See Law Com no 271, para 16.28.
[3] Law Com no 271, para 16.29.

15.86 The third offence does not relate to circumstances where, for example, a conveyancer makes a mistaken alteration (whether intentionally or recklessly). It does relate to circumstances where the conveyancer intentionally or recklessly makes a change which the conveyancer does not have the authority to make (for example, where the conveyancer's authority is limited by the network access agreement) or where an individual makes a change where that individual has no authority to alter the register.

TRANSITIONAL

15.87 Where a dispute arose prior to 13 October 2003, whether from an objection to an application or out of a 'warning' off of a caution against dealings, the registrar must deal with, and continue to deal with, the dispute in the same manner that he would have done under the LRR 1925 (Land Registration Act 2002 (Transitional Provisions) Order 2003, SI 2003/1953, art 6). The dispute will therefore remain with the registrar and will be subject to the same provisions it would have been had the LRA 2002 not come into force and will not be transferred to the adjudicator.

15.88 Where an objection is made after 13 October 2003 to an application made before that date the dispute will be governed by the new provisions (Land Registration Act 2002 (Transitional Provisions) Order 2003, SI 2003/1953, art 7).

15.89 A decision by the registrar that an objection is groundless, where the decision is made before 13 October 2003 or where the decision is in respect of an application pending before the that day, the old rules should be appealed under the old rules. Similarly any decision or order made under the provisions of the old rules should be appealed under those rules (Land Registration Act 2002 (Transitional Provisions) Order 2003, SI 2003/1953, art 8).

15.90 Any proceedings instituted before 13 October 2003 but not concluded before that date will continue until concluded as if the LRA 2002 had not been passed (Land Registration Act 2002 (Transitional Provisions) Order 2003, SI 2003/1953, art 9).

APPENDIX 1

OVERRIDING INTERESTS REQUIRED TO BE DISCLOSED

As set out in paras 4.14, 4.18 and 5.19 above, on an application for first registration or for registration of a disposition of registered land, the applicant is required to disclose overriding interests within LRA 2002, Sch 1 or Sch 3, as the case may be, of which he has knowledge. By virtue of LRA 2002 s 33 and LRR 2003, rr 28 and 57, there are some overriding interests which are not required to be disclosed. This Appendix sets out two consolidated lists of the interests required to be disclosed, one relating to applications for first registration, and one relating to applications for registration of a disposition of registered land. They are consolidated in that they show the combined effect of the relevant legislation.

A: DISCLOSURE ON FIRST REGISTRATION

(LRA 2002, ss 33, 71(a), 90(4), Sch 1, and LRR 2003, r 28(1) and (2))

Interests to be disclosed are in bold, *but subject to the exceptions which are shown in italics.*

On a first registration application the following must be disclosed if the applicant knows about them, they affect the estate being registered, and they are not obvious from the documents he submits in support of the application (LRR 2003, r 28(1), (2)(b))—

- **any lease granted after 12 October 2003 for a term of seven years or less** (LRA 2002, Sch 1 para 1) *subject to the following exceptions: a lease for three years or less;[1] a PPP lease;[2] a lease which was granted, out of a freehold or leasehold with more than seven years to run, to take effect in possession more than three months after the date of grant;[3] a lease granted pursuant to the right to buy;[4] a lease granted in circumstances where the Housing Act 1985, s 171A applies (a disposal by a landlord which leads to a person no longer being a secure tenant);[5] a lease which has a year or less to run at the time of the application;[6]*
- **any lease for a term of more than three years and not exceeding 21 years which was granted before 13 October 2003** *other than a PPP lease,[7] a lease which has a year or less to run at the time of the application, a lease granted pursuant to the Housing Act 1985, Pt 5 (the right to buy), and a lease granted in circumstances where the Housing Act 1985, s 171A applied (a disposal by a landlord which leads to a person no longer being a secure tenant);[8]*
- **any interest belonging to a person in actual occupation** (LRA 2002, Sch 1, para 2)[9] *subject to the following exceptions: a beneficial interest under a trust of land[10] or under a Settled Land Act 1925 settlement;[11] a restrictive covenant between*

landlord and tenant so far as relating to the demised premises;[12] a lease granted for three years or less, or which is within LRA 2002, Sch 1, para 1 and has a year or less left to run at the time of the application;[13]

- **where the disposition was or is made before 13 October 2006, interests acquired under the Limitation Act 1980 before 13 October 2003;**[14]
- **any legal easement or profit a prendre** (LRA 2002, Sch 1, para 3);
- **customary rights, certain rights to mines and minerals created before 1925, franchises, manorial rights, rights to rents reserved by the Crown on grant of a freehold, non-statutory rights in respect of embankments and sea or river walls, rights to payment in lieu of tithes, and chancel repair obligations** (LRA 2002, Sch 1, paras 4–14 and the LRA 2002 (Transitional Provisions) (No 2) Order 2003, SI 2003/2431, art 2).[15]

---

[1] These are not capable of being noted on the register (LRA 2002, s 33(b)), and so are excepted from the disclosure requirement (LRR 2003, r 28(2)(a)).

[2] For PPP leases see paras 12.26 and 12.27, and the LRA 2002, s 90. They are overriding interests (LRA 2002, s 90(5)) but are not capable of being recorded on the register and are excluded from disclosure to the registrar on first registration by the LRR 2003, r 28(2)(a) by reference to the LRA 2002, s 90(4).

[3] These are registrable leases which are excluded from the LRA 2002, Sch 1, para 1 by that para by reference to the LRA 2002, s 4(1)(d).

[4] Ie a lease granted pursuant to the Housing Act 1985, Pt 5 out of an unregistered legal estate. These are registrable leases excluded from the LRA 2002, Sch 1, para 1 by that para by reference to the LRA 2002, s 4(1)(e).

[5] These are registrable leases excluded from the LRA 2002, Sch 1, para 1 by that para by reference to the LRA 2002, s 4(1)(f).

[6] These are excepted from disclosure on first registration by the LRR 2003, r 28(2)(e).

[7] See footnote 2 above.

[8] Ie a lease which immediately before the LRA 2002, Sch 1 came into force fell within the LRA 1925, s 70(1)(k) as substituted by LRA 1986, s 4(1): LRA 2002, Sch 12, para 12, treating such interests as included in the LRA 2002, Sch 1, para 1. The exclusion of leases granted for three years or less derives from the LRA 2002, s 33(b) (see the LRR 2003, r 28(2)(a)), and that of leases with a year or less to run from LRR 2003, r 28(2)(e). The exception of the Housing Act 1985 leases is because they were excluded from being overriding interests by Housing Act 1985, s 154(7) and Sch 9A, para 3.

[9] See para 7.9. This category includes any lease, registrable or not, which is not within any of the exceptions mentioned in this sub-paragraph, and is owned by someone in actual occupation of the land comprised in the lease, and also includes any adverse possession rights of a person in actual occupation.

[10] Such an interest can be overriding when the person entitled to it is in actual occupation, but it cannot be noted on the register (LRA 2002, s 33(a)) and so is excepted from disclosure on first registration (LRR 2003, r 28(2)(a)).

[11] An interest under Settled Land Act 1925 is excepted both from the possibility of being overriding under the LRA 2002, Sch 1, para 2 (by para 2 itself) and from being noted on the register (LRA 2002, s 33(a)).

[12] Such an interest is not capable of being noted on the register: LRA 2002, s 33(c).

[13] For the last mentioned two exceptions see the LRA 2002, s 33(b) and LRR 2003, r 28(2)(e). There are some other, more esoteric, exceptions, but they are in practice unlikely to be rights or interests owned by persons in actual occupation: see the LRA 2002, ss 33(d) and (e) and 87(3), and the LRR 2003, r 28(2)(c), (d).

[14] LRA 2002, Sch 12, para 7 adds this category to the LRA 2002, Sch 1.

15 Subject to the exceptions in the LRA 2002, s 33(d) and (e) and the LRR 2003, r 28(2)(c) and (d), and also subject to the point that after 12 October 2013 there will be no obligation to disclose franchises, manorial rights, rights to rents reserved by the Crown on grant of a freehold, non-statutory rights in respect of embankments and sea or river walls, rights to payment in lieu of tithes, and obligations to repair chancels, because they then cease to be overriding interests (LRA 2002, s 117(1), the LRA 2002 (Transitional Provisions) (No 2) Order 2003, SI 2003/2431, art 2).

B: DISCLOSURE AFTER A DISPOSITION OF REGISTERED LAND

(LRA 2002, ss 33, 71(b), 90(4), Sch 3, and LRR 2003, r 57(1), (2))

Interests to be disclosed are in bold, *but subject to the exceptions which are shown in italics.* <u>Categories included or excluded which are not in the list in Part A are underlined.</u>

On an application to register a disposition of a registered estate the following interests are required to be disclosed if the applicant knows about them and they affect the registered estate (LRR 2003, r 57(1), and they are not already noted on the register of the title to that estate—[1]

- **any lease granted after 12 October 2003 for a term of seven years or less** (LRA 2002, Sch 3, para 1) *subject to the following exceptions: a lease for three years or less;[2] a PPP lease;[3] a lease granted to take effect in possession more than three months after the date of grant;[4] a lease granted pursuant to the right to buy;[5] a lease granted in circumstances where the Housing Act 1985, s 171A applies (a disposal by a landlord which leads to a person no longer being a secure tenant);[6]* <u>*a lease under which possession is discontinuous which was granted out of the land after it became registered;*[7]</u> *a lease which has a year or less to run at the time of the application;[8]*

- **any lease for a term of more than three years and not exceeding 21 years which was granted before 13 October 2003,** *other than a PPP lease,[9] a lease which has a year or less to run at the time of the application, a lease granted pursuant to the Housing Act 1985, Pt 5 (the right to buy), and a lease granted in circumstances where the Housing Act 1985, s 171A applied (a disposal by a landlord which leads to a person no longer being a secure tenant);[10]*

- **any interest belonging to a person in actual occupation** (LRA 2002, Sch 3, para 2)[11] *subject to the following exceptions: a beneficial interest under a trust of land[12] or under a Settled Land Act 1925 settlement;[13]* <u>*a lease granted to take effect in possession more than three months after the date of grant, which had not taken effect in possession at the date of the disposition*</u> (LRA 2002, Sch 3, para 2(d));[14] <u>*any interest or right of a person in actual occupation who did not disclose it when he could reasonably have been expected to do so when asked before the disposition, or whose occupation was not obvious at the time of the disposition and was not known to*</u>

the disponee;[15] *a restrictive covenant between landlord and tenant so far as relating to the demised premises;*[16] *a lease which is not required to be registered and was granted for three years or less, or a lease within the LRA 2002, Sch 1, para 1 with a year or less left to run at the time of the application;*[17]

- **an interest of someone in receipt of rents and profits of the land which was an overriding interest under LRA 1925, s 70(1)(g) on 12 October 2003 by virtue of receipt of rents and profits,** *unless he failed to disclose it when asked, or it would after 12 October 2003 have ceased to be overriding by virtue of receipt of rents and profits if LRA 1925 had continued in force* (LRA 2002, Sch 12, para 8, which adds this category to the LRA 2002, Sch 3 as para 2A);

- **where the disposition is one made before 13 October 2006, interests acquired under the Limitation Act 1980 before 13 October 2003** (LRA 2002, Sch 12, para 11 adds this category to the LRA 2002, Sch 3);

- **any legal easement or profit a prendre**, *but, with effect from 13 October 2006, with the exception of any legal easement or profit (not registered under the Commons Registration Act 1965) not obvious and not known to the disponee at the time of the disposition, and not exercised in the previous year* (LRA 2002, Sch 3 para 3);[18]

- **an equitable easement or profit or prendre which was an overriding interest on 12 October 2003** (LRA 2002, Sch 12, para 9);

- **customary rights, certain rights to mines and minerals created before 1925, franchises, manorial rights, rights to rents reserved by the Crown on grant of a freehold, non-statutory rights in respect of embankments and sea or river walls, rights to payment in lieu of tithes, and chancel repair obligations** (LRA 2002, Sch 3, paras 4–14 and the LRA 2002 (Transitional Provisions) (No 2) Order 2003, SI 2003/2431, art 2).[19]

---

[1]   There is no express exception for interests already noted on the register, and strictly speaking an interest does not cease to be within LRA 2002, Sch 3 if it is noted on the register, but such an exception is implicit because there is no point in requiring disclosure of interests already noted on the register, and interests which are noted on the register cease to have priority by virtue of falling within Sch 3 (s 29(3)).

[2]   This is the combined effect of the LRR 2003, r 57(2)(a) and the LRA 2002, s 33(b). These are overriding interests but ones not capable of being noted on the register, and so are excepted from the disclosure requirement.

[3]   For PPP leases see paras 12.26 and 12.27, and the LRA 2002, s 90. They are overriding interests which may not be noted in the register (LRA 2002, s 90(4) and (5)), and are excluded from disclosure by the LRR 2003, r 57(2)(a) by reference to the LRA 2002, s 90(4).

[4]   These are registrable leases, granted after 12 October 2003, which are excluded from the LRA 2002, Sch 3, para 1 by that para by the exception for a grant within the LRA 2002, s 4(1)(d) and (in relation to those granted out of a registered estate) by reference to grants which are registrable.

5 Ie a lease granted pursuant to the Housing Act 1985, Pt 5. These are registrable leases excluded from the LRA 2002, Sch 3, para 1 by that para by the exception for a grant within the LRA 2002, s 4(1)(e) and (in relation to those granted out of a registered estate) by the reference in the LRA 2002, Sch 3, para 1 to grants which are registrable.

6 These are registrable leases excluded from the LRA 2002, Sch 3, para 1 by that para by reference to the LRA 2002, s 4(1)(f) and (in relation to those granted out of a registered estate) by the reference in the LRA 2002, Sch 3, para 1 to grants which are registrable.

7 Such a lease is not subject to compulsory registration when granted from unregistered land (see the LRA 2002, s 4) but is a registrable disposition when granted out of registered land (see the LRA 2002, s 27), and is thus within the LRA 2002, Sch 1, para 1 but not within the LRA 2002, Sch 3, para 1.

8 These are excepted from disclosure on first registration by the LRR 2003, r 57(2)(d).

9 See footnote 3 above.

10 Ie a lease which immediately before 13 October 2003 fell within the LRA 1925, s 70(1)(k) as substituted by the LRA 1986, s 4(1): LRA 2002, Sch 12, para 12, treating such interests as included in the LRA 2002, Sch 3, para 1. This category of disclosable interest is subject to the exceptions in the LRA 2002, s 33(b) (leases granted for three years or less)—see the LRR 2003, r 57(2)(a)—and the LRR 2003, r 57(2)(d) (leases with a year or less to run). The exception of the Housing Act 1985 leases is because they were excluded from being overriding interests by Housing Act 1985, s 154(7) and Sch 9A, para 3.

11 See paras 7.67 et seq. This category will include any adverse possession rights of a person in actual occupation and any lease, registrable or not, which is not within any of the exceptions here noted, and is owned by someone in actual occupation of the land comprised in the lease.

12 Such an interest can be overriding when the person entitled to it is in actual occupation, but it cannot be noted on the register (LRA 2002, s 33(a)) and so is excepted from disclosure on first registration (LRR 2003, r 28(2)(a)).

13 An interest under a Settled Land Act 1925 settlement is excepted both from the possibility of being overriding under the LRA 2002, Sch 3, para 2 (by para 2 itself) and from being noted on the register (LRA 2002, s 33(a)).

14 Such a lease also falls outside the LRA 2002, Sch 3, para 1 because it is registrable.

15 LRA 2002, Sch 3, exception in para 2(b) and (c).

16 Such an interest is not capable of being noted on the register: LRA 2002, s 33(c).

17 For the last mentioned two exceptions see the LRA 2002, s 33(b) and the LRR 2003, r 57(2)(d). There are some other, more esoteric exceptions, but they are in practice unlikely to be rights or interests owned by persons in actual occupation: see the LRA 2002, ss 33(d) and (e) and 87(3), and the LRR 2003, r 57(2)(b), (c).

18 The exception is deferred for three years by the LRA 2002, Sch 12, para 10.

19 Subject to the exceptions in LRA 2002, s 33(d) and (e) and LRR 2003, r 57(2)(b) and (c), and also subject to the point that after 12 October 2013 there will be no obligation to disclose franchises, manorial rights, rights to rents reserved by the Crown on grant of a freehold, non-statutory rights in respect of embankments and sea or river walls, rights to payment in lieu of tithes, and obligations to repair chancels, because they then cease to be overriding interests (LRA 2002, s 117(1), the LRA 2002 (Transitional Provisions) (No 2) Order 2003, SI 2003/2431, art 2).

Appendix 2

Law of Property Act 1925 (extracts)

Land Registration Act 2002

Land Registration Rules 2003, SI 2003/1417

Land Registration (Proper Office) Order 2003, SI 2003/2040

Land Registration Fee Order 2004, SI 2004/595

Land Registration Act 2002 (Commencement No 1) Order 2003, SI 2003/935

Land Registration Act 2002 (Commencement No 2) Order 2003, SI 2003/1028

Land Registration Act 2002 (Commencement No 3) Order 2003, SI 2003/1612

Land Registration Act 2002 (Commencement No 4) Order 2003, SI 2003/1725

Land Registration Act 2002 (Transitional Provisions) Order 2003, SI 2003/1953

Land Registration Act 2002 (Transitional Provisions) (No 2) Order 2003, SI 2003/2431

Land Registration (Referral to the Adjudicator to HM Land Registry) Rules 2003, SI 2003/2114

Adjudicator to Her Majesty's Land Registry (Practice and Procedure) Rules 2003, SI 2003/2171

Land Registration (Acting Chief Land Registrar) Regulations 2003, SI 2003/2281

Land Registration (Acting Adjudicator) Regulations 2003, SI 2003/2342

Law of Property Act 1925

(15 & 16 Geo 5 c 20)

PART I
GENERAL PRINCIPLES AS TO LEGAL ESTATES,
EQUITABLE INTERESTS AND POWERS

1 Legal estates and equitable interests

(1)   The only estates in land which are capable of subsisting or of being conveyed or created at law are—

    (a)   An estate in fee simple absolute in possession;

    (b)   A term of years absolute.

(2)   The only interests or charges in or over land which are capable of subsisting or of being conveyed or created at law are—

    (a)   An easement, right, or privilege in or over land for an interest equivalent to an estate in fee simple absolute in possession or a term of years absolute;

    (b)   A rentcharge in possession issuing out of or charged on land being either perpetual or for a term of years absolute;

    (c)   A charge by way of legal mortgage;

    (d)   . . . and any other similar charge on land which is not created by an instrument;

    (e)   Rights of entry exercisable over or in respect of a legal term of years absolute, or annexed, for any purpose, to a legal rentcharge.

(3)   All other estates, interests, and charges in or over land take effect as equitable interests.

(4)   The estates, interests, and charges which under this section are authorised to subsist or to be conveyed or created at law are (when subsisting or conveyed or created at law) in this Act referred to as "legal estates," and have the same incidents as legal estates subsisting at the commencement of this Act; and the owner of a legal estate is referred to as "an estate owner" and his legal estate is referred to as his estate.

(5)   A legal estate may subsist concurrently with or subject to any other legal estate in the same land in like manner as it could have done before the commencement of this Act.

(6)   A legal estate is not capable of subsisting or of being created in an undivided share in land or of being held by an infant.

(7)   Every power of appointment over, or power to convey or charge land or any interest therein, whether created by a statute or other instrument or implied by law, and whether created before or after the commencement of this Act (not being a power vested in a legal mortgagee or an estate owner in right of his estate and exercisable by him or by another person in his name and on his behalf), operates only in equity.

(8)–(10) . . .

Amendments: Sub-s (2): words omitted repealed by the Finance Act 1963, s 73(8)(b), Sch 14, Pt IV and the Tithe Act 1936, s 48(3), Sch 9.
Sub-ss (8)–(10): not reproduced.
References: See paras 4.10, 5.16, 5.18, 12.1.

PART XII
CONSTRUCTION, JURISDICTION, AND GENERAL PROVISIONS

205 General definitions

(1)   In this Act unless the context otherwise requires, the following expressions have the meanings hereby assigned to them respectively, that is to say—

(i)–(ix) . . .

(x)"Legal estates" mean the estates, interests and charges, in or over land (subsisting or created at law) which are by this Act authorised to subsist or to be created as legal estates; "equitable interests" mean all the other interests and charges in or over land *or in the proceeds of sale thereof*; an equitable interest "capable of subsisting as a legal estate" means such as could validly subsist or be created as a legal estate under this Act;

(xi)–(xv) . . .

(xvi)"Mortgage" includes any charge or lien on any property for securing money or money's worth; "legal mortgage" means a mortgage by demise or subdemise or a charge by way of legal mortgage and "legal mortgagee" has a corresponding meaning; "mortgage money" means money or money's worth secured by a mortgage; "mortgagor" includes any person from time to time deriving title under the original mortgagor or entitled to redeem a mortgage according to his estate interest or right in the mortgaged property; "mortgagee" includes a chargee by way of legal mortgage and any person from time to time deriving title under the original mortgagee; and "mortgagee in possession" is, for the purposes of this Act, a mortgagee who, in right of the mortgage, has entered into and is in possession of the mortgaged property; and "right of redemption" includes an option to repurchase only if the option in effect creates a right of redemption;

(xvii)–(xxvi) . . .

(xxvii)"Term of years absolute" means a term of years (taking effect either in possession or in reversion whether or not at a rent) with or without impeachment for waste, subject or not to another legal estate, and either certain or liable to determination by notice, re-entry, operation of law, or by a provision for cesser on redemption, or in any other event (other than the dropping of a life, or the determination of a determinable life interest); but does not include any term of years determinable with life or lives or with the cesser of a determinable life interest, nor, if created after the commencement of this Act, a term of years which is not expressed to take effect in possession within twenty-one years after the creation thereof where required by this Act to take effect within that period; and in this definition the expression "term of years" includes a term for less than a year, or for a year or years and a fraction of a year or from year to year;

(xxviii)–(xxxi) . . .

(1A)–(3) . . .

Amendments: Sub-s (1): words in italics in para (x) repealed by the Trusts of Land and Appointment of Trustees Act 1996, s 25(2), Sch 4 subject to savings contained in ss 3, 18(3), 25(5) of the 1996 Act. Sub-ss (1)(i)–(ix), (xi)–(xv), (xvii)–(xxvi), (xxviii)–(xxxi), sub-ss (1A)–(3): not reproduced.
References: See para 8.7.

209 Short title, commencement, extent

(1) This Act may be cited as the Law of Property Act 1925.

(2) . . .

(3) This Act extends to England and Wales only.

Amendments: Sub-s (2): repealed by the Statute Law Revision Act 1950.

Land Registration Act 2002

(2002 c 9)

ARRANGEMENT OF SECTIONS

PART 1
PRELIMINARY

PART 5
CHARGES

Relative priority

Powers as chargee

Realisation of security

Miscellaneous

PART 6
REGISTRATION: GENERAL

Registration as proprietor

Boundaries

Quality of title

Alteration of register

Information etc

Applications

An Act to make provision about land registration; and for connected purposes

[26 February 2002]

Parliamentary debates
House of Lords:
2nd Reading 3 July 2001: 626 HL Official Report (5th series) col 776.
Committee Stage 17 July 2001: 626 HL Official Report (5th series) col 1384; 19 July 2001: 626 HL Official Report (5th series) col 1600.
Report Stage 30 October 2001: 627 HL Official Report (5th series) col 1301.
3rd Reading 8 November 2001: 628 HL Official Report (5th series) col 307.
House of Commons:
2nd Reading in Committee 29 November 2001 HC Official Report, SC (Land Registration Bill).
Committee Stage 11, 13 December 2001: HC Official Report, SC D (Land Registration Bill).
Remaining Stages 11 February 2002: 380 HC Official Report (6th series) col 23.

PART 1
PRELIMINARY

1 Register of title

(1)   There is to continue to be a register of title kept by the registrar.

(2)   Rules may make provision about how the register is to be kept and may, in particular, make provision about—
  (a)   the information to be included in the register,
  (b)   the form in which information included in the register is to be kept, and
  (c)   the arrangement of that information.

Definitions: For "register" and "registrar" see s 132(1).
References: See paras 1.13, 2.1.

2 Scope of title registration

This Act makes provision about the registration of title to—
  (a)   unregistered legal estates which are interests of any of the following kinds—
    (i)   an estate in land,
    (ii)   a rentcharge,
    (iii) a franchise,
    (iv)   a profit à prendre in gross, and
    (v)   any other interest or charge which subsists for the benefit of, or is a charge on, an interest the title to which is registered; and
  (b)   interests capable of subsisting at law which are created by a disposition of an interest the title to which is registered.

Definitions: For "charge", "land", "legal estate" and "registered" see s 132(1).

PART 2
FIRST REGISTRATION OF TITLE

CHAPTER 1
FIRST REGISTRATION

Voluntary registration

3 When title may be registered

(1)   This section applies to any unregistered legal estate which is an interest of any of the following kinds—
      (a)   an estate in land,
      (b)   a rentcharge,
      (c)   a franchise, and
      (d)   a profit à prendre in gross.

(2)   Subject to the following provisions, a person may apply to the registrar to be registered as the proprietor of an unregistered legal estate to which this section applies if—
      (a)   the estate is vested in him, or
      (b)   he is entitled to require the estate to be vested in him.

(3)   Subject to subsection (4), an application under subsection (2) in respect of a leasehold estate may only be made if the estate was granted for a term of which more than seven years are unexpired.

(4)   In the case of an estate in land, subsection (3) does not apply if the right to possession under the lease is discontinuous.

(5)   A person may not make an application under subsection (2)(a) in respect of a leasehold estate vested in him as a mortgagee where there is a subsisting right of redemption.

(6)   A person may not make an application under subsection (2)(b) if his entitlement is as a person who has contracted to buy under a contract.

(7)   If a person holds in the same right both—
      (a)   a lease in possession, and
      (b)   a lease to take effect in possession on, or within a month of, the end of the lease in possession,
then, to the extent that they relate to the same land, they are to be treated for the purposes of this section as creating one continuous term.

Definitions: For "land", "legal estate", "registered" and "registrar" see s 132(1).
References: See paras 5.9, 6.9, 6.37, 6.51, 7.4, 12.2, 12.7.

Compulsory registration

4 When title must be registered

(1)   The requirement of registration applies on the occurrence of any of the following events—
      (a)   the transfer of a qualifying estate—

(i) for valuable or other consideration, by way of gift or in pursuance of an order of any court, or

(ii) by means of an assent (including a vesting assent);

(b) the transfer of an unregistered legal estate in land in circumstances where section 171A of the Housing Act 1985 (c 68) applies (disposal by landlord which leads to a person no longer being a secure tenant);

(c) the grant out of a qualifying estate of an estate in land—

(i) for a term of years absolute of more than seven years from the date of the grant, and

(ii) for valuable or other consideration, by way of gift or in pursuance of an order of any court;

(d) the grant out of a qualifying estate of an estate in land for a term of years absolute to take effect in possession after the end of the period of three months beginning with the date of the grant;

(e) the grant of a lease in pursuance of Part 5 of the Housing Act 1985 (the right to buy) out of an unregistered legal estate in land;

(f) the grant of a lease out of an unregistered legal estate in land in such circumstances as are mentioned in paragraph (b);

(g) the creation of a protected first legal mortgage of a qualifying estate.

(2) For the purposes of subsection (1), a qualifying estate is an unregistered legal estate which is—

(a) a freehold estate in land, or

(b) a leasehold estate in land for a term which, at the time of the transfer, grant or creation, has more than seven years to run.

(3) In subsection (1)(a), the reference to transfer does not include transfer by operation of law.

(4) Subsection (1)(a) does not apply to—

(a) the assignment of a mortgage term, or

(b) the assignment or surrender of a lease to the owner of the immediate reversion where the term is to merge in that reversion.

(5) Subsection (1)(c) does not apply to the grant of an estate to a person as a mortgagee.

(6) For the purposes of subsection (1)(a) and (c), if the estate transferred or granted has a negative value, it is to be regarded as transferred or granted for valuable or other consideration.

(7) In subsection (1)(a) and (c), references to transfer or grant by way of gift include transfer or grant for the purpose of—

(a) constituting a trust under which the settlor does not retain the whole of the beneficial interest, or

(b) uniting the bare legal title and the beneficial interest in property held under a trust under which the settlor did not, on constitution, retain the whole of the beneficial interest.

(8) For the purposes of subsection (1)(g)—

(a) a legal mortgage is protected if it takes effect on its creation as a mortgage to be protected by the deposit of documents relating to the mortgaged estate, and

(b) a first legal mortgage is one which, on its creation, ranks in priority ahead of any other mortgages then affecting the mortgaged estate.

(9)   In this section—
"land" does not include mines and minerals held apart from the surface;
"vesting assent" has the same meaning as in the Settled Land Act 1925 (c 18).

Definitions: For "court" see s 132(3)(a); for "land", "legal estate", "legal mortgage", "mines and minerals", "term of years absolute" and "valuable consideration" see s 132(1) (and for "land" note also sub-s (9) above).
References: See paras 4.2, 5.2–5.7, 6.1, 6.3–6.8, 8.3–8.6.

---

5 Power to extend section 4

(1)   The Lord Chancellor may by order—
  (a)   amend section 4 so as to add to the events on the occurrence of which the requirement of registration applies such relevant event as he may specify in the order, and
  (b)   make such consequential amendments of any provision of, or having effect under, any Act as he thinks appropriate.

(2)   For the purposes of subsection (1)(a), a relevant event is an event relating to an unregistered legal estate which is an interest of any of the following kinds—
  (a)   an estate in land,
  (b)   a rentcharge,
  (c)   a franchise, and
  (d)   a profit à prendre in gross.

(3)   The power conferred by subsection (1) may not be exercised so as to require the title to an estate granted to a person as a mortgagee to be registered.

(4)   Before making an order under this section the Lord Chancellor must consult such persons as he considers appropriate.

Definitions: For "land", "legal estate", "registered" and "requirement of registration" see s 132(1).
References: See paras 5.8, 12.2.

---

6 Duty to apply for registration of title

(1)   If the requirement of registration applies, the responsible estate owner, or his successor in title, must, before the end of the period for registration, apply to the registrar to be registered as the proprietor of the registrable estate.

(2)   If the requirement of registration applies because of section 4(1)(g)—
  (a)   the registrable estate is the estate charged by the mortgage, and
  (b)   the responsible estate owner is the owner of that estate.

(3)   If the requirement of registration applies otherwise than because of section 4(1)(g)—
  (a)   the registrable estate is the estate which is transferred or granted, and
  (b)   the responsible estate owner is the transferee or grantee of that estate.

(4)   The period for registration is 2 months beginning with the date on which the relevant event occurs, or such longer period as the registrar may provide under subsection (5).

(5)   If on the application of any interested person the registrar is satisfied that there is good reason for doing so, he may by order provide that the period for registration ends on such later date as he may specify in the order.

(6) Rules may make provision enabling the mortgagee under any mortgage falling within section 4(1)(g) to require the estate charged by the mortgage to be registered whether or not the mortgagor consents.

Definitions: For "registered", "registrar" and "requirement of registration" see s 132(1).
References: See paras 4.9–4.12.

7 Effect of non-compliance with section 6

(1) If the requirement of registration is not complied with, the transfer, grant or creation becomes void as regards the transfer, grant or creation of a legal estate.

(2) On the application of subsection (1)—
  (a) in a case falling within section 4(1)(a) or (b), the title to the legal estate reverts to the transferor who holds it on a bare trust for the transferee, and
  (b) in a case falling within section 4(1)(c) to (g), the grant or creation has effect as a contract made for valuable consideration to grant or create the legal estate concerned.

(3) If an order under section 6(5) is made in a case where subsection (1) has already applied, that application of the subsection is to be treated as not having occurred.

(4) The possibility of reverter under subsection (1) is to be disregarded for the purposes of determining whether a fee simple is a fee simple absolute.

Definitions: For "legal estate", "requirement of registration" and "valuable consideration" see s 132(1).
References: See paras 4.10, 5.4, 5.5, 6.7, 6.54.

8 Liability for making good void transfers etc

If a legal estate is retransferred, regranted or recreated because of a failure to comply with the requirement of registration, the transferee, grantee or, as the case may be, the mortgagor—
  (a) is liable to the other party for all the proper costs of and incidental to the retransfer, regrant or recreation of the legal estate, and
  (b) is liable to indemnify the other party in respect of any other liability reasonably incurred by him because of the failure to comply with the requirement of registration.

Definitions: For "legal estate" and "requirement of registration" see s 132(1).
References: See paras 4.10, 5.5, 8.3.

Classes of title

9 Titles to freehold estates

(1) In the case of an application for registration under this Chapter of a freehold estate, the classes of title with which the applicant may be registered as proprietor are—
  (a) absolute title,
  (b) qualified title, and
  (c) possessory title;
and the following provisions deal with when each of the classes of title is available.

(2)   A person may be registered with absolute title if the registrar is of the opinion that the person's title to the estate is such as a willing buyer could properly be advised by a competent professional adviser to accept.

(3)   In applying subsection (2), the registrar may disregard the fact that a person's title appears to him to be open to objection if he is of the opinion that the defect will not cause the holding under the title to be disturbed.

(4)   A person may be registered with qualified title if the registrar is of the opinion that the person's title to the estate has been established only for a limited period or subject to certain reservations which cannot be disregarded under subsection (3).

(5)   A person may be registered with possessory title if the registrar is of the opinion—

> (a)   that the person is in actual possession of the land, or in receipt of the rents and profits of the land, by virtue of the estate, and
>
> (b)   that there is no other class of title with which he may be registered.

Definitions: For "land", "registered" and "registrar" see s 132(1).
References: See paras 5.11–5.13, 5.15, 6.40.

---

10 Titles to leasehold estates

(1)   In the case of an application for registration under this Chapter of a leasehold estate, the classes of title with which the applicant may be registered as proprietor are—

> (a)   absolute title,
> (b)   good leasehold title,
> (c)   qualified title, and
> (d)   possessory title;

and the following provisions deal with when each of the classes of title is available.

(2)   A person may be registered with absolute title if—

> (a)   the registrar is of the opinion that the person's title to the estate is such as a willing buyer could properly be advised by a competent professional adviser to accept, and
>
> (b)   the registrar approves the lessor's title to grant the lease.

(3)   A person may be registered with good leasehold title if the registrar is of the opinion that the person's title to the estate is such as a willing buyer could properly be advised by a competent professional adviser to accept.

(4)   In applying subsection (2) or (3), the registrar may disregard the fact that a person's title appears to him to be open to objection if he is of the opinion that the defect will not cause the holding under the title to be disturbed.

(5)   A person may be registered with qualified title if the registrar is of the opinion that the person's title to the estate, or the lessor's title to the reversion, has been established only for a limited period or subject to certain reservations which cannot be disregarded under subsection (4).

(6)   A person may be registered with possessory title if the registrar is of the opinion—

> (a)   that the person is in actual possession of the land, or in receipt of the rents and profits of the land, by virtue of the estate, and
>
> (b)   that there is no other class of title with which he may be registered.

Definitions: For "land", "registered" and "registrar" see s 132(1).
References: See paras 6.11–6.14, 6.18, 6.40.

Effect of first registration

11 Freehold estates

(1)   This section is concerned with the registration of a person under this Chapter as the proprietor of a freehold estate.

(2)   Registration with absolute title has the effect described in subsections (3) to (5).

(3)   The estate is vested in the proprietor together with all interests subsisting for the benefit of the estate.

(4)   The estate is vested in the proprietor subject only to the following interests affecting the estate at the time of registration—

(a)   interests which are the subject of an entry in the register in relation to the estate,

(b)   unregistered interests which fall within any of the paragraphs of Schedule 1, and

(c)   interests acquired under the Limitation Act 1980 (c 58) of which the proprietor has notice.

(5)   If the proprietor is not entitled to the estate for his own benefit, or not entitled solely for his own benefit, then, as between himself and the persons beneficially entitled to the estate, the estate is vested in him subject to such of their interests as he has notice of.

(6)   Registration with qualified title has the same effect as registration with absolute title, except that it does not affect the enforcement of any estate, right or interest which appears from the register to be excepted from the effect of registration.

(7)   Registration with possessory title has the same effect as registration with absolute title, except that it does not affect the enforcement of any estate, right or interest adverse to, or in derogation of, the proprietor's title subsisting at the time of registration or then capable of arising.

Definitions: For "register" see s 132(1).
References: See paras 5.11–5.13, 10.6–10.8, 10.51, 13.21, 13.32, 14.15.

12 Leasehold estates

(1)   This section is concerned with the registration of a person under this Chapter as the proprietor of a leasehold estate.

(2)   Registration with absolute title has the effect described in subsections (3) to (5).

(3)   The estate is vested in the proprietor together with all interests subsisting for the benefit of the estate.

(4)   The estate is vested subject only to the following interests affecting the estate at the time of registration—

(a) implied and express covenants, obligations and liabilities incident to the estate,

(b) interests which are the subject of an entry in the register in relation to the estate,

(c) unregistered interests which fall within any of the paragraphs of Schedule 1, and

(d) interests acquired under the Limitation Act 1980 (c 58) of which the proprietor has notice.

(5)   If the proprietor is not entitled to the estate for his own benefit, or not entitled solely for his own benefit, then, as between himself and the persons beneficially entitled to the estate, the estate is vested in him subject to such of their interests as he has notice of.

(6)   Registration with good leasehold title has the same effect as registration with absolute title, except that it does not affect the enforcement of any estate, right or interest affecting, or in derogation of, the title of the lessor to grant the lease.

(7)   Registration with qualified title has the same effect as registration with absolute title except that it does not affect the enforcement of any estate, right or interest which appears from the register to be excepted from the effect of registration.

(8)   Registration with possessory title has the same effect as registration with absolute title, except that it does not affect the enforcement of any estate, right or interest adverse to, or in derogation of, the proprietor's title subsisting at the time of registration or then capable of arising.

Definitions: For "register" see s 132(1).
References: See paras 6.11–6.14, 6.40, 10.6–10.8, 10.51, 14.15.

Dependent estates

13 Appurtenant rights and charges

Rules may—

(a) make provision for the registration of the proprietor of a registered estate as the proprietor of an unregistered legal estate which subsists for the benefit of the registered estate;

(b) make provision for the registration of a person as the proprietor of an unregistered legal estate which is a charge on a registered estate.

Definitions: For "charge", "legal estate" and "registered estate" see s 132(1).
References: See paras 6.15, 8.6.

Supplementary

14 Rules about first registration

Rules may—

(a) make provision about the making of applications for registration under this Chapter;

(b) make provision about the functions of the registrar following the making of such an application, including provision about—

(i)   the examination of title, and

(ii)   the entries to be made in the register where such an application is approved;

(c)   make provision about the effect of any entry made in the register in pursuance of such an application.

Definitions: For "register" and "registrar" see s 132(1).

CHAPTER 2
CAUTIONS AGAINST FIRST REGISTRATION

15 Right to lodge

(1)   Subject to subsection (3), a person may lodge a caution against the registration of title to an unregistered legal estate if he claims to be—

(a)   the owner of a qualifying estate, or

(b)   entitled to an interest affecting a qualifying estate.

(2)   For the purposes of subsection (1), a qualifying estate is a legal estate which—

(a)   relates to land to which the caution relates, and

(b)   is an interest of any of the following kinds—

(i)   an estate in land,

(ii)   a rentcharge,

(iii)   a franchise, and

(iv)   a profit à prendre in gross.

(3)   No caution may be lodged under subsection (1)—

(a)   in the case of paragraph (a), by virtue of ownership of—

(i)   a freehold estate in land, or

(ii)   a leasehold estate in land granted for a term of which more than seven years are unexpired;

(b)   in the case of paragraph (b), by virtue of entitlement to such a leasehold estate as is mentioned in paragraph (a)(ii) of this subsection.

(4)   The right under subsection (1) is exercisable by application to the registrar.

Definitions: For "land", "legal estate" and "registrar" see s 132(1); for "an interest affecting an estate or charge" see s 132(3)(b).
Transitional provisions: See s 134, Sch 12, paras 14, 15.
References: See paras 4.3–4.5, 12.2, 12.3.

16 Effect

(1)   Where an application for registration under this Part relates to a legal estate which is the subject of a caution against first registration, the registrar must give the cautioner notice of the application and of his right to object to it.

(2)   The registrar may not determine an application to which subsection (1) applies before the end of such period as rules may provide, unless the cautioner has exercised his right to object to the application or given the registrar notice that he does not intend to do so.

(3)   Except as provided by this section, a caution against first registration has no effect and, in particular, has no effect on the validity or priority of any interest of the cautioner in the legal estate to which the caution relates.

(4)   For the purposes of subsection (1), notice given by a person acting on behalf of an applicant for registration under this Part is to be treated as given by the registrar if—

(a)   the person is of a description provided by rules, and

(b)   notice is given in such circumstances as rules may provide.

Definitions: For "caution against first registration" see s 132(1); for "the cautioner" see s 22; for "legal estate" and "registrar" see s 132(1); for "right to object to an application" see s 132(3)(c).
References: See paras 2.25, 4.8.

17 Withdrawal

The cautioner may withdraw a caution against first registration by application to the registrar.

Definitions: For "caution against first registration" see s 132(1); for "the cautioner" see s 22; for "registrar" see s 132(1).
References: See para 4.7.

18 Cancellation

(1)   A person may apply to the registrar for cancellation of a caution against first registration if he is—

(a)   the owner of the legal estate to which the caution relates, or

(b)   a person of such other description as rules may provide.

(2)   Subject to rules, no application under subsection (1)(a) may be made by a person who—

(a)   consented in such manner as rules may provide to the lodging of the caution, or

(b)   derives title to the legal estate by operation of law from a person who did so.

(3)   Where an application is made under subsection (1), the registrar must give the cautioner notice of the application and of the effect of subsection (4).

(4)   If the cautioner does not exercise his right to object to the application before the end of such period as rules may provide, the registrar must cancel the caution.

Definitions: For "caution against first registration" see s 132(1); for "the cautioner" see s 22; for "legal estate" and "registrar" see s 132(1); for "right to object to an application" see s 132(3)(c).
References: See para 4.7.

19 Cautions register

(1)   The registrar must keep a register of cautions against first registration.

(2)   Rules may make provision about how the cautions register is to be kept and may, in particular, make provision about—

(a)   the information to be included in the register,

(b)   the form in which information included in the register is to be kept, and

(c)   the arrangement of that information.

Definitions: For "caution against first registration" and "registrar" see s 132(1).
References: See paras 4.6, 4.7.

20 Alteration of register by court

(1)   The court may make an order for alteration of the cautions register for the purpose of—
   (a)   correcting a mistake, or
   (b)   bringing the register up to date.

(2)   An order under subsection (1) has effect when served on the registrar to impose a duty on him to give effect to it.

(3)   Rules may make provision about—
   (a)   the circumstances in which there is a duty to exercise the power under subsection (1),
   (b)   the form of an order under that subsection, and
   (c)   service of such an order.

Definitions: For "cautions register" see s 132(1); for "court" see s 132(3)(a); for "registrar" see s 132(1).
References: See paras 4.7, 15.74.

21 Alteration of register by registrar

(1)   The registrar may alter the cautions register for the purpose of—
   (a)   correcting a mistake, or
   (b)   bringing the register up to date.

(2)   Rules may make provision about—
   (a)   the circumstances in which there is a duty to exercise the power under subsection (1),
   (b)   how the cautions register is to be altered in exercise of that power,
   (c)   applications for the exercise of that power, and
   (d)   procedure in relation to the exercise of that power, whether on application or otherwise.

(3)   Where an alteration is made under this section, the registrar may pay such amount as he thinks fit in respect of any costs reasonably incurred by a person in connection with the alteration.

Definitions: For "cautions register" and "registrar" see s 132(1).
References: See para 4.7.

22 Supplementary

In this Chapter, "the cautioner", in relation to a caution against first registration, means the person who lodged the caution, or such other person as rules may provide.

Definitions: For "caution against first registration" see s 132(1).
References: See paras 4.7, 4.8.

PART 3
DISPOSITIONS OF REGISTERED LAND

Powers of disposition

23 Owner's powers

(1) Owner's powers in relation to a registered estate consist of—
    (a) power to make a disposition of any kind permitted by the general law in relation to an interest of that description, other than a mortgage by demise or sub-demise, and
    (b) power to charge the estate at law with the payment of money.

(2) Owner's powers in relation to a registered charge consist of—
    (a) power to make a disposition of any kind permitted by the general law in relation to an interest of that description, other than a legal sub-mortgage, and
    (b) power to charge at law with the payment of money indebtedness secured by the registered charge.

(3) In subsection (2)(a), "legal sub-mortgage" means—
    (a) a transfer by way of mortgage,
    (b) a sub-mortgage by sub-demise, and
    (c) a charge by way of legal mortgage.

Definitions: For "charge", "legal mortgage", "registered charge" and "registered estate" see s 132(1).
References: See paras 5.16, 5.29, 5.33, 6.19, 8.7, 8.12, 8.34, 9.31.

24 Right to exercise owner's powers

A person is entitled to exercise owner's powers in relation to a registered estate or charge if he is—
    (a) the registered proprietor, or
    (b) entitled to be registered as the proprietor.

Definitions: For "registered", "registered charge" and "registered estate" see s 132(1).
References: See paras 5.16, 5.24, 5.30, 5.33, 6.19.

25 Mode of exercise

(1) A registrable disposition of a registered estate or charge only has effect if it complies with such requirements as to form and content as rules may provide.

(2) Rules may apply subsection (1) to any other kind of disposition which depends for its effect on registration.

Definitions: For "registered charge", "registered estate" and "registrable disposition" see s 132(1).
References: See paras 2.37, 5.16, 6.19, 8.9, 9.10, 9.31.

26 Protection of disponees

(1) Subject to subsection (2), a person's right to exercise owner's powers in relation to a registered estate or charge is to be taken to be free from any limitation affecting the validity of a disposition.

(2) Subsection (1) does not apply to a limitation—
    (a) reflected by an entry in the register, or
    (b) imposed by, or under, this Act.

(3) This section has effect only for the purpose of preventing the title of a disponee being questioned (and so does not affect the lawfulness of a disposition).

Definitions: For "register", "registered charge" and "registered estate" see s 132(1).
References: See paras 5.26, 6.19, 6.45, 7.41, 7.43, 10.6.

Registrable dispositions

27 Dispositions required to be registered

(1) If a disposition of a registered estate or registered charge is required to be completed by registration, it does not operate at law until the relevant registration requirements are met.

(2) In the case of a registered estate, the following are the dispositions which are required to be completed by registration—
    (a) a transfer,
    (b) where the registered estate is an estate in land, the grant of a term of years absolute—
        (i) for a term of more than seven years from the date of the grant,
        (ii) to take effect in possession after the end of the period of three months beginning with the date of the grant,
        (iii) under which the right to possession is discontinuous,
        (iv) in pursuance of Part 5 of the Housing Act 1985 (c 68) (the right to buy), or
        (v) in circumstances where section 171A of that Act applies (disposal by landlord which leads to a person no longer being a secure tenant),
    (c) where the registered estate is a franchise or manor, the grant of a lease,
    (d) the express grant or reservation of an interest of a kind falling within section 1(2)(a) of the Law of Property Act 1925 (c 20), other than one which is capable of being registered under the Commons Registration Act 1965 (c 64),
    (e) the express grant or reservation of an interest of a kind falling within section 1(2)(b) or (e) of the Law of Property Act 1925, and
    (f) the grant of a legal charge.

(3) In the case of a registered charge, the following are the dispositions which are required to be completed by registration—
    (a) a transfer, and
    (b) the grant of a sub-charge.

(4) Schedule 2 to this Act (which deals with the relevant registration requirements) has effect.

(5) This section applies to dispositions by operation of law as it applies to other dispositions, but with the exception of the following—
    (a) a transfer on the death or bankruptcy of an individual proprietor,
    (b) a transfer on the dissolution of a corporate proprietor, and
    (c) the creation of a legal charge which is a local land charge.

(6)   Rules may make provision about applications to the registrar for the purpose of meeting registration requirements under this section.

(7)   In subsection (2)(d), the reference to express grant does not include grant as a result of the operation of section 62 of the Law of Property Act 1925 (c 20).

Definitions: For "land", "registered charge", "registered estate", "registrar", "sub-charge" and "term of years absolute" see s 132(1).
References: See paras 4.11, 5.16,–5.18, 5.22, 5.29, 5.32, 5.33, 6.19–6.21, 6.43, 8.7, 9.11–9.15, 12.4, 12.9, 12.13.

Effect of dispositions on priority

28 Basic rule

(1)   Except as provided by sections 29 and 30, the priority of an interest affecting a registered estate or charge is not affected by a disposition of the estate or charge.

(2)   It makes no difference for the purposes of this section whether the interest or disposition is registered.

Definitions: For "registered", "registered charge" and "registered estate" see s 132(1); for "an interest affecting an estate" see s 132(3)(b).
References: See paras 5.21–5.23, 6.34, 6.35, 7.17, 7.18, 7.64.

29 Effect of registered dispositions: estates

(1)   If a registrable disposition of a registered estate is made for valuable consideration, completion of the disposition by registration has the effect of postponing to the interest under the disposition any interest affecting the estate immediately before the disposition whose priority is not protected at the time of registration.

(2)   For the purposes of subsection (1), the priority of an interest is protected—
    (a)   in any case, if the interest—
        (i)   is a registered charge or the subject of a notice in the register,
        (ii)   falls within any of the paragraphs of Schedule 3, or
        (iii)   appears from the register to be excepted from the effect of registration, and
    (b)   in the case of a disposition of a leasehold estate, if the burden of the interest is incident to the estate.

(3)   Subsection (2)(a)(ii) does not apply to an interest which has been the subject of a notice in the register at any time since the coming into force of this section.

(4)   Where the grant of a leasehold estate in land out of a registered estate does not involve a registrable disposition, this section has effect as if—
    (a)   the grant involved such a disposition, and
    (b)   the disposition were registered at the time of the grant.

Definitions: For "land", "register", "registered", "registered charge", "registered estate", "registrable disposition" and "valuable consideration" see s 132(1); for "an interest affecting an estate" see s 132(3)(b).
References: See paras 5.21, 6.34–6.38, 7.17, 7.18, 10.6, 10.51.

30 Effect of registered dispositions: charges

(1)   If a registrable disposition of a registered charge is made for valuable consideration, completion of the disposition by registration has the effect of postponing to the interest under the disposition any interest affecting the charge immediately before the disposition whose priority is not protected at the time of registration.

(2)   For the purposes of subsection (1), the priority of an interest is protected—
    (a)   in any case, if the interest—
        (i)   is a registered charge or the subject of a notice in the register,
        (ii)   falls within any of the paragraphs of Schedule 3, or
        (iii)   appears from the register to be excepted from the effect of registration, and
    (b)   in the case of a disposition of a charge which relates to a leasehold estate, if the burden of the interest is incident to the estate.

(3)   Subsection (2)(a)(ii) does not apply to an interest which has been the subject of a notice in the register at any time since the coming into force of this section.

Definitions: For "register", "registered charge", "registrable disposition" and "valuable consideration" see s 132(1); for "an interest affecting an estate or charge" see s 132(3)(b).
References: See paras 7.17, 7.18, 8.33, 8.34, 10.6, 10.51.

31 Inland Revenue charges

The effect of a disposition of a registered estate or charge on a charge under section 237 of the Inheritance Tax Act 1984 (c 51) (charge for unpaid tax) is to be determined, not in accordance with sections 28 to 30 above, but in accordance with sections 237(6) and 238 of that Act (under which a purchaser in good faith for money or money's worth takes free from the charge in the absence of registration).

Definitions: For "charge", "registered charge" and "registered estate" see s 132(1).
References: See para 7.19.

PART 4
NOTICES AND RESTRICTIONS

Notices

32 Nature and effect

(1)   A notice is an entry in the register in respect of the burden of an interest affecting a registered estate or charge.

(2)   The entry of a notice is to be made in relation to the registered estate or charge affected by the interest concerned.

(3)   The fact that an interest is the subject of a notice does not necessarily mean that the interest is valid, but does mean that the priority of the interest, if valid, is protected for the purposes of sections 29 and 30.

Definitions: For "register", "registered charge" and "registered estate" see s 132(1); for "an interest affecting an estate or charge" see s 132(3)(b).
References: See paras 6.22, 7.20.

33 Excluded interests

No notice may be entered in the register in respect of any of the following—
- (a) an interest under—
  - (i) a trust of land, or
  - (ii) a settlement under the Settled Land Act 1925 (c 18),
- (b) a leasehold estate in land which—
  - (i) is granted for a term of years of three years or less from the date of the grant, and
  - (ii) is not required to be registered,
- (c) a restrictive covenant made between a lessor and lessee, so far as relating to the demised premises,
- (d) an interest which is capable of being registered under the Commons Registration Act 1965 (c 64), and
- (e) an interest in any coal or coal mine, the rights attached to any such interest and the rights of any person under section 38, 49 or 51 of the Coal Industry Act 1994 (c 21).

Definitions: For "register" and "registered" see s 132(1).
References: See paras 4.14, 5.19, 6.22, 6.37, 6.41, 6.42, 7.23, 9.30, 10.4, Appendix 1.

34 Entry on application

(1) A person who claims to be entitled to the benefit of an interest affecting a registered estate or charge may, if the interest is not excluded by section 33, apply to the registrar for the entry in the register of a notice in respect of the interest.

(2) Subject to rules, an application under this section may be for—
- (a) an agreed notice, or
- (b) a unilateral notice.

(3) The registrar may only approve an application for an agreed notice if—
- (a) the applicant is the relevant registered proprietor, or a person entitled to be registered as such proprietor,
- (b) the relevant registered proprietor, or a person entitled to be registered as such proprietor, consents to the entry of the notice, or
- (c) the registrar is satisfied as to the validity of the applicant's claim.

(4) In subsection (3), references to the relevant registered proprietor are to the proprietor of the registered estate or charge affected by the interest to which the application relates.

Definitions: For "register", "registered", "registered charge", "registered estate" and "registrar" see s 132(1); for "an interest affecting an estate or charge" see s 132(3)(b).
References: See paras 7.24, 7.28, 7.29.

35 Unilateral notices

(1) If the registrar enters a notice in the register in pursuance of an application under section 34(2)(b) ("a unilateral notice"), he must give notice of the entry to—
- (a) the proprietor of the registered estate or charge to which it relates, and
- (b) such other persons as rules may provide.

(2)   A unilateral notice must—
    (a)   indicate that it is such a notice, and
    (b)   identify who is the beneficiary of the notice.

(3)   The person shown in the register as the beneficiary of a unilateral notice, or such other person as rules may provide, may apply to the registrar for the removal of the notice from the register.

Definitions: For "register", "registered charge", "registered estate" and "registrar" see s 132(1).
References: See paras 7.35, 7.36.

36 Cancellation of unilateral notices

(1)   A person may apply to the registrar for the cancellation of a unilateral notice if he is—
    (a)   the registered proprietor of the estate or charge to which the notice relates, or
    (b)   a person entitled to be registered as the proprietor of that estate or charge.

(2)   Where an application is made under subsection (1), the registrar must give the beneficiary of the notice notice of the application and of the effect of subsection (3).

(3)   If the beneficiary of the notice does not exercise his right to object to the application before the end of such period as rules may provide, the registrar must cancel the notice.

(4)   In this section—
    "beneficiary", in relation to a unilateral notice, means the person shown in the register as the beneficiary of the notice, or such other person as rules may provide;
    "unilateral notice" means a notice entered in the register in pursuance of an application under section 34(2)(b).

Definitions: For "register", "registered" and "registrar" see s 132(1); for "right to object to an application" see s 132(3)(c).
References: See paras 7.24, 7.36.

37 Unregistered interests

(1)   If it appears to the registrar that a registered estate is subject to an unregistered interest which—
    (a)   falls within any of the paragraphs of Schedule 1, and
    (b)   is not excluded by section 33,
he may enter a notice in the register in respect of the interest.

(2)   The registrar must give notice of an entry under this section to such persons as rules may provide.

Definitions: For "register", "registered estate" and "registrar" see s 132(1).
References: See paras 4.15, 7.24, 7.26.

38 Registrable dispositions

Where a person is entered in the register as the proprietor of an interest under a disposition falling within section 27(2)(b) to (e), the registrar must also enter a notice in the register in respect of that interest.

Definitions: For "register" and "registrar" see s 132(1).
References: See paras 5.32, 6.27, 7.24.

39 Supplementary

Rules may make provision about the form and content of notices in the register.

Definitions: For "register" see s 132(1).

Restrictions

40 Nature

(1)   A restriction is an entry in the register regulating the circumstances in which a disposition of a registered estate or charge may be the subject of an entry in the register.

(2)   A restriction may, in particular—
(a)   prohibit the making of an entry in respect of any disposition, or a disposition of a kind specified in the restriction;
(b)   prohibit the making of an entry—
(i)   indefinitely,
(ii)   for a period specified in the restriction, or
(iii)   until the occurrence of an event so specified.

(3)   Without prejudice to the generality of subsection (2)(b)(iii), the events which may be specified include—
(a)   the giving of notice,
(b)   the obtaining of consent, and
(c)   the making of an order by the court or registrar.

(4)   The entry of a restriction is to be made in relation to the registered estate or charge to which it relates.

Definitions: For "court" see s 132(3)(a); for "register", "registered charge", "registered estate" and "registrar" see s 132(1).
References: See paras 7.40, 7.41.

41 Effect

(1)   Where a restriction is entered in the register, no entry in respect of a disposition to which the restriction applies may be made in the register otherwise than in accordance with the terms of the restriction, subject to any order under subsection (2).

(2)   The registrar may by order—
(a)   disapply a restriction in relation to a disposition specified in the order or dispositions of a kind so specified, or

(b)   provide that a restriction has effect, in relation to a disposition specified in the order or dispositions of a kind so specified, with modifications so specified.

(3)   The power under subsection (2) is exercisable only on the application of a person who appears to the registrar to have a sufficient interest in the restriction.

Definitions: For "register" and "registrar" see s 132(1).
References: See paras 7.40, 7.57.

42 Power of registrar to enter

(1)   The registrar may enter a restriction in the register if it appears to him that it is necessary or desirable to do so for the purpose of—
(a)   preventing invalidity or unlawfulness in relation to dispositions of a registered estate or charge,
(b)   securing that interests which are capable of being overreached on a disposition of a registered estate or charge are overreached, or
(c)   protecting a right or claim in relation to a registered estate or charge.

(2)   No restriction may be entered under subsection (1)(c) for the purpose of protecting the priority of an interest which is, or could be, the subject of a notice.

(3)   The registrar must give notice of any entry made under this section to the proprietor of the registered estate or charge concerned, except where the entry is made in pursuance of an application under section 43.

(4)   For the purposes of subsection (1)(c), a person entitled to the benefit of a charging order relating to an interest under a trust shall be treated as having a right or claim in relation to the trust property.

Definitions: For "register", "registered charge", "registered estate" and "registrar" see s 132(1).
References: See paras 7.42, 7.47, 10.63, 15.9.

43 Applications

(1)   A person may apply to the registrar for the entry of a restriction under section 42(1) if—
(a)   he is the relevant registered proprietor, or a person entitled to be registered as such proprietor,
(b)   the relevant registered proprietor, or a person entitled to be registered as such proprietor, consents to the application, or
(c)   he otherwise has a sufficient interest in the making of the entry.

(2)   Rules may—
(a)   require the making of an application under subsection (1) in such circumstances, and by such person, as the rules may provide;
(b)   make provision about the form of consent for the purposes of subsection (1)(b);
(c)   provide for classes of person to be regarded as included in subsection (1)(c);
(d)   specify standard forms of restriction.

(3)   If an application under subsection (1) is made for the entry of a restriction which is not in a form specified under subsection (2)(d), the registrar may only approve the application if it appears to him—

    (a)   that the terms of the proposed restriction are reasonable, and

    (b)   that applying the proposed restriction would—

        (i)   be straightforward, and

        (ii)   not place an unreasonable burden on him.

(4)   In subsection (1), references to the relevant registered proprietor are to the proprietor of the registered estate or charge to which the application relates.

Definitions: For "registered charge", "registered estate" and "registrar" see s 132(1).
References: See paras 7.43, 7.46, 10.6.

44 Obligatory restrictions

(1)   If the registrar enters two or more persons in the register as the proprietor of a registered estate in land, he must also enter in the register such restrictions as rules may provide for the purpose of securing that interests which are capable of being overreached on a disposition of the estate are overreached.

(2)   Where under any enactment the registrar is required to enter a restriction without application, the form of the restriction shall be such as rules may provide.

Definitions: For "land", "register", "registered estate" and "registrar" see s 132(1).
References: See paras 4.15, 5.20, 7.48, 10.12.

45 Notifiable applications

(1)   Where an application under section 43(1) is notifiable, the registrar must give notice of the application, and of the right to object to it, to—

    (a)   the proprietor of the registered estate or charge to which it relates, and

    (b)   such other persons as rules may provide.

(2)   The registrar may not determine an application to which subsection (1) applies before the end of such period as rules may provide, unless the person, or each of the persons, notified under that subsection has exercised his right to object to the application or given the registrar notice that he does not intend to do so.

(3)   For the purposes of this section, an application under section 43(1) is notifiable unless it is—

    (a)   made by or with the consent of the proprietor of the registered estate or charge to which the application relates, or a person entitled to be registered as such proprietor,

    (b)   made in pursuance of rules under section 43(2)(a), or

    (c)   an application for the entry of a restriction reflecting a limitation under an order of the court or registrar, or an undertaking given in place of such an order.

Definitions: For "court" see s 132(3)(a); for "registered charge", "registered estate" and "registrar" see s 132(1); for "right to object to an application" see s 132(3)(c).
References: See paras 7.54, 10.6, 10.14.

46 Power of court to order entry

(1)   If it appears to the court that it is necessary or desirable to do so for the purpose of protecting a right or claim in relation to a registered estate or charge, it may make an order requiring the registrar to enter a restriction in the register.

(2)   No order under this section may be made for the purpose of protecting the priority of an interest which is, or could be, the subject of a notice.

(3)   The court may include in an order under this section a direction that an entry made in pursuance of the order is to have overriding priority.

(4)   If an order under this section includes a direction under subsection (3), the registrar must make such entry in the register as rules may provide.

(5)   The court may make the exercise of its power under subsection (3) subject to such terms and conditions as it thinks fit.

Definitions: For "court" see s 132(3)(a); for "register", "registered charge", "registered estate" and "registrar" see s 132(1).
References: See paras 7.55, 7.56, 15.74.

47 Withdrawal

A person may apply to the registrar for the withdrawal of a restriction if—
> (a)   the restriction was entered in such circumstances as rules may provide, and
> (b)   he is of such a description as rules may provide.

Definitions: For "registrar" see s 132(1).
References: See para 7.61.

PART 5
CHARGES

Relative priority

48 Registered charges

(1)   Registered charges on the same registered estate, or on the same registered charge, are to be taken to rank as between themselves in the order shown in the register.

(2)   Rules may make provision about—
> (a)   how the priority of registered charges as between themselves is to be shown in the register, and
> (b)   applications for registration of the priority of registered charges as between themselves.

Definitions: For "register", "registered charge" and "registered estate" see s 132(1).
References: See para 8.14.

49 Tacking and further advances

(1)   The proprietor of a registered charge may make a further advance on the security of the charge ranking in priority to a subsequent charge if he has not received from the subsequent chargee notice of the creation of the subsequent charge.

(2)   Notice given for the purposes of subsection (1) shall be treated as received at the time when, in accordance with rules, it ought to have been received.

(3)   The proprietor of a registered charge may also make a further advance on the security of the charge ranking in priority to a subsequent charge if—
    (a)   the advance is made in pursuance of an obligation, and
    (b)   at the time of the creation of the subsequent charge the obligation was entered in the register in accordance with rules.

(4)   The proprietor of a registered charge may also make a further advance on the security of the charge ranking in priority to a subsequent charge if—
    (a)   the parties to the prior charge have agreed a maximum amount for which the charge is security, and
    (b)   at the time of the creation of the subsequent charge the agreement was entered in the register in accordance with rules.

(5)   Rules may—
    (a)   disapply subsection (4) in relation to charges of a description specified in the rules, or
    (b)   provide for the application of that subsection to be subject, in the case of charges of a description so specified, to compliance with such conditions as may be so specified.

(6)   Except as provided by this section, tacking in relation to a charge over registered land is only possible with the agreement of the subsequent chargee.

Definitions: For "charge", "register", "registered charge" and "registered land" see s 132(1).
References: See paras 8.16, 8.20.

50 Overriding statutory charges: duty of notification

If the registrar enters a person in the register as the proprietor of a charge which—
    (a)   is created by or under an enactment, and
    (b)   has effect to postpone a charge which at the time of registration of the statutory charge is—
        (i)   entered in the register, or
        (ii)   the basis for an entry in the register,

he must in accordance with rules give notice of the creation of the statutory charge to such person as rules may provide.

Definitions: For "charge", "register" and "registrar" see s 132(1).
References: See paras 8.21, 14.32.

Powers as chargee

51 Effect of completion by registration

On completion of the relevant registration requirements, a charge created by means of a registrable disposition of a registered estate has effect, if it would not otherwise do so, as a charge by deed by way of legal mortgage.

Definitions: For "charge", "legal mortgage", "registered estate" and "registrable disposition" see s 132(1).
References: See paras 8.7, 8.22.

52 Protection of disponees

(1)   Subject to any entry in the register to the contrary, the proprietor of a registered charge is to be taken to have, in relation to the property subject to the charge, the powers of disposition conferred by law on the owner of a legal mortgage.

(2)   Subsection (1) has effect only for the purpose of preventing the title of a disponee being questioned (and so does not affect the lawfulness of a disposition).

Definitions: For "legal mortgage", "register" and "registered charge" see s 132(1).
References: See para 8.22.

53 Powers as sub-chargee

The registered proprietor of a sub-charge has, in relation to the property subject to the principal charge or any intermediate charge, the same powers as the sub-chargor.

Definitions: For "charge", "registered" and "sub-charge" see s 132(1).
References: See para 8.36.

Realisation of security

54 Proceeds of sale: chargee's duty

For the purposes of section 105 of the Law of Property Act 1925 (c 20) (mortgagee's duties in relation to application of proceeds of sale), in its application to the proceeds of sale of registered land, a person shall be taken to have notice of anything in the register immediately before the disposition on sale.

Definitions: For "register" and "registered land" see s 132(1).
References: See para 8.24.

55 Local land charges

A charge over registered land which is a local land charge may only be realised if the title to the charge is registered.

Definitions: For "charge", "registered" and "registered land" see s 132(1).
References: See para 8.27.

Miscellaneous

56 Receipt in case of joint proprietors

Where a charge is registered in the name of two or more proprietors, a valid receipt for the money secured by the charge may be given by—
    (a)   the registered proprietors,

   (b)   the survivors or survivor of the registered proprietors, or
   (c)   the personal representative of the last survivor of the registered
         proprietors.

Definitions: For "charge" and "registered" see s 132(1).
References: See para 8.29.

57 Entry of right of consolidation

Rules may make provision about entry in the register of a right of consolidation in relation to a registered charge.

Definitions: For "register" and "registered charge" see s 132(1).
References: See para 8.25.

PART 6
REGISTRATION: GENERAL

Registration as proprietor

58 Conclusiveness

   (1)   If, on the entry of a person in the register as the proprietor of a legal estate, the legal estate would not otherwise be vested in him, it shall be deemed to be vested in him as a result of the registration.

   (2)   Subsection (1) does not apply where the entry is made in pursuance of a registrable disposition in relation to which some other registration requirement remains to be met.

Definitions: For "legal estate", "register" and "registrable disposition" see s 132(1).
References: See paras 2.2, 2.3, 5.24, 5.25, 5.33, 5.34, 12.4, 12.9, 12.13.

59 Dependent estates

   (1)   The entry of a person in the register as the proprietor of a legal estate which subsists for the benefit of a registered estate must be made in relation to the registered estate.

   (2)   The entry of a person in the register as the proprietor of a charge on a registered estate must be made in relation to that estate.

   (3)   The entry of a person in the register as the proprietor of a sub-charge on a registered charge must be made in relation to that charge.

Definitions: For "charge", "legal estate", "register", "registered charge", "registered estate" and "sub-charge" see s 132(1).
References: See paras 2.8, 8.7, 9.11.

Boundaries

60 Boundaries

(1)   The boundary of a registered estate as shown for the purposes of the register is a general boundary, unless shown as determined under this section.

(2)   A general boundary does not determine the exact line of the boundary.

(3)   Rules may make provision enabling or requiring the exact line of the boundary of a registered estate to be determined and may, in particular, make provision about—

    (a)   the circumstances in which the exact line of a boundary may or must be determined,

    (b)   how the exact line of a boundary may be determined,

    (c)   procedure in relation to applications for determination, and

    (d)   the recording of the fact of determination in the register or the index maintained under section 68.

(4)   Rules under this section must provide for applications for determination to be made to the registrar.

Definitions: For "register", "registered estate" and "registrar" see s 132(1).
References: See para 2.14.

61 Accretion and diluvion

(1)   The fact that a registered estate in land is shown in the register as having a particular boundary does not affect the operation of accretion or diluvion.

(2)   An agreement about the operation of accretion or diluvion in relation to a registered estate in land has effect only if registered in accordance with rules.

Definitions: For "land", "register", "registered" and "registered estate" see s 132(1).
References: See paras 2.18, 2.19.

Quality of title

62 Power to upgrade title

(1)   Where the title to a freehold estate is entered in the register as possessory or qualified, the registrar may enter it as absolute if he is satisfied as to the title to the estate.

(2)   Where the title to a leasehold estate is entered in the register as good leasehold, the registrar may enter it as absolute if he is satisfied as to the superior title.

(3)   Where the title to a leasehold estate is entered in the register as possessory or qualified the registrar may—

    (a)   enter it as good leasehold if he is satisfied as to the title to the estate, and

    (b)   enter it as absolute if he is satisfied both as to the title to the estate and as to the superior title.

(4)   Where the title to a freehold estate in land has been entered in the register as possessory for at least twelve years, the registrar may enter it as absolute if he is satisfied that the proprietor is in possession of the land.

(5)   Where the title to a leasehold estate in land has been entered in the register as possessory for at least twelve years, the registrar may enter it as good leasehold if he is satisfied that the proprietor is in possession of the land.

(6)   None of the powers under subsections (1) to (5) is exercisable if there is outstanding any claim adverse to the title of the registered proprietor which is made by virtue of an estate, right or interest whose enforceability is preserved by virtue of the existing entry about the class of title.

(7)   The only persons who may apply to the registrar for the exercise of any of the powers under subsections (1) to (5) are—
>   (a)   the proprietor of the estate to which the application relates,
>   (b)   a person entitled to be registered as the proprietor of that estate,
>   (c)   the proprietor of a registered charge affecting that estate, and
>   (d)   a person interested in a registered estate which derives from that estate.

(8)   In determining for the purposes of this section whether he is satisfied as to any title, the registrar is to apply the same standards as those which apply under section 9 or 10 to first registration of title.

(9)   The Lord Chancellor may by order amend subsection (4) or (5) by substituting for the number of years for the time being specified in that subsection such number of years as the order may provide.

Definitions: For "land", "proprietor in possession of land", "register", "registered", "registered charge", "registered estate" and "registrar" see s 132(1).
References: See paras 5.15, 6.18.

---

63 Effect of upgrading title

(1)   On the title to a registered freehold or leasehold estate being entered under section 62 as absolute, the proprietor ceases to hold the estate subject to any estate, right or interest whose enforceability was preserved by virtue of the previous entry about the class of title.

(2)   Subsection (1) also applies on the title to a registered leasehold estate being entered under section 62 as good leasehold, except that the entry does not affect or prejudice the enforcement of any estate, right or interest affecting, or in derogation of, the title of the lessor to grant the lease.

Definitions: For "registered" see s 132(1).
References: See paras 5.15, 6.18.

---

64 Use of register to record defects in title

(1)   If it appears to the registrar that a right to determine a registered estate in land is exercisable, he may enter the fact in the register.

(2)   Rules may make provision about entries under subsection (1) and may, in particular, make provision about—
>   (a)   the circumstances in which there is a duty to exercise the power conferred by that subsection,

(b)   how entries under that subsection are to be made, and
(c)   the removal of such entries.

Definitions: For "land", "register", "registered estate" and "registrar" see s 132(1).
References: See paras 5.15, 6.65, 15.9.

Alteration of register

65 Alteration of register

Schedule 4 (which makes provision about alteration of the register) has effect.

Information etc

66 Inspection of the registers etc

(1)   Any person may inspect and make copies of, or of any part of—
    (a)   the register of title,
    (b)   any document kept by the registrar which is referred to in the register of title,
    (c)   any other document kept by the registrar which relates to an application to him, or
    (d)   the register of cautions against first registration.

(2)   The right under subsection (1) is subject to rules which may, in particular—
    (a)   provide for exceptions to the right, and
    (b)   impose conditions on its exercise, including conditions requiring the payment of fees.

Definitions: For "registrar" see s 132(1).
References: See paras 2.66, 2.68, 3.55, 4.6, 5.31, 15.75.

---

67 Official copies of the registers etc

(1)   An official copy of, or of a part of—
    (a)   the register of title,
    (b)   any document which is referred to in the register of title and kept by the registrar,
    (c)   any other document kept by the registrar which relates to an application to him, or
    (d)   the register of cautions against first registration,
is admissible in evidence to the same extent as the original.

(2)   A person who relies on an official copy in which there is a mistake is not liable for loss suffered by another by reason of the mistake.

(3)   Rules may make provision for the issue of official copies and may, in particular, make provision about—
    (a)   the form of official copies,
    (b)   who may issue official copies,
    (c)   applications for official copies, and
    (d)   the conditions to be met by applicants for official copies, including conditions requiring the payment of fees.

Definitions: For "registrar" see s 132(1).
References: See paras 2.64, 2.71, 15.75.

68 Index

(1)   The registrar must keep an index for the purpose of enabling the following matters to be ascertained in relation to any parcel of land—
>   (a)   whether any registered estate relates to the land,
>   (b)   how any registered estate which relates to the land is identified for the purposes of the register,
>   (c)   whether the land is affected by any, and, if so what, caution against first registration, and
>   (d)   such other matters as rules may provide.

(2)   Rules may—
>   (a)   make provision about how the index is to be kept and may, in particular, make provision about—
>   (i)   the information to be included in the index,
>   (ii)   the form in which information included in the index is to be kept, and
>   (iii)   the arrangement of that information;
>   (b)   make provision about official searches of the index.

Definitions: For "caution against first registration", "land", "register", "registered estate" and "registrar" see s 132(1).
References: See paras 2.20, 4.6.

69 Historical information

(1)   The registrar may on application provide information about the history of a registered title.

(2)   Rules may make provision about applications for the exercise of the power conferred by subsection (1).

(3)   The registrar may—
>   (a)   arrange for the provision of information about the history of registered titles, and
>   (b)   authorise anyone who has the function of providing information under paragraph (a) to have access on such terms as the registrar thinks fit to any relevant information kept by him.

Definitions: For "registered" and "registrar" see s 132(1).
References: See para 15.75.

70 Official searches

Rules may make provision for official searches of the register, including searches of pending applications for first registration, and may, in particular, make provision about—
>   (a)   the form of applications for searches,
>   (b)   the manner in which such applications may be made,
>   (c)   the form of official search certificates, and
>   (d)   the manner in which such certificates may be issued.

Definitions: For "register" see s 132(1).

Applications

71 Duty to disclose unregistered interests

Where rules so provide—

(a) a person applying for registration under Chapter 1 of Part 2 must provide to the registrar such information as the rules may provide about any interest affecting the estate to which the application relates which—

    (i) falls within any of the paragraphs of Schedule 1, and

    (ii) is of a description specified by the rules;

(b) a person applying to register a registrable disposition of a registered estate must provide to the registrar such information as the rules may provide about any unregistered interest affecting the estate which—

    (i) falls within any of the paragraphs of Schedule 3, and

    (ii) is of description specified by the rules.

Definitions: For "registered estate", "registrable disposition" and "registrar" see s 132(1); for "an interest affecting an estate or charge" see s 132(3)(b).
References: See paras 4.14, 5.19, 5.21, 6.22, Appendix 1.

72 Priority protection

(1) For the purposes of this section, an application for an entry in the register is protected if—

(a) it is one to which a priority period relates, and

(b) it is made before the end of that period.

(2) Where an application for an entry in the register is protected, any entry made in the register during the priority period relating to the application is postponed to any entry made in pursuance of it.

(3) Subsection (2) does not apply if—

(a) the earlier entry was made in pursuance of a protected application, and

(b) the priority period relating to that application ranks ahead of the one relating to the application for the other entry.

(4) Subsection (2) does not apply if the earlier entry is one to which a direction under section 46(3) applies.

(5) The registrar may defer dealing with an application for an entry in the register if it appears to him that subsection (2) might apply to the entry were he to make it.

(6) Rules may—

(a) make provision for priority periods in connection with—

    (i) official searches of the register, including searches of pending applications for first registration, or

    (ii) the noting in the register of a contract for the making of a registrable disposition of a registered estate or charge;

(b) make provision for the keeping of records in relation to priority periods and the inspection of such records.

(7) Rules under subsection (6)(a) may, in particular, make provision about—

(a) the commencement and length of a priority period,

(b)   the applications for registration to which such a period relates,

(c)   the order in which competing priority periods rank, and

(d)   the application of subsections (2) and (3) in cases where more than one priority period relates to the same application.

Definitions: For "register", "registered charge", "registered estate", "registrable disposition" and "registrar" see s 132(1).
References: See paras 5.21, 5.30, 7.82, 7.83, 7.86.

73 Objections

(1)   Subject to subsections (2) and (3), anyone may object to an application to the registrar.

(2)   In the case of an application under section 18, only the person who lodged the caution to which the application relates, or such other person as rules may provide, may object.

(3)   In the case of an application under section 36, only the person shown in the register as the beneficiary of the notice to which the application relates, or such other person as rules may provide, may object.

(4)   The right to object under this section is subject to rules.

(5)   Where an objection is made under this section, the registrar—
(a)   must give notice of the objection to the applicant, and
(b)   may not determine the application until the objection has been disposed of.

(6)   Subsection (5) does not apply if the objection is one which the registrar is satisfied is groundless.

(7)   If it is not possible to dispose by agreement of an objection to which subsection (5) applies, the registrar must refer the matter to the adjudicator.

(8)   Rules may make provision about references under subsection (7).

Definitions: For "adjudicator", "register" and "registrar" see s 132(1); for "right to object to an application" see s 132(3)(c).
References: See paras 2.55, 2.84, 4.7, 4.8, 7.36–7.38, 13.6, 15.5, 15.7, 15.19, 15.27, 15.28.

74 Effective date of registration

An entry made in the register in pursuance of—
(a)   an application for registration of an unregistered legal estate, or
(b)   an application for registration in relation to a disposition required to be completed by registration,

has effect from the time of the making of the application.

Definitions: For "register" see s 132(1).
References: See paras 4.11, 5.20, 5.21, 13.31, 15.4.

Proceedings before the registrar

75 Production of documents

(1)   The registrar may require a person to produce a document for the purposes of proceedings before him.

(2)   The power under subsection (1) is subject to rules.

(3)   A requirement under subsection (1) shall be enforceable as an order of the court.

(4)   A person aggrieved by a requirement under subsection (1) may appeal to a county court, which may make any order which appears appropriate.

Definitions: For "court" and "registrar" see s 132(1).
References: See paras 7.80, 15.12, 15.19, 15.20.

76 Costs

(1)   The registrar may make orders about costs in relation to proceedings before him.

(2)   The power under subsection (1) is subject to rules which may, in particular, make provision about—
  (a)   who may be required to pay costs,
  (b)   whose costs a person may be required to pay,
  (c)   the kind of costs which a person may be required to pay, and
  (d)   the assessment of costs.

(3)   Without prejudice to the generality of subsection (2), rules under that subsection may include provision about—
  (a)   costs of the registrar, and
  (b)   liability for costs thrown away as the result of neglect or delay by a legal representative of a party to proceedings.

(4)   An order under subsection (1) shall be enforceable as an order of the court.

(5)   A person aggrieved by an order under subsection (1) may appeal to a county court, which may make any order which appears appropriate.

Definitions: For "court" see s 132(3)(a); for "registrar" see s 132(1).
References: See paras 15.15, 15.18–15.20, 15.79.

Miscellaneous

77 Duty to act reasonably

(1)   A person must not exercise any of the following rights without reasonable cause—
  (a)   the right to lodge a caution under section 15,
  (b)   the right to apply for the entry of a notice or restriction, and
  (c)   the right to object to an application to the registrar.

(2)   The duty under this section is owed to any person who suffers damage in consequence of its breach.

Definitions: For "registrar" see s 132(1); for "right to object to an application" see s 132(3)(c).
References: See paras 2.56, 15.77.

78 Notice of trust not to affect registrar

The registrar shall not be affected with notice of a trust.

Definitions: For "registrar" see s 132(1).
References: See para 10.4.

PART 7
SPECIAL CASES

The Crown

79 Voluntary registration of demesne land

(1)   Her Majesty may grant an estate in fee simple absolute in possession out of demesne land to Herself.

(2)   The grant of an estate under subsection (1) is to be regarded as not having been made unless an application under section 3 is made in respect of the estate before the end of the period for registration.

(3)   The period for registration is two months beginning with the date of the grant, or such longer period as the registrar may provide under subsection (4).

(4)   If on the application of Her Majesty the registrar is satisfied that there is a good reason for doing so, he may by order provide that the period for registration ends on such later date as he may specify in the order.

(5)   If an order under subsection (4) is made in a case where subsection (2) has already applied, that application of the subsection is to be treated as not having occurred.

Definitions: For "demesne land" and "registrar" see s 132(1).
References: See paras 5.9, 12.19, 12.21, 13.28.

80 Compulsory registration of grants out of demesne land

(1)   Section 4(1) shall apply as if the following were included among the events listed—

    (a)   the grant by Her Majesty out of demesne land of an estate in fee simple absolute in possession, otherwise than under section 79;

    (b)   the grant by Her Majesty out of demesne land of an estate in land—

        (i)   for a term of years absolute of more than seven years from the date of the grant, and

        (ii)   for valuable or other consideration, by way of gift or in pursuance of an order of any court.

(2)   In subsection (1)(b)(ii), the reference to grant by way of gift includes grant for the purpose of constituting a trust under which Her Majesty does not retain the whole of the beneficial interest.

(3)   Subsection (1) does not apply to the grant of an estate in mines and minerals held apart from the surface.

(4)   The Lord Chancellor may by order—

(a)   amend this section so as to add to the events in subsection (1) such events relating to demesne land as he may specify in the order, and

(b)   make such consequential amendments of any provision of, or having effect under, any Act as he thinks appropriate.

(5)   In its application by virtue of subsection (1), section 7 has effect with the substitution for subsection (2) of—

"(2)   On the application of subsection (1), the grant has effect as a contract made for valuable consideration to grant the legal estate concerned".

Definitions: For "court" see s 132(3)(a); for "demesne land", "land", "legal estate", "mines and minerals", "term of years absolute" and "valuable consideration" see s 132(1).
References: See paras 5.2, 6.5, 12.21.

81 Demesne land: cautions against first registration

(1)   Section 15 shall apply as if demesne land were held by Her Majesty for an unregistered estate in fee simple absolute in possession.

(2)   The provisions of this Act relating to cautions against first registration shall, in relation to cautions lodged by virtue of subsection (1), have effect subject to such modifications as rules may provide.

Definitions: For "caution against first registration" and "demesne land" see s 132(1).
References: See para 12.20.

82 Escheat etc

(1)   Rules may make provision about—

(a)   the determination of a registered freehold estate in land, and

(b)   the registration of an unregistered freehold legal estate in land in respect of land to which a former registered freehold estate in land related.

(2)   Rules under this section may, in particular—

(a)   make provision for determination to be dependent on the meeting of such registration requirements as the rules may specify;

(b)   make provision for entries relating to a freehold estate in land to continue in the register, notwithstanding determination, for such time as the rules may provide;

(c)   make provision for the making in the register in relation to a former freehold estate in land of such entries as the rules may provide;

(d)   make provision imposing requirements to be met in connection with an application for the registration of such an unregistered estate as is mentioned in subsection (1)(b).

Definitions: For "land", "legal estate", "register" and "registered" see s 132(1).

83 Crown and Duchy land: representation

(1) With respect to a Crown or Duchy interest, the appropriate authority—
   (a) may represent the owner of the interest for all purposes of this Act,
   (b) is entitled to receive such notice as that person is entitled to receive under this Act, and
   (c) may make such applications and do such other acts as that person is entitled to make or do under this Act.

(2) In this section—
   "the appropriate authority" means—
   (a) in relation to an interest belonging to Her Majesty in right of the Crown and forming part of the Crown Estate, the Crown Estate Commissioners;
   (b) in relation to any other interest belonging to Her Majesty in right of the Crown, the government department having the management of the interest or, if there is no such department, such person as Her Majesty may appoint in writing under the Royal Sign Manual;
   (c) in relation to an interest belonging to Her Majesty in right of the Duchy of Lancaster, the Chancellor of the Duchy;
   (d) in relation to an interest belonging to the Duchy of Cornwall, such person as the Duke of Cornwall, or the possessor for the time being of the Duchy of Cornwall, appoints;
   (e) in relation to an interest belonging to a government department, or held in trust for Her Majesty for the purposes of a government department, that department;
   "Crown interest" means an interest belonging to Her Majesty in right of the Crown, or belonging to a government department, or held in trust for Her Majesty for the purposes of a government department;
   "Duchy interest" means an interest belonging to Her Majesty in right of the Duchy of Lancaster, or belonging to the Duchy of Cornwall;
   "interest" means any estate, interest or charge in or over land and any right or claim in relation to land.

Definitions: For "charge" and "land" see s 132(1).

84 Disapplication of requirements relating to Duchy land

Nothing in any enactment relating to the Duchy of Lancaster or the Duchy of Cornwall shall have effect to impose any requirement with respect to formalities or enrolment in relation to a disposition by a registered proprietor.

Definitions: For "registered" see s 132(1).

85 Bona vacantia

Rules may make provision about how the passing of a registered estate or charge as bona vacantia is to be dealt with for the purposes of this Act.

Definitions: For "registered charge" and "registered estate" see s 132(1).

Pending actions etc

86 Bankruptcy

(1)   In this Act, references to an interest affecting an estate or charge do not include a petition in bankruptcy or bankruptcy order.

(2)   As soon as practicable after registration of a petition in bankruptcy as a pending action under the Land Charges Act 1972 (c 61), the registrar must enter in the register in relation to any registered estate or charge which appears to him to be affected a notice in respect of the pending action.

(3)   Unless cancelled by the registrar in such manner as rules may provide, a notice entered under subsection (2) continues in force until—
　　(a)   a restriction is entered in the register under subsection (4), or
　　(b)   the trustee in bankruptcy is registered as proprietor.

(4)   As soon as practicable after registration of a bankruptcy order under the Land Charges Act 1972, the registrar must, in relation to any registered estate or charge which appears to him to be affected by the order, enter in the register a restriction reflecting the effect of the Insolvency Act 1986 (c 45).

(5)   Where the proprietor of a registered estate or charge is adjudged bankrupt, the title of his trustee in bankruptcy is void as against a person to whom a registrable disposition of the estate or charge is made if—
　　(a)   the disposition is made for valuable consideration,
　　(b)   the person to whom the disposition is made acts in good faith, and
　　(c)   at the time of the disposition—
　　　　(i)   no notice or restriction is entered under this section in relation to the registered estate or charge, and
　　　　(ii)   the person to whom the disposition is made has no notice of the bankruptcy petition or the adjudication.

(6)   Subsection (5) only applies if the relevant registration requirements are met in relation to the disposition, but, when they are met, has effect as from the date of the disposition.

(7)   Nothing in this section requires a person to whom a registrable disposition is made to make any search under the Land Charges Act 1972.

Definitions: For "charge", "register", "registered", "registered charge", "registered estate", "registrable disposition", "registrar" and "valuable consideration" see s 132(1); for "an interest affecting an estate or charge" see s 132(3)(b).
References: See para 5.23.

---

87 Pending land actions, writs, orders and deeds of arrangement

(1)   Subject to the following provisions, references in this Act to an interest affecting an estate or charge include—
　　(a)   a pending land action within the meaning of the Land Charges Act 1972,
　　(b)   a writ or order of the kind mentioned in section 6(1)(a) of that Act (writ or order affecting land issued or made by any court for the purposes of enforcing a judgment or recognisance),
　　(c)   an order appointing a receiver or sequestrator, and
　　(d)   a deed of arrangement.

(2)   No notice may be entered in the register in respect of—
      (a)   an order appointing a receiver or sequestrator, or
      (b)   a deed of arrangement.

(3)   None of the matters mentioned in subsection (1) shall be capable of falling within paragraph 2 of Schedule 1 or 3.

(4)   In its application to any of the matters mentioned in subsection (1), this Act shall have effect subject to such modifications as rules may provide.

(5)   In this section, "deed of arrangement" has the same meaning as in the Deeds of Arrangement Act 1914 (c 47).

Definitions: For "charge" and "register" see s 132(1); for "court" see s 132(3)(a); for "an interest affecting an estate or charge" see s 132(3)(b).
References: See paras 6.46, 10.6, 15.75.

Miscellaneous

88 Incorporeal hereditaments

In its application to—
      (a)   rentcharges,
      (b)   franchises,
      (c)   profits à prendre in gross, or
      (d)   manors,
this Act shall have effect subject to such modification as rules may provide.

References: See para 12.5.

89 Settlements

(1)   Rules may make provision for the purposes of this Act in relation to the application to registered land of the enactments relating to settlements under the Settled Land Act 1925 (c 18).

(2)   Rules under this section may include provision modifying any of those enactments in its application to registered land.

(3)   In this section, "registered land" means an interest the title to which is, or is required to be, registered.

Definitions: For "registered" see s 132(1).
References: See paras 10.16, 10.33.

90 PPP leases relating to transport in London

(1)   No application for registration under section 3 may be made in respect of a leasehold estate in land under a PPP lease.

(2)   The requirement of registration does not apply on the grant or transfer of a leasehold estate in land under a PPP lease.

(3)   For the purposes of section 27, the following are not dispositions requiring to be completed by registration—

(a)   the grant of a term of years absolute under a PPP lease;

(b)   the express grant of an interest falling within section 1(2) of the Law of Property Act 1925 (c 20), where the interest is created for the benefit of a leasehold estate in land under a PPP lease.

(4)   No notice may be entered in the register in respect of an interest under a PPP lease.

(5)   Schedules 1 and 3 have effect as if they included a paragraph referring to a PPP lease.

(6)   In this section, "PPP lease" has the meaning given by section 218 of the Greater London Authority Act 1999 (c 29) (which makes provision about leases created for public-private partnerships relating to transport in London).

Definitions: For "land", "register" and "term of years absolute" see s 132(1).
References: See paras 12.26, 12.27.

PART 8
ELECTRONIC CONVEYANCING

91 Electronic dispositions: formalities

(1)   This section applies to a document in electronic form where—
    (a)   the document purports to effect a disposition which falls within subsection (2), and
    (b)   the conditions in subsection (3) are met.

(2)   A disposition falls within this subsection if it is—
    (a)   a disposition of a registered estate or charge,
    (b)   a disposition of an interest which is the subject of a notice in the register, or
    (c)   a disposition which triggers the requirement of registration,
which is of a kind specified by rules.

(3)   The conditions referred to above are that—
    (a)   the document makes provision for the time and date when it takes effect,
    (b)   the document has the electronic signature of each person by whom it purports to be authenticated,
    (c)   each electronic signature is certified, and
    (d)   such other conditions as rules may provide are met.

(4)   A document to which this section applies is to be regarded as—
    (a)   in writing, and
    (b)   signed by each individual, and sealed by each corporation, whose electronic signature it has.

(5)   A document to which this section applies is to be regarded for the purposes of any enactment as a deed.

(6)   If a document to which this section applies is authenticated by a person as agent, it is to be regarded for the purposes of any enactment as authenticated by him under the written authority of his principal.

(7)   If notice of an assignment made by means of a document to which this section applies is given in electronic form in accordance with rules, it is to be regarded for the purposes of any enactment as given in writing.

(8)   The right conferred by section 75 of the Law of Property Act 1925 (c 20) (purchaser's right to have the execution of a conveyance attested) does not apply to a document to which this section applies.

(9)   If subsection (4) of section 36A of the Companies Act 1985 (c 6) (execution of documents) applies to a document because of subsection (4) above, subsection (6) of that section (presumption of due execution) shall have effect in relation to the document with the substitution of "authenticated" for "signed".

[(9A) If subsection (3) of section 29C of the Industrial and Provident Societies Act 1965 (execution of documents) applies to a document because of subsection (4) above, subsection (5) of that section (presumption of due execution) shall have effect in relation to the document with the substitution of "authenticated" for "signed".]

(10) In this section, references to an electronic signature and to the certification of such a signature are to be read in accordance with section 7(2) and (3) of the Electronic Communications Act 2000 (c 7).

Definitions: For "register", "registered charge", "registered estate" and "requirement of registration" see s 132(1).
Amendments: Sub-s (9A) inserted by the Co-operatives and Community Benefit Societies Act 2003, s 5(8).
References: See paras 3.14–3.16, 3.25, 3.29.

92 Land registry network

(1)   The registrar may provide, or arrange for the provision of, an electronic communications network for use for such purposes as he thinks fit relating to registration or the carrying on of transactions which—
    (a)   involve registration, and
    (b)   are capable of being effected electronically.

(2)   Schedule 5 (which makes provision in connection with a network provided under subsection (1) and transactions carried on by means of such a network) has effect.

Definitions: For "registrar" see s 132(1).

93 Power to require simultaneous registration

(1)   This section applies to a disposition of—
    (a)   a registered estate or charge, or
    (b)   an interest which is the subject of a notice in the register,
where the disposition is of a description specified by rules.

(2)   A disposition to which this section applies, or a contract to make such a disposition, only has effect if it is made by means of a document in electronic form and if, when the document purports to take effect—
    (a)   it is electronically communicated to the registrar, and
    (b)   the relevant registration requirements are met.

(3)   For the purposes of subsection (2)(b), the relevant registration requirements are—

    (a)   in the case of a registrable disposition, the requirements under Schedule 2, and

    (b)   in the case of any other disposition, or a contract, such requirements as rules may provide.

(4)   Section 27(1) does not apply to a disposition to which this section applies.

(5)   Before making rules under this section the Lord Chancellor must consult such persons as he considers appropriate.

(6)   In this section, "disposition", in relation to a registered charge, includes postponement.

Definitions: For "register", "registered charge", "registered estate" "registrable disposition" and "registrar" see s 132(1) (and for "registrable disposition" note sub-s (6) above).
References: See paras 2.41, 3.56, 3.57.

94 Electronic settlement

The registrar may take such steps as he thinks fit for the purpose of securing the provision of a system of electronic settlement in relation to transactions involving registration.

Definitions: For "registrar" see s 132(1).

95 Supplementary

Rules may—

    (a)   make provision about the communication of documents in electronic form to the registrar;

    (b)   make provision about the electronic storage of documents communicated to the registrar in electronic form.

Definitions: For "registrar" see s 132(1).

PART 9
ADVERSE POSSESSION

96 Disapplication of periods of limitation

(1)   No period of limitation under section 15 of the Limitation Act 1980 (c 58) (time limits in relation to recovery of land) shall run against any person, other than a chargee, in relation to an estate in land or rentcharge the title to which is registered.

(2)   No period of limitation under section 16 of that Act (time limits in relation to redemption of land) shall run against any person in relation to such an estate in land or rentcharge.

(3)   Accordingly, section 17 of that Act (extinction of title on expiry of time limit) does not operate to extinguish the title of any person where, by virtue of this section, a period of limitation does not run against him.

Definitions: For "land" and "registered" see s 132(1).
References: See paras 13.7, 13.8.

97 Registration of adverse possessor

Schedule 6 (which makes provision about the registration of an adverse possessor of an estate in land or rentcharge) has effect.

References: See para 13.7.

98 Defences

(1)   A person has a defence to an action for possession of land if—
      (a)   on the day immediately preceding that on which the action was brought he was entitled to make an application under paragraph 1 of Schedule 6 to be registered as the proprietor of an estate in the land, and
      (b)   had he made such an application on that day, the condition in paragraph 5(4) of that Schedule would have been satisfied.

(2)   A judgment for possession of land ceases to be enforceable at the end of the period of two years beginning with the date of the judgment if the proceedings in which the judgment is given were commenced against a person who was at that time entitled to make an application under paragraph 1 of Schedule 6.

(3)   A person has a defence to an action for possession of land if on the day immediately preceding that on which the action was brought he was entitled to make an application under paragraph 6 of Schedule 6 to be registered as the proprietor of an estate in the land.

(4)   A judgment for possession of land ceases to be enforceable at the end of the period of two years beginning with the date of the judgment if, at the end of that period, the person against whom the judgment was given is entitled to make an application under paragraph 6 of Schedule 6 to be registered as the proprietor of an estate in the land.

(5)   Where in any proceedings a court determines that—
      (a)   a person is entitled to a defence under this section, or
      (b)   a judgment for possession has ceased to be enforceable against a person by virtue of subsection (4),
the court must order the registrar to register him as the proprietor of the estate in relation to which he is entitled to make an application under Schedule 6.

(6)   The defences under this section are additional to any other defences a person may have.

(7)   Rules may make provision to prohibit the recovery of rent due under a rentcharge from a person who has been in adverse possession of the rentcharge.

Definitions: For "court" see s 132(3)(a); for "land", "register", "registered" and "registrar" see s 132(1).
References: See paras 13.6, 13.32, 15.74.

PART 10
LAND REGISTRY

Administration

99 The land registry

(1)   There is to continue to be an office called Her Majesty's Land Registry which is to deal with the business of registration under this Act.

(2)   The land registry is to consist of—
   (a)   the Chief Land Registrar, who is its head, and
   (b)   the staff appointed by him;

and references in this Act to a member of the land registry are to be read accordingly.

(3)   The Lord Chancellor shall appoint a person to be the Chief Land Registrar.

(4)   Schedule 7 (which makes further provision about the land registry) has effect.

References: See para 2.1.

100 Conduct of business

(1)   Any function of the registrar may be carried out by any member of the land registry who is authorised for the purpose by the registrar.

(2)   The Lord Chancellor may by regulations make provision about the carrying out of functions during any vacancy in the office of registrar.

(3)   The Lord Chancellor may by order designate a particular office of the land registry as the proper office for the receipt of applications or a specified description of application.

(4)   The registrar may prepare and publish such forms and directions as he considers necessary or desirable for facilitating the conduct of the business of registration under this Act.

Definitions: For "member of the land registry" see s 99; for "registrar" see s 132(1).
References: See para 2.1, 2.49, 7.83, 7.87.

101 Annual report

(1)   The registrar must make an annual report on the business of the land registry to the Lord Chancellor.

(2)   The registrar must publish every report under this section and may do so in such manner as he thinks fit.

(3)   The Lord Chancellor must lay copies of every report under this section before Parliament.

Definitions: For "registrar" see s 132(1).

Fees and indemnities

102 Fee orders

The Lord Chancellor may with the advice and assistance of the body referred to in section 127(2) (the Rule Committee), and the consent of the Treasury, by order—
> (a) prescribe fees to be paid in respect of dealings with the land registry, except under section 69(3)(b) or 105;
> (b) make provision about the payment of prescribed fees.

103 Indemnities

Schedule 8 (which makes provision for the payment of indemnities by the registrar) has effect.

References: See para 8.21.

Miscellaneous

104 General information about land

The registrar may publish information about land in England and Wales if it appears to him to be information in which there is legitimate public interest.

Definitions: For "land" and "registrar" see s 132(1).

105 Consultancy and advisory services

(1) The registrar may provide, or arrange for the provision of, consultancy or advisory services about the registration of land in England and Wales or elsewhere.

(2) The terms on which services are provided under this section by the registrar, in particular terms as to payment, shall be such as he thinks fit.

Definitions: For "land" and "registrar" see s 132(1).

106 Incidental powers: companies

(1) If the registrar considers it expedient to do so in connection with his functions under section 69(3)(a), 92(1), 94 or 105(1) or paragraph 10 of Schedule 5, he may—
> (a) form, or participate in the formation of, a company, or
> (b) purchase, or invest in, a company.

(2) In this section—
> "company" means a company within the meaning of the Companies Act 1985 (c 6);
> "invest" means invest in any way (whether by acquiring assets, securities or rights or otherwise).

(3) This section is without prejudice to any powers of the registrar exercisable otherwise than by virtue of this section.

Definitions: For "registrar" see s 132(1).

PART 11
ADJUDICATION

107 The adjudicator

(1)   The Lord Chancellor shall appoint a person to be the Adjudicator to Her Majesty's Land Registry.

(2)   To be qualified for appointment under subsection (1), a person must have a 10 year general qualification (within the meaning of section 71 of the Courts and Legal Services Act 1990 (c 41)).

(3)   Schedule 9 (which makes further provision about the adjudicator) has effect.

108 Jurisdiction

(1)   The adjudicator has the following functions—
    (a)   determining matters referred to him under section 73(7), and
    (b)   determining appeals under paragraph 4 of Schedule 5.

(2)   Also, the adjudicator may, on application, make any order which the High Court could make for the rectification or setting aside of a document which—
    (a)   effects a qualifying disposition of a registered estate or charge,
    (b)   is a contract to make such a disposition, or
    (c)   effects a transfer of an interest which is the subject of a notice in the register.

(3)   For the purposes of subsection (2)(a), a qualifying disposition is—
    (a)   a registrable disposition, or
    (b)   a disposition which creates an interest which may be the subject of a notice in the register.

(4)   The general law about the effect of an order of the High Court for the rectification or setting aside of a document shall apply to an order under this section.

Definitions: For "adjudicator", "register", "registered charge", "registered estate" and "registrable disposition" see s 132(1).
References: See paras 13.6, 15.26, 15.30, 15.34.

109 Procedure

(1)   Hearings before the adjudicator shall be held in public, except where he is satisfied that exclusion of the public is just and reasonable.

(2)   Subject to that, rules may regulate the practice and procedure to be followed with respect to proceedings before the adjudicator and matters incidental to or consequential on such proceedings.

(3)   Rules under subsection (2) may, in particular, make provision about—
    (a)   when hearings are to be held,
    (b)   requiring persons to attend hearings to give evidence or to produce documents,
    (c)   the form in which any decision of the adjudicator is to be given,

(d) payment of costs of a party to proceedings by another party to the proceedings, and

(e) liability for costs thrown away as the result of neglect or delay by a legal representative of a party to proceedings.

Definitions: For "adjudicator" see s 132(1).
References: See para 7.37.

110 Functions in relation to disputes

(1) In proceedings on a reference under section 73(7), the adjudicator may, instead of deciding a matter himself, direct a party to the proceedings to commence proceedings within a specified time in the court for the purpose of obtaining the court's decision on the matter.

(2) Rules may make provision about the reference under subsection (1) of matters to the court and may, in particular, make provision about—

(a) adjournment of the proceedings before the adjudicator pending the outcome of the proceedings before the court, and

(b) the powers of the adjudicator in the event of failure to comply with a direction under subsection (1).

(3) Rules may make provision about the functions of the adjudicator in consequence of a decision on a reference under section 73(7) and may, in particular, make provision enabling the adjudicator to determine, or give directions about the determination of—

(a) the application to which the reference relates, or

(b) such other present or future application to the registrar as the rules may provide.

(4) If, in the case of a reference under section 73(7) relating to an application under paragraph 1 of Schedule 6, the adjudicator determines that it would be unconscionable because of an equity by estoppel for the registered proprietor to seek to dispossess the applicant, but that the circumstances are not such that the applicant ought to be registered as proprietor, the adjudicator—

(a) must determine how the equity due to the applicant is to be satisfied, and

(b) may for that purpose make any order that the High Court could make in the exercise of its equitable jurisdiction.

Definitions: For "adjudicator" see s 132(1); for "court" see s 132(3)(a); for "registered" and "registrar" see s 132(1).
References: See paras 15.40, 15.76.

111 Appeals

(1) Subject to subsection (2), a person aggrieved by a decision of the adjudicator may appeal to the High Court.

(2) In the case of a decision on an appeal under paragraph 4 of Schedule 5, only appeal on a point of law is possible.

(3) If on an appeal under this section relating to an application under paragraph 1 of Schedule 6 the court determines that it would be unconscionable because of an equity by estoppel for the registered proprietor to seek to dispossess

the applicant, but that the circumstances are not such that the applicant ought to be registered as proprietor, the court must determine how the equity due to the applicant is to be satisfied.

Definitions: For "adjudicator" see s 132(1); for "court" see s 132(3)(a); for "registered" see s 132(1).
References: See para 15.68

112 Enforcement of orders etc

A requirement of the adjudicator shall be enforceable as an order of the court.

Definitions: For "adjudicator" see s 132(1); for "court" see s 132(3)(a).

113 Fees

The Lord Chancellor may by order—
    (a)   prescribe fees to be paid in respect of proceedings before the adjudicator;
    (b)   make provision about the payment of prescribed fees.

Definitions: For "adjudicator" see s 132(1).

114 Supplementary

Power to make rules under this Part is exercisable by the Lord Chancellor.

PART 12
MISCELLANEOUS AND GENERAL

Miscellaneous

115 Rights of pre-emption

(1)   A right of pre-emption in relation to registered land has effect from the time of creation as an interest capable of binding successors in title (subject to the rules about the effect of dispositions on priority).

(2)   This section has effect in relation to rights of pre-emption created on or after the day on which this section comes into force.

Definitions: For "registered land" see s 132(1).
References: See paras 11.8–11.10.

116 Proprietary estoppel and mere equities

It is hereby declared for the avoidance of doubt that, in relation to registered land, each of the following—
    (a)   an equity by estoppel, and
    (b)   a mere equity,
has effect from the time the equity arises as an interest capable of binding successors in title (subject to the rules about the effect of dispositions on priority).

Definitions: For "registered land" see s 132(1).
References: See paras 11.14, 11.18.

117 Reduction in unregistered interests with automatic protection

(1)   Paragraphs 10 to 14 of Schedules 1 and 3 shall cease to have effect at the end of the period of ten years beginning with the day on which those Schedules come into force.

(2)   If made before the end of the period mentioned in subsection (1), no fee may be charged for—
    (a)   an application to lodge a caution against first registration by virtue of an interest falling within any of paragraphs 10 to 14 of Schedule 1, or
    (b)   an application for the entry in the register of a notice in respect of an interest falling within any of paragraphs 10 to 14 of Schedule 3.

Definitions: For "caution against first registration" and "register" see s 132(1).
References: See paras 7.14, 12.12, 12.15, 12.17.

118 Power to reduce qualifying term

(1)   The Lord Chancellor may by order substitute for the term specified in any of the following provisions—
    (a)   section 3(3),
    (b)   section 4(1)(c)(i) and (2)(b),
    (c)   section 15(3)(a)(ii),
    (d)   section 27(2)(b)(i),
    (e)   section 80(1)(b)(i),
    (f)   paragraph 1 of Schedule 1,
    (g)   paragraphs 4(1), 5(1) and 6(1) of Schedule 2, and
    (h)   paragraph 1 of Schedule 3,
such shorter term as he thinks fit.

(2)   An order under this section may contain such transitional provision as the Lord Chancellor thinks fit.

(3)   Before making an order under this section, the Lord Chancellor must consult such persons as he considers appropriate.

References: See paras 6.1, 6.8, 6.21, 6.22, 9.11.

119 Power to deregister manors

On the application of the proprietor of a registered manor, the registrar may remove the title to the manor from the register.

Definitions: For "register", "registered" and "registrar" see s 132(1).
References: See para 12.14.

120 Conclusiveness of filed copies etc

(1)   This section applies where—
    (a)   a disposition relates to land to which a registered estate relates, and

(b)   an entry in the register relating to the registered estate refers to a document kept by the registrar which is not an original.

(2)   As between the parties to the disposition, the document kept by the registrar is to be taken—

(a)   to be correct, and

(b)   to contain all the material parts of the original document.

(3)   No party to the disposition may require production of the original document.

(4)   No party to the disposition is to be affected by any provision of the original document which is not contained in the document kept by the registrar.

Definitions: For "land", "register", "registered estate" and "registrar" see s 132(1).
References: See paras 2.75, 6.28.

121 Forwarding of applications to registrar of companies

The Lord Chancellor may by rules make provision about the transmission by the registrar to the registrar of companies (within the meaning of the Companies Act 1985 (c 6)) of applications under—

(a)   Part 12 of that Act (registration of charges), or

(b)   Chapter 3 of Part 23 of that Act (corresponding provision for oversea companies).

Definitions: For "registrar" see s 132(1).

122 Repeal of Land Registry Act 1862

(1)   The Land Registry Act 1862 (c 53) shall cease to have effect.

(2)   The registrar shall have custody of records of title made under that Act.

(3)   The registrar may discharge his duty under subsection (2) by keeping the relevant information in electronic form.

(4)   The registrar may on application provide a copy of any information included in a record of title made under that Act.

(5)   Rules may make provision about applications for the exercise of the power conferred by subsection (4).

Definitions: For "registrar" see s 132(1).

Offences etc

123 Suppression of information

(1)   A person commits an offence if in the course of proceedings relating to registration under this Act he suppresses information with the intention of—

(a)   concealing a person's right or claim, or

(b)   substantiating a false claim.

(2)   A person guilty of an offence under this section is liable—
  (a)   on conviction on indictment, to imprisonment for a term not exceeding two years or to a fine;
  (b)   on summary conviction, to imprisonment for a term not exceeding six months or to a fine not exceeding the statutory maximum, or to both.

References: See paras 4.18, 15.19, 15.84, 15.85.

124   Improper alteration of the registers

(1)   A person commits an offence if he dishonestly induces another—
  (a)   to change the register of title or cautions register, or
  (b)   to authorise the making of such a change.

(2)   A person commits an offence if he intentionally or recklessly makes an unauthorised change in the register of title or cautions register.

(3)   A person guilty of an offence under this section is liable—
  (a)   on conviction on indictment, to imprisonment for a term not exceeding 2 years or to a fine;
  (b)   on summary conviction, to imprisonment for a term not exceeding six months or to a fine not exceeding the statutory maximum, or to both.

(4)   In this section, references to changing the register of title include changing a document referred to in it.

Definitions: For "cautions register" see s 132(1).
References: See para 15.84.

125   Privilege against self-incrimination

(1)   The privilege against self-incrimination, so far as relating to offences under this Act, shall not entitle a person to refuse to answer any question or produce any document or thing in any legal proceedings other than criminal proceedings.

(2)   No evidence obtained under subsection (1) shall be admissible in any criminal proceedings under this Act against the person from whom it was obtained or that person's spouse.

Land registration rules

126   Miscellaneous and general powers

Schedule 10 (which contains miscellaneous and general land registration rule-making powers) has effect.

127   Exercise of powers

(1)   Power to make land registration rules is exercisable by the Lord Chancellor with the advice and assistance of the Rule Committee.

(2)   The Rule Committee is a body consisting of—

  (a)   a judge of the Chancery Division of the High Court nominated by the Lord Chancellor,
  (b)   the registrar,
  (c)   a person nominated by the General Council of the Bar,
  (d)   a person nominated by the Council of the Law Society,
  (e)   a person nominated by the Council of Mortgage Lenders,
  (f)   a person nominated by the Council of Licensed Conveyancers,
  (g)   a person nominated by the Royal Institution of Chartered Surveyors,
  (h)   a person with experience in, and knowledge of, consumer affairs, and
  (i)   any person nominated under subsection (3).

(3)   The Lord Chancellor may nominate to be a member of the Rule Committee any person who appears to him to have qualifications or experience which would be of value to the committee in considering any matter with which it is concerned.

Definitions: For "land registration rules" and "registrar" see s 132(1).
References: See para 1.17.

Supplementary

128 Rules, regulations and orders

(1)   Any power of the Lord Chancellor to make rules, regulations or orders under this Act includes power to make different provision for different cases.

(2)   Any power of the Lord Chancellor to make rules, regulations or orders under this Act is exercisable by statutory instrument.

(3)   A statutory instrument containing—

  (a)   regulations under section 100(2), or
  (b)   an order under section 100(3), 102 or 113,

is to be laid before Parliament after being made.

(4)   A statutory instrument containing—

  (a)   land registration rules,
  (b)   rules under Part 11 or section 121,
  (c)   regulations under paragraph 5 of Schedule 9, or
  (d)   an order under section 5(1), 62(9), 80(4), 118(1) or 130,

is subject to annulment in pursuance of a resolution of either House of Parliament.

(5)   Rules under section 93 or paragraph 1, 2 or 3 of Schedule 5 shall not be made unless a draft of the rules has been laid before and approved by resolution of each House of Parliament.

Definitions: For "land registration rules" see s 132(1).

129 Crown application

This Act binds the Crown.

130 Application to internal waters

This Act applies to land covered by internal waters of the United Kingdom which are—

    (a)   within England or Wales, or

    (b)   adjacent to England or Wales and specified for the purposes of this section by order made by the Lord Chancellor.

References: See para 5.9, 12.19.

131 "Proprietor in possession"

(1)   For the purposes of this Act, land is in the possession of the proprietor of a registered estate in land if it is physically in his possession, or in that of a person who is entitled to be registered as the proprietor of the registered estate.

(2)   In the case of the following relationships, land which is (or is treated as being) in the possession of the second-mentioned person is to be treated for the purposes of subsection (1) as in the possession of the first-mentioned person—

    (a)   landlord and tenant;

    (b)   mortgagor and mortgagee;

    (c)   licensor and licensee;

    (d)   trustee and beneficiary.

(3)   In subsection (1), the reference to entitlement does not include entitlement under Schedule 6.

Definitions: For "land", "registered" and "registered estate" see s 132(1).
References: See paras 4.7, 14.18.

132 General interpretation

(1)   In this Act—

"adjudicator" means the Adjudicator to Her Majesty's Land Registry;

"caution against first registration" means a caution lodged under section 15;

"cautions register" means the register kept under section 19(1);

"charge" means any mortgage, charge or lien for securing money or money's worth;

"demesne land" means land belonging to Her Majesty in right of the Crown which is not held for an estate in fee simple absolute in possession;

"land" includes—

    (a)   buildings and other structures,

    (b)   land covered with water, and

    (c)   mines and minerals, whether or not held with the surface;

"land registration rules" means any rules under this Act, other than rules under section 93, Part 11, section 121 or paragraph 1, 2 or 3 of Schedule 5;

"legal estate" has the same meaning as in the Law of Property Act 1925 (c 20);

"legal mortgage" has the same meaning as in the Law of Property Act 1925;

"mines and minerals" includes any strata or seam of minerals or substances in or under any land, and powers of working and getting any such minerals or substances;

"registrar" means the Chief Land Registrar;

"register" means the register of title, except in the context of cautions against first registration;

"registered" means entered in the register;

"registered charge" means a charge the title to which is entered in the register;

"registered estate" means a legal estate the title to which is entered in the register, other than a registered charge;

"registered land" means a registered estate or registered charge;

"registrable disposition" means a disposition which is required to be completed by registration under section 27;

"requirement of registration" means the requirement of registration under section 4;

"sub-charge" means a charge under section 23(2)(b);

"term of years absolute" has the same meaning as in the Law of Property Act 1925 (c 20);

"valuable consideration" does not include marriage consideration or a nominal consideration in money.

(2)   In subsection (1), in the definition of "demesne land", the reference to land belonging to Her Majesty does not include land in relation to which a freehold estate in land has determined, but in relation to which there has been no act of entry or management by the Crown.

(3)   In this Act—

    (a)   references to the court are to the High Court or a county court,

    (b)   references to an interest affecting an estate or charge are to an adverse right affecting the title to the estate or charge, and

    (c)   references to the right to object to an application to the registrar are to the right under section 73.

Transitional provisions: See s 134, Sch 12, para 16.

Final provisions

133 Minor and consequential amendments

Schedule 11 (which makes minor and consequential amendments) has effect.

References: See para 5.17.

---

134 Transition

(1)   The Lord Chancellor may by order make such transitional provisions and savings as he thinks fit in connection with the coming into force of any of the provisions of this Act.

(2)   Schedule 12 (which makes transitional provisions and savings) has effect.

(3)   Nothing in Schedule 12 affects the power to make transitional provisions and savings under subsection (1); and an order under that subsection may modify any provision made by that Schedule.

135 Repeals

The enactments specified in Schedule 13 (which include certain provisions which are already spent) are hereby repealed to the extent specified there.

References: See para 1.14.

136 Short title, commencement and extent

(1) This Act may be cited as the Land Registration Act 2002.

(2) This Act shall come into force on such day as the Lord Chancellor may by order appoint, and different days may be so appointed for different purposes.

(3) Subject to subsection (4), this Act extends to England and Wales only.

(4) Any amendment or repeal by this Act of an existing enactment, other than—

    (a) section 37 of the Requisitioned Land and War Works Act 1945 (c 43), and

    (b) Schedule 2A to the Building Societies Act 1986 (c 53),

has the same extent as the enactment amended or repealed.

SCHEDULES

SCHEDULE 1

Sections 11 and 12

UNREGISTERED INTERESTS WHICH OVERRIDE FIRST REGISTRATION

Leasehold estates in land

1 A leasehold estate in land granted for a term not exceeding seven years from the date of the grant, except for a lease the grant of which falls within section 4(1) (d), (e) or (f).

Interests of persons in actual occupation

2 An interest belonging to a person in actual occupation, so far as relating to land of which he is in actual occupation, except for an interest under a settlement under the Settled Land Act 1925 (c 18).

Easements and profits à prendre

3 A legal easement or profit à prendre.

Customary and public rights

4 A customary right.

5 A public right.

Local land charges

6 A local land charge.

Mines and minerals

7 An interest in any coal or coal mine, the rights attached to any such interest and the rights of any person under section 38, 49 or 51 of the Coal Industry Act 1994 (c 21).

8 In the case of land to which title was registered before 1898, rights to mines and minerals (and incidental rights) created before 1898.

9 In the case of land to which title was registered between 1898 and 1925 inclusive, rights to mines and minerals (and incidental rights) created before the date of registration of the title.

Miscellaneous

10 *A franchise.*

11 A manorial right.

12 A right to rent which was reserved to the Crown on the granting of any freehold estate (whether or not the right is still vested in the Crown).

13 A non-statutory right in respect of an embankment or sea or river wall.

14 A right to payment in lieu of tithe.

Definitions: For "land" and "mines and minerals" see s 132(1).
Amendments: Paras 10–14 shall cease to have effect at the end of the period of ten years beginning with the day on which this Schedule comes into force; see s 117(1).
Transitional provisions: See Sch 12, paras 7, 12, 13.
References: See paras 6.47, 6.49–6.51, 6.57, 6.58, 6.60–6.62, 7.7–7.16, 10.52, 10.53, 11.4, 12.8, 12. 15, 12.17, 13.22, 13.31, 13.32, Appendix 1.

SCHEDULE 2

Section 27

REGISTRABLE DISPOSITIONS: REGISTRATION REQUIREMENTS

PART 1
REGISTERED ESTATES

Introductory

1 This Part deals with the registration requirements relating to those dispositions of registered estates which are required to be completed by registration.

Transfer

2—(1) In the case of a transfer of whole or part, the transferee, or his successor in title, must be entered in the register as the proprietor.

(2)   In the case of a transfer of part, such details of the transfer as rules may provide must be entered in the register in relation to the registered estate out of which the transfer is made.

Lease of estate in land

3—(1) This paragraph applies to a disposition consisting of the grant out of an estate in land of a term of years absolute.

(2)   In the case of a disposition to which this paragraph applies—
    (a)   the grantee, or his successor in title, must be entered in the register as the proprietor of the lease, and
    (b)   a notice in respect of the lease must be entered in the register.

Lease of franchise or manor

4—(1) This paragraph applies to a disposition consisting of the grant out of a franchise or manor of a lease for a term of more than seven years from the date of the grant.

(2)   In the case of a disposition to which this paragraph applies—
    (a)   the grantee, or his successor in title, must be entered in the register as the proprietor of the lease, and
    (b)   a notice in respect of the lease must be entered in the register.

5—(1) This paragraph applies to a disposition consisting of the grant out of a franchise or manor of a lease for a term not exceeding seven years from the date of the grant.

(2)   In the case of a disposition to which this paragraph applies, a notice in respect of the lease must be entered in the register.

Creation of independently registrable legal interest

6—(1) This paragraph applies to a disposition consisting of the creation of a legal rentcharge or profit à prendre in gross, other than one created for, or for an interest equivalent to, a term of years absolute not exceeding seven years from the date of creation.

(2)   In the case of a disposition to which this paragraph applies—

    (a)   the grantee, or his successor in title, must be entered in the register as the proprietor of the interest created, and

    (b)   a notice in respect of the interest created must be entered in the register.

(3)   In sub-paragraph (1), the reference to a legal rentcharge or profit à prendre in gross is to one falling within section 1(2) of the Law of Property Act 1925 (c 20).

Creation of other legal interest

7—(1) This paragraph applies to a disposition which—

    (a)   consists of the creation of an interest of a kind falling within section 1(2)(a), (b) or (e) of the Law of Property Act 1925, and

    (b)   is not a disposition to which paragraph 4, 5 or 6 applies.

(2)   In the case of a disposition to which this paragraph applies—

    (a)   a notice in respect of the interest created must be entered in the register, and

    (b)   if the interest is created for the benefit of a registered estate, the proprietor of the registered estate must be entered in the register as its proprietor.

(3)   Rules may provide for sub-paragraph (2) to have effect with modifications in relation to a right of entry over or in respect of a term of years absolute.

Creation of legal charge

8 In the case of the creation of a charge, the chargee, or his successor in title, must be entered in the register as the proprietor of the charge.

PART 2
REGISTERED CHARGES

Introductory

9 This Part deals with the registration requirements relating to those dispositions of registered charges which are required to be completed by registration.

Transfer

10 In the case of a transfer, the transferee, or his successor in title, must be entered in the register as the proprietor.

Creation of sub-charge

11 In the case of the creation of a sub-charge, the sub-chargee, or his successor in title, must be entered in the register as the proprietor of the sub-charge.

Definitions: For "charge", "land", "register", "registered charge", "registered estate", "sub-charge" and "term of years absolute" see s 132(1).
References: See paras 2.3, 2.4, 5.18, 5.24, 5.33, 6.16, 6.27, 6.43, 6.44, 6.60, 12.4, 12.9, 12.13.

SCHEDULE 3

Sections 29 and 30

UNREGISTERED INTERESTS WHICH OVERRIDE REGISTERED DISPOSITIONS

Leasehold estates in land

1 A leasehold estate in land granted for a term not exceeding seven years from the date of the grant, except for—

(a) a lease the grant of which falls within section 4(1)(d), (e) or (f);

(b) a lease the grant of which constitutes a registrable disposition.

Interests of persons in actual occupation

2 An interest belonging at the time of the disposition to a person in actual occupation, so far as relating to land of which he is in actual occupation, except for—

(a) an interest under a settlement under the Settled Land Act 1925 (c 18);

(b) an interest of a person of whom inquiry was made before the disposition and who failed to disclose the right when he could reasonably have been expected to do so;

(c) an interest—

(i) which belongs to a person whose occupation would not have been obvious on a reasonably careful inspection of the land at the time of the disposition, and

(ii) of which the person to whom the disposition is made does not have actual knowledge at that time;

(d) a leasehold estate in land granted to take effect in possession after the end of the period of three months beginning with the date of the grant and which has not taken effect in possession at the time of the disposition.

Easements and profits à prendre

3—(1) A legal easement or profit à prendre, except for an easement, or a profit à prendre which is not registered under the Commons Registration Act 1965 (c 64), which at the time of the disposition—

(a) is not within the actual knowledge of the person to whom the disposition is made, and

(b) would not have been obvious on a reasonably careful inspection of the land over which the easement or profit is exercisable.

(2) The exception in sub-paragraph (1) does not apply if the person entitled to the easement or profit proves that it has been exercised in the period of one year ending with the day of the disposition.

Customary and public rights

4 A customary right.

5 A public right.

Local land charges

6 A local land charge.

Mines and minerals

7 An interest in any coal or coal mine, the rights attached to any such interest and the rights of any person under section 38, 49 or 51 of the Coal Industry Act 1994 (c 21).

8 In the case of land to which title was registered before 1898, rights to mines and minerals (and incidental rights) created before 1898.

9 In the case of land to which title was registered between 1898 and 1925 inclusive, rights to mines and minerals (and incidental rights) created before the date of registration of the title.

Miscellaneous

10 *A franchise.*

11 *A manorial right.*

12 *A right to rent which was reserved to the Crown on the granting of any freehold estate (whether or not the right is still vested in the Crown).*

13 *A non-statutory right in respect of an embankment or sea or river wall.*

14 *A right to payment in lieu of tithe.*

Amendments: Paras 10–14 shall cease to have effect at the end of the period of ten years beginning with the day on which this Schedule comes into force; see s 117(2)(b).
Transitional provisions: See Sch 12, paras 8–13 to this Act.
References: See paras 4.11, 6.20–6.22, 6.37–6.39, 6.43, 6.44, 6.46, 6.47, 6.49–6.51, 6.53, 6.55–6.59, 6.60–6.62, 7.62–7.81, 10.52, 10.53, 10.59, 11.4, 12.8, 12.15, 12.17, 13.22.

SCHEDULE 4

Section 65

ALTERATION OF THE REGISTER

Introductory

1 In this Schedule, references to rectification, in relation to alteration of the register, are to alteration which—

    (a)   involves the correction of a mistake, and

    (b)   prejudicially affects the title of a registered proprietor.

Alteration pursuant to a court order

2—(1) The court may make an order for alteration of the register for the purpose of—

    (a)   correcting a mistake,

    (b)   bringing the register up to date, or

    (c)   giving effect to any estate, right or interest excepted from the effect of registration.

    (2)   An order under this paragraph has effect when served on the registrar to impose a duty on him to give effect to it.

3—(1) This paragraph applies to the power under paragraph 2, so far as relating to rectification.

    (2)   If alteration affects the title of the proprietor of a registered estate in land, no order may be made under paragraph 2 without the proprietor's consent in relation to land in his possession unless—

    (a)   he has by fraud or lack of proper care caused or substantially contributed to the mistake, or

    (b)   it would for any other reason be unjust for the alteration not to be made.

    (3)   If in any proceedings the court has power to make an order under paragraph 2, it must do so, unless there are exceptional circumstances which justify its not doing so.

    (4)   In sub-paragraph (2), the reference to the title of the proprietor of a registered estate in land includes his title to any registered estate which subsists for the benefit of the estate in land.

4 Rules may—

    (a)   make provision about the circumstances in which there is a duty to exercise the power under paragraph 2, so far as not relating to rectification;

    (b)   make provision about the form of an order under paragraph 2;

    (c)   make provision about service of such an order.

Alteration otherwise than pursuant to a court order

5 The registrar may alter the register for the purpose of—
- (a) correcting a mistake,
- (b) bringing the register up to date,
- (c) giving effect to any estate, right or interest excepted from the effect of registration, or
- (d) removing a superfluous entry.

6—(1) This paragraph applies to the power under paragraph 5, so far as relating to rectification.

(2) No alteration affecting the title of the proprietor of a registered estate in land may be made under paragraph 5 without the proprietor's consent in relation to land in his possession unless—
- (a) he has by fraud or lack of proper care caused or substantially contributed to the mistake, or
- (b) it would for any other reason be unjust for the alteration not to be made.

(3) If on an application for alteration under paragraph 5 the registrar has power to make the alteration, the application must be approved, unless there are exceptional circumstances which justify not making the alteration.

(4) In sub-paragraph (2), the reference to the title of the proprietor of a registered estate in land includes his title to any registered estate which subsists for the benefit of the estate in land.

7 Rules may—
- (a) make provision about the circumstances in which there is a duty to exercise the power under paragraph 5, so far as not relating to rectification;
- (b) make provision about how the register is to be altered in exercise of that power;
- (c) make provision about applications for alteration under that paragraph, including provision requiring the making of such applications;
- (d) make provision about procedure in relation to the exercise of that power, whether on application or otherwise.

Rectification and derivative interests

8 The powers under this Schedule to alter the register, so far as relating to rectification, extend to changing for the future the priority of any interest affecting the registered estate or charge concerned.

Costs in non-rectification cases

9—(1) If the register is altered under this Schedule in a case not involving rectification, the registrar may pay such amount as he thinks fit in respect of any costs or expenses reasonably incurred by a person in connection with the alteration which have been incurred with the consent of the registrar.

(2) The registrar may make a payment under sub-paragraph (1) notwithstanding the absence of consent if—
- (a) it appears to him—
  - (i) that the costs or expenses had to be incurred urgently, and
  - (ii) that it was not reasonably practicable to apply for his consent, or
- (b) he has subsequently approved the incurring of the costs or expenses.

Definitions: For "court" see s 132(3)(a); for "land", "register", "registered charge", "registered estate" and "registrar" see s 132(1); for "an interest affecting an estate or charge" see s 132(3)(b).
References: See paras 14.4–14.22.

SCHEDULE 5

Section 92

LAND REGISTRY NETWORK

Access to network

1—(1) A person who is not a member of the land registry may only have access to a land registry network under authority conferred by means of an agreement with the registrar.

(2)   An agreement for the purposes of sub-paragraph (1) ("network access agreement") may authorise access for—

     (a)   the communication, posting or retrieval of information,

     (b)   the making of changes to the register of title or cautions register,

     (c)   the issue of official search certificates,

     (d)   the issue of official copies, or

     (e)   such other conveyancing purposes as the registrar thinks fit.

(3)   Rules may regulate the use of network access agreements to confer authority to carry out functions of the registrar.

(4)   The registrar must, on application, enter into a network access agreement with the applicant if the applicant meets such criteria as rules may provide.

Terms of access

2—(1) The terms on which access to a land registry network is authorised shall be such as the registrar thinks fit, subject to sub-paragraphs (3) and (4), and may, in particular, include charges for access.

(2)   The power under sub-paragraph (1) may be used, not only for the purpose of regulating the use of the network, but also for—

     (a)   securing that the person granted access uses the network to carry on such qualifying transactions as may be specified in, or under, the agreement,

     (b)   such other purpose relating to the carrying on of qualifying transactions as rules may provide, or

     (c)   enabling network transactions to be monitored.

(3)   It shall be a condition of a network access agreement which enables the person granted access to use the network to carry on qualifying transactions that he must comply with any rules for the time being in force under paragraph 5.

(4)   Rules may regulate the terms on which access to a land registry network is authorised.

Termination of access

3—(1) The person granted access by a network access agreement may terminate the agreement at any time by notice to the registrar.

(2)   Rules may make provision about the termination of a network access agreement by the registrar and may, in particular, make provision about—

     (a)   the grounds of termination,

     (b)   the procedure to be followed in relation to termination, and

     (c)   the suspension of termination pending appeal.

(3)   Without prejudice to the generality of sub-paragraph (2)(a), rules under that provision may authorise the registrar to terminate a network access agreement if the person granted access—

     (a)   fails to comply with the terms of the agreement,

     (b)   ceases to be a person with whom the registrar would be required to enter into a network access agreement conferring the authority which the agreement confers, or

     (c)   does not meet such conditions as the rules may provide.

Appeals

4—(1) A person who is aggrieved by a decision of the registrar with respect to entry into, or termination of, a network access agreement may appeal against the decision to the adjudicator.

(2) On determining an appeal under this paragraph, the adjudicator may give such directions as he considers appropriate to give effect to his determination.

(3) Rules may make provision about appeals under this paragraph.

Network transaction rules

5—(1) Rules may make provision about how to go about network transactions.

(2) Rules under sub-paragraph (1) may, in particular, make provision about dealings with the land registry, including provision about—
   (a) the procedure to be followed, and
   (b) the supply of information (including information about unregistered interests).

Overriding nature of network access obligations

6 To the extent that an obligation not owed under a network access agreement conflicts with an obligation owed under such an agreement by the person granted access, the obligation not owed under the agreement is discharged.

Do-it-yourself conveyancing

7—(1) If there is a land registry network, the registrar has a duty to provide such assistance as he thinks appropriate for the purpose of enabling persons engaged in qualifying transactions who wish to do their own conveyancing to do so by means of the network.

(2) The duty under sub-paragraph (1) does not extend to the provision of legal advice.

Presumption of authority

8 Where—
   (a) a person who is authorised under a network access agreement to do so uses the network for the making of a disposition or contract, and
   (b) the document which purports to effect the disposition or to be the contract—
      (i) purports to be authenticated by him as agent, and
      (ii) contains a statement to the effect that he is acting under the authority of his principal,
he shall be deemed, in favour of any other party, to be so acting.

Management of network transactions

9—(1) The registrar may use monitoring information for the purpose of managing network transactions and may, in particular, disclose such information to persons authorised to use the network, and authorise the further disclosure of information so disclosed, if he considers it is necessary or desirable to do so.

(2) The registrar may delegate his functions under sub-paragraph (1), subject to such conditions as he thinks fit.

(3) In sub-paragraph (1), "monitoring information" means information provided in pursuance of provision in a network access agreement included under paragraph 2(2)(c).

Supplementary

10 The registrar may provide, or arrange for the provision of, education and training in relation to the use of a land registry network.

11—(1) Power to make rules under paragraph 1, 2 or 3 is exercisable by the Lord Chancellor.

(2) Before making such rules, the Lord Chancellor must consult such persons as he considers appropriate.

(3) In making rules under paragraph 1 or 3(2)(a), the Lord Chancellor must have regard, in particular, to the need to secure—
- (a) the confidentiality of private information kept on the network,
- (b) competence in relation to the use of the network (in particular for the purpose of making changes), and
- (c) the adequate insurance of potential liabilities in connection with use of the network.

12 In this Schedule—
> "land registry network" means a network provided under section 92(1);
> "network access agreement" has the meaning given by paragraph 1(2);
> "network transaction" means a transaction carried on by means of a land registry network;
> "qualifying transaction" means a transaction which—
> - (a) involves registration, and
> - (b) is capable of being effected electronically.

Definitions: For "adjudicator" and "cautions register" see s 132(1); for "member of the land registry" see s 99; for "registrar" see s 132(1).
References: See paras 3.19–3.21, 3.23, 3.24, 3.29, 3.32, 3.34.

SCHEDULE 6

Section 97

REGISTRATION OF ADVERSE POSSESSOR

Right to apply for registration

1—(1) A person may apply to the registrar to be registered as the proprietor of a registered estate in land if he has been in adverse possession of the estate for the period of ten years ending on the date of the application.

(2) A person may also apply to the registrar to be registered as the proprietor of a registered estate in land if—
- (a) he has in the period of six months ending on the date of the application ceased to be in adverse possession of the estate because of eviction by the registered proprietor, or a person claiming under the registered proprietor,
- (b) on the day before his eviction he was entitled to make an application under sub-paragraph (1), and
- (c) the eviction was not pursuant to a judgment for possession.

(3) However, a person may not make an application under this paragraph if—
- (a) he is a defendant in proceedings which involve asserting a right to possession of the land, or
- (b) judgment for possession of the land has been given against him in the last two years.

(4) For the purposes of sub-paragraph (1), the estate need not have been registered throughout the period of adverse possession.

Notification of application

2—(1) The registrar must give notice of an application under paragraph 1 to—
- (a) the proprietor of the estate to which the application relates,
- (b) the proprietor of any registered charge on the estate,
- (c) where the estate is leasehold, the proprietor of any superior registered estate,
- (d) any person who is registered in accordance with rules as a person to be notified under this paragraph, and
- (e) such other persons as rules may provide.

(2) Notice under this paragraph shall include notice of the effect of paragraph 4.

Treatment of application

3—(1) A person given notice under paragraph 2 may require that the application to which the notice relates be dealt with under paragraph 5.

(2) The right under this paragraph is exercisable by notice to the registrar given before the end of such period as rules may provide.

4 If an application under paragraph 1 is not required to be dealt with under paragraph 5, the applicant is entitled to be entered in the register as the new proprietor of the estate.

5—(1) If an application under paragraph 1 is required to be dealt with under this paragraph, the applicant is only entitled to be registered as the new proprietor of the estate if any of the following conditions is met.

(2) The first condition is that—
    (a) it would be unconscionable because of an equity by estoppel for the registered proprietor to seek to dispossess the applicant, and
    (b) the circumstances are such that the applicant ought to be registered as the proprietor.

(3) The second condition is that the applicant is for some other reason entitled to be registered as the proprietor of the estate.

(4) The third condition is that—
    (a) the land to which the application relates is adjacent to land belonging to the applicant,
    (b) the exact line of the boundary between the two has not been determined under rules under section 60,
    (c) for at least ten years of the period of adverse possession ending on the date of the application, the applicant (or any predecessor in title) reasonably believed that the land to which the application relates belonged to him, and
    (d) the estate to which the application relates was registered more than one year prior to the date of the application.

(5) In relation to an application under paragraph 1(2), this paragraph has effect as if the reference in sub-paragraph (4)(c) to the date of the application were to the day before the date of the applicant's eviction.

Right to make further application for registration

6—(1) Where a person's application under paragraph 1 is rejected, he may make a further application to be registered as the proprietor of the estate if he is in adverse possession of the estate from the date of the application until the last day of the period of two years beginning with the date of its rejection.

(2) However, a person may not make an application under this paragraph if—
    (a) he is a defendant in proceedings which involve asserting a right to possession of the land,
    (b) judgment for possession of the land has been given against him in the last two years, or
    (c) he has been evicted from the land pursuant to a judgment for possession.

7 If a person makes an application under paragraph 6, he is entitled to be entered in the register as the new proprietor of the estate.

Restriction on applications

8—(1) No one may apply under this Schedule to be registered as the proprietor of an estate in land during, or before the end of twelve months after the end of, any period in which the existing registered proprietor is for the purposes of the Limitation (Enemies and War Prisoners) Act 1945 (8 & 9 Geo 6 c 16)—
    (a) an enemy, or
    (b) detained in enemy territory.

(2)   No-one may apply under this Schedule to be registered as the proprietor of an estate in land during any period in which the existing registered proprietor is—

    (a)   unable because of mental disability to make decisions about issues of the kind to which such an application would give rise, or

    (b)   unable to communicate such decisions because of mental disability or physical impairment.

(3)   For the purposes of sub-paragraph (2), "mental disability" means a disability or disorder of the mind or brain, whether permanent or temporary, which results in an impairment or disturbance of mental functioning.

(4)   Where it appears to the registrar that sub-paragraph (1) or (2) applies in relation to an estate in land, he may include a note to that effect in the register.

Effect of registration

9—(1) Where a person is registered as the proprietor of an estate in land in pursuance of an application under this Schedule, the title by virtue of adverse possession which he had at the time of the application is extinguished.

(2)   Subject to sub-paragraph (3), the registration of a person under this Schedule as the proprietor of an estate in land does not affect the priority of any interest affecting the estate.

(3)   Subject to sub-paragraph (4), where a person is registered under this Schedule as the proprietor of an estate, the estate is vested in him free of any registered charge affecting the estate immediately before his registration.

(4)   Sub-paragraph (3) does not apply where registration as proprietor is in pursuance of an application determined by reference to whether any of the conditions in paragraph 5 applies.

Apportionment and discharge of charges

10—(1) Where—

    (a)   a registered estate continues to be subject to a charge notwithstanding the registration of a person under this Schedule as the proprietor, and

    (b)   the charge affects property other than the estate,

the proprietor of the estate may require the chargee to apportion the amount secured by the charge at that time between the estate and the other property on the basis of their respective values.

(2)   The person requiring the apportionment is entitled to a discharge of his estate from the charge on payment of—

    (a)   the amount apportioned to the estate, and

    (b)   the costs incurred by the chargee as a result of the apportionment.

(3)   On a discharge under this paragraph, the liability of the chargor to the chargee is reduced by the amount apportioned to the estate.

(4)   Rules may make provision about apportionment under this paragraph, in particular, provision about—

    (a)   procedure,

    (b)   valuation,

    (c)   calculation of costs payable under sub-paragraph (2)(b), and

    (d)   payment of the costs of the chargor.

Meaning of "adverse possession"

11—(1) A person is in adverse possession of an estate in land for the purposes of this Schedule if, but for section 96, a period of limitation under section 15 of the Limitation Act 1980 (c 58) would run in his favour in relation to the estate.

(2)   A person is also to be regarded for those purposes as having been in adverse possession of an estate in land—

(a)   where he is the successor in title to an estate in the land, during any period of adverse possession by a predecessor in title to that estate, or

(b)   during any period of adverse possession by another person which comes between, and is continuous with, periods of adverse possession of his own.

(3)   In determining whether for the purposes of this paragraph a period of limitation would run under section 15 of the Limitation Act 1980, there are to be disregarded—

(a)   the commencement of any legal proceedings, and

(b)   paragraph 6 of Schedule 1 to that Act.

Trusts

12 A person is not to be regarded as being in adverse possession of an estate for the purposes of this Schedule at any time when the estate is subject to a trust, unless the interest of each of the beneficiaries in the estate is an interest in possession.

Crown foreshore

13—(1) Where—

(a)   a person is in adverse possession of an estate in land,

(b)   the estate belongs to Her Majesty in right of the Crown or the Duchy of Lancaster or to the Duchy of Cornwall, and

(c)   the land consists of foreshore,

paragraph 1(1) is to have effect as if the reference to ten years were to sixty years.

(2)   For the purposes of sub-paragraph (1), land is to be treated as foreshore if it has been foreshore at any time in the previous ten years.

(3)   In this paragraph, "foreshore" means the shore and bed of the sea and of any tidal water, below the line of the medium high tide between the spring and neap tides.

Rentcharges

14 Rules must make provision to apply the preceding provisions of this Schedule to registered rentcharges, subject to such modifications and exceptions as the rules may provide.

Procedure

15 Rules may make provision about the procedure to be followed pursuant to an application under this Schedule.

Definitions: For "charge", "land", "register", "registered", "registered charge", "registered estate" and "registrar" see s 132(1); for "an interest affecting an estate or charge" see s 132(3)(b).
References: See paras 2.25, 2.27, 10.64–10.66, 13.6–13.9, 13.11, 13.12, 13.14, 13.18–13.21, 13.23–13.25, 13.27, 13.29, 13.32, 15.29.

SCHEDULE 7

Section 99

THE LAND REGISTRY

Holding of office by Chief Land Registrar

1—(1) The registrar may at any time resign his office by written notice to the Lord Chancellor.

(2)   The Lord Chancellor may remove the registrar from office if he is unable or unfit to discharge the functions of office.

(3)   Subject to the above, a person appointed to be the registrar is to hold and vacate office in accordance with the terms of his appointment and, on ceasing to hold office, is eligible for reappointment.

Remuneration etc of Chief Land Registrar

2—(1) The Lord Chancellor shall pay the registrar such remuneration, and such travelling and other allowances, as the Lord Chancellor may determine.

(2)   The Lord Chancellor shall—
   (a)   pay such pension, allowances or gratuities as he may determine to or in respect of a person who is or has been the registrar, or
   (b)   make such payments as he may determine towards provision for the payment of a pension, allowances or gratuities to or in respect of such a person.

(3)   If, when a person ceases to be the registrar, the Lord Chancellor determines that there are special circumstances which make it right that the person should receive compensation, the Lord Chancellor may pay to the person by way of compensation a sum of such amount as he may determine.

Staff

3—(1) The registrar may appoint such staff as he thinks fit.

(2)   The terms and conditions of appointments under this paragraph shall be such as the registrar, with the approval of the Minister for the Civil Service, thinks fit.

Indemnity for members

4 No member of the land registry is to be liable in damages for anything done or omitted in the discharge or purported discharge of any function relating to land registration, unless it is shown that the act or omission was in bad faith.

Seal

5 The land registry is to continue to have a seal and any document purporting to be sealed with it is to be admissible in evidence without any further or other proof.

Documentary evidence

6 The Documentary Evidence Act 1868 (c 37) has effect as if—
   (a)   the registrar were included in the first column of the Schedule to that Act,
   (b)   the registrar and any person authorised to act on his behalf were mentioned in the second column of that Schedule, and
   (c)   the regulations referred to in that Act included any form or direction issued by the registrar or by any such person.

7 (*Amends the House of Commons Disqualification Act 1975, Sch 1, Pt III, and the Northern Ireland Assembly Disqualification Act 1975, Sch 1, Pt III.*)

Definitions: For "member of the land registry" see s 99; for "registrar" see s 132(1).
References: See para 2.1.

SCHEDULE 8

Section 103

INDEMNITIES

Entitlement

1—(1) A person is entitled to be indemnified by the registrar if he suffers loss by reason of—
   (a)   rectification of the register,
   (b)   a mistake whose correction would involve rectification of the register,

     (c)   a mistake in an official search,

     (d)   a mistake in an official copy,

     (e)   a mistake in a document kept by the registrar which is not an original and is referred to in the register,

     (f)   the loss or destruction of a document lodged at the registry for inspection or safe custody,

     (g)   a mistake in the cautions register, or

     (h)   failure by the registrar to perform his duty under section 50.

(2)   For the purposes of sub-paragraph (1)(a)—

     (a)   any person who suffers loss by reason of the change of title under section 62 is to be regarded as having suffered loss by reason of rectification of the register, and

     (b)   the proprietor of a registered estate or charge claiming in good faith under a forged disposition is, where the register is rectified, to be regarded as having suffered loss by reason of such rectification as if the disposition had not been forged.

(3)   No indemnity under sub-paragraph (1)(b) is payable until a decision has been made about whether to alter the register for the purpose of correcting the mistake; and the loss suffered by reason of the mistake is to be determined in the light of that decision.

Mines and minerals

2 No indemnity is payable under this Schedule on account of—

     (a)   any mines or minerals, or

     (b)   the existence of any right to work or get mines or minerals,

unless it is noted in the register that the title to the registered estate concerned includes the mines or minerals.

Costs

3—(1) In respect of loss consisting of costs or expenses incurred by the claimant in relation to the matter, an indemnity under this Schedule is payable only on account of costs or expenses reasonably incurred by the claimant with the consent of the registrar.

(2)   The requirement of consent does not apply where—

     (a)   the costs or expenses must be incurred by the claimant urgently, and

     (b)   it is not reasonably practicable to apply for the registrar's consent.

(3)   If the registrar approves the incurring of costs or expenses after they have been incurred, they shall be treated for the purposes of this paragraph as having been incurred with his consent.

4—(1) If no indemnity is payable to a claimant under this Schedule, the registrar may pay such amount as he thinks fit in respect of any costs or expenses reasonably incurred by the claimant in connection with the claim which have been incurred with the consent of the registrar.

(2)   The registrar may make a payment under sub-paragraph (1) notwithstanding the absence of consent if—

     (a)   it appears to him—

        (i)   that the costs or expenses had to be incurred urgently, and

        (ii)   that it was not reasonably practicable to apply for his consent, or

     (b)   he has subsequently approved the incurring of the costs or expenses.

Claimant's fraud or lack of care

5—(1) No indemnity is payable under this Schedule on account of any loss suffered by a claimant—

     (a)   wholly or partly as a result of his own fraud, or

     (b)   wholly as a result of his own lack of proper care.

(2)   Where any loss is suffered by a claimant partly as a result of his own lack of proper care, any indemnity payable to him is to be reduced to such extent as is fair having regard to his share in the responsibility for the loss.

(3)   For the purposes of this paragraph any fraud or lack of care on the part of a person from whom the claimant derives title (otherwise than under a disposition for valuable consideration which is registered or protected by an entry in the register) is to be treated as if it were fraud or lack of care on the part of the claimant.

Valuation of estates etc

6 Where an indemnity is payable in respect of the loss of an estate, interest or charge, the value of the estate, interest or charge for the purposes of the indemnity is to be regarded as not exceeding—

(a)   in the case of an indemnity under paragraph 1(1)(a), its value immediately before rectification of the register (but as if there were to be no rectification), and

(b)   in the case of an indemnity under paragraph 1(1)(b), its value at the time when the mistake which caused the loss was made.

Determination of indemnity by court

7—(1) A person may apply to the court for the determination of any question as to—

(a)   whether he is entitled to an indemnity under this Schedule, or

(b)   the amount of such an indemnity.

(2)   Paragraph 3(1) does not apply to the costs of an application to the court under this paragraph or of any legal proceedings arising out of such an application.

Time limits

8 For the purposes of the Limitation Act 1980 (c 58)—

(a)   a liability to pay an indemnity under this Schedule is a simple contract debt, and

(b)   the cause of action arises at the time when the claimant knows, or but for his own default might have known, of the existence of his claim.

Interest

9 Rules may make provision about the payment of interest on an indemnity under this Schedule, including—

(a)   the circumstances in which interest is payable, and

(b)   the periods for and rates at which it is payable.

Recovery of indemnity by registrar

10—(1) Where an indemnity under this Schedule is paid to a claimant in respect of any loss, the registrar is entitled (without prejudice to any other rights he may have)—

(a)   to recover the amount paid from any person who caused or substantially contributed to the loss by his fraud, or

(b)   for the purpose of recovering the amount paid, to enforce the rights of action referred to in sub-paragraph (2).

(2)   Those rights of action are—

(a)   any right of action (of whatever nature and however arising) which the claimant would have been entitled to enforce had the indemnity not been paid, and

(b)   where the register has been rectified, any right of action (of whatever nature and however arising) which the person in whose favour the register has been rectified would have been entitled to enforce had it not been rectified.

(3)   References in this paragraph to an indemnity include interest paid on an indemnity under rules under paragraph 9.

Interpretation

11—(1) For the purposes of this Schedule, references to a mistake in something include anything mistakenly omitted from it as well as anything mistakenly included in it.

(2)   In this Schedule, references to rectification of the register are to alteration of the register which—

(a)   involves the correction of a mistake, and

(b)   prejudicially affects the title of a registered proprietor.

Definitions: For "cautions register" and "charge" see s 132(1); for "court" see s 132(3)(a); for "mines and minerals", "register", "registered", "registered charge", "registered estate", "registrar" and "valuable consideration" see s 132(1).
References: See paras 14.32, 14.37–14.40, 14.43–14.46, 14.50–14.53, 15.78.

SCHEDULE 9

Section 107

THE ADJUDICATOR

Holding of office

1—(1) The adjudicator may at any time resign his office by written notice to the Lord Chancellor.

(2)   The Lord Chancellor may remove the adjudicator from office on the ground of incapacity or misbehaviour.

(3)   Section 26 of the Judicial Pensions and Retirement Act 1993 (c 8) (compulsory retirement at 70, subject to the possibility of annual extension up to 75) applies to the adjudicator.

(4)   Subject to the above, a person appointed to be the adjudicator is to hold and vacate office in accordance with the terms of his appointment and, on ceasing to hold office, is eligible for reappointment.

Remuneration

2—(1) The Lord Chancellor shall pay the adjudicator such remuneration, and such other allowances, as the Lord Chancellor may determine.

(2)   The Lord Chancellor shall—

(a)   pay such pension, allowances or gratuities as he may determine to or in respect of a person who is or has been the adjudicator, or

(b)   make such payments as he may determine towards provision for the payment of a pension, allowances or gratuities to or in respect of such a person.

(3)   Sub-paragraph (2) does not apply if the office of adjudicator is a qualifying judicial office within the meaning of the Judicial Pensions and Retirement Act 1993.

(4)   If, when a person ceases to be the adjudicator, the Lord Chancellor determines that there are special circumstances which make it right that the person should receive compensation, the Lord Chancellor may pay to the person by way of compensation a sum of such amount as he may determine.

Staff

3—(1) The adjudicator may appoint such staff as he thinks fit.

(2)   The terms and conditions of appointments under this paragraph shall be such as the adjudicator, with the approval of the Minister for the Civil Service, thinks fit.

Conduct of business

4—(1) Subject to sub-paragraph (2), any function of the adjudicator may be carried out by any member of his staff who is authorised by him for the purpose.

(2)   In the case of functions which are not of an administrative character, sub-paragraph (1) only applies if the member of staff has a 10 year general qualification (within the meaning of section 71 of the Courts and Legal Services Act 1990 (c 41)).

5 The Lord Chancellor may by regulations make provision about the carrying out of functions during any vacancy in the office of adjudicator.

Finances

6 The Lord Chancellor shall be liable to reimburse expenditure incurred by the adjudicator in the discharge of his functions.

7 The Lord Chancellor may require the registrar to make payments towards expenses of the Lord Chancellor under this Schedule.

8 (*Amends the Tribunals and Inquiries Act 1992, Sch 1.*)

9 (*Amends the House of Commons Disqualification Act 1975, Sch 1, Pt I, and the Northern Ireland Assembly Disqualification Act 1975, Sch 1, Pt I.*)

Definitions: For "adjudicator" and "registrar" see s 132(1).
References: See paras 15.24, 15.25.

SCHEDULE 10

Section 126

MISCELLANEOUS AND GENERAL POWERS

PART 1
MISCELLANEOUS

Dealings with estates subject to compulsory first registration

1—(1) Rules may make provision—
- (a)   applying this Act to a pre-registration dealing with a registrable legal estate as if the dealing had taken place after the date of first registration of the estate, and
- (b)   about the date on which registration of the dealing is effective.

(2)   For the purposes of sub-paragraph (1)—
- (a)   a legal estate is registrable if a person is subject to a duty under section 6 to make an application to be registered as the proprietor of it, and
- (b)   a pre-registration dealing is one which takes place before the making of such an application.

Regulation of title matters between sellers and buyers

2—(1) Rules may make provision about the obligations with respect to—
- (a)   proof of title, or
- (b)   perfection of title,

of the seller under a contract for the transfer, or other disposition, for valuable consideration of a registered estate or charge.

(2)   Rules under this paragraph may be expressed to have effect notwithstanding any stipulation to the contrary.

Implied covenants

3 Rules may—
- (a) make provision about the form of provisions extending or limiting any covenant implied by virtue of Part 1 of the Law of Property (Miscellaneous Provisions) Act 1994 (c 36) (implied covenants for title) on a registrable disposition;
- (b) make provision about the application of section 77 of the Law of Property Act 1925 (c 20) (implied covenants in conveyance subject to rents) to transfers of registered estates;
- (c) make provision about reference in the register to implied covenants, including provision for the state of the register to be conclusive in relation to whether covenants have been implied.

Land certificates

4 Rules may make provision about—
- (a) when a certificate of registration of title to a legal estate may be issued,
- (b) the form and content of such a certificate, and
- (c) when such a certificate must be produced or surrendered to the registrar.

PART 2
GENERAL

Notice

5—(1) Rules may make provision about the form, content and service of notice under this Act.

(2) Rules under this paragraph about the service of notice may, in particular—
- (a) make provision requiring the supply of an address for service and about the entry of addresses for service in the register;
- (b) make provision about—
  - (i) the time for service,
  - (ii) the mode of service, and
  - (iii) when service is to be regarded as having taken place.

Applications

6 Rules may—
- (a) make provision about the form and content of applications under this Act;
- (b) make provision requiring applications under this Act to be supported by such evidence as the rules may provide;
- (c) make provision about when an application under this Act is to be taken as made;
- (d) make provision about the order in which competing applications are to be taken to rank;
- (e) make provision for an alteration made by the registrar for the purpose of correcting a mistake in an application or accompanying document to have effect in such circumstances as the rules may provide as if made by the applicant or other interested party or parties.

Statutory statements

7 Rules may make provision about the form of any statement required under an enactment to be included in an instrument effecting a registrable disposition or a disposition which triggers the requirement of registration.

Residual power

8 Rules may make any other provision which it is expedient to make for the purposes of carrying this Act into effect, whether similar or not to any provision which may be made under the other powers to make land registration rules.

Definitions: For "land registration rules", "legal estate", "register", "registered", "registered charge", "registered estate", "registrable disposition", "registrar", "requirement of registration" and "valuable consideration" see s 132(1).
References: See paras 2.61, 4.11, 5.30, 6.26, 6.30.

SCHEDULE 11

Section 133

MINOR AND CONSEQUENTIAL AMENDMENTS

Settled Land Act 1925 (c 18)

1 Section 119(3) of the Settled Land Act 1925 ceases to have effect.

Law of Property Act 1925 (c 20)

2—(1) The Law of Property Act 1925 is amended as follows.

(2) In section 44, after subsection (4) there is inserted—

"(4A) Subsections (2) and (4) of this section do not apply to a contract to grant a term of years if the grant will be an event within section 4(1) of the Land Registration Act 2002 (events which trigger compulsory first registration of title)."

(3) In that section, in subsection (5), for "the last three preceding subsections" there is substituted "subsections (2) to (4) of this section".

(4) In that section, at the end there is inserted—

"(12) Nothing in this section applies in relation to registered land or to a term of years to be derived out of registered land."

(5) In section 84(8), the words from ", but" to the end are omitted.

(6) In section 85(3), for the words from the beginning to the second "or" there is substituted "Subsection (2) does not apply to registered land, but, subject to that, this section applies whether or not the land is registered land and whether or not".

(7) In section 86(3), for the words from the beginning to the second "or" there is substituted "Subsection (2) does not apply to registered land, but, subject to that, this section applies whether or not the land is registered land and whether or not".

(8) In section 87, at the end there is inserted—

"(4) Subsection (1) of this section shall not be taken to be affected by section 23(1)(a) of the Land Registration Act 2002 (under which owner's powers in relation to a registered estate do not include power to mortgage by demise or sub-demise)."

(9) In section 94(4), for the words from "registered" to the end there is substituted "on registered land".

(10) In section 97, for "Land Registration Act 1925" there is substituted "Land Registration Act 2002".

(11) In section 115(10), for the words from "charge" to the end there is substituted "registered charge (within the meaning of the Land Registration Act 2002)".

(12) In section 125(2), for the words from "(not being" to "1925)" there is substituted "(not being registered land)".

(13) In section 205(1)(xxii)—

(a) for "Land Registration Act 1925" there is substituted "Land Registration Act 2002;", and

(b) the words from ", and" to the end are omitted.

3 In section 43(2) of the Administration of Estates Act 1925, for "Land Registration Act 1925" there is substituted "Land Registration Act 2002".

Requisitioned Land and War Works Act 1945 (c 43)

4—(1) Section 37 of the Requisitioned Land and War Works Act 1945 is amended as follows.

(2)   In subsection (2), for "Land Registration Act 1925" there is substituted "Land Registration Act 2002".

(3)   Subsection (3) ceases to have effect.

Law of Property (Joint Tenants) Act 1964 (c 63)

5 In section 3 of the Law of Property (Joint Tenants) Act 1964, for the words from "any land" to the end there is substituted "registered land".

Gas Act 1965 (c 36)

6—(1) The Gas Act 1965 is amended as follows.

(2)   In section 12(3), for "Land Registration Act 1925" there is substituted "Land Registration Act 2002".

(3)   In sections 12(4) and 13(6), for the words from "be deemed" to the end there is substituted—

> "(a) for the purposes of the Land Charges Act 1925, be deemed to be a charge affecting land falling within Class D(iii), and
> (b) for the purposes of the Land Registration Act 2002, be deemed to be an equitable easement."

Commons Registration Act 1965 (c 64)

7—(1) The Commons Registration Act 1965 is amended as follows.

(2)   In sections 1(1), (2) and (3), 4(3) and 8(1), for "under the Land Registration Acts 1925 and 1936" there is substituted "in the register of title".

(3)   In section 9, for "the Land Registration Acts 1925 and 1936" there is substituted "in the register of title".

(4)   In section 12 (in both places), for "under the Land Registration Acts 1925 and 1936" there is substituted "in the register of title".

(5)   In section 22, in subsection (1), there is inserted at the appropriate place—

> ""register of title" means the register kept under section 1 of the Land Registration Act 2002;".

(6)   In that section, in subsection (2), for "under the Land Registration Acts 1925 and 1936" there is substituted "in the register of title".

Leasehold Reform Act 1967 (c 88)

8—(1) The Leasehold Reform Act 1967 is amended as follows.

(2)   In section 5(5)—
> (a) for "an overriding interest within the meaning of the Land Registration Act 1925" there is substituted "regarded for the purposes of the Land Registration Act 2002 as an interest falling within any of the paragraphs of Schedule 1 or 3 to that Act", and
> (b) for "or caution under the Land Registration Act 1925" there is substituted "under the Land Registration Act 2002".

(3)   In Schedule 4, in paragraph 1(3)—
    (a)   for paragraph (a) there is substituted—
        "(a)   the covenant may be the subject of a notice in the register of title kept under the Land Registration Act 2002, if apart from this subsection it would not be capable of being the subject of such a notice; and", and
    (b)   in paragraph (b), for "notice of the covenant has been so registered, the covenant" there is substituted "a notice in respect of the covenant has been entered in that register, it".

Law of Property Act 1969 (c 59)

9 In section 24(1) of the Law of Property Act 1969, for "Land Registration Act 1925" there is substituted "Land Registration Act 2002".

Land Charges Act 1972 (c 61)

10—(1) The Land Charges Act 1972 is amended as follows.

(2)   In section 14(1), for the words from "Land Registration" to the end there is substituted "Land Registration Act 2002".

(3)   In section 14(3)—
    (a)   for the words from "section 123A" to "register)" there is substituted "section 7 of the Land Registration Act 2002 (effect of failure to comply with requirement of registration)", and
    (b)   for "that section" there is substituted "section 6 of that Act".

(4)   In section 17(1), in the definition of "registered land", for "Land Registration Act 1925" there is substituted "Land Registration Act 2002".

Consumer Credit Act 1974 (c 39)

11 In section 177(1) and (6) of the Consumer Credit Act 1974, for "Land Registration Act 1925" there is substituted "Land Registration Act 2002".

Solicitors Act 1974 (c 47)

12—(1) The Solicitors Act 1974 is amended as follows.

(2)   In sections 22(1) and 56(1)(f), for "Land Registration Act 1925" there is substituted "Land Registration Act 2002".

(3)   Section 75(b) ceases to have effect.

Local Land Charges Act 1975 (c 76)

13 In section 10(3)(b)(ii) of the Local Land Charges Act 1975, for "under the Land Registration Act 1925" there is substituted "in the register of title kept under the Land Registration Act 2002".

Rent Act 1977 (c 42)

14 In section 136(b) of the Rent Act 1977, for the words from "charge" to the end there is substituted "registered charge (within the meaning of the Land Registration Act 2002)".

Charging Orders Act 1979 (c 53)

15 In section 3(2) and (6) of the Charging Orders Act 1979, for "Land Registration Act 1925" there is substituted "Land Registration Act 2002".

Highways Act 1980 (c 66)

16 Section 251(5) of the Highways Act 1980 ceases to have effect.

Inheritance Tax Act 1984 (c 51)

17 In section 238(3) of the Inheritance Tax Act 1984, for paragraph (a) there is substituted—
  "(a) in relation to registered land—
        (i)   if the disposition is required to be completed by registration, the time of registration, and
        (ii) otherwise, the time of completion,".

Housing Act 1985 (c 68)

18—(1) The Housing Act 1985 is amended as follows.

  (2) In section 37(5), for the words from "and" to the end there is substituted—

      "(5A) Where the Chief Land Registrar approves an application for registration of—
        (a) a disposition of registered land, or
        (b) the disponee's title under a disposition of unregistered land,

      and the instrument effecting the disposition contains a covenant of the kind mentioned in subsection (1), he must enter in the register a restriction reflecting the limitation imposed by the covenant".

  (3) In section 154(5), for "Land Registration Acts 1925 to 1971" there is substituted "Land Registration Act 2002".

  (4) In section 157(7), for the words from "the appropriate" to the end there is substituted "a restriction in the register of title reflecting the limitation".

  (5) In section 165(6), for "section 83 of the Land Registration Act 1925" there is substituted "Schedule 8 to the Land Registration Act 2002".

  (6) In Schedule 9A, in paragraph 2(2), for the words from the beginning to "the disponor" there is substituted "Where on a qualifying disposal the disponor's title to the dwelling-house is not registered, the disponor".

  (7) In that Schedule, for paragraph 4 there is substituted—

      "4—(1) This paragraph applies where the Chief Land Registrar approves an application for registration of—
        (a) a disposition of registered land, or
        (b) the disponee's title under a disposition of unregistered land,

      and the instrument effecting the disposition contains the statement required by paragraph 1.

      (2) The Chief Land Registrar must enter in the register—
        (a) a notice in respect of the rights of qualifying persons under this Part in relation to dwelling-houses comprised in the disposal, and
        (b) a restriction reflecting the limitation under section 171D(2) on subsequent disposal."

  (8) In that Schedule, for paragraph 5(2) there is substituted—

      "(2) If the landlord's title is registered, the landlord shall apply for the entry in the register of—
        (a) a notice in respect of the rights of the qualifying person or persons under the provisions of this Part, and
        (b) a restriction reflecting the limitation under section 171D(2) on subsequent disposal."

  (9) In that Schedule, paragraph 5(3) ceases to have effect.

  (10) In that Schedule, in paragraph 6, for sub-paragraph (1) there is substituted—

      "(1) The rights of a qualifying person under this Part in relation to the qualifying dwelling house shall not be regarded as falling within Schedule 3 to the Land Registration Act 2002 (and so are liable to be postponed under section 29 of that Act, unless protected by means of a notice in the register)."

(11) In that Schedule, in paragraph 9(2), for "Land Registration Acts 1925 to 1986" there is substituted "Land Registration Act 2002".

(12) In Schedule 17, in paragraph 2(2), for "Land Registration Acts 1925 to 1971" there is substituted "Land Registration Act 2002".

(13) In Schedule 20, in paragraph 17(2), for "Land Registration Acts 1925 to 1986" there is substituted "Land Registration Act 2002".

Building Societies Act 1986 (c 53)

19—(1) In Schedule 2A to the Building Societies Act 1986, paragraph 1 is amended as follows.

(2) In sub-paragraph (2), for "charge or incumbrance registered under the Land Registration Act 1925" there is substituted "registered charge (within the meaning of the Land Registration Act 2002)".

(3) Sub-paragraph (4) ceases to have effect.

(4) In sub-paragraph (5), the definition of "registered land" and the preceding "and" cease to have effect.

Landlord and Tenant Act 1987 (c 31)

20 In sections 24(8) and (9), 28(5), 30(6) and 34(9) of the Landlord and Tenant Act 1987, for "Land Registration Act 1925" there is substituted "Land Registration Act 2002".

Diplomatic and Consular Premises Act 1987 (c 46)

21—(1) The Diplomatic and Consular Premises Act 1987 is amended as follows.

(2) In section 5, after the definition of the expression "diplomatic premises" there is inserted—

> ""land" includes buildings and other structures, land covered with water and any estate, interest, easement, servitude or right in or over land,".

(3) In Schedule 1, in paragraph 1—
   (a) before the definition of the expression "the registrar" there is inserted—

> ""registered land" has the same meaning as in the Land Registration Act 2002;", and

   (b) the words from "and expressions" to the end are omitted.

Criminal Justice Act 1988 (c 33)

22—(1) The Criminal Justice Act 1988 is amended as follows.

(2) In section 77(12)—
   (a) for "Land Registration Act 1925" there is substituted "Land Registration Act 2002", and
   (b) in paragraph (a), at the end there is inserted ", except that no notice may be entered in the register of title under the Land Registration Act 2002 in respect of such orders".

(3) In section 79(1) and (4), for "Land Registration Act 1925" there is substituted "Land Registration Act 2002".

Housing Act 1988 (c 50)

23—(1) The Housing Act 1988 is amended as follows.

(2) In section 81, in subsection (9)(c), for "Land Registration Acts 1925 to 1986" there is substituted "Land Registration Act 2002".

(3) In that section, for subsection (10) there is substituted—

"(10) Where the Chief Land Registrar approves an application for registration of—
(a) a disposition of registered land, or
(b) the approved person's title under a disposition of unregistered land,

and the instrument effecting the disposition contains the statement required by subsection (1) above, he shall enter in the register a restriction reflecting the limitation under this section on subsequent disposal."

(4) In section 90(4), for "Land Registration Act 1925" there is substituted "Land Registration Act 2002".

(5) In section 133, in subsection (8)—
(a) for the words "conveyance, grant or assignment" there is substituted "transfer or grant",
(b) for the words "section 123 of the Land Registration Act 1925" there is substituted "section 4 of the Land Registration Act 2002", and
(c) in paragraph (c), for "Land Registration Acts 1925 to 1986" there is substituted "Land Registration Act 2002".

(6) In that section, for subsection (9) there is substituted—

"(9) Where the Chief Land Registrar approves an application for registration of—
(a) a disposition of registered land, or
(b) a person's title under a disposition of unregistered land,

and the instrument effecting the original disposal contains the statement required by subsection (3)(d) above, he shall enter in the register a restriction reflecting the limitation under this section on subsequent disposal."

Local Government and Housing Act 1989 (c 42)

24—(1) Section 173 of the Local Government and Housing Act 1989 is amended as follows.

(2) In subsection (8)—
(a) for the words "conveyance, grant or assignment" there is substituted "transfer or grant",
(b) for the words "section 123 of the Land Registration Act 1925" there is substituted "section 4 of the Land Registration Act 2002", and
(c) in paragraph (c), for "Land Registration Acts 1925 to 1986" there is substituted "Land Registration Act 2002".

(3) For subsection (9) there is substituted—

"(9) Where the Chief Land Registrar approves an application for registration of—
(a) a disposition of registered land, or
(b) a person's title under a disposition of unregistered land,

and the instrument effecting the initial transfer contains the statement required by subsection (3) above, he shall enter in the register a restriction reflecting the limitation under this section on subsequent disposal."

Water Resources Act 1991 (c 57)

25—(1) Section 158 of the Water Resources Act 1991 is amended as follows.

(2) In subsection (5)—
(a) for paragraphs (a) and (b) there is substituted—
"(a) the agreement may be the subject of a notice in the register of title under the Land Registration Act 2002 as if it were an interest affecting the registered land;
(b) the provisions of sections 28 to 30 of that Act (effect of dispositions of registered land on priority of adverse interests) shall apply as if the agreement were such an interest;", and
(b) in paragraph (c), for "where notice of the agreement has been so registered," there is substituted "subject to the provisions of those sections,".

(3)   In subsection (6), for "Land Registration Act 1925" there is substituted "Land Registration Act 2002".

Access to Neighbouring Land Act 1992 (c 4)

26—(1) The Access to Neighbouring Land Act 1992 is amended as follows.

(2)   In section 4(1), for "Land Registration Act 1925" there is substituted "Land Registration Act 2002".

(3)   In section 5, in subsection (4)—
>   (a)   in paragraph (b), for "notice or caution under the Land Registration Act 1925" there is substituted "notice under the Land Registration Act 2002", and
>   (b)   for "entry, notice or caution" there is substituted "entry or notice".

(4)   In that section, for subsection (5) there is substituted—

> "(5)   The rights conferred on a person by or under an access order shall not be capable of falling within paragraph 2 of Schedule 1 or 3 to the Land Registration Act 2002 (overriding status of interest of person in actual occupation)."

(5)   In that section, in subsection (6), for "Land Registration Act 1925" there is substituted "Land Registration Act 2002".

Further and Higher Education Act 1992 (c 13)

27 In Schedule 5 to the Further and Higher Education Act 1992, in paragraph 6(1)—
>   (a)   for "Land Registration Acts 1925 to 1986" there is substituted "Land Registration Act 2002", and
>   (b)   for "those Acts" there is substituted "that Act".

Judicial Pensions and Retirement Act 1993 (c 8)

28 In Schedule 5 to the Judicial Pensions and Retirement Act 1993, there is inserted at the end—

> "Adjudicator to Her Majesty's Land Registry"

Charities Act 1993 (c 10)

29—(1) The Charities Act 1993 is amended as follows.

(2)   In section 37, for subsections (7) and (8) there is substituted—

> "(7)   Where the disposition to be effected by any such instrument as is mentioned in subsection (1)(b) or (5)(b) above will be—
>   (a) a registrable disposition, or
>   (b) a disposition which triggers the requirement of registration,
> the statement which, by virtue of subsection (1) or (5) above, is to be contained in the instrument shall be in such form as may be prescribed by land registration rules.

>   (8)   Where the registrar approves an application for registration of—
>   (a) a disposition of registered land, or
>   (b) a person's title under a disposition of unregistered land,
> and the instrument effecting the disposition contains a statement complying with subsections (5) and (7) above, he shall enter in the register a restriction reflecting the limitation under section 36 above on subsequent disposal."

(3)   In that section, in subsection (9)—
>   (a)   for "the restriction to be withdrawn" there is substituted "the removal of the entry", and
>   (b)   for "withdraw the restriction" there is substituted "remove the entry".

(4)   In that section, in subsection (11), for "Land Registration Act 1925" there is substituted "Land Registration Act 2002".

(5)   In section 39, in subsection (1), at the end there is inserted "by land registration rules".

(6)   In that section, for subsections (1A) and (1B) there is substituted—

"(1A) Where any such mortgage will be one to which section 4(1)(g) of the Land Registration Act 2002 applies—
  (a) the statement required by subsection (1) above shall be in such form as may be prescribed by land registration rules; and
  (b) if the charity is not an exempt charity, the mortgage shall also contain a statement, in such form as may be prescribed by land registration rules, that the restrictions on disposition imposed by section 36 above apply to the land (subject to subsection (9) of that section).

(1B) Where—
  (a) the registrar approves an application for registration of a person's title to land in connection with such a mortgage as is mentioned in subsection (1A) above,
  (b) the mortgage contains statements complying with subsections (1) and (1A) above, and
  (c) the charity is not an exempt charity,

the registrar shall enter in the register a restriction reflecting the limitation under section 36 above on subsequent disposal.

(1C) Section 37(9) above shall apply in relation to any restriction entered under subsection (1B) as it applies in relation to any restriction entered under section 37(8)."

(7)   In that section, in subsection (6), for the words from "and subsections" to the end there is substituted "and subsections (1) to (1B) above shall be construed as one with the Land Registration Act 2002".

Leasehold Reform, Housing and Urban Development Act 1993 (c 28)

30—(1) The Leasehold Reform, Housing and Urban Development Act 1993 is amended as follows.

(2)   In sections 34(10) and 57(11), for the words from "rules" to the end there is substituted "land registration rules under the Land Registration Act 2002".

(3)   In section 97, in subsection (1)—
  (a) for "an overriding interest within the meaning of the Land Registration Act 1925" there is substituted "capable of falling within paragraph 2 of Schedule 1 or 3 to the Land Registration Act 2002", and
  (b) for "or caution under the Land Registration Act 1925" there is substituted "under the Land Registration Act 2002".

(4)   In that section, in subsection (2), for "Land Registration Act 1925" there is substituted "Land Registration Act 2002".

Law of Property (Miscellaneous Provisions) Act 1994 (c 36)

31—(1) The Law of Property (Miscellaneous Provisions) Act 1994 is amended as follows.

(2)   In section 6 (cases in which there is no liability under covenants implied by virtue of Part 1 of that Act), at the end there is inserted—

"(4) Moreover, where the disposition is of an interest the title to which is registered under the Land Registration Act 2002, that person is not liable under any of those covenants for anything (not falling within subsection (1) or (2)) which at the time of the disposition was entered in relation to that interest in the register of title under that Act."

(3)   In section 17(3)—
  (a) in paragraph (c), for the words from "any" to the end there is substituted "the Adjudicator to Her Majesty's Land Registry", and

(b) for "section 144 of the Land Registration Act 1925" there is substituted "the Land Registration Act 2002".

Drug Trafficking Act 1994 (c 37)

32—(1) The Drug Trafficking Act 1994 is amended as follows.

(2) In section 26(12)—
   (a) for "Land Registration Act 1925" there is substituted "Land Registration Act 2002", and
   (b) in paragraph (a), at the end there is inserted ", except that no notice may be entered in the register of title under the Land Registration Act 2002 in respect of such orders".

(3) In section 28(1) and (4), for "Land Registration Act 1925" there is substituted "Land Registration Act 2002".

Landlord and Tenant (Covenants) Act 1995 (c 30)

33—(1) The Landlord and Tenant (Covenants) Act 1995 is amended as follows.

(2) In sections 3(6) and 15(5)(b), for "Land Registration Act 1925" there is substituted "Land Registration Act 2002".

(3) In section 20, in subsection (2), for the words from "rules" to the end there is substituted "land registration rules under the Land Registration Act 2002".

(4) In that section, in subsection (6)—
   (a) for "an overriding interest within the meaning of the Land Registration Act 1925" there is substituted "capable of falling within paragraph 2 of Schedule 1 or 3 to the Land Registration Act 2002", and
   (b) for "or caution under the Land Registration Act 1925" there is substituted "under the Land Registration Act 2002".

Family Law Act 1996 (c 27)

34—(1) The Family Law Act 1996 is amended as follows.

(2) In section 31(10)—
   (a) for "Land Registration Act 1925" there is substituted "Land Registration Act 2002", and
   (b) for paragraph (b) there is substituted—

   "(b) a spouse's matrimonial home rights are not to be capable of falling within paragraph 2 of Schedule 1 or 3 to that Act."

(3) In Schedule 4, in paragraph 4(6), for "section 144 of the Land Registration Act 1925" there is substituted "by land registration rules under the Land Registration Act 2002".

Housing Act 1996 (c 52)

35 In section 13(5) of the Housing Act 1996, for the words from "if" to the end there is substituted "if the first disposal involves registration under the Land Registration Act 2002, the Chief Land Registrar shall enter in the register of title a restriction reflecting the limitation".

Education Act 1996 (c 56)

36 In Schedule 7 to the Education Act 1996, in paragraph 11—
   (a) in sub-paragraph (a), for "Land Registration Acts 1925 to 1986" there is substituted "Land Registration Act 2002", and
   (b) in sub-paragraphs (b) and (c), for "those Acts" there is substituted "that Act".

School Standards and Framework Act 1998 (c 31)

37 In Schedule 22 to the School Standards and Framework Act 1998, in paragraph 9(1)—
   (a) in paragraph (a), for "Land Registration Acts 1925 to 1986" there is substituted "Land Registration Act 2002", and
   (b) in paragraphs (b) and (c), for "those Acts" there is substituted "that Act".

38 In Schedule 4 to the Terrorism Act 2000, in paragraph 8(1)—
- (a) for "Land Registration Act 1925" there is substituted "Land Registration Act 2002", and
- (b) in paragraph (a), at the end there is inserted ", except that no notice may be entered in the register of title under the Land Registration Act 2002 in respect of such orders".

Finance Act 2000 (c 17)

39 In section 128 of the Finance Act 2000—
- (a) in subsection (2), for the words from "rule" to the end there is substituted "land registration rules under the Land Registration Act 2002", and
- (b) in subsection (8)(a), for "Land Registration Act 1925" there is substituted "Land Registration Act 2002".

International Criminal Court Act 2001 (c 17)

40 In Schedule 6 to the International Criminal Court Act 2001, in paragraph 7(1)—
- (a) for "Land Registration Act 1925" there is substituted "Land Registration Act 2002", and
- (b) in paragraph (a), at the end there is inserted ", except that no notice may be entered in the register of title under the Land Registration Act 2002 in respect of such orders".

SCHEDULE 12

Section 134

TRANSITION

Existing entries in the register

1 Nothing in the repeals made by this Act affects the validity of any entry in the register.

2—(1) This Act applies to notices entered under the Land Registration Act 1925 (c 21) as it applies to notices entered in pursuance of an application under section 34(2)(a).

(2) This Act applies to restrictions and inhibitions entered under the Land Registration Act 1925 as it applies to restrictions entered under this Act.

(3) Notwithstanding their repeal by this Act, sections 55 and 56 of the Land Registration Act 1925 shall continue to have effect so far as relating to cautions against dealings lodged under that Act[, but with the substitution of the words in section 55(1) from "prescribed" to "served" of the words "period prescribed under paragraph 2(4) of Schedule 12 to the Land Registration Act 2002".]

(4) Rules may make provision about cautions against dealings entered under the Land Registration Act 1925.

(5) In this paragraph, references to the Land Registration Act 1925 include a reference to any enactment replaced (directly or indirectly) by that Act.

3 An entry in the register which, immediately before the repeal of section 144(1)(xi) of the Land Registration Act 1925, operated by virtue of rule 239 of the Land Registration Rules (SI 1925/1093) as a caution under section 54 of that Act shall continue to operate as such a caution.

Existing cautions against first registration

4 Notwithstanding the repeal of section 56(3) of the Land Registration Act 1925, that provision shall continue to have effect in relation to cautions against first registration lodged under that Act, or any enactment replaced (directly or indirectly) by that Act.

Pending applications

5 Notwithstanding the repeal of the Land Registration Act 1925, that Act shall continue to have effect in relation to an application for the entry in the register of a notice, restriction, inhibition or caution against dealings which is pending immediately before the repeal of the provision under which the application is made.

6 Notwithstanding the repeal of section 53 of the Land Registration Act 1925, subsections (1) and (2) of that section shall continue to have effect in relation to an application to lodge a caution against first registration which is pending immediately before the repeal of those provisions.

Former overriding interests

7 For the period of three years beginning with the day on which Schedule 1 comes into force, it has effect with the insertion after paragraph 14 of—

"15 A right acquired under the Limitation Act 1980 before the coming into force of this Schedule."

8 Schedule 3 has effect with the insertion after paragraph 2 of—

"2A—(1) An interest which, immediately before the coming into force of this Schedule, was an overriding interest under section 70(1)(g) of the Land Registration Act 1925 by virtue of a person's receipt of rents and profits, except for an interest of a person of whom inquiry was made before the disposition and who failed to disclose the right when he could reasonably have been expected to do so.

(2) Sub-paragraph (1) does not apply to an interest if at any time since the coming into force of this Schedule it has been an interest which, had the Land Registration Act 1925 (c 21) continued in force, would not have been an overriding interest under section 70(1)(g) of that Act by virtue of a person's receipt of rents and profits."

9—(1) This paragraph applies to an easement or profit à prendre which was an overriding interest in relation to a registered estate immediately before the coming into force of Schedule 3, but which would not fall within paragraph 3 of that Schedule if created after the coming into force of that Schedule.

(2) In relation to an interest to which this paragraph applies, Schedule 3 has effect as if the interest were not excluded from paragraph 3.

10 For the period of three years beginning with the day on which Schedule 3 comes into force, paragraph 3 of the Schedule has effect with the omission of the exception.

11 For the period of three years beginning with the day on which Schedule 3 comes into force, it has effect with the insertion after paragraph 14 of—

"15 A right under paragraph 18(1) of Schedule 12."

12 Paragraph 1 of each of Schedules 1 and 3 shall be taken to include an interest which immediately before the coming into force of the Schedule was an overriding interest under section 70(1)(k) of the Land Registration Act 1925.

13 Paragraph 6 of each of Schedules 1 and 3 shall be taken to include an interest which immediately before the coming into force of the Schedule was an overriding interest under section 70(1)(i) of the Land Registration Act 1925 and whose status as such was preserved by section 19(3) of the Local Land Charges Act 1975 (c 76) (transitional provision in relation to change in definition of "local land charge").

Cautions against first registration

14—(1) For the period of two years beginning with the day on which section 15 comes into force, it has effect with the following omissions—
    (a) in subsection (1), the words "Subject to subsection (3),", and
    (b) subsection (3).

(2)   Any caution lodged by virtue of sub-paragraph (1) which is in force immediately before the end of the period mentioned in that sub-paragraph shall cease to have effect at the end of that period, except in relation to applications for registration made before the end of that period.

(3)   This paragraph does not apply to section 15 as applied by section 81.

15—(1) As applied by section 81, section 15 has effect for the period of ten years beginning with the day on which it comes into force, or such longer period as rules may provide, with the omission of subsection (3)(a)(i).

(2)   Any caution lodged by virtue of sub-paragraph (1) which is in force immediately before the end of the period mentioned in that sub-paragraph shall cease to have effect at the end of that period, except in relation to applications for registration made before the end of that period.

16 This Act shall apply as if the definition of "caution against first registration" in section 132 included cautions lodged under section 53 of the Land Registration Act 1925 (c 21).

Applications under section 34 or 43 by cautioners

17 Where a caution under section 54 of the Land Registration Act 1925 is lodged in respect of a person's estate, right, interest or claim, he may only make an application under section 34 or 43 above in respect of that estate, right, interest or claim if he also applies to the registrar for the withdrawal of the caution.

Adverse possession

18—(1) Where a registered estate in land is held in trust for a person by virtue of section 75(1) of the Land Registration Act 1925 immediately before the coming into force of section 97, he is entitled to be registered as the proprietor of the estate.

(2)   A person has a defence to any action for the possession of land (in addition to any other defence he may have) if he is entitled under this paragraph to be registered as the proprietor of an estate in the land.

(3)   Where in an action for possession of land a court determines that a person is entitled to a defence under this paragraph, the court must order the registrar to register him as the proprietor of the estate in relation to which he is entitled under this paragraph to be registered.

(4)   Entitlement under this paragraph shall be disregarded for the purposes of section 131(1).

(5)   Rules may make transitional provision for cases where a rentcharge is held in trust under section 75(1) of the Land Registration Act 1925 immediately before the coming into force of section 97.

Indemnities

19—(1) Schedule 8 applies in relation to claims made before the commencement of that Schedule which have not been settled by agreement or finally determined by that time (as well as to claims for indemnity made after the commencement of that Schedule).

(2)   But paragraph 3(1) of that Schedule does not apply in relation to costs and expenses incurred in respect of proceedings, negotiations or other matters begun before 27 April 1997.

Implied indemnity covenants on transfers of pre-1996 leases

20—(1) On a disposition of a registered leasehold estate by way of transfer, the following covenants are implied in the instrument effecting the disposition, unless the contrary intention is expressed—
- (a)   in the case of a transfer of the whole of the land comprised in the registered lease, the covenant in sub-paragraph (2), and
- (b)   in the case of a transfer of part of the land comprised in the lease—
  - (i)   the covenant in sub-paragraph (3), and

(ii) where the transferor continues to hold land under the lease, the covenant in sub-paragraph (4).

(2) The transferee covenants with the transferor that during the residue of the term granted by the registered lease the transferee and the persons deriving title under him will—

(a) pay the rent reserved by the lease,

(b) comply with the covenants and conditions contained in the lease, and

(c) keep the transferor and the persons deriving title under him indemnified against all actions, expenses and claims on account of any failure to comply with paragraphs (a) and (b).

(3) The transferee covenants with the transferor that during the residue of the term granted by the registered lease the transferee and the persons deriving title under him will—

(a) where the rent reserved by the lease is apportioned, pay the rent apportioned to the part transferred,

(b) comply with the covenants and conditions contained in the lease so far as affecting the part transferred, and

(c) keep the transferor and the persons deriving title under him indemnified against all actions, expenses and claims on account of any failure to comply with paragraphs (a) and (b).

(4) The transferor covenants with the transferee that during the residue of the term granted by the registered lease the transferor and the persons deriving title under him will—

(a) where the rent reserved by the lease is apportioned, pay the rent apportioned to the part retained,

(b) comply with the covenants and conditions contained in the lease so far as affecting the part retained, and

(c) keep the transferee and the persons deriving title under him indemnified against all actions, expenses and claims on account of any failure to comply with paragraphs (a) and (b).

(5) This paragraph does not apply to a lease which is a new tenancy for the purposes of section 1 of the Landlord and Tenant (Covenants) Act 1995 (c 30).

Definitions: For "court" see s 132(3)(a); for "register" and "registered" see s 132(1).
Amendments: Words in para 2 inserted by the Land Registration Act 2002 (Transitional Provisions) Order 2003, SI 2003/1953, art 17.

SCHEDULE 13

Section 135

REPEALS

Short title and chapter	Extent of Repeal
Land Registry Act 1862 (c 53).	The whole Act.
Settled Land Act 1925 (c 18).	Section 119(3).
Law of Property Act 1925 (c 20).	In section 84(8), the words from ", but" to the end.
	In section 205(1)(xxii), the words from ", and" to the end.
Land Registration Act 1925 (c 21).	The whole Act.
Law of Property (Amendment) Act 1926 (c 11).	Section 5.
Land Registration Act 1936 (c 26).	The whole Act.

Short title and chapter	Extent of Repeal
Requisitioned Land and War Works Act 1945 (c 43).	Section 37(3).
Mental Health Act 1959 (c 72).	In Schedule 7, the entry relating to the Land Registration Act 1925.
Charities Act 1960 (c 58).	In Schedule 6, the entry relating to the Land Registration Act 1925.
Civil Evidence Act 1968 (c 64).	In the Schedule, the entry relating to the Land Registration Act 1925.
Post Office Act 1969 (c 48).	In Schedule 4, paragraph 27.
Law of Property Act 1969 (c 59).	Section 28(7).
Land Registration and Land Charges Act 1971 (c 54).	The whole Act.
Superannuation Act 1972 (c 11).	In Schedule 6, paragraph 16.
Local Government Act 1972 (c 70).	In Schedule 29, paragraph 26.
Solicitors Act 1974 (c 47).	Section 75(b).
Finance Act 1975 (c 7).	In Schedule 12, paragraph 5.
Local Land Charges Act 1975 (c 76).	Section 19(3).
	In Schedule 1, the entry relating to the Land Registration Act 1925.
Endowments and Glebe Measure 1976 (No 4).	In Schedule 5, paragraph 1.
Administration of Justice Act 1977 (c 38).	Sections 24 and 26.
Charging Orders Act 1979 (c 53).	Section 3(3).
	Section 7(4).
Limitation Act 1980 (c 58).	In section 17, paragraph (b) and the preceding "and".
Highways Act 1980 (c 66).	Section 251(5).
Matrimonial Homes and Property Act 1981 (c 24).	Section 4.
Administration of Justice Act 1982 (c 53).	Sections 66 and 67 and Schedule 5.
Mental Health Act 1983 (c 20).	In Schedule 4, paragraph 6.
Capital Transfer Tax Act 1984 (c 51).	In Schedule 8, paragraph 1.
Administration of Justice Act 1985 (c 61).	In section 34, in subsection (1), paragraph (b) and the preceding "and" and, in subsection (2), paragraph (b).
	In Schedule 2, paragraph 37(b).
Insolvency Act 1985 (c 65).	In Schedule 8, paragraph 5.

Short title and chapter	Extent of Repeal
Housing Act 1985 (c 68).	Section 36(3).
	Section 154(1), (6) and (7).
	Section 156(3).
	Section 168(5).
	In Schedule 9A, paragraphs 2(1), 3 and 5(3).
Land Registration Act 1986 (c 26).	Sections 1 to 4.
Insolvency Act 1986 (c 45).	In Schedule 14, the entry relating to the Land Registration Act 1925.
Building Societies Act 1986 (c 53).	In Schedule 2A, in paragraph 1, sub-paragraph (4) and, in sub-paragraph (5), the definition of "registered land" and the preceding "and".
	In Schedule 18, paragraph 2.
	In Schedule 21, paragraph 9(b).
Patronage (Benefices) Measure 1986 (No 3).	Section 6.
Landlord and Tenant Act 1987 (c 31).	Section 28(6).
	In Schedule 4, paragraphs 1 and 2.
Diplomatic and Consular Premises Act 1987 (c 46).	In Schedule 1, in paragraph 1, the words from "and expressions" to the end.
Land Registration Act 1988 (c 3).	The whole Act.
Criminal Justice Act 1988 (c 33).	Section 77(13).
	In Schedule 15, paragraphs 6 and 7.
Housing Act 1988 (c 50).	In Schedule 11, paragraph 2(3).
Finance Act 1989 (c 26).	Sections 178(2)(e) and 179(1)(a)(iv).
Courts and Legal Services Act 1990 (c 41).	In Schedule 10, paragraph 3.
	In Schedule 17, paragraph 2.
Access to Neighbouring Land Act 1992 (c 23).	Section 5(2) and (3).
Leasehold Reform, Housing and Urban Development Act 1993 (c 28).	Section 97(3).
	In Schedule 21, paragraph 1.
Coal Industry Act 1994 (c 21).	In Schedule 9, paragraph 1.
Law of Property (Miscellaneous Provisions) Act 1994 (c 36).	In Schedule 1, paragraph 2.
Drug Trafficking Act 1994 (c 37).	Section 26(13).
	In Schedule 1, paragraph 1.
Family Law Act 1996 (c 27).	Section 31(11).
	In Schedule 8, paragraph 45.

Short title and chapter	Extent of Repeal
Trusts of Land and Appointment of Trustees Act 1996 (c 47).	In Schedule 3, paragraph 5.
Housing Act 1996 (c 52).	Section 11(4).
Housing Grants, Construction and Regeneration Act 1996 (c 53).	Section 138(3).
Land Registration Act 1997 (c 2).	Sections 1 to 3 and 5(4) and (5). In Schedule 1, paragraphs 1 to 6.
Greater London Authority Act 1999 (c 29).	Section 219.
Terrorism Act 2000 (c 11).	In Schedule 4, paragraph 8(2) and (3).
Trustee Act 2000 (c 29).	In Schedule 2, paragraph 26.
International Criminal Court Act 2001 (c 17).	In Schedule 6, paragraph 7(2).

Land Registration Rules 2003

(SI 2003/1417)

Made: 19 May 2003.
Authority: Land Registration Act 2002, ss 1(2), 6(6), 13(a), (b), 14(a), (b), 16(2), 18(1)(b), (2), (4), 19(2), 20(3)(a)–(c), 21(2)(a)–(d), 22, 25(1), 27(6), 34(2), 35(3), 36(3), (4), 37(2), 39, 43(2)(a)–(d), 44(2), 45(2), 46(4), 47(a), (b), 48(2)(a), (b), 49(2), (3)(b), (4)(b), 50, 57, 60(3), (4), 61(2), 64(2), 66(2), 67(3), 68(1)(d), (2)(a), (b), 69(2), 70, 71(a), (b), 72(6)(a), (b), 73(2), (3), (4), 75(2), 76(2), 81(2), 82, 86(3), 87(4), 89, 95(a), 98(7), Sch 2, paras 2(2), 7(3), Sch 4, paras 4(a)–(c), 7(a)–(d), Sch 6, paras 2(1)(d), 3(2), 14, 15, Sch 8, para 9, Sch 10, paras 1(1)(a), (b), 3(a), (b), (c), 5, 6(a)–(e), 7, 8, Sch 12, paras 2(4), 18(5); Charities Act 1993, ss 37(7), 39(1), (1A); Leasehold Reform, Housing and Urban Development Act 1993, ss 34(10), 57(1); Family Law Act 1996, Sch 4, para 4(4).
Commencement: 13 October 2003 (ie the day on which the Land Registration Act 2002, s 1 comes into force).

ARRANGEMENT OF RULES

PART 5
CAUTIONS AGAINST FIRST REGISTRATION

PART 6
REGISTERED LAND: APPLICATIONS, DISPOSITIONS AND MISCELLANEOUS ENTRIES

Applications

Registrable dispositions—Form

Execution by an attorney

Covenants

PART 15
GENERAL PROVISIONS

Preliminary

1 Citation and commencement

These rules may be cited as the Land Registration Rules 2003 and shall come into force on the day that section 1 of the Act comes into force.

References: See para 6.27.

PART 1
THE REGISTER OF TITLE

2 Form and arrangement of the register of title

(1) The register of title may be kept in electronic or paper form, or partly in one form and partly in the other.

(2) Subject to rule 3, the register of title must include an individual register for each registered estate which is—
    (a) an estate in land, or
    (b) a rentcharge, franchise, manor or profit a prendre in gross,

vested in a proprietor.

References: See paras 2.5, 2.6.

---

3 Individual registers and more than one registered estate, division and amalgamation

(1) The registrar may include more than one registered estate in an individual register if the estates are of the same kind and are vested in the same proprietor.

(2) On first registration of a registered estate, the registrar may open an individual register for each separate area of land affected by the proprietor's registered estate as he designates.

(3) Subsequently, the registrar may open an individual register for part of the registered estate in a registered title and retain the existing individual register for the remainder—
    (a) on the application of the proprietor of the registered estate and of any registered charge over it, or
    (b) if he considers it desirable for the keeping of the register of title, or
    (c) on the registration of a charge of part of the registered estate comprised in the registered title.

(4) The registrar may amalgamate two or more registered titles, or add an estate which is being registered for the first time to an existing registered title, if the estates are of the same kind and are vested in the same proprietor—
    (a) on the application of the proprietor of the registered estate and of any registered charge over it, or
    (b) if he considers it desirable for the keeping of the register of title.

(5)   Where the registrar has divided a registered title under paragraph (3)(b) or amalgamated registered titles or an estate on first registration with a registered title under paragraph (4)(b) he—

    (a)   must notify the proprietor of the registered estate and any registered charge, unless they have agreed to such action, and

    (b)   may make a new edition of any individual register or make entries on any individual register to reflect the division or amalgamation.

References: See para 2.6.

4 Arrangement of individual registers

(1)   Each individual register must have a distinguishing number, or series of letters and numbers, known as the title number.

(2)   Each individual register must consist of a property register, a proprietorship register and, where necessary, a charges register.

(3)   An entry in an individual register may be made by reference to a plan or other document; in which case the registrar must keep the original or a copy of the document.

(4)   Whenever the registrar considers it desirable, he may make a new edition of any individual register so that it contains only the subsisting entries, rearrange the entries in the register or alter its title number.

References: See para 2.7.

5 Contents of the property register

The property register of a registered estate must contain—

    (a)   a description of the registered estate which in the case of a registered estate in land, rentcharge or registered franchise which is an affecting franchise must refer to a plan based on the Ordnance Survey map and known as the title plan;

    (b)   where appropriate, details of—

        (i)   the inclusion or exclusion of mines and minerals in or from the registration under rule 32,

        (ii)   easements, rights, privileges, conditions and covenants benefiting the registered estate and other similar matters,

        (iii)   all exceptions arising on enfranchisement of formerly copyhold land, and

        (iv)   any other matter required to be entered in any other part of the register which the registrar considers may more conveniently be entered in the property register, and

    (c)   such other matters as are required to be entered in the property register by these rules.

References: See paras 2.7, 2.13.

6 Property register of a registered leasehold estate

(1)   The property register of a registered leasehold estate must also contain sufficient particulars of the registered lease to enable that lease to be identified.

(2)   If the lease contains a provision that prohibits or restricts dispositions of the leasehold estate, the registrar must make an entry in the property register stating that all estates, rights, interests, powers and remedies arising on or by reason of a disposition made in breach of that prohibition or restriction are excepted from the effect of registration.

References: See paras 2.7, 6.27.

7 Property register of a registered estate in a rentcharge, a franchise or a profit a prendre in gross

The property register of a registered estate in a rentcharge, franchise or a profit a prendre in gross must, if the estate was created by an instrument, also contain sufficient particulars of the instrument to enable it to be identified.

References: See para 2.7.

8 Contents of the proprietorship register

(1)   The proprietorship register of a registered estate must contain, where appropriate—
- (a)   the class of title,
- (b)   the name of the proprietor of the registered estate including, where the proprietor is a company registered under the Companies Acts, or a limited liability partnership incorporated under the Limited Liability Partnerships Act 2000, its registered number,
- (c)   an address for service of the proprietor of the registered estate in accordance with rule 198,
- (d)   restrictions under section 40 of the Act, including one entered under section 86(4) of the Act, in relation to the registered estate,
- (e)   notices under section 86(2) of the Act in relation to the registered estate,
- (f)   positive covenants by a transferor or transferee and indemnity convenants by a transferee entered under rules 64 or 65,
- (g)   details of any modification of the covenants implied by paragraphs 20(2) and (3) of Schedule 12 to the Act entered under rule 66,
- (h)   details of any modification of the covenants implied under the Law of Property (Miscellaneous Provisions) Act 1994 entered under rule 67(6),
- (i)   where the class of title is possessory, the name of the first proprietor of the registered estate and, where that proprietor is a company registered under the Companies Acts, or a limited liability partnership incorporated under the Limited Liability Partnerships Act 2000, its registered number, and
- (j)   such other matters as are required to be entered in the proprietorship register by these rules.

(2)   On first registration and on a subsequent change of proprietor, the registrar whenever practicable will enter in the proprietorship register the price paid or value declared and such entry will remain until there is a change of proprietor, or some other change in the register of title which the registrar considers would result in the entry being misleading.

References: See paras 2.7, 5.13.

9 Contents of the charges register

The charges register of a registered estate must contain, where appropriate—
- (a)   details of leases, charges, and any other interests which adversely affect the registered estate subsisting at the time of first registration of the estate or created thereafter,
- (b)   any dealings with the interests referred to in paragraph (a), or affecting their priority, which are capable of being noted on the register,
- (c)   sufficient details to enable any registered charge to be identified,
- (d)   the name of the proprietor of any registered charge including, where the proprietor is a company registered under the Companies Acts, or a limited liability partnership incorporated under the Limited Liability Partnerships Act 2000, its registered number,
- (e)   an address for service of the proprietor of any registered charge in accordance with rule 198,
- (f)   restrictions under section 40 of the Act, including one entered under section 86(4) of the Act, in relation to a registered charge,
- (g)   notices under section 86(2) of the Act in relation to a registered charge, and
- (h)   such other matters affecting the registered estate or any registered charge as are required to be entered in the charges register by these rules.

References: See paras 2.7, 4.15, 6.39, 6.48.

PART 2
INDICES

10 Index to be kept under section 68 of the Act

(1)   The index to be kept under section 68 of the Act must comprise—
- (a)   an index map from which it is possible to ascertain, in relation to a parcel of land, whether there is—
  - (i)   a pending application for first registration (other than of title to a relating franchise),
  - (ii)   a pending application for a caution against first registration (other than where the subject of the caution is a relating franchise),
  - (iii)   a registered estate in land,
  - (iv)   a registered rentcharge,
  - (v)   a registered profit a prendre in gross,
  - (vi)   a registered affecting franchise, or

(vii) a caution against first registration (other than where the subject of the caution is a relating franchise),

and, if there is such a registered estate or caution, the title number, and

(b) an index of verbal descriptions of—

(i) pending applications for first registration of title to relating franchises,

(ii) pending applications for cautions against first registration where the subject of the caution is a relating franchise,

(iii) registered franchises which are relating franchises,

(iv) registered manors, and

(v) cautions against first registration where the subject of the caution is a relating franchise,

and the title numbers of any such registered estates and cautions, arranged by administrative area.

(2) The information required to be shown in the index to be kept under section 68 is to be entered by the registrar in the index as soon as practicable.

References: See para 2.21.

11 Index of proprietors' names

(1) Subject to paragraph (2), the registrar must keep an index of proprietors' names, showing for each individual register the name of the proprietor of the registered estate and the proprietor of any registered charge together with the title number.

(2) Until every individual register is held in electronic form, the index need not contain the name of any corporate or joint proprietor of an estate or of a charge registered as proprietor prior to 1st May 1972.

(3) A person may apply in Form PN1 for a search to be made in the index in respect of either his own name or the name of some other person in whose property he can satisfy the registrar that he is interested generally (for instance as trustee in bankruptcy or personal representative).

(4) On receipt of such an application the registrar must make the search and supply the applicant with details of every entry in the index relating to the particulars given in the application.

References: See paras 2.23, 8.8.

12 The day list

(1) The registrar must keep a record (known as the day list) showing the date and time at which every pending application under the Act or these rules was made and of every application for an official search with priority under rule 147.

(2) The entry of notice of an application for an official search with priority must remain on the day list until the priority period conferred by the entry has ceased to have effect.

(3) Where the registrar proposes to alter the register without having received an application he must enter his proposal on the day list and, when so entered, the

proposal will have the same effect for the purposes of rules 15 and 20 as if it were an application to the registrar made at the date and time of its entry.

(4)   In this rule the term "pending application" does not include an application within Part 13, other than an application that the registrar designate a document an exempt information document under rule 136.

References: See paras 2.24, 15.4.

PART 3
APPLICATIONS: GENERAL PROVISIONS

13 Form AP1

(1)   Any application made under the Act or these rules for which no other application form is prescribed must be made in Form AP1.

(2)   Paragraph (1) does not apply to—
    (a)   an application to remove from the register the name of a deceased joint registered proprietor,
    (b)   applications made under rule 14, or
    (c)   outline applications as defined in rule 54.

References: See paras 2.43, 5.19, 13.30.

14 Electronic delivery of applications

Any application to which rule 15 applies (other than an outline application under rule 54) may during the currency of any notice given under Schedule 2, and subject to and in accordance with the limitations contained in that notice, be delivered by electronic means and the applicant shall provide, in such order as may be required by that notice, such of the particulars required for an application of that type as are appropriate in the circumstances and as are required by the notice.

15 Time at which applications are taken to be made

(1)   An application received on a business day is to be taken as made at the earlier of—
    (a)   the time of the day that notice of it is entered in the day list, or
    (b)
        (i)   midnight marking the end of the day it was received if the application was received before 12 noon, or
        (ii)   midnight marking the end of the next business day after the day it was received if the application was received at or after 12 noon.

(2)   An application received on a day which is not a business day is to be taken as made at the earlier of—
    (a)   the time of a business day that notice of it is entered in the day list, or
    (b)   midnight marking the end of the next business day after the day it was received.

(3)   In this rule an application is received when it is delivered—
    (a)   to the designated proper office in accordance with an order under section 100(3) of the Act, or

    (b)   to the registrar in accordance with a written arrangement as to delivery made between the registrar and the applicant or between the registrar and the applicant's conveyancer, or

    (c)   to the registrar under the provisions of any relevant notice given under Schedule 2.

(4)   This rule does not apply to applications under Part 13, other than an application that the registrar designate a document an exempt information document under rule 136.

References: See paras 2.45, 2.49, 2.50, 5.20, 7.87.

16 Applications not in order

(1)   If an application is not in order the registrar may raise such requisitions as he considers necessary, specifying a period (being not less than twenty business days) within which the applicant must comply with the requisitions.

(2)   If the applicant fails to comply with the requisitions within that period, the registrar may cancel the application or may extend the period when this appears to him to be reasonable in the circumstances.

(3)   If an application appears to the registrar to be substantially defective, he may reject it on delivery or he may cancel it at any time thereafter.

(4)   Where a fee for an application is paid by means of a cheque and the registrar becomes aware, before that application has been completed, that the cheque has not been honoured, the application may be cancelled.

References: See paras 2.37, 2.53.

17 Additional evidence and enquiries

If the registrar at any time considers that the production of any further documents or evidence or the giving of any notice is necessary or desirable, he may refuse to complete or proceed with an application, or to do any act or make any entry, until such documents, evidence or notices have been supplied or given.

References: See para 2.54.

18 Continuation of application on a transfer by operation of law

If, before an application has been completed, the whole of the applicant's interest is transferred by operation of law, the application may be continued by the person entitled to that interest in consequence of that transfer.

19 Objections

(1)   Subject to paragraph (5), an objection under section 73 of the Act to an application must be made by delivering to the registrar at the appropriate office a written statement signed by the objector or his conveyancer.

(2)   The statement must—

    (a)   state that the objector objects to the application,

(b) state the grounds for the objection, and

(c) give the full name of the objector and an address to which communications may be sent.

(3) Subject to paragraph (5), the written statement referred to in paragraph (1) must be delivered—

(a) in paper form, or

(b) to the electronic address, or

(c) to the fax number.

(4) In paragraph (3) the reference to the electronic address and the fax number is to the electronic address or fax number for the appropriate office specified in a direction by the registrar under section 100(4) of the Act as that to be used for delivery of objections.

(5) Where a person is objecting to an application in response to a notice given by the registrar, he may alternatively do so in the manner and to the address stated in the notice as provided by rule 197(1)(c).

(6) In this rule the appropriate office is the same office as the proper office, designated under an order under section 100(3) of the Act, for the receipt of an application relating to the land in respect of which the objection is made, but on the assumption that if the order contains exceptions none of the exceptions apply to that application.

References: See paras 2.55, 15.6.

20 Completion of applications

(1) Any entry in, removal of an entry from or alteration of the register pursuant to an application under the Act or these rules has effect from the time of the making of the application.

(2) This rule does not apply to the applications mentioned in section 74 of the Act.

References: See paras 2.44, 2.47, 15.4.

PART 4
FIRST REGISTRATION

21 First registration—application by mortgagee

A mortgagee under a mortgage falling within section 4(1)(g) of the Act may make an application in the name of the mortgagor for the estate charged by the mortgage to be registered whether or not the mortgagor consents.

References: See paras 5.2, 5.9, 6.4, 8.3.

22 Registration of a proprietor of a charge falling within section 4(1)(g) of the Act

(1) This rule applies to an application for first registration made—

(a) under rule 21, or

(b)   by the owner of an estate that is subject to a legal charge falling within section 4(1)(g) of the Act.

(2)   The registrar must enter the mortgagee of the legal charge falling within section 4(1)(g) of the Act as the proprietor of that charge if he is satisfied of that person's entitlement.

References: See paras 4.15, 8.3.

23 First registration—application form

(1)   Subject to paragraph (2), an application for first registration must be made in Form FR1.

(2)   Where Her Majesty applies for the first registration of an estate under section 79 of the Act, Form FR1 must be used with such modifications to it as are appropriate and have been approved by the registrar.

References: See paras 4.13, 7.5, 13.31.

24 Documents to be delivered with a first registration application

(1)   Unless the registrar otherwise directs, every application for first registration must be accompanied by—
    (a)   sufficient details, by plan or otherwise (subject to rules 25 and 26), so that the land can be identified clearly on the Ordnance Survey map,
    (b)   in the case of a leasehold estate, the lease, if in the control of the applicant, and a certified copy,
    (c)   all deeds and documents relating to the title that are in the control of the applicant,
    (d)   a list in duplicate in Form DL of all the documents delivered.

(2)   On an application to register a rentcharge, franchise or profit a prendre in gross, the land to be identified under paragraph (1)(a) is the land affected by that estate or to which it relates.

References: See paras 4.13, 4.18, 6.10.

25 First registration of mines and minerals

When applying for first registration of an estate in mines and minerals held apart from the surface, the applicant must provide—
    (a)   a plan of the surface under which the mines and minerals lie,
    (b)   any other sufficient details by plan or otherwise so that the mines and minerals can be identified clearly, and
    (c)   full details of rights incidental to the working of the mines and minerals.

References: See para 4.13.

26 First registration of cellars, flats, tunnels etc

(1)   Subject to paragraph (2), unless all of the land above and below the surface is included in an application for first registration the applicant must provide a plan of the surface on under or over which the land to be registered lies, and sufficient information to define the vertical and horizontal extents of the land.

(2)   This rule does not apply where only mines and minerals are excluded from the application.

References: See para 4.13.

27 First registration application where title documents are unavailable

An application for first registration by a person who is unable to produce a full documentary title must be supported by evidence—

    (a)   to satisfy the registrar that the applicant is entitled to apply under section 3(2) of the Act or required to apply under section 6(1) of the Act, and

    (b)   where appropriate, to account for the absence of documentary evidence of title.

References: See para 4.13.

28 Duty to disclose unregistered interests that override first registration

(1)   Subject to paragraph (2), a person applying for first registration must provide information to the registrar about any of the interests that fall within Schedule 1 to the Act that—

    (a)   are within the actual knowledge of the applicant, and

    (b)   affect the estate to which the application relates,

in Form DI.

(2)   The applicant is not required to provide information about—

    (a)   an interest that under section 33 or 90(4) of the Act cannot be protected by notice,

    (b)   an interest that is apparent from the deeds and documents of title accompanying the application under rule 24,

    (c)   a public right,

    (d)   a local land charge,

    (e)   a leasehold estate in land if—

        (i)   it is within paragraph 1 of Schedule 1 to the Act, and

        (ii)   at the time of the application, the term granted by the lease has one year or less to run.

(3)   In this rule and in Form FR1, a "disclosable overriding interest" is an interest that the applicant must provide information about under paragraph (1).

(4)   Where the applicant provides information about a disclosable overriding interest under this rule, the registrar may enter a notice in the register in respect of that interest.

References: See paras 4.14, 4.18, 7.5, Appendix 1.

29 First registration—examination of title

In examining the title shown by the documents accompanying an application for first registration the registrar may have regard to any examination of title by a conveyancer prior to the application and to the nature of the property.

References: See para 4.13.

30 Searches and enquiries by the registrar

In examining title on an application for first registration the registrar may—
- (a) make searches and enquiries and give notices to other persons,
- (b) direct that searches and enquiries be made by the applicant,
- (c) advertise the application.

References: See para 4.13.

31 First registration—foreshore

(1) Where it appears to the registrar that any land included in an application for first registration comprises foreshore, he must serve a notice of that application on—
- (a) the Crown Estate Commissioners in every case,
- (b) the Chancellor of the Duchy of Lancaster in the case of land in the county palatine of Lancaster,
- (c) the appropriate person in the case of land in the counties of Devon and Cornwall and in the Isles of Scilly and in the case of land within the jurisdiction of the Port of London Authority, and
- (d) the Port of London Authority in the case of land within its jurisdiction.

(2) A notice under paragraph (1) must provide a period ending at 12 noon on the twentieth business day after the date of issue of the notice in which to object to the application.

(3) A notice need not be served under paragraph (1) where, if it was served, it would result in it being served on the applicant for first registration.

(4) In this rule—
"the appropriate person" means such person as the Duke of Cornwall, or the possessor for the time being of the Duchy of Cornwall, appoints,
"foreshore" has the meaning given by paragraph 13(3) of Schedule 6 to the Act.

References: See para 4.13.

32 Mines and minerals—note as to inclusion or exclusion

Where, on first registration of an estate in land which comprises or includes the land beneath the surface, the registrar is satisfied that the mines and minerals are included in or excluded from the applicant's title he must make an appropriate note in the register.

References: See para 4.15, 4.16.

33 First registration—entry of beneficial rights

(1) The benefit of an appurtenant right may be entered in the register at the time of first registration if—
- (a) on examination of the title, or

> (b)   on receipt of a written application providing details of the right and evidence of its existence,

the registrar is satisfied that the right subsists as a legal estate and benefits the registered estate.

(2)   If the registrar is not satisfied that the right subsists as a legal interest benefiting the registered estate, he may enter details of the right claimed in the property register with such qualification as he considers appropriate.

References: See paras 4.16.

34   First registration—registration of a proprietor of a legal mortgage not within rule 22 or rule 38

(1)   The registrar must enter the mortgagee of a legal mortgage to which this rule applies as the proprietor of that charge if on first registration of the legal estate charged by that charge he is satisfied of that person's entitlement.

(2)   This rule applies to a legal mortgage—
> (a)   which is either—
>> (i)   a charge on the legal estate that is being registered, or
>> (ii)   is a charge on such charge, and
> (b)   which is not a charge falling within rule 22 or rule 38.

35   First registration—entry of burdens

(1)   On first registration the registrar must enter a notice in the register of the burden of any interest which appears from his examination of the title to affect the registered estate.

(2)   This rule does not apply to—
> (a)   an interest that under section 33 or 90(4) of the Act cannot be protected by notice,
> (b)   a public right,
> (c)   a local land charge,
> (d)   an interest which appears to the registrar to be of a trivial or obvious character, or the entry of a notice in respect of which would be likely to cause confusion or inconvenience.

References: See paras 4.15, 6.39.

36   First registration—note as to rights of light and air

On first registration, if it appears to the registrar that an agreement prevents the acquisition of rights of light or air for the benefit of the registered estate, he may make an entry in the property register of that estate.

References: See para 4.15.

37 First registration—notice of lease

(1)   Subject to paragraph (2), before completing an application for registration of a leasehold estate with absolute title, the registrar must give notice of the application to the proprietor of the registered reversion.

(2)   This rule only applies where—
    (a)   at the time of the grant of the lease—
        (i)   the reversion was not registered, or
        (ii)   the reversion was registered but the grant of the lease was not required to be completed by registration,
    (b)   the lease is not noted in the register of the registered reversion, and
    (c)   it is not apparent from the application that the proprietor of the registered reversion consents to the registration.

(3)   On completing registration of the leasehold estate, the registrar must enter notice of the lease in the register of the registered reversion.

(4)   In this rule, "the reversion" refers to the estate that is the immediate reversion to the lease that is the subject of the application referred to in paragraph (1) and "registered reversion" refers to such estate when it is a registered estate.

References: See paras 4.13, 6.16.

38 Application of the Act to dealings prior to first registration

(1)   If, while a person is subject to a duty under section 6 of the Act to make an application to be registered as proprietor of a legal estate, there is a dealing with that estate, then the Act applies to that dealing as if the dealing had taken place after the date of first registration of that estate.

(2)   The registration of any dealing falling within paragraph (1) that is delivered for registration with the application made pursuant to section 6 has effect from the time of the making of that application.

References: See para 4.11.

PART 5
CAUTIONS AGAINST FIRST REGISTRATION

39 Definitions

In this Part—
        "cautioner" has the same meaning as in section 22 of the Act (read with rule 52),
        "cautioner's register" is the register so named in rule 41(2) the contents of which are described in rule 41(5),
        "relevant interest" means the interest claimed by the cautioner in the unregistered legal estate to which the caution against first registration relates.

40 Form and arrangement of the cautions register

(1)   The cautions register may be kept in electronic or paper form, or partly in one form and partly in the other.

(2) Subject to paragraph (3), the cautions register will comprise an individual caution register for each caution against the registration of title to an unregistered estate.

(3) On registration of a caution, the registrar may open an individual caution register for each separate area of land affected by the caution as he designates.

References: See para 4.6.

41 Arrangement of individual caution registers

(1) Each individual caution register will have a distinguishing number, or series of letters and numbers, known as the caution title number.

(2) Each individual caution register will be in two parts called the caution property register and the cautioner's register.

(3) The caution property register will contain—
    (a) a description of the legal estate to which the caution relates, and
    (b) a description of the relevant interest.

(4) Where the legal estate to which the caution relates is an estate in land, a rentcharge, or an affecting franchise, the description will refer to a caution plan, which plan will be based on the Ordnance Survey map.

(5) The cautioner's register will contain—
    (a) the name of the cautioner including, where the cautioner is a company registered under the Companies Acts, or a limited liability partnership incorporated under the Limited Liability Partnerships Act 2000, its registered number,
    (b) an address for service in accordance with rule 198, and
    (c) where appropriate, details of any person consenting to the lodging of the caution under rule 47.

References: See paras 4.5, 4.6, 4.8.

42 Caution against first registration—application

An application for a caution against first registration must be made in Form CT1 and contain sufficient details, by plan or otherwise, so that the extent of the land to which the caution relates can be identified clearly on the Ordnance Survey map.

References: See para 4.3.

43 Withdrawal of a caution against first registration—application

An application to withdraw a caution against first registration must be made in Form WCT and, if the application is made in respect of part only of the land to which the individual caution register relates, it must contain sufficient details, by plan or otherwise, so that the extent of that part can be identified clearly on the Ordnance Survey map.

References: See paras 4.6, 4.7.

44 Cancellation of a caution against first registration—application

(1)   Subject to paragraph (5), an application for the cancellation of a caution against first registration must be in Form CCT.

(2)   Where the application is made in respect of part only of the land to which the individual caution register relates, it must contain sufficient details, by plan or otherwise, so that the extent of that part can be identified clearly on the Ordnance Survey map.

(3)   Where a person applies under section 18(1)(a) of the Act or rule 45(a) or (b)(ii), evidence to satisfy the registrar that he is entitled to apply must accompany the application.

(4)   Where the applicant, or a person from whom the applicant derives title to the legal estate by operation of law, has consented to the lodging of the caution, evidence of the facts referred to in rule 46 must accompany the application.

(5)   Where an application is made for the cancellation of a caution against first registration by Her Majesty by virtue of rule 45(b)(i), Form CCT must be used with such modifications to it as are appropriate and have been approved by the registrar.

References: See para 4.7.

45 Other persons who may apply to cancel a caution against first registration

In addition to the owner of the legal estate to which the caution relates—
  (a)   the owner of a legal estate derived out of that estate, and
  (b)   where the land to which the caution relates is demesne land,
    (i)   Her Majesty, or
    (ii)   the owner of a legal estate affecting the demesne land,

may apply under section 18(1)(b) of the Act for cancellation of a caution against first registration.

References: See para 15.71.

46 Application for cancellation of a caution against first registration by a person who originally consented

A person to whom section 18(2) of the Act applies may make an application for cancellation of a caution against first registration only if—
  (a)   the relevant interest has come to an end, or
  (b)   the consent referred to in section 18(2) was induced by fraud, misrepresentation, mistake or undue influence or given under duress.

References: See para 4.7.

47 Consent to registration of a caution against first registration

For the purposes of section 18(2) of the Act a person consents to the lodging of a caution against first registration if before the caution is entered in the cautions register—

    (a)   he has confirmed in writing that he consents to the lodging of the caution, and

    (b)   that consent is produced to the registrar.

References: See para 4.7.

48 Alteration of the cautions register by the court

(1)   If in any proceedings the court decides that the cautioner does not own the relevant interest, or only owns part, or that such interest either wholly or in part did not exist or has come to an end, the court must make an order for alteration of the cautions register under section 20(1) of the Act.

(2)   An order for alteration of the cautions register must state the caution title number of the individual caution register affected, describe the alteration that is to be made, and direct the registrar to make the alteration.

(3)   For the purposes of section 20(2) of the Act an order for alteration of the cautions register may only be served on the registrar by making an application for him to give effect to the order.

References: See paras 4.7, 14.24, 14.25, 15.74.

49 Alteration of the cautions register by the registrar

If the registrar is satisfied that the cautioner does not own the relevant interest, or only owns part, or that such interest did not exist or has come to an end wholly or in part, he must on application alter the cautions register under section 21(1) of the Act.

References: See paras 4.7, 14.24.

50 Applications to the registrar to alter the cautions register and service of notice

(1)   A person who wishes the registrar to alter the cautions register under section 21(1) of the Act must request the registrar to do so by an application, which must include—

    (a)   written details of the alteration required and of the grounds on which the application is made, and

    (b)   any supporting document.

(2)   Before the registrar alters the cautions register under section 21(1) of the Act he must serve a notice on the cautioner giving details of the application, unless the registrar is satisfied that service of the notice is unnecessary.

References: See paras 4.7, 14.24.

51 Alteration of the cautions register—alteration of cautioner

(1)   A person who claims that the whole of the relevant interest described in an individual caution register is vested in him by operation of law as successor to the cautioner may apply for the register to be altered under section 21(1) of the Act to show him as cautioner in the cautioner's register in place of the cautioner.

(2)   If the registrar does not serve notice under rule 50(2) or if the cautioner does not object within the time specified in the notice, the registrar must give effect to the application.

References: See paras 4.7, 14.26.

52 Definition of "the cautioner"

For the purpose of Chapter 2 of Part 2 and section 73(2) of the Act, the other person referred to in sections 22 and 73(2) of the Act shall be the person for the time being shown as cautioner in the cautioner's register, where that person is not the person who lodged the caution against first registration.

References: See paras 4.7, 4.8.

53 The prescribed periods under section 16(2) and section 18(4) of the Act

(1)   The period for the purpose of section 16(2) and section 18(4) of the Act is the period ending at 12 noon on the fifteenth business day after the date of issue of the notice under section 16(1) or section 18(3) of the Act, as the case may be, or such longer period as the registrar may allow following a request under paragraph (2), provided that the longer period never exceeds a period ending at 12 noon on the thirtieth business day after the date of issue of the notice.

(2)   The request referred to in paragraph (1) is one by the cautioner to the registrar setting out why the longer period referred to in that paragraph should be allowed.

(3)   If a request is received under paragraph (2), the registrar may, if he considers it appropriate, seek the views of the person who applied for registration or cancellation, as the case may be, and if, after considering any such views and all other relevant matters, he is satisfied that a longer period should be allowed he may allow such period (not exceeding a period ending at 12 noon on the thirtieth business day after the date of issue of the notice) as he considers appropriate, whether or not the period is the same as any period requested by the cautioner.

(4)   A request under paragraph (2) must be made before the period ending at 12 noon on the fifteenth business day after the date of issue of the notice has expired.

References: See paras 4.7, 4.8.

PART 6
REGISTERED LAND: APPLICATIONS, DISPOSITIONS AND MISCELLANEOUS ENTRIES

Applications

54 Outline applications

(1)   An outline application is an application made in accordance with this rule.

(2)   Subject to Schedule 2, any application may be made by outline application if it satisfies the following conditions—
- (a)   the application must not be—
  - (i)   an application which can be protected by an official search with priority within the meaning of rule 147,
  - (ii)   an application for first registration,
  - (iii)   an application for a caution against first registration or in respect of the cautions register,
  - (iv)   an application dealing with part only of the land in a registered title, whether or not also involving any other registered title,
  - (v)   an application under Part 13, and
- (b)   the right, interest or matter the subject of the application must exist at the time the application is made.

(3)   During the currency of any notice given under Schedule 2, and subject to and in accordance with the limitations contained in that notice, an outline application may be made by—
- (a)   an oral application,
- (b)   telephone, or
- (c)   electronic means.

(4)   An outline application must contain the following particulars when made—
- (a)   the title number(s) affected,
- (b)   if there is only one proprietor or applicant for first registration and that person is an individual, his surname, otherwise the proprietor's or such applicant's full name or the full name of one of the proprietors or such applicants, as appropriate,
- (c)   the nature of the application,
- (d)   the name of the applicant,
- (e)   the name and address of the person or firm lodging the application,
- (f)   any other particulars specified in any notice made under Schedule 2.

(5)   Every outline application must be allocated an official reference number and must be identified on the day list as such and must be marked with the date and time at which the application is taken as made and the registrar must acknowledge receipt of any outline application by notifying the applicant, as soon as practicable, of the official reference number allocated to it.

(6)   Without prejudice to the power of the registrar to cancel an application under rule 16, the outline application must be cancelled by the registrar unless there is delivered at the appropriate office before the expiry of the reserved period the relevant application form prescribed by these rules, duly completed in respect of the outline application, quoting the official reference number of the outline application and accompanied by the appropriate documentation and the prescribed fee.

(7)   If the outline application has been cancelled before the form required by paragraph (6) is delivered at the appropriate office, the registrar shall accept the form as an application in its own right.

(8)   In this rule the "appropriate office" is the same office as the proper office, designated under an order under section 100(3) of the Act, for the receipt of an application relating to the land in respect of which the outline application is made, but on the assumption that if the order contains exceptions none of the exceptions apply to the application.

(9)   In this rule "reserved period" means the period expiring at 12 noon on the fourth business day following the day that the outline application was taken as made.

References: See paras 2.47, 2.48.

55 Priority of applications

(1)   Where two or more applications relating to the same registered title are under the provisions of rule 15 taken as having been made at the same time, the order in which, as between each other, they rank in priority shall be determined in the manner prescribed by this rule.

(2)   Where the applications are made by the same applicant, they rank in such order as he may specify.

(3)   Where the applications are not made by the same applicant, they rank in such order as the applicants may specify that they have agreed.

(4)   Where the applications are not made by the same applicant, and the applicants have not specified the agreed order of priority, the registrar must notify the applicants that their applications are regarded as having been delivered at the same time and request them to agree, within a specified time (being not less than fifteen business days), their order of priority.

(5)   Where the parties fail within the time specified by the registrar to indicate the order of priority of their applications the registrar must propose the order of priority and serve notice on the applicants of his proposal.

(6)   Any notice served under paragraph (5) must draw attention to the right of any applicant who does not agree with the registrar's proposal to object to another applicant's application under the provisions of section 73 of the Act.

(7)   Where one transaction is dependent upon another the registrar must assume (unless the contrary appears) that the applicants have specified that the applications will have priority so as to give effect to the sequence of the documents effecting the transactions.

References: See para 2.46, 4.11, 5.20.

56 Dispositions affecting two or more registered titles

(1)   A disposition affecting two or more registered titles may, on the written request of the applicant, be registered as to some or only one of the registered titles.

(2)   The applicant may later apply to have the disposition registered as to any of the other registered titles affected by it.

57 Duty to disclose unregistered interests that override registered dispositions

(1)   Subject to paragraph (2), a person applying to register a registrable disposition of a registered estate must provide information to the registrar about any of the interests that fall within Schedule 3 to the Act that—

      (a)   are within the actual knowledge of the applicant, and
      (b)   affect the estate to which the application relates,

in Form DI.

(2)   The applicant is not required to provide information about—

(a)   an interest that under section 33 or 90(4) of the Act cannot be protected by notice,

(b)   a public right,

(c)   a local land charge, or

(d)   a leasehold estate in land if—

(i)   it is within paragraph 1 of Schedule 3 to the Act, and

(ii)   at the time of the application, the term granted by the lease has one year or less to run.

(3)   In this rule and in Form AP1, a "disclosable overriding interest" is an interest that the applicant must provide information about under paragraph (1).

(4)   The applicant must produce to the registrar any documentary evidence of the existence of a disclosable overriding interest that is under his control.

(5)   Where the applicant provides information about a disclosable overriding interest under this rule, the registrar may enter a notice in the register in respect of that interest.

References: See paras 4.18, 5.19, Appendix 1.

Registrable dispositions — Form

58 Form of transfer of registered estates

A transfer of a registered estate must be in Form TP1, TP2, TP3, TR1, TR2, TR5, AS1 or AS3, as appropriate.

References: See paras 2.37, 5.17.

59 Transfers by way of exchange

(1)   Where any registered estate is transferred wholly or partly in consideration of a transfer of another estate, the transaction must be effected by a transfer in one of the forms prescribed by rule 58.

(2)   A receipt for the equality money (if any) must be given in the receipt panel and the following provision must be included in the additional provisions panel—

"This transfer is in consideration of a transfer (*or* conveyance, *or as appropriate*,) of (*brief description of property exchanged*) dated today [*if applicable*, and of the sum stated above paid for equality of exchange].".

References: See para 5.17.

60 Transfer of leasehold land, the rent being apportioned or land exonerated

(1)   A transfer of a registered leasehold estate in land which contains a legal apportionment of or exoneration from the rent reserved by the lease must include the following statement in the additional provisions panel, with any necessary alterations and additions—

"Liability for the payment of [*if applicable* the previously apportioned rent of (*amount*) being part of] the rent reserved by the registered lease is apportioned between the Transferor and the Transferee as follows—

(*amount*) shall be payable out of the Property and the balance shall be payable out of the land remaining in title number (*title number of retained land*) or

the whole of that rent shall be payable out of the Property and none of it shall be payable out of the land remaining in title number (*title number of retained land*) or

the whole of that rent shall be payable out of the land remaining in title number (*title number of retained land*) and none of it shall be payable out of the Property".

(2)   Where in a transfer of part of a registered leasehold estate which is held under an old tenancy that part is, without the consent of the lessor, expressed to be exonerated from the entire rent, and the covenants in paragraph 20(4) of Schedule 12 to the Act are included, that paragraph shall apply as if—

(a)   the reference in paragraph 20(4)(a) to the rent apportioned to the part retained were to the entire rent, and

(b)   the covenants in paragraphs 20(4)(b) and (c) extended to a covenant to pay the entire rent.

(3)   Where in a transfer of part of a registered leasehold estate which is held under an old tenancy that part is, without the consent of the lessor, expressed to be subject to or charged with the entire rent, and the covenants in paragraph 20(3) of Schedule 12 to the Act are included, that paragraph shall apply as if—

(a)   the reference in paragraph 20(3)(a) to the rent apportioned to the part transferred were to the entire rent, and

(b)   the covenants in paragraphs 20(3)(b) and (c) extended to a covenant to pay the entire rent.

References: See paras 6.29, 6.31.

Execution by an attorney

61 Documents executed by attorney

(1)   If any document executed by an attorney is delivered to the land registry, there must be produced to the registrar—

(a)   the instrument creating the power, or

(b)   a copy of the power by means of which its contents may be proved under section 3 of the Powers of Attorney Act 1971, or

(c)   a document which under section 4 of the Evidence and Powers of Attorney Act 1940 or section 7(3) of the Enduring Powers of Attorney Act 1985 is sufficient evidence of the contents of the power, or

(d)   a certificate by a conveyancer in Form 1.

(2)   If an order under section 8 of the Enduring Powers of Attorney Act 1985 has been made with respect to a power or the donor of the power or the attorney appointed under it, the order must be produced to the registrar.

(3)   In this rule, "power" means the power of attorney.

References: See para 5.19.

62 Evidence of non-revocation of power more than 12 months old

(1)   If any transaction between a donee of a power of attorney and the person dealing with him is not completed within 12 months of the date on which the power came into operation, the registrar may require the production of evidence to satisfy him that the power had not been revoked at the time of the transaction.

(2)   The evidence that the registrar may require under paragraph (1) may consist of or include a statutory declaration by the person who dealt with the attorney or a certificate given by that person's conveyancer in Form 2.

References: See para 5.19.

63 Evidence in support of power delegating trustees' functions to a beneficiary

(1)   If any document executed by an attorney to whom functions have been delegated under section 9 of the Trusts of Land and Appointment of Trustees Act 1996 is delivered to the registrar, the registrar may require the production of evidence to satisfy him that the person who dealt with the attorney—

(a)   did so in good faith, and

(b)   had no knowledge at the time of the completion of the transaction that the attorney was not a person to whom the functions of the trustees in relation to the land to which the application relates could be delegated under that section.

(2)   The evidence that the registrar may require under paragraph (1) may consist of or include a statutory declaration by the person who dealt with the attorney or a certificate given by that person's conveyancer either in Form 3 or, where evidence of non-revocation is also required pursuant to rule 62, in Form 2.

References: See para 5.19.

Covenants

64 Positive covenants

(1)   The registrar may make an appropriate entry in the proprietorship register of any positive covenant that relates to a registered estate given by the proprietor or any previous proprietor of that estate.

(2)   Any entry made under paragraph (1) must, where practicable, refer to the instrument that contains the covenant.

(3)   If it appears to the registrar that a covenant referred to in an entry made under paragraph (1) does not bind the current proprietor of the registered estate, he must remove the entry.

References: See paras 5.20, 9.33.

65 Indemnity covenants

(1)   The registrar may make an appropriate entry in the proprietorship register of an indemnity covenant given by the proprietor of a registered estate in respect of

any restrictive covenant or other matter that affects that estate or in respect of a positive covenant that relates to that estate.

(2)   Any entry made under paragraph (1) must, where practicable, refer to the instrument that contains the indemnity covenant.

(3)   If it appears to the registrar that a covenant referred to in an entry made under paragraph (1) does not bind the current proprietor of the registered estate, he must remove the entry.

References: See paras 5.20, 9.33.

66 Modification of implied covenants in transfer of land held under an old tenancy

Where a transfer of a registered leasehold estate which is an old tenancy modifies or negatives any covenants implied by paragraphs 20(2) and (3) of Schedule 12 to the Act, an entry that the covenants have been so modified or negatived must be made in the register.

References: See paras 6.31.

67 Covenants implied under Part I of the Law of Property (Miscellaneous Provisions) Act 1994 and under the Law of Property Act 1925

(1)   Subject to paragraph (2), a registrable disposition may be expressed to be made either with full title guarantee or with limited title guarantee and, in the case of a disposition which is effected by an instrument in the Welsh language, the appropriate Welsh expression specified in section 8(4) of the 1994 Act may be used.

(2)   In the case of a registrable disposition to which section 76 of the LPA 1925 applies by virtue of section 11(1) of the 1994 Act—

(a)   a person may be expressed to execute, transfer or charge as beneficial owner, settlor, trustee, mortgagee, or personal representative of a deceased person or under an order of the court, and the document effecting the disposition may be framed accordingly, and

(b)   any covenant implied by virtue of section 76 of the LPA 1925 in such a disposition will take effect as though the disposition was expressly made subject to—

(i)   all charges and other interests that are registered at the time of the execution of the disposition and affect the title of the covenantor,

(ii)   any of the matters falling within Schedule 3 to the Act of which the purchaser has notice and subject to which it would have taken effect, had the land been unregistered.

(3)   The benefit of any covenant implied under sections 76 and 77 of the LPA 1925 or either of them will, on and after the registration of the disposition in which it is implied, be annexed and incident to and will go with the registered proprietorship of the interest for the benefit of which it is given and will be capable of being enforced by the proprietor for the time being of that interest.

(4)   The provisions of paragraphs (2)(b) and (3) are in addition to and not in substitution for the other provisions relating to covenants contained in the LPA 1925.

(5)   Except as provided in paragraph (6), no reference to any covenant implied by virtue of Part I of the 1994 Act, or by section 76 of the LPA 1925 as applied by section 11(1) of the 1994 Act, shall be made in the register.

(6)   A reference may be made in the register where a registrable disposition of leasehold land limits or extends the covenant implied under section 4 of the 1994 Act.

(7)   In this rule "the LPA 1925" means the Law of Property Act 1925 and "the 1994 Act" means the Law of Property (Miscellaneous Provisions) Act 1994.

References: See paras 5.17, 6.26, 6.30, 9.34.

68 Additional provisions as to implied covenants

(1)   A document effecting a registrable disposition which contains a provision limiting or extending any covenant implied by virtue of Part I of the Law of Property (Miscellaneous Provisions) Act 1994 must include a statement referring to the section of that Act in which the covenant is set out.

(2)   The statement required by paragraph (1) must be in one of the following forms—

(a)   "The covenant set out in section (*number*) of the Law of Property (Miscellaneous Provisions) Act 1994 shall [not] extend to .... ", or

(b)   "The [transferor or lessor] shall not be liable under any of the covenants set out in section (*number*) of the Law of Property (Miscellaneous Provisions) Act 1994".

References: See paras 5.17, 9.34.

69 Transfer of registered estate subject to a rentcharge

(1)   Where the covenants set out in Part VII or Part VIII of Schedule 2 to the LPA 1925 are included in a transfer, the references to "the grantees", "the conveyance" and "the conveying parties" shall be treated as references to the transferees, the transfer and the transferors respectively.

(2)   Where in a transfer to which section 77(1)(B) of the LPA 1925 does not apply, part of a registered estate affected by a rentcharge is, without the consent of the owner of the rentcharge, expressed to be exonerated from the entire rent, and the covenants in paragraph (ii) of Part VIII of Schedule 2 to the LPA 1925 are included, that paragraph shall apply as if—

(a)   any reference to the balance of the rent were to the entire rent, and

(b)   the words ",other than the covenant to pay the entire rent," were omitted.

(3)   Where in a transfer to which section 77(1)(B) of the LPA 1925 does not apply, part of a registered estate affected by a rentcharge is, without the consent of the owner of the rentcharge, expressed to be subject to or charged with the entire rent, and the covenants in paragraph (i) of Part VIII of Schedule 2 to the LPA 1925 are included, that paragraph shall apply as if—

(a)   any reference to the apportioned rent were to the entire rent, and

(b)   the words "(other than the covenant to pay the entire rent)" were omitted.

(4)   On a transfer of a registered estate subject to a rentcharge—

    (a)   any covenant implied by section 77(1)(A) or (B) of the LPA 1925 may be modified or negatived, and

    (b)   any covenant included in the transfer may be modified,

by adding suitable words to the transfer.

(5)   In this rule "the LPA 1925" means the Law of Property Act 1925.

References: See paras 5.17.

Mines or minerals

70 Description of land where mines or minerals situated

(1)   This rule applies where—

    (a)   a registered estate in land includes any mines or minerals but there is no note in the register that the title to the registered estate includes the mines or minerals, and

    (b)   it is appropriate (for instance, because of a registrable disposition of part of the registered estate, or on a sub-division or amalgamation of a registered title) when describing the registered estate to do so by reference to the land where the mines or minerals are or may be situated.

(2)   After the description required to be made in the property register under rule 5(a) the registrar may make an entry to the effect that the description is an entry made under that rule and is not a note that the registered estate includes the mines or minerals to which paragraph 2 of Schedule 8 to the Act refers.

71 Note as to inclusion of mines or minerals in the registered estate

(1)   This rule applies where a registered estate includes any mines or minerals but there is no note in the register to that effect and the registered proprietor of the registered estate applies for a note to be entered that the registered estate includes the mines or minerals or specified mines or minerals.

(2)   An application for the entry of the note must be accompanied by evidence to satisfy the registrar that the mines or minerals were vested in the applicant for first registration of the registered estate at the time of first registration and were so vested in the same capacity as the remainder of the estate in land then sought to be registered.

(3)   If the registrar is satisfied that mines or minerals were so vested in that applicant he must enter the appropriate note.

References: See para 4.16.

Miscellaneous entries

72 Register entries arising from transfers and charges of part

(1)   Subject to paragraphs (3) and (4), on a transfer or charge of part of the registered estate in a registered title the following entries must be made in the individual register of that registered title—

    (a)   an entry in the property register referring to the removal of the estate comprised in the transfer or charge, and

    (b)   entries relating to any rights, covenants, provisions, and other matters created by the transfer or charge which the registrar considers affect the retained or uncharged registered estate.

(2)   Subject to paragraph (4), on a transfer or charge of part of the registered estate in a registered title entries will be made in the individual register of the registered title comprising the part transferred or charged relating to any rights, covenants, provisions, and other matters created by the transfer or charge which the registrar considers affect the transferred or charged part.

(3)   The registrar may, instead of making the entry referred to in paragraph (1)(a), make a new edition of the registered title out of which the transfer or charge is made and, if the registrar considers it desirable, he may allot a new title number to that registered title.

(4)   This rule only applies to a charge of part of a registered estate in a registered title if the registrar decides that the charged part will be comprised in a separate registered title from the uncharged part.

References: See para 5.18.

73 Application for register entries for express appurtenant rights over unregistered land

(1)   A proprietor of a registered estate who claims the benefit of a legal easement or profit a prendre which has been expressly granted over an unregistered legal estate may apply for it to be registered as appurtenant to his estate.

(2)   The application must be accompanied by the grant and evidence of the grantor's title to the unregistered estate.

(3)   In paragraph (1) the reference to express grant does not include a grant as a result of the operation of section 62 of the Law of Property Act 1925.

References: See para 9.15.

74 Application for register entries for implied or prescriptive appurtenant rights

(1)   A proprietor of a registered estate who claims the benefit of a legal easement or profit a prendre, which has been acquired otherwise than by express grant, may apply for it to be registered as appurtenant to his estate.

(2)   The application must be accompanied by evidence to satisfy the registrar that the right subsists as a legal estate appurtenant to the applicant's registered estate.

(3)   In paragraph (1) the reference to an acquisition otherwise than by express grant includes acquired as a result of the operation of section 62 of the Law of Property Act 1925.

References: See para 9.16.

75 Qualified register entries for appurtenant rights

(1)   This rule applies where a proprietor of a registered estate makes an application under rule 73 or rule 74 and the registrar is not satisfied that the right claimed subsists as a legal estate appurtenant to the applicant's registered estate.

(2)   The registrar may enter details of the right claimed in the property register with such qualification as he considers appropriate.

References: See para 9.16.

76 Note as to rights of light or air

If it appears to the registrar that an agreement prevents the acquisition of rights of light or air for the benefit of the registered estate, he may make an entry in the property register of that estate.

77 No entry on reversionary title of a right of entry in lease

Where a right of re-entry is contained in a lease the registrar need not make any entry regarding such right in the registered title of the reversionary estate.

References: See paras 6.26, 6.27.

78 Note of variation of lease etc on register

An application to register the variation of a lease or other disposition of a registered estate or a registered charge which has been completed by registration must be accompanied by the instrument (if any) effecting the variation and evidence to satisfy the registrar that the variation has effect at law.

References: See para 6.63.

79 Determination of registered estates

(1)   An application to record in the register the determination of a registered estate must be accompanied by evidence to satisfy the registrar that the estate has determined.

(2)   Subject to paragraph (3), if the registrar is satisfied that the estate has determined, he must close the registered title to the estate and cancel any notice in any other registered title relating to it.

(3)   Where an entry is made under rule 173 the registrar need not close the registered title to the estate until a freehold legal estate in land in respect of the land in which such former estate subsisted has been registered.

References: See paras 6.64, 12.24.

PART 7
NOTICES

80 Certain interests to be protected by agreed notices

A person who applies for the entry of a notice in the register must apply for the entry of an agreed notice where the application is for—

    (a)   a matrimonial home rights notice,

    (b)   an inheritance tax notice,

    (c)   a notice in respect of an order under the Access to Neighbouring Land Act 1992,

    (d)   a notice of any variation of a lease effected by or under an order under section 38 of the Landlord and Tenant Act 1987 (including any variation as modified by an order under section 39(4) of that Act),

    (e)   a notice in respect of a—

        (i)   public right, or

        (ii)   customary right.

References: See para 7.29.

81 Application for an agreed notice

(1)   Subject to paragraph (2), an application for the entry in the register of an agreed notice (including an agreed notice in respect of any variation of an interest protected by a notice) must be—

    (a)   made in Form AN1,

    (b)   accompanied by the order or instrument (if any) giving rise to the interest claimed or, if there is no such order or instrument, such other details of the interest claimed as satisfy the registrar as to the nature of the applicant's claim, and

    (c)   accompanied, where appropriate, by—

        (i)   the consent referred to in section 34(3)(b) of the Act, and, where appropriate, evidence to satisfy the registrar that the person applying for, or consenting to the entry of, the notice is entitled to be registered as the proprietor of the registered estate or charge affected by the interest to which the application relates, or

        (ii)   evidence to satisfy the registrar as to the validity of the applicant's claim.

(2)   Paragraph (1) does not apply to an application for the entry of a matrimonial home rights notice made under rule 82.

References: See paras 6.70, 7.30.

82 Application for a matrimonial home rights notice or its renewal

(1)   An application under section 31(10)(a) or section 32 of, and paragraph 4(3)(b) of Schedule 4 to, the Family Law Act 1996 for the entry of an agreed notice in the register must be in Form MH1.

(2)   An application to renew the registration of a matrimonial home rights notice or a matrimonial home rights caution under section 32 of, and paragraph 4(3)(a) of Schedule 4 to, the Family Law Act 1996 must be in Form MH2.

(3)   An application in Form MH1, where the application is made under section 32 of, and paragraph 4(3)(b) of Schedule 4 to, the Family Law Act 1996, or in Form MH2 must be accompanied by—

(a)   an office copy of the section 33(5) order, or

(b)   a conveyancer's certificate that he holds an office copy of the section 33(5) order.

References: See para 7.31.

83 Application for entry of a unilateral notice

An application for the entry in the register of a unilateral notice must be in Form UN1.

References: See para 7.35.

84 Entry of a notice in the register

(1)   A notice under section 32 of the Act must be entered in the charges register of the registered title affected.

(2)   The entry must identify the registered estate or registered charge affected and, where the interest protected by the notice only affects part of the registered estate in a registered title, it must contain sufficient details, by reference to a plan or otherwise, to identify clearly that part.

(3)   In the case of a notice (other than a unilateral notice), the entry must give details of the interest protected.

(4)   In the case of a notice (other than a unilateral notice) of a variation of an interest protected by a notice, the entry must give details of the variation.

(5)   In the case of a unilateral notice, the entry must give such details of the interest protected as the registrar considers appropriate.

References: See paras 7.32, 7.33.

85 Removal of a unilateral notice

(1)   An application for the removal of a unilateral notice from the register under section 35(3) of the Act must be in Form UN2.

(2)   The personal representative or trustee in bankruptcy of the person shown in the register as the beneficiary of a unilateral notice may apply under section 35(3) of the Act; and if he does he must provide evidence to satisfy the registrar as to his appointment as personal representative or trustee in bankruptcy.

(3)   If the registrar is satisfied that the application is in order he must remove the notice.

References: See para 7.39.

86 Cancellation of a unilateral notice

(1)   An application to cancel a unilateral notice under section 36 of the Act must be made in Form UN4.

(2)   An application made under section 36(1)(b) of the Act must be accompanied by—

   (a)   evidence to satisfy the registrar of the applicant's entitlement to be registered as the proprietor of the estate or charge to which the unilateral notice the subject of the application relates, or

   (b)   a conveyancer's certificate that the conveyancer is satisfied that the applicant is entitled to be registered as the proprietor of the estate or charge to which the unilateral notice the subject of the application relates.

(3)   The period referred to in section 36(3) of the Act is the period ending at 12 noon on the fifteenth business day after the date of issue of the notice or such longer period as the registrar may allow following a request under paragraph (4), provided that the longer period never exceeds a period ending at 12 noon on the thirtieth business day after the issue of the notice.

(4)   The request referred to in paragraph (3) is one by the beneficiary to the registrar setting out why the longer period referred to in that paragraph should be allowed.

(5)   If a request is received under paragraph (4) the registrar may, if he considers it appropriate, seek the views of the person who applied for cancellation and if after considering any such views and all other relevant matters he is satisfied that a longer period should be allowed he may allow such period (not exceeding a period ending at 12 noon on the thirtieth business day after the issue of the notice) as he considers appropriate, whether or not the period is the same as any period requested by the beneficiary.

(6)   A request under paragraph (4) must be made before the period ending at 12 noon on the fifteenth business day after the date of issue of the notice under section 36(2) of the Act has expired.

(7)   A person entitled to be registered as the beneficiary of a notice under rule 88 may object to an application under section 36(1) of the Act for cancellation of that notice and the reference to the beneficiary in section 36(3) includes such a person.

References: See para 7.36.

87 Cancellation of a notice (other than a unilateral notice or a matrimonial home rights notice)

(1)   An application for the cancellation of a notice (other than a unilateral notice or a matrimonial home rights notice) must be in Form CN1 and be accompanied by evidence to satisfy the registrar of the determination of the interest.

(2)   Where a person applies for cancellation of a notice in accordance with paragraph (1) and the registrar is satisfied that the interest protected by the notice has come to an end, he must cancel the notice or make an entry in the register that the interest so protected has come to an end.

(3)   If the interest protected by the notice has only come to an end in part, the registrar must make an appropriate entry.

References: See para 7.34.

88 Registration of a new or additional beneficiary of a unilateral notice

(1)   A person entitled to the benefit of an interest protected by a unilateral notice may apply to be entered in the register in place of, or in addition to, the registered beneficiary.

(2)   An application under paragraph (1) must be—
   (a)   in Form UN3, and
   (b)   accompanied by evidence to satisfy the registrar of the applicant's title to the interest protected by the unilateral notice.

(3)   Subject to paragraph (4), if an application is made in accordance with paragraph (2) and the registrar is satisfied that the interest protected by the unilateral notice is vested—
   (a)   in the applicant, the registrar must enter the applicant in the register in place of the registered beneficiary, or
   (b)   in the applicant and the registered beneficiary, the registrar must enter the applicant in addition to the registered beneficiary.

(4)   Except where one of the circumstances specified in paragraph (5) applies, the registrar must serve notice of the application on the registered beneficiary before entering the applicant in the register.

(5)   The registrar is not obliged to serve notice on the registered beneficiary if—
   (a)   the registered beneficiary signs Form UN3 or otherwise consents to the application, or
   (b)   the applicant is the registered beneficiary's personal representative and evidence of his title to act accompanies the application.

(6)   In this rule, "registered beneficiary" means the person shown in the register as the beneficiary of the notice at the time an application is made under paragraph (1).

References: See para 7.38.

89 Notice of unregistered interests

(1)   If the registrar enters a notice of an unregistered interest under section 37(1) of the Act, he must give notice—
   (a)   subject to paragraph (2), to the registered proprietor, and
   (b)   subject to paragraph (3), to any person who appears to the registrar to be entitled to the interest protected by the notice or whom the registrar otherwise considers appropriate.

(2)   The registrar is not obliged to give notice to a registered proprietor under paragraph (1)(a) who applies for entry of the notice or otherwise consents to an application to enter the notice.

(3)   The registrar is not obliged to give notice to a person referred to in paragraph (1)(b) if—
   (a)   that person applied for the entry of the notice or consented to the entry of the notice, or
   (b)   that person's name and his address for service under rule 198 are not set out in the individual register in which the notice is entered.

References: See para 7.26.

90 Application for entry of a notice under paragraph 5(2) or, in certain cases, paragraph 7(2)(a) of Part 1 of Schedule 2 to the Act

An application to meet the registration requirements under—

      (a)   paragraph 5(2) of Part 1 of Schedule 2 to the Act, or

      (b)   paragraph 7(2)(a) of that Part, where the interest is created for the benefit of an unregistered estate,

must be made in Form AP1.

References: See para 9.11.

PART 8
RESTRICTIONS

91 Standard forms of restriction

(1) The forms of restriction set out in Schedule 4 are standard forms of restriction prescribed under section 43(2)(d) of the Act.

(2) The word "conveyancer", where it appears in any of the standard forms of restriction, has the same meaning as in these rules.

(3) The word "registered", where it appears in any of the standard forms of restriction in relation to a disposition, means completion of the registration of that disposition by meeting the relevant registration requirements under section 27 of the Act.

References: See paras 7.43, 7.44.

92 Application for a restriction and the prescribed period under section 45(2) of the Act

(1) Subject to paragraphs (5), (6), (7) and (8) an application for a restriction to be entered in the register must be made in Form RX1.

(2) The application must be accompanied by—

      (a)   full details of the required restriction,

      (b)   if the restriction—

            (i)   requires notice to be given to a person,

            (ii)   requires a person's consent or certificate, or

            (iii)   is a standard form of restriction that refers to a named person,

      that person's address for service,

      (c)   if the application is made with the consent of the relevant registered proprietor, or a person entitled to be registered as such proprietor, and that consent is not given in Form RX1, the relevant consent,

      (d)   if the application is made by or with the consent of a person entitled to be registered as the relevant registered proprietor, evidence to satisfy the registrar of his entitlement, and

      (e)   if the application is made by a person who claims that he has a sufficient interest in the making of the entry, the statement referred to in paragraph (3) signed by the applicant or his conveyancer.

(3)   The statement required under paragraph (2)(e) must either—
  (a)   give details of the applicant's interest in the making of the entry of the required restriction, or
  (b)   if the interest is one of those specified in rule 93, state which of them.

(4)   If requested to do so, an applicant within paragraph (2)(e) must supply further evidence to satisfy the registrar that he has a sufficient interest.

(5)   The registrar may accept a certificate given by a conveyancer that the conveyancer is satisfied that the person making or consenting to the application is entitled to be registered as the relevant proprietor, and that either—
  (a)   the conveyancer holds the originals of the documents that contain evidence of that person's entitlement, or
  (b)   an application for registration of that person as proprietor is pending at the land registry.

(6)   If an application is made with the consent of the relevant registered proprietor, or a person entitled to be registered as such proprietor, the registrar may accept a certificate given by a conveyancer that the conveyancer holds the relevant consent.

(7)   Paragraph (1) of this rule does not apply where—
  (a)   a person applies for the entry of a standard form of restriction in the additional provisions panel of Form TP1, TP2, TP3, TR1, TR2, TR3, TR4, TR5, AS1, AS2 or AS3,
  (b)   a person applies for the entry of a standard form of restriction in panel 7 of Form CH1, or
  (c)   a person applies for the entry of a standard form of restriction in an approved charge.

(8)   This rule does not apply to an application to the registrar to give effect to an order of the court made under section 46 of the Act.

(9)   The period for the purpose of section 45(2) of the Act is the period ending at 12 noon on the fifteenth business day after the date of issue of the notice under section 45(1) or, if more than one such notice is issued, the date of issue of the latest notice.

(10)   In this rule "approved charge" means a charge, the form of which (including the application for the restriction) has first been approved by the registrar.

References: See paras 7.49, 7.50, 10.6.

93 Persons regarded as having a sufficient interest to apply for a restriction

The following persons are to be regarded as included in section 43(1)(c) of the Act—
  (a)   any person who has an interest in a registered estate held under a trust of land where a sole proprietor or a survivor of joint proprietors (unless a trust corporation) will not be able to give a valid receipt for capital money, and who is applying for a restriction in Form A to be entered in the register of that registered estate,

(b)   any person who has a sufficient interest in preventing a contravention of section 6(6) or section 6(8) of the Trusts of Land and Appointment of Trustees Act 1996 and who is applying for a restriction in order to prevent such a contravention,

(c)   any person who has an interest in a registered estate held under a trust of land where the powers of the trustees are limited by section 8 of the Trusts of Land and Appointment of Trustees Act 1996, and who is applying for a restriction in Form B to be entered in the register of that registered estate,

(d)   any person who has an interest in the due administration of the estate of a deceased person, where—

    (i)   the personal representatives of the deceased hold a registered estate on a trust of land created by the deceased's will and the personal representatives' powers are limited by section 8 of the Trusts of Land and Appointment of Trustees Act 1996, and

    (ii)   he is applying for a restriction in Form C to be entered in the register of that registered estate,

(e)   the donee of a special power of appointment in relation to registered land affected by that power,

(f)   the Charity Commissioners in relation to registered land held upon charitable trusts,

(g)   the Church Commissioners, the Parsonages Board or the Diocesan Board of Finance if applying for a restriction—

    (i)   to give effect to any arrangement which is made under any enactment or Measure administered by or relating to the Church Commissioners, the Parsonages Board or the Diocesan Board of Finance, or

    (ii)   to protect any interest in registered land arising under any such arrangement or statute,

(h)   any person with the benefit of a freezing order or an undertaking given in place of a freezing order, who is applying for a restriction in Form AA or BB,

(i)   any person who has applied for a freezing order and who is applying for a restriction in Form CC or DD,

(j)   a trustee in bankruptcy who has an interest in a beneficial interest in registered land held under a trust of land, and who is applying for a restriction in Form J to be entered in the register of that land,

(k)   any person with the benefit of a charging order over a beneficial interest in registered land held under a trust of land who is applying for a restriction in Form K to be entered in the register of that land,

(l)   a person who has obtained a restraint order under—

    (i)   paragraph 5(1) or 5(2) of Schedule 4 to the Terrorism Act 2000, or

    (ii)   section 41 of the Proceeds of Crime Act 2002,

and who is applying for a restriction in Form EE or FF,

(m)   a person who has applied for a restraint order under the provisions referred to in paragraph (1) and who is applying for a restriction in Form GG or HH,

(n)   a person who has obtained an acquisition order under section 28 of the Landlord and Tenant Act 1987 and who is applying for a restriction in Form L or N,

    (o)   a person who has applied for an acquisition order under section 28 of the Landlord and Tenant Act 1987 and who is applying for a restriction in Form N,

    (p)   a person who has obtained a vesting order under section 26(1) or 50(1) of the Leasehold Reform, Housing and Urban Development Act 1993 and who is applying for a restriction in Form L or N,

    (q)   a person who has applied for a vesting order under section 26(1) or 50(1) of the Leasehold Reform, Housing and Urban Development Act 1993 and who is applying for a restriction in Form N,

    (r)   the International Criminal Court where it applies for a restriction—

        (i)   in Form AA or BB to give effect to a freezing order under Schedule 6 to the International Criminal Court Act 2001, or

        (ii)   in Form CC or DD to protect an application for such a freezing order,

    (s)   a receiver or a sequestrator appointed by order who applies for a restriction in Form L or N,

    (t)   a trustee under a deed of arrangement who applies for a restriction in Form L or N,

    (u)   a person who has obtained an interim receiving order under section 246 of the Proceeds of Crime Act 2002 and who is applying for a restriction in Form EE or FF, and

    (v)   a person who has applied for an interim receiving order under section 246 of the Proceeds of Crime Act 2002 and who is applying for a restriction in Form GG or HH.

References: See paras 7.51, 10.6, 10.63.

94 When an application for a restriction must be made

(1)   A proprietor of a registered estate must apply for a restriction in Form A where—

    (a)   the estate becomes subject to a trust of land, other than on a registrable disposition, and the proprietor or the survivor of joint proprietors will not be able to give a valid receipt for capital money, or

    (b)   the estate is held on a trust of land and, as a result of a change in the trusts, the proprietor or the survivor of joint proprietors will not be able to give a valid receipt for capital money.

(2)   A sole or last surviving trustee of land held on a trust of land must, when applying to register a disposition of a registered estate in his favour or to be registered as proprietor of an unregistered estate, at the same time apply for a restriction in Form A.

(3)   Subject to paragraph (6), a personal representative of a deceased person who holds a registered estate on a trust of land created by the deceased's will, or on a trust of land arising under the laws of intestacy which is subsequently varied, and whose powers have been limited by section 8 of the Trusts of Land and Appointment of Trustees Act 1996, must apply for a restriction in Form C.

(4)   Subject to paragraphs (6) and (7), a proprietor of a registered estate must apply for a restriction in Form B where—

    (a)   a declaration of trust of that estate imposes limitations on the powers of the trustees under section 8 of the Trusts of Land and Appointment of Trustees Act 1996, or

    (b)   a change in the trusts on which that estate is held imposes limitations or changes the limitations on the powers of the trustees under section 8 of the Trusts of Land and Appointment of Trustees Act 1996.

(5)   Subject to paragraphs (6) and (7), an applicant for first registration of a legal estate held on a trust of land where the powers of the trustees are limited by section 8 of the Trusts of Land and Appointment of Trustees Act 1996 must at the same time apply for a restriction in Form B.

(6)   Paragraphs (3), (4) and (5) do not apply to legal estates held on charitable, ecclesiastical or public trusts.

(7)   Paragraphs (4) and (5) apply not only where the legal estate is held by the trustees, but also where it is vested in the personal representatives of a sole or last surviving trustee.

(8)   An application for a restriction must be made where required by paragraphs (2) or (3) of rule 176 or paragraph (2) of rule 178.

References: See paras 7.53, 10.12, 10.14, 10.15.

95 Form of obligatory restrictions

(1)   The form of any restriction that the registrar is obliged to enter under any enactment shall be—

    (a)   as specified in these rules,

    (b)   as required by the relevant enactment, or

    (c)   in other cases, such form as the registrar may direct having regard to the provisions of the relevant enactment.

(2)   The form of the restriction required under—

    (a)   section 44(1) of the Act is Form A,

    (b)   section 37(5A) of the Housing Act 1985 is Form U,

    (c)   section 157(7) of the Housing Act 1985 is Form V,

    (d)   section 81(10) of the Housing Act 1988 is Form X,

    (e)   section 133 of the Housing Act 1988 is Form X,

    (f)   paragraph 4 of Schedule 9A to the Housing Act 1985 is Form W,

    (g)   section 173(9) of the Local Government and Housing Act 1989 is Form X, and

    (h)   section 13(5) of the Housing Act 1996 is Form Y.

References: See paras 4.15, 7.48, 10.12.

96 Application for an order that a restriction be disapplied or modified

(1)   An application to the registrar for an order under section 41(2) of the Act must be made in Form RX2.

(2)   The application must—
    (a)   state whether the application is to disapply or to modify the restriction and, if the latter, give details of the modification requested,
    (b)   explain why the applicant has a sufficient interest in the restriction to make the application,
    (c)   give details of the disposition or the kind of dispositions that will be affected by the order, and
    (d)   state why the applicant considers that the registrar should make the order.

(3)   If requested to do so, the applicant must supply further evidence to satisfy the registrar that he should make the order.

(4)   The registrar may make such enquiries and serve such notices as he thinks fit in order to determine the application.

(5)   A note of the terms of any order made by the registrar under section 41(2) of the Act must be entered in the register.

References: See para 7.58.

97 Application to cancel a restriction

(1)   An application to cancel a restriction must be made in Form RX3.

(2)   The application must be accompanied by evidence to satisfy the registrar that the restriction is no longer required.

(3)   If the registrar is satisfied that the restriction is no longer required, he must cancel the restriction.

References: See paras 7.60, 10.25.

98 Application to withdraw a restriction from the register

(1)   An application to withdraw a restriction must be made in Form RX4 and accompanied by the consents required under paragraphs (2) to (5).

(2)   Subject to paragraphs (3), (4) and (5) an application to withdraw a restriction may only be made by or with the consent of all persons who appear to the registrar to have an interest in the restriction.

(3)   An application to withdraw a restriction that requires the consent of a specified person may only be made by or with the consent of that person.

(4)   An application to withdraw a restriction that requires notice to be given to a specified person may only be made by or with the consent of that person.

(5)   An application to withdraw a restriction that requires a certificate to be given by a specified person may only be made by or with the consent of that person.

(6)   No application may be made to withdraw a restriction—
    (a)   that is entered under section 42(1)(a) of the Act and reflects some limitation on the registered proprietor's powers of disposition imposed by statute or the general law,
    (b)   that is entered in the register following an application under rule 94,
    (c)   that the registrar is under an obligation to enter in the register,

(d)　that reflects a limitation under an order of the court or registrar, or an undertaking given in place of such an order,

(e)　that is entered pursuant to a court order under section 46 of the Act.

(7)　The registrar may accept a certificate given by a conveyancer that the conveyancer holds any consents required.

References: See para 7.61.

99 Cancellation of a restriction relating to a trust

When registering a disposition of a registered estate, the registrar must cancel a restriction entered for the purpose of protecting an interest, right or claim arising under a trust of land if he is satisfied that the registered estate is no longer subject to that trust of land.

References: See para 7.59.

100 Entry following a direction of the court regarding overriding priority in connection with a restriction

(1)　Any entry in the register required under section 46(4) of the Act shall be in such form as the registrar may determine so as to ensure that the priority of the restriction ordered by the court is apparent from the register.

(2)　Where the making of the entry is completed by the registrar during the priority period of an official search which was delivered before the making of the application for the entry, he must give notice of the entry to the person who applied for the official search or, if a conveyancer or other agent applied on behalf of that person, to that agent, unless he is satisfied that such notice is unnecessary.

References: See para 7.55, 15.74.

PART 9
CHARGES

101 How ranking of registered charges as between themselves to be shown on register

Subject to any entry in the individual register to the contrary, for the purpose of section 48(1) of the Act the order in which registered charges are entered in an individual register shows the order in which the registered charges rank as between themselves.

References: See para 8.14.

102 Alteration of priority of registered charges

(1)　An application to alter the priority of registered charges, as between themselves, must be made by or with the consent of the proprietor or a person entitled to be registered as the proprietor of any registered charge whose priority is adversely affected by the alteration, but no such consent is required from a person who has executed the instrument which alters the priority of the charges.

(2)   The registrar may accept a conveyancer's certificate confirming that the conveyancer holds any necessary consents.

(3)   The registrar must make an entry in the register in such terms as the registrar considers appropriate to give effect to the application.

References: See para 8.14.

103 Form of charge of registered estate

A legal charge of a registered estate may be made in Form CH1.

References: See paras 2.37, 5.17, 8.9.

104 Application for registration of the title to a local land charge

An application to register the title to a charge over registered land which is a local land charge must be supported by evidence of the charge.

References: See para 8.27.

105 Overriding statutory charges

(1)   An applicant for registration of a statutory charge that has the effect mentioned in section 50 of the Act must lodge Form SC with the application.

(2)   If the applicant satisfies the registrar that the statutory charge has the priority specified in that Form SC, the registrar must make an entry showing that priority in the charges register of the affected registered title.

(3)   If the applicant does not satisfy the registrar as mentioned in paragraph (2) but the registrar considers that the applicant has an arguable case, the registrar may make an entry in the charges register of the affected registered title that the applicant claims the priority specified in that Form SC.

(4)   If the registrar makes an entry under paragraph (3) the registrar must give notice of the entry to the persons mentioned in rule 106(1) (subject to rule 106(2)).

(5)   Where an entry has been made under paragraph (3)—
    (a)   the proprietor of the statutory charge which gave rise to the entry, or
    (b)   the proprietor of a charge entered in the charges register of the affected registered title which, subject to the effect of the entry, would rank in priority to or have equal priority with that statutory charge under rule 101,

may apply for the entry to be removed or to be replaced by an entry of the kind referred to in paragraph (2).

(6)   Paragraph (5)(b) includes the proprietor of a statutory charge entered in the charges register of the affected registered title which has had an entry made in respect of it under paragraph (3) claiming priority over the statutory charge referred to in paragraph (5)(a).

(7)   An applicant under paragraph (5) must provide evidence to satisfy the registrar that the registrar should take the action sought by the applicant under that paragraph.

(8)   Before taking the action sought by the applicant under paragraph (5), the registrar must give notice of the application to any proprietors within that paragraph (other than the applicant).

References: See para 8.21.

---

106 Service of notice of overriding statutory charges

(1)   The registrar shall give notice under section 50 of the Act to—
- (a)   the registered proprietor of a registered charge, and
- (b)   subject to paragraph (2), any person who appears to the registrar to be entitled to a charge protected by a notice,

entered in the charges register of the affected registered title at the time of registration of the statutory charge.

(2)   The registrar shall not be obliged to give notice to a person referred to in paragraph (1)(b) if that person's name and his address for service under rule 198 are not set out in the individual register in which the notice is entered.

References: See para 8.21.

---

107 Further advances—notice of creation of subsequent charge

(1)   A notice given for the purposes of section 49(1) of the Act by one of the methods mentioned in paragraph (2) ought to have been received at the time shown in the table in paragraph (4).

(2)   The methods referred to in paragraph (1) are—
- (a)   by post, to the postal address, whether or not in the United Kingdom, entered in the register as the prior chargee's address for service, or
- (b)   by leaving the notice at that address, or
- (c)   by sending to the box number at the relevant document exchange entered in the register as an additional address for service of the prior chargee, or
- (d)   by electronic transmission to the electronic address entered in the register as an additional address for service of the prior chargee, or
- (e)   where paragraph (3) applies, by post, document exchange, fax or electronic transmission to the address, box number or fax number provided.

(3)   This paragraph applies where the prior chargee has provided to the subsequent chargee a postal address, document exchange box number, fax number, e-mail or other electronic address, and stated in writing to the subsequent chargee that notices to the prior chargee under section 49(1) of the Act may be sent to that address, box number or fax number.

(4)   For the purposes of section 49(2) of the Act a notice sent in accordance with paragraph (2) or (3) ought to have been received at the time shown in the table below—

Method of delivery	Time of receipt
Post to an address in the United Kingdom	The second working day after posting
Leaving at a postal address	The working day after it was left
Post to an address outside the United Kingdom	The seventh working day after posting
Document exchange	On the second working day after it was left at the sender's document exchange
Fax	The working day after transmission
Electronic transmission to an electronic address entered in the register as an address for service or e-mail or other electronic means of delivery under paragraph (3)	The second working day after transmission

(5)   A notice posted or transmitted after 1700 hours on a working day or posted or transmitted on a day which is not a working day is to be treated as having been posted or transmitted on the next working day.

(6)   In this rule—

"post" means pre-paid delivery by a postal service which seeks to deliver documents within the United Kingdom no later than the next working day in all or the majority of cases, and to deliver outside the United Kingdom within such a period as is reasonable in all the circumstances,

"prior chargee" means the proprietor of a registered charge to whom notice is being given under section 49(1) of the Act,

"subsequent chargee" means the chargee giving notice under section 49(1) of the Act,

"working day" means any day from Monday to Friday (inclusive) which is not Christmas Day, Good Friday or any other day either specified or declared by proclamation under section 1 of the Banking and Financial Dealings Act 1971 or appointed by the Lord Chancellor.

References: See para 8.17.

108 Obligations to make further advances

(1)   The proprietor of a registered charge or a person applying to be so registered, who is under an obligation to make further advances on the security of that charge, may apply to the registrar for such obligation to be entered in the register for the purposes of section 49(3) of the Act.

(2)   Except as provided in paragraph (3), the application must be made in Form CH2.

(3)   Form CH2 need not be used if the application is contained in panel 7 of Form CH1, or in a charge received for registration where the form of that charge has been approved by the registrar.

(4)   The registrar must make an entry in the register in such terms as he considers appropriate to give effect to an application under this rule.

References: See para 8.18.

109 Agreement of maximum amount of security

(1)   Where the parties to a legal charge which is a registered charge or which is a registrable disposition have agreed a maximum amount for which the charge is security, the proprietor of the registered charge or a person applying to be registered as proprietor of the registrable disposition may apply to the registrar for such agreement to be entered in the register under section 49(4) of the Act.

(2)   The application must be made in Form CH3.

(3)   The registrar must make an entry in the register in such terms as he considers appropriate to give effect to an application under this rule.

References: See para 8.19.

110 Consolidation of registered charges

(1)   A chargee who has a right of consolidation in relation to a registered charge may apply to the registrar for an entry to be made in respect of that right in the individual register in which the charge is registered.

(2)   The application must be made in Form CC.

(3)   The registrar must make an entry in the individual register in such terms as he considers appropriate to give effect to an application under this rule.

References: See para 8.25.

111 Certificate of registration of company charges

(1)   When making an application for the registration of a charge created by a company registered under the Companies Acts, a limited liability partnership incorporated under the Limited Liability Partnerships Act 2000, or a Northern Ireland company, the applicant must produce to the registrar—
  (a)   a certificate issued under section 401 of the 1985 Act that the charge has been registered under section 395 of that Act, or
  (b)   (in the case of a charge created by a company registered in Scotland) a certificate issued under section 418 of the 1985 Act that the charge has been registered under section 410 of that Act, or
  (c)   (in the case of a charge created by a Northern Ireland company) a certificate issued under article 409 of the 1986 Order that the charge has been registered under article 403 of that Order.

(2)   If the applicant does not produce the certificate required by paragraph (1) with the application for registration of the charge, the registrar must enter a note in

the register that the charge is subject to the provisions of section 395 or section 410 of the 1985 Act, or article 403 of the 1986 Order (as appropriate).

    (3)   In this rule—

"the 1985 Act" means the Companies Act 1985,

"the 1986 Order" means the Companies (NI) Order 1986,

"Northern Ireland" company means a company formed and registered under the 1986 Order or a company formed and registered, or deemed to have been registered, in Northern Ireland under the former Northern Ireland Companies Acts,

"former Northern Ireland Companies Acts" means the Joint Stock Companies Acts, the Companies Act 1862, the Companies (Consolidation) Act 1908, the Companies Act (Northern Ireland) 1932 and the Companies Acts (Northern Ireland) 1960 to 1983,

"Joint Stock Companies Acts" means the Joint Stock Companies Act 1856, the Joint Stock Companies Act 1857, the Joint Stock Banking Companies Act 1857 and the Act to enable Joint Stock Banking Companies to be formed on the principle of limited liability, or any one or more of those Acts (as the case may require), but does not include the Joint Stock Companies Act 1844.

112 Foreclosure—registration requirements

    (1)   Subject to paragraph (3), an application by a person who has obtained an order for foreclosure absolute to be entered in the register as proprietor of the registered estate in respect of which the charge is registered must be accompanied by the order.

    (2)   The registrar must—

        (a)   cancel the registration of the charge in respect of which the order was made,

        (b)   cancel all entries in respect of interests over which the charge has priority, and

        (c)   enter the applicant as proprietor of the registered estate.

    (3)   The registrar may accept a conveyancer's certificate confirming that the conveyancer holds the order for foreclosure absolute or an office copy of it.

References: See para 8.26.

113 Variation of the terms of a registered charge

    (1)   An application to register an instrument varying the terms of a registered charge must be made—

        (a)   by, or with the consent of, the proprietor of the registered charge and the proprietor of the estate charged, and

        (b)   with the consent of the proprietor, or a person entitled to be registered as proprietor, of every other registered charge of equal or inferior priority that is prejudicially affected by the variation,

but no such consent is required from a person who has executed the instrument.

    (2)   The registrar may accept a conveyancer's certificate confirming that the conveyancer holds any necessary consents.

(3)   If the registrar is satisfied that the proprietor of any other registered charge of equal or inferior priority to the varied charge that is prejudicially affected by the variation is bound by it, he shall make a note of the variation in the register.

(4)   If the registrar is not so satisfied, he may make an entry in the register that an instrument which is expressed to vary the terms of the registered charge has been entered into.

References: See para 8.11.

114 Discharges and releases of registered charges

(1)   Subject to rule 115, a discharge of a registered charge must be in Form DS1.

(2)   Subject to rule 115, a release of part of the registered estate in a registered title from a registered charge must be in Form DS3.

(3)   Any discharge or release in Form DS1 or DS3 must be executed as a deed or authenticated in such other manner as the registrar may approve.

(4)   Notwithstanding paragraphs (1) and (2) and rule 115, the registrar is entitled to accept and act upon any other proof of satisfaction of a charge that he may regard as sufficient.

(5)   An application to register a discharge in Form DS1 must be made in Form AP1 or DS2 and an application to register a release in Form DS3 must be made in Form AP1.

References: See para 8.29.

115 Discharges and releases of registered charges in electronic form

(1)   During the currency of a notice given under Schedule 2 and subject to and in accordance with the limitations contained in such notice, notification of—
  (a)   the discharge of, or
  (b)   the release of part of a registered estate in a registered title form, a registered charge may be delivered to the registrar in electronic form.

(2)   Notification of discharge or release of part given in accordance with paragraph (1) shall be regarded as having the same effect as a discharge in Form DS1, or a release of part in Form DS3, as appropriate, executed in accordance with rule 114 by or on behalf the person who has delivered it to the registrar.

References: See para 8.30.

116 Transfer of a registered charge

A transfer of a registered charge must be in Form TR3, TR4 or AS2, as appropriate.

References: See para 8.33.

PART 10
BOUNDARIES

117 Definition

In this Part, except in rule 121, "boundary" includes part only of a boundary.

References: See para 2.15.

118 Application for the determination of the exact line of a boundary

(1)   A proprietor of a registered estate may apply to the registrar for the exact line of the boundary of that registered estate to be determined.

(2)   An application under paragraph (1) must be made in Form DB and be accompanied by—
- (a)   a plan, or a plan and a verbal description, identifying the exact line of the boundary claimed and showing sufficient surrounding physical features to allow the general position of the boundary to be drawn on the Ordnance Survey map, and
- (b)   evidence to establish the exact line of the boundary.

References: See para 2.15.

119 Procedure on an application for the determination of the exact line of a boundary

(1)   Where the registrar is satisfied that—
- (a)   the plan, or plan and verbal description, supplied in accordance with rule 118(2)(a) identifies the exact line of the boundary claimed,
- (b)   the applicant has shown an arguable case that the exact line of the boundary is in the position shown on the plan, or plan and verbal description, supplied in accordance with rule 118(2)(a), and
- (c)   he can identify all the owners of the land adjoining the boundary to be determined and has an address at which each owner may be given notice,

he must give the owners of the land adjoining the boundary to be determined (except the applicant) notice of the application to determine the exact line of the boundary and of the effect of paragraph (6).

(2)   Where the evidence supplied in accordance with rule 118(2)(b) includes an agreement in writing as to the exact line of the boundary with an owner of the land adjoining the boundary, the registrar need not give notice of the application to that owner.

(3)   Subject to paragraph (4), the time fixed by the notice to the owner of the land to object to the application shall be the period ending at 12 noon on the twentieth business day after the date of issue of the notice or such longer period as the registrar may decide before the issue of the notice.

(4)   The period set for the notice under paragraph (3) may be extended for a particular recipient of the notice by the registrar following a request by that recipient, received by the registrar before that period has expired, setting out why an extension should be allowed.

(5)   If a request is received under paragraph (4) the registrar may, if he considers it appropriate, seek the views of the applicant and if, after considering any such views and all other relevant matters, he is satisfied that a longer period should be allowed he may allow such period as he considers appropriate, whether or not the period is the same as any period requested by the recipient of the notice.

(6)   Unless any recipient of the notice objects to the application to determine the exact line of the boundary within the time fixed by the notice (as extended under paragraph (5), if applicable), the registrar must complete the application.

(7)   Where the registrar is not satisfied as to paragraph (1)(a), (b) and (c), he must cancel the application.

(8)   In this rule, the "owner of the land" means—
> (a)   a person entitled to apply to be registered as the proprietor of an unregistered legal estate in land under section 3 of the Act,
> (b)   the proprietor of any registered estate or charge affecting the land, and
> (c)   if the land is demesne land, Her Majesty.

References: See para 2.15.

120 Completion of application for the exact line of a boundary to be determined

(1)   Where the registrar completes an application under rule 118, he must—
> (a)   make an entry in the individual register of the applicant's registered title and, if appropriate, in the individual register of any superior or inferior registered title, and any registered title affecting the other land adjoining the determined boundary, stating that the exact line of the boundary is determined under section 60 of the Act, and
> (b)   subject to paragraph (2), add to the title plan of the applicant's registered title and, if appropriate, to the title plan of any superior or inferior registered title, and any registered title affecting the other land adjoining the determined boundary, such particulars of the exact line of the boundary as he considers appropriate.

(2)   Instead of, or as well as, adding particulars of the exact line of the boundary to the title plans mentioned in paragraph (1)(b), the registrar may make an entry in the individual registers mentioned in paragraph (1)(a) referring to any other plan showing the exact line of the boundary.

References: See para 2.15.

121 Relationship between determined and undetermined parts of a boundary

Where the exact line of part of the boundary of a registered estate has been determined, the ends of that part of the boundary are not to be treated as determined for the purposes of adjoining parts of the boundary the exact line of which has not been determined.

References: See para 2.15.

122 Determination of the exact line of a boundary without application

(1) This rule applies where—
    (a) there is—
        (i) a transfer of part of a registered estate in land, or
        (ii) the grant of a term of years absolute which is a registrable disposition of part of a registered estate in land,
    (b) there is a common boundary, and
    (c) there is sufficient information in the disposition to enable the registrar to determine the exact line of the common boundary.

(2) The registrar may determine the exact line of the common boundary and if he does he must—
    (a) make an entry in the individual registers of the affected registered titles stating that the exact line of the common boundary is determined under section 60 of the Act, and
    (b) subject to paragraph (3), add to the title plan of the disponor's affected registered title (whether or not the disponor is still the proprietor of that title, or still entitled to be registered as proprietor of that title) and to the title plan of the registered title under which the disposition is being registered, such particulars of the exact line of the common boundary as he considers appropriate.

(3) Instead of, or as well as, adding particulars of the exact line of the common boundary to the title plans mentioned in paragraph (2)(b), the registrar may make an entry in the individual registers of the affected registered titles referring to the description of the common boundary in the disposition.

(4) In this rule—
    "common boundary" means any boundary of the land disposed of by a disposition which adjoins land in which the disponor at the date of the disposition had a registered estate in land or of which such disponor was entitled to be registered as proprietor, and
    "disposition" means a transfer or grant mentioned in paragraph (1)(a).

References: See para 2.16.

123 Agreement about accretion or diluvion

(1) An application to register an agreement about the operation of accretion or diluvion in relation to a registered estate in land must be made by, or be accompanied by the consent of, the proprietor of the registered estate and of any registered charge, except that no such consent is required from a person who is party to the agreement.

(2) On registration of such an agreement the registrar must make a note in the property register that the agreement is registered for the purposes of section 61(2) of the Act.

References: See para 2.19.

PART 11
QUALITY OF TITLE

124 Application to upgrade title under section 62 of the Act

(1)   An application for the registrar to upgrade title under section 62 of the Act must be made in Form UT1.

(2)   An application referred to in paragraph (1) must, except where made under sections 62(2), (4) or (5) of the Act, be accompanied by such documents as will satisfy the registrar as to the title.

(3)   An application under section 62(2) of the Act must be accompanied by—
  (a)   such documents as will satisfy the registrar as to any superior title which is not registered,
  (b)   where any superior title is registered with possessory, qualified or good leasehold title, such evidence as will satisfy the registrar that that title qualifies for upgrading to absolute title, and
  (c)   evidence of any consent to the grant of the lease required from—
    (i)   any chargee of any superior title, and
    (ii)   any superior lessor.

(4)   An application under section 62(3)(b) of the Act must, in addition to the documents referred to in paragraph (2), be accompanied by the documents listed at paragraph (3)(a) to (c).

(5)   An application by a person entitled to be registered as the proprietor of the estate to which the application relates must be accompanied by evidence of that entitlement.

(6)   An application by a person interested in a registered estate which derives from the estate to which the application relates must be accompanied by—
  (a)   details of the interest, and
  (b)   where the interest is not apparent from the register, evidence to satisfy the registrar of the applicant's interest.

References: See paras 2.11, 5.15, 6.18.

125 Use of register to record defects in title

(1)   An entry under section 64 of the Act that a right to determine a registered estate in land is exercisable shall be made in the property register.

(2)   An application for such an entry must be supported by evidence to satisfy the registrar that the applicant has the right to determine the registered estate and that the right is exercisable.

(3)   Subject to paragraph (4), the registrar must make the entry on receipt of an application which relates to a right to determine the registered estate on non-payment of a rentcharge.

(4)   Before making an entry under this rule the registrar must give notice of the application to the proprietor of the registered estate to which the application relates and the proprietor of any registered charge on that estate.

(5)   A person may apply to the registrar for removal of the entry if he is—
  (a)   the person entitled to determine the registered estate,
  (b)   the proprietor of the registered estate to which the entry relates,

> (c)   a person entitled to be registered as proprietor of that estate, or
> (d)   any other person whom the registrar is satisfied has an interest in the removal of the entry.

(6)   An application for removal of the entry must be supported by evidence to satisfy the registrar that the right to determine the registered estate is not exercisable.

References: See paras 2.12, 6.65.

PART 12
ALTERATIONS AND CORRECTIONS

126 Alteration under a court order—not rectification

(1)   Subject to paragraphs (2) and (3), if in any proceedings the court decides that—

> (a)   there is a mistake in the register,
> (b)   the register is not up to date, or
> (c)   there is an estate, right or interest excepted from the effect of registration that should be given effect to,

it must make an order for alteration of the register under the power given by paragraph 2(1) of Schedule 4 to the Act.

(2)   The court is not obliged to make an order if there are exceptional circumstances that justify not doing so.

(3)   This rule does not apply to an alteration of the register that amounts to rectification.

References: See para 14.6.

127 Court order for alteration of the register—form and service

(1)   An order for alteration of the register must state the title number of the title affected and the alteration that is to be made, and must direct the registrar to make the alteration.

(2)   Service on the registrar of an order for alteration of the register must be made by making an application for the registrar to give effect to the order, accompanied by the order.

References: See para 14.7.

128 Alteration otherwise than pursuant to a court order—notice and enquiries

(1)   Subject to paragraph (5), this rule applies where an application for alteration of the register has been made, or where the registrar is considering altering the register without an application having been made.

(2)   The registrar must give notice of the proposed alteration to—

> (a)   the registered proprietor of any registered estate,
> (b)   the registered proprietor of any registered charge, and

(c)   subject to paragraph (3), any person who appears to the registrar to be entitled to an interest protected by a notice,

where that estate, charge or interest would be affected by the proposed alteration, unless he is satisfied that such notice is unnecessary.

(3)   The registrar is not obliged to give notice to a person referred to in paragraph (2)(c) if that person's name and his address for service under rule 198 are not set out in the individual register in which the notice is entered.

(4)   The registrar may make such enquiries as he thinks fit.

(5)   This rule does not apply to alteration of the register in the specific circumstances covered by any other rule.

References: See para 14.9.

129 Alteration otherwise than under a court order—evidence

Unless otherwise provided in these rules, an application for alteration of the register (otherwise than under a court order) must be supported by evidence to justify the alteration.

130 Correction of mistakes in an application or accompanying document

(1)   This rule applies to any alteration made by the registrar for the purpose of correcting a mistake in any application or accompanying document.

(2)   The alteration will have effect as if made by the applicant or other interested party or parties—

(a)   in the case of a mistake of a clerical or like nature, in all circumstances,

(b)   in the case of any other mistake, only if the applicant and every other interested party has requested, or consented to, the alteration.

References: See para 14.28.

PART 13
INFORMATION ETC

Interpretation of this Part

131 Definitions

In this Part—

"commencement date" means the date of commencement of this Part,

"edited information document" means, where the registrar has designated a document an exempt information document, the edited copy of that document lodged under rule 136(2)(b),

"exempt information document" means the original and copies of a document so designated under rule 136(3),

"prejudicial information" means—

(a)   information that relates to an individual who is the applicant under rule 136 and if disclosed to other persons (whether to the public generally or specific persons) would, or would be likely to, cause substantial unwarranted damage or substantial unwarranted distress to the applicant or another, or

(b)   information that if disclosed to other persons (whether to the public generally or specific persons) would, or would be likely to, prejudice the commercial interests of the applicant under rule 136,

"priority period" means—

(a)   where the application for an official search is entered on the day list before the date referred to in rule 216(3), the period beginning at the time when that application is entered on the day list and ending at midnight marking the end of the thirtieth business day thereafter, and

(b)   where the application for an official search is entered on the day list on or after the date referred to in rule 216(3), the period beginning at the time when that application is entered on the day list and ending at midnight marking the end of the thirty sixth business day thereafter,

"protectable disposition" means a registrable disposition (including one by virtue of rule 38) of a registered estate or registered charge made for valuable consideration,

"purchaser" means a person who has entered into or intends to enter into a protectable disposition as disponee,

"registrable estate or charge" means the legal estate and any charge which is sought to be registered as a registered estate or registered charge in an application for first registration,

"search from date" means—

(a)   the date stated on an official copy of the individual register of the relevant registered title, as the date on which the entries shown on that official copy were subsisting,

(b)   the date stated at the time of an access by remote terminal, where provided for under these rules, to the individual register of the relevant registered title as the date on which the entries accessed were subsisting,

"transitional period" means the period of two years beginning with the commencement date,

"transitional period document" means—

(a)   a lease or charge or a copy lease or charge kept by the registrar since before the commencement date, where an entry referring to the lease or charge was made in the register of title before the commencement date, or

(b)   any other document kept by the registrar which is not referred to in the register of title but relates to an application to the registrar and was received by the registrar before the commencement date.

References: See paras 2.77, 6.67.

Delivery of applications and issuing of certificates

132 Delivery of applications and issuing of certificates by electronic and other means

(1)   During the currency of a relevant notice given under Schedule 2, and subject to and in accordance with the limitations contained in that notice, any application under this Part may be made by delivering the application to the registrar by any means of communication other than post, document exchange or

personal delivery, and the applicant must provide, in such order as may be required by that notice, such of the particulars required for an application of that type as are appropriate in the circumstances and as are required by the notice.

(2)   During the currency of a relevant notice given under Schedule 2, and subject to and in accordance with the limitations contained in that notice, any certificates and other results of applications and searches under this Part may be issued by any means of communication other than post, document exchange or personal delivery.

(3)   Except where otherwise provided in this Part, where information is issued under paragraph (2) it must be to like effect to that which would have been provided had the information been issued in paper form.

Inspection and copying

133 Inspection and copying

(1)   This rule applies to the right to inspect and make copies of the registers and documents under section 66(1) of the Act.

(2)   There is excepted from the right—
    (a)   any exempt information document,
    (b)   any edited information document which has been replaced by another edited information document under rule 136(6),
    (c)   any Form EX1A,
    (d)   any Form CIT,
    (e)   any Form to which Form CIT has been attached under rule 140(3) or (4), and
    (f)   any document or copy of any document prepared by the registrar in connection with an application in a Form to which Form CIT has been attached under rule 140(3) or (4).

(3)   Subject to rule 132(1), an application under section 66 of the Act must be in Form PIC.

(4)   Where inspection and copying under this rule takes place at an office of the land registry it must be undertaken in the presence of a member of the land registry.

(5)   In paragraph (2) the references to Form EX1A and Form CIT and Forms to which Form CIT has been attached include any equivalent information provided under rule 132 and the reference to an application in a Form to which Form CIT has been attached includes an equivalent application made by virtue of rule 132.

References: See para 2.81.

Official copies

134 Application for official copies of a registered title, the cautions register or for a certificate of inspection of the title plan

(1)   A person may apply for—
    (a)   an official copy of an individual register,
    (b)   an official copy of any title plan referred to in an individual register,
    (c)   an official copy of an individual caution register and any caution plan referred to in it, and
    (d)   a certificate of inspection of any title plan.

(2)   Subject to rule 132(1), an application under paragraph (1) must be in Form OC1.

(3)   A separate application must be made in respect of each registered title or individual caution register.

(4)   Where, notwithstanding paragraph (3), an application is in respect of more than one registered title or individual caution register, but the applicant fails to provide a title number, or the title number provided does not relate to any part of the property in respect of which the application is made, the registrar may—
- (a)   deal with the application as if it referred only to one of the title numbers relating to the property,
- (b)   deal with the application as if it referred to all of the title numbers relating to the property, or
- (c)   cancel the application.

(5)   In paragraph (4) the reference to title number includes in the case of an individual caution register a caution title number.

(6)   Where the registrar deals with the application under paragraph (4)(b), the applicant is to be treated as having made a separate application in respect of each of the registered titles or each of the individual caution registers.

(7)   An official copy of an individual caution register and any caution plan referred to in it must be issued disregarding any application or matter that may affect the subsistence of the caution.

References: See paras 2.64, 15.75.

135 Application for official copies of documents referred to in the register of title and other documents kept by the registrar

(1)   Subject to paragraphs (2) and (3), a person may apply for an official copy of—
- (a)   any document referred to in the register of title and kept by the registrar,
- (b)   any other document kept by the registrar that relates to an application to him.

(2)   There is excepted from paragraph (1)—
- (a)   any exempt information document,
- (b)   any edited information document which has been replaced by another edited information document under rule 136(6),
- (c)   any Form EX1A,
- (d)   any Form CIT,
- (e)   any Form to which Form CIT has been attached under rule 140(3) or (4), and
- (f)   any document or copy of any document prepared by the registrar in connection with an application in a Form to which Form CIT has been attached under rule 140(3) or (4).

(3)   During the transitional period, paragraph (1) is also subject to rule 139.

(4)   Subject to rule 132(1), an application under paragraph (1) must be made in Form OC2.

(5)   In paragraph (2) the references to Form EX1A and Form CIT and Forms to which Form CIT has been attached include any equivalent information provided under rule 132 and the reference to an application in a Form to which Form CIT has been attached includes an equivalent application made by virtue of rule 132.

References: See paras 2.64, 6.66, 15.75.

Exempt information documents

136 Application that the registrar designate a document an exempt information document

(1)   A person may apply for the registrar to designate a relevant document an exempt information document if he claims that the document contains prejudicial information.

(2)   Subject to rule 132(1), an application under paragraph (1) must—
    (a)   be made in Form EX1 and EX1A, and
    (b)   include a copy of the relevant document which excludes the prejudicial information and which is certified as being a true copy of the relevant document from which copy this information has been excluded.

(3)   Subject to paragraph (4), provided that the registrar is satisfied that the applicant's claim is not groundless he must designate the relevant document an exempt information document.

(4)   Where the registrar considers that designating the document an exempt information document could prejudice the keeping of the register, he may cancel the application.

(5)   Where a document is an exempt information document, the registrar may make an appropriate entry in the individual register of any affected registered title.

(6)   Where a document is an exempt information document and a further application is made under paragraph (1) which would, but for the existing designation, have resulted in its being so designated, the registrar must prepare another edited information document which excludes—
    (a)   the information excluded from the existing edited information document, and
    (b)   any further information excluded from the edited information document lodged by the applicant.

(7)   In this rule a "relevant document" is a document—
    (a)   referred to in the register of title, or one that relates to an application to the registrar, the original or a copy of which is kept by the registrar, or

(b)   that will be referred to in the register of title as a result of an application (the "accompanying application") made at the same time as an application under this rule, or that relates to the accompanying application, the original or a copy of which will be or is for the time being kept by the registrar.

References: See paras 2.79, 2.80, 6.66–6.68.

137 Application for an official copy of an exempt information document

(1)   A person may apply for an official copy of an exempt information document.

(2)   Subject to rule 132(1), application under paragraph (1) must be made in Form EX2.

(3)   The registrar must give notice of an application under paragraph (1) to the person who made the relevant application under rule 136(1) unless he is satisfied that such notice is unnecessary or impracticable.

(4)   If the registrar decides that—
(a)   none of the information excluded from the edited information document is prejudicial information, or
(b)   although all or some of the information excluded is prejudicial information, the public interest in providing an official copy of the exempt information document to the applicant outweighs the public interest in not doing so,

then he must provide an official copy of the exempt information document to the applicant.

(5)   Where the registrar has decided an application under paragraph (1) on the basis that none of the information is prejudicial information, he must remove the designation of the document as an exempt information document and any entry made in respect of the document under rule 136(5).

References: See paras 2.82–2.84, 6.66, 6.67.

138 Application for removal of the designation of a document as an exempt information document

(1)   Where a document is an exempt information document, the person who applied for designation under rule 136(1) may apply for the designation to be removed.

(2)   Subject to rule 132(1), an application made under paragraph (1) must be in Form EX3.

(3)   Subject to paragraph (4), where the registrar is satisfied that the application is in order, he must remove the designation of the document as an exempt information document and remove any entry made in respect of the document under rule 136(5).

(4)   Where—
(a)   the document has been made an exempt information document under more than one application,

    (b)   an application under paragraph (1) is made by fewer than all of the applicants under rule 136(1), and

    (c)   the registrar is satisfied that the application is in order,

the registrar must replace the existing edited information document with one that excludes only the information excluded both from that edited information document and the edited information documents lodged under rule 136(2)(b) by those applicants not applying under paragraph (1).

References: See para 2.82.

Transitional period documents

139 Inspection, copying and official copies of transitional period documents

(1)   Subject to paragraph (2) and rule 140(2), during the transitional period a person may only inspect and make copies of, or of any part of, a transitional period document or obtain an official copy of a transitional period document at the registrar's discretion.

(2)   Where a transitional period document is an exempt information document, paragraph (1) does not apply.

References: See paras 2.86, 6.66.

Inspection, official copies and searches of the index of proprietors' names in connection with court proceedings, insolvency and tax liability

140 Application in connection with court proceedings, insolvency and tax liability

(1)   In this rule, a qualifying applicant is a person referred to in column 1 of Schedule 5 who gives the registrar the appropriate certificate referred to in column 2 of the Schedule or, where rule 132 applies, an equivalent certificate in accordance with a notice given under Schedule 2.

(2)   A qualifying applicant may apply—

    (a)   to inspect or make copies of any document (including a form) within rule 133(2) and, during the transitional period, any transitional period document,

    (b)   for official copies of any document (including a form) within rule 135(2) and, during the transitional period, any transitional period document, and

    (c)   for a search in the index of proprietors' names in respect of the name of a person specified in the application.

(3)   Subject to rule 132(1), an application under paragraph (2) must be made in Form PIC, OC2 or PN1, as appropriate, with Form CIT attached.

(4)   A qualifying applicant who applies—

    (a)   to inspect and make copies of registers and documents not within paragraph (2)(a) under section 66 of the Act,

    (b)   for official copies of registers and plans under rule 134(1) and of documents not within paragraph (2)(b) under rule 135,

    (c)   for an historical edition of a registered title under rule 144,

    (d)   for an official search of the index map under rule 145, or

(e)   for an official search of the index of relating franchises and manors under rule 146,

may attach Form CIT to the Form PIC, OC1, OC2, HC1, SIM or SIF, as appropriate, used in the application.

(5)   In Form CIT and Schedule 5, references to tax are references to any of the taxes mentioned in the definition of tax in section 118(1) of the Taxes Management Act 1970.

References: See para 2.87, 15.75.

Information about the day list, electronic discharges of registered charges and title plans

141 Day list information

(1)   In this rule "day list information" means information kept by the registrar under rule 12.

(2)   A person may only apply for the day list information relating to a specified title number during the currency of a relevant notice given under Schedule 2, and subject to and in accordance with the limitations contained in the notice.

(3)   The registrar must provide the day list information in the manner specified in the relevant notice.

(4)   Unless otherwise stated by the registrar, the day list information provided must be based on the entries subsisting in the day list immediately before the information is provided.

(5)   The registrar is not required to disclose under this rule details of an application under rule 136.

142 Enquiry as to discharge of a charge by electronic means

(1)   A person may apply in respect of a specified registered title for confirmation of receipt by the registrar of notification of—
  (a)   the discharge of a registered charge given by electronic means, or
  (b)   the release of part of a registered estate from a registered charge given by electronic means.

(2)   An application under paragraph (1) may only be made during the currency of a relevant notice given under Schedule 2, and subject to and in accordance with the limitations contained in the notice.

(3)   The registrar is not required to disclose under this rule any information concerning a notification once the entries of the registered charge to which it relates have been cancelled from the relevant registered title, or the affected part of it.

143 Certificate of inspection of title plan

(1)   Where a person has applied under rule 134 for a certificate of inspection of a title plan, on completion of the inspection the registrar must issue a certificate of inspection.

(2)   Subject to rule 132(2), the certificate of inspection must be issued by the registrar in Form CI or to like effect.

Historical information

144 Application for an historical edition of a registered title kept by the registrar in electronic form

(1)   A person may apply for a copy of—
  (a)   the last edition for a specified day, or
  (b)   every edition for a specified day,
of a registered title, and of a registered title that has been closed, kept by the registrar in electronic form.

(2)   Subject to rule 132(1), an application under paragraph (1) must be made in Form HC1.

(3)   Subject to paragraph (4), if an application under paragraph (1) is in order and the registrar is keeping in electronic form an edition of the registered title for the day specified in the application, he must issue—
  (a)   if the application is under paragraph (1)(a), subject to rule 132(2), a paper copy of the edition of the registered title at the end of that day, or
  (b)   if the application is under paragraph (1)(b), subject to rule 132(2), a paper copy of the edition of the registered title at the end of that day and any prior edition kept in electronic form of the registered title for that day.

(4)   Where only part of the edition of the registered title requested is kept by the registrar in electronic form he must issue, subject to rule 132(2), a paper copy of that part.

References: See paras 2.73, 15.75.

Official searches of the index kept under section 68 of the Act

145 Searches of the index map

(1)   Any person may apply for an official search of the index map.

(2)   Subject to rule 132(1), an application under paragraph (1) must be made in Form SIM.

(3)   If the registrar so requires, an applicant must provide a copy of an extract from the Ordnance Survey map on the largest scale published showing the land to which the application relates.

(4)   If an application under paragraph (1) is in order, subject to rule 132(2), a paper certificate must be issued including such information specified in Part 1 of Schedule 6 as the case may require.

146 Searches of the index of relating franchises and manors

(1)   Any person may apply for an official search of the index of relating franchises and manors.

(2)   Subject to rule 132(1), an application under paragraph (1) must be made in Form SIF.

(3)   If an application under paragraph (1) is in order, subject to rule 132(2), a paper certificate must be issued including such information specified in Part 2 of Schedule 6 as the case may require.

Official searches with priority

147 Application for official search with priority by purchaser

(1)   A purchaser may apply for an official search with priority of the individual register of a registered title to which the protectable disposition relates.

(2)   Where there is a pending application for first registration, the purchaser of a protectable disposition which relates to that pending application may apply for an official search with priority in relation to that pending application.

(3)   Subject to rule 132(1), an application for an official search with priority must be made in Form OS1 or Form OS2, as appropriate.

(4)   Where the application is made in Form OS2 and an accompanying plan is required, unless the registrar allows otherwise, the plan must be delivered in duplicate.

References: See paras 7.82, 7.83.

148 Entry on day list of application for official search with priority

(1)   An application for an official search with priority is to be taken as having been made on the date and at the time of the day notice of it is entered on the day list.

(2)   Paragraph (3) has effect where—
   (a)   an application for an official search is in order, and
   (b)   the applicant has not withdrawn the official search.

(3)   Subject to paragraph (4), the entry on the day list of notice of an application for an official search with priority confers a priority period on an application for an entry in the register in respect of the protectable disposition to which the official search relates.

(4)   Paragraph (3) does not apply if the application for an official search with priority is cancelled subsequently because it is not in order.

References: See para 7.83.

149 Issue of official search certificate with priority

(1)   If an application for an official search with priority is in order an official search certificate with priority must be issued giving the result of the search as at the date and time that the application was entered on the day list.

(2)   An official search certificate with priority relating to a registered estate or to a pending application for first registration may, at the registrar's discretion, be issued in one or both of the following ways—

(a)   in paper form, or

(b)   under rule 132(2).

(3)   Subject to paragraph (4), an official search certificate issued under paragraph (2) must include such information as specified in Part 3 or Part 4 of Schedule 6 as the case may require and may be issued by reference to an official copy of the individual register of the relevant registered title.

(4)   If an official search certificate is to be, or has been, issued in paper form under paragraph (2)(a), another official search certificate issued under paragraph (2)(b) in respect of the same application need only include the information specified at A, F, G and H of Part 3 and A, H and I of Part 4 of Schedule 6, as the case may require.

References: See para 7.84.

150 Withdrawal of official search with priority

(1)   Subject to paragraph (2), a person who has made an application for an official search with priority of a registered title or in relation to a pending first registration application, may withdraw that official search by application to the registrar.

(2)   An application under paragraph (1) cannot be made if an application for an entry in the register in respect of the protectable disposition made pursuant to the official search has been made and completed.

(3)   Once an official search has been withdrawn under paragraph (1) rule 148(3) shall cease to apply in relation to it.

References: See para 7.83.

151 Protection of an application on which a protected application is dependent

(1)   Subject to paragraph (4), paragraph (2) has effect where an application for an entry in the register is one on which an official search certificate confers a priority period and there is a prior registrable disposition affecting the same registered land, on which that application is dependent.

(2)   An application for an entry in the register in relation to that prior registrable disposition is for the purpose of section 72(1)(a) of the Act an application to which a priority period relates.

(3)   The priority period referred to in paragraph (2) is a period expiring at the same time as the priority period conferred by the official search referred to in paragraph (1).

(4)   Paragraph (2) does not have effect unless both the application referred to in paragraph (1) and the application referred to in paragraph (2) are—

(a)   made before the end of that priority period, and

(b)   in due course completed by registration.

References: See para 7.85.

152 Protection of an application relating to a pending application for first registration on which a protected application is dependent

(1)   Subject to paragraphs (4) and (5), paragraph (2) has effect where—

    (a)   there is a pending application for first registration,

    (b)   there is a pending application for an entry in the register on which an official search confers a priority period,

    (c)   there is an application for registration of a prior registrable disposition affecting the same registrable estate or charge as the pending application referred to in sub-paragraph (b),

    (d)   the pending application referred to in sub-paragraph (b) is dependent on the application referred to in sub-paragraph (c), and

    (e)   the application referred to in sub-paragraph (c) is subject to the pending application for first registration referred to in sub-paragraph (a).

(2)   An application for an entry in the register in relation to the prior registrable disposition referred to in paragraph (1)(c) is for the purpose of section 72(1)(a) of the Act an application to which a priority period relates.

(3)   The priority period referred to in paragraph (2) is a period expiring at the same time as the priority period conferred by the official search referred to in paragraph (1)(b).

(4)   Paragraph (2) does not have effect unless the pending application for first registration referred to in paragraph (1)(a) is in due course completed by registration of all or any part of the registrable estate.

(5)   Paragraph (2) does not have effect unless both the pending application on which an official search confers priority referred to in paragraph (1)(b) and the application relating to the prior registrable disposition referred to in paragraph (1)(c) are—

    (a)   made before the end of that priority period, and

    (b)   in due course completed by registration.

References: See para 7.85.

153 Priority of concurrent applications for official searches with priority and concurrent official search certificates with priority

(1)   Where two or more official search certificates with priority relating to the same registrable estate or charge or to the same registered land have been issued and are in operation, the certificates take effect, as far as relates to the priority conferred, in the order of the times at which the applications for official search with priority were entered on the day list, unless the applicants agree otherwise.

(2)   Where one transaction is dependent upon another the registrar must assume (unless the contrary appears) that the applicants for official search with priority have agreed that their applications have priority so as to give effect to the sequence of the documents effecting the transactions.

References: See para 7.86.

154 Applications lodged at the same time as the priority period expires

(1)   Where an official search with priority has been made in respect of a registered title and an application relating to that title is taken as having been made at the same time as the expiry of the priority period relating to that search, the time of the making of that application is to be taken as within that priority period.

(2)   Where an official search with priority has been made in respect of a pending application for first registration and a subsequent application relating to a registrable estate which is subject to that pending application for first registration, or was so subject before completion of the registration of that registrable estate, is taken as having been made at the same time as the expiry of the priority period relating to that search, the time of the making of that subsequent application is to be taken as within that priority period.

References: See para 7.87.

Official searches without priority

155 Application for official search without priority

(1)   A person may apply for an official search without priority of an individual register of a registered title.

(2)   Subject to rule 132(1), an application for an official search without priority must be made in Form OS3.

(3)   Where the application is in Form OS3 and an accompanying plan is required, unless the registrar allows otherwise, the plan must be delivered in duplicate.

156 Issue of official search certificate without priority

(1)   If an application for an official search without priority is in order, an official search certificate without priority must be issued.

(2)   An official search certificate without priority may, at the registrar's discretion, be issued in one or both of the following ways—

(a)   in paper form, or
(b)   under rule 132(2).

(3)   Subject to paragraph (4), an official search certificate without priority issued under paragraph (2) must include such information specified in Part 3 of Schedule 6 as the case may require and may be issued by reference to an official copy of the individual register of the relevant registered title.

(4)   If an official certificate of search is to be, or has been, issued in paper form under paragraph (2)(a), another official search certificate issued under paragraph (2)(b) in respect of the same application need only include the information specified at A, F, G and H of Part 3 of Schedule 6, as the case may require.

Request for information

157 Information requested by telephone, oral or remote terminal application for an official search

(1) If an application under rule 147(3) or rule 155(2) has been made by telephone or orally by virtue of rule 132(1) in respect of a registered title, the registrar may, before or after the official search has been completed, at his discretion, inform the applicant, by telephone or orally, whether or not—

    (a)   there have been any relevant adverse entries made in the individual register since the search from date given in the application, or

    (b)   there is any relevant entry subsisting on the day list.

(2) If an application under rule 147(3) has been made by telephone or orally by virtue of rule 132(1) in respect of a legal estate subject to a pending application for first registration, the registrar may, before or after the official search has been completed, at his discretion, inform the applicant, by telephone or orally, whether or not there is any relevant entry subsisting on the day list.

(3) If an application under rule 147(3) or rule 155(2) has been made to the land registry computer system from a remote terminal by virtue of rule 132(1), the registrar may, before or after the official search has been completed, at his discretion, inform the applicant, by a transmission to the remote terminal, whether or not—

    (a)   in the case of an official search of a registered title, there have been any relevant entries of the kind referred to in paragraph (1)(a) or (b), or

    (b)   in the case of an official search of a legal estate subject to a pending application for first registration, there have been any relevant entries of the kind referred to in paragraph (2).

(4) Under this rule the registrar need not provide the applicant with details of any relevant entries.

Official searches for the purpose of the Family Law Act 1996 and information requests

158 Application for official search for the purpose of the Family Law Act 1996 by a mortgagee

(1) A mortgagee of land comprised in a registered title that consists of or includes all or part of a dwelling-house may apply for an official search certificate of the result of a search of the relevant individual register for the purpose of section 56(3) of the Family Law Act 1996.

(2) Subject to rule 132(1), an application under paragraph (1) must be made in Form MH3.

159 Issue of official search certificate result following an application made by a mortgagee for the purpose of section 56(3) of the Family Law Act 1996

(1) An official search certificate giving the result of a search in respect of an application made under rule 158 may, at the registrar's discretion, be issued in one or both of the following ways—

    (a)   in paper form, or

    (b)   under rule 132(2).

(2)   Subject to paragraph (3), an official search certificate issued under paragraph (1) must include the information specified in Part 5 of Schedule 6.

(3)   If an official search certificate is to be, or has been, issued under paragraph (1)(a), another official search certificate issued under rule 132(2) by virtue of paragraph (1)(b) in respect of the same application need only include the information specified at A, E and F of Part 5 of Schedule 6.

160 Information requested by an applicant for an official search for the purpose of the Family Law Act 1996

If an application has been made under rule 158 the registrar may, at his discretion, during the currency of a relevant notice given under Schedule 2, and in accordance with the limitations contained in that notice, before the official search has been completed, inform the applicant, by any means of communication, whether or not—

      (a)   a matrimonial home rights notice or matrimonial home rights caution has been entered in the individual register of the relevant registered title, or

      (b)   there is a pending application for the entry of a matrimonial home rights notice entered on the day list.

PART 14
MISCELLANEOUS AND SPECIAL CASES

Dispositions by operation of law within section 27(5) of the Act

161 Applications to register dispositions by operation of law which are registrable dispositions

(1)   Subject to paragraphs (2) and (3), an application to register a disposition by operation of law which is a registrable disposition must be accompanied by sufficient evidence of the disposition.

(2)   Where a vesting order has been made, it must accompany the application.

(3)   Where there is a vesting declaration to which section 40 of the Trustee Act 1925 applies, the application must be accompanied by the deed of appointment or retirement, and—

      (a)   a certificate from the conveyancer acting for the persons making the appointment or effecting the retirement that they are entitled to do so, or

      (b)   such other evidence to satisfy the registrar that the persons making the appointment or effecting the retirement are entitled to do so.

References: See para 5.23.

Death of proprietor

162 Transfer by a personal representative

(1)   An application to register a transfer by a personal representative, who is not already registered as proprietor, must be accompanied by the original grant of probate or letters of administration showing him as the personal representative.

(2)   The registrar shall not be under a duty to investigate the reasons a transfer of registered land by a personal representative of a deceased sole proprietor or last surviving joint proprietor is made nor to consider the contents of the will and, provided the terms of any restriction on the register are complied with, he must assume, whether he knows of the terms of the will or not, that the personal representative is acting correctly and within his powers.

References: See para 5.23.

163 Registration of a personal representative

(1)   An application by a personal representative to become registered as proprietor of a registered estate or registered charge—

  (a)   in place of a deceased sole proprietor or the last surviving joint proprietor, or

  (b)   jointly with another personal representative who is already so registered, or

  (c)   in place of another personal representative who is already registered as proprietor,

must be accompanied by the evidence specified in paragraph (2).

(2)   Subject to paragraph (3), the evidence that must accompany an application under paragraph (1) is—

  (a)   the original grant of probate or letters of administration of the deceased proprietor showing the applicant as his personal representative, or

  (b)   a court order appointing the applicant as the deceased's personal representative, or

  (c)   (where a conveyancer is acting for the applicant) a certificate given by the conveyancer that he holds the original or an office copy of such grant of probate, letters of administration or court order.

(3)   An application under paragraph (1)(c) must be accompanied by evidence to satisfy the registrar that the appointment of the personal representative whom the applicant is replacing has been terminated.

(4)   When registering a personal representative of a deceased proprietor, the registrar must add the following after the personal representative's name—

  "executor *or* executrix (*or* administrator *or* administratrix) of [name] deceased".

(5)   Before registering another personal representative as a result of an application made under paragraph (1)(b) the registrar must serve notice upon the personal representative who is registered as proprietor.

References: See para 5.23.

164 Death of joint proprietor

An application for alteration of the register by the removal from the register of the name of a deceased joint proprietor of a registered estate or registered charge must be accompanied by evidence of his death.

Bankruptcy of proprietor

165 Bankruptcy notice

(1)   The bankruptcy notice in relation to a registered estate must be entered in the proprietorship register and the bankruptcy notice in relation to a registered charge must be entered in the charges register in the following form—

> "BANKRUPTCY NOTICE entered under section 86(2) of the Land Registration Act 2002 in respect of a pending action, as the title of the [proprietor of the registered estate] *or* [the proprietor of the charge dated..........referred to above] appears to be affected by a petition in bankruptcy against [*name of debtor*], presented in the [*name*] Court (Court Reference Number..........) (Land Charges Reference Number PA..........).".

(2)   The registrar must give notice of the entry of a bankruptcy notice to the proprietor of the registered estate or registered charge to which it relates.

(3)   In this rule, "bankruptcy notice" means the notice which the registrar must enter in the register under section 86(2) of the Act.

References: See para 5.23.

166 Bankruptcy restriction

(1)   The bankruptcy restriction in relation to a registered estate must be entered in the proprietorship register and the bankruptcy restriction in relation to a registered charge must be entered in the charges register in the following form—

> "BANKRUPTCY RESTRICTION entered under section 86(4) of the Land Registration Act 2002, as the title of [the proprietor of the registered estate] *or* [the proprietor of the charge dated..........referred to above] appears to be affected by a bankruptcy order made by the [*name*] Court (Court Reference Number..........) against [*name of debtor*] (Land Charges Reference Number WO..........).
>
> [No disposition of the registered estate] *or* [No disposition of the charge] is to be registered until the trustee in bankruptcy of the property of the bankrupt is registered as proprietor of the [registered estate] *or* [charge].".

(2)   The registrar must give notice of the entry of a bankruptcy restriction to the proprietor of the registered estate or registered charge to which it relates.

(3)   In this rule, "bankruptcy restriction" means the restriction which the registrar must enter in the register under section 86(4) of the Act.

References: See para 5.23.

167 Action of the registrar in relation to bankruptcy entries

(1)   Where the registrar is satisfied that—
  (a)   the bankruptcy order has been annulled, or
  (b)   the bankruptcy petition has been dismissed or withdrawn with the court's permission, or

(c)   the bankruptcy proceedings do not affect or have ceased to affect the registered estate or registered charge in relation to which a bankruptcy notice or bankruptcy restriction has been entered on the register,

he must as soon as practicable cancel any bankruptcy notice or bankruptcy restriction which relates to that bankruptcy order, to that bankruptcy petition or to those proceedings from the register.

(2)   Where it appears to the registrar that there is doubt as to whether the debtor or bankrupt is the same person as the proprietor of the registered estate or registered charge in relation to which a bankruptcy notice or bankruptcy restriction has been entered, he must as soon as practicable take such action as he considers necessary to resolve the doubt.

(3)   In this rule—

    "bankruptcy notice" means the notice which the registrar must enter in the register under section 86(2) of the Act, and

    "bankruptcy restriction" means the restriction which the registrar must enter in the register under section 86(4) of the Act.

168 Registration of trustee in bankruptcy

(1)   Where—
    (a)   a proprietor has had a bankruptcy order made against him, or
    (b)   an insolvency administration order has been made in respect of a deceased proprietor,

and the bankrupt's or deceased's registered estate or registered charge has vested in the trustee in bankruptcy, the trustee may apply for the alteration of the register by registering himself in place of the bankrupt or deceased proprietor.

(2)   The application must be supported by, as appropriate—
    (a)   the bankruptcy order relating to the bankrupt or the insolvency administration order relating to the deceased's estate, and
    (b)   a certificate signed by the trustee that the registered estate or registered charge is comprised in the bankrupt's estate or deceased's estate, and
    (c)   where the official receiver is the trustee, a certificate by him to that effect, and, where the trustee is another person, the evidence referred to in paragraph (3).

(3)   The evidence referred to at paragraph (2)(c) is—
    (a)   his certificate of appointment as trustee by the meeting of the bankrupt's or deceased debtor's creditors, or
    (b)   his certificate of appointment as trustee by the Secretary of State, or
    (c)   the order of the court appointing him trustee.

(4)   In this rule, "insolvency administration order" has the same meaning as in section 385(1) of the Insolvency Act 1986.

169 Trustee in bankruptcy vacating office

(1)   This rule applies where—
    (a)   a trustee in bankruptcy, who has been registered as proprietor, vacates his office, and
    (b)   the official receiver or some other person has been appointed the trustee of the relevant bankrupt's estate, and

(c) the official receiver or that person applies to be registered as proprietor in place of the former trustee.

(2) The application referred to in paragraph (1)(c) must be supported by the evidence required by rule 168(2)(c).

170 Description of trustee in register

Where the official receiver or another trustee in bankruptcy is registered as proprietor, the words "Official Receiver and trustee in bankruptcy of [name]" or "Trustee in bankruptcy of [name]" must be added to the register, as appropriate.

Overseas insolvency proceedings

171 Proceedings under the EC Regulation on insolvency proceedings

(1) A relevant person may apply for a note of a judgement opening insolvency proceedings to be entered in the register.

(2) An application under paragraph (1) must be accompanied by such evidence as the registrar may reasonably require.

(3) Following an application under paragraph (1) if the registrar is satisfied that the judgement opening insolvency proceedings has been made he may enter a note of the judgement in the register.

(4) In this rule—
"judgement opening insolvency proceedings" means a judgement opening proceedings within the meaning of article 3(1) of the Regulation,
"Regulation" means Council Regulation (EC) No 1346/2000,
"relevant person" means any person or body authorised under the provisions of article 22 of the Regulation to request or require an entry to be made in the register in respect of the judgement opening insolvency proceedings the subject of the application.

Pending land actions, writs and orders

172 Benefit of pending land actions, writs and orders

(1) For the purposes of section 34(1) of the Act, a relevant person shall be treated as having the benefit of the pending land action, writ or order, as appropriate.

(2) In determining whether a person has a sufficient interest in the making of an entry of a restriction under section 43(1)(c) of the Act, a relevant person shall be treated as having the benefit of the pending land action, writ or order, as appropriate.

(3) In this rule, "a relevant person" means a person (or his assignee or chargee, if appropriate) who is taking any action or proceedings which are within section 87(1)(a) of the Act, or who has obtained a writ or order within section 87(1)(b) of the Act.

References: See para 10.6.

The Crown

173 Escheat etc

(1)   Where a registered freehold estate in land has determined, the registrar may enter a note of that fact in the property register and in the property register of any inferior affected registered title.

(2)   Where the registrar considers that there is doubt as to whether a registered freehold estate in land has determined, the entry under paragraph (1) must be modified by a statement to that effect.

References: See para 12.24.

Church of England

174 Entry of Incumbent on a transfer to the Church Commissioners

(1)   Where by virtue of any Act or Measure a transfer to the Church Commissioners has the effect, subject only to being completed by registration, of vesting any registered land either immediately or at a subsequent time in an incumbent or any other ecclesiastical corporation sole, the registrar must register the incumbent or such other ecclesiastical corporation as proprietor upon receipt of—

 (a)   an application,
 (b)   the transfer to the Church Commissioners, and
 (c)   a certificate by the Church Commissioners in Form 4.

(2)   The certificate in Form 4 may be given either in the transfer or in a separate document.

(3)   In this rule, "Measure" means a Measure of the National Assembly of the Church of England or of the General Synod of the Church of England.

175 Entry of Church Commissioners etc as proprietor

(1)   When any registered land is transferred to or (subject only to completion by registration) vested in the Church Commissioners, any ecclesiastical corporation, aggregate or sole, or any other person, by—

 (a)   a scheme of the Church Commissioners, or
 (b)   an instrument taking effect on publication in the London Gazette made pursuant to any Act or Measure relating to or administered by the Church Commissioners, or
 (c)   any transfer authorised by any such Act or Measure,

the registrar must, on application, register the Church Commissioners, such ecclesiastical corporation or such other person as proprietor.

(2)   The application must be accompanied by—

 (a)   a certificate by the Church Commissioners in Form 5, and
 (b)   (i)   a copy of the London Gazette publishing the instrument, or
    (ii)   the transfer (if any).

(3)   The certificate in Form 5 may be given either in the transfer or in a separate document.

(4)   In this rule, "Measure" means a Measure of the National Assembly of the Church of England or of the General Synod of the Church of England.

Charities

176 Non-exempt charities—restrictions

(1)   The restriction which the registrar is required by section 37(8) or section 39(1B) of the Charities Act 1993 to enter in the register where one of those subsections applies must be the appropriate restriction.

(2)   Any of the following applications must, if they relate to a registered or unregistered estate held by or in trust for a non-exempt charity, be accompanied by an application for entry of the appropriate restriction unless, in the case of a registered estate, that restriction is already in the register—

    (a)   an application for first registration of an unregistered estate unless the disposition which triggers the requirement of registration is effected by an instrument containing the statement set out in rule 179(b) or rule 180(2)(b) or (c),

    (b)   an application to register a transfer of a registered estate unless the disposition is effected by an instrument containing the statement set out in rule 179(b),

    (c)   an application under rule 161 to register the vesting of a registered estate in a person other than the proprietor of that estate.

(3)   Where a registered estate is held by or in trust for a corporation and the corporation becomes a non-exempt charity, the charity trustees must apply for entry of the appropriate restriction.

(4)   In this rule "the appropriate restriction" means a restriction in Form E.

References: See paras 10.40, 10.41, 10.45.

177 Registration of trustees incorporated under Part VII of the Charities Act 1993

In any registrable disposition in favour of charity trustees incorporated under Part VII of the Charities Act 1993 they must be described as "a body corporate under Part VII of the Charities Act 1993" and the application to register the disposition must be accompanied by the certificate granted by the Charity Commissioners under section 50 of that Act.

178 Registration of official custodian

(1)   An application to register the official custodian as proprietor of a registered estate or a registered charge must be accompanied by—

    (a)   an order of the court made under section 21(1) of the Charities Act 1993, or

    (b)   an order of the Charity Commissioners made under sections 16 or 18 of the Charities Act 1993.

(2)   Where the estate or charge is vested in the official custodian by virtue of an order under section 18 of the Charities Act 1993, an application to register him as proprietor (whether under Chapter 1 of Part 2 of the Act or following a registrable disposition) must be accompanied by an application for the entry of a restriction in Form F.

(3)   Where the official custodian is registered as proprietor of a registered estate or a registered charge, except where the estate or charge is vested in him by virtue of an order under section 18 of the Charities Act 1993, the address of the charity trustees or, where the registered estate or registered charge is held on behalf of a charity which is a corporation, the address of the charity, must be entered in the register as his address for service under rule 198.

References: See paras 10.41, 10.49.

179 Statements to be contained in dispositions in favour of a charity

The statement required by section 37(5) of the Charities Act 1993 must, in an instrument to which section 37(7) of that Act applies, be in one of the following forms—

(a)   "The land transferred (*or as the case may be*) will, as a result of this transfer (*or as the case may be*) be held by (or in trust for) (*charity*), an exempt charity."

(b)   "The land transferred (*or as the case may be*) will, as a result of this transfer (*or as the case may be*) be held by (*or* in trust for) (*charity*), a non-exempt charity, and the restrictions on disposition imposed by section 36 of the Charities Act 1993 will apply to the land (subject to section 36(9) of that Act).".

References: See para 10.47.

180 Statements to be contained in dispositions by a charity

(1)   The statement required by section 37(1) of the Charities Act 1993 must, in an instrument to which section 37(7) of that Act applies, be in one of the following forms—

(a)   "The land transferred (*or as the case may be*) is held by [(*proprietors*) in trust for] (*charity*), an exempt charity."

(b)   "The land transferred (*or as the case may be*) is held by [(*proprietors*) in trust for] (*charity*), a non-exempt charity, but this transfer (*or as the case may be*) is one falling within paragraph ((a), (b) or (c) *as the case may be*) of section 36(9) of the Charities Act 1993."

(c)   "The land transferred (*or as the case may be*) is held by [(*proprietors*) in trust for] (*charity*), a non-exempt charity, and this transfer (*or as the case may be*) is not one falling within paragraph (a), (b) or (c) of section 36(9) of the Charities Act 1993, so that the restrictions on disposition imposed by section 36 of that Act apply to the land.".

(2)   The statement required by section 39(1) of the Charities Act 1993 must, in a mortgage which is a registrable disposition or to which section 4(1)(g) of the Act applies, be in one of the following forms—

(a)   "The land charged is held by (*or* in trust for) (*charity*), an exempt charity."

(b)   "The land charged is held by (*or* in trust for) (*charity*), a non-exempt charity, but this charge (*or* mortgage) is one falling within section 38(5) of the Charities Act 1993."

(c)   "The land charged is held by (*or* in trust for) (*charity*), a non-exempt charity, and this charge (*or* mortgage) is not one falling within section 38(5) of the Charities Act 1993, so that the restrictions imposed by section 38 of that Act apply.".

(3)   The statement required by section 39(1A)(b) of the Charities Act 1993 must be in the following form—

"The restrictions on disposition imposed by section 36 of the Charities Act 1993 also apply to the land (subject to section 36(9) of that Act).".

References: See para 10.37.

Companies and other corporations

181 Registration of companies and limited liability partnerships

(1)   Where a company registered in England and Wales or Scotland under the Companies Acts applies to be registered as proprietor of a registered estate or of a registered charge, the application must state the company's registered number.

(2)   If the company is a registered social landlord within the meaning of the Housing Act 1996, the application must also contain or be accompanied by a certificate to that effect.

(3)   If the company is an unregistered housing association within the meaning of the Housing Associations Act 1985 and the application relates to grant-aided land as defined in Schedule 1 to that Act, the application must also contain or be accompanied by a certificate to that effect.

(4)   Where a limited liability partnership incorporated under the Limited Liability Partnerships Act 2000 applies to be registered as proprietor of a registered estate or of a registered charge, the application must state the limited liability partnership's registered number.

References: See paras 4.13, 5.19.

182 Registration of trustees of charitable, ecclesiastical or public trust

(1)   Subject to paragraph (4), where a corporation or body of trustees holding on charitable, ecclesiastical or public trusts applies to be registered as proprietor of a registered estate or registered charge, the application must be accompanied by the document creating the trust.

(2)   If the registered estate or registered charge to which the application relates is held on trust for a registered social landlord within the meaning of the Housing Act 1996, the application must also contain or be accompanied by a certificate to that effect.

(3)   If the registered estate or registered charge to which the application relates is held on trust for an unregistered housing association within the meaning of the Housing Associations Act 1985 and is grant-aided land as defined in Schedule 1 to that Act, the application must also contain or be accompanied by a certificate to that effect.

(4)   Paragraph (1) of this rule does not apply in the case of a registered estate or a registered charge held by or in trust for a non-exempt charity.

References: See paras 4.13, 5.19.

183 Registration of other corporations

(1)   Where a corporation aggregate, to which rules 181 and 182 do not apply, makes an application to be registered as proprietor of a registered estate or registered charge the application must also be accompanied by evidence of the extent of its powers to hold and sell, mortgage, lease and otherwise deal with land and, in the case of a charge, to lend money on mortgage.

(2)   The evidence must include the charter, statute, rules, memorandum and articles of association or other documents constituting the corporation, together with such further evidence as the registrar may require.

(3)   If the corporation is a registered social landlord within the meaning of the Housing Act 1996, the application must contain or be accompanied by a certificate to that effect.

(4)   If the corporation is an unregistered housing association within the meaning of the Housing Associations Act 1985 and the application relates to grant-aided land as defined in Schedule 1 to that Act, the application must contain or be accompanied by a certificate to that effect.

References: See paras 4.13, 5.19.

184 Administration orders and liquidation of a company

(1)   Paragraph (2) applies where a company which is the registered proprietor of a registered estate or registered charge is the subject of an administration order made under the Insolvency Act 1986.

(2)   Upon the application of the company's administrator, supported by the order, the registrar must make an entry in the individual register of the relevant registered title as to the making of the order and the appointment of the administrator.

(3)   Paragraphs (4) and (5) apply where a company which is the registered proprietor of a registered estate or registered charge is in liquidation.

(4)   Upon the application of the company's liquidator, the registrar must make an entry in the individual register of the relevant registered title as to the appointment of the liquidator.

(5)   The application under paragraph (4) must be supported by the order, appointment by the Secretary of State or resolution under which the liquidator was appointed and such other evidence as the registrar may require.

References: See para 5.23.

185 Note of dissolution of a corporation

Where a corporation shown in an individual register as the proprietor of the registered estate or of a registered charge has been dissolved, the registrar may enter a note of that fact in the proprietorship register or in the charges register, as appropriate.

References: See paras 5.23, 12.25.

Settlements

186 Settlements

Schedule 7 (which makes provision for the purposes of the Act in relation to the application to registered land of the enactments relating to settlements under the Settled Land Act 1925) has effect.

Adverse possession

187 Interpretation

Where the application is to be registered as proprietor of a registered rentcharge, the references in rules 188, 189, 190, 192 and 193 to Schedule 6 to the Act are to Schedule 6 as applied by rule 191.

188 Applications for registration—procedure

(1)   An application under paragraphs 1 or 6 of Schedule 6 to the Act must be in Form ADV1 and be accompanied by—

   (a)   a statutory declaration made by the applicant not more than one month before the application is taken to have been made, together with any supporting statutory declarations, to provide evidence of adverse possession of the registered estate in land or rentcharge against which the application is made for a period which if it were to continue from the date of the applicant's statutory declaration to the date of the application would be—

      (i)   where the application is under paragraph 1, of not less than ten years (or sixty years, if paragraph 13 of Schedule 6 to the Act applies) ending on the date of the application, or

      (ii)   where the application is under paragraph 6, of not less than two years beginning with the date of rejection of the original application under paragraph 1 and ending on the date of the application,

   (b)   any additional evidence which the applicant considers necessary to support the claim.

(2)   The statutory declaration by an applicant in support of an application under paragraph 1 of Schedule 6 to the Act must also—

   (a)   exhibit a plan enabling the extent of the land to be identified on the Ordnance Survey map, unless the application is to be registered as proprietor of a registered rentcharge,

   (b)   if reliance is placed on paragraph 1(2) of Schedule 6 to the Act, contain the facts relied upon with any appropriate exhibits,

   (c)   contain confirmation that paragraph 1(3) of Schedule 6 to the Act does not apply,

(d)   where the application is to be registered as proprietor of a registered rentcharge, contain confirmation that the proprietor of the registered rentcharge has not re-entered the land out of which the rentcharge issues,

(e)   contain confirmation that to the best of his knowledge the restriction on applications in paragraph 8 of Schedule 6 to the Act does not apply,

(f)   contain confirmation that to the best of his knowledge the estate or rentcharge is not, and has not been during any of the period of alleged adverse possession, subject to a trust (other than one where the interest of each of the beneficiaries is an interest in possession),

(g)   if, should a person given notice under paragraph 2 of Schedule 6 to the Act require the application to be dealt with under paragraph 5 of that Schedule, it is intended to rely on one or more of the conditions set out in paragraph 5 of Schedule 6 to the Act, contain the facts supporting such reliance.

(3)   The statutory declaration by an applicant in support of an application under paragraph 6 of Schedule 6 to the Act must also—

(a)   exhibit a plan enabling the extent of the land to be identified on the Ordnance Survey map, unless the application is to be registered as proprietor of a registered rentcharge or the extent is the same as in the previous rejected application,

(b)   contain full details of the previous rejected application,

(c)   contain confirmation that to the best of his knowledge the restriction on applications in paragraph 8 of Schedule 6 to the Act does not apply,

(d)   contain confirmation that to the best of his knowledge the estate or rentcharge is not, and has not been during any of the period of alleged adverse possession, subject to a trust (other than one where the interest of each of the beneficiaries is an interest in possession),

(e)   contain confirmation that paragraph 6(2) of Schedule 6 to the Act does not apply, and

(f)   where the application is to be registered as proprietor of a registered rentcharge, contain confirmation that the proprietor of the registered rentcharge has not re-entered the land out of which the rentcharge issues.

References: See para 13.13.

189 Time limit for reply to a notice of an application

The period for the purpose of paragraph 3(2) of Schedule 6 to the Act is the period ending at 12 noon on the sixty-fifth business day after the date of issue of the notice.

References: See paras 2.27, 13.16.

190 Notice under paragraph 3(2) of Schedule 6 to the Act

(1)   A notice to the registrar under paragraph 3(2) of Schedule 6 to the Act from a person given a registrar's notice must be—

(a)   in Form NAP, and

(b)   given to the registrar in the manner and at the address stated in the registrar's notice.

(2)   Form NAP must accompany a registrar's notice.

(3)   In this rule a "registrar's notice" is a notice given by the registrar under paragraph 2 of Schedule 6 to the Act.

References: See para 13.16.

191 Adverse possession of rentcharges

Schedule 6 to the Act applies to the registration of an adverse possessor of a registered rentcharge in the modified form set out in Schedule 8.

192 Adverse possession of a rentcharge; non-payment of rent

(1)   This rule applies where—
- (a)   a person is entitled to be registered as proprietor of a registered rentcharge under Schedule 6 to the Act, and
- (b)   if that person were so registered he would not be subject to a registered charge or registered lease or other interest protected in the register, and
- (c)   that person's adverse possession is based on non-payment of rent due under the registered rentcharge.

(2)   Where paragraph (1) applies the registrar must—
- (a)   close the whole of the registered title of the registered rentcharge, or
- (b)   cancel the registered rentcharge, if the registered title to it also comprises other rentcharges.

193 Prohibition of recovery of rent after adverse possession of a rentcharge

(1)   When—
- (a)   a person has been registered as proprietor of a rentcharge, or
- (b)   the registered title to a rentcharge has been closed, or
- (c)   a registered rentcharge has been cancelled, where the registered title also comprises other rentcharges,

following an application made under Schedule 6 to the Act, and, if appropriate, closure or cancellation under rule 192, no previous registered proprietor of the rentcharge may recover any rent due under the rentcharge from a person who has been in adverse possession of the rentcharge.

(2)   Paragraph (1) applies whether the adverse possession arose either as a result of non-payment of the rent or by receipt of the rent from the person liable to pay it.

194 Registration as a person entitled to be notified of an application for adverse possession

(1)   Any person who can satisfy the registrar that he has an interest in a registered estate in land or a registered rentcharge which would be prejudiced by the registration of any other person as proprietor of that estate under Schedule 6 to the Act or as proprietor of a registered rentcharge under that Schedule as applied by rule 191 may apply to be registered as a person to be notified under paragraph 2(1)(d) of Schedule 6.

(2)   An application under paragraph (1) must be made in Form ADV2.

(3)   The registrar must enter the name of the applicant in the proprietorship register as a person entitled to be notified under paragraph 2 of Schedule 6 to the Act.

References: See paras 2.27, 13.14, 13.15.

Indemnity; interest on

195 Payment of interest on an indemnity

(1)   Subject to paragraph (4), interest is payable on the amount of any indemnity paid under Schedule 8 to the Act for the period specified in paragraph (2) at the rate specified in paragraph (3).

(2)   Interest is payable—
   (a)   where paragraph 1(1)(a) of Schedule 8 applies, from the date of the rectification to the date of payment,
   (b)   where any other sub-paragraph of paragraph 1(1) of Schedule 8 applies, from the date the loss is suffered by reason of the relevant mistake, loss, destruction or failure to the date of payment,

but excluding any period or periods where the registrar or the court is satisfied that the claimant has not taken reasonable steps to pursue with due diligence the claim for indemnity or, where relevant, the application for rectification.

(3)   Interest is payable at the applicable rate or rates set for court judgement debts.

(4)   Interest is payable in respect of an indemnity on account of costs or expenses within paragraph 3 of Schedule 8 from the date when the claimant pays them to the date of payment.

(5)   A reference in this rule to a period from a date to the date of payment excludes the former date but includes the latter date.

References: See paras 14.48.

Statements under the Leasehold Reform, Housing and Urban Development Act 1993

196 Statements in transfers or conveyances and leases under the Leasehold Reform, Housing and Urban Development Act 1993

(1)   The statement required by section 34(10) of the Leasehold Reform, Housing and Urban Development Act 1993 to be contained in a conveyance executed for the purposes of Chapter I of Part I of that Act must be in the following form:

> "This conveyance (or transfer) is executed for the purposes of Chapter I of Part I of the Leasehold Reform, Housing and Urban Development Act 1993.".

(2) The statement required by section 57(11) of the Leasehold Reform, Housing and Urban Development Act 1993 to be contained in any new lease granted under section 56 of that Act must be in the following form:

> "This lease is granted under section 56 of the Leasehold Reform, Housing and Urban Development Act 1993.".

PART 15
GENERAL PROVISIONS

Notices and addresses for Service

197 Content of notice

(1) Every notice given by the registrar must—
  (a) fix the time within which the recipient is to take any action required by the notice,
  (b) state what the consequence will be of a failure to take such action as is required by the notice within the time fixed,
  (c) state the manner in which any reply to the notice must be given and the address to which it must be sent.

(2) Except where otherwise provided by these rules, the time fixed by the notice will be the period ending at 12 noon on the fifteenth business day after the date of issue of the notice.

References: See paras 2.34, 2.35.

198 Address for service of notice

(1) A person who is (or will as a result of an application be) a person within paragraph (2) must give the registrar an address for service to which all notices and other communications to him by the registrar may be sent, as provided by paragraph (3).

(2) The persons referred to in paragraph (1) are—
  (a) the registered proprietor of a registered estate or registered charge,
  (b) the registered beneficiary of a unilateral notice,
  (c) a cautioner named in an individual caution register,
  (d) a person whose name and address is required to be included in a standard restriction set out in Schedule 4 or whose consent or certificate is required, or upon whom notice is required to be served by the registrar or another person, under any other restriction,
  (e) a person entitled to be notified of an application for adverse possession under rule 194,
  (f) a person who objects to an application under section 73 of the Act,
  (g) a person who gives notice to the registrar under paragraph 3(2) of Schedule 6 to the Act, and
  (h) any person who while dealing with the registrar in connection with registered land or a caution against first registration is requested by the registrar to give an address for service.

(3) A person within paragraph (1) must give the registrar an address for service which is a postal address, whether or not in the United Kingdom.

(4)   A person within paragraph (1) may give the registrar one or two additional addresses for service, provided that he may not have more than three addresses for service, and the address or addresses must be—
  (a)   a postal address, whether or not in the United Kingdom, or
  (b)   subject to paragraph (7), a box number at a United Kingdom document exchange, or
  (c)   an electronic address.

(5)   Subject to paragraphs (3) and (4) a person within paragraph (1) may give the registrar a replacement address for service.

(6)   A cautioner who is entered in the register of title in respect of a caution against dealings under section 54 of the Land Registration Act 1925 may give the registrar a replacement or additional address for service provided that—
  (a)   he may not have more than three addresses for service,
  (b)   one of his addresses for service must be a postal address, whether or not in the United Kingdom, and
  (c)   all of his addresses for service must be such addresses as are mentioned in paragraph (4).

(7)   The box number referred to at paragraph (4)(b) must be at a United Kingdom document exchange to which delivery can be made on behalf of the land registry under arrangements already in existence between the land registry and a service provider at the time the box number details are provided to the registrar under this rule.

(8)   In this rule an electronic address means—
  (a)   an e-mail address, or
  (b)   any other form of electronic address specified in a direction under paragraph (9).

(9)   If the registrar is satisfied that a form of electronic address, other than an e-mail address, is a suitable form of address for service he may issue a direction to that effect.

(10)   A direction under paragraph (9) may contain such conditions or limitations or both as the registrar considers appropriate.

(11)   A person within paragraph (2)(d) shall be treated as having complied with any duty imposed on him under paragraph (1) where rule 92(2)(b) has been complied with.

References: See paras 2.27–2.30.

199 Service of notice

(1)   All notices which the registrar is required to give may be served—
  (a)   by post, to any postal address in the United Kingdom entered in the register as an address for service,
  (b)   by post, to any postal address outside the United Kingdom entered in the register as an address for service,
  (c)   by leaving the notice at any postal address in the United Kingdom entered in the register as an address for service,
  (d)   by directing the notice to the relevant box number at any document exchange entered in the register as an address for service,

  (e) by electronic transmission to the electronic address entered in the register as an address for service,

  (f) subject to paragraph (3), by fax, or

  (g) by any of the methods of service given in sub-paragraphs (a), (b), (c) and (d) to any other address where the registrar believes the addressee is likely to receive it.

(2) In paragraph (1) references to an address or box number "entered in the register as an address for service" include an address for service given under rule 198(2)(h), whether or not it is entered in the register.

(3) The notice may be served by fax if the recipient has informed the registrar in writing—

  (a) that the recipient is willing to accept service of the notice by fax, and

  (b) of the fax number to which it should be sent.

(4) Service of a notice which is served in accordance with this rule shall be regarded as having taken place at the time shown in the table below—

Method of service	Time of service
Post to an address in the United Kingdom	The second working day after posting
Leaving at a postal address	The working day after it was left
Post to an address outside the United Kingdom	The seventh working day after posting
Document exchange	On the second working day after it was left at the registrar's document exchange
Fax	The working day after transmission
Electronic transmission to an electronic address	The second working day after transmission

(5) In this rule "post" means pre-paid delivery by a postal service which seeks to deliver documents within the United Kingdom no later than the next working day in all or the majority of cases, and to deliver outside the United Kingdom within such a period as is reasonable in all the circumstances.

(6) In paragraphs (4) and (5), "working day" means any day from Monday to Friday (inclusive) which is not Christmas Day, Good Friday or any other day either specified or declared by proclamation under section 1 of the Banking and Financial Dealings Act 1971 or appointed by the Lord Chancellor.

References: See paras 2.29, 2.33.

Specialist assistance

200 Use of specialist assistance by the registrar

(1) The registrar may refer to an appropriate specialist—

(a)   the examination of the whole or part of any title lodged with an application for first registration, or

(b)   any question or other matter which arises in the course of any proceedings before the registrar and which, in his opinion, requires the advice of an appropriate specialist.

(2)   The registrar may act upon the advice or opinion of an appropriate specialist to whom he has referred a matter under paragraph (1).

(3)   In this rule, "appropriate specialist" means a person who the registrar considers has the appropriate knowledge, experience and expertise to advise on the matter referred to him.

References: See para 15.21.

Proceedings before the registrar

201   Production of documents

(1)   The registrar may only exercise the power conferred on him by section 75(1) of the Act if he receives from a person who is a party to proceedings before him a request that he should require a document holder to produce a document for the purpose of those proceedings.

(2)   The request must be made—
   (a)   in paper form in Form PRD1 delivered to such office of the land registry as the registrar may direct, or
   (b)   during the currency of a relevant notice given under Schedule 2, and subject to and in accordance with the limitations contained in the notice, by delivering the request to the registrar, by any means of communication, other than as mentioned in sub-paragraph (a).

(3)   The registrar must give notice of the request to the document holder.

(4)   The address for the document holder provided in Form PRD1 is to be regarded for the purpose of rule 199 as an address for service given under rule 198(2)(h).

(5)   The notice must give the document holder a period ending at 12 noon on the twentieth business day after the issue of the notice, or such other period as the registrar thinks appropriate, to deliver a written response to the registrar by the method and to the address stated in the notice.

(6)   The response must—
   (a)   state whether or not the document holder opposes the request,
   (b)   if he does, state in full the grounds for that opposition,
   (c)   give an address to which communications may be sent, and
   (d)   be signed by the document holder or his conveyancer.

(7)   The registrar must determine the matter on the basis of the request and any response submitted to him and, subject to paragraph (8), he may make the requirement by sending a notice in Form PRD2 to the document holder if he is satisfied that—
   (a)   the document is in the control of the document holder, and
   (b)   the document may be relevant to the proceedings, and
   (c)   disclosure of the document is necessary in order to dispose fairly of the proceedings or to save costs,

and he is not aware of any valid ground entitling the document holder to withhold the document.

(8)   The registrar may, as a condition of making the requirement, provide that the person who has made the request should pay the reasonable costs incurred in complying with the requirement by the document holder.

(9)   In this rule, "document holder" means the person who is alleged to have control of a document which is the subject of a request under paragraph (1).

References: See paras 15.12, 15.13, 15.19.

---

202 Costs

(1)   A person who has incurred costs in relation to proceedings before the registrar may request the registrar to make an order requiring a party to those proceedings to pay the whole or part of those costs.

(2)   The registrar may only order a party to proceedings before him to pay costs where those costs have been occasioned by the unreasonable conduct of that party in relation to the proceedings.

(3)   Subject to paragraph (5), a request for the payment of costs must be made by delivering to the registrar a written statement in paper form by 12 noon on the twentieth business day after the completion of the proceedings to which the request relates.

(4)   The statement must—
  (a)   identify the party against whom the order is sought and include an address where notice may be served on that party,
  (b)   state in full the grounds for the request,
  (c)   give an address to which communications may be sent, and
  (d)   be signed by the person making the request or his conveyancer.

(5)   During the currency of a relevant notice given under Schedule 2, and subject to and in accordance with the limitations contained in the notice, a request under this rule may also be made by delivering the written statement to the registrar, by any means of communication, other than as mentioned in paragraph (3).

(6)   The registrar must give notice of the request to the party against whom the order is sought at the address provided under paragraph (4)(a) and if that party has an address for service in an individual register that relates to the proceedings, at that address.

(7)   An address for a party provided under paragraph (4)(a) is to be regarded for the purpose of rule 199 as if it was an address for service given under rule 198(2)(h).

(8)   The notice must give the recipient a period ending at 12 noon on the twentieth business day after the issue of the notice, or such other period as the registrar thinks appropriate, to deliver a written response to the registrar by the method and to the address stated in the notice.

(9)   The response must—
  (a)   state whether or not the recipient opposes the request,
  (b)   if he does, state in full the grounds for that opposition,
  (c)   give an address to which communications may be sent, and
  (d)   be signed by the recipient or his conveyancer.

(10) The registrar must determine the matter on the basis of: the written request and any response submitted to him, all the circumstances including the conduct of the parties, and the result of any enquiries he considers it necessary to make.

(11) The registrar must send to all parties his written reasons for any order he makes under paragraph (1).

(12) An order under paragraph (1) may—
- (a) require a party against whom it is made to pay to the requesting party the whole or such part as the registrar thinks fit of the costs incurred in the proceedings by the requesting party,
- (b) specify the sum to be paid or require the costs to be assessed by the court (if not otherwise agreed), and specify the basis of the assessment to be used by the court.

References: See paras 15.15–15.18.

Retention and return of documents

203 Retention of documents on completion of an application

(1) Subject to paragraphs (2) to (5), on completion of any application the registrar may retain all or any of the documents that accompanied the application and must return all other such documents to the applicant or as otherwise specified in the application.

(2) When making an application, an applicant or his conveyancer may request the return of all or any of the documents accompanying the application.

(3) Except on an application for first registration, a person making a request under paragraph (2) must deliver with the application certified copies of the documents which are the subject of the request.

(4) On an application for first registration, a person making a request under paragraph (2) for the return of any statutory declaration, subsisting lease, subsisting charge or the latest document of title must deliver with the application certified copies of any such documents as are the subject of the request, but shall not be required to deliver copies of any other documents.

(5) Subject to the delivery of any certified copies required under paragraphs (3) or (4), the registrar must comply with any request made under paragraph (2).

(6) The registrar may destroy any document retained under paragraph (1) if he is satisfied that either—
- (a) he has made and retained a sufficient copy of the document, or
- (b) further retention of the document is unnecessary.

(7) If the registrar considers that he no longer requires delivery of certified copies of documents, or classes of documents, under this rule he may, in such manner as he thinks appropriate for informing persons who wish to make applications, give notice to that effect and on and after the date specified in such notice—
- (a) the requirement under this rule to deliver certified copies of the documents covered by the notice no longer applies, and
- (b) the registrar may amend any Schedule 1 form to reflect that fact.

(8)   In paragraph (4) the "latest document of title" means the document vesting the estate sought to be registered in the applicant or where the estate vested in the applicant by operation of law the most recent document that vested the estate in a predecessor of the applicant.

References: See para 6.27.

204 Request for the return of certain documents

(1)   This rule applies to all documents on which any entry in the register of title is or was founded and which are kept by the registrar on the relevant date.

(2)   During the period of 5 years beginning with the relevant date any person who delivered a document to the registrar may request the return of that document.

(3)   Where at the time of the delivery of the document the person delivering the document was the registered proprietor, or was applying to become the registered proprietor, of any registered estate or registered charge in respect of which the entry referred to in paragraph (1) was made, a person who is at the date of the request the registered proprietor of any part of the same registered estate or registered charge may make a request under paragraph (2) for the document to be returned to him.

(4)   Subject to paragraph (5), if, at the date of the request under paragraph (2), the document is kept by the registrar he must return it to the person making the request.

(5)   If the registrar receives more than one request under paragraph (2) in respect of the same document, he may either retain the document or, in his discretion, return it to one of the persons making a request.

(6)   At the end of the period mentioned in paragraph (2) if there is no outstanding request in relation to the document the registrar may destroy any document if he is satisfied that—
   (a)   he has retained a copy of the document, or
   (b)   further retention of the document is unnecessary.

(7)   Where a request is made for the return of a document after the end of the period mentioned in paragraph (2), the registrar may treat the request as a request under paragraph (2).

(8)   The "relevant date" for the purpose of this rule is the date on which these rules come into force.

205 Release of documents kept by the registrar

The registrar may release any document retained under rule 203(1) or to which rule 204 applies upon such terms, if any, for its return as he considers appropriate.

Forms

206 Use of forms

(1)   Subject to paragraph (4) and to rules 208 and 209, the Schedule 1 forms must be used where required by these rules and must be prepared in accordance with the requirements of rules 210 and 211.

(2)   Subject to paragraph (4) and to rules 208 and 209, except where these rules require the use of a Schedule 1 form, the Schedule 3 forms must be used in all

matters to which they refer, or are capable of being applied or adapted, with such alterations and additions as are desired and the registrar allows.

(3)   Subject to rule 208(2), the forms of execution in Schedule 9 must be used in the execution of dispositions in the scheduled forms in the cases for which they are provided, or are capable of being applied or adapted, with such alterations and additions, if any, as the registrar may allow.

(4)   A requirement in these rules to use a scheduled form is subject, where appropriate, to the provisions in these rules relating to the making of applications and issuing results of applications other than in paper form, during the currency of a notice given under Schedule 2.

References: See para 2.36.

207 Adaptation of certain Schedule 1 forms to provide for direct debit

(1)   This rule applies where—
   (a)   a Schedule 1 form has a payment of fee panel which does not provide for payment by direct debit, and
   (b)   a fee order made under section 102 of the Act and sections 2 and 3 of the Public Offices Fees Act 1879 permits, where there is an agreement with the registrar, payment by direct debit of the fee for the matter in respect of which that form is prescribed, and
   (c)   the registrar intends to enter into an agreement under the fee order which will enable a person to pay that fee by direct debit.

(2)   Where paragraph (1) applies the registrar may amend the payment of fee panel of the affected form to include provision for payment by direct debit and make any consequential amendments to the form.

(3)   Where a form has been amended under paragraph (2) a person not paying by direct debit may use the form as amended or as unamended.

References: See para 5.17.

208 Welsh language forms

(1)   Where the registrar, in exercise of his powers under section 100(4) of the Act, publishes an instrument as the Welsh language version of a scheduled form, the instrument shall be regarded as being in the scheduled form.

(2)   In place of the form of execution provided by Schedule 9, an instrument referred to in paragraph (1) may be executed using a form of execution approved by the registrar as the Welsh language version of the Schedule 9 form.

(3)   An instrument containing a statement approved by the registrar as the Welsh language version of a statement prescribed by these rules shall be regarded as containing the prescribed statement.

(4)   An instrument containing a provision approved by the registrar as the Welsh language version of a provision prescribed by these rules shall be regarded as containing the prescribed provision.

209 Use of non-prescribed forms

(1)   This rule applies where—

(a)   an application should be accompanied by a scheduled form and a person wishes to make an application relying instead upon an alternative document that is not the relevant scheduled form, and

(b)   it is not possible for that person to obtain and lodge the relevant scheduled form (duly executed, if appropriate) at the land registry or it is only possible to do so at unreasonable expense.

(2)   Such a person may make a request to the registrar, either before or at the time of making the application which should be accompanied by the relevant scheduled form, that he be permitted to rely upon the alternative document.

(3)   The request must contain evidence to satisfy the registrar as mentioned in paragraph (1)(b) and include the original, or, if the request is made before the application, a copy, of the alternative document.

(4)   If, after considering the request, the registrar is satisfied as mentioned at paragraph (1)(b) and that neither the rights of any person nor the keeping of the register are likely to be materially prejudiced by allowing the alternative document to be relied upon instead of the relevant scheduled form, he may permit such reliance.

(5)   If the registrar allows the request it may be on condition that the person making the request provides other documents or evidence in support of the application.

(6)   This rule is without prejudice to any of the registrar's powers under the Act.

References: See paras 2.38, 2.39.

210 Documents in a Schedule 1 form

(1)   Subject to rule 211, any application or document in one of the Schedule 1 forms must—

(a)   be printed on durable A4 size paper,

(b)   be reproduced as set out in the Schedule as to its wording, layout, ruling, font and point size, and

(c)   contain all the information required in an easily legible form.

(2)   Where on a Schedule 1 form (other than Form DL) any panel is insufficient in size to contain the required insertions, and the method of production of the form does not allow the depth of the panel to be increased, the information to be inserted in the panel must be continued on a continuation sheet in Form CS.

(3)   When completing a Schedule 1 form containing an additional provisions panel, any statement, certificate or application required or permitted by these rules to be included in the form for which the form does not otherwise provide and any additional provisions desired by the parties must be inserted in that panel or a continuation of it.

(4)   Where the form consists of more than one sheet of paper, or refers to an attached plan or a continuation sheet, all the sheets and any plan must be securely fastened together.

References: See para 2.36.

211 Electronically produced forms

(1)   Where the method of production of a Schedule 1 form permits—

- (a)   the depth of a panel may be increased or reduced to fit the material to be comprised in it, and a panel may be divided at a page break,
- (b)   instructions in italics may be omitted,
- (c)   inapplicable certificates and statements may be omitted,
- (d)   the plural may be used instead of the singular and the singular instead of the plural,
- (e)   panels which would contain only the panel number and the panel heading may be omitted, but such omission must not affect the numbering of subsequent panels,
- (f)   "X" boxes may be omitted where all inapplicable statements and certificates have been omitted,
- (g)   the sub-headings in an additional provisions panel may be added to, amended, repositioned or omitted,
- (h)   "Seller" may be substituted for "Transferor" and "Buyer" for "Transferee" in a transfer on sale,
- (i)   the vertical lines which define the left and right boundaries of the panel may be omitted.

References: See para 2.36.

212 Documents where no form is prescribed

(1)   Documents for which no form is prescribed must be in such form as the registrar may direct or allow.

(2)   A document prepared under this rule must not bear the number of a Schedule 1 form.

(3)   A document affecting a registered title must refer to the title number.

References: See paras 2.36, 6.19, 6.24.

Documents accompanying applications

213 Identification of part of the registered title dealt with

(1)   Subject to paragraphs (4) and (5) of this rule, a document lodged at the land registry dealing with part of the land in a registered title must have attached to it a plan identifying clearly the land dealt with.

(2)   Where the document is a disposition, the disponor must sign the plan.

(3)   Where the document is an application, the applicant must sign the plan.

(4)   If the land dealt with is identified clearly on the title plan of the registered title, it may instead be described by reference to that title plan.

(5)   Where a disposition complies with this rule, the application lodged in respect of it need not.

References: See para 2.52.

214 Lodging of copy instead of an original document

(1)   Subject to paragraphs (2), (3) and (4), where a rule requires that an application be accompanied by an original document (for instance, a grant of representation) the applicant may, instead of lodging the original, lodge a certified or office copy of that document.

(2)   This rule does not apply to—
   (a)   any document required to be lodged under Part 4,
   (b)   a scheduled form,
   (c)   a document that is a registrable disposition.

(3)   This rule does not apply also where the registrar considers that the circumstances are such that the original of a document should be lodged and the applicant has possession, or the right to possession, of that original document.

(4)   Where this rule permits a certified or office copy of a document to be lodged the registrar may permit an uncertified copy of the document to be lodged instead.

References: See para 2.51.

215 Documents and other evidence in support of an application

(1)   This rule applies where—
   (a)   the lodging of a document (not being a scheduled form) or other evidence in support of an application is required by these rules, and
   (b)   the document or other evidence is in the particular case unnecessary or the purpose of the lodging of the document or other evidence can be achieved by another document or other evidence.

(2)   An applicant may request the registrar to be relieved of the requirement.

(3)   The request must contain evidence to satisfy the registrar as mentioned in paragraph (1)(b).

(4)   If, after considering the request, the registrar is satisfied as mentioned at paragraph (1)(b) and that neither the rights of any person nor the keeping of the register are likely to be materially prejudiced by relieving the applicant of the requirement, he may so relieve the applicant.

(5)   If the registrar allows the request it may be on condition that the applicant provides other documents or evidence in support of the application.

(6)   This rule is without prejudice to any of the registrar's powers under the Act.

References: See para 2.51.

Land registry—when open to public

216 Days on which the Land Registry is open to the public

(1)   Subject to paragraph (2), the land registry shall be open to the public daily except on Saturdays, Sundays, Christmas Day, Good Friday or any other day either specified or declared by proclamation under section 1 of the Banking and Financial Dealings Act 1971 or appointed by the Lord Chancellor.

(2)   If the registrar is satisfied that adequate arrangements have been made or will be in place for opening the land registry to the public on Saturdays, he may, in such manner as he considers appropriate, give notice to that effect.

(3)   On and after the date specified in any notice given pursuant to paragraph (2), paragraph (1) shall have effect as though the word "Saturdays" had been omitted.

(4)   The date referred to in paragraph (3) must be at least eight weeks after the date of the notice.

(5)   On and after the date specified in any notice given pursuant to paragraph (2), the periods in column 3 in the table below are substituted for the periods in column 2 in that table in the rules to which they relate.

(1) Rule	*(2) Prescribed period before any notice given under rule 216(2) takes effect*	*(3) Prescribed period after any notice given under rule 216(2) takes effect*
16(1)	Twenty business days	twenty-four business days
31(2)	the twentieth business day	the twenty-fourth business day
53(1)	the fifteenth business day	the eighteenth business day
53(1)	the thirtieth business day	the thirty-sixth business day
53(3)	the thirtieth business day	the thirty-sixth business day
53(4)	the fifteenth business day	the eighteenth business day
54(9)	the fourth business day	the fourth business day
55(4)	fifteen business days	eighteen business days
86(3)	the fifteenth business day	the eighteenth business day
86(3)	the thirtieth business day	the thirty-sixth business day
86(5)	the thirtieth business day	the thirty-sixth business day
86(6)	the fifteenth business day	the eighteenth business day
92(9)	the fifteenth business day	the eighteenth business day
119(3)	the twentieth business day	the twenty-fourth business day
189	the sixty-fifth business day	the seventy-eighth business day
197(2)	the fifteenth business day	the eighteenth business day
201(5)	the twentieth business day	the twenty-fourth business day
202(3)	the twentieth business day	the twenty-fourth business day
202(8)	the twentieth business day	the twenty-fourth business day
218	the fifteenth business day	the eighteenth business day

References: See para 4.7.

Interpretation

217 General Interpretation

(1)　In these rules—

"the Act" means the Land Registration Act 2002,

"affecting franchise" means a franchise which relates to a defined area of land and is an adverse right affecting, or capable of affecting, the title to an estate or charge,

"business day" means a day when the land registry is open to the public under rule 216,

"caution plan" has the meaning given by rule 41(4),

"caution title number" has the meaning given by rule 41(1),

"certified copy" means a copy of a document which a conveyancer, or such other person as the registrar may permit, has certified on its face to be a true copy of the original and endorsed with his name and address, and the reference to a conveyancer includes where the document is one referred to in—

(a)　rule 168(2)(a) or 168(3), the bankrupt's trustee in bankruptcy or the official receiver,

(b)　rule 184(2), the company's administrator,

(c)　rule 184(5), the company's liquidator,

"charges register" is the register so named in rule 4 the contents of which are described in rule 9,

"charity" and "charity trustees" have the same meaning as in sections 96 and 97(1) of the Charities Act 1993 respectively,

"Companies Acts" means the Companies Act 1985, any Act amending or replacing that Act and any former enactment relating to companies,

"control" in relation to a document of which a person has control means physical possession, or the right to possession, or right to take copies of the document,

"conveyancer" means—

(a)　a solicitor, or

(b)　a licensed conveyancer within the meaning of section 11(2) of the Administration of Justice Act 1985, or

(c)　a fellow of the Institute of Legal Executives,

and a reference to a person's conveyancer is a reference to a solicitor, licensed conveyancer or fellow of the Institute of Legal Executives who is acting on that person's behalf,

"day list" has the same meaning given by rule 12,

"exempt charity" has the same meaning as in section 96 of the Charities Act 1993 and "non-exempt charity" means a charity which is not an exempt charity,

"index map" has the meaning given by rule 10(1)(a),

"index of proprietors' names" has the meaning given by rule 11(1),

"index of relating franchises and manors" is the index described in rule 10(1)(b),

"individual caution register" is the register so named in rule 41(1) the arrangement of which is described in rule 41(2),

"individual register" is the register so named in rule 2 the contents and arrangement of which are described in rules 3 and 4, "inheritance tax notice" means a notice in respect of an Inland Revenue charge arising under Part III of the Finance Act 1975 or section 237 of the Inheritance Tax Act 1984,

"matrimonial home rights caution" means a caution registered under the Matrimonial Homes Act 1967 before 14 February 1983,

"matrimonial home rights notice" means a notice registered under section 31(10)(a) or section 32 of, and paragraph 4(3)(a) or 4(3)(b) of Schedule 4 to, the Family Law Act 1996, or section 2(8) or section 5(3)(b) of the Matrimonial Homes Act 1983 or section 2(7) or section 5(3)(b) of the Matrimonial Homes Act 1967,

"official custodian" means the official custodian for charities,

"old tenancy" means a tenancy as defined in section 28 of the Landlord and Tenant (Covenants) Act 1995 which is not a new tenancy as defined in section 1 of that Act,

"overseas company" means a company incorporated outside Great Britain,

"property register" is the register so named in rule 4 the contents of which are described in rules 5, 6 and 7,

"proprietorship register" is the register so named in rule 4 the contents of which are described in rule 8,

"registered title" means an individual register and any title plan referred to in that register,

"relating franchise" means a franchise which is not an affecting franchise,

"Schedule 1 form" means a form in Schedule 1,

"Schedule 3 form" means a form in Schedule 3,

"scheduled form" means a Schedule 1 form or a Schedule 3 form,

"section 33(5) order" means an order made under section 33(5) of the Family Law Act 1996,

"statutory declaration" includes affidavit,

"title number" has the meaning given by rule 4,

"title plan" has the meaning given by rule 5,

"trust corporation" has the same meaning as in the Settled Land Act 1925,

"trusts" in relation to a charity has the same meaning as in section 97(1) of the Charities Act 1993,

"unregistered company" means a body corporate to which section 718(1) of the Companies Act 1985 applies.

(2)   Subject to paragraph (3), a reference in these rules to a form by letter, or by number, or by a combination of both is to a scheduled form.

(3)   A reference in these rules to Forms A to Y and Forms AA to HH (in each case inclusive) is to the standard form of restriction bearing that letter in Schedule 4.

PART 16
TRANSITIONAL

Cautions against dealings

218 Definitions

In this Part—

"the 1925 Act" means the Land Registration Act 1925,

"caution" means a caution entered in the register of title under section 54 of the 1925 Act,

"cautioner" includes his personal representative,

"the notice period" is the period ending at 12 noon on the fifteenth business day, or ending at 12 noon on such later business day as the registrar may allow, after the date of issue of the notice.

References: See para 10.50.

219 Consent under a caution

Any consent given under section 55 or 56 of the 1925 Act must be in writing signed by the person giving it or his conveyancer.

References: See para 10.50.

220 Notice under section 55(1) of the 1925 Act and under rule 223(3)

(1)   Rule 199 applies to the method of service of a notice under section 55(1) of the 1925 Act and under rule 223(3).

(2)   The notice period applies to a notice served under section 55(1) of the 1925 Act and to one served under rule 223(3).

References: See paras 7.88, 10.50.

221 Cautioner showing cause

(1)   This rule applies where notice is served under section 55(1) of the 1925 Act or rule 223(3).

(2)   At any time before expiry of the notice period, the cautioner may show cause why the registrar should not give effect to the application that resulted in the notice being served.

(3)   To show cause, the cautioner must—
   (a)   deliver to the registrar, in the manner and to the address stated in the notice, a written statement signed by the cautioner or his conveyancer setting out the grounds relied upon, and
   (b)   show that he has a fairly arguable case for the registrar not to give effect to the application that resulted in the notice being served.

(4)   If, after reading the written statement, and after making any enquiries he thinks necessary, the registrar is satisfied that cause has been shown, he must order that the caution is to continue until withdrawn or otherwise disposed of under these rules or the Act.

(5)   Where the registrar makes an order under paragraph (4)—
   (a)   the registrar must give notice to the applicant and the cautioner that he has made the order and of the effect of sub-paragraph (b),
   (b)   the cautioner is to be treated as having objected under section 73 of the Act to the application that resulted in notice being served, and
   (c)   the notice given by the registrar under sub-paragraph (a) to the applicant is to be treated as notice given under section 73(5)(a) of the Act.

(6)   If after service of the notice under section 55(1) of the 1925 Act or rule 223(3) the application that resulted in the notice being served is cancelled, withdrawn or otherwise does not proceed, the registrar must make an order that the caution will continue to have effect, unless he has already done so or the caution has been cancelled.

References: See paras 7.88, 10.50.

222 Withdrawal of a caution by the cautioner

(1)   The cautioner may at any time apply to withdraw his caution in Form WCT.

(2)   The form must be signed by the cautioner or his conveyancer.

References: See paras 7.88, 8.32, 10.50.

223 Cancellation of a caution—application by the proprietor etc

(1)   A person may apply to the registrar for the cancellation of a caution if he is—
    (a)   the proprietor of the registered estate or a registered charge to which the caution relates, or
    (b)   a person who, but for the existence of the caution, would be entitled to be registered as the proprietor of that estate or charge.

(2)   An application for the cancellation of a caution must be in Form CCD.

(3)   Where application is made under this rule, the registrar must give the cautioner notice of the application.

(4)   Following the expiry of the notice period, unless the registrar makes an order under rule 221(4), the registrar must cancel the entry of the caution.

References: See paras 7.88, 8.32, 10.50.

Rentcharges and adverse possession

224 Registered rentcharges held in trust under section 75(1) of the 1925 Act on commencement

Where a rentcharge is held in trust under section 75(1) of the Land Registration Act 1925 immediately before the coming into force of section 97 of the Act, the beneficiary of the trust may apply—
    (a)   to be registered as proprietor of the rentcharge, or
    (b)   for the registration of the rentcharge to be cancelled.

Rule 11

SCHEDULE 1

SCHEDULE 1 FORMS REFERRED TO IN RULES 206, 207 AND 210

The Forms themselves are not reproduced. Their numbers and descriptions are listed below. The forms can be obtained from law stationers or downloaded from the Land Registry's website at www.landregistry.gov.uk/publications/.

Title	LR Rules 2003 Forms
FORM ADV1	Application for registration of a person in adverse possession under Schedule 6 to the Land Registration Act 2002
FORM ADV2	Application to be registered as a person to be notified of an application for adverse possession
FORM AN1	Application to enter an agreed notice
FORM AP1	Application to change the register
FORM AS1	Assent of whole of registered title(s)
FORM AS2	Assent of charge
FORM AS3	Assent of part of registered title(s)
FORM CC	Entry of a note of consolidation of charges
FORM CCD	Application to cancel a caution against dealings
FORM CCT	Application to cancel a caution against first registration
FORM CH1	Legal charge of a registered estate
FORM CH2	Application to enter an obligation to make further advances
FORM CH3	Application to note agreed maximum amount of security
FORM CI	Certificate of inspection of title plan
FORM CIT	Application in connection with court proceedings, insolvency and tax liability
FORM CN1	Application to cancel notice of an unregistered lease or rentcharge
FORM CS	Continuation sheet for use with application and disposition forms
FORM CT1	Caution against First Registration
FORM DB	Application to determine the exact line of a boundary
FORM DI	Disclosable overriding interests
FORM DL	List of documents
FORM DS1	Cancellation of entries relating to a registered charge
FORM DS2	Application to cancel entries relating to a registered charge
FORM DS3	Release of part of the land from a registered charge
FORM EX1	Application for the registrar to designate a document as an exempt information document
FORM EX1A	Reasons for exemption in support of an application to designate a document as an exempt information document
FORM EX2	Application for official copy of an exempt information document
FORM EX3	Application to remove the designation of a document as an exempt information document
FORM FR1	First Registration application

Title	LR Rules 2003 Forms
FORM HC1	Application for copies of historical edition(s) of the register/title plan held in electronic form
FORM MH1	Application for Registration of a Notice of Matrimonial Home Rights
FORM MH2	Application for Renewal of Registration of a Notice or a Caution in respect of Matrimonial Home Rights
FORM MH3	Application by Mortgagee for Official Search in respect of Matrimonial Home Rights
FORM NAP	Notice to the registrar in respect of an adverse possession application
FORM OC1	Application for official copies of register/plan or certificate in Form CI
FORM OC2	Application for official copies of documents only
FORM OS1	Application by purchaser for official search with priority of the whole of the land in a registered title or a pending first registration application
FORM OS2	Application by purchaser for official search with priority of part of the land in a registered title or a pending first registration application
FORM OS3	Application for official search without priority of the land in a registered title
FORM PIC	Application for a personal inspection under section 66 of the Land Registration Act 2002
FORM PN1	Application for a search in the Index of Proprietors' Names
FORM PRD1	Request for the production of documents
FORM PRD2	Notice to produce a document
FORM RX1	Application to enter a restriction
FORM RX2	Application for an order that a restriction be disapplied or modified
FORM RX3	Application to cancel a restriction
FORM RX4	Application to withdraw a restriction
FORM SC	Application for noting the overriding priority of a statutory charge
FORM SIF	Application for an official search of the index of relating franchises and manors
FORM SIM	Application for an official search of the index map
FORM TP1	Transfer of part of registered title(s)
FORM TP2	Transfer of part of registered title(s) under power of sale
FORM TP3	Transfer of portfolio of titles
FORM TR1	Transfer of whole of registered title(s)
FORM TR2	Transfer of whole of registered title(s) under power of sale

Title	LR Rules 2003 Forms
FORM TR3	Transfer of charge
FORM TR4	Transfer of a portfolio of charges
FORM TR5	Transfer of portfolio of whole titles
FORM UN1	Application to enter a unilateral notice
FORM UN2	Application to remove a unilateral notice
FORM UN3	Application to be registered as beneficiary of an existing unilateral notice
FORM UN4	Application for the cancellation of a unilateral notice
FORM UT1	Application for upgrading of title
FORM WCT	Application to withdraw a caution

References: See paras 2.36, 2.37, 2.43, 6.24.

SCHEDULE 2

Rule 14

NOTICES PUBLICISING ARRANGEMENTS FOR ELECTRONIC AND OTHER MODES OF DELIVERY OF APPLICATIONS AND OTHER MATTERS

1. If the registrar is satisfied that adequate arrangements have been made or will be in place for dealing with the applications and other matters specified in paragraph 2 by means other than post, document exchange or personal delivery, he may, in such manner as he thinks appropriate, give notice publicising the arrangements.

2. The applications and other matters referred to in paragraph 1 are—
    (a)   an application by electronic means under rule 14,
    (b)   an outline application under rule 54,
    (c)   a notification of discharge or release of a registered charge under rule 115,
    (d)   an application and the result of an application or search under Part 13 to which rule 132 applies,
    (e)   information requested by an applicant for an official search for the purpose of the Family Law Act 1996 under rule 160,
    (f)   a request to the registrar that he require a person to produce documents under rule 201(2)(b),
    (g)   a request for an order requiring a party to proceedings before the registrar to pay costs under rule 202(5).

3. Subject to paragraphs 4, 5 and 6, a notice given under paragraph 1 will be current from the time specified in the notice until the time, if any, specified in the notice or if no expiry date is specified in the notice, indefinitely.

4. A notice given under paragraph 1 may from time to time be varied, suspended, withdrawn, renewed or replaced by a further notice.

5. If and so long as owing the breakdown or other unavailability of facilities or data involved in giving effect to the arrangements made for dealing with applications covered by a notice given under paragraph 1, such arrangements cease, in whole or in part, to be effective, the notice shall cease, to the necessary extent, to be treated as current.

6. Paragraph 5 will apply despite the absence of a variation, suspension or withdrawal of the notice under paragraph 4.

7. The provisions referred to in paragraph 2 will not prevent the registrar, at his discretion, from refusing to accept an application or request made, or to issue a result, under any of those provisions in an individual case.

References: See paras 2.41, 2.48, 2.72.

SCHEDULE 3

Rule 61

SCHEDULE 3 FORMS REFERRED TO IN RULE 206

Form 1—Certificate as to execution of power of attorney (rule 61)

Date of power of attorney: ....

Donor of power
of attorney: ....

Donee of power
of attorney: ....

I/We ....of
....

certify that

—the power of attorney ("the power") is in existence [and is made under (*state statutory provision under which the power is made if applicable*)],

—the power is dated (*insert date*),

—I am/we are satisfied that the power is validly executed as a deed and authorises the attorney to execute the document on behalf of the donor of that power, and

—I/we hold [the instrument creating the power] *or* [a copy of the power by means of which its contents may be proved under section 3 of the Powers of Attorney Act 1971] *or* [a document which under section 4 of the Evidence and Powers of Attorney Act 1940 or section 7(3) of the Enduring Powers of Attorney Act 1985 is sufficient evidence of the contents of the power].

Signature of
conveyancer ....Date ....

Form 2—Statutory declaration/certificate as to non-revocation for powers more than 12 months old at the date of the disposition for which they are used (rule 62)

Date of power of attorney: ....

Donor of power of
attorney: ....

I/We ....
of..

do solemnly and sincerely [declare] *or* [certify] that at the time of completion of the

.... to me/us/my client/I/we/my client had no knowledge—

—of a revocation of the power, or

—of the death or bankruptcy of the donor or, if the donor is a corporate body, its winding up or dissolution, or

—of any incapacity of the donor where the power is not a valid enduring power, or

Where the power is in the form prescribed for an enduring power—

—that the power was not in fact a valid enduring power, or

—of an order or direction of the Court of Protection which revoked the power, or

—of the bankruptcy of the attorney, or

Where the power was given under section 9 of the Trusts of Land and Appointment of Trustees Act 1996—

—of an appointment of another trustee of the land in question, or

—of any other event which would have the effect of revoking the power, or

—of any lack of good faith on the part of the person(s) who dealt with the attorney, or

—that the attorney was not a person to whom the functions of the trustees could be delegated under section 9 of the Trusts of Land and Appointment of Trustees Act 1996, or

Where the power is expressed to be given by way of security—

—that the power was not in fact given by way of security, or

—of any revocation of the power with the consent of the attorney

—of any other event which would have had the effect of revoking the power.

Where a certificate is given—

Signature of
conveyancer..Date....................................; or

Where a Statutory Declaration is made—

And I/we make this solemn declaration conscientiously believing the same to be true and by virtue of the provisions of the Statutory Declarations Act 1835.

Signature of
Declarant(s) ....Date ....

DECLARED at ....before me, a person entitled to administer oaths.

Name...

Address..

Qualification...

Signature..

Form 3—Statutory declaration/certificate in support of power delegating trustees' functions to a beneficiary (rule 63)

Date of power of attorney: ....

Donor of power of
attorney:...

I/We...of
....

do solemnly and sincerely [declare] *or* [certify] that at the time of completion of the...................................to me/us/my client/I/we/my client had no knowledge—

—of any lack of good faith on the part of the person(s) who dealt with the attorney, or

—that the attorney was not a person to whom the functions of the trustees could be delegated under section 9 of the Trusts of Land and Appointment of Trustees Act 1996.

Where a certificate is given—

Signature of conveyancer .... Date ...., or

Where a Statutory Declaration is made—

And I/we make this solemn declaration conscientiously believing the same to be true and by virtue of the provisions of the Statutory Declarations Act 1835.

Signature of
Declarant(s).. Date ....

DECLARED at .... before me, a person entitled to administer oaths.

Name...

Address...

Qualification...

Signature..

Form 4—Certificate as to Vesting in an Incumbent or other Ecclesiastical Corporation (rule 174)

(*Date*). This is to certify that the registered estate (*or* registered charge *or* that part of the registered estate) comprised in a [*describe the transfer*] under the provisions of [*state the Act or Measure*] (if such transfer were a conveyance under such Act or Measure), vests in the incumbent of............................(*or* the bishop of.................................*as the case may be*) and his successors immediately (*or as the case may be*) upon the happening of the event following, namely, the [*state event*]

(To be sealed by the Church Commissioners)

Form 5—The Like Certificate under rule 175

(*Date*). This is to certify that the [*describe Scheme, instrument or transfer, &c*] operates to vest immediately (*or* on publication in the "London Gazette", *or at some subsequent period, as the case may be*), the registered estate (*or* registered charge *or* that part of the registered estate [*include description by reference to a plan or to the register if possible*]) in the [*describe the corporation or person*].

(To be sealed by the Church Commissioners)

Form 6—Transfer where the Tenant for Life is already registered as proprietor (rule 186 and paragraph 5 of Schedule 7)

(*Date*). Pursuant to a trust deed of even date herewith, [made between AB (*name of tenant for life*) and CD and EF (*names of trustees of the Settlement*)], I, the said AB, hereby declares as follows—

(a)   The land is vested in me upon the trusts from time to time affecting it by virtue of the said trust deed.

[(b)   The said CD and EF are the trustees of the Settlement.

(c)   The following powers relating to land are expressly conferred by the said trust deed in extension of those conferred by the settled Land Act 1925 (*fill in the powers, if any*).]

(d)   I have the power to appoint new trustees of the Settlement.

(To be executed as a deed)

References: See para 10.22.

SCHEDULE 4

Rule 91

STANDARD FORMS OF RESTRICTION

Form A (Restriction on dispositions by sole proprietor)

No disposition by a sole proprietor of the registered estate (except a trust corporation) under which capital money arises is to be registered unless authorised by an order of the court.

Form B (Dispositions by trustees—certificate required)

No disposition [*or specify details*] by the proprietors of the registered estate is to be registered unless they make a statutory declaration, or their conveyancer gives a certificate, that the disposition [*or specify details*] is in accordance with [*specify the disposition creating the trust*] or some variation thereof referred to in the declaration or certificate.

Form C (Dispositions by personal representatives—certificate required)

No disposition by [*name*], the [executor *or* administrator] of [*name*] deceased, other than a transfer as personal representative, is to be registered unless he makes a statutory declaration, or his conveyancer gives a certificate, that the disposition is in accordance with the terms [of the will of the deceased or the law relating to intestacy as varied by a deed dated *specify details of deed or specify appropriate details*] or [some variation *or* further variation] thereof referred to in the declaration or certificate, or is necessary for the purposes of administration.

Form D (Parsonage, church or churchyard land)

No disposition of the registered estate is to be registered unless made in accordance with [the Parsonages Measure 1938 (*in the case of parsonage land*) or the New Parishes Measure 1943 (*in the case of church or churchyard land*)] or some other Measure or authority.

Form E (Non-exempt charity—certificate required)

No disposition by the proprietor of the registered estate to which section 36 or section 38 of the Charities Act 1993 applies is to be registered unless the instrument contains a certificate complying with section 37(2) or section 39(2) of that Act as appropriate.

Form F (Land vested in official custodian on trust for non-exempt charity—authority required)

No disposition executed by the trustees of [*charity*] in the name and on behalf of the proprietor shall be registered unless the transaction is authorised by an order of the court or of the Charity Commissioners, as required by section 22(3) of the Charities Act 1993.

Form G (Tenant for life as registered proprietor of settled land, where there are trustees of the settlement)

No disposition is to be registered unless authorised by the Settled Land Act 1925, or by any extension of those statutory powers in the settlement, and no disposition under which capital money arises is to be registered unless the money is paid to (*name*) of (*address*) and (*name*) of (*address*), (the trustees of the settlement, who may be a sole trust corporation or, if individuals, must number at least two but not more than four) or into court.

Note—If applicable under the terms of the settlement, a further provision may be added that no transfer of the mansion house (shown on an attached plan or otherwise adequately described to enable it to be fully identified on the Ordnance Survey map or title plan) is to be registered without the consent of the named trustees or an order of the court.

Form H (Statutory owners as trustees of the settlement and registered proprietors of settled land)

No disposition is to be registered unless authorised by the Settled Land Act 1925, or by any extension of those statutory powers in the settlement, and, except where the sole proprietor is a trust corporation, no disposition under which capital money arises is to be registered unless the money is paid to at least two proprietors.

Note—This restriction does not apply where the statutory owners are not the trustees of the settlement.

Form I (Tenant for life as registered proprietor of settled land—no trustees of the settlement)

No disposition under which capital money arises, or which is not authorised by the Settled Land Act 1925 or by any extension of those statutory powers in the settlement, is to be registered.

Form J (Trustee in bankruptcy and beneficial interest—certificate required)

No disposition of the [registered estate *or* registered charge dated [*date*]] is to be registered without a certificate signed by the applicant for registration or his conveyancer that written notice of the disposition was given to [*name of trustee in bankruptcy*] (the trustee in bankruptcy of [*name of bankrupt person*]) at [*address for service*].

Form K (Charging order affecting beneficial interest—certificate required)

No disposition of the [registered estate or registered charge dated [*date*]] is to be registered without a certificate signed by the applicant for registration or his conveyancer that written notice of the disposition was given to [*name of person with the benefit of the charging order*] at [*address for service*], being the person with the benefit of [an interim] [a final] charging order on the beneficial interest of (*name of judgement debtor*) made by the (*name of court*) on (*date*) (*Court reference . . . .*).

Form L (Disposition by registered proprietor of a registered estate or proprietor of charge—certificate required)

No disposition [or specify details] of the registered estate [(other than a charge)] by the proprietor of the registered estate [, or by the proprietor of any registered charge,] is to be registered without a certificate

[signed by [*name*] of [*address*] (or [his conveyancer] *or specify appropriate details*)]

or

[signed on behalf of [*name*] of [*address*] by [its secretary or conveyancer *or specify appropriate details*]]

that the provisions of [*specify clause, paragraph or other particulars*] of [*specify details*] have been complied with.

Form M (Disposition by registered proprietor of registered estate or proprietor of charge—certificate of registered proprietor of specified title number required)

No disposition [*or specify details*] of the registered estate [(other than a charge)] by the proprietor of the registered estate [or by the proprietor of any registered charge] is to be registered without a certificate signed by the proprietor for the time being of the estate registered under title number [*title number*] [(or his conveyancer *or specify appropriate details*)] or, if appropriate, signed on such proprietor's behalf by [its secretary or conveyancer *or specify appropriate details*], that the provisions of [*specify clause, paragraph or other particulars*] of [*specify details*] have been complied with.

Form N (Disposition by registered proprietor of registered estate or proprietor of charge—consent required)

No disposition [*or specify details*] of the registered estate [(other than a charge)] by the proprietor of the registered estate [or by the proprietor of any registered charge] is to be registered without a written consent

[signed by [*name*] of [*address*] (or [his conveyancer] *or specify appropriate details*)]

or

[signed on behalf of [*name*] of [*address*] by [its secretary or conveyancer *or specify appropriate details*]].

Form O (Disposition by registered proprietor of registered estate or proprietor of charge—consent of registered proprietor of specified title number required)

No disposition [*or specify details*] of the registered estate [(other than a charge)] by the proprietor of the registered estate [or by the proprietor of any registered charge] is to be registered without a written consent signed by the proprietor for the time being of the estate registered under title number [*title number*], [(or his conveyancer, *or specify appropriate details*)] or, if appropriate, signed on such proprietor's behalf by [its secretary or conveyancer *or specify appropriate details*].

Form P (Disposition by registered proprietor of registered estate or proprietor of charge—consent of proprietor of specified charge required)

No disposition [*or specify details*] of the registered estate [(other than a charge)] by the proprietor of the registered estate [or by the proprietor of any registered charge] is to be registered without a written consent signed by the proprietor for the time being of the charge dated [*date*] in favour of [*chargee*] referred to in the charges register [(or his conveyancer *or specify appropriate details*)] or, if appropriate, signed on such proprietor's behalf by [its secretary or conveyancer *or specify appropriate details*].

Form Q (Disposition by registered proprietor of registered estate or proprietor of charge—consent of personal representative required)

No disposition [*or specify details*] of [the registered estate *or* the registered charge dated [*date*] (referred to above)] by the proprietor [of the registered estate *or* of that registered charge] is to be registered after the death of [*name of the current proprietor(s) whose personal representative's consent will be required*] without the written consent of the personal representatives of the deceased.

Form R (Disposition by registered proprietor of registered estate or proprietor of charge—evidence of compliance with club rules required)

No disposition [*or specify details*] of the registered estate [(other than a charge)] by the proprietor of the registered estate [or by the proprietor of any registered charge] is to be registered unless authorised by the rules of the [*name of club*] of [*address*] as evidenced [by a resolution of its members or by a certificate signed by its secretary or conveyancer [*or specify appropriate details*]].

Form S (Disposition by proprietor of charge—certificate of compliance required)

No disposition [*or specify details*] by the proprietor of the registered charge dated [*date*] (referred to above) is to be registered without a certificate

[signed by [*name*] of [*address*] (or [his conveyancer] *or specify appropriate details*)]

or

[signed on behalf of [*name*] of [*address*] by [its secretary or conveyancer *or specify appropriate details*],

that the provisions of [*specify clause, paragraph or other particulars*] of [*specify details*] have been complied with.

Form T (Disposition by proprietor of charge—consent required)

No disposition [*or specify details*] by the proprietor of the registered charge dated [*date*] (referred to above) is to be registered without a written consent

[signed by [*name*] of [*address*] (or [his conveyancer] *or specify appropriate details*)]

or

[signed on behalf of [*name*] of [*address*] by [its secretary or conveyancer *or specify appropriate details*].

Form U (Section 37 of the Housing Act 1985)

No transfer or lease by the proprietor of the registered estate or by the proprietor of any registered charge is to be registered unless a certificate by [*specify relevant local authority*] is given that the transfer or lease is made in accordance with section 37 of the Housing Act 1985.

Form V (Section 157 of the Housing Act 1985)

No transfer or lease by the proprietor of the registered estate or by the proprietor of any registered charge is to be registered unless a certificate by [*specify relevant local authority or housing association etc*] is given that the transfer or lease is made in accordance with section 157 of the Housing Act 1985.

Form W (Paragraph 4 of Schedule 9A to the Housing Act 1985)

No disposition (except a transfer) of a qualifying dwellinghouse (except to a qualifying person or persons) is to be registered without the consent of the Secretary of State given under section 171D(2) of the Housing Act 1985 as it applies by virtue of the Housing (Preservation of Right to Buy) Regulations 1993.

Form X (Section 81 or 133 of the Housing Act 1988 or section 173 of the Local Government and Housing Act 1989)

No disposition by the proprietor of the registered estate or in exercise of the power of sale or leasing in any registered charge (except an exempt disposal as defined by section 81(8) of the Housing Act 1988) is to be registered without the consent of the Secretary of State to that disposition under the provisions of (*as appropriate* [section 81 of that Act] *or* [section 133 of that Act] *or* [section 173 of the Local Government and Housing Act 1989]).

Form Y (Section 13 of the Housing Act 1996)

No transfer or lease by the proprietor of the registered estate or by the proprietor of any registered charge is to be registered unless a certificate by [*specify relevant registered social landlord*] is given that the transfer or lease is made in accordance with section 13 of the Housing Act 1996.

Form AA (freezing order on the registered estate)

Under an order of the (*name of court*) made on (*date*) (*claim no*) no disposition by the proprietor of the registered estate is to be registered except under a further order of the Court.

Form BB (freezing order on charge)

Under an order of the (*name of court*) made on (*date*) (*claim no*) no disposition by the proprietor of the charge is to be registered except under a further order of the Court.

Form CC (application for freezing order on the registered estate)

Pursuant to an application made on (*date*) to the (*name of court*) for a freezing order to be made under (*statutory provision*) no disposition by the proprietor of the registered estate is to be registered except with the consent of (*name of the person applying*) or under a further order of the Court.

Form DD (application for freezing order on charge)

Pursuant to an application made on (*date*) to the (*name of the court*) for a freezing order to be made under (*statutory provision*) no disposition by the proprietor of the registered charge dated (*date*) (referred to above) is to be registered except with the consent of (*name of the person applying*) or under a further order of the Court.

Form EE (restraint order or interim receiving order on the registered estate)

Under (*as appropriate* [a restraint order] *or* [an interim receiving order]) made under (*statutory provision*) on (*date*) (*claim no*) no disposition by the proprietor of the registered estate is to be registered without the consent of (*name of the prosecutor or other person who applied for the order*) or under a further order of the Court.

Form FF (restraint order or interim receiving order on charge)

Under (*as appropriate* [a restraint order] *or* [an interim receiving order]) made under (*statutory provision*) on (*date*) (*claim no*) no disposition by the proprietor of the registered charge dated (*date*) (referred to above) is to be registered without the consent of (*name of the prosecutor or other person who applied for the order*) or under a further order of the Court.

Form GG (application for restraint order or interim receiving order on the registered estate)

Pursuant to an application for (*as appropriate* [a restraint order] *or* [an interim receiving order]) to be made under (*statutory provision*) and under any order made as a result of that application, no disposition by the proprietor of the registered estate is to be registered without the consent of (*name of the prosecutor or other person applying*) or under a further order of the Court.

Form HH (application for restraint order or interim receiving order on charge)

Pursuant to an application for (*as appropriate* [a restraint order] *or* [an interim receiving order]) to be made under (*statutory provision*) and under any order made as a result of that application no disposition by the proprietor of the registered charge dated (*date*) (referred to above) is to be registered without the consent of (*name of the prosecutor or other person applying*) or under a further order of the Court.

References: See paras 7.42–7.44, 10.13, 10.21, 10.41.

SCHEDULE 5

Rule 140

APPLICATIONS IN CONNECTION WITH COURT PROCEEDINGS, INSOLVENCY AND TAX LIABILITY—QUALIFYING APPLICANTS AND APPROPRIATE CERTIFICATES

Column 1	Column 2
Status of applicant	*Certificate in Form CIT*
An **Administrator** appointed for the purposes of the Insolvency Act 1986	Certificate K
An **Administrator** appointed under section 13 of the Criminal Justice (Scotland) Act 1987	Certificate J
A **Chief Officer of Police** or a police officer authorised to apply on behalf of a Chief Officer	Certificate A
	Certificate B
	Certificate C
	Certificate D
	Certificate E
	Certificate G
A person commissioned by the **Commissioners of Customs and Excise**	Certificate C
	Certificate D

Column 1	Column 2
	Certificate E
	Certificate H
A person authorised to apply by the **Commissioners of Inland Revenue**	Certificate E

Column 1	Column 2
A person authorised to apply by the **Commissioners of Inland Revenue** and having the consent of a General or Special Commissioner to make the application	Certificate L
A **constable**	Certificate H
The **Director of the Assets Recovery Agency** or a member of the Assets Recovery Agency authorised to apply on behalf of the Director	Certificate H
	Certificate I
	Certificate M
The **Director of Public Prosecutions** or a member of the Crown Prosecution Service authorised to apply on behalf of the Director	Certificate A
	Certificate B
	Certificate C
	Certificate D
	Certificate E
The **Director of the Serious Fraud Office** or a member of the Serious Fraud Office authorised to apply on behalf of the Director	Certificate A
	Certificate B
	Certificate E
The **Director-General of the Security Service** or a member of the Security Service authorised to apply on behalf of the Director-General	Certificate F
A **Liquidator** appointed for the purposes of the Insolvency Act 1986	Certificate K
The **Lord Advocate** or a person conducting a prosecution in Scotland on behalf of the Lord Advocate	Certificate C
	Certificate D
The **Official Assignee** for bankruptcy for Northern Ireland or the **Official Assignee** for company liquidations for Northern Ireland	Certificate K
An **Official Receiver** for the purposes of the Insolvency Act 1986	Certificate K

Column 1	Column 2
A **Receiver** appointed under the Criminal Justice Act 1988, the Drug Trafficking Act 1994 or the Proceeds of Crime Act 2002	Certificate J
The **Scottish Ministers** or a person named by them	Certificate I
A person authorised by the **Secretary of State for the Department of Trade and Industry**	Certificate A
	Certificate B
	Certificate E

Column 1	Column 2
A person authorised by the **Secretary of State for Work and Pensions**	Certificate A
	Certificate B
A **trustee in bankruptcy**, being either a trustee in bankruptcy of a person adjudged bankrupt in England and Wales or Northern Ireland or a permanent or interim trustee in the sequestration of a debtor's estate in Scotland	Certificate K

References: See paras 2.87, 15.75.

SCHEDULE 6

Rule 145

INFORMATION TO BE INCLUDED IN CERTAIN RESULTS OF OFFICIAL SEARCHES

PART 1
INFORMATION TO BE INCLUDED IN THE RESULT OF AN OFFICIAL SEARCH OF THE INDEX MAP

A. The date and time of the official search certificate

B. A description of the land searched

C. The reference (if any) of the applicant or the person to whom the search is being sent: limited to 25 characters including spaces

D. Whether there is—
- (i) a pending application for first registration (other than of title to a relating franchise)
- (ii) a pending application for a caution against first registration (other than where the subject of the caution is a relating franchise)
- (iii) a registered estate in land
- (iv) a registered rentcharge
- (v) a registered profit a prendre in gross
- (vi) a registered affecting franchise, or
- (vii) a caution against first registration (other than where the subject of the caution is a relating franchise)

and, if there is such a registered estate or caution, the title number

PART 2
INFORMATION TO BE INCLUDED IN THE RESULT OF AN OFFICIAL SEARCH OF THE INDEX OF RELATING FRANCHISES AND MANORS

A. The date and time of the official search certificate

B. The administrative area(s) searched

C. The reference (if any) of the applicant or the person to whom the search is being sent: limited to 25 characters including spaces

D. Whether there is a verbal description of—
- (i) a pending application for first registration of title to a relating franchise
- (ii) a pending application for a caution against first registration where the subject of the caution is a relating franchise
- (iii) a registered franchise which is a relating franchise
- (iv) a registered manor, or
- (v) a caution against first registration where the subject of the caution is a relating franchise

and the title numbers of any such registered estates and cautions arranged by administrative area

PART 3
INFORMATION TO BE INCLUDED IN THE RESULT OF AN OFFICIAL SEARCH OF AN INDIVIDUAL REGISTER OF A REGISTERED TITLE

A. The title number

B. The date and time of the official search certificate

C. If the official search certificate is part of a registered title, a short description of the property or plot number on the approved estate plan

D. The applicant's name

E. The applicant's, or his agent's, reference (if any): limited to 25 characters including spaces

F. Details of any relevant adverse entries made in the individual register since the end of the day specified in the application as the search from date

G. Notice of the entry of any relevant pending application affecting the registered title entered on the day list (other than an application to designate a document as an exempt information document under rule 136)

H. Notice of the entry of any relevant official search the priority period of which has not expired

I. If the official search is with priority, the date and time at which the priority expires

J. If the official search is without priority, a statement that the certificate will not confer on the applicant priority for any registrable disposition

PART 4
INFORMATION TO BE INCLUDED IN THE RESULT OF AN OFFICIAL SEARCH WITH PRIORITY IN RELATION TO A PENDING APPLICATION FOR FIRST REGISTRATION

A. The title number allotted to the pending application for first registration

B. The date and time of the official search certificate

C. If the official search is of part, a short description of the property

D. The applicant's name

E. The applicant's, or his agent's, reference (if any): limited to 25 characters including spaces

F. The full name of the person who has applied for first registration

G. The date and time at which the pending application for first registration was entered on the day list

H. Notice of the entry of any relevant pending application affecting the estate sought to be registered and entered on the day list subsequent to the date and time at which the pending application for first registration was entered on the day list (other than an application to designate a document as an exempt information document under rule 136)

I. Notice of the entry of any relevant official search the priority period of which has not expired affecting the pending application for first registration

J. The date and time at which priority expires

PART 5
INFORMATION TO BE INCLUDED IN THE RESULT OF AN OFFICIAL SEARCH BY A MORTGAGEE FOR THE PURPOSE OF SECTION 56(3) OF THE FAMILY LAW ACT 1996

A. The title number

B. The date and time of the official search certificate

C. The mortgagee's name

D. The mortgagee's, or his agent's, reference (if any): limited to 25 characters including spaces

E. Whether, at the date of the official search certificate, a matrimonial home rights notice or matrimonial home rights caution has been registered against the registered title searched and if so the date of registration and the name of the person in whose favour the notice or caution was registered

F. Whether there is a pending application for the entry of a matrimonial home rights notice entered on the day list

---

References: See paras 7.84, 15.4.

SCHEDULE 7

Rule 186

SETTLEMENTS

General

1. Registered land which is settled land must be registered in the name of the tenant for life or the statutory owner.

First registration—restriction required

2. An application for first registration of an unregistered legal estate which is settled land must be accompanied by an application for entry of a restriction in Form G, H, or I, as appropriate.

Standard forms of restriction applicable to settled land

3.—(1) The restrictions in Forms G, H and I apply respectively to the various cases referred to in those forms, and may be modified as the registrar sees fit according to the circumstances.

(2) Where one of the restrictions referred to in sub-paragraph (1) should have been entered in the register and has not been, any person who has an interest in the settled land and who applies for such restriction shall be regarded as included in section 43(1)(c) of the Act.

(3) Subject to paragraphs 8 and 14, the restrictions referred to in sub-paragraph (1) are binding on the proprietor during his life, but do not affect a disposition by his personal representatives.

Transfer of land into settlement

4.—(1) A transfer of registered land into settlement must include the following provisions, with any necessary alterations and additions—

"The Transferor and the Transferee declare that—

(a)   the property is vested in the Transferee upon the trusts declared in a trust deed dated (date) and made between (*parties*),

(b)   the trustees of the settlement are (*names of trustees*),

(c)   the power of appointment of new trustees is vested in (*name*),

(d)   the following powers relating to land are expressly conferred by the trust deed in addition to those conferred by the Settled Land Act 1925: (*insert additional powers*).

or if the tenant for life is a minor and the transferees are the statutory owner—

(a)   the property is vested in the Transferee as statutory owner under a trust deed dated (*date*) and made between (*parties*),

(b)   the tenant for life is (*name*), a minor, who was born on (*date*),

(c)   the trustees of the settlement are (*names*),

(d)   during the minority of the tenant for life the power of appointment of new trustees is vested in the Transferee,

(e)   the following powers relating to land are expressly conferred by the trust deed in addition to those conferred by the Settled Land Act 1925: (*insert additional powers*).".

(2)   An application for the registration of a transfer of registered land into settlement must be accompanied by an application for entry of a restriction in Form G, H or I, as appropriate.

(3)   When the registrar receives the application he must register the transferee named in the transfer as the proprietor of the registered land and enter the appropriate restriction in the register.

Registered land brought into settlement

5. Where registered land has been settled and the existing registered proprietor is the tenant for life under the settlement, the registered proprietor must—

(a)   make a declaration in Form 6, and

(b)   apply for the entry of a restriction in Form G, modified if appropriate.

Registered land bought with capital money

6.—(1) Where registered land is acquired with capital money the transfer must be in one of the forms prescribed by rule 206 and must include the following provisions, with any necessary alterations and additions—

"The Transferee declares that—

(a)   the consideration has been paid out of capital money,

(b)   the Property is vested in the Transferee upon the trusts declared in a trust deed dated (*date*) and made between (*parties*),

(c)   the trustees of the settlement are (*names of trustees*),

(d)   the power of appointment of new trustees is vested in (*name*),

(e)   the following powers relating to land are expressly conferred by the trust deed in addition to those conferred by the Settled Land Act 1925: (*set out additional powers*).".

(2)   An application for registration of the transfer must be accompanied by an application for entry of a restriction in Form G, H or I, as appropriate.

Duty to apply for restrictions when registered land is settled

7.—(1) Where registered land is settled land the proprietor, or (if there is no proprietor) the per.sonal representatives of a deceased proprietor, must apply to the registrar for the entry of such restrictions (in addition to a restriction in Form G, H or I) as may be appropriate to the case.

(2)   The application must state that the restrictions applied for are required for the protection of the beneficial interests and powers under the settlement.

(3)   Subject to section 43(3) of the Act, the registrar must enter such restrictions without inquiry as to the terms of the settlement.

(4)   Nothing in this rule affects the rights and powers of personal representatives for purposes of administration.

Proprietor ceasing in his lifetime to be the tenant for life

8. Where a registered proprietor ceases in his lifetime to be a tenant for life and has not become absolutely entitled to the registered land—

(a)   he must transfer the land to his successor in tile, or, if the successor is a minor, to the statutory owner, and

(b)   on the registration of the successor in title or statutory owner as proprietor, the trustees of the settlement, if the settlement continues, must apply for such alteration in the restrictions as may be required for the protection of the beneficial interests and powers under the settlement.

Tenant for life or statutory owner entitled to have the settled land vested in him

9. Where a tenant for life or statutory owner who, if the registered land were not registered, would be entitled to have the settled land vested in him, is not the registered proprietor, the registered proprietor must at the cost of the trust estate execute such transfers as may be required for giving effect on the register to the rights of such tenant for life or statutory owner.

Registration of statutory owner during a minority otherwise than on death

10.—(1) If a minor becomes entitled in possession (or will become entitled in possession on attaining full age) to registered land otherwise than on a death, the statutory owner during the minority is entitled to require the settled land to be transferred to him and to be registered as proprietor accordingly.

(2)   The transfer to the statutory owner—

(a)   must be in Form TR1, and

(b)   must not refer to the settlement.

(3)   An application to register the transfer must be accompanied by an application for entry of a restriction in Form H.

Registration of special personal representatives

11.—(1) Where—

(a)   land was settled before the death of the sole or last surviving joint registered proprietor and not by his will, and

(b)   the settlement continues after his death,

the personal representatives in whom the registered land vests under the Administration of Estates Act 1925 may apply to be registered as proprietor in place of the deceased proprietor.

(2)   The application must be accompanied by the grant of probate or letters of administration of the deceased proprietor limited to the settled land.

(3)   The personal representatives must be registered in place of the deceased proprietor and the following added after his name—

"special executor or executrix (or administrator or administratrix) of [*name*], deceased.".

Transfer on the death of the tenant for life

12.—(1) Where the settlement continues after the death of the proprietor who was the tenant for life—

(a)   an application to register a transfer by the personal representatives to the person next entitled to the registered land which is settled land must be accompanied by—

      (i)   if the personal representatives are not already registered, the grant of probate or letters of administration of the deceased proprietor limited to the settled land,

      (ii)   a transfer in Form AS1 or AS2, as appropriate,

    (iii) an application for entry of a restriction in Form G or H, as appropriate.

  (b)   The transfer must contain the following provisions with any necessary alterations or additions—

"The Personal Representatives and the Transferee declare that—

    (a)   the Property is vested in the Transferee upon the trusts declared in [a trust deed dated (*date*) and made between (*parties*)] or [the will of (*name of deceased*) proved on (*date*)],

    (b)   the trustees of the settlement are (*names of trustees*),

    (c)   the power of appointment of new trustees is vested in (*name*),

    (d)   the following powers relating to land are expressly conferred by the will in addition to those conferred by the Settled Land Act 1925: (*set out additional powers*).".

(2)   Where the settlement ends on the death of the proprietor, an application to register a transfer by the personal representatives to the person entitled must be accompanied by—

    (a)   if the personal representatives are not already registered, the grant of probate or letters of administration of the deceased proprietor,

    (b)   Form RX3 for cancellation of the restriction entered on the register relating to the settlement.

(3)   The registrar shall not be under a duty to investigate the reasons any transfer is made by the personal representatives or consider the contents of the will and, provided the terms of any restriction on the register are complied with, he must assume, whether he knows of the terms of the will or not, that the personal representatives are acting correctly and within their powers.

Minority where settlement arises under a will or intestacy

13.—(1) Where a settlement is created or arises under the will or intestacy of a person who died before 1st January 1997—

    (a)   The personal representatives under the will or intestacy under which the settlement is created or arises must, during a minority, be registered as proprietors and will have all the powers conferred by the Settled Land Act 1925 on the tenant for life and on the trustees of the settlement.

    (b)   When a minor becomes beneficially entitled to an estate in fee simple or a term of years absolute in the registered land, or would, if he were of full age, be or have the powers of a tenant for life, the personal representatives must (unless they are themselves the statutory owner) during the minority give effect on the register to the directions of the statutory owner.

    (c)   In particular, the statutory owner shall, after administration is completed as respects the registered land, direct the personal representatives to apply for a restriction in Form H.

(2)   The application for the restriction in form H must be made by the personal representatives.

(3)   On an application by the personal representatives under sub-paragraph (2), the registrar shall be under no duty to consider or call for any information concerning—

    (a)   the reason the application is made, or

    (b)   the terms of the will or the devolution under the intestacy, or

    (c)   whether the direction by the statutory owner was actually given or not, or its terms, and whether he has notice of those matters or not, he must assume that the personal representatives are acting according to the directions given and that the directions were given by the statutory owner and were correct.

(4)   A disponee dealing with the personal representatives who complies with the restriction entered under sub-paragraph (2) is not concerned to see or enquire whether any directions have been given by the statutory owner with regard to the disposition to him.

(5)   Where under subsection (3) of section 19 of the Settled Land Act 1925 there is a tenant for life of full age, he shall be entitled to be registered as proprietor during any minority referred to in that subsection, but subject to the restrictions in Forms G or I, as appropriate.

(6)   Nothing in this paragraph shall affect the right of a statutory owner to be registered as proprietor.

Discharge of registered land from beneficial interests and powers under a settlement

14. Where the trustees of a settlement desire to discharge registered land from the beneficial interests and powers under the settlement they may do so by any document sufficient to discharge it.

Discharge from liability in respect of beneficial interests and powers under a settlement

15. Where a proprietor or the personal representatives of a deceased proprietor has or have, in good faith, complied with the requirements of this Schedule in executing a transfer of settled land or discharge of trustees and in applying for the appropriate restrictions that may be required for the protection of the beneficial interests and powers under a settlement—

(a)   he is or they are absolutely discharged from all liability in respect of the equitable interests and powers taking effect under the settlement, and

(b)   he is or they are entitled to be kept indemnified at the cost of the trust estate from all liabilities affecting the settled land.

Interpretation

16.—(1) In this Schedule—

"capital" money has the same meaning as in the Settled Land Act 1925,

"personal representatives" includes the special personal representatives for the purposes of any settled land where they have been appointed in relation to that land,

"settled land" has the same meaning as in the Settled Land Act 1925,

"settlement" has the same meaning as in the Settled Land Act 1925,

"statutory owner" has the same meaning as in the Settled Land Act 1925,

"tenant for life" has the same meaning as in the Settled Land Act 1925,

"transfer" includes an assent and a vesting assent,

"trustees of the settlement" has the same meaning as in the Settled Land Act 1925,

"vesting assent" has the same meaning as in the Settled Land Act 1925.

(2)   References in this Schedule to the "tenant for life" shall, where the context admits, be read as referring to the tenant for life, statutory owner, or personal representatives who is or are entitled to be registered.

(3)   Nothing in this Schedule modifies the provisions of section 2 of the Trusts of Land and Appointment of Trustees Act 1996 concerning settlements in relation to their application to registered land (as defined in section 89(3) of the Act).

References: See paras 10.16, 10.17, 10.21, 10.22, 10.25, 10.27–10.29, 10.32, 10.33.

SCHEDULE 8

Rule 191

MODIFIED FORM OF SCHEDULE 6 TO THE ACT APPLICABLE TO REGISTERED RENTCHARGES

SCHEDULE 6
REGISTRATION OF ADVERSE POSSESSOR

Right to apply for registration

1.—(1) A person may apply to the registrar to be registered as the proprietor of a registered rentcharge if he has been in adverse possession of the registered rentcharge for the period of ten years ending on the date of the application.

(2)   However, a person may not make an application under this paragraph if—

    (a)   he is a defendant in proceedings by the registered proprietor of the registered rentcharge for recovery of the rent or to enter into possession of the land out of which the registered rentcharge issues,

    (b)   judgement in favour of the registered proprietor of the registered rentcharge in respect of proceedings of the nature mentioned in sub-paragraph (2)(a) has been given against him in the last two years, or

    (c)   the registered proprietor of the registered rentcharge of which that person was in adverse possession has entered into possession of the land out of which the registered rentcharge issues.

(3)   For the purposes of sub-paragraph (1), the registered rentcharge need not have been registered throughout the period of adverse possession.

Notification of application

2.—(1) The registrar must give notice of an application under paragraph 1 to—

    (a)   the proprietor of the registered rentcharge to which the application relates,

    (b)   the proprietor of any registered charge on the registered rentcharge,

    (c)   where the registered rentcharge is leasehold, the proprietor of any superior registered rentcharge,

    (d)   any person who is registered in accordance with rules as a person to be notified under this paragraph, and

    (e)   such other persons as rules may provide.

(2)   Notice under this paragraph shall include notice of the effect of paragraph 4.

Treatment of application

3.—(1) A person given notice under paragraph 2 may require that the application to which the notice relates be dealt with under paragraph 5.

(2)   The right under this paragraph is exercisable by notice to the registrar given before the end of such period as rules may provide.

4. If an application under paragraph 1 is not required to be dealt with under paragraph 5, the applicant is entitled to be entered in the register as the new proprietor of the registered rentcharge.

5.—(1) If an application under paragraph 1 is required to be dealt with under this paragraph, the applicant is only entitled to be registered as the new proprietor of the registered rentcharge if either of the following conditions is met.

(2)   The first condition is that—

    (a)   it would be unconscionable because of an equity by estoppel for the registered proprietor to seek to assert his title to the registered rentcharge against the applicant, and

    (b)   the circumstances are such that the applicant ought to be registered as the proprietor.

(3) The second condition is that the applicant is for some other reason entitled to be registered as the proprietor of the registered rentcharge.

Right to make further application for registration

6.—(1) Where a person's application under paragraph 1 is rejected, he may make a further application to be registered as the proprietor of the registered rentcharge if he is in adverse possession of the registered rentcharge from the date of the application until the last day of the period of two years beginning with the date of its rejection.

(2) However, a person may not make an application under this paragraph if—

    (a) he is a defendant in proceedings by the registered proprietor of the registered rentcharge for recovery of the rent or to enter into possession of the land out of which the registered rentcharge issues,

    (b) judgement in favour of the registered proprietor of the registered rentcharge in respect of proceedings of the nature mentioned in sub-paragraph (2)(a) has been given against him in the last two years, or

    (c) the registered proprietor of the registered rentcharge of which that person was in adverse possession has entered into possession of the land out of which the registered rentcharge issues.

7. If a person makes an application under paragraph 6, he is entitled to be entered in the register as the new proprietor of the registered rentcharge.

Restriction on applications

8.—(1) No one may apply under this Schedule to be registered as the proprietor of a registered rentcharge during, or before the end of twelve months after the end of, any period in which the existing registered proprietor is for the purposes of the Limitation (Enemies and War Prisoners) Act 1945 (8 & 9 Geo 6 c 16)—

    (a) an enemy, or

    (b) detained in enemy territory.

(2) No-one may apply under this Schedule to be registered as the proprietor of a registered rentcharge during any period in which the existing registered proprietor is—

    (a) unable because of mental disability to make decisions about issues of the kind to which such an application would give rise, or

    (b) unable to communicate such decisions because of mental disability or physical impairment.

(3) For the purposes of sub-paragraph (2), mental disability means a disability or disorder of the mind or brain, whether permanent or temporary, which results in an impairment or disturbance of mental functioning.

(4) Where it appears to the registrar that sub-paragraph (1) or (2) applies in relation to a registered rentcharge, he may include a note to that effect in the register.

Effect of registration

9.—(1) Where a person is registered as the proprietor of a registered rentcharge in pursuance of an application under this Schedule, the title by virtue of adverse possession which he had at the time of the application is extinguished.

(2) Subject to sub-paragraph (3), the registration of a person under this Schedule as the proprietor of a registered rentcharge does not affect the priority of any interest affecting the registered rentcharge.

(3) Subject to sub-paragraph (4), where a person is registered under this Schedule as the proprietor of a registered rentcharge, the registered rentcharge is vested in him free of any registered charge affecting the registered rentcharge immediately before his registration.

(4) Sub-paragraph (3) does not apply where registration as proprietor is in pursuance of an application determined by reference to whether either of the conditions in paragraph 5 applies.

Apportionment and discharge of charges

10.—(1) Where—

- (a) a registered rentcharge continues to be subject to a charge notwithstanding the registration of a person under this Schedule as the proprietor, and
- (b) the charge affects property other than the registered rentcharge,

the proprietor of the registered rentcharge may require the chargee to apportion the amount secured by the charge at that time between the registered rentcharge and the other property on the basis of their respective values.

(2) The person requiring the apportionment is entitled to a discharge of his registered rentcharge from the charge on payment of—

- (a) the amount apportioned to the registered rentcharge, and
- (b) the costs incurred by the chargee as a result of the apportionment.

(3) On a discharge under this paragraph, the liability of the chargor to the chargee is reduced by the amount apportioned to the registered rentcharge.

(4) Rules may make provision about apportionment under this paragraph, in particular, provision about—

- (a) procedure,
- (b) valuation,
- (c) calculation of costs payable under sub-paragraph (2)(b), and
- (d) payment of the costs of the chargor.

Meaning of "adverse possession"

11.—(1) A person is in adverse possession of a registered rentcharge for the purposes of this Schedule if, but for section 96, a period of limitation under section 15 of the Limitation Act 1980 (c 58) would run in his favour in relation to the registered rentcharge.

(2) A person is also to be regarded for those purposes as having been in adverse possession of a registered rentcharge—

- (a) where he is the successor in title to the registered rentcharge, during any period of adverse possession by a predecessor in title to that registered rentcharge, or
- (b) during any period of adverse possession by another person which comes between, and is continuous with, periods of adverse possession of his own.

(3) In determining whether for the purposes of this paragraph a period of limitation would run under section 15 of the Limitation Act 1980, there are to be disregarded—

- (a) the commencement of any legal proceedings, and
- (b) paragraph 6 of Schedule 1 to that Act.

Trusts

12. A person is not to be regarded as being in adverse possession of a registered rentcharge for the purposes of this Schedule at any time when the registered rentcharge is subject to a trust, unless the interest of each of the beneficiaries in the registered rentcharge is an interest in possession.

References: See para 12.50.

SCHEDULE 9

Rule 206(3)

FORMS OF EXECUTION

Note: All dispositions other than assents must be executed as a deed. In the case of an assent the words "as a deed" may be omitted.

Land Registration Rules 2003, Sch 9

A. Where the instrument is to be executed personally by an individual—

Signed as a deed by (*full name of individual*) in the presence of:

Signature

Signature of witness...
Name (in BLOCK CAPITALS)
....

Address...
....
....

B. Where the instrument is to be executed by an individual directing another to sign on his behalf—

Signed as a deed by (*full name of person signing*) at the direction and on behalf of (*full name of individual*) in [his][her] presence and in the presence of:

Sign here the name of the individual and your own name,   *eg:* John Smith by Jane Brown

Signature of first witness ....
Name (in BLOCK CAPITALS)
....

Address...
....
....

Signature of second witness...
Name (in BLOCK CAPITALS)
....

Address...
....
....

C. Where the instrument is to be executed by a company registered under the Companies Acts, or an unregistered company, using its common seal—

The common seal of (*name of company*) was affixed in the presence of:

Common seal of company

....
Signature of director
....
Signature of secretary

D. Where the instrument is to be executed by a company registered under the Companies Acts, or an unregistered company, without using a common seal—

Signed as a deed by (*name of company*)
acting by [a director and its secretary]
[two directors]

Signature
Director
Signature
[Secretary][Director]

E. Where the instrument is to be executed on behalf of an overseas company without using a common seal—

Signed as a deed on behalf of (*name
of company*), a company incorporated
in (*territory*), by (*full name(s) of
person(s) signing*), being [a] person[s]
who, in accordance with the laws of that
territory, [is][are] acting under the
authority of the company.

Signature(s)
Authorised [signatory][signatories]

Note: In the case of an overseas company having a common seal, the form of execution appropriate to a company registered under the Companies Acts may be used, with such adaptations as may be necessary, in place of execution by a person or persons acting under the authority of the company.

F. Where the instrument is to be executed by a limited liability partnership incorporated under the Limited Liability Partnerships Act 2000, without using a common seal—

Signed as a deed by (*name of limited
liability partnership*) acting by two
members

Signature
Member
Signature
Member

References: See paras 2.36, 5.17.

Land Registration (Proper Office) Order 2003

(SI 2003/2040)

Made: 2 August 2003.
Authority: Land Registration Act 2002, s 100(3).
Commencement: 13 October 2003.

1 Citation and commencement

This Order may be cited as the Land Registration (Proper Office) Order 2003 and shall come into force on 13th October 2003.

2 Applications to which this Order applies

(1)   This Order applies to any application to the registrar except an application delivered to the registrar—
  (a)   in accordance with a written arrangement as to delivery made between the registrar and the applicant or between the registrar and the applicant's conveyancer, or
  (b)   under the provisions of any relevant notice given under Schedule 2 to the Land Registration Rules 2003.

(2)   In this article "conveyancer" means—
  (a)   a solicitor, or
  (b)   a licensed conveyancer within the meaning of section 11(2) of the Administration of Justice Act 1985, or
  (c)   a fellow of the Institute of Legal Executives.

3 Designation of the proper office

The proper office for the receipt of an application to which this Order applies is any office of the land registry specified in column 1 of the Schedule which is opposite an administrative area shown in column 2 of the Schedule in which the land to which that application relates is wholly or partly situated.

SCHEDULE

Article 3

Column 1 Office of the land registry	Column 2 Administrative Area
Land Registry, Birkenhead (Old Market) Office	Merseyside Staffordshire Stoke-on-Trent
Land Registry, Birkenhead (Rosebrae) Office	Cheshire Halton Hammersmith and Fulham Kensington and Chelsea Warrington

Column 1	Column 2
Office of the land registry	*Administrative Area*
Land Registry, Coventry Office	West Midlands
	Worcestershire
Land Registry, Croydon Office	Bexley
	Bromley
	Croydon
	Kingston upon Thames
	Merton
	Sutton
Land Registry, Durham (Boldon) Office	Cumbria
	Surrey
Land Registry, Durham (Southfield) Office	Darlington
	Durham
	Hartlepool
	Middlesbrough
	Northumberland
	Redcar and Cleveland
	Stockton-on-Tees
	Tyne and Wear
Land Registry, Gloucester Office	Bracknell Forest
	Bristol
	Gloucestershire
	Oxfordshire
	Reading
	Slough
	South Gloucestershire
	Warwickshire
	West Berkshire
	Windsor and Maidenhead
	Wokingham
Land Registry, Harrow Office	Brent
	Camden
	City of Westminster
	The City of London
	Harrow
	Islington
	The Inner Temple and the Middle Temple

Land Registration (Proper Office) Order 2003, Schedule

Column 1	Column 2
Office of the land registry	Administrative Area
Land Registry, Kingston Upon Hull Office	Kingston upon Hull
	Lincolnshire
	Norfolk
	North East Lincolnshire
	North Lincolnshire
	Suffolk
Land Registry, Lancashire	Blackburn with Darwen
	Blackpool
	Lancashire
Land Registry, Leicester Office	Buckinghamshire
	Leicester
	Leicestershire
	Milton Keynes
	Northamptonshire
	Rutland
Land Registry, Lytham Office	Greater Manchester
	Land Registry, Nottingham (East) Office
	Nottingham
	Nottinghamshire
	South Yorkshire
Land Registry, Nottingham (West) Office	Derby
	Derbyshire
	West Yorkshire
Land Registry, Peterborough Office	Bedfordshire
	Cambridgeshire
	Essex
	Luton
	Peterborough
	Southend-on-Sea
	Thurrock
Land Registry, Plymouth Office	Bath and North East Somerset
	Cornwall
	Devon
	Isles of Scilly
	North Somerset
	Plymouth

Column 1	Column 2	
Office of the land registry	Administrative Area	
Land Registry, Plymouth Office—*contd*	Somerset:	Sedgemoor
		Taunton Deane
		West Somerset
	Torbay	
Land Registry, Portsmouth Office	Brighton and Hove	
	East Sussex	
	Hampshire:	East Hampshire
		Havant
	Isle of Wight	
	Portsmouth	
	West Sussex	
Land Registry, Stevenage Office	Barking and Dagenham	
	Hackney	
	Havering	
	Hertfordshire	
	Newham	
	Redbridge	
	Tower Hamlets	
	Waltham Forest	
Land Registry, Swansea Office	Cofrestrfa Tir Swyddfa	
	Abertawe	
	Barnet	
	Ealing	
	Enfield	
	Harringey	
	Hillingdon	
	Hounslow	
Land Registry, Telford Office	Greenwich	
	Herefordshire	
	Lambeth	
	Lewisham	
	Richmond upon Thames	
	Shropshire	
	Southwark	
	The Wrekin	
	Wandsworth	

Land Registration (Proper Office) Order 2003, Schedule

Column 1	Column 2
Office of the land registry	*Administrative Area*
Land Registry, Tunbridge Wells Office	Kent Medway
Land Registry, Wales Office Cofrestrfa Tir Swyddfa Cymru	All counties and county boroughs in Wales

Land Registry, Weymouth Office	Bournemouth
	Dorset
	Hampshire: Basingstoke & Deane
	                               Eastleigh
	                               Fareham
	                               Gosport
	                               Hart
	                               New Forest
	                               Rushmoor
	                               Test Valley
	                               Winchester
	Poole
	Somerset: Mendip
	                               South Somerset
	Southampton
	Swindon
	Wiltshire

Land Registry, York Office	East Riding of Yorkshire North Yorkshire York

References: See paras 2.49, 2.50.

Land Registration Fee Order 2004

(SI 2004/595)

Made: 3rd March 2004
Authority: Land Registration Act 2002, s 102
Commencement: 1 April 2004

PART 1
GENERAL

1 Citation, commencement and interpretation

(1)   This Order may be cited as the Land Registration Fee Order 2004 and shall come into force on 1st April 2004.

(2)   In this Order unless the context otherwise requires—

"account holder" means a person or firm holding a credit account,

"the Act" means the Land Registration Act 2002,

"charge" includes a sub-charge,

"credit account" means an account authorised by the registrar under article 14(1),

"large scale application" is as defined in article 6(1),

"monetary consideration" means a consideration in money or money's worth (other than a nominal consideration or a consideration consisting solely of a covenant to pay money owing under a mortgage),

"premium" means the amount or value of any monetary consideration given by the lessee as part of the same transaction in which a lease is granted by way of fine, premium or otherwise, but, where a registered leasehold estate of substantially the same land is surrendered on the grant of a new lease, the premium for the new lease shall not include the value of the surrendered lease,

"profit" means a profit a prendre in gross,

"rent" means the largest amount of annual rent the lease reserves within the first five years of its term that can be quantified at the time an application to register the lease is made,

"the rules" means the Land Registration Rules 2003 and a rule referred to by number means the rule so numbered in the rules,

"Scale 1" means Scale 1 in Schedule 1,

"Scale 2" means Scale 2 in Schedule 2,

"scale fee" means a fee payable in accordance with a scale set out in Schedule 1 or 2 whether or not reduced in accordance with article 2(6),

"scale fee application" means an application which attracts a scale fee, or which would attract such a fee but for the operation of article 6,

"share", in relation to land, means an interest in that land under a trust of land,

"surrender" includes a surrender not made by deed,

"voluntary application" means an application for first registration (other than for the registration of title to a rentcharge, a franchise or a profit) which is not made wholly or in part pursuant to section 4 of the Act (when title must be registered).

[(2A) In this Order, the terms: "a commonhold"; "commonhold association"; "common parts"; "commonhold community statement"; "commonhold land"; "commonhold unit"; "developer"; "termination application" and "unit-holder" have the same meaning as they have in the Commonhold and Leasehold Reform Act 2002.]

(3)　Expressions used in this Order have, unless the contrary intention appears, the meaning which they bear in the rules.

Amendment: Para (2A): inserted by SI 2004/1833, arts 2, 3.

PART 2
SCALE FEES

2 Applications for first registration and applications for registration of a lease by an original lessee

(1)　The fee for an application for first registration of an estate in land is payable under Scale 1 on the value of the estate in land comprised in the application assessed under article 7 unless the application is—

　　(a)　for the registration of title to a lease by the original lessee or his personal representative, where paragraph (2) applies,

　　(b)　a voluntary application, where paragraph (6) applies, or

　　(c)　a large scale application, where article 6 applies.

(2)　The fee for an application for the registration of title to the grant of a lease by the original lessee or his personal representative is payable under Scale 1—

　　(a)　on an amount equal to the sum of the premium and the rent, or

　　(b)　where

　　　　(i)　there is no premium, and

　　　　(ii)　either there is no rent or the rent cannot be quantified at the time the application is made,

　　on the value of the lease assessed under article 7 subject to a minimum fee of £40,

unless either of the circumstances in paragraph (3) applies.

(3)　Paragraph (2) shall not apply if the application is—

　　(a)　a voluntary application, where paragraph (6) applies, or

　　(b)　a large scale application, where article 6 applies.

(4)　The fee for an application for the first registration of a rentcharge is £40.

(5)　The fee for an application for the first registration of a franchise or a profit is payable under Scale 1 on the value of the franchise or the profit assessed under article 7.

(6)　The fee for a voluntary application is the fee which would otherwise be payable under paragraphs (1) and (2) for applications to which those paragraphs apply reduced by 25 per cent and, where the reduced fee would be a figure which includes pence, the fee must be adjusted to the nearest £10.

(7)   In paragraph (2) "lease" means—
    (a)   a lease which grants an estate in land whether or not the grant is a registrable disposition, or
    (b)   a lease of a franchise, profit or manor the grant of which is a registrable disposition.

3 Transfers of registered estates for monetary consideration, etc

(1)   Subject to paragraphs (2), (3) and (4), the fee for an application for the registration of—
    (a)   a transfer of a registered estate for monetary consideration,
    (b)   a transfer for the purpose of giving effect to a disposition for monetary consideration of a share in a registered estate, or
    (c)   a surrender of a registered leasehold estate for monetary consideration, other than a surrender to which paragraph (3) of Schedule 4 applies,
is payable under Scale 1 on the amount or value of the consideration.

(2)   Paragraph (1) shall not apply if the application is—
    (a)   a large scale application, where article 6 applies, or
    (b)   for the registration of a transfer of a matrimonial home made pursuant to an order of the court, where article 4(1)(h) applies.

(3)   Where a sale and sub-sale of a registered estate are made by separate deeds of transfer, a separate fee is payable for each deed of transfer.

(4)   Where a single deed of transfer gives effect to a sale and a sub-sale of the same registered estate a single fee is assessed upon the greater of the monetary consideration given by the purchaser and the monetary consideration given by the sub-purchaser.

(5)   The fee for an application to cancel an entry in the register of notice of an unregistered lease which has determined is payable under Scale 1 on the value of the lease immediately before its determination assessed under article 7.

4 Transfers of registered estates otherwise than for monetary consideration, etc

(1)   Unless the application is a large scale application (where article 6 applies), the fee for an application for the registration of—
    (a)   a transfer of a registered estate otherwise than for monetary consideration (unless paragraph (2) applies),
    (b)   a surrender of a registered leasehold estate otherwise than for monetary consideration,
    (c)   a transfer of a registered estate by operation of law on death or bankruptcy, of an individual proprietor,
    (d)   an assent of a registered estate (including a vesting assent),
    (e)   an appropriation of a registered estate,
    (f)   a vesting order or declaration to which section 27(5) of the Act applies,
    (g)   an alteration of the register, or

> (h)   a transfer of a matrimonial home (being a registered estate) made pursuant to an order of the Court,

is payable under Scale 2 on the value of the registered estate which is the subject of the application, assessed under article 7, but after deducting from it the amount secured on the registered estate by any charge subject to which the registration takes effect.

(2)   Where a transfer of a registered estate otherwise than for monetary consideration is for the purpose of giving effect to the disposition of a share in a registered estate, the fee for an application for its registration is payable under Scale 2 on the value of that share.

5 Charges of registered estates or registered charges

(1)   The fee for an application for the registration of a charge is payable under Scale 2 on the amount of the charge assessed under article 8 unless it is an application to which paragraphs (2), (3) or (4) apply.

(2)   No fee is payable for an application to register a charge lodged with or before the completion of [either a scale fee application or an application to which paragraph (17) in Part 1 of Schedule 3 applies] ("the primary application") that will result in the chargor being registered as proprietor of the registered estate included in the charge unless—

> (a)   the charge includes a registered estate which is not included in the primary application, where paragraph (4) applies, or
> (b)   the primary application is a voluntary application, in which case this paragraph shall apply only if the application to register the charge accompanies the primary application.

(3)   No fee is to be paid for an application to register a charge made by a predecessor in title of the applicant that is lodged with or before completion of an application for first registration of the estate included in the charge.

(4)   Where a charge also includes a registered estate which is not included in the primary application ("the additional property") any fee payable under Scale 2 is to be assessed on an amount calculated as follows:

$$\frac{\text{Value of the additional property}}{\text{Value of all the property included in the charge}} \times \text{Amount secured by the charge}$$

(5)   The fee for an application for the registration of—

> (a)   the transfer of a registered charge for monetary consideration, or
> (b)   a transfer for the purpose of giving effect to a disposition for monetary consideration of a share in a registered charge,

is payable under Scale 2 on the amount or value of the consideration.

(6)   The fee for an application for the registration of the transfer of a registered charge otherwise than for monetary consideration is payable under Scale 2 on—

> (a)   the amount secured by the registered charge at the time of the transfer or,

(b) where the transfer relates to more than one charge, the aggregate of the amounts secured by the registered charges at the time of the transfer.

(7) The fee for an application for the registration of a transfer for the purpose of giving effect to a disposition otherwise than for monetary consideration of a share in a registered charge is payable under Scale 2 on—

(a) the proportionate part of the amount secured by the registered charge at the time of the transfer, or,

(b) where the transfer relates to more than one charge, the proportionate part of the aggregate of the amounts secured by the registered charges at the time of the transfer.

(8) This article takes effect subject to article 6 (large scale applications).

Amendment: Para (2): words in square brackets substituted by SI 2004/1833, arts 2, 4.

6 Large scale applications, etc

(1) In this article—

(a) "land unit" means—

(i) the land registered under a single title number other than, in the case of an application to register a charge, any estate under any title number which is included in a primary application within the meaning of article 5(2), or

(ii) on a first registration application, a separate area of land not adjoining any other unregistered land affected by the same application.

(b) "large scale application" means a scale fee application which relates to 20 or more land units, other than [an application to register a disposition by the developer affecting the whole or part of the freehold estate in land which has been registered as a freehold estate in commonhold land, or a low value application],

(c) "low value application" means a scale fee application, other than an application for first registration, where the value of the land or the amount of the charge to which it relates (as the case may be) does not exceed £30,000.

(2) The fee for a large scale application is the greater of—

(a) the scale fee, and

(b) a fee calculated on the following basis—

(i) where the application relates to not more than 500 land units, £10 for each land unit, or

(ii) where the application relates to more than 500 land units, £5,000 plus £5 for each land unit in excess of 500, up to a maximum of £40,000.

(3) If a large scale application is a voluntary application, the fee payable under this article is reduced in accordance with article 2(6).

Amendment: Para (1): in sub-para (b) words in square brackets substituted by SI 2004/1833, arts 2, 5.

PART 3
VALUATION

7 Valuation (first registration and registered estates)

(1)   The value of the estate in land, franchise, profit, manor or share is the maximum amount for which it could be sold in the open market free from any charge—

    (a)   in the case of a surrender, at the date immediately before the surrender, and

    (b)   in any other case, at the date of the application.

(2)   As evidence of the amount referred to in paragraph (1), the registrar may require a written statement signed by the applicant or his conveyancer or by any other person who, in the registrar's opinion, is competent to make the statement.

(3)   Where an application for first registration is made on—

    (a)   the purchase of a leasehold estate by the reversioner,

    (b)   the purchase of a reversion by the leaseholder, or

    (c)   any other like occasion,

and an unregistered interest is determined, the value of the land is the combined value of the reversionary and determined interests assessed in accordance with paragraphs (1) and (2).

8 Valuation (charges)

(1)   On an application for registration of a charge, the amount of the charge is—

    (a)   where the charge secures a fixed amount, that amount,

    (b)   where the charge secures further advances and the maximum amount that can be advanced or owed at any one time is limited, that amount,

    (c)   where the charge secures further advances and the total amount that can be advanced or owed at any one time is not limited, the value of the property charged,

    (d)   where the charge is by way of additional or substituted security or by way of guarantee, an amount equal to the lesser of—

        (i) the amount secured or guaranteed, and

        (ii) the value of the property charged,

    (e)   where the charge secures an obligation or liability which is contingent upon the happening of a future event ("the obligation"), and is not a charge to which sub-paragraph (d) applies, an amount equal to—

        (i) the maximum amount or value of the obligation, or

        (ii) if that maximum amount is greater than the value of the property charged, or is not limited by the charge, or cannot be calculated at the time of the application, the value of the property charged.

(2)   Where a charge of a kind referred to in paragraph (1)(a) or (1)(b) is secured on unregistered land or other property as well as on a registered estate or registered charge, the fee is payable on an amount calculated as follows—

$$\frac{\text{Value of the registered estate or registered charge}}{\text{Value of all the property charged}} \times \text{Amount of the charge}$$

(3)   Where one deed contains two or more charges made by the same chargor to secure the same debt, the deed is to be treated as a single charge, and the fee for registration of the charge is to be paid on the lesser of—

(a)   the amount of the whole debt, and

(b)   an amount equal to the value of the property charged.

(4)   Where one deed contains two or more charges to secure the same debt not made by the same chargor, the deed is to be treated as a separate single charge by each of the chargors and a separate fee is to be paid for registration of the charge by each chargor on the lesser of—

(a)   the amount of the whole debt, and

(b)   an amount equal to the value of the property charged by that chargor.

(5)   In this article "value of the property charged" means the value of the registered estate or the amount of the registered charge or charges affected by the application to register the charge, less the amount secured by any prior registered charges.

PART 4
FIXED FEES AND EXEMPTIONS

9 Fixed fees

(1)   Subject to paragraph (2) [and (3)] and to article 10, the fees for the applications and services specified in Schedule 3 shall be those set out in that Schedule.

(2)   The fee for an application under rule 140 shall be the aggregate of the fees payable for the services provided, save that the maximum fee for any one application shall be £200.

[(3)   Where an application is one specified in paragraphs (1), (2) or (10) in Part 1 of Schedule 3 affecting the whole or part of the freehold estate in land which has been registered as a freehold estate in commonhold land registered in the name of the developer under more than one title number, the fee is to be assessed as if the application affects only one title.]

Amendments: Para (1): words in square brackets inserted by SI 2004/1833, arts 2, 6(1), (2).
Para (3): inserted by SI 2004/1833, arts 2, 6(1), (3).

10 Exemptions

No fee is payable for any of the applications and services specified in Schedule 4.

PART 5
GENERAL AND ADMINISTRATIVE PROVISIONS

11 Cost of surveys, advertisements and special enquiries

The applicant is to meet the costs of any survey, advertisement or other special enquiry that the registrar requires to be made or published in dealing with an application.

12 Applications not otherwise referred to

Upon an application for which no other fee is payable under this Order and which is not exempt from payment, there shall be paid a fee of £40.

13 Method of payment

(1) Except where the registrar otherwise permits, every fee shall be paid by means of a cheque or postal order crossed and made payable to the Land Registry.

(2) Where there is an agreement with the applicant, a fee may be paid by direct debit to such bank account of the Land Registry as the registrar may from time to time direct.

(3) Where the amount of the fee payable on an application is immediately quantifiable, the fee shall be payable on delivery of the application.

(4) Where the amount of the fee payable on an application is not immediately quantifiable, the applicant shall pay the sum of £40 towards the fee when the application is made and shall lodge at the same time an undertaking to pay on demand the balance of the fee due, if any.

(5) Where an outline application is made, the fee payable shall be the fee payable under paragraph (9) of Part 1 of Schedule 3 in addition to the fee otherwise payable under this Order.

14 Credit accounts

(1) Any person or firm may, if authorised by the registrar, use a credit account in accordance with this article for the payment of fees for applications and services of such kind as the registrar shall from time to time direct.

(2) To enable the registrar to consider whether or not a person or firm applying to use a credit account may be so authorised, that person or firm shall supply the registrar with such information and evidence as the registrar may require to satisfy him of the person or firm's fitness to hold a credit account and the ability of the person or firm to pay any amounts which may become due from time to time under a credit account.

(3) To enable the registrar to consider from time to time whether or not an account holder may continue to be authorised to use a credit account, the account holder shall supply the registrar, when requested to do so, with such information and evidence as the registrar may require to satisfy him of the account holder's continuing fitness to hold a credit account and the continuing ability of the account holder to pay any amounts which may become due from time to time under the account holder's credit account.

(4) Where an account holder makes an application where credit facilities are available to him, he may make a request, in such manner as the registrar directs, for the appropriate fee to be debited to the account holder's credit account, but the registrar shall not be required to accept such a request where the amount due on the account exceeds the credit limit applicable to the credit account, or would exceed it if the request were to be accepted.

(5)   Where an account holder makes an application where credit facilities are available to him, and the application is accompanied neither by a fee nor a request for the fee to be debited to his account, the registrar may debit the fee to his account.

(6)   A statement of account shall be sent by the registrar to each account holder at the end of each calendar month or such other interval as the registrar shall direct.

(7)   The account holder must pay any sums due on his credit account before the date and in the manner specified by the registrar.

(8)   The registrar may at any time and without giving reasons terminate or suspend any or all authorisations given under paragraph (1).

(9)   In this article "credit limit" in relation to a credit account authorised for use under paragraph (1) means the maximum amount (if any) which is to be due on the account at any time, as notified by the registrar to the account holder from time to time, by means of such communication as the registrar considers appropriate.

15 Revocation

The Land Registration Fee Order 2003 is revoked.

SCHEDULE 1

Articles 2 & 3

SCALE 1

NOTE 1: Where the amount or value is a figure which includes pence, it must be rounded down to the nearest £1.

NOTE 2: The third column, which sets out the reduced fee payable where article 2(6) (voluntary registration: reduced fees) applies, is not part of the scale.

Amount or value	Fee	Reduced fee where article 2(6) (voluntary registration: reduced fees) applies
£	£	£
0–50,000	40	30
50,001–80,000	60	45
80,001–100,000	100	75
100,001–200,000	150	110
200,001–500,000	220	165
500,001–1,000,000	420	315
1,000,001 and over	700	525

SCHEDULE 2

Articles 4 & 5

SCALE 2

NOTE: Where the amount or value is a figure which includes pence, it must be rounded down to the nearest £1.

Amount or value £	Fee £
0–100,000	40
100,001–200,000	50
200,001–500,000	70
500,001–1,000,000	100
1,000,001 and over	200

SCHEDULE 3

Articles 9 & 13

PART 1
FIXED FEE APPLICATIONS

Fee

(1) To register:

(a) a standard form of restriction contained in Schedule 4 to the rules, or

(b) a notice (other than a notice to which section 117(2)(b) of the Act applies), or

(c) a new or additional beneficiary of a unilateral notice

—total fee for up to three registered titles affected £40

—additional fee for each subsequent registered title affected £20

Provided that no such fee is payable if, in relation to each registered title affected, the application is accompanied by a scale fee application or another application which attracts a fee under this paragraph.

(2) To register a restriction in a form not contained in Schedule 4 to the rules—for each registered title £80

(3) To register a caution against first registration (other than a caution to which section 117(2)(a) of the Act applies) £40

(4) To alter a cautions register—for each individual cautions register £40

(5) To close or partly close a registered leasehold or a registered rentcharge title other than on surrender—for each registered title closed or partly closed £40

Provided that no such fee is payable if the application is accompanied by a scale fee application.

(6) To upgrade from one class of registered title to another £40

Provided that no such fee is payable if the application for upgrading is accompanied by a scale fee application.

(7) To cancel an entry in the register of notice of an unregistered rentcharge which has determined—for each registered title affected £40

Fee

Provided that no such fee is payable if the application is accompanied by a scale fee application.

(8) To enter or remove a record of a defect in title pursuant to section 64(1) of the Act £40

Provided that no such fee is payable if the application is accompanied by a scale fee application.

(9) An outline application made under rule 54:

(a) where delivered directly to the registrar's computer system by means of a remote terminal £2

(b) where delivered by any other permitted means £4

Such fee is payable in addition to any other fee which is payable in respect of the application.

(10) For an order in respect of a restriction under section 41(2) of the Act—for each registered title affected £40

(11) To register a person in adverse possession of a registered estate—for each registered title affected £100

(12) For registration as a person entitled to be notified of an application for adverse possession—for each registered title affected £40

(13) For the determination of the exact line of a boundary under rule 118—for each registered title affected £80

[(14) To register a freehold estate in land as a freehold estate in commonhold land which is not accompanied by a statement under section 9(1)(b) of the Commonhold and Leasehold Reform Act 2002:

(a) up to 20 commonhold units £40

(b) for every 20 commonhold units, or up to 20 commonhold units, thereafter £10

(15) To add land to a commonhold:

(a) adding land to the common parts title £40

(b) adding land to a commonhold unit £40

(c) adding commonhold units

up to 20 commonhold units £40

for every 20 commonhold units, or up to 20 commonhold units, thereafter. £10

(16) To apply for a freehold estate in land to cease to be registered as a freehold estate in commonhold land during the transitional period, as defined in the Commonhold and Leasehold Reform Act 2002 £40

(17) To register a freehold estate in land as a freehold estate in commonhold land, which is accompanied by a statement under section 9(1)(b) of the Commonhold and Leasehold Reform Act 2002

for each commonhold unit converted £40

		Fee
(18)	To register an amended commonhold community statement which changes the extent of the common parts or any commonhold unit:	
	for the common parts	£40
	for up to three commonhold units	£40
	for each subsequent commonhold unit	£20
	Provided that no such fee shall be payable if, in relation to each registered title affected, the application is accompanied by a scale fee application or another application that attracts a fee under this Part.	
(19)	To register an amended commonhold community statement, which does not change the extent of a registered title within the commonhold	£40
	Provided that no such fee shall be payable if, in relation to each registered title affected, the application is accompanied by a scale fee application or another application that attracts a fee under this Part.	
(20)	To register an alteration to the Memorandum or Articles of Association of a commonhold association	£40
(21)	To make a termination application	£40
(22)	To note the surrender of a development right under section 58 of the Commonhold and Leasehold Reform Act 2002	£40]

Amendment: Paras (14)–(22) inserted by SI 2004/1833, arts 2, 7.

PART 2
SERVICES—INSPECTION AND COPYING

(1)	Inspection of the following, including in each case the making of a copy, on any one occasion when a person gains access to the registrar's computer system by means of a remote terminal by virtue of rule 132:	
	(a) for each individual register	£2
	(b) for each title plan	£2
	(c) for any or all of the documents referred to in an individual register (other than the documents referred to in paragraph (7) below)	£2
	[(ca) for the register of a commonhold common parts title	£2]
	(d) for each individual caution register	£2
	(e) for each caution plan	£2
	(f) for any other document kept by the registrar which relates to an application to him—for each document	£2
(2)	Inspection (otherwise than under paragraph (1)):	
	(a) for each individual register	£4
	(b) for each title plan	£4
	(c) for any or all of the documents referred to in an individual register (other than the documents referred to in paragraph (7))	£4

[(ca) for the register of a commonhold common parts title £4]

(d) for each individual caution register £4

(e) for each caution plan £4

(f) for any other document kept by the registrar which relates to an application to him—for each document £4

(3) Official copy in respect of a registered title:

(a) for each individual register

(i) where an official copy in electronic form is requested from a remote terminal by virtue of a notice under rule 132 £2

(ii) where an official copy in paper form is requested by any permitted means £4

(b) for each title plan

(i) where an official copy in electronic form is requested from a remote terminal by virtue of a notice under rule 132 £2

(ii) where an official copy in paper form is requested by any permitted means £4

[(c) for each commonhold common parts register and title plan

(i) where an official copy in electronic form is requested from a remote terminal by virtue of a notice under rule 132 £2

(ii) where an official copy in paper form is requested by any permitted means £4]

(4) Official copy in respect of a cautions register

(a) for each individual caution register

(i) where an official copy in electronic form is requested from a remote terminal by virtue of a notice under rule 132 £2

(ii) where an official copy in paper form is requested by any permitted means £4

(b) for each caution plan

(i) where an official copy in electronic form is requested from a remote terminal by virtue of a notice under rule 132 £2

(ii) where requested by any other permitted means £4

(5) Official copy of any or all of the documents referred to in an individual register (other than documents referred to in paragraph (7))—for each registered title

(a) where an official copy in electronic form is requested from a remote terminal by virtue of a notice under rule 132 £2

(b) where requested by any other permitted means £4

(6) Official copy of any other document kept by the registrar which relates to an application to him—for each document

(a) where an official copy in electronic form is requested from a remote terminal by virtue of a notice under rule 132 £2

(b) where an official copy in paper form is requested by any permitted means £4

(7) Where permitted (being unavailable as of right) inspection or official copy (or both) of a transitional period document—for each document £8

(8) Copy of an historical edition of a registered title (or part of the edition where rule 144(4) applies)—for each title £8

(9) Subject to paragraph (14) of Schedule 4, application to the registrar to ascertain the title number or numbers (if any) under which the estate is registered where the applicant seeks to inspect or to be supplied with an official copy of an individual register or of a title plan and the applicant has not supplied a title number, or the title number supplied does not relate to any part of the land described by the applicant—for each title number in excess of ten disclosed £4

Amendments: Para (1): sub-para (ca) inserted by SI 2004/1833, arts 2, 8(1), (2).
Para (2): sub-para (ca) inserted by SI 2004/1833, arts 2, 8(1), (3).
Para (3): sub-para (c) inserted by SI 2004/1833, arts 2, 8(1), (4).

PART 3
SERVICES—SEARCHES

(1) An official search of an individual register or of a pending first registration application made to the registrar by means of a remote terminal communicating with the registrar's computer system by virtue of rule 132—for each title £2

(2) An official search of an individual register by a mortgagee for the purpose of section 56(3) of the Family Law Act 1996 made to the registrar by means of a remote terminal communicating with the registrar's computer system by virtue of rule 132—for each title £2

(3) An official search of an individual register or of a pending first registration application other than as described in paragraphs (1) and (2)—for each title £4

(4) The issue of a certificate of inspection of a title plan—for each registered title affected £4

(5) Subject to paragraph (15) of Schedule 4, an official search of the index map—for each registered title in excess of ten in respect of which a result is given £4

(6) Search of the index of proprietors' names—for each name £10

(7) An official search of the index of relating franchises and manors—for each administrative area:

(a) where the application is made by means of a remote terminal communicating with the registrar's computer system by virtue of rule 132 £2

(b) where the application is made by any other permitted means £4

PART 4
SERVICES—OTHER INFORMATION

(1) Application to be supplied with the name and address of the registered proprietor of a registered title identified by its postal address—for each application £4

(2) Application for return of a document under rule 204 £8

(3)   Application that the registrar designate a document an exempt   £20
        information document

(4)   Application for an official copy of an exempt information document   £40
        under rule 137

SCHEDULE 4

Article 10

EXEMPTIONS

No fee is payable for:

(1)   reflecting a change in the name, address or description of a registered proprietor or other person referred to in the register, or in the cautions register, or changing the description of a property,

(2)   giving effect in the register to a change of proprietor where the registered estate or the registered charge, as the case may be, has become vested without further assurance (other than on the death or bankruptcy of a proprietor) in some person by the operation of any statute (other than the Act), statutory instrument or scheme taking effect under any statute or statutory instrument,

(3)   registering the surrender of a registered leasehold estate where the surrender is consideration or part consideration for the grant of a new lease to the registered proprietor of substantially the same premises as were comprised in the surrendered lease and where a scale fee is paid for the registration of the new lease,

(4)   registering a discharge of a registered charge,

(5)   registering a matrimonial home rights notice, or renewal of such a notice, or renewal of a matrimonial home rights caution under the Family Law Act 1996,

(6)   entering in the register the death of a joint proprietor,

(7)   cancelling the registration of a notice, (other than a notice in respect of an unregistered lease or unregistered rentcharge), caution against first registration, caution against dealings, including a withdrawal of a deposit or intended deposit, inhibition, restriction, or note,

(8)   the removal of the designation of a document as an exempt information document,

(9)   approving an estate layout plan or any draft document with or without a plan,

(10)   an order by the registrar (other than an order under section 41(2) of the Act),

(11)   deregistering a manor,

(12)   an entry in the register of a note of the dissolution of a corporation,

(13)   registering a restriction in form A in Schedule 4 to the rules,

(14)   an application to ascertain the title number or numbers (if any) under which the estate is registered where the applicant seeks to inspect or to be supplied with an official copy of an individual register or of a title plan and the applicant has not supplied a title number, or the title number supplied does not relate to any part of the land described by the applicant, provided the number of registered titles supplied does not exceed ten,

(15)   an official search of the index map where either no part of the land to which the search relates is registered, or, where the whole or part is registered, the number of registered titles disclosed does not exceed ten,

(16)   an application for day list information on any one occasion when a person gains access to the registrar's computer system by means of a remote terminal communicating with the registrar's computer system by virtue of rule 132,

(17) an application to lodge a caution against first registration or to make a register entry where in either case the application relates to rights in respect of the repair of a church chancel.

Land Registration Act 2002 (Commencement No 1) Order 2003

(SI 2003/935)

Made: 21 March 2003.
Authority: Land Registration Act 2002, s 136(2).

1 This Order may be cited as the Land Registration Act 2002 (Commencement No 1) Order 2003.

2 Sections 128 to 132, 134(1) and 136 of the Land Registration Act 2002 shall come into force on 4th April 2003.

Land Registration Act 2002 (Commencement No 2) Order 2003

(SI 2003/1028)

Made: 2 April 2003.
Authority: Land Registration Act 2002, s 136(2).

1 This Order may be cited as the Land Registration Act 2002 (Commencement No 2) Order 2003.

2 The following provisions of the Land Registration Act 2002 shall come into force on 28th April 2003—
    (a) section 107 and Schedule 9; and
    (b) paragraph 28 of Schedule 11 and, so far as it relates to that paragraph, section 133.

Land Registration Act 2002 (Commencement No 3) Order 2003

(SI 2003/1612)

Made: 16 June 2003.
Authority: Land Registration Act 2002, s 136(2).

1 This Order may be cited as the Land Registration Act 2002 (Commencement No 3) Order 2003.

2 Section 102 of the Land Registration Act 2002 shall come into force on 27th June 2003.

Land Registration Act 2002 (Commencement No 4) Order 2003

(SI 2003/1725)

Made: 8 July 2003.
Authority: Land Registration Act 2002, s 136(2).

1 This Order may be cited as the Land Registration Act 2002 (Commencement No 4) Order 2003.

2—(1) Subject to paragraph (2), all the provisions of the Land Registration Act 2002 ("the Act") not already in force shall come into force on 13th October 2003.

(2) The following provisions of the Act shall come into force on 13th October 2004—
   (a) section 98(1);
   (b) paragraph 5(4) and (5) of Schedule 6 and, to the extent that it relates thereto, section 97.

References: See para 13.32.

Land Registration Act 2002 (Transitional Provisions) Order 2003

(SI 2003/1953)

Made: 10 July 2003.
Authority: Land Registration Act 2002, s 134.
Commencement: 13 October 2003 (ie the day on which the Land Registration Act 2002, s 1 comes into force).

Preliminary

1 Citation, commencement and interpretation

(1) This Order may be cited as the Land Registration Act 2002 (Transitional Provisions) Order 2003 and shall come into force on the day that section 1 of the Act comes into force.

(2) In this Order—
   "the 1925 Act" means the Land Registration Act 1925,
   "the 1925 Rules" means the Land Registration Rules 1925,
   "the 1972 Rules" means the Land Registration (Souvenir Land) Rules 1972,
   "the 1991 Rules" means the Land Registration (Open Register) Rules 1991,

"the 1993 Rules" means the Land Registration (Official Searches) Rules 1993,
"the 2003 Rules" means the Land Registration Rules 2003,
"the Act" means the Land Registration Act 2002,
"commencement" means the day when section 1 of the Act comes into force,
"the Regulations" means the Land Registration (Conduct of Business) Regulations 2000.

General and administrative

2 Chief Land Registrar

The person holding the office of Chief Land Registrar immediately before commencement shall continue to be the Chief Land Registrar notwithstanding that he has not been appointed under section 99(3) of the Act.

References: See para 2.1.

---

3 Extension of effect of statutory provisions—first registration, dealings, etc

(1)   Notwithstanding the repeal of the 1925 Act, that Act shall continue to have effect in relation to any application referred to in paragraph (2) that is pending immediately before commencement.

(2)   Paragraph (1) applies to—
    (a)   an application for the first registration of land,
    (b)   any other application (whether or not being one within paragraphs 5 or 6 of Schedule 12 to the Act) that, if completed, would result in a change to the register.

(3)   Paragraph (1) is subject to articles 5, 7 and 24.

References: See para 4.12.

---

4 Extension of effect of statutory provisions for the purpose of the Order

Notwithstanding the repeal of the 1925 Act, that Act shall continue in force to the extent necessary to enable the remaining provisions of this Order to have effect.

5 Notices

(1)   The 2003 Rules apply to the giving of—
    (a)   any notice under this Order, and
    (b)   any notice under the 1925 Act, as continued under Schedule 12 to the Act or article 3, other than a notice to which paragraph (3) applies.

(2)   Section 79 of the 1925 Act does not apply to any notice to which paragraph (1)(b) applies.

(3)   Subject to the modification referred to in paragraph (4), sub-sections (1) and (2) of section 30 of the 1925 Act apply to any notice required to be given under sub-section (1) of that section, as continued under article 3.

(4)   The modification referred to in paragraph (3) is the omission of the words "by registered post" from section 30(1) of the 1925 Act.

References: See para 4.12.

Disputes, objections, appeals and proceedings

6 Hearing of existing disputes

(1)   This article applies to any pending application in relation to which there is, immediately before commencement, a dispute to which rule 299(1) of the 1925 Rules applies that has not been finally disposed of.

(2)   For the purposes of paragraph (1) there is a dispute to which rule 299(1) of the 1925 Rules applies where—

    (a)   in relation to a caution lodged under section 54 of the 1925 Act or rule 215(2) of the 1925 Rules, an application has been lodged that has resulted in the notice referred to in rule 218 of the 1925 Rules being issued before commencement, provided that (whether before or after commencement) the registrar is satisfied that cause has been shown under rule 219(3) of the 1925 Rules, and

    (b)   in the case of any other pending application, a person has, before commencement, objected to the application under rule 298(1) of the 1925 Rules, provided that the registrar is satisfied subsequently that the objection cannot be treated as groundless under rule 298(4) of the 1925 Rules.

(3)   Neither the objection that has led to the dispute, nor any subsequent objection to the same application, shall constitute an objection for the purpose of section 73 of the Act.

(4)   The registrar must deal with or continue to deal with the existing dispute and any dispute resulting from any subsequent objection to the same application, in accordance with rule 299 of the 1925 Rules and, where appropriate, the Land Registration (Hearings Procedure) Rules 2000 until the dispute has been finally disposed of.

(5)   Subject to the modifications referred to in paragraph (6), the Regulations shall continue to apply in relation to any dispute referred to in paragraph (1) to enable relevant acts of the registrar to which those regulations relate to be done or continue to be done by a person nominated by the registrar under the Regulations.

(6)   The modifications referred to in paragraph (5) are—

    (a)   substitution of the following sub-paragraph for regulation 2(d) of the Regulations—

        "(d) "qualified officer" means a member of staff of the land registry who holds a 10 year general qualification within the meaning of section 71 of the Courts and Legal Services Act 1990; and",

    (b)   substitution of the words "qualified officer" for the words "qualified registrar" where they occur in regulations 3(1), 5(1) and 6(1) of the Regulations,

    (c)   substitution of the word "person" for the word "registrar" where it occurs in regulations 3(2), 5(2) and 6(2) of the Regulations, and

    (d)   substitution of the words "qualified officer" for the word "registrar" where it occurs in regulations 5(3) and 6(3) of the Regulations.

References: See para 15.87.

7 Objection after commencement

(1)   This article applies to any application that is pending immediately before commencement in relation to which an objection is made after commencement that is not an objection to which article 6(3) applies.

(2)   Notwithstanding paragraph 5 of Schedule 12 to the Act, the objection shall constitute an objection to which section 73 of the Act applies.

References: See para 15.88.

8 Appeals

Rule 300 of the 1925 Rules (Appeal to the court) shall continue to have effect in relation to—

    (a)   any decision by the registrar under rule 298(4) of the 1925 Rules that an objection is groundless (whether the decision is made before commencement, or after commencement in relation to an application that is pending immediately before commencement), and

    (b)   any decision or order by the registrar under rule 299 of the 1925 Rules (whether made before commencement, or after commencement in relation to a dispute to which article 6 applies).

References: See para 15.89.

9 Legal Proceedings

(1)   This article applies to any proceedings which were instituted before commencement but which have not been concluded immediately before commencement.

(2)   Any proceedings to which paragraph (1) applies may be continued until concluded, whether by final determination by the court or otherwise, as if the 2002 Act had not been passed.

(3)   Where in any proceedings the court gives judgement or makes an order, or has already done so before commencement, and the effect of the judgement or order is to require an entry or cancellation to be made in the register or the register to be rectified or altered, then the proceedings shall not be treated as concluded for the purpose of paragraphs (1) and (2) until the entry or cancellation has been made, or the register rectified or altered, as required by the court.

(4)   Paragraphs (2) and (3) have effect without prejudice to the need for any order of the court or alteration of the register made after commencement to comply with rule 127 of the 2003 Rules.

(5)   In this article—
"court" has the same meaning as in the 1925 Act, and
"proceedings" means any proceedings within the jurisdiction of the court by
   virtue of a provision of the 1925 Act.

References: See para 15.90.

Souvenir land

10 Souvenir land—application of articles and definitions

(1)   Articles 11, 12 and 13 apply where—
   (a)   there is in force in relation to registered land immediately before
          commencement a declaration by the registrar under rule 3 of the
          1972 Rules, and
   (b)   particulars of the declaration have been entered in the register under
          rule 6 of those rules.

(2)   In articles 11, 12 and 13—
"declaration" means the declaration by the registrar under rule 3 of the 1972
   Rules,
"proprietor" in relation to souvenir land means the registered proprietor or,
   where the registered proprietor has died, been made bankrupt or,
   being a corporate body, has been dissolved, the person who would be
   entitled to be registered as proprietor in his place but for any
   unregistered transaction effected after the declaration was made,
"souvenir land" means the registered land subject to a declaration,
"third party" means a person other than the proprietor.

11 Souvenir land—restriction on dispositions

(1)   Where any unregistered transaction with souvenir land has been effected
after the declaration was made and has resulted in one or more third parties
becoming entitled to apply to be registered as proprietor of any part or parts of the
land, the proprietor must not dispose of that land otherwise than in a manner that
gives effect in the register to the interests of the third parties.

(2)   The particulars of a declaration entered in the individual register of any
souvenir land shall take effect after commencement as if there were a restriction in
the proprietorship register in the following terms—

"No disposition is to be registered without the consent of the person or
persons (if any) entitled to apply to be registered as proprietor of the land
disposed of, or any part of it, as the result of any unregistered transaction
effected since [*date*] being the date when a declaration made under rule 3 of
the Land Registration (Souvenir Land) Rules 1972 was noted in the register.".

(3)   The registrar may amend the registered title to any souvenir land so as to
substitute for the particulars of the declaration a restriction in the terms set out in
paragraph (2).

12 Application to cancel entries relating to souvenir land

(1)   A proprietor who claims that there has been no unregistered transaction
with the souvenir land, or a particular part of the land, after the declaration was

made, so that no third party has become entitled to be registered as proprietor of it, may apply in Form RX3 in Schedule 1 to the 2003 Rules in relation to that land to cancel in the register the particulars of the declaration or, where the registrar has registered a restriction in substitution for those particulars under article 11(3), that restriction.

(2)   If the registrar is satisfied that there has been no such transaction as is referred to in paragraph (1), he must—

  (a)   where the application relates to the whole of the land in a registered title, cancel the relevant entry in the register,

  (b)   where the application relates to part only of the land in a registered title, give effect to the application in the register in such manner as he thinks appropriate.

13 Application for registration by a third party

(1)   This article applies where, in relation to any souvenir land, a third party is able to satisfy the registrar that one or more unregistered transactions have been effected since the declaration was made and that, as a result of them and any other events that have taken place—

  (a)   the registered estate is now vested in him, or

  (b)   a legal estate derived (whether directly or indirectly) out of the land is vested in him, or

  (c)   a legal estate such as is referred to in sub-paragraph (a) or (b) has been transferred to him (either directly or indirectly) by the person in whom it has become vested.

(2)   The third party may apply to be registered as the proprietor of a legal estate if that estate is one to which section 3 of the Act would apply if the estate were an unregistered estate within that section.

(3)   Before determining an application under paragraph (2), the registrar must give notice of it to the person named in the proprietorship register as proprietor unless that person has consented to the application.

Cautions

14 Cautions against first registration

(1)   In relation to a caution against first registration lodged for registration before commencement, Part 5 of the 2003 Rules applies with the modifications set out in paragraph (2).

(2)   The modifications referred to in paragraph (1) are—

  (a)   paragraphs (2) to (5) of rule 41 do not apply,

  (b)   in rule 51(1) of the 2003 Rules, the omission of the word "cautioner's".

References: See para 4.5.

15 Cautions against conversion

(1)   This article applies where, immediately before commencement, there is an entry in respect of a caution lodged under rule 215(2) of the 1925 Rules in the register of any title.

(2)   In the event of an application to upgrade the title under any of subsections (1) to (5) of section 62 of the Act, the registrar shall, before determining the application, give notice of it to the person named in the entry referred to in paragraph (1).

(3)   Where the person to whom notice is given, or any person deriving title under that person, responds to the notice by claiming any estate, right or interest in the land in the title, then, to the extent that the estate, right or interest subsists and is otherwise enforceable against the land, the claim is to be treated for the purpose of section 62(6) of the Act as one for an estate right or interest whose enforceability is preserved by virtue of the existing entry about the class of title.

16 Mortgage cautions

(1)   Subject to this article, mortgage cautions and sub-mortgage cautions entered in the register shall continue to have the same effect after commencement as they had immediately before commencement.

(2)   Subject to paragraphs (3) and (4), the registrar must cancel a mortgage caution or a sub-mortgage caution where—
- (a)   the cautioner, or some other person who can satisfy the registrar that he is entitled to the benefit of the protected mortgage or protected sub-mortgage, makes an application to withdraw it in Form WCT in Schedule 1 to the 2003 Rules, or
- (b)   evidence is produced that satisfies the registrar, that the protected mortgage or protected sub-mortgage has been discharged, or
- (c)   an application is made to register the protected mortgage, and any protected sub-mortgage, under section 27 of the Act and the registrar approves the application.

(3)   Where there is a sub-mortgage caution entered in the register and application is made to cancel the relevant mortgage caution under sub-paragraph (a) or (b) of paragraph (2), the registrar must give notice of the application to the sub-mortgage cautioner.

(4)   An application to register a protected mortgage under section 27(2)(f) of the Act must comply with the 2003 Rules and be accompanied by—
- (a)   the original deed creating the protected mortgage, and
- (b)   where title to the protected mortgage is vested in someone other than the cautioner, the documents proving devolution of title to the applicant.

(5)   When registering a protected mortgage, the registrar must make an entry showing that it has priority in relation to other entries in the register from the date that the mortgage caution was entered in the register.

(6)   Where application is made to register a disposition of the registered estate or registered charge affected by a mortgage caution or sub-mortgage caution, the registrar must—
- (a)   give notice of the application to the cautioner,
- (b)   retain the mortgage caution or sub-mortgage caution in the register unless it is to be cancelled in accordance with paragraph (2).

(7)   In this article—
"cautioner" means the person named in a mortgage caution or sub-mortgage caution,

> > "mortgage caution" means a caution entered in the register in a specially prescribed form under section 106 of the 1925 Act as originally enacted,
> > "protected mortgage" means the mortgage that is protected by a mortgage caution,
> > "protected sub-mortgage" means the sub-mortgage that is protected by a sub-mortgage caution,
> > "sub-mortgage caution" means a sub-mortgage caution to which rule 228 of the 1925 Rules applied before commencement.

17 Modification of paragraph 2(3) of Schedule 12 to the Act

Paragraph 2(3) of Schedule 12 to the Act shall have the effect as if there were inserted at the end ", but with the substitution for the wolds in section 55(1) from "prescribed" to "served" of the words "period prescribed under paragraph 2(4) of Schedule 12 to the Land Registration Act 2002". ".

18 Non-standard restrictions in approved instruments

(1)   This article applies where a person applies in an approved instrument to enter a restriction in the register and the registrar considers that there is a standard form of restriction which is to like or similar effect to the restriction applied for (or would be but for the fact that it does not purport to restrict the entry of a notice).

(2)   Where this article applies—
> (a)   the registrar must enter in the register the standard form of restriction referred to in paragraph (1) instead of the restriction applied for,
> (b)   the application is to be treated as though it was an application for entry in the register of a standard form of restriction, and
> (c)   rule 92(1) of the 2003 rules does not apply to the application.

(3)   In this article—
> "approved instrument" means a charge, or transfer—
> > (a)   which contains the application for the restriction applied for (whether in the body of the instrument or, in the case of a charge, in an incorporated document within the meaning of rule 139 of the 1925 Rules),
> > (b)   the form of which (including the application for the restriction) has been approved by the registrar before commencement as capable of being accepted for registration, and
> > (c)   in relation to which the approval referred to in sub-paragraph (b) has not been withdrawn, and
> "standard form of restriction" means one referred to in rule 91 of the 2003 Rules.

References: See para 8.13.

Outline applications

19 Outline applications

(1)   This article applies where, immediately before commencement—
> (a)   there is in force a notice given under rule 83A(9) of the 1925 Rules that allows an outline application to be delivered in respect of any category of application (including, for the avoidance of doubt, a caution to which rule 215 of those rules applies),

> (b) an outline application has been validly delivered in relation to such an application,
>
> (c) the reserved period referred to in rule 83A(8) of the 1925 Rules has not expired, and
>
> (d) the form required by rule 83A(6) of the 1925 Rules has not been lodged.

(2)   Notwithstanding the repeal of the 1925 Act, the registrar must give effect to the application in the register as of the time at which the outline application was delivered, provided the applicant lodges the appropriate form required by rule 83A(6) of the 1925 Rules at the appropriate office before expiry of the reserved period referred to in rule 83A(8) of those rules and the application otherwise complies with those rules.

(3)   In paragraph (2), "appropriate office" means the office of the land registry that, immediately before commencement, would have been the proper office within the meaning of rule 1(5A) of the 1925 Rules.

Matrimonial home rights cautions

20 Matrimonial home rights cautions

(1)   The registrar shall not be required, on the application of the proprietor of the registered estate affected, to serve the notice referred to in rule 223 of the 2003 Rules in relation to a matrimonial caution except upon production of—

> (a) a release in writing of the matrimonial home rights protected by the matrimonial caution, or
>
> (b) a statutory declaration that, as to the whole or any part of the land to which the matrimonial caution relates, no charge under section 2 of the Matrimonial Homes Act 1967, section 2 of the Matrimonial Homes Act 1983 or section 31 of the Family Law Act 1996 has ever arisen or, if such a charge has arisen, it is no longer subsisting.

(2)   In this article "matrimonial caution" means a caution registered under section 2(7) of the Matrimonial Homes Act 1967 before 14th February 1983 which remains in the register after commencement.

Index of relating franchises and manors

21 Index of relating franchises and manors

(1)   As soon as practicable after commencement, the registrar must take such steps as he considers appropriate to create the index of relating franchises and manors from the material parts of the index map maintained by the registrar under rule 8 of the 1925 Rules and other relevant information under his control in such a form that it complies with rule 10(1)(b).

(2)   Rule 10(1)(b) shall not have effect until the index of relating franchises and manors has been created so as to comply with it.

(3)   Until the index of relating franchises and manors has been created so as to comply with rule 10(1)(b), the registrar must ensure that official certificates of the result of searches of the index of relating franchises and manors issued in accordance with rule 146(3) of the 2003 Rules contain the same information as if the index of relating franchises and manors had been so created.

(4)　In this article—
　　"index of relating franchises and manors" means the index to be kept under
　　　　rule 10(1)(b), and
　　"rule 10(1)(b)" means rule 10(1)(b) of the 2003 Rules.

Compulsory first registration

22　Dispositions void under section 123A of the 1925 Act

(1)　After commencement, a void disposition is to be treated for all purposes as an event to which the requirement of registration applied and as a transfer, grant or creation that has become void as a result of the application of section 7(1) of the Act.

(2)　In this article "void disposition" means a disposition of unregistered land that, before commencement, has become void as a result of the application of section 123A(5) of the 1925 Act.

References: See para 4.12.

23　Other dispositions affected by section 123A of the 1925 Act

(1)　Subject to paragraph (2), a relevant disposition is to be treated for all purposes after commencement as an event to which the requirement of registration applies.

(2)　For the purposes of section 6(4) of the Act, the period for registration is the period that expires at the end of the applicable period referred to in section 123A(3) of the 1925 Act, or such longer period as the registrar may provide under section 6(5) of the Act.

(3)　In this article "relevant disposition" means a disposition of unregistered land where—
　　(a)　before commencement section 123A of the 1925 Act applied to it,
　　(b)　no application to register the relevant legal estate in accordance with section 123A(2) of the 1925 Act had been made before commencement, and
　　(c)　immediately before commencement the applicable period referred to in section 123A(3) of the 1925 Act had not expired.

References: See para 4.12.

Land and charge certificates

24　Abolition of land and charge certificates

(1)　Notwithstanding paragraph 5 of Schedule 12 to the Act, Part V of the 1925 Act shall cease to apply in relation to any application that is pending immediately before commencement.

(2)　Rules 203 and 204 of the 2003 Rules do not apply to—
　　(a)　any land certificate or charge certificate held by the registrar immediately before commencement, or
　　(b)　any land certificate or charge certificate lodged in connection with any application, including any application that is pending immediately before commencement, or
　　(c)　any document incorporated in any land certificate or charge certificate.

(3)   The registrar may destroy—
    (a)   any land certificate or charge certificate held by him or which comes into his possession,
    (b)   any document incorporated in such a land certificate or charge certificate.

(4)   Paragraph (3) applies notwithstanding an entry in the register to which paragraph 3 of Schedule 12 to the Act applies but without prejudice to the continuing effect of such an entry.

References: See para 2.62.

Obligation to make further advances

25 Obligation to make further advances

Where, immediately before commencement, an obligation to make a further advance is noted in the register under section 30(3) of the 1925 Act, the obligation is to be treated after commencement as entered in the register according to rules for the purpose of section 49(3)(b) of the Act.

References: See para 8.18.

Forms

26 Period of grace for use of old forms

(1)   Subject to paragraph (3), an applicant may use in place of any new form the relevant old form—
    (a)   for the period of 3 months following commencement, and
    (b)   thereafter, where use of the relevant old form is expressly required by law or under the terms of a valid contract entered into before commencement.

(2)   Where the relevant old form is used in accordance with paragraph (1) the 2003 Rules apply to the use of that form as they would apply to the use of the new form.

(3)   Where there is an entry in Column 3 in the Schedule, paragraph (1) only applies to the use of the relevant old form—
    (a)   where the entry limits use of the relevant old form to particular cases, in those cases specified in the entry, and
    (b)   where the entry places an additional requirement on the applicant, if the applicant complies with that requirement.

(4)   In this article—
    "new form" means a form prescribed by the 2003 Rules that is referred to in Column 1 in the Schedule, and
    "relevant old form" in relation to any particular new form means the form prescribed by the 1925 Rules, the 1991 Rules, the 1993 Rules or the Land Registration (Matrimonial Home Rights) Rules 1997 (as the case may be) that is shown against the new form in Column 2 in the Schedule.

References: See para 14.31.

27 Exclusion of Forms 112A, 112B and 112C from inspection or copying

Rules 133(2) and 135(2) of the 2003 Rules apply to any Form 112A, Form 112B or Form 112C, as lodged under the 1991 Rules or article 26, as they apply to any Form CIT.

Official searches and official copies

28 Priority of unexpired official searches

(1)   This article applies to an official search with priority made before commencement under the 1993 Rules whose priority period has not expired at commencement.

(2)   Section 72 of the Act and rules 151 to 154 of the 2003 Rules (as appropriate) shall apply to the official search as if it had been made under Part 13 of the 2003 Rules but with the priority period being that which applied to it under the 1993 Rules.

29 Office copies issued before commencement

Office copies of and extracts from the register and of and from documents, to which section 113 of the 1925 Act applied before commencement, are to be treated for all purposes after commencement as official copies to which section 67 of the Act applies.

SCHEDULE

Article 26

Column 1	Column 2	Column 3
New form	**Relevant old form**	**Requirements or limitations**
AP1	AP1	*Requirements—* (1) Where a fee is payable then the applicant must lodge with the form a cheque or postal order for the requisite fee or a request in writing for the fee to be paid by Direct Debit under an authorised agreement with the land registry. (2) The full name of the person applying to change the register must be inserted in the form. (3) Where the application is to register a registrable disposition, but there are no disclosable overriding interests, the form must include a statement to that effect, or be accompanied by such a statement in writing signed by the applicant.
AS1	AS1	
AS2	AS2	
AS3	AS3	

Column 1	Column 2	Column 3
New form	**Relevant old form**	**Requirements or limitations**
CH1	113	*Requirement—*
		Where a fee is payable then the applicant must lodge with the form a cheque or postal order for the requisite fee or a request in writing for the fee to be paid by Direct Debit under an authorised agreement with the land registry.
CI	102	
CIT	112A, or 112B, or 112C	*Limitation—*
		The relevant old form may only be used where it is signed by a qualifying applicant (within the meaning of rule 140 of the 2003 Rules) who is able to complete one or more of the certificates contained in the particular form.
CN1	CN1	*Limitation—*
		The relevant old form may only be used where application is made to cancel notice of an unregistered lease or rentcharge.
		Requirement—
		Where a fee is payable then the applicant must lodge with the form a cheque or postal order for the requisite fee or a request in writing for the fee to be paid by Direct Debit under an authorised agreement with the land registry.
CT1	CT1	*Limitation—*
		The relevant old form may not be used
		(a) Where the estate affected by the caution is a rentcharge, a franchise or a profit a prendre in gross, or
		(b) Where the applicant wishes to provide a certificate by a conveyancer as to the cautioner's interest in place of a statutory declaration.
		Requirements—
		(1) The applicant must lodge with the form a cheque or postal order for the fee payable or a request in writing for the fee to be paid by Direct Debit under an authorised agreement with the land registry.
		(2) Where the estate affected by the caution is a lease, the applicant must add a note as to whether or not the lease is discontinuous.
DL	DL	*Requirement—*
		The applicant must leave panels 2 and 3 of the relevant old form blank and use the accompanying application form to provide the relevant information.
DS1	DS1	
DS2	DS2	*Requirement—*
		The full name of the applicant must be inserted in the form.
DS3	DS3	

Column 1	Column 2	Column 3
New form	**Relevant old form**	**Requirements or limitations**
FR1	FR1	*Requirements—* (1) The applicant must lodge with the form a cheque or postal order for the fee payable or a request in writing for the fee to be paid by Direct Debit under an authorised agreement with the land registry. (2) The full name of the applicant must be inserted in the form. (3) Where there are no disclosable overriding interests, the form must include a statement to that effect, or be accompanied by such a statement in writing signed by the applicant.
MH1	MH1	*Limitation—* The relevant old form may not be used where the applicant wishes to provide a certificate by a conveyancer as to the existence of an order made under section 33(5) of the Family Law Act 1996.
MH2	MH2	*Limitation—* The relevant old form may not be used where the applicant wishes to provide a certificate by a conveyancer as to the existence of an order made under section 33(5) of the Family Law Act 1996.
MH3	MH3	
OC1	109	*Requirements—* (1) Where a title number is not quoted and the application relates to a caution against first registration, a rentcharge, a franchise, a profit a prendre in gross or a manor, panel 6 of the relevant old form must be amended accordingly. (2) Where the applicant wishes to apply for a certificate of inspection of a title plan, the words "Form 102" in panel 3 of the relevant old form must be amended to read "Form CI".
OC2	110	*Limitation—* The relevant old form may not be used to apply for an official copy of any document that is not referred to in the register.
OS1	94A	
OS2	94B	
OS3	94C	
PIC	111	*Limitation—* The relevant old form may not be used to apply for personal inspection of any document that is not referred to in the register.
PN1	104	
SIM	96	
TP1	TP1	
TP2	TP2	
TP3	TP3	

Column 1	Column 2	Column 3
New form	**Relevant old form**	**Requirements or limitations**
TR1	TR1	
TR2	TR2	
TR3	TR3	
TR4	TR4	
WCT	WCT	

Land Registration Act 2002 (Transitional Provisions) (No 2) Order 2003

(SI 2003/2431)

Made: 14 September 2003.
Authority: Land Registration Act 2002, s 134.
Commencement: 13 October 2003.

1 Citation, commencement and interpretation

(1)   This Order may be cited as the Land Registration Act 2002 (Transitional Provisions) (No 2) Order 2003 and shall come into force on 13th October 2003.

(2)   In this Order "the Act" means the Land Registration Act 2002.

2 A right in respect of the repair of a church chancel

(1)   For the period of ten years beginning with the day on which Schedule 1 to the Act comes into force, it has effect with the insertion at the end of—

"**16**. A right in respect of the repair of a church chancel."

(2)   For the period of ten years beginning with the day on which Schedule 3 to the Act comes into force, it has effect with the insertion at the end of—

"**16**. A right in respect of the repair of a church chancel."

References: See para 7.14.

Land Registration (Referral to the Adjudicator to HM Land Registry) Rules 2003

(SI 2003/2114)

Made: 2 August 2003.
Authority: Land Registration Act 2002, s 73(8).
Commencement: 13 October 2003.

1 Citation and commencement

These rules may be cited as the Land Registration (Referral to the Adjudicator to HM Land Registry) Rules 2003 and shall come into force on 13 October 2003.

2 Interpretation

In these rules—

"the Act" means the Land Registration Act 2002;

"business day" means a day when the land registry is open to the public under rule 216 of the Land Registration Rules 2003;

"disputed application" means an application to the registrar under the Act to which an objection has been made;

"objection" means an objection made under section 73 of the Act;

"the parties" means the person who has made the disputed application and the person who has made an objection to that application.

3 Procedure for referral to the adjudicator

(1) When the registrar is obliged to refer a matter to the adjudicator under section 73(7) of the Act, he must as soon as practicable—

(a) prepare a case summary containing the information set out in paragraph (2),

(b) send a copy of the case summary to the parties,

(c) give the parties an opportunity to make comments on the contents of the case summary in the manner, to the address, and within the time specified by him, and

(d) inform the parties in writing that the case summary together with copies of the documents listed in it will be sent to the adjudicator with the notice referred to in rule 5(2).

(2) The case summary must contain the following information—

(a) the names of the parties,

(b) the addresses of the parties,

(c) details of their legal or other representatives (if any),

(d) a summary of the core facts,

(e) details of the disputed application,

(f) details of the objection to that application,

(g) a list of any documents that will be copied to the adjudicator, and

(h) anything else that the registrar may consider to be appropriate.

(3) The registrar may amend the case summary as he considers appropriate having considered any written comments made to him by the parties under paragraph (1)(c).

4 Parties' addresses

(1) If the address of a party set out in the case summary does not comply with paragraph (2), that party must provide the registrar with one that does.

(2) An address complies with this paragraph if it—

(a) is a postal address in England and Wales, and

(b) is either that of the party or of his representative.

5 Notice of referral to the adjudicator

(1)　This rule applies—
- (a)　when the registrar has considered any written comments made by the parties under rule 3(1)(c), or
- (b)　if he has not received any comments from the parties within the time specified under rule 3(1)(c), on the expiry of that period, and
- (c)　when he has amended the case summary, if appropriate, under rule 3(3).

(2)　The registrar must as soon as practicable—
- (a)　send to the adjudicator a written notice, accompanied by the documents set out in paragraph (3), informing him that the matter is referred to him under section 73(7) of the Act,
- (b)　inform the parties in writing that the matter has been referred to the adjudicator, and
- (c)　send the parties a copy of the case summary prepared under rule 3 in the form sent to the adjudicator.

(3)　The notice sent to the adjudicator under paragraph (2)(a) must be accompanied by—
- (a)　the case summary prepared under rule 3 amended, if appropriate, by the registrar under rule 3(3), and
- (b)　copies of the documents listed in that case summary.

6 Specified time periods

(1)　For the purposes of rule 3(1)(c), the time specified by the registrar must not end before 12 noon on the fifteenth business day after the date on which the registrar sends the copy of the case summary to the relevant party under rule 3(1)(b) or such earlier time as the parties may agree.

(2)　On and after the date specified in any notice given pursuant to rule 216(2) of the Land Registration Rules 2003, paragraph (1) shall have effect with the substitution of the words "eighteenth business day" for the words "fifteenth business day".

References: See para 15.28.

Adjudicator to Her Majesty's Land Registry (Practice and Procedure) Rules 2003

(SI 2003/2171)

Made: 14 August 2003.
Authority: Land Registration Act 2002, ss 109(2), 109(3), 110(2), 110(3), 114, 128(1) and 128(2).
Commencement: 13 October 2003.

1 Citation and Commencement

These Rules may be cited as the Adjudicator to Her Majesty's Land Registry (Practice and Procedure) Rules 2003 and shall come into force on 13th October 2003.

PART 1
INTRODUCTION

2 Interpretation

(1)　In these Rules—

"applicant" means the party whom the adjudicator designates as such under rule 5 or under rule 24, or the party who makes a rectification application;

"hearing" means a sitting of the adjudicator for the purpose of enabling the adjudicator to reach or announce a substantive decision, but does not include a sitting of the adjudicator solely in the exercise of one or more of the following powers—

(a)　to consider an application, representation or objection made in the interim part of the proceedings;

(b)　to reach a substantive decision without an oral hearing; or

(c)　to consider whether to grant permission to appeal a decision or to stay the implementation of a decision pending the outcome of an appeal;

"matter" means the subject of either a reference or a rectification application;

"office copy" means an official copy of a document held or issued by a public authority;

"original application" means the application originally made to the registrar that resulted in a reference;

"proceedings" means, except in the expression "court proceedings", the proceedings of the matter before the adjudicator but does not include any negotiations, communications or proceedings that occurred prior to the reference or rectification application;

"record of matters" means a record of references, rectification applications and certain other applications and decisions, kept in accordance with these Rules and in particular in accordance with rule 46;

"rectification application" means an application made to rectify or set aside a document under section 108(2) for determination of the matter by the adjudicator;

"reference" means a reference from the registrar to the adjudicator under section 73(7) for determination of the matter by the adjudicator;

"respondent" means the party or parties who the adjudicator designates as such under rule 5 or rule 24, or the party or parties making an objection to a rectification application;

"substantive decision" means a decision of the adjudicator on the matter or on any substantive issue that arises in it but does not include any direction in interim parts of the proceedings or any order as to costs or any order as to costs thrown away;

"substantive order" means an order or direction that records and gives effect to a substantive decision;

"the Act" means the Land Registration Act 2002 and a reference to a section by number alone is a reference to a section of the Act;

"witness statement" means a written statement signed by a witness containing the evidence that the witness intends to give; and

"working day" means any day other than a Saturday or Sunday, Christmas Day, Good Friday or any other bank holiday.

(2)   In these Rules a person has a document or other material in his possession or control if—
    (a)   it is in his physical possession;
    (b)   he has a right to possession of it; or
    (c)   he has a right to inspect or take copies of it.

3 The overriding objective

(1)   The overriding objective of these Rules is to enable the adjudicator to deal with matters justly.

(2)   Dealing with a matter justly includes, so far as is practicable—
    (a)   ensuring that the parties are on an equal footing;
    (b)   saving expense;
    (c)   dealing with the matter in ways that are proportionate—
       (i)   to the value of the land or other interests involved;
       (ii)   to the importance of the matter;
       (iii)   to the complexity of the issues in the matter; and
       (iv)   to the financial position of each party; and
    (d)   ensuring that the matter is dealt with expeditiously and fairly.

(3)   The adjudicator must seek to give effect to the overriding objective when he—
    (a)   exercises any power given to him by these Rules; or
    (b)   interprets these Rules.

(4)   The parties are required to help the adjudicator to further the overriding objective.

References: See para 15.37, 15.38.

PART 2
REFERENCES TO THE ADJUDICATOR

4 Scope of this Part

The rules in this Part apply to references.

5 Notice of receipt by the adjudicator of a reference

Following receipt by the adjudicator of a reference, the adjudicator must—
    (a)   enter the particulars of the reference in the record of matters; and
    (b)   serve on the parties notice in writing of—
       (i)   the fact that the reference has been received by the adjudicator;
       (ii)   the date when the adjudicator received the reference;
       (iii)   the matter number allocated to the reference;
       (iv)   the name and any known address and address for service of the parties to the proceedings; and
       (v)   which party will be the applicant for the purposes of the proceedings and which party or parties will be the respondent.

6 Direction to commence court proceedings under section 110(1)

Where the adjudicator intends to direct a party to commence court proceedings under section 110(1), the parties may make representations or objections but any representations or objections must be concerned with one or more of the following—

    (a)   whether the adjudicator should make such a direction;
    (b)   which party should be directed to commence court proceedings;
    (c)   the time within which court proceedings should commence; and
    (d)   the questions the court should determine.

References: See para 15.41.

7 Notification to the adjudicator of court proceedings following a direction to commence court proceedings under section 110(1)

(1)   In this Part—

"the date that the matter before the court is finally disposed of" means the earliest date by which the court proceedings relating to the matter or on the relevant part (including any court proceedings on or in consequence of an appeal) have been determined and any time for appealing or further appealing has expired;

"the relevant part" means the part of the matter in relation to which the adjudicator has directed a party under section 110(1) to commence court proceedings; and

"the final court order" means the order made by the court that records the court's final determination (on appeal or otherwise).

(2)   A party who has been directed to commence court proceedings under section 110(1) must serve on the adjudicator—

    (a)   within 14 days of the commencement of the court proceedings, a written notice stating—
        (i)   that court proceedings have been issued in accordance with directions given by the adjudicator;
        (ii)   the date of issue of the court proceedings;
        (iii)   the names and any known addresses of the parties to the court proceedings;
        (iv)   the name of the court at which the court proceedings will be heard; and
        (v)   the case number allocated to the court proceedings;
    (b)   within 14 days of the date of the court's decision on any application for an extension of time, a copy of that decision; and
    (c)   within 14 days of the date that the matter before the court is finally disposed of, a copy of the final court order.

References: See para 15.43.

8 Adjournment of proceedings before the adjudicator following a direction to commence court proceedings on the whole of the matter under section 110(1)

(1)   This rule applies where the adjudicator has directed a party under section 110(1) to commence court proceedings for the court's decision on the whole of the matter.

(2)   Once he has received notice under rule 7(2)(a) that court proceedings have been issued, the adjudicator must adjourn all of the proceedings before him pending the outcome of the court proceedings.

(3)   Once he has received a copy of the final court order and unless the court directs otherwise, the adjudicator must close the proceedings before him without making a substantive decision.

References: See para 15.42.

9 Adjournment of proceedings before the adjudicator following a direction to commence court proceedings on part of the matter under section 110(1)

(1)   This rule applies where the adjudicator has directed a party under section 110(1) to commence court proceedings for the court's decision on the relevant part.

(2)   Once he has received notice under rule 7(2)(a) that court proceedings have been issued in relation to the relevant part, the adjudicator—
>   (a)   must adjourn the proceedings before him in relation to the relevant part, pending the outcome of the court proceedings; and
>   (b)   unless the court directs otherwise, must not make a substantive decision on the relevant part.

(3)   Once he has received a copy of the final court order on the relevant part and unless the court directs otherwise, the adjudicator must close the proceedings before him in relation to the relevant part without making a substantive decision on that relevant part.

(4)   The adjudicator may adjourn the proceedings in relation to any other part of the matter before him pending the outcome of the court proceedings.

(5)   While the court proceedings are still ongoing, the party directed to commence court proceedings must notify the court of any substantive decision made by the adjudicator within 14 days of service on that party of the substantive decision.

References: See para 15.42.

10 Notification where court proceedings are commenced otherwise than following a direction to commence court proceedings under section 110(1)

Where a party commences or has commenced court proceedings otherwise than following a direction under section 110(1) and those court proceedings concern or relate to the matter before the adjudicator, that party must serve—
>   (a)   on the adjudicator within 14 days of the commencement of the court proceedings or, if later, within 7 days of service on that party of notification of the reference under rule 5(b), a written notice stating—
>   (i)   that court proceedings have been issued;
>   (ii)   the way and the extent to which the court proceedings concern or relate to the matter before the adjudicator;
>   (iii)   the date of issue of the court proceedings;
>   (iv)   the names and any known addresses of the parties to the court proceedings;
>   (v)   the name of the court at which the court proceedings will be heard; and
>   (vi)   the case number allocated to the court proceedings;

    (b)   on the adjudicator within 14 days of the date that the matter before the court is finally disposed of, a copy of the final court order; and

    (c)   on the court within 14 days of service on that party of such a decision, a copy of any substantive decision made by the adjudicator on the matter.

References: See para 15.45.

11 Adjournment of proceedings before the adjudicator where court proceedings are commenced otherwise than following a direction to commence court proceedings under section 110(1)

Where court proceedings are commenced otherwise than following a direction to commence court proceedings under section 110(1), the adjudicator may adjourn the whole or part of the proceedings before him pending the outcome of the court proceedings.

References: See para 15.45.

12 Applicant's statement of case and documents

Unless otherwise directed by the adjudicator, the applicant must serve on the adjudicator and each of the other parties within 28 days of service of the notification of the reference under rule 5(b)—

    (a)   his statement of case which must be in accordance with rule 14; and

    (b)   a copy of all of the documents listed in the list of documents contained in his statement of case in accordance with rule 47.

References: See para 15.47.

13 Respondent's statement of case and documents

The respondent must serve on the adjudicator and each of the other parties within 28 days of service of the applicant's statement of case—

    (a)   his statement of case which must be in accordance with rule 14; and

    (b)   a copy of all of the documents listed in the list of documents contained in his statement of case in accordance with rule 47.

References: See para 15.47.

14 Statement of case

(1)   Where under these Rules a party is required to provide a statement of case, that statement of case must be in writing and must include—

    (a)   the name of the party and confirmation of the party's address for service;

    (b)   the party's reasons for supporting or objecting to the original application;

    (c)   the facts on which the party intends to rely in the proceedings;

    (d)   a list of documents in accordance with rule 47 on which the party intends to rely in the proceedings; and

    (e)   a list of witnesses that the party intends to call to give evidence in support of the party's case.

(2)   If in relation to part only of the matter—

    (a)   a party has been directed to commence or has commenced court proceedings; or

    (b)   the adjudicator has adjourned proceedings before him,

the adjudicator may direct that the statement of case should contain the information specified in paragraphs (1)(b) to (1)(e) inclusive only in relation to the part of the matter that is not before the court for the court's decision or has not been adjourned before the adjudicator.

References: See para 15.48.

PART 3
RECTIFICATION APPLICATION TO THE ADJUDICATOR TO RECTIFY OR SET ASIDE DOCUMENTS

15 Scope of this Part

The rules in this Part apply to rectification applications.

16 Form and contents of a rectification application

(1)   A rectification application must—

    (a)   be made in writing;

    (b)   be dated and signed by the applicant or the applicant's duly authorised representative;

    (c)   be addressed to the adjudicator;

    (d)   include the following information—

        (i)   the name and address of the person or persons against whom the order is sought;

        (ii)   details of the remedy being sought;

        (iii)   the grounds on which the rectification application is based;

        (iv)   in accordance with rule 47 a list of documents on which the party intends to rely to support the rectification application;

        (v)   a list of witnesses that the party intends to call to give evidence in support of the rectification application; and

        (vi)   the applicant's name and address for service;

    (e)   include the following copies—

        (i)   a copy of each of the documents listed in the party's list of documents; and

        (ii)   a copy of the document to which the rectification application relates, or if a copy is not available, details of the document, which must include if available, its nature, its date, the parties to it and any version number or other similar identification number or code that it has; and

    (f)   be served on the adjudicator.

(2)   Following receipt by the adjudicator of a rectification application, the adjudicator must enter the particulars of the rectification application in the record of matters.

(3)   If, having considered the rectification application and made any enquiries he thinks necessary, the adjudicator is satisfied that it is groundless, he must reject the rectification application.

References: See paras 15.33, 15.49.

17 Notice of a rectification application

(1)   This rule does not apply where the adjudicator has rejected a rectification application under rule 16(3).

(2)   Where a rectification application has been received by the adjudicator, he must serve on the person against whom the order is sought and on any other person who, in the opinion of the adjudicator, should be a party to the proceedings—
    (a)   written notice of the rectification application; and
    (b)   a copy of the rectification application.

(3)   The adjudicator must specify in the notice under paragraph (2)(a) that if a party receiving the notice has any objection to the rectification application and that party wishes to lodge an objection, he must lodge his objection within 28 days of service of the notice under paragraph (2)(a).

References: See para 15.33.

18 Objection to a rectification application

A person lodges an objection under rule 17(3) if within 28 days of service of the notice under rule 17(2)(a) he serves—
    (a)   on the adjudicator—
        (i)   a written statement addressed to the adjudicator and dated and signed by the person lodging the objection or his duly authorised representative setting out the grounds for the objection;
        (ii)   in accordance with rule 47 a list of documents on which the party intends to rely to support his objection;
        (iii)   a copy of each of the documents listed in the list of documents;
        (iv)   a written list of witnesses that the party intends to call to give evidence in support of the objection; and
        (v)   written confirmation of his name and address for service; and
    (b)   on the other parties a copy of all the information and documents served on the adjudicator under sub-paragraph (a).

References: See paras 15.33, 15.50.

PART 4
PREPARATION FOR DETERMINATION OF REFERENCES AND RECTIFICATION APPLICATIONS

19 Scope of this Part

This Part sets out the procedure for the preparation for the determination of references and rectification applications.

20 Directions

The adjudicator may at any time, on the application of a party or otherwise, give directions, including (but not limited to) such as are provided for in these Rules, to enable the parties to prepare for the hearing or to assist the adjudicator to conduct the proceedings or to determine the whole or part of the matter or any question of dispute in the proceedings without a hearing.

References: See para 15.51, 15.52.

21 Form of directions

(1)   Any direction made by the adjudicator must be—
    (a)   in writing;
    (b)   dated; and
    (c)   except in the case of requirement notices under rule 28, served by him on—
       (i)   every party to the proceedings;
      (ii)   where the person who made the application, representation or objection that resulted in the direction was not a party, that person; and
      (iii)   where the direction requires the registrar to take action, the registrar.

(2)   Directions containing a requirement must include a statement of the possible consequences of failure to comply with the requirement within any time limit specified by these Rules, or imposed by the adjudicator.

(3)   Directions requiring a party to provide or produce a document or any other material may require the party to provide or produce it to the adjudicator or to another party or both.

22 Consolidating proceedings

Where a reference or rectification application is related to another reference or rectification application and in the opinion of the adjudicator it is appropriate or practicable to do so, the adjudicator may direct that any or all of those related references or rectification applications be dealt with together.

References: See para 15.52.

23 Intention to appear

The adjudicator may give directions requiring a party to state whether that party intends to—
    (a)   attend or be represented at the hearing; and
    (b)   call witnesses.

24 Addition and substitution of parties

(1)   The adjudicator may give one or more of the following directions—
    (a)   that any person be added as a new party to the proceedings, if it appears to the adjudicator desirable for that person to be made a party;

   (b) that any person cease to be a party to the proceedings, if it appears to the adjudicator that it is not desirable for that person to remain a party; and

   (c) that a new party be substituted for an existing party, if—

     (i) the existing party's interest or liability has passed to the new party; and

    (ii) it appears to the adjudicator desirable to do this to enable him to resolve the whole or part of the matter or any question of dispute in the proceedings.

(2) If the adjudicator directs that a new party is to be added to the proceedings, the adjudicator must specify—

   (a) whether the new party is added as an applicant or a respondent; and

   (b) how the new party is to be referred to.

(3) Each new party must be given a single identification that should be in accordance with the order in which they joined the proceedings, for example "second applicant" or "second respondent".

(4) If the adjudicator directs that a new party is to be substituted for an existing party, the adjudicator must specify which party the new party is to substitute, for example "respondent" or "second applicant".

(5) The adjudicator must serve on each new party a copy of each of the following—

   (a) the applicant's statement of case and copy documents served on the adjudicator under rule 12 or the applicant's rectification application served on the adjudicator under rule 16(1); and

   (b) the respondent's statement of case and copy documents served on the adjudicator under rule 13 or the documents and information served by the respondent on the adjudicator under rule 18(a).

(6) If the new party is added to or substituted for parties to proceedings on a reference, the new party must serve on the adjudicator and each of the other parties within 28 days of service on him of the documents specified in paragraph (5)—

   (a) his statement of case which must be in accordance with rule 14; and

   (b) copies of documents contained in his list of documents, which must be in accordance with rule 47.

(7) If the new party is added to or substituted for parties to proceedings on a rectification application, the new party must serve on the adjudicator and each of the other parties, within 28 days of service on him of the documents specified in paragraph (5)—

   (a) if the new party is added or substituted as an applicant, his rectification application which must be in accordance with rule 16(1); or

   (b) if the new party is added or substituted as a respondent, his objection to the rectification application which must be in accordance with rule 18(a).

(8) If a continuing party wishes to respond to the documents specified in paragraph (6) or (7), he may apply to the adjudicator for leave to do so.

(9) If the adjudicator grants the requested leave to respond, the adjudicator must require the party requesting leave to respond to serve a copy of his response on the adjudicator and all other parties.

(10) Following the addition or substitution of parties and if it is necessary to do so, the adjudicator may give consequential directions, including for—

    (a)   the preparation and updating of a list of parties;

    (b)   the delivery and service of documents; and

    (c)   the waiver of the requirement to supply copies of documents listed in the new party's list of documents where copies have already been served on the adjudicator in the course of the proceedings.

References: See para 15.52.

25 Further information, supplementary statements and further responses to statements of case

The adjudicator may give directions requiring a party to provide one or more of the following—

    (a)   a statement of the facts in dispute or issues to be decided;

    (b)   a statement of the facts on which that party intends to rely and the allegations he intends to make;

    (c)   a summary of the arguments on which that party intends to rely; and

    (d)   such further information, responses to statements of case or supplementary statements as may reasonably be required for the determination of the whole or part of the matter or any question in dispute in the proceedings.

References: See para 15.52.

26 Witness statements

The adjudicator may give directions requiring a party to provide a witness statement made by any witness on whose evidence that party intends to rely in the proceedings.

References: See para 15.52.

27 Disclosure and inspection of documents

(1) Any document or other material supplied to the adjudicator or to a party under this rule or under rule 28 may only be used for the purpose of the proceedings in which it was disclosed.

(2) The adjudicator may give directions requiring a party who has a document or other material in his possession or control—

    (a)   to deliver to the adjudicator the original or a copy of that document or other material and, if the adjudicator thinks necessary, to supply copies of that document or material to another party; or

    (b)   to permit another party to inspect and take copies of that document or other material and specifying the time and place for disclosure and inspection of that document or other material.

References: See para 15.52.

28 Requirement notices

(1)   The adjudicator may, at any time, require the attendance of any person to give evidence or to produce any document or other material specified by the adjudicator which is in that person's possession or control.

(2)   The adjudicator must make any such requirement in a requirement notice.

(3)   The requirement notice must be in the form specified by the adjudicator provided that the requirement notice—

  (a)   is in writing;
  (b)   identifies the person who must comply with the requirement;
  (c)   identifies the matter to which the requirement relates;
  (d)   states the nature of the requirement being imposed by the adjudicator;
  (e)   specifies the time and place at which the adjudicator requires the person to attend and, if appropriate, produce any document or other material; and
  (f)   includes a statement of the possible consequences of failure to comply with the requirement notice.

(4)   The party on whose behalf it is issued must serve the requirement notice.

(5)   Subject to paragraph (6) a requirement notice will be binding only if, not less than 7 working days before the time that the person is required to attend—

  (a)   the requirement notice is served on that person; and
  (b)   except in the case where that person is a party to the proceedings, the necessary expenses of his attendance are offered and (unless he has refused the offer of payment of his expenses) paid to him.

(6)   At any time before the time that the person is required to attend, that person and the party on whose behalf the requirement notice is issued may substitute a shorter period for the period of 7 working days specified in paragraph (5) by—

  (a)   agreeing in writing such shorter period; and
  (b)   before the time that the person is required to attend, serving a copy of that agreement on the adjudicator.

(7)   Where a requirement has been imposed on a person under paragraph (1), that person may apply to the adjudicator for the requirement to be varied or set aside.

(8)   Any application made under paragraph (7) must be made to the adjudicator before the time when the person is to comply with the requirement to which the application under paragraph (7) relates.

References: See para 15.52.

29 Estimate of length of hearing

The adjudicator may require the parties to provide an estimate of the length of the hearing.

References: See para 15.52.

30 Site inspections

(1)   In this rule—

"the appropriate party" is the party who is in occupation or has ownership or control of the property;

"the property" is the land or premises that the adjudicator wishes to inspect for the purposes of determining the whole or part of the matter; and

"a request for entry" is a written request from the adjudicator to the appropriate party, requesting permission for the adjudicator to enter onto and inspect the property and such a request may include a request to be accompanied by one or more of—

(a)   another party;

(b)   such number of the adjudicator's officers or staff as he considers necessary; and

(c)   if a member of the Council on Tribunals informs the adjudicator that he wishes to attend the inspection, that member.

(2)   The adjudicator, at any time for the purpose of determining the whole or part of the matter, may serve a request for entry on an appropriate party.

(3)   The request for entry must specify a time for the entry that, unless otherwise agreed in writing by the appropriate party, must be not earlier than 7 days after the date of service of the request for entry.

(4)   The adjudicator must serve a copy of the request for entry on any party (other than the appropriate party) and any member of the Council on Tribunals named in the request for entry and, if reasonably practicable to do so in the circumstances, must notify them of any change in the time specified.

(5)   If the adjudicator makes a request for entry and the appropriate party withholds or refuses his consent to the whole or part of the request without reasonable excuse, the adjudicator may take such refusal into account when making his substantive decision.

(6)   If a request for entry includes a request for a member of the Council on Tribunals to accompany the adjudicator and the appropriate party consents to the presence of that member, then that member shall be entitled to attend the site inspection but must not take an active part in the inspection.

References: See para 15.52.

31 Preliminary issues

(1)   At any time and on the application of a party or of his own motion, the adjudicator may dispose of any matter or matters that are in dispute as a preliminary issue.

(2)   If in the opinion of the adjudicator the decision on the preliminary issue will dispose of the whole of the matter then the decision on the preliminary issue must be—

(a)   made in accordance with the provisions in these Rules on substantive decisions; and

(b)   treated as a substantive decision.

References: See para 15.52.

PART 5
HEARINGS AND SUBSTANTIVE DECISIONS

32 Scope of this Part

This Part sets out the procedure for determination of references and rectification applications, the format of substantive decisions and substantive orders and rules on costs.

33 Substantive decision without a hearing

(1)   There is a presumption that a substantive decision is made following a hearing.

(2)   Subject to paragraph (1), the adjudicator may make a substantive decision without a hearing if—

(a)   he is satisfied that there is no important public interest consideration that requires a hearing in public; and

(b)   unless paragraph (3) applies, he has served written notice on the parties in accordance with these Rules that he intends to make a substantive decision without a hearing or that he has received an application requesting that the substantive decision be made without a hearing and—

(i)   the parties agree to the substantive decision being made without a hearing; or

(ii)   the parties fail to object within the specified period for objection to the substantive decision being made without a hearing.

(3)   The adjudicator is not required to serve notice under paragraph (2)(b) if all parties have requested the adjudicator to make the substantive decision without a hearing.

References: See para 15.62.

34 Notice of hearing

(1)   Where the adjudicator is to hold a hearing, he must serve written notice of his intention to hear on such parties as he considers necessary.

(2)   The adjudicator must specify in the notice under paragraph (1), the date, time and location of the hearing.

(3)   The adjudicator must serve the notice under paragraph (1)—

(a)   no later than 28 days before the hearing; or

(b)   before the expiry of such shorter notice period as agreed by all the parties on whom he intends to serve notice under paragraph (1).

References: See para 15.57.

35 Representation at the hearing

(1)   At the hearing a party may conduct his case himself or, subject to paragraph (2), be represented or assisted by any person, whether or not legally qualified.

(2)   If, in any particular case, the adjudicator is satisfied that there is sufficient reason for doing so, he may refuse to permit a particular person to represent or assist a party at the hearing.

References: See para 15.59.

36 Publication of hearings

The adjudicator must publish details of all listed hearings at the office of the adjudicator and, if different, the venue at which the hearing is to take place.

References: See para 15.57.

37 Attendance at hearings by members of the Council on Tribunals

A member of the Council on Tribunals shall be entitled to attend any hearing of the adjudicator whether or not it is in private, but shall take no part in the hearing or in the deliberations on the matter.

38 Absence of parties

(1)   If any party does not attend and is not represented at any hearing of which notice has been served on him in accordance with these Rules, the adjudicator—
      (a)   may proceed with the hearing and reach a substantive decision in that party's absence if—
          (i)   the adjudicator is not satisfied that any reasons given for the absence are justified;
         (ii)   the absent party consents; or
       (iii)   it would be unjust to adjourn the hearing; or
      (b)   must otherwise adjourn the hearing.

(2)   Following a decision by the adjudicator under paragraph (1) to proceed with or adjourn the hearing, the adjudicator may make such consequential directions as he sees fit.

References: See para 15.60.

39 Substantive decision of the adjudicator

(1)   Where there is a hearing, the substantive decision of the adjudicator may be given orally at the end of the hearing or reserved.

(2)   A substantive decision of the adjudicator, whether made at a hearing or without a hearing, must be recorded in a substantive order.

(3)   The adjudicator may not vary or set aside a substantive decision.

References: See paras 15.63, 15.64.

40 Substantive orders and written reasons

(1)   A substantive order must—
      (a)   be in writing;
      (b)   be dated;

(c) be signed by the adjudicator;
(d) state the substantive decision that has been reached;
(e) state any steps that must be taken to give effect to that substantive decision; and
(f) state the possible consequences of a party's failure to comply with the substantive order within any specified time limits.

(2) The substantive order must be served by the adjudicator on—
(a) every party to the proceedings; and
(b) where the substantive order requires the registrar to take action, the registrar.

(3) A substantive order requiring a party to provide or produce a document or any other material may require the party to provide or produce it to any or all of the adjudicator, the registrar or another party.

(4) Unless the adjudicator directs otherwise, the substantive order must be publicly available.

(5) Where the substantive order is publicly available, the adjudicator may provide copies of it to the public on request.

(6) The adjudicator must give in writing to all parties his reasons for—
(a) his substantive decision; and
(b) any steps that must be taken to give effect to that substantive decision.

(7) The adjudicator's reasons referred to in paragraph (6) need not be given in the substantive order.

References: See para 15.63.

41 Substantive orders on a reference that include requirements on the registrar

(1) Where the adjudicator has made a substantive decision on a reference, the substantive order giving effect to that substantive decision may include a requirement on the registrar to—
(a) give effect to the original application in whole or in part as if the objection to that original application had not been made; or
(b) cancel the original application in whole or in part.

(2) A requirement on the registrar under this rule may include—
(a) a condition that a specified entry be made on the register of any title affected; or
(b) a requirement to reject any future application of a specified kind by a named party to the proceedings—
(i) unconditionally; or
(ii) unless that party satisfies specified conditions.

42 Costs

(1) In this rule—
(a) "all the circumstances" are all the circumstances of the proceedings and include—
(i) the conduct of the parties during (but not prior to) the proceedings;
(ii) whether a party has succeeded on part of his case, even if he has not been wholly successful; and

      (iii)   any representations made to the adjudicator by the parties; and
   (b)   the conduct of the parties during the proceedings includes—
      (i)   whether it was reasonable for a party to raise, pursue or contest a particular allegation or issue;
      (ii)   the manner in which a party has pursued or defended his case or a particular allegation or issue; and
      (iii)   whether a party who has succeeded in his case in whole or in part exaggerated his case.

(2)   The adjudicator may, on the application of a party or of his own motion, make an order as to costs.

(3)   In deciding what order as to costs (if any) to make, the adjudicator must have regard to all the circumstances.

(4)   An order as to costs may—
   (a)   require a party to pay the whole or such part of the costs of another party and—
      (i)   specify a fixed sum or proportion to be paid; or
      (ii)   specify that the costs are to be assessed by the adjudicator if not agreed; and
   (b)   specify the time within which the costs are to be paid.

(5)   An order as to costs must be recorded in a costs order.

(6)   A costs order must—
   (a)   be in writing;
   (b)   be dated;
   (c)   be signed by the adjudicator;
   (d)   state the order as to costs; and
   (e)   be served by the adjudicator on the parties.

(7)   Where the costs are to be assessed by the adjudicator, he may assess the costs—
   (a)   on the standard basis; or
   (b)   on the indemnity basis,
but in either case the adjudicator will not allow costs that have been unreasonably incurred or are unreasonable in amount.

(8)   The adjudicator must inform the parties of the basis on which he will be assessing the costs.

(9)   Where the amount of the costs are to be assessed on the standard basis, the adjudicator must—
   (a)   only allow costs which are proportionate to the matters in issue; and
   (b)   resolve any doubt that he may have as to whether costs were reasonably incurred or reasonable and proportionate in favour of the paying party.

(10) In deciding whether costs assessed on the standard basis were either proportionately and reasonably incurred or proportionate and reasonable in amount, the adjudicator must have regard to all the circumstances.

(11) Where the amount of the costs are to be assessed on the indemnity basis, the adjudicator must resolve any doubt that he may have as to whether costs were reasonably incurred or were reasonable in amount in favour of the paying party.

(12) In deciding whether costs assessed on the indemnity basis were either reasonably incurred or reasonable in amount, the adjudicator must have regard to all the circumstances.

(13) Once the adjudicator has assessed the costs, he must serve on the parties written notice—

    (a)   of the amount which must be paid;

    (b)   by whom and to whom the amount must be paid; and

    (c)   if appropriate, the time by when the amount must be paid.

References: See para 15.65, 15.66.

43 Costs thrown away

(1)   In this rule—

"costs thrown away" means costs of the proceedings resulting from any neglect or delay of the legal representative during (but not prior to) the proceedings and which—

    (a)   have been incurred by a party; or

    (b)   have been—

        (i)   paid by a party to another party; or

        (ii) awarded to a party,

under an order made under rule 42;

"an order as to costs thrown away" means an order requiring the legal representative concerned to meet the whole or part of the costs thrown away; and

"the legal representative" means the legally qualified representative of a party.

(2)   The adjudicator may, on the application of a party or otherwise, make an order as to costs thrown away provided the adjudicator is satisfied that—

    (a)   a party has incurred costs of the proceedings unnecessarily as a result of the neglect or delay of the legal representative; and

    (b)   it is just in all the circumstances for the legal representative to compensate the party who has incurred or paid the costs thrown away, for the whole or part of those costs.

(3)   If the adjudicator has received an application for or proposes to make an order as to costs thrown away, he may give directions to the parties and the legal representative about the procedure to be followed to ensure that the issues are dealt with in a way that is fair and as simple and summary as the circumstances permit.

(4)   An order as to costs thrown away may—

    (a)   specify the amount of costs to be paid by the legal representative; and

    (b)   if the adjudicator considers it appropriate, specify the time within which the costs are to be paid.

(5)   An order as to costs thrown away must be recorded in a costs thrown away order.

(6)   A costs thrown away order must—

    (a)   be in writing;

(b)   be dated;

(c)   be signed by the adjudicator;

(d)   state the order as to costs thrown away; and

(e)   be served by the adjudicator on the parties and the legal representative.

References: See para 15.67.

PART 6
APPEALS FROM ADJUDICATOR

44 Scope of this Part

This Part contains provisions in relation to appeals to the High Court of decisions by the adjudicator and includes provisions about the adjudicator staying implementation of his decision pending the outcome of an appeal.

45 Appeals to the High Court

(1)   Where a party is granted permission to appeal, the adjudicator may, of his own motion or on the application of a party, stay the implementation of the whole or part of his decision pending the outcome of the appeal.

(2)   A party who wishes to apply to the adjudicator to stay the implementation of the whole or part of a decision pending the outcome of the appeal must make such an application to the adjudicator at the same time that he applies to the adjudicator for permission to appeal.

(3)   Where a party applies under paragraph (2) to the adjudicator to stay implementation of the whole or part of a decision, that party must at the same time provide reasons for the application.

(4)   Before reaching a decision as to whether to grant permission to appeal a decision or to stay implementation of a decision, the adjudicator must allow the parties the opportunity to make representations or objections.

(5)   The adjudicator must serve written notice on the parties of any decision that he makes as to whether to grant permission to appeal or to stay the implementation of the whole or part of his decision pending the outcome of the appeal.

(6)   Where the adjudicator's decision to grant permission to appeal or to stay implementation of a decision relates to a decision contained in a substantive order, the adjudicator must serve on the registrar a copy of the notice under paragraph (5).

(7)   The notice under paragraph (5) must—

(a)   be in writing;

(b)   be dated;

(c)   specify the decision made by the adjudicator;

(d)   include the adjudicator's reasons for his decision; and

(e)   be signed by the adjudicator.

PART 7
GENERAL

46 Record of matters

(1)   The adjudicator must keep at his principal office a record of matters that records the particulars of all—

    (a)   references;

    (b)   rectification applications;

    (c)   substantive decisions; and

    (d)   all applications and decisions made under rule 45.

(2)   Subject to paragraph (3), the record of matters must be open to the inspection of any person without charge at all reasonable hours on working days.

(3)   Where the adjudicator is satisfied that it is just and reasonable to do so, the adjudicator may exclude from inspection any information contained in the record of matters.

(4)   Depending on all the circumstances, it may be just and reasonable for the adjudicator to exclude from inspection any information contained in the record of matters if it is in the interest of morals, public order, national security, juveniles or the protection of the private lives of the parties to the proceedings, or where the adjudicator considers that publicity would prejudice the interests of justice.

References: See para 15.63.

---

47 List of documents and documents

(1)   For the purposes of these Rules, a list of documents must be in writing and must contain the following information where available in relation to each document—

    (a)   a brief description of the nature of the document;

    (b)   whether the document is in the possession or control of the party;

    (c)   whether the document is an original, a copy certified to be a true copy of the original, an office copy or another type of copy;

    (d)   the date of the document;

    (e)   the document parties or the original author and recipient of the document; and

    (f)   the version number or similar identification number or code of the document.

(2)   Unless the adjudicator otherwise permits, where a document provided for the purposes of the proceedings is or contains a coloured map, plan or drawing, any copy provided of that map, plan or drawing must be in the same colours as the map, plan or drawing of which it is a copy (so for example, where a plan shows the boundary of a property in red, a copy of the plan must also show the boundary in red).

48 Evidence

(1)   The adjudicator may require any witness to give evidence on oath or affirmation and for that purpose there may be administered an oath or affirmation in due form.

(2)   No person may be compelled to give any evidence or produce any document or other material that that person could not be compelled to give or produce on a trial of an action in a court of law in England and Wales.

49 Expert evidence

No party may call an expert, or submit an expert's report as evidence, without the adjudicator's permission.

50 Service of documents

(1)   A party's address for service must be a postal address in England and Wales.

(2)   The address for service in paragraph (1) must be either that of the party or of the party's representative who has been appointed as his representative for the purposes of the proceedings.

(3)   A party's address for service remains that party's address for service for the purposes of these Rules unless and until he serves on the adjudicator and the other parties notice of a different address for service.

(4)   Any document to be served on or delivered to any person (other than the adjudicator) under these Rules may only be served—
  (a)   by first class post to his postal address given as his address for service;
  (b)   by leaving it at his address for service;
  (c)   subject to paragraph (5), by document exchange;
  (d)   subject to paragraph (6), by fax;
  (e)   subject to paragraph (7), by email; or
  (f)   where no address for service has been given, by post to or leaving it at his registered office, principal place of business, head or main office or last known address, as appropriate.

(5)   A document may be served on any person other than the adjudicator by document exchange in England and Wales if, in advance, the recipient has informed the adjudicator and all parties in writing—
  (a)   that the recipient is willing to accept service by document exchange; and
  (b)   of the box number at the document exchange to which the documents should be addressed.

(6)   A document may be served by fax on any person other than the adjudicator, to a fax number at the address for service for that person if, in advance, the recipient has informed the adjudicator and all parties in writing—
  (a)   that the recipient is willing to accept service by fax; and
  (b)   of the fax number to which the documents should be sent.

(7)   A document may be served by email on any person other than the adjudicator, if, in advance, the recipient has informed the adjudicator and all parties in writing—
  (a)   that the recipient is willing to accept service by email;
  (b)   of the email address to which documents should be sent, which shall be deemed to be at the recipient's address for service; and
  (c)   if the recipient wishes to so specify, the format in which documents must be sent.

(8)   Any document addressed to the adjudicator must be sent—
  (a)   by first class post to an address specified by the adjudicator; or

      (b)   by such other method as the adjudicator may specify, including document exchange, fax or email.

(9)   Where under paragraph (8)(b) the adjudicator specifies another method of service, the adjudicator may—

      (a)   specify that that method may be used generally or only in relation to a certain document or documents;

      (b)   specify that the specified method is no longer available or substitute that specified method with another specified method; and

      (c)   make such directions in relation to the use of the specified method as he deems appropriate.

(10) Any document served on an unincorporated body may be sent to its secretary, manager or similar officer duly authorised to accept such service.

(11) Any document which is served in accordance with this rule shall be regarded as having been served on the day shown in the table below—

Method of service	Day of service
First class post to a postal address within England and Wales	The second working day after it was posted.
Leaving it at a postal address within England and Wales	The working day after it was left.
Document exchange within England and Wales	The second working day after it was left at the document exchange.
Fax	The working day after it was transmitted.
Email	The working day after it was transmitted.

(12) The adjudicator may direct that service under these Rules of any document may be dispensed with and in those circumstances may make such consequential directions as he deems appropriate.

51 Applications, actions by the adjudicator of his own motion, notification, representations and objections

(1)   This rule does not apply to Part 3 and rule 45.

(2)   An application to the adjudicator must—

      (a)   be in writing;

      (b)   state the name of the person applying or on whose behalf the application is made;

      (c)   be addressed to the adjudicator;

      (d)   state the nature of the application;

      (e)   state the reason or reasons for the application; and

      (f)   if any of the parties or persons who would be affected by the application consent to it, either—

          (i)   be signed by all the parties or persons who consent or their duly authorised representatives; or

         (ii)   have attached to it a copy of their written consent.

(3)   The adjudicator may dispense with any or all of the requirements under paragraph (2)—

(a) in relation to an application made to the adjudicator at a time when all persons who would be affected by the application are present before the adjudicator; or

(b) if the adjudicator otherwise considers it appropriate or practicable to do so.

(4) For the purposes of paragraph (2)(f), the written consent referred to in that paragraph may be in the form of a letter, fax or email.

(5) If an application is not consented to by all persons who will be affected by the application then, subject to paragraph (10), the adjudicator must serve written notice on persons who have not consented to the application but who would be affected by it.

(6) In the notice under paragraph (5) the adjudicator must state—
(a) that the application has been made;
(b) details of the application;
(c) that the person has a right to make written objections to or representations about the application; and
(d) the period within which such objections or representations must be lodged with the adjudicator.

(7) If the adjudicator intends to act of his own motion under these Rules then, subject to paragraph (10), he must serve written notice of his intention on all persons who will be affected by the action.

(8) In the notice under paragraph (7) the adjudicator must state—
(a) that the adjudicator intends to take action of his own motion;
(b) the action the adjudicator intends to take;
(c) that a person has a right to make written objections or representations to the action that the adjudicator intends to take; and
(d) the period within which such objections or representations must be lodged with the adjudicator.

(9) A person lodges an objection or representation if within the specified period he serves—
(a) on the adjudicator a written statement setting out the grounds for his objection or representation; and
(b) on all the other persons who will be affected by the action a copy of the written statement served on the adjudicator under sub-paragraph (a).

(10) The adjudicator shall not be required to serve notice under paragraphs (5) and (7) if, in the circumstances, he does not consider it appropriate or practicable to do so.

(11) Paragraph (10) does not apply to notices required to be served by rule 33.

References: See paras 15.54, 15.55.

---

52 Consideration by the adjudicator of applications (including applications for directions), representations and objections

(1) In relation to any application, representation or objection made to the adjudicator, unless—
(a) the adjudicator is satisfied that it is frivolous or vexatious; or

(b) it is received by the adjudicator after the expiry of any time limit specified for making that application, representation or objection,

the adjudicator must consider all applications, representations or objections made to him.

(2) If an application, representation or objection is received by the adjudicator after the expiry of any time limit specified for making it, the adjudicator may consider the application, representation or objection, but he is not bound to do so.

(3) In considering any application, representation or objection, the adjudicator must make all enquiries he thinks necessary and must, if required by these Rules or if he considers it necessary, give the person making the application, representation or objection and the parties or other persons who will be affected by it the opportunity to appear before him or to submit written representations.

(4) The adjudicator may decide to accept or reject an application, representation or objection in whole or in part.

(5) Following his consideration of any applications, representations or objections that are made to him, the adjudicator must notify the person who made the application, representation or objection and the parties and any other persons who will be affected by it, of his decision in accordance with these Rules.

References: See para 15.56.

53 Adjournment

In addition to the powers and obligations to adjourn proceedings contained in Part 2 and rule 38, the adjudicator may adjourn the whole or part of the proceedings when and to the extent that he feels it reasonable to do so.

54 Power to vary or set aside directions

Subject to these Rules, the adjudicator may at any time, on the application of a party or otherwise, vary or set aside directions made under these Rules.

55 Failure to comply with a direction

(1) Where a party has failed to comply with a direction given by the adjudicator (including a direction to commence court proceedings under section 110(1)) the adjudicator may impose a sanction on the defaulting party—
(a) on the application of any other party; or
(b) of his own motion.

(2) Where the defaulting party was the person who made (or has been substituted for or added to the party who made) the original application, the sanction may include requiring the registrar to cancel the original application in whole or in part.

(3) Where the defaulting party was a person who objected to (or has been substituted for or added to the party who objected to) the original application, the sanction may include requiring the registrar to give effect to the original application in whole or in part as if the objection had not been made.

(4) A sanction that includes either of the requirements on the registrar under paragraph (2) or (3) shall be treated as the substantive decision on that matter.

(5) If the sanction does not include either of the requirements on the registrar under paragraph (2) or (3), the adjudicator must serve written notice on the parties of his decision as to what if any sanctions are imposed, and he may make consequential directions.

References: See paras 15.44, 15.53.

56 Errors of procedure

Where, before the adjudicator has made his final substantive order in relation to a matter, there has been an error of procedure such as a failure to comply with a rule—

  (a)   the error does not invalidate any step taken in the proceedings, unless the adjudicator so orders; and

  (b)   the adjudicator may make an order or take any other step that he considers appropriate to remedy the error.

57 Accidental slips or omissions

The adjudicator may at any time amend an order or direction to correct a clerical error or other accidental slip or omission.

58 Time and place

If the adjudicator deems it appropriate to do so, he may alter—

  (a)   any time limit specified in these Rules;

  (b)   any time limit set by the adjudicator; or

  (c)   the date, time or location appointed for a hearing or for any other appearance of the parties before him.

References: See para 15.53.

59 Calculation of time

(1) Where a period of time for doing an act is specified by these Rules or by a direction of the adjudicator, that period is to be calculated—

  (a)   excluding the day on which the period begins; and

  (b)   unless otherwise specified, by reference to calendar days.

(2) Where the time specified by these Rules or by a direction of the adjudicator for doing an act ends on a day which is not a working day, that act is done in time if it is done on the next working day.

60 Representation of parties

(1) If a party who was previously unrepresented appoints a representative or, having been represented, appoints a replacement representative, that party must, as soon as reasonably practicable following the appointment, notify the adjudicator and the other parties in writing—

  (a)   of the fact that he has appointed a representative or replacement representative;

  (b)   the name and contact details of the representative or replacement representative;

    (c)   whether the representative or replacement representative has been authorised by the party to accept service of documents; and

    (d)   if the representative or replacement representative has been authorised to accept service, the address for service.

(2)   If a party who was previously represented ceases to be represented, that party must, as soon as reasonably practicable following the ending of his representation, notify the adjudicator and the other parties in writing—

    (a)   of the fact that he is no longer represented; and

    (b)   where the party's address for service had previously been the address of the representative, the party's new address for service.

61 Independence of adjudicator's staff

When undertaking a non-administrative function of the adjudicator on the adjudicator's authorisation, a member of the adjudicator's staff is not subject to the direction of the Lord Chancellor or any other person or body.

References: See para 15.25.

Land Registration (Acting Chief Land Registrar) Regulations 2003

(SI 2003/2281)

Made: 4 September 2003.
Authority: Land Registration Act 2002, s 100(2).
Commencement: 13 October 2003.

---

1 Citation and commencement

These Regulations may be cited as the Land Registration (Acting Chief Land Registrar) Regulations 2003 and shall come into force on 13th October 2003.

2 Appointment

(1)   The Lord Chancellor may appoint a person to carry out the functions of the registrar during any vacancy in that office.

(2)   The person appointed under paragraph (1) must, at the time of appointment, be a member of the land registry and also a member of the Senior Civil Service.

(3)   Subject to paragraph (4), the person appointed shall carry out the functions of the registrar during any vacancy.

(4)   An appointment under paragraph (1) shall cease if the person appointed—

    (a)   ceases to be a member of the land registry, or

    (b)   resigns his appointment under paragraph (1) by giving notice in writing to the Lord Chancellor, or

    (c)   has his appointment revoked by the Lord Chancellor on the grounds of being unable or unfit to discharge the functions of the registrar.

(5)   For the purpose of paragraph (2), a person is to be treated as a member of the Senior Civil Service if, at the time of his appointment, he holds a Civil Service grade which is, or is equivalent to, a grade at any time covered by the Senior Civil Service.

Land Registration (Acting Adjudicator) Regulations 2003

(SI 2003/2342)

Made: 8 September 2003.
Authority: Land Registration Act 2002, Sch 9, para 5.
Commencement: 13 October 2003.

1 Citation and commencement

These Regulations may be cited as the Land Registration (Acting Adjudicator) Regulations 2003 and shall come into force on 13th October 2003.

2 Appointment

(1)   The Lord Chancellor may, in order to facilitate the disposal of the business of the adjudicator, appoint a person to carry out the functions of the adjudicator during any vacancy in that office.

(2)   To be qualified for appointment under paragraph (1), a person must hold the office of district judge (as defined in section 74(1) of the Courts and Legal Services Act 1990).

(3)   The person appointed shall carry out the functions of the adjudicator during the vacancy, unless within that period, he:—
  (a)   dies; or
  (b)   resigns by giving notice in writing to the Lord Chancellor; or
  (c)   is removed by the Lord Chancellor on the grounds of incapacity or misbehaviour.

3 Functions

Every person appointed, whilst acting under these Regulations, shall have all the jurisdiction and powers of the person appointed to the office of adjudicator pursuant to section 107 of the Land Registration Act 2002.

Index